GREAT EVENTS
FROM
HISTORY II

GREAT EVENTS FROM HISTORY II

Arts and Culture
Series

Volume 3
1937-1954

Edited by
FRANK N. MAGILL

SALEM PRESS
Pasadena, California   Englewood Cliffs, New Jersey

Library of Congress Cataloging-in-Publication Data
Great events from history II. Arts and culture series / edited by Frank N. Magill.
    p.   cm.
Includes bibliographical references and index.
    1. Arts, Modern—20th century. 2. Arts and so-
ciety—History—20th century. I. Magill, Frank Northen,
1907-   . II. Title: Great events from history. 2. Arts
and culture series.

NX456.G72   1993
700′.9′04—dc20
ISBN 0-89356-807-4 (set)   93-28381
ISBN 0-89356-810-4 (volume 3)   CIP

PRINTED IN THE UNITED STATES OF AMERICA

LIST OF EVENTS IN VOLUME III

HITLER ORGANIZES AN EXHIBITION DENOUNCING MODERN ART

Category of event: Art
Time: July 19-November 30, 1937
Locale: Hofgarten Arcades, Munich, Germany

A display of modern art confiscated by the Nazis from German museums and labeled "degenerate" foreshadowed the later purging of artists by Adolf Hitler's regime

Principal personages:
ADOLF HITLER (1889-1945), the Nazi dictator who opposed modern art, from which he believed Germany needed to be cleansed
JOSEPH GOEBBELS (1897-1945), the Nazi minister of propaganda who was responsible for overseeing German cultural life
ADOLF ZIEGLER (1892-1959), the president of the Reich Chamber of Visual Arts and the organizer of the Degenerate Art Exhibition and the Great German Art Exhibition
OTTO DIX (1891-1969), an artist and World War I veteran whose work was attacked by the Nazis
GEORGE GROSZ (1893-1959), an artist who satirized German economic and political life during the Weimar Republic
WASSILY KANDINSKY (1866-1944), an expressionist painter derided by the Nazis
EMIL NOLDE (EMIL HANSEN, 1867-1956), an expressionist painter whose Nazi Party membership did not protect his work from confiscation

Summary of Event

The Degenerate Art Exhibition was opened in Munich on July 19, 1937, by Adolf Ziegler, the president of the Reich Chamber of Visual Arts, one day after Adolf Hitler had dedicated the city's House of German Art and the first of eight official "Great German Art Exhibitions." Speaking in the city where the Nazi movement was born and shortly before the height of his prewar success, Hitler described the House of German Art as a temple for an eternal German art that would not welcome modern art. Ziegler's speech, which summarized thoughts previously articulated by Hitler and his minions, condemned modern art as "the monstrous offspring of insanity, impudence, ineptitude, and sheer degeneracy." These complementary speeches and exhibits clarified the role of art in the Third Reich, establishing the parameters for what would be officially promoted as well as making clear what would be condemned, removed from public view, and then concealed or destroyed.

Visitors to the Degenerate Art Exhibition saw displayed in a calculatedly defamatory manner more than 650 modern paintings, prints, books, and sculptures that had been hastily removed from thirty-two public museums in Germany by Ziegler, with the authorization of Nazi propaganda chief Joseph Goebbels. Some paintings were stripped of their frames, and the labels that provided information about each work, including its original purchase price, were often erroneous and simply tacked or pasted in place. Scattered haphazardly throughout the exhibit were phrases and slogans denigrating modern art, quotations by avant-garde artists taken out of context and selected so as to seem threatening or ridiculous, and passages about the nature of art and its place in Nazi Germany by Hitler and other party functionaries. The exhibition appeared crowded, jumbled, and claustrophobic—an effect the organizers wished to impress upon the viewer, for the event reflected a concept of modern art as both degenerate and the product of artistic incompetence. In the opinion of Hitler, the modern art that had flourished in Germany before World War I and then during the 1920's was a symptom not only of political and cultural decline but also of racial, physical, and mental pathology.

Art confiscated for the Degenerate Art Exhibition was arranged in nine loosely thematic groups. Visitors saw first Ludwig Gies's *Crucified Christ*, a war memorial that had once hung in Lübeck Cathedral and that the Nazis branded a horror, and then Emil Nolde's multipaneled altarpiece *The Life of Christ*, both of which purportedly mocked Christianity. Next came paintings by Jewish artists such as Marc Chagall and Ludwig Meidner. The third room housed more than seventy pieces, among them nudes by Karl Hofer, Ernst Ludwig Kirchner, and Otto Mueller headed "An Insult to German Womanhood," images of World War I labeled "Deliberate Sabotage of National Defense," and portrayals of peasants by Kirchner and Karl Schmidt-Rottluff that were identified as "German Farmers—A Yiddish View." Singled out for ridicule was Dadaist art; on the so-called Dada wall, works by Kurt Schwitters and Paul Klee appeared beneath a quotation from George Grosz and against a backdrop copied from an abstract but hardly Dada painting by Wassily Kandinsky. Similar displays filled the remaining rooms. Prominent were townscapes by Lyonel Feininger, compositions by professors and teachers of art who allegedly were corrupting German youth, etchings by Otto Dix, and miscellaneous works by Klee, Schmidt-Rottluff, Grosz, and Max Beckmann, among others. In the lobby stood Otto Freundlich's "The New Man," which was reproduced on the cover of the exhibition guide.

The names of the 112 artists exhibited testify to the dynamism of modern German art during the first third of the twentieth century; the artists listed represented movements as diverse as the Bauhaus style, cubism, Dadaism, expressionism, the New Objectivity, and abstractionism. Artists represented with ten or more works, excluding those named above, included Erich Heckel, Oskar Kokoschka, Max Pechstein, and Christian Rohlfs. The selection criteria, however, remain obscure. Despite the Nazi insistence that modern art was foreign, Jewish, or left-wing in inspiration, only six artists were Jewish, and non-German artists were rare. Troublesome was the inclusion of works by the expressionist Franz Marc, who had been killed in World War I; the German Officers' Federation protested the use of his work, and his *Tower of Blue Horses* was removed from the exhibit. Likewise controversial was the presence of works by Nolde, a Nazi Party member whose art had once found favor with such high officials as Goebbels. The case of the sculptor Rudolf Belling was particularly ironic; Belling had two works shown in the Degenerate Art Exhibition, while his bronze of the boxer Max Schmeling stood in the nearby Great German Art Exhibition.

More than two million people visited the Degenerate Art Exhibition, making it the most popular exhibit of modern art ever; fewer than a fifth as many viewers attended the Great German Art Exhibit. Between February, 1938, and April, 1941, the Degenerate Art Exhibition traveled to twelve cities in Germany and Austria, usually under the patronage of local branches of the Nazi Party. Though the traveling exhibition was changed and reduced in size from the Munich showing, it also attracted large audiences, with attendance in excess of 100,000 in Berlin, Düsseldorf, Hamburg, and Vienna, and a total of more than one million additional viewers. Added in Düsseldorf was an exhibit of "degenerate music" that excoriated jazz, so-called Jewish music, and the compositions of Arnold Schoenberg, Igor Stravinsky, and Kurt Weill, to name but a few. A catalog accompanied the touring exhibition, although none was available for the original in Munich. The catalog juxtaposed a programmatic statement and excerpts from Hitler's speeches with quotations from the exhibit's walls and photographs of exhibited works. Readers were invited, in one notorious instance, to view three drawings and guess which was by an inmate of an insane asylum and which were by a modern artist.

Impact of Event

The Degenerate Art Exhibition and the Great German Art Exhibition cannot be understood apart from Hitler's ideas concerning art. According to his worldview, the Nazi movement stood at the forefront of a cultural revolution destined to usher in a creative new age, that of the thousand-year Reich, and the arts were to play a formative role in the revolution's genesis. Nazi doctrine held that artistic creativity and inspiration originated in the *Volkgemeinschaft*, the racial community, and that the duty of the artist was to express what Hitler called the essential character of that people or community; the artist's task was therefore not to create images for other artists to admire but rather to present an ideal for the people to emulate. Further, said Hitler, art should embody eternal values and be easily understood and appreciated by the average person. However specific their formulation by the Nazis, these ideas derived from racist concepts long in circulation and from an ongoing debate that had set in opposition so-called pure German art and modern art.

The brand of art favored by the Nazis was made evident at the Great German Art Exhibition. Displayed were almost nine hundred paintings and sculptures by Arno Breker, Josef Thorak, Ziegler, and other politically acceptable artists. Landscapes, idealized men and women, farmers and artisans, portraits of Nazi officials, and images of public buildings or works predominated. The large number of male and female nudes achieved what George L. Mosse has called "beauty without sensuality." Also shown was "In the Beginning Was the Word," an image by Hermann Otto Hoyer of Hitler speaking before his earliest followers. Notable by their absence were urban scenes and any art that raised questions or stimulated thought. In brief, the

Great German Art Exhibition presented idealized images of Nazi ideology, just as the Degenerate Art Exhibition summarized, again with images, not only what the Nazi regime rejected as diseased but also what it intended to purge from German cultural life.

The Munich Degenerate Art Exhibition completed a series of attacks launched by Hitler and his government after 1933 upon artists, teachers, collectors, museum administrators, and critics connected with avant-garde movements. Such actions had been anticipated by a 1933 report by Goebbels that had proposed a five-point program for the purge of modern art and were in keeping with the Nazi policy of *Gleichschaltung*, the goal of which was ideological and administrative control of all German associations, institutions, and aspects of individual life. Artists whose work was categorized as degenerate—including, for the most part, those even remotely associated with expressionism, the German defeat in World War I, the Weimar Republic, Jewishness, Marxism, or abstract art—were excluded from membership in the Reich Chamber of Culture and therefore forbidden to practice their profession. Likewise, the modern wing of the National Gallery in Berlin was closed in 1936, the same year that Goebbels banned art criticism.

Not content merely to silence modern artists and their advocates, the Nazis organized between 1933 and 1937 nearly a dozen exhibitions slandering modern art and gave the shows such titles as "The Chamber of Horrors" and "Images of Cultural Bolshevism." Indeed, the prototype for the 1937 Degenerate Art Exhibition may have been a Dresden exhibition of the same title organized in 1933 and shown at eight other locations, including the 1935 Nazi Party rally at Nuremberg. Before long, though, ridicule gave way to a systematic purge. While the Degenerate Art Exhibition still hung in Munich, a committee appointed by Goebbels and headed by Ziegler undertook additional confiscations, and some sixteen thousand pieces of modern art by more than a thousand artists were seized and removed to Berlin for storage. A few hundred, including a self-portrait by Vincent van Gogh, were sold abroad at auctions or exchanged between 1939 and 1941. Approximately five thousand other works of art were reportedly burned at the central fire department in Berlin in March, 1939, while thousands more simply vanished.

The fate of the artists classified as degenerate by the Third Reich was similarly grim. Those who were able, including Beckmann, Feininger, or Grosz, left Germany. Others, including Kircher, committed suicide; Freundlich and others died in concentration camps. Many, including Nolde, retreated into silence after having lost their teaching or other public positions. Following the end of World War II, those who survived often resumed their work, taking on teaching and administrative positions both in the East and the West.

In the long term, of course, the Nazis failed. The Thousand Year Reich lasted but twelve years, and its creators succeeded neither in imposing their ideology and their concept of art on Germany and Europe nor in purging Germany of modern art. Museum visitors today are thus able to view paintings and sculptures by the expressionists, the New Objectivitists, the Surrealists, and the members of other schools attacked by the Nazis. In contrast, the officially sanctioned art of the Third Reich is all but unknown. Nevertheless, the Degenerate Art Exhibition should be not forgotten, for it is an example of what is possible when a government manipulates for its own purposes the bewilderment or the discomfort felt by many in the presence of modern art.

Bibliography

Adam, Peter. *Art of the Third Reich.* New York: Harry N. Abrams, 1992. Understanding the Degenerate Art Exhibition is impossible without an understanding of the exhibit's context, the official Nazi art discussed and reproduced in this book.

Barron, Stephanie, ed. *Degenerate Art: The Fate of the Avant-Garde in Nazi Germany.* New York: Harry N. Abrams, 1991. Essential source; its ten essays by mostly German authors include a complete re-creation of the exhibit, photographs of works exhibited, a facsimile and translation of the 1937 catalog, and an outstanding bibliography of literature, mostly in German.

Crockett, Dennis. "The Most Famous Painting of the 'Golden Twenties'? Otto Dix and the *Trench* Affair." *Art Journal* 51 (Spring, 1992): 72-80. Solid discussion of the controversy raised during the Weimar period by a painting shown at the Degenerate Art Exhibition.

Dunlop, Ian. *The Shock of the New: Seven Historic Exhibitions of Modern Art.* New York: American Heritage Press, 1972. The final chapter deals with the Degenerate Art Exhibition; extensive quotes from German documents and reviews in the German press make this a valuable source.

Grosshans, Henry. *Hitler and the Artists.* New York: Holmes & Meier, 1983. A general account of the development of Hitler's ideas on art and culture, with a chapter on the Degenerate Art Exhibition.

Hinz, Berthold. *Art in the Third Reich.* Translated by Robert Kimber and Rita Kimber. New York: Pantheon Books, 1979. Well-illustrated study, with chapters that treat the Great German Exhibition, the Degenerate Art Exhibition, and Nazi concepts of art.

Sax, Benjamin, and Dieter Kuntz, eds. *Inside Hitler's Germany: A Documentary History of the Third Reich.* Lexington, Mass.: D. C. Heath, 1992. Contains a translation of Hitler's speech opening the House of German Art.

Robert W. Brown

Cross-References

Avant-Garde Artists in Dresden Form Die Brücke (1905), p. 134; Der Blaue Reiter Abandons Representation in Art (1911), p. 275; Kandinsky Publishes His Views on Abstraction in Art (1912), p. 320; The Soviet Union Bans Abstract Art (1922), p. 544; The New Objectivity Movement Is Introduced (1925), p. 631; The Nazis Ban Nolde's Paintings (1941), p. 1217; Wiesel's *Night* Recalls the Holocaust (1956), p. 1700.

THE BALLET RUSSE DE MONTE CARLO
FINDS NEW LEADERSHIP

Category of event: Dance
Time: 1938
Locale: New York, New York

French critic René Blum and Russian impresario Sergei Denham joined in managing a new Ballet Russe de Monte Carlo that helped to popularize ballet in America through frequent touring

Principal personages:
RENÉ BLUM (1884-1944), a French impresario and art critic who took over the management of Sergei Diaghilev's Ballets Russes, eventually renaming it the Ballet Russe de Monte Carlo in partnership with Sergei Denham
SERGEI DENHAM (1897-1970), a Russian impresario whose direction of the Ballet Russe de Monte Carlo helped to popularize ballet in America
LÉONIDE MASSINE (LEONID MIASSIN, 1896-1979), a French dancer originally from the Diaghilev company who served as the widely acclaimed choreographer for the Ballet Russe de Monte Carlo
COLONEL WASSILI DE BASIL (VASILY VOSKRESENSKY, 1888-1951), a Cossack officer who briefly joined Blum in leading the Ballet Russe de Monte Carlo until moving to form his own company of dancers
MICHEL FOKINE (1880-1942), a Russian choreographer whose revolutionary ideas about the dance helped to modernize ballet
GEORGE BALANCHINE (GEORGI MELITONOVITCH BALANCHIVADZE, 1904-1983), a Russian choreographer who contributed works to the Ballet Russe de Monte Carlo before beginning a long association with the New York City Ballet

Summary of Event

The Ballet Russe de Monte Carlo, aggressively promoted as "The One and Only," was synonymous with glamorous stars, sumptuous decor, and brilliant dancing for nearly a quarter of a century. An itinerant company with roots torn by war and internal intrigue, the Ballet Russe created its own family from the American public at large. Rather than being elitist, inapproachable bearers of high art, the company infiltrated remote corners of the United States, appearing in high-school auditoriums as well as big-city opera houses. The Ballet Russe de Monte Carlo created a mass audience for ballet with success unmatched by fledgling American companies during the same period. Its contribution to the evolution of twentieth century theatrical dance is significant.

Beginning in 1938, impresarios René Blum and Sergei Denham together guided the group's progress. Blum, formerly Monte Carlo Opera Ballet director, managed the remains of Sergei Diaghilev's legendary Ballets Russes after Diaghilev's death in 1929. Denham, a Russian banker transplanted to New York, was vice-president of a sponsoring organization called Universal Art (formerly known as World Art). This organization wished to assemble a new company for French choreographer Léonide Massine. Denham turned to Blum.

For roughly forty thousand dollars, Blum sold the rights to the valuable Monte Carlo name and elements of the Diaghilev repertory to Universal Art (backed by millionaire Julius Fleischmann). By arrangement, the Ballets Russes continued its annual spring season in Monte Carlo and its U.S. touring under Universal's management and financial support. Denham assumed the role of business director of the company—renamed Ballet Russe de Monte Carlo—while Blum remained its artistic director and Massine its choreographer and principal dancer. (In fact, to Blum's chagrin, the company was widely known as "Massine's Ballet Russe.") Its debut performance was given on April 5, 1938, in Monte Carlo, and on October 12, 1938, the company first appeared in New York City.

The Ballet Russe de Monte Carlo led by Blum, Denham, and Massine was one in a series of incarnations of the Ballet Russe name. The success of Blum and Denham's partnership followed the deterioration of Blum's earlier efforts to preserve the legendary company created by Diaghilev. Blum initially assumed direction of the Ballets Russes in the country of its patron, the Prince of Monaco. In 1932, Russian Colonel Wassili de Basil joined him in his efforts to salvage the dissipated Diaghilev spirit. With new ballets by George Balanchine and Massine, this earlier company created a sensation during its tours of Europe and, in 1933, America.

Blum and de Basil proved incompatible as partners, however. They split the group into two separate enterprises in 1936 with great hostility, dividing repertory, trademarks, costumes, even dancers. Thriving on intrigue and confusion, de Basil changed the name of his reorganized company six times in less than eight years. Common appellations were "De Basil's Ballet Russe" or the "Original Ballet Russe." Litigation over rights of ownership to the ballets continued into the late 1940's, as did the rivalry between the two companies. These so-called Ballet Wars, often fought across continents, generated tremendous publicity. Newspapers from Europe to the Americas carried frequent updates on the squabbles and traced the dancers' shifting loyalties.

Indeed, in addition to the exotic company name, the popularity of Blum and Denham's company hinged upon the star appeal of its dancers. At its inception, the Ballet Russe de Monte Carlo took with it or hired such foreign favorites as Alexandra Danilova, Alicia Markova, Eugenie Delarova, Mia Slavenska, Tamara Toumanova, Serge Lifar, Michel Panieff, Marc Platoff, and Frederic Franklin. Among those lost to de Basil were premier danseur David Lichine and "baby ballerinas" (Balanchine's prodigies) Tatiana Riabouchinska and Irina Baronova.

Both Ballet Russe companies continued to tour Europe and North and South America with immense, if independent, success. The partnership undertaken by

Blum and Denham ushered in golden years for the new Ballet Russe de Monte Carlo, as their travels took them from New York to Boston, Toronto to Los Angeles, Kansas City to Seattle. The company was met by welcoming audiences, impressive box-office returns, and daily reviews. Many historians recall that theaters advertised "standing room only" as much as a month before the company's arrival in a given town.

Though its official headquarters was in Monte Carlo, the Ballet Russe became a permanent fixture at New York's Metropolitan Opera House as a result of the onset of World War II in 1939. With European tours impossible, the company performed frequently throughout the United States and Canada. With new Russian dancers unavailable, Blum and Denham began to hire Americans. Many of them, seeking a share of the company's alluring image, at first adopted Russian stage names.

Although many of his previous works were retained by de Basil through court action, Massine created new choreographic masterpieces for the Ballet Russe de Monte Carlo. Favoring the avant-garde and surreal, Massine often commissioned modern artists such as Henri Matisse and Salvador Dalí to create the decor for his ballets. The company came to be associated with colorful, flamboyant, even outrageous results.

Blum and Denham employed the Diaghilev "formula" for an evening's concert, presenting three of four stylistically or thematically different ballets on one program. One critic compared the Ballet Russe to a three-ring circus in which an audience could pick its pleasure from a variety of interesting acts. Entertainment value aside, the company's repertoire was the subject of serious and intense scrutiny by patrons who were beginning to gain a critical understanding of ballet.

Despite continued success, the Ballet Russe de Monte Carlo soon faced new political and artistic realities. The horrifying state of affairs in Europe dealt a severe blow to the dance company in America. Many dancers worried about families overseas, and some even joined the service. Most distressingly, while his company was touring the United States in 1941, Blum tragically decided to visit France instead. He was arrested by Nazi police in December and sent to the concentration camp at Auschwitz, where he died nine months later.

The prewar glamour of the Ballet Russe, replete with its images of Russian exoticism, started to fade. Indeed, external upheaval seemed to coincide with a change in the company's internal artistic philosophy. The new "modern" dance was rising to the forefront of American stages, as choreographers such as Martha Graham and Doris Humphrey sought to translate into movement the emotion of inherently national or personal themes. For example, dances were created about the Great Depression and unemployment or about the American frontier, freedom, and equality. Denham responded to this outside impetus by inviting the young American dancer Agnes de Mille to create a work for the Ballet Russe in 1942. The result was *Rodeo*, a spirited depiction of Western ranch life.

Massine stayed with the group until 1943, when he left to form yet another offshoot company, Ballet Russe Highlights. Denham then appealed to Balanchine to rejuvenate his company. In contrast to the idiosyncratic ballets of Massine, Balanchine composed "neoclassic" ballets that were closely related to their music and structurally complex. He remained with the company until 1946, when he left to join Lincoln Kirstein in the formation of Ballet Society. These initial years of the Ballet Russe de Monte Carlo, guided by Blum and Denham with artistic direction by Massine and Balanchine, were profoundly instrumental in raising the American public's interest in the art of ballet.

Impact of Event

Blum and Denham's Ballet Russe de Monte Carlo made the United States excited about ballet. This was no small achievement, as the country was only slowly gaining an understanding of dance as legitimate entertainment and even art. The way had been paved by the frequent tours of Anna Pavlova's company and Diaghilev's Ballets Russes in the 1910's and 1920's. These dancers introduced the United States to the glamour and artistry of a European and Russian tradition that, until their visits, was mostly unfamiliar to Americans. The Ballet Russe de Monte Carlo capitalized on that earlier introduction, performing often enough to help a mass audience cultivate its tastes and emerging aesthetic values. The Ballet Russe's greatest asset was its familiarity to the public and its recognizable brand of showmanship.

Under Blum and Denham, the company preserved the Diaghilev mystique and kept the lauded Russian tradition before a star-struck public's eye. In so doing, however, it reinforced the notion that ballet was essentially a Russian art form. While some considered this a negative influence, it had the positive effect of elevating artistic standards for rising national and regional groups that struggled to compete with the Ballet Russe's established fame. Regardless of its international orientation, the Ballet Russe de Monte Carlo helped to establish ballet on a permanent, professional basis in the United States.

Probably the best-known choreographer of the decade, Massine created some of his finest pieces for the Ballet Russe de Monte Carlo. *Gaîeté Parisienne*, which premiered in 1938, featured fun-loving cancan dancers and madcap waiters in a Paris music hall. Massine also produced a 1930's series of notable symphonic ballets set to the music of such composers as Hector Berlioz, Ludwig van Beethoven, and Johannes Brahms. *Rouge et Noir* (1939), with music by Dmitri Shostakovich, incorporated color-drenched settings and costumes by Matisse. Described as "a vast mural in motion," the ballet was a discordant allegory representing the forces of destiny in shaping a man's life.

De Mille made a different kind of contribution to the Ballet Russe de Monte Carlo, affecting both the company and its audiences. *Rodeo*, which premiered to dozens of curtain calls, was the Ballet Russe's first truly notable attempt to incorporate American themes (although Massine had tried to do this on several occasions as well). *Rodeo* also employed an American composer, Aaron Copland, and American designer Oliver Smith.

Depicting a naïve cowgirl's fervent crush on a Kansas City cowboy, *Rodeo* was based on a realistic theme and believable characters—a true departure from the traditional ballet fantasies of swans, princes, and spirits. That this tribute to life in the United States could find success in the repertory of the Ballet Russe signified a new era in the company's history and the growing popularity of ballet as an American art form.

For his part, Balanchine brought an extensive repertory with him to the Ballet Russe de Monte Carlo. Among them were older works such as *Mozartiana* (1933) and *Serenade* (1935); recent works including the 1941 *Concerto barocco* (created for another fledgling company, the American Ballet); and new works, such as *Danses concertantes* (1944), choreographed especially for the Ballet Russe. Over the next two decades, choreographers including Frederick Ashton, Ruth Page, Ruthanna Boris, and Bronislava Nijinska added works to the repertory as well.

The Ballet Russe noticed the effects of other performing groups trying to build an audience at the same time. Often the company appeared in the same city or even the same theater with Kirstein's Ballet Caravan, a company that overtly attempted a nationalistic outlook. In other instances, the repertory of the Blum/Denham group overlapped with Colonel de Basil's Original Ballet. In their last parallel season, 1940-1941, the two companies both boasted versions of *Giselle*, *L'Après-midi d'un faune*, *Petrushka*, *Swan Lake*, and *Schéhérazade*. Presenter Sol Hurok, who then managed both Ballet Russe groups, ignored the coincidence because tickets continued to sell. Quite possibly, audiences did not distinguish between the two companies with similar names and repertoire; on the other hand, the presence and popularity of one company probably enhanced that of the other.

Under the guidance of Denham, the Ballet Russe de Monte Carlo remained active until 1962 (roughly a decade longer than de Basil's group). During that time, it became an essentially American company, both in its travels and its repertory. It partly preserved the spirit of the Diaghilev legend while absorbing some of the qualities of its new homeland in the process. Although after Massine's and then Balanchine's departure the company lacked definite artistic coherence, its very existence helped the American public to make (as one dancer remarked) "a habit out of art."

Bibliography

Amberg, George. *Ballet in America*. New York: Duell, Sloan and Pearce, 1949. An older publication, this provides three detailed chapters on the succession of companies called the Ballet Russe. All are useful; Blum and Denham's group is discussed in a chapter entitled "The Ballet Russe II-Massine's Ballet Russe." Appendix provides a comprehensive list of the company's repertoire.

Anderson, Jack. *The One and Only: The Ballet Russe de Monte Carlo*. New York: Dance Horizons, 1981. An excellent resource. The most complete volume devoted to the company that Blum, Denham, and Massine began. Traces the company through birth, reorganization, and final performances. Contains well-researched information, extensive notes, rosters of repertoire and dancers, and important primary source material.

Clarke, Mary, and Clement Crisp. "History of Ballet: Twentieth Century." In *The History of Dance*. New York: Crown, 1981. While this attempts to cover an obviously enormous topic in a comparatively small number of pages, it provides a helpful chronological sequence of developments in the art of ballet. The origins of the Ballet Russe and its implications are discussed in detail. Good for putting the company into the context of other dance events.

Massine, Léonide. *My Life in Ballet*. Edited by Phyllis Hartnoll. New York: St. Martin's Press, 1968. A complex autobiography of the choreographer, with heavy emphasis on descriptions of works. The influence of Sergei Diaghilev on the author is stressed. Contains an alphabetical catalog of ballets.

Maynard, Olga. "The Companies: Ballet Russe de Monte Carlo." In *The American Ballet*. Philadelphia: Macrae Smith Company, 1959. A look at the evolution of theatrical dance in the United States, with a section devoted to Blum and Denham's Ballet Russe. Describes company history, repertory, and dancers in detail.

Alecia C. Townsend

Cross-References

Duncan Interprets Chopin in Her Russian Debut (1904), p. 113; Pavlova First Performs Her Legendary Solo *The Dying Swan* (1907), p. 187; Diaghilev's Ballets Russes Astounds Paris (1909), p. 241; Fokine's *Les Sylphides* Introduces Abstract Ballet (1909), p. 247; *The Firebird* Premieres in Paris (1910), p. 269; *L'Après-midi d'un faune* Causes an Uproar (1912), p. 332; *The Rite of Spring* Stuns Audiences (1913), p. 373; Balanchine's *Serenade* Inaugurates American Ballet (1934), p. 974; Balanchine and Kirstein Make New York a World Center for Ballet (1946), p. 1301.

AMERICAN SCIENCE FICTION ENJOYS ITS GOLDEN AGE

Categories of event: Literature and journalism
Time: 1938-1950
Locale: The United States

The entry of scientifically trained writers and editors into the science-fiction magazine market significantly increased the quality of the genre, making the 1940's the Golden Age of American science fiction

Principal personages:

JOHN W. CAMPBELL, JR. (1910-1971), an engineer turned science-fiction writer who, as editor of *Astounding*, launched the careers of virtually all the great writers of the period

ISAAC ASIMOV (1920-1992), a scientist, science writer, and science-fiction writer first published, by Campbell, at the age of eighteen

ROBERT A. HEINLEIN (1907-1988), the most popular writer of the Golden Age, controversial for the strong political views in his fiction

THEODORE STURGEON (1918-1985), the most conscious prose stylist of the Golden Age, known for taking science fiction beyond various taboos

A. E. VAN VOGT (1912-   ), an influential writer of the 1940's whose ideas about non-Aristotelian logic form the premise for his stories, most with superhuman protagonists

Summary of Event

The story of America's Golden Age of science fiction is the story of the "pulp" magazines. Until the end of the 1940's, there was little science fiction in book form. Novels usually were serialized in the pulps, cheap magazines named for the rough, cheap, pulpy newsprint on which they were printed. The pulps were the major forum for adventure stories of the mystery, detective, Wild West, or sea adventure types. In the beginning, science fiction simply followed the established pulp adventure formula.

The roots of the Golden Age can be dated quite specifically. In April of 1926, the first magazine devoted exclusively to science fiction appeared: *Amazing Stories*, edited by Hugo Gernsback. To be sure, science fiction appeared in other periodicals, and Gernsback's science and technology monthlies, such as *Modern Electrics*, had published and encouraged science stories as early as 1911. In *Amazing Stories*, however, science fiction for the first time could find its own identity without competing with other forms of fiction. Gernsback's ideal was a fiction that combined literary skill with scientific plausibility. That ideal was not achieved for another decade, and then by another editor.

In September of 1937, a young engineer who had been publishing science fiction in *Amazing Stories* since 1930 (though Gernsback was no longer editor) was invited to take over as editor of a magazine with a similar title, *Astounding Stories.* His name was John W. Campbell, Jr., and he remained at the helm of the magazine through two name changes, until his death in 1971. He introduced more talented writers than any other editor of the period.

The writers who dominated science fiction's Golden Age of the 1940's were almost all first published by Campbell: Lester del Rey and L. Ron Hubbard in 1938; Isaac Asimov, Robert A. Heinlein, Fritz Leiber, Theodore Sturgeon, and A. E. van Vogt in 1939; C. M. Cornbluth in 1940; Hal Clement in 1942; Arthur C. Clarke in 1946; Poul Anderson in 1947; and Judith Merril in 1948. The few science-fiction writers of any stature who did not come through Campbell's stable in the 1940's— James Blish, Ray Bradbury, and Damon Knight—were influenced by those who did.

What made this period a Golden Age were Campbell's high editorial standards. By what he bought, Campbell told readers and writers what the new measure of science fiction would be. More important, he did not buy the scientifically absurd travesties scornfully dubbed "space opera" by science-fiction fans. In editorials and letters pages, his principles were articulated more directly: solid scientific plausibility and the same basic standards of literary quality set by any other genre.

Four writers who delivered both, and who came to dominate the genre, owed their start to Campbell. Their first stories in *Astounding* appeared in the same year, 1939. The first was Isaac Asimov, whose short story "Marooned Off Vesta" appeared in the March, 1939, issue. As a chemistry major at Columbia University preparing for graduate school, Asimov was confident of the scientific quality of his writing. Under Campbell's guidance, he soon developed a literary craftsmanship to match. Campbell's influence can be seen in Asimov's two most important contributions to science fiction: the three laws of robotics and the psychohistory that is the basis of his *Foundation* series. The three laws explained how robots would be governed in their relationships with humans. Psychohistory, involving prediction of the future and guidance of its course through human psychology, was born out of a discussion Asimov had with Campbell about Edward Gibbon's *The Decline and Fall of the Roman Empire* (1776-1788).

The second Campbell find of 1939 was Robert A. Heinlein, an older man who also had done graduate study in the sciences. His major contribution of the Golden Age, the "future history" concept, also owed much to Campbell's influence. Campbell had noticed that many of Heinlein's stories referred to the same characters and events, as if Heinlein had a coherent picture of a possible future. He had, and Campbell began referring to Heinlein's "future history" in the February, 1941, *Astounding*, eventually publishing an outline of it.

Campbell's influence on his third discovery of 1939, Theodore Sturgeon, may have been primarily a negative one. Campbell represented the moral taboos against which Sturgeon would later struggle to break free. Sturgeon's Golden Age work stayed within Campbell's guidelines, but the language and style of his stories of the 1940's pushed the limits of science fiction. Sturgeon was the first true stylist of American science fiction, with an ear for the sound and rhythm of prose. Sturgeon made science fiction sing without endangering its value as story or science.

A. E. van Vogt, the last science-fiction giant to emerge in 1939, is the only one of the four whose influence has not lasted. His novel *Slan*, serialized in *Astounding* in 1940, introduced the first of a series of superhuman heroes persecuted by an inferior majority who feared them. The stories were tremendously popular until it became uncomfortably obvious that they presented an ugly potential for science-fiction writers and readers to see themselves as just such misfits with a supposed superiority. Nevertheless, van Vogt remained one of Campbell's most popular writers through the end of the Golden Age.

Impact of Event

Although the beginning of the Golden Age was signaled by the advent of John Campbell as editor, its end was not a matter of Campbell stepping down, for he remained an influential editor until his last issue of *Analog* (formerly *Astounding*) in December, 1971. Several developments conspired, however, to lessen Campbell's influence, most of which had nothing to do with the nature of science fiction.

An obvious influence is World War II. Campbell lost his best writers to the war effort. The most scientifically gifted were assigned to war-related scientific research; Asimov and Heinlein, in fact, worked in the same laboratory in Philadelphia. Moreover, the government appropriated more than Campbell's writers. The war effort needed paper, and science fiction, like all literary fields, lost many magazine titles during the war. In 1941, there were twenty major science-fiction magazines; by the end of the war, there were seven.

The influence of a watershed event like World War II is not, of course, limited to personnel and paper. As Asimov pointed out in his essays on the Golden Age, a single moment at the end of the war changed the world's attitude toward science fiction forever. That was the world's abrupt entry into the atomic age, when atomic bombs were dropped on Hiroshima and Nagasaki. Suddenly, everything the science-fiction writers had suggested about atomic power became horribly real. The concurrent fight for Hitler's rocket scientists and the subsequent race with the Soviets to get into space quickly made the American public aware that science had caught up with fiction.

Another boom time for science fiction came immediately after the war. The major writers from before the war began writing again, and several new writers appeared. Many influential British science-fiction magazines appeared in 1946, emulating (and sometimes reprinting) the best stories of the American Golden Age. Arthur C. Clarke was published in these British pulps, although his first publication was in Campbell's *Astounding* in 1946.

The American magazines that had survived the war were stronger than ever, but new developments in publishing occurred in the last years of the Golden Age that would end the pulp magazines' exclusive hold on science fiction. The first was the advent of paperback publishing during the war. Many publishing houses at that time produced inexpensive newsprint versions of their best-selling titles, with spaces on the back cover for addressing. The intent was for civilians to buy them and mail them to servicemen overseas. The paperback form, without the address labels, remained after the war, and science fiction found a home in the paperback industry.

The end of the 1940's also saw Golden Age science fiction published for the first time in hardcover form, as short-story anthologies and novels previously serialized in the pulps. Four small presses specializing in science fiction sprang up in the 1940's: Advent, Fantasy, Gnome, and the horror-story publisher Arkham House. When these houses proved that it was economically feasible to publish science fiction outside pulp magazines, Doubleday became the first major "mainstream" publisher to try it. Charles Scribner's Sons launched a series of "boys' books" by Robert A. Heinlein, beginning with *Rocket Ship Galileo* in 1947.

For the most part, paperback and hardcover science fiction continued the style and themes of the Golden Age. Hugo Gernsback's emphasis on gadgets had changed to John Campbell's focus on people. The scope of stories broadened, however, following the Golden Age. Instead of reading about individuals encountering new ideas and technologies, readers began to see stories about the effects of those ideas and technologies on society at large. To put it another way, the science of science fiction had been drawn from the physical sciences in the Golden Age. In the second half of the twentieth century, it would be drawn from the social sciences, including anthropology, sociology, and psychology.

To some extent, Heinlein and Asimov, both Campbell-trained Golden Age writers, had anticipated this shift. From the beginning, many of Heinlein's stories dealt with psychological issues. Heinlein complained that editors were rejecting such stories for lack of "scientific" content. Asimov's *Foundation* series, similarly, had sociological and psychological premises in its use of psychohistory. Both Heinlein and Asimov, however, were trained in the physical sciences and always had some of that orientation in their stories.

The rise of two new and different science-fiction magazines, *Fantasy and Science Fiction* (Fall, 1949) and *Galaxy* (October, 1950), proclaimed the end of the Golden Age by taking science fiction in a new direction. A greater emphasis on prose style, the courting of mainstream writers, and an aim at a more adult audience characterized these two titles. Although it differed in many respects from the science fiction that preceded it, this newer fiction still showed the influence of the Golden Age, in which a successful balance was found between science and fiction.

Bibliography

Aldiss, Brian W. *Billion Year Spree.* New York: Schocken Books, 1973. A history of science fiction that takes into account concurrent movements in literature outside the field. Written by an important science-fiction writer of the later "New Wave" movement who is not blinded by nostalgia for the Golden Age.

Asimov, Isaac. *Asimov on Science Fiction.* New York: Avon Books, 1981. A collection of periodical essays, mostly editorials from Asimov's science-fiction magazine. Chapters are arranged by topic. Two chapters deal with the Golden Age in general, and two specifically with Campbell.

Fiedler, Leslie A., ed. *In Dreams Awake*. New York: Dell Books, 1975. A critical anthology of short stories, with helpful introductions to each section. Both the general introduction and the introduction to the Golden Age section contain vital insights regarding the period. Fiedler is the most important mainstream critic to write on the Golden Age.

Moskowitz, Sam. *Seekers of Tomorrow*. New York: Ballantine, 1967. A series of critical biographies of the major writers in science fiction up to the mid-1960's. Chapters on Asimov, Campbell, Heinlein, Sturgeon, and van Vogt are included. Moskowitz, the editor of Gernsback's last science-fiction magazine, knew most of the major writers professionally.

Wingrove, David. *The Science Fiction Source Book*. New York: Van Nostrand, 1984. The bulk of this book is an encyclopedia of science-fiction writers, rarely with more than one hundred words per entry. A brief history of science fiction by Brian W. Aldiss opens the book, and an essay on science-fiction magazines by Wingrove appears as an appendix. Both essays provide insight into the Golden Age.

John R. Holmes

Cross-References

Le Voyage dans la lune Introduces Special Effects (1902), p. 57; Lang Expands the Limits of Filmmaking with *Metropolis* (1927), p. 707; Huxley's *Brave New World* Reflects Fears About the Future (1932), p. 896; *Nineteen Eighty-Four* Portrays Total-itarianism and Mind Control (1949), p. 1421; Tolkien Publishes *The Lord of the Rings* (1954), p. 1607; Heinlein Publishes *Stranger in a Strange Land* (1961), p. 1883; Syndication Turns *Star Trek* into a Cult Classic (1972), p. 2260; The *Star Wars* Trilogy Redefines Special Effects (1977), p. 2391; Scott's *Blade Runner* Is a Visual Masterpiece (1982), p. 2486; *E.T.: The Extraterrestrial* Breaks Box-Office Records (1982), p. 2491.

OUR TOWN OPENS ON BROADWAY

Category of event: Theater
Time: February 4, 1938
Locale: New York, New York

Thornton Wilder's Our Town *opened on Broadway, signaling an American revolt against traditional "box set" staging that kept spectators at a distance from the play*

Principal personages:
> THORNTON WILDER (1897-1975), an American man of letters then best-known for his novels
> JED HARRIS (JACOB HOROWITZ, 1900-1979), an ambitious and successful producer

Summary of Event

Having achieved worldwide recognition at the early age of thirty with his second published novel, *The Bridge of San Luis Rey* (1927), Thornton Wilder, who had been fond of the theater since childhood, harbored an ambition to write plays. By the age of forty, Wilder had published two additional novels to somewhat mixed reviews and had begun to set his sights and expectations on the stage. As early as 1931, he had published a volume of collected short plays, and since then he had translated and adapted at least two European plays for performance on the Broadway stage for such recognized performers as Katharine Cornell and Ruth Gordon. Many of Wilder's good friends, including Gordon and her then-consort Jed Harris, were Broadway theater people, and Wilder, along with most of his students at the University of Chicago, then saw the theater as the most rewarding outlet (personally and professionally, if not financially) then available to creative writers.

Although not born to wealth, Wilder had acquired, with the unexpected success of his second novel, sufficient means and income not only to buy a house for his parents and siblings but also to travel wherever he pleased, with added remuneration along the way for lectures and other public appearances. While traveling in Europe, he had kept his eyes and ears open to various developments in the arts, particularly in the theater.

As a student at Yale University recently mustered out of stateside service during World War I, Wilder had been impressed by the minimalist, "theatricalist" staging of the French director Jacques Copeau, then on worldwide tour with the repertory company he had founded in 1913 at the Théâtre du Vieux-Colombier in Paris. While traveling through Europe in the mid-1930's, Wilder had reexperienced both French theatricalism (recently refreshed by the import of plays by Luigi Pirandello of Italy) and German expressionism; he had also discussed the elements of literary art at great length with the American expatriate poet and theorist Gertrude Stein, whom he first met when Stein came to Chicago as a visiting lecturer. Drawing eclectically from such "foreign" influences, as well as upon his own earlier experiments in playwriting, Wilder in late 1936 conceived and subsequently developed what would in time be seen as the quintessential American play, which would eventually be seen and heard by a larger worldwide audience than any previous American play.

Its plotting grounded in classical and medieval literature, *Our Town* highlights life and death in a New England town between 1899 and 1913. Time and place, however, soon recede into the background; spectators see a bare stage that remains to be furnished by their imaginations, with only occasional help from the Stage Manager, Wilder's one-man adaptation of the classical Greek chorus. Ladders and shelving are moved about the bare stage by the actors to simulate houses, rooms, and furniture; many props, though, are left to be imagined.

Years earlier, Wilder had accorded to his Yale and Broadway acquaintance Jed Harris the rights of refusal to his first full-length play. In fact, Wilder in 1937 had two such efforts in his briefcase: *Our Town* and *The Merchant of Yonkers* (which was reworked as 1954's *The Matchmaker* and later became the source of the 1964 musical comedy *Hello, Dolly!*). Harris, already well known for his devotion to the bottom line, was quick to choose *Our Town*, because it offered him and his actors, yet to be chosen, an easy compromise between creative freedom and practical economy. Harris had long sought to combine art with craft and profit. *Our Town*, perhaps a bit exotic for the prevailing Broadway taste, nevertheless opened at the Morosco Theater on Broadway early in 1938, with future film star Martha Scott in the pivotal role of Emily Webb.

Our Town got off to a slow start, but it gained momentum as the months passed. Failing to acquire the New York Drama Critics Circle Award for which it was nominated, the play nevertheless won the 1938 Pulitzer Prize for drama, with several amateur and student groups quite literally waiting in the wings for performance rights to be released in the spring of 1939. In 1940, *Our Town* was successfully filmed in Hollywood from a screenplay prepared free of charge by Wilder himself, who had rejected an earlier scenario written by playwright Lillian Hellman.

Impact of Event

A quarter century after its less-than-spectacular debut, *Our Town* had become perhaps the best-read and most frequently performed text in American dramatic history, known at least by name to most literate Americans and respected and performed by theater professionals in Europe. More than a few American theatergoers versed also in the European tradition yet jaded by repeated exposure to bad productions of *Our Town* in American high schools, where countless prom queens sought to play Emily, would first rediscover the play's abiding virtues through the medium of European productions, not only in a foreign country but also in a foreign language. After fifty years, the place of *Our Town* in the worldwide dramatic repertory was even more secure, proving the wisdom and foresight implicit in Wilder's apparently peculiar blend of foreign and domestic elements.

Unlike many of his predecessors and contemporaries writing for the Broadway stage, Wilder in *Our Town* rejected the somber, detailed realism of plot and staging, itself a European legacy most frequently associated with the work of the Norwegian Henrik Ibsen, whose work Wilder had himself translated and adapted for the stage. Breaking with recently hallowed tradition, following even more recent German and French trends that harked back to the ancient Greeks, Wilder presented his archetypal town, Grover's Corners, New Hampshire, as less fictional than mythical; the town is constructed and furnished through the collaboration of the play's spectators, who contribute their imaginations in order to make the play succeed as an act of communication.

"Do any human beings ever realize life while they live it?—every, every minute?" wonders Emily Webb Gibbs, dead in childbirth at age twenty-six. Emily is allowed by the Stage Manager to reexperience one full day in her short life, and she chooses her twelfth birthday, February 11, 1899. The Stage Manager replies to her question in the negative, adding, after a pause, "The saints and poets, maybe—they do some." The deceptive homespun simplicity of Wilder's carefully crafted dialogue earmarks the play as quintessentially American, but it also misleads some observers to find in the play only nostalgia and sentimentality. What Wilder has done, however, is to place each human life against the broadest possible background—described elsewhere in the play as "The Mind of God"—highlighting both the unique and the universal elements implicit in all human experience. The American audience for which he was writing is thus "repatriated" into the world community of theater, at once giving and receiving; thus does *Our Town* remain in the dramatic repertory, often revived in New York and elsewhere, despite the grumblings of those who still regard the play as sentimental.

The 1940 film version of the play, notable mainly for its impact upon the Hollywood career of William Holden, who starred as George Gibbs, was recirculated some forty years later on videotape. A somewhat ill-advised television musical from the mid-1950's, starring Frank Sinatra as the Stage Manager, remains in the collective American memory primarily as a consequence of its theme song, "Love and Marriage," performed and recorded by Sinatra. Televised productions of *Our Town*, without music, would continue well past Wilder's death in 1975, as would live productions both domestic and foreign. In the meantime, the creative freedom exercised by Wilder in *Our Town* would help to open up the American stage to greater measures of spectator participation. By the late 1960's, many American productions, on and off Broadway, were performed with few or no props and frequently on three-dimensional "thrust" stages, which were all but unknown to American audiences before their use for *Our Town* productions during the 1950's.

Beneath the surface of Wilder's plays, especially *Our Town*, lies an intelligent acquaintance with developing psychoanalytic theory. Wilder's biographers have documented his meetings during the 1930's with pioneer psychiatrist Sigmund Freud and Wilder's public denunciation of the elderly, terminally ill doctor's mistreatment by the Nazis. In retrospect, however, Wilder's theater seems to bear an even stronger imprint from Freud's erstwhile colleague Carl Gustav Jung's explorations of myth and the collective unconscious. In any case, Wilder, through the contemplation of death, managed in *Our Town* to breathe fresh life into the mainstream of American theater, and his contribution still survives him.

Bibliography

Burbank, Rex. *Thornton Wilder.* New York: Twayne, 1961. 2d ed. Boston: Twayne, 1978. Among the first full-length studies of Wilder's work, Burbank's volume remains authoritative, if not definitive; second edition may rely too much on Richard Goldstone's volume.

Cowley, Malcolm. *A Second Flowering.* New York: Viking, 1973. Cowley devotes a useful, perceptive chapter to Wilder's "universality" and its sources.

Goldstein, Malcolm. *The Art of Thornton Wilder.* Lincoln: University of Nebraska Press, 1965. A reader's guide to Wilder's novels and plays, notable for its brevity and insights.

Goldstone, Richard. *Thornton Wilder: An Intimate Portrait.* New York: E. P. Dutton, 1975. Prepared over the course of many years, originally planned—or presented—as a work of literary criticism, Goldstone's volume appeared in print shortly before Wilder's death, and much against Wilder's wishes. Wilder questioned Goldstone's critical talents, seriously opposed biographical studies of persons still living, and in effect forced a cancellation of Goldstone's original contract with Harper & Row, Wilder's own longtime publisher. Goldstone, meanwhile, had obtained access to a number of letters and other documents unavailable elsewhere. The published result, repudiated by its subject (who refused to read it), remains flawed but useful in places.

Haberman, Donald. *The Plays of Thornton Wilder: A Critical Study.* Middletown, Conn.: Wesleyan University Press, 1967. Revised from a Yale doctoral dissertation, Haberman's thematic study remains fresh and provocative, reaching back toward sources and forward toward results.

Harrison, Gilbert A. *The Enthusiast.* New York: Ticknor & Fields, 1983. A full-scale biography of Wilder, begun after his death and somewhat better grounded than Goldstone's, although short on literary analysis. Authoritative on production history of *Our Town.*

David B. Parsell

Cross-References

Freud Inaugurates a Fascination with the Unconscious (1899), p. 19; Jung Publishes *Psychology of the Unconscious* (1912), p. 309; Pirandello's *Six Characters in Search of an Author* Premieres (1921), p. 534; Sartre and Camus Give Dramatic Voice to Existential Philosophy (1940's), p. 1174; *Waiting for Godot* Expresses the Existential Theme of Absurdity (1953), p. 1573.

WELLES BROADCASTS *THE WAR OF THE WORLDS*

Category of event: Television and radio
Time: October 30, 1938
Locale: New York, New York

Orson Welles terrified thousands with his radio broadcast of The War of the Worlds, *proving the power of the medium in the hands of a genius*

Principal personages:
ORSON WELLES (1915-1985), a "boy genius" actor and director
JOHN HOUSEMAN (1902-1988), an actor, director, and acting teacher who worked with Welles
HOWARD KOCH (1902-   ), a scriptwriter and playwright

Summary of Event

On October 30, 1938, as newspaper headlines and radio news broadcasts carried threats of a coming world war, a Sunday night radio drama sent thousands of Americans into panic, hysteria, and flight. The young Orson Welles and his Mercury Theatre had already acquired a reputation in New York for unusual productions either under the aegis of the Federal Theatre Project or begun while he worked for the project. Welles staged a modern-dress *Julius Caesar* with characters in uniforms resembling those of German and Italian soldiers and a memorable production of *Macbeth* with an African-American cast. When Congress canceled funding for the Federal Theatre Project's production of Marc Blitzstein's political musical *The Cradle Will Rock* and the unpaid theater owners locked the doors, directors Welles and John Houseman led the cast and audience to a hastily rented theater down the street, making headlines and creating the first production of their new Mercury Theatre in 1937.

In the fall of 1938, Mercury Theatre had a broadcast spot on the Columbia Broadcasting System (CBS) opposite Edgar Bergen and Charlie McCarthy on the National Broadcasting Company (NBC) network. The theater company presented dramatic versions of classic stories. Welles decided, on the eve of All Hallows' Eve, to update H. G. Wells's novel *The War of the Worlds* (1898). As writer Howard Koch wrote later, nothing much of the original story, set in England in the nineteenth century, could be used except the invasion of the Martians and the subsequent destruction the "alien beings" wrought.

Koch had only days to write the script. Welles told him to use the format of a news broadcast. Without knowledge of the format of radio in the 1930's, it is difficult to understand how listeners could have been so gullible as to be fooled by the show; such knowledge illuminates how the Mercury Theatre broadcast could be so convincing.

Airtime had to be filled with sounds. An easy way to fill "dead" time, particularly at night, was to broadcast live dance music from hotel ballrooms across the country. Listeners were conditioned to interruptions of these programs for news bulletins. Commercial time slots were shorter and more flexible in their scheduling. Today, a viewer switching major network television channels during a commercial break simply finds more commercials. In 1938, a radio listener might have found another program in progress. The Mercury Theatre's fairly small audience was augmented on the first Chase and Sanborn commercial break by listeners from the Edgar Bergen and Charlie McCarthy show and others who tuned in in the midst of a Martian invasion.

These station switchers and other late arrivals missed the opening announcement: "The Columbia Broadcasting System and its affiliated stations present Orson Welles and the Mercury Theatre on the Air in a radio play by Howard Koch suggested by the H. G. Wells novel *The War of the Worlds.*" This was followed by the show's musical theme and the introduction of the "director of the Mercury Theatre and star of these broadcasts, Orson Welles." His lead-in to the script of "Invasion from Mars" was followed by a "weather report," and by what purported to be live dance orchestra music from downtown New York. The music was interrupted almost immediately by a bulletin announcing the "explosion of incandescent gas" on Mars, the result of the takeoffs of the invading vehicles.

The time left for the presentation of the entire invasion, after commercials and the introduction, was only forty-five minutes. This included events from the takeoffs from Mars to the spread of destruction across the United States and the ultimate destruction of the Martians, "slain, after all man's defenses had failed, by the humblest thing that God in His wisdom put upon this earth," to Orson Welles's closing line, "if your doorbell rings and nobody's there, that was no Martian . . . it's Halloween." Of an estimated six million listeners, approximately one million believed that Martians had landed. Thousands did not wait to hear that the aliens had been destroyed by bacteria or that the broadcast was the "radio version of dressing up in a sheet and saying 'Boo!' " as Welles said at the end of the show. Those thousands fled in their cars, called friends and families to warn them, rushed to churches, guarded property with guns, and headed for Grover's Mill, New Jersey, where "the Martians had landed," to lend a hand in the defense.

Meanwhile, at the CBS studio in New York, the actors were unaware of problems until the telephone rang as the closing theme played. Police officers entered and escorted the Mercury Theatre players out a back entrance. Although for several days it appeared that Orson Welles, in particular, was in serious trouble, good sense prevailed at last. The show had been announced as an adaptation, and it was clear that no one connected with it had intended to create a panic or had dreamed that listeners would confuse it with reality. Dorothy Thompson, an important political columnist of the day, wrote a supportive column, helping to calm the overreaction.

Headlines in major newspapers on October 31 indicated the seriousness of the panic of the night before. The headline of the *New York Daily News* proclaimed

"Fake Radio 'War' Stirs Terror Through U.S." *The New York Times* headed a front-page article "Radio Listeners in Panic, Taking War Drama as Fact." The piece was four columns in length, with four more columns on page 4 giving examples of reactions from all the New York City boroughs and upstate New York. The story ended with a statement from CBS "pointing out that the fictional character of the broadcast had been announced four times and had been previously publicized." Orson Welles was quoted as expressing "profound regret" and commenting that he had "hesitated about presenting it . . . because 'it was our thought that perhaps people might be bored or annoyed at hearing a tale so improbable.'"

Impact of Event

At the end of the broadcast season, Welles and some of his company went to Hollywood. Welles directed and starred in the classic film *Citizen Kane* (1941). He followed that success by directing *The Magnificent Ambersons* (1942), treasured by film buffs for its then-unusual camera angles. He was never to have such Hollywood success again, although he acted in a number of films and directed several more.

In *The Stranger* (1946, actor and director), costarring Loretta Young and Edward G. Robinson, he played a Nazi hiding under a false identity in a small American town. *The Lady from Shanghai* (1948, actor and director), in which he costarred with Rita Hayworth, is remembered for its climactic scene in a maze of mirrors. *Touch of Evil* (1958, actor and director) is considered to be cinematically innovative for its opening scene, shot in one long take as the camera takes the audience through the street of the town. This "long take" opening has since been used in any number of films, including the opening scene of *The Player* (1992).

Welles acted in a number of later films, his most memorable performance perhaps being in *The Third Man* (1949), in which his presence was always announced by the theme song, played solely on a theremin. Perhaps the best known of the many subsequent films in which he had acting roles were *Compulsion* (1959), based on the Leopold and Loeb case; *Moby Dick* (1956), in which he played Father Mapple in a tour de force scene, preaching to the crew of the *Pequod* before they sailed; *The Long Hot Summer* (1958); *Is Paris Burning?* (1966); *A Man for All Seasons* (1966); *Casino Royale* (1967); *Catch-22* (1970); and *Treasure Island* (1972). *Macbeth* (1948, actor and director) was a perhaps undeserved failure, as was his Falstaff film *Chimes at Midnight* (1966, actor and director), the title taken from William Shakespeare, who created the character of Falstaff. Self-exiled to Europe, where he worked for a number of years, he was "forgiven" by Hollywood in 1970, when he received an Academy Award for "supreme artistry and versatility in the creation of motion pictures." He received a life achievement award from the American Film Institute in 1975. Younger television audiences know Welles from frequent appearances on Johnny Carson's *The Tonight Show*, on which he told interesting stories and performed magic tricks (he was a skilled magician), and from a popular commercial for a winemaker in which he assured the audience that "we will sell no wine before its time."

John Houseman, codirector of Mercury Theatre, also followed Welles to Hollywood and produced a number of films including *The Blue Dahlia* (1946), *Julius Caesar* (1953), *Executive Suite* (1954), *Lust for Life* (1956), and *This Property Is Condemned* (1966). He acted in several films during this period, and for a number of years he taught acting at Juilliard in New York City, training a number of students who became immensely successful. It was his role, however, as a law professor in *The Paper Chase* (1973), followed by the same role in the popular television dramatic series based on the film, that made his face and voice so familiar to the general public that he was cast in a series of television commercials for an investment firm.

Through his work with the Federal Theatre Project, his own Mercury Theatre, and his film work, both as director and actor, Orson Welles left a permanent creative mark on American theatrical entertainment. Ironically, what may live longest with the general public is his "panic broadcast." In the 1980's, a television docudrama recreated the broadcast, interwoven with the fictional stories of characters who listened to it. Woody Allen included it in the film *Radio Days* (1987). In 1970, scriptwriter Howard Koch wrote a book about the experience, *The Panic Broadcast: Portrait of an Event.*

Two years after the Mercury Theatre broadcast, Princeton professor Hadley Cantril, funded by the Rockefeller Foundation, studied the reaction of selected interviewees who had been frightened by it. He published the results in *The Invasion from Mars* (1940). Not to be discounted was the political and economic environment of the times. The broadcast came during the last years of the Great Depression. On the eve of World War II, Americans were accustomed to listening to news broadcast from Europe; they heard Adolf Hitler himself speaking to the German people and their answering cry of "Sieg Heil!" They saw newsreels of German troops. They had vicariously experienced the Spanish Civil War, in which the fascist forces had "tested the guns" for the invasions of Poland, Czechoslovakia, Holland, Belgium, and France. Americans thus had reason to be apprehensive. Their hearts jumped when they heard "we interrupt this program."

A wit said at the time that the panic happened because "all the intelligent people were listening to Charlie McCarthy." It was not that simple. The people taken in were a cross-section of the American citizenry. Many of them missed the opening announcement and had swung into wild action before the repetition of the announcement at the commercial break. Many made some attempt to check, calling neighbors or family. If those people were not home, the callers' fears were confirmed. If they could not get through to an authority because others were trying to make similar calls, the busy signal confirmed the fear. Some listeners did switch stations and realized the truth. Others who switched reasoned that the other stations just had not received word yet. Some of the more eschatological thought that the invasion was the justified end of the world. One man was pleased; he hoped his mother-in-law would be scared to death. Another interviewee said that, when he was convinced of the reality of the "invasion," he was struck by "how pretty all things on earth seemed."

Professor Cantril concluded that anxiety about impending war was a less important cause than the "highly disturbed economic conditions many Americans have experienced for the past decade, the consequent unemployment, the prolonged discrepancies between family incomes, the inability of both young and old to plan for the future [that] have engendered a widespread feeling of insecurity." Americans had become highly suggestible, he added.

Those who grew up on the medium of radio might add that listening enlarged the powers of the imagination, and that Orson Welles had a voice made for radio. The influence of television seems to be more subliminal, a sort of delayed reaction to sound bites and commercials, as Americans see anew each presidential election year.

Mars, the red planet of war, still holds a fascination for most people, who were disappointed when a planetary probe found no evidence of life. Scientists continue to listen for sounds of intelligent life in the universe; many people believe that the occasional UFO sightings are of craft from outer space. The frightening extraterrestrial has become, to some, a friendly character such as "E.T." Others continue to be thrilled by portrayals of menacing aliens in popular books and films. The broadcast of *The War of the Worlds* illustrated an ongoing willingness and ability to believe.

Bibliography

Brady, Frank. *Citizen Welles: A Biography of Orson Welles.* New York: Scribner, 1989. Contains a large section on *The War of the Worlds* broadcast and its aftermath. Primary and secondary bibliographies, index.

Cantril, Hadley. *The Invasion from Mars.* Princeton, N.J.: Princeton University Press, 1940. An account of the public panic, followed by Cantril's funded study of some of the listeners and his conclusions. Includes the broadcast script.

Houseman, John. *Run-Through.* New York: Simon & Schuster, 1972. Houseman writes entertainingly about his own career, which included work with Welles in the Federal Theatre Project and Mercury Theatre, including the famous broadcast. He also recounts their parting in Hollywood.

Koch, Howard. *As Time Goes By: Memoirs of a Writer.* New York: Harcourt Brace Jovanovich, 1979. Koch's autobiography includes an account of his involvement with John Houseman, Orson Welles, and the Mercury Theatre. Koch is most famous for writing *Casablanca* (1942) with Philip and Julius Epstein, and he draws his title from that experience.

_____. *The Panic Broadcast: Portrait of an Event.* Boston: Little, Brown, 1970. An account by the scriptwriter for the broadcast of the origin of the script, the night of the broadcast, and the results of the broadcast. Contains the script, photographs of the studio performance, reproductions of news accounts, and cartoons about the broadcast.

Katherine Lederer

Cross-References

Radio Programming Dominates Home Leisure (1930's), p. 828; The Federal Theatre Project Promotes Live Theater (1935), p. 989; American Science Fiction Enjoys Its Golden Age (1938), p. 1094; Welles's *Citizen Kane* Breaks with Traditional Filmmaking (1941), p. 1200; The *Star Wars* Trilogy Redefines Special Effects (1977), p. 2391.

THE CLASSIC *THE WIZARD OF OZ* OPENS

Category of event: Motion pictures
Time: 1939
Locale: Hollywood, California

On August 15, 1939, The Wizard of Oz premiered in Hollywood at Grauman's Chinese Theater, catapulting Judy Garland into stardom and beginning a lasting love affair with audiences

Principal personages:
MERVYN LEROY (1900-1987), a film director and producer
ARTHUR FREED (1894-1973), a producer and songwriter who worked as Leroy's assistant on *The Wizard of Oz*
VICTOR FLEMING (1883-1949), the principal director of *The Wizard of Oz*
JUDY GARLAND (FRANCES GUMM, 1922-1969), a singer and actor who starred in *The Wizard of Oz*
RAY BOLGER (1904-1987), a song-and-dance man who played the Scarecrow in *The Wizard of Oz*
JACK HALEY (1899-1979), the actor who played the Tin Woodman in *The Wizard of Oz*
BERT LAHR (IRVING LAHRHEIM, 1895-1967), an actor and vaudevillian whose performance as the Cowardly Lion in *The Wizard of Oz* received great acclaim

Summary of Event

Samuel Goldwyn sold the film rights to L. Frank Baum's classic 1900 children's book *The Wizard of Oz* to Metro-Goldwyn-Mayer (MGM) for seventy-five thousand dollars on June 3, 1938. The studio had, however, been preparing to film the story for several months previous to the sale. As early as January, 1938, Mervyn Leroy had entrusted William Cannon with the task of preparing the story for the screen; the first of the twelve screenwriters who worked on the script was Irving Brecher. Others included Herman Mankiewicz, Ogden Nash, Noel Langley, Herbert Fields, Samuel Hoffenstein, Florence Ryerson, and Edgar Allan Woolf; Langley, Ryerson, and Woolf received screen credit. Harold Arlen and Edgar Harburg wrote the music and lyrics; they had been hired in May. The model for both the writers and for the composers was Walt Disney's *Snow White and the Seven Dwarfs* (1937), which had been extremely successful just a year earlier. From the beginning, though, MGM did not apparently expect to make much money on the live-action fantasy. Instead this was to be the studio's "prestige picture" for the year.

When the film began production, Norman Taurog was the director, but he left within a short time to direct the Mickey Rooney vehicle *The Adventures of Huckleberry Finn* (1939). Richard Thorpe, director of a few *Tarzan* films, followed briefly, then for seven days came George Cukor. Cukor, like his successor Victor Fleming, left *The Wizard of Oz* to work on *Gone with the Wind* (1939). Finally, King Vidor completed the sequences in Kansas that begin and end the film. On-screen credit went to Victor Fleming as the film's director, and it seems clear that he did the lion's share of the director's work. Yet the many writers, directors, producers, and assorted others who worked on the film show just how much of a collaborative effort filmmaking was in the large studios of the 1930's and 1940's.

Much of the film's appeal stems from the performances of its stars, but these, too, changed before the final version was cut. At the outset, Louis B. Mayer attempted to borrow Shirley Temple from Twentieth Century-Fox to play the role of Dorothy, but Fox head Darryl Zanuck refused. The alternative was Judy Garland, the choice of both Leroy and his assistant Arthur Freed. Garland was sixteen years old and more mature than the Dorothy of the book, but with tight-fitting brassiere and pigtails, she began to look the part. At first, the Scarecrow and the Tin Woodman were to be played by Buddy Ebsen and Ray Bolger, respectively, but after much complaining by Bolger, the two actors changed roles. Before long, Ebsen developed an allergy to the makeup needed to play the Tin Woodman, and he was replaced by Jack Haley. The part of the Cowardly Lion was apparently always intended for Bert Lahr. Gale Sondergaard tested for the part of the Wicked Witch, but the role eventually went to Margaret Hamilton. A number of actors were considered for the role of the Wizard. Leroy wanted Ed Wynn, but he turned the part down because he thought it was too small (Wynn based his decision on an early version of the script in which the Wizard's part was considerably smaller than in the final version). Others mentioned for the part included Wallace Beery, W. C. Fields, Hugh Herbert, and Charles Winninger. The final choice was Frank Morgan.

Production began in the fall of 1938 and was completed in the spring of 1939. Several features of the final film are noteworthy: the wardrobe and makeup, the special effects, and the music. The head of the MGM wardrobe department was Gilbert Adrian, and his counterpart in makeup was Jack Dawn. To give the effect of a straw man, the makeup people fashioned a light mask of baked rubber made to simulate burlap. For the Tin Woodman, a suit of buckram covered over with metallic cloth painted silver served to give the illusion of a tin man. Bert Lahr wore fifty pounds of genuine lion skins. Virtually all the characters endured many changes in costume and makeup. For example, the witch's costume at various times included sequins and cowled headdress, fright wig and false nose, several hairstyles, and green skin. For the diminutive Munchkins who populate the land of Oz, Adrian and Dawn concocted costumes and makeup that would make these already small people appear even smaller than they were. Oversized belts, hats, buttons, and so on accentuated the smallness of the Munchkins. The Munchkin makeup required wigs, prosthetic items, and skullcaps. Dawn organized an assembly line to manage the makeup of the Munchkins, a kind of real-life echo of the sprucing up of the Cowardly Lion, Scarecrow, Tin Woodman, and Dorothy that takes place in Emerald City in the film.

Equally complex were the special effects. The film contains many fantastic effects: a tornado that sweeps Dorothy and her dog Toto into the land of Oz, a good witch who travels in a bubble, flying monkeys, talking and apple-throwing trees, a flying witch, a huge spectral appearance by the Wizard, and a melting witch. In charge of special effects for the picture was A. Arnold (Buddy) Gillespie, and he and his cohorts used five of the six types of special effects available at the time: miniatures, back projection, optical effects, matte painting, and full-scale mechanical effects. Some of the flying monkeys were full-scale effects; various types of rear and front projection created the effects of the Wizard's disembodied head and the head of the witch in her large crystal ball. The witch on her broomstick writing in the sky was a miniature; the witch was, in reality, three-eighths of an inch high, and her broomstick was a hypodermic needle filled with milk and dye. Matte painting was used to create the panorama of Emerald City and parts of the witch's castle. Other effects included the Cowardly Lion's swishing tail, which was controlled by a man on a catwalk with a fishing pole the line of which was attached to the tail; dry ice and an elevator simulated the melting witch. Elevators proved dangerous, and Margaret Hamilton, the wicked witch, was injured using one in her departure from Munchkinland near the beginning of the film. On the second take, the flames that accompanied her departure set alight her hat and broom, and her face and right hand were burned. She left the set for six weeks.

Perhaps the most complicated effect in the film was the tornado. The tornado was a muslin sock connected to a slot in a floor and to a steel gantry at the top of a stage. The gantry had a small car that could zigzag horizontally. From the bottom, fuller's earth and compressed air were fed into the tornado to create the illusion of a great wind whipping up dust as it crossed the prairie. Eight-by-four panels of glass with cotton balls pasted on them served to heighten the effect of a stormy sky. Once photographed, the film of the tornado was projected to form a backdrop for the actors scurrying to shelter.

Special effects, wardrobe, and makeup all went into the creation of the film's magic, but improvements in technology have allowed filmmakers, if not to better the effects of *The Wizard of Oz*, at least to provide more spectacular ones. In addition to its effects, however, *The Wizard of Oz* contained a stunning musical score. From romantic ballads to jaunty dance numbers to ebullient celebratory choruses, the music and songs were various and vibrant. The score was the creation of Harold Arlen (music) and Edgar Harburg (lyrics), and their genius provided not only memorable songs and tunes but also songs that were integrated with the plot development. "Somewhere over the Rainbow," for example, clearly sets the wistful tone for a young girl whose life is as uneventful as the sepia-colored print of the scene indicates. The lyrics prepare viewers for Oz as a dream world ("a land that I heard of once in a lullaby") and a land of color ("skies are blue," "troubles melt like lemon drops," "bluebirds," and, of course, the rainbow image itself). Dorothy's longing for color, adventure, and release found expression in the song. In a similar way, the songs of the Scarecrow, Tin Woodman, and Cowardly Lion filled in their personalities. Unlike other musicals of the 1930's, *The Wizard of Oz* contained no large-scale production numbers that existed merely for their own sake. The closest the film came to such a scene was in the Lion's "King of the Forest" number; even that song, however, indicated the Cowardly Lion's inner goodness. The scene also served to provide a playful interlude before the climactic encounter with the Wizard.

Such lively music and words deserved equally lively choreography, and in this, too, the film excelled. Leroy wanted Busby Berkeley to handle the dance numbers, but Bobby Connolly came from Warner Bros. to take over as dance director. His dance numbers were visually imaginative. The sprightly nursery rhyme effect of "The Wicked Witch Is Dead" sequence far outshone similar sequences in Laurel and Hardy's *Babes in Toyland* (1934), and Ray Bolger's floppy footwork as the Scarecrow became justly famous. Interestingly, much of Bolger's first dance was cut to keep the film from running too long.

The completed film was a triumph of cinematic art that demonstrated how the collaboration of many people could produce a serendipitous masterpiece. Released near the end of 1939, *The Wizard of Oz* summed up much of what went on in the films of the 1930's. The Depression-weary lives of middle Americans were visible in the opening and closing sequences in Kansas, while the lavish worlds of escape Hollywood was famous for producing in the decade appeared in the colorful Oz sequences. Both the fantasy and the "reality" in the film expressed the need for self-reliance and cooperation; all one needs, the film implied, is a little ingenuity and pluck to succeed. In a year in which high romance was the order of the day— witness such 1939 productions as *Gone with the Wind, Stagecoach, Ninotchka, Destry Rides Again, Only Angels Have Wings*, and *Mr. Smith Goes to Washington—The Wizard of Oz* provided romance enough for everyone.

Impact of Event

The film was more successful than anyone involved with its making expected. Shortly after its release, the market was flooded with *The Wizard of Oz* memorabilia: party masks, rag dolls, wooden dolls, rubber dolls, Valentine cards, stationery, dart games. Such merchandise continued to sell decades later; clearly, the public, in North America and around the world, took the film to its heart.

It also took Judy Garland to its heart; the film had a profound impact on her career. She signed her first contract with MGM on September 27, 1935, only three months after her thirteenth birthday. *The Wizard of Oz* was her eighth film and the one that catapulted her to worldwide fame. For her role in the film, she won a special Academy Award as the best juvenile performer of the year. The honor was well deserved; Garland played her part with a conviction and a depth of feeling that struck a chord in audiences. MGM knew it had a star on its hands, and the studio's story department set about finding musical properties for her. In the next two years, she starred in seven films. As late as 1968 (six months before she died), Garland guest-hosted a television talk show and was surprised by the appearance of Margaret Hamilton. Garland asked her wicked witch adversary from *The Wizard of Oz* to "Laugh! Just do that wicked, mean laugh!" Hamilton did as she was asked, and the audience went wild.

The television audience's reaction stands as testimony to the continuing hold of the film on viewers. Beginning in 1956, *The Wizard of Oz* began appearing regularly on television. The Columbia Broadcasting System (CBS) first aired it on Saturday, November 3; it was the first film MGM sold to network television. CBS ran it, using a variety of guest hosts (including Bert Lahr, Red Skelton, Richard Boone, Dick Van Dyke, and Danny Kaye), until 1967, when the National Broadcasting Company (NBC) bought the rights. In 1976, CBS reclaimed the rights, and the film continues to appear each year. In 1980, *The Wizard of Oz* appeared on videocassette for the first time; in 1989, a special fiftieth-anniversary videocassette appeared.

The Wizard of Oz has also had an impact on American films. Such films as *Alice Doesn't Live Here Anymore* (1975), *Star Wars* (1977), *E.T.: The Extraterrestrial* (1982), *Gremlins* (1984), and *Good Morning, Vietnam* (1987) all pay homage to the 1939 film. Robert Altman paid silent tribute to the film in *Brewster McCloud* (1970) when he tracked his camera to the feet of the character played by Margaret Hamilton (she has just been killed); she is wearing ruby slippers. In 1978, Diana Ross starred in *The Wiz*, an all-black urban version of *The Wizard of Oz* adapted from the Broadway hit of 1975. Two other film versions of Oz stories also appeared: the animated *Journey Back to Oz* (released in 1974, although made in 1964), and *Return to Oz* (1985).

The Wizard of Oz is probably the most familiar film in history. What MGM referred to in 1939 as the film's "kindly philosophy" has not gone out of fashion. Audiences young and old continue to seek escape to fantastic worlds in motion pictures, looking for places where good always triumphs over evil and people get what they desire.

Bibliography

Billman, Carol. " 'I've Seen the Movie': Oz Revisited." In *Children's Novels and the Movies*, edited by Douglas Street. New York: Frederick Ungar, 1983. A comparison of the book with the film. Argues that the film reduces the clutter of the book and simplifies the plot and that the visual splendor of the film helps it to surpass the book, despite the fact that both are moralistic. Notes that the artificiality of the effects adds to the film's (and Oz's) fantastic quality.

Fricke, John, Jay Scarfone, and William Stillman. *"The Wizard of Oz": The Official Fiftieth Anniverary Pictorial History.* New York: Warner Books, 1989. A detailed account of the making of *The Wizard of Oz* and its subsequent impact. Filled with rare photographs of the players and professionals associated with MGM, of Oz memorabilia and merchandise, and of memos and letters related to the film and its creation. Bibliography.

Harmetz, Aljean. *The Making of "The Wizard of Oz."* New York: Alfred A. Knopf, 1977. A detailed account of how a major studio worked in the heyday of the Hollywood studio system. Many interviews with the people who worked on the film, and many behind-the-scenes photographs. A more complete account of the special effects than in the Fricke, Scarfone, and Stillman volume. Index and bibliography.

Langley, Noel, Florence Ryerson, and Edgar Allan Woolf. *"The Wizard of Oz" : The Screenplay.* New York: Delta, 1989. The first publication of the entire film script, including the addition of scenes and songs cut from the final version. Introduction and notes by Michael Patrick Hearne. Contains film stills and other photographs. Hearne's introduction chronicles, in brief, the making of the film.

McClelland, Doug. *Down the Yellow Brick Road.* New York: Pyramid Books, 1976. Tells the story of the legends behind the making of the film. For a general audience rather than for aficionados. Many film stills.

Roderick McGillis

Cross-References

Le Voyage dans la lune Introduces Special Effects (1902), p. 57; Hollywood Enters Its Golden Age (1930's), p. 822; Lubitsch's *The Merry Widow* Opens New Vistas for Film Musicals (1934), p. 941; Disney Releases *Snow White and the Seven Dwarfs* (1937), p. 1053; *Gone with the Wind* Premieres (1939), p. 1154; The *Star Wars* Trilogy Redefines Special Effects (1977), p. 2391; *E.T.: The Extraterrestrial* Breaks Box-Office Records (1982), p. 2491.

FORD DEFINES THE WESTERN IN *STAGECOACH*

Category of event: Motion pictures
Time: 1939
Locale: The United States

John Ford's Stagecoach *combined realistic characterizations, dramatic special effects, and impressive location filming to define the Western as both popular culture and serious art form*

Principal personages:

JOHN FORD (SEAN O'FEENEY, 1895-1973), the director of more than one hundred feature films

JOHN WAYNE (MARION MICHAEL MORRISON, 1907-1979), an actor who attained stardom with his performance in *Stagecoach*

CLAIRE TREVOR (1909-   ), an actress who played both character and glamour roles in the 1930's and 1940's

THOMAS MITCHELL (1892-1962), a stage actor whose versatility was evident in many films

YAKIMA CANUTT (1895-1986), a rodeo cowboy who turned to a long career as a Hollywood stuntman and stunt director

WALTER WANGER (WALTER FEUCHTWANGER, 1894-1968), an independent producer and sometime executive at several Hollywood studios

Summary of Event

The camera seemed to jump forward toward the young cowboy standing by the roadside. The cowboy held a Winchester rifle in one hand and a saddle in the other, and his rugged face suddenly filled the screen with a compelling mixture of confidence and vulnerability. In this single shot, less than ten seconds in duration, director John Ford notified his audience and film critics that *Stagecoach* was no ordinary Western and that John Wayne was no ordinary film personality.

The film's content involved much more than cowboys, Apaches, chases and shootouts. Dudley Nichols' screenplay was based on Ernest Haycox's short story "The Last Stage to Lordsburg," which appeared originally in *Collier's* magazine. Nichols placed the emphasis on both pathos and humor to underline the human feelings and personal struggles of his protagonists. An outlaw with a conscience and a prostitute with a yearning for respectability established a poignant ambiguity in the film's two main characters. Nichols' screenplay and Ford's direction stressed the interaction of nine people thrown together in a perilous journey from the frontier town of Tonto to Lordsburg. In their cramped quarters, the passengers were divided into two classes. The elite consisted of the pompous, overbearing banker Gatewood (Berton Churchill), the suave Southern gentleman-gambler Hatfield (John Carradine), and the pregnant wife of an Army officer, Lucy Mallory (Louise Platt). Of a lower social standing than this trio were the prostitute Dallas (Claire Trevor), the outlaw Ringo (John Wayne) in custody of Sheriff Wilcox (George Bancroft), the bumbling whiskey drummer Peacock (Donald Meek), and the buffoonish, verbose stage driver Buck (Andy Devine). Thomas Mitchell won an Academy Award for his performance as an alcoholic doctor, Doc Boone, fallen from the grace of professional respectability because of his drinking.

The story line had a strong populist bent. By the end of the film, the self-righteous Gatewood was arrested for embezzlement, Hatfield died in an Apache attack, and Lucy Mallory discovered her indebtedness to her social inferiors, as Doc Boone, Dallas, and Ringo helped her through childbirth. The wrongly accused Ringo revealed his physical prowess, strength of character, and sense of justice as he saved the stagecoach from the Apaches and then, with the blessing of Sheriff Wilcox, wreaked vengeance on the wastrel Plummer brothers, the murderers of his father and brother. The film thus upended the social pyramid. Right-minded Ringo and good-hearted Dallas, their characters redeemed, rode off together on a buckboard to his ranch in Mexico, while Gatewood went to jail.

In a time of autocratic studio bosses and meddlesome producers, Ford was fortunate to have Walter Wanger finance the film as an independent production through United Artists. Wanger allowed Ford considerable latitude as director, and Ford used this opportunity well. The visual imagery was impressive, as Ford captured the large vistas of Monument Valley with sweeping camera angles and deep-focus shots. In the confinements of the stagecoach and the way station, the camera helped to establish class distinctions through the physical and emotional distance between the characters. Except for the use of Monument Valley, however, none of these devices was original with *Stagecoach*. Therefore, many film critics and historians in recent decades have seen Ford's work as less innovative than the contemporary critical and public response indicated. Within these limits, however, it must be noted that *Stagecoach* was an exceptional achievement in a specific set of circumstances. Ford's accomplishment was to bring so many new techniques into one film, which was, after all, a Western—a genre that had become a cliché-ridden, low-budget, mass-produced Hollywood staple during the Depression years. Ford's directorial virtuosity surprised and stimulated audiences and critics, who had come to expect little innovative artistry in Westerns.

Ford had a good ear for folk and popular music and worked well with Richard Hageman, whose Academy Award-winning score offered carefully selected tunes drawn from America's rural traditions. The film's songs varied from Stephen Foster's "Jeanie with the Light Brown Hair" to honky-tonk tunes typical of frontier saloons and bordellos. Hageman's music helped to establish the film's sympathy for Dallas and Ringo and appealed to a broad public taste for symphonic versions of familiar tunes.

Stagecoach launched John Wayne to more than stardom; he became the archetypal Western hero whose film persona assumed mythic proportions in popular culture. Wayne had broken into motion pictures in 1926 as a stunt man and had made a series of generally unimpressive Westerns and other action-adventure films. By the mid-1930's, he had steady work as the lead in cowboy films for Monogram and Republic, two of Hollywood's minor studios. Fortunately for Wayne, he made a favorable impression on Ford, who sensed the lanky ex-collegiate football player's potential as a dominant screen personality. Wayne and Ford worked well together on *Stagecoach*. Even a casual viewing of the film indicates that the actor's laconic voice and commanding presence somehow combined with a sincerity and an occasional suggestion of vulnerability to create a powerful personal image. Ford's camera captured all these qualities in Wayne's rendition of Johnny Ringo.

Few directors in motion-picture history have had the leeway granted to director Ford by producer Wanger, and even fewer have been able to translate an opportunity for creative expression into such a large financial and artistic success. The story itself was a reflection of Ford's sympathy for the common people, a perspective also brought to the screen in his films *The Grapes of Wrath* (1940) and *How Green Was My Valley* (1941). Ford's personal touch was especially visible in *Stagecoach*, a major event in his career and in the history of Hollywood Westerns.

Impact of Event

Stagecoach rescued the Western from the wilderness of quickly made, often hackneyed B-films and the pristine Arcadia of music and dance inhabited by the singing cowboy. These two types of films had their strengths and their loyal fans, but the mix of cinematic creativity and social realism in *Stagecoach* set a standard for quality and box-office appeal that even the most profit-oriented studio could not ignore.

Yet Ford's work was so unique for the time that few producers and directors attempted to copy *Stagecoach*. Instead, they began to explore the genre with feature attractions as vehicles for established stars, proven directors, and the new technology of Technicolor. "Its enormous popularity was understandable," wrote film historian William K. Everson, adding that "What was surprising was that none of its immediate offspring even attempted to duplicate its artistic standards, but were content to be big 'shows.'" Examples abounded in the early 1940's. Director Raoul Walsh reunited Wayne and Trevor in *Dark Command* (1940) for Republic Pictures. William Wyler's *The Westerner* (1940) starred Gary Cooper and Walter Brennan for United Artists, and Fritz Lang's *Western Union* (1941) featured Robert Young, Randolph Scott, and Technicolor for Twentieth Century-Fox.

Ford's use of Monument Valley prodded other directors to film on location in the broad expanses of the American West. Among the many following in Ford's footsteps were Raoul Walsh, who placed Errol Flynn on the rolling plains to film George Custer's fatal blunders in *They Died with Their Boots On* (1941). King Vidor's *Duel in the Sun* (1946) presented the spectacle of a massive cattle drive, and George Stevens captured the grandeur of the Grand Tetons in *Shane* (1953).

Stuntman and second-unit director Yakima Canutt made a major contribution to *Stagecoach* in the film's exciting chase sequence, which also gave a major boost to his own career. Canutt was already a Hollywood veteran in 1939, but *Stagecoach* put his services in great demand. Westerns and other types of films as well began to use more complex and difficult stunts that called for the skills and experience of Canutt. He continued to be active as a stuntman into the 1940's and worked as a stunt director for many years thereafter. His later films included *Ben Hur* (1959) and *El Cid* (1961).

In *Stagecoach*, Ford elicited a strong performance from John Wayne, at the time a little-known performer. From the release of *Stagecoach* when he was thirty-two until his death in 1979, Wayne projected the image of the iron-willed, two-fisted man of action with an unerring sense of justice. The hero of the common folk in *Stagecoach*, he starred as an Army officer in Ford's cavalry trilogy and made a deep imprint on the public mind with his roles as courageous soldiers in several films about World War II. Because of his immense popularity over four decades, Wayne had a larger symbolic importance than most Hollywood stars. Known as a political conservative in his last years, Wayne also had another side to his image: the champion of the underdog, especially in his first major characterization as Johnny Ringo and in later Westerns such as *True Grit* (1969), *The Cowboys* (1972), and *The Shootist* (1976).

Stagecoach made John Ford the master of the mature Western. His direction of *My Darling Clementine* in 1946 brought the shootout at the O.K. Corral to the screen in impressive fashion, but he enjoyed even greater success with his cavalry trilogy *Fort Apache* (1948), *She Wore a Yellow Ribbon* (1949), and *Rio Grande* (1950). John Wayne appeared as the central character in all three films. In comparison with Wayne's roles in the B-Westerns of the 1930's, these characters were far from one-dimensional cowboys. In particular, *Rio Grande* explored the troubled relationship between professional commitment to military discipline and the importance of wife and family. In the end, the brutality of the frontier was decisive; the dominant male patriarch discovered that he needed his wife and that his son could stand on his own.

While critics and historians continue to debate the precise place of *Stagecoach* in the evolution of serious cinema, the film itself remains a durable and impressive contribution to American motion-picture history. Ford successfully combined popular culture with high culture through his creative use of camera, visual imagery, and character. Other directors such as Orson Welles, Akira Kurosawa, and Kihado Okamoto, as well as numerous film commentators such as William K. Everson and Andrew Sarris, have testified to the lasting importance of *Stagecoach* as a serious achievement in motion-picture history.

Bibliography

Bogdanovich, Peter. *John Ford.* Berkeley: University of California Press, 1968. Lengthy interviews with Ford that cover his career. Only brief comments on *Stagecoach*, but important for Ford's sometimes blunt and unexpected opinions on his own films.
Edgerton, Gary. "A Reappraisal of John Wayne." *Films in Review* 37 (May, 1986): 282-289. Emphasizes Wayne's instinctive appeal to American audiences as the

embodiment of the nineteenth century ideal of rugged honesty.

Everson, William K. *A Pictorial History of the Western Film.* New York: Citadel Press, 1969. Well-written general survey with carefully chosen illustrations from film stills and posters. Chapters 10 and 11 are especially helpful in assessing the Hollywood background for *Stagecoach* and the film's impact on the motion-picture industry of the 1940's and 1950's.

Fenin, George N., and William K. Everson. *The Western, from Silents to the Seventies.* Rev. ed. New York: Grossman, 1973. Greater factual detail and analytical depth than the previous citation, with more text and fewer illustrations. Chapters 9 through 13 cover the period from 1920 to 1950, ranging from the big studio productions to the action B-Westerns and singing cowboy films that were typical of the 1930's.

Gallagher, Tag. *John Ford: The Man and His Films.* Berkeley: University of California Press, 1986. Thorough academic treatment of Ford and his work. Clearly written, though with some technical language. Pages 143 to 162 contain an analysis of *Stagecoach*; Gallagher also discusses the film throughout the text in comparison with other Ford films. Covers Ford's private life as well as his Hollywood career. Careful research reflected in extensive and informative footnotes and filmography.

Place, J. A. *The Western Films of John Ford.* Secaucus, N.J.: Citadel Press, 1974. Useful compendium of Ford's Westerns, with descriptive commentary and representative illustrations.

Parks, Rita. *The Western Hero in Film and Television: Mass Media Mythology.* Ann Arbor, Mich.: UMI Research Press, 1982. Broad, interpretive analysis of the cowboy hero that provides the literary and sociological setting for *Stagecoach* in American popular culture—from the frontier folk tales of the nineteenth century to the Hollywood films of the interwar years to the television Westerns of the 1950's and 1960's.

Sarris, Andrew. *The John Ford Movie Mystery.* Bloomington: Indiana University Press, 1975. Incisive, stimulating overview of Ford's contributions as director and as social and political commentator.

Stowell, Peter. *John Ford.* Boston, Mass.: Twayne, 1986. Sophisticated assessment of Ford's films within the context of American culture and history. Chapter 2 deals with *Stagecoach* in the development of the American frontier myth, and chapter 6 explores Ford's use of narrative structure in that film and in *The Searchers* (1956).

Zolotow, Maurice. *Shooting Star: A Biography of John Wayne.* New York: Simon & Schuster, 1974. Detailed, pioneering biography based on interviews and some private archives. Nicely written; includes anecdotes and insights into Wayne's personality. Much material on the Wayne-Ford relationship, including the production of *Stagecoach*.

John A. Britton

Cross-References

The Great Train Robbery Introduces New Editing Techniques (1903), p. 79; Grey's

BILL MONROE AND THE BLUE GRASS BOYS DEFINE BLUEGRASS MUSIC

Category of event: Music
Time: 1939-1949
Locale: Grand Ole Opry, Nashville, Tennessee

Bill Monroe and the Blue Grass Boys' innovative style of playing led to the development of a new genre, bluegrass music

Principal personages:

BILL MONROE (1911-   ), a country and bluegrass singer-songwriter who altered the tempo, key, pitch, and instrumentation of traditional country music to inspire the creation of a new style

CHARLIE MONROE (1903-1974), the senior partner in the duo known as the Monroe Brothers, the first professional group in which Bill was involved

LESTER FLATT (1914-1979), a singer, songwriter, guitarist, and emcee in Monroe's most celebrated band

EARL SCRUGGS (1924-   ), a master of the five-string banjo who revolutionized the three-finger style of banjo playing to make it one of the most distinguishing characteristics of bluegrass music

Summary of Event

In October of 1939, George D. "Judge" Hay, the creator and producer of *The Grand Ole Opry,* invited Bill Monroe and the Blue Grass Boys to audition for a spot on the prestigious radio broadcast. Although Monroe lacked the experience and name recognition of such Opry stars as Roy Acuff, he was confident that his Blue Grass Boys were ready for the task. His opinion was proved correct when, at the conclusion of the band's audition, the Opry's representatives, Judge Hay and David Stone, offered Monroe what was in essence a lifetime appointment to the Opry's slate of performers.

Insight into the unique Monroe sound is best obtained by examining one of the audition numbers performed by the Blue Grass Boys, "Mule Skinner Blues." This popular Jimmy Rodgers song, which became one of Monroe's top show pieces, provides excellent commentary on the innovator's musical ingenuity. Monroe took Rodgers' newfangled "blue yodel" and rhythmically reshaped it by increasing the tempo to a fiery speed and significantly elevating the vocal pitch to fit his high tenor voice. In short, Bill Monroe fused a popular hillbilly song with the older string-band sound, and in the process, he inspired the creation of a new style of music.

After his successful audition for Judge Hay, Monroe selected "Mule Skinner Blues" as his inaugural piece *The Grand Ole Opry.* According to observers, when the curtain went up, the audience and Opry regulars alike, including stars such as Roy

Acuff, Uncle Dave Macon, and Pee Wee King, were awed by the furious tempo of the Blue Grass Boys. Band member Cleo Davis later observed that the audience "couldn't think as fast as we played."

Without question, Bill Monroe and the Blue Grass Boys were perceived by their contemporaries as being new, unique, and exciting, but it would be erroneous to credit any single individual with having been the inventor of a genre of music. Does Bill Monroe merit the title "Father of Bluegrass Music"? Yes, but the story is complex, and there were several plateaus and numerous personages involved in the evolution of the music. The Monroe Brothers, Bill and Charlie, performed as a duo in the mid-1930's; the Monroe Brothers were followed in 1939 by Bill's first group of Blue Grass Boys, who awed folks at the Grand Ole Opry. In 1945, Monroe put together his most celebrated band, including Lester Flatt, Earl Scruggs, Chubby Wise, and Cedric Rainwater. The new band provided increased refinement and new instrumentation for Monroe's creation. Although bluegrass evolved through several stages and involved a host of contributors, through it all, Bill Monroe remained the guiding and inspirational force.

Born on September 13, 1911, near Rosine, Kentucky, William Smith Monroe was the youngest child in a musical family of six. From his earliest youth, Bill loved the fiddle and guitar, but he was relegated to the mandolin in the family band, as his older brothers, Birch and Charlie, had prior claims to Bill's instruments of choice. One of the greatest musical influences in Bill's early life was his uncle, Pendleton Vandiver, a fiddler who played at dances in the area. As a boy, Bill provided guitar rhythm for his uncle and, in the process, gained valuable insight into the capabilities of the fiddle. Monroe also acknowledged the virtuosity of black guitarist and fiddler Arnold Schultz as being one of the molding forces in his music. As a result of the influences of Vandiver, Schultz, and, later, Clayton McMichen, Monroe kept his mandolin in tune with his bands' fiddles—an important ingredient in the ultimate development of the Monroe sound.

When Bill turned eighteen, he moved north to join brothers Birch and Charlie, who were working in oil refineries in East Chicago. The brothers supplemented their income by performing as an acoustic trio for the WLS National Barn Dance road show. Although the Depression years were extremely difficult for the Monroe brothers, in 1933 Charlie and Bill decided to leave their day jobs to become full-time musicians. The Monroe Brothers, as they were billed, worked for the Southern-based "Crazy Water Crystal Barn Dance," and they developed a considerable following in the South and Midwest. The duo began their recording career in February, 1936, and by 1938, they had recorded sixty songs for Victor Records that were released on the Bluebird label. Perhaps the most significant accomplishment of Bill Monroe during his tenure with Charlie was the proficiency he gained on the mandolin, transforming it into a popular solo instrument.

After six years of performing as the Monroe Brothers, Bill left the family band in 1938 in hopes of perfecting his own musical ideas, something he could not do with his older brother as boss. In search of a new partner, Bill ran an advertisement in an

Atlanta newspaper that resulted in the hiring of Cleo Davis as his new guitarist and lead singer. As the duo's repertoire expanded beyond the songs of the Monroe Brothers, Bill advertised for additional band members, and he eventually hired bassist Amos Garen and fiddler Art Wooten. Monroe named the expanded band Bill Monroe and the Blue Grass Boys in honor of his home state of Kentucky. Throughout 1939, Monroe labored endlessly, tutoring Cleo Davis on how to do his guitar runs and Wooten on how to bow his fiddle. In addition to his emphasis on speed and clarity, Monroe forced his members to play in unconventional keys. His band was the first to play in B-flat, B-natural, and E, and when Monroe moved up to a B-flat or B, he went beyond the capabilities of most fiddlers and guitarists. In the process of perfecting his new sound, Monroe also established higher standards of professionalism for acoustic musicians.

Another contribution of Monroe's 1939 band was the utilization of the string bass, an instrument popularized by jazz musicians, in country music. Although Monroe was not the first to use a string bass in his band—Roy Acuff and a few others were experimenting with the integration of the bass into their music—after the grand success of the Blue Grass Boys at the Opry in 1939, the bass became a mainstay in all bluegrass and country bands.

Perhaps the most significant new Blue Grass Boy was Art Wooten, the first in a long line of Monroe's world-class fiddlers that included Tony Magness, Gordon Terry, Chubby Wise, Kenny Baker, Bobby Hicks, Charlie Cline, Howdy Forrester, Benny Martin, and "Tater" Tate. The fiddle was not only critical to the new instrumentals he was perfecting, but it also influenced Monroe's unique vocal quality, which is often described as a "high-lonesome" sound. The high-lonesome sound became another characteristic that helped to define bluegrass music.

Guitarist Cleo Davis proved to be an able replacement for Charlie Monroe. He worked with the band through their first appearance on *The Grand Ole Opry*, but he departed before their first recording session in 1940. Davis had a worthy list of successors that included Clyde Moody, Pete Pyle, Lester Flatt, Jimmy Martin, Edd Mayfield, Del McCoury, Wayne Lewis, Tom Ewing, and others. By October of 1939, Monroe had fused his hard-driving tempo with the high-lonesome sound, and the result was the style that proved so successful on *The Grand Ole Opry*.

Although Bill experienced great success following his debut at the Opry, the World War II years were difficult for all bands. Not only did the military draft make retaining a band quite difficult, the implementation of gas rationing and other federal restrictions greatly reduced the size of audiences. In an attempt to carry the music to the people, Bill organized his own traveling tent show in 1943, and it proved to be a major success. The tent show was a combined minstrel and vaudeville show that included comedy, jug players, harmonica players, and even a baseball team. Using such unorthodox techniques, Monroe, an ingenious businessman, attracted record crowds, kept his music alive, and weathered the war years in good financial shape.

In the postwar era, Monroe assembled his most renowned band, which included the five-string banjo wizard Earl Scruggs; Scruggs added the final ingredient that was to distinguish bluegrass as a unique form of music. Scruggs, a native of Cleveland County, North Carolina, who had played for Lost John Miller and the Allied Kentuckians, was encouraged by Jim Shumate, a Monroe band fiddler, to audition for a position with the Blue Grass Boys. Fearful of losing his regular job, Scruggs was reluctant, but Shumate arranged for the audition. There was also doubt among the Blue Grass Boys as to whether or not a banjo should be added to the band; Monroe had already experimented with a banjo player, David "Stringbean" Akeman, in 1942, but Akeman's old-time style of play was incompatible with the band's rapid-fire tempo. Scruggs appeared for his audition and played an old standard, "Sally Goodin," which he followed with a new song entitled "Dear Old Dixie." Lester Flatt, who had opposed the addition of a banjoist, was so dumbfounded that he recommended to Monroe that Scruggs be hired whatever the cost.

Scruggs utilized a three-fingered (thumb, index, middle) picking style that was indigenous to western North Carolina. Although he did not invent the three-fingered technique, Scruggs certainly refined and revolutionized the style. His banjo solos at the Opry made him an instant star, and his style of banjo playing became a permanent part of the Monroe sound.

It would be hard to exaggerate the impact of Earl Scruggs on Bill Monroe's band, but it is a mistake to conclude, as some critics have, that the banjo is the first requirement of bluegrass. Clearly, Monroe assigned a greater importance to the fiddle and mandolin. It would also be a mistake to minimize the importance of singer, songwriter, and guitarist Lester Flatt, who sang lead on many Monroe recordings and who contributed a number of hit songs to the band's repertoire, including "Why Did You Wander," and "Will You Be Loving Another Man." Fiddler Chubby Wise was also important to this model bluegrass band, as he perpetuated the extremely high standards set by his predecessors for bluegrass fiddling. It is also clear that bassist Howard Watts (who used the stage name "Cedric Rainwater") complemented the virtuosity of the other band members.

Impact of Event

By 1948, the Monroe innovation was clearly being transformed from the "Monroe sound" into the musical genre of bluegrass. This transformation was signaled by an ever-increasing number of Monroesque bands appearing across the country. Rather than being flattered by this newly emerging school of imitators, though, Monroe was enraged; he considered the copying to be equivalent to stealing corn from another man's crib. He was understandably disturbed in 1948 when three of his Blue Grass Boys—Flatt, Scruggs, and Rainwater—left to form their own band, Lester Flatt, Earl Scruggs, and the Foggy Mountain Boys. Monroe had lost numerous band members since 1939, but this was the first time a group had left to go into direct competition with him. Their sound, as well as much of their repertoire, was without question the creation of Bill Monroe. Other imitators included Ralph and Carter Stanley (the Stanley Brothers), who had a singer and mandolin player, Darrell "Pee Wee" Lambert, who was a Bill Monroe clone. When the Stanley Brothers were signed by

Columbia Records in 1948, Monroe moved from Columbia to Decca, being totally intolerant of his imitators. Other bands imitating the Monroe sound were Wilma Lee and Stoney Cooper, the Bailey Brothers, the Briarhoppers, and the Blue River Boys.

Although some of Monroe's resentment was justified—as when Wilma Lee and Stoney Cooper recorded and released Monroe's "Wicked Path of Sin" before he could release it himself—with the increasing number of bands aping his music, bluegrass was becoming more than a personalized sound. Bluegrass was becoming a musical genre, and the future of the music was becoming more secure. By 1965, Bill Monroe came to realize the significance of his contribution, and the resentment he formerly expressed for his competitors ended. Formal recognition of Bill Monroe's contribution to bluegrass music came in September, 1991, when he was selected by his peers and fans to be one of the first three inductees into the International Bluegrass Music Association's Hall of Honor.

Bibliography

Kochman, Marilyn, ed. *The Big Book of Bluegrass.* New York: Quill, 1984. A heavily illustrated text with historical notes, artist interviews, and personal notes. Special attention is given to the patriarchs of bluegrass and current innovators. Should be used with caution; contains errors.

Malone, Bill C. *Country Music U.S.A.: A Fifty-Year History.* Austin: University of Texas Press, 1968. A scholarly book that is useful for placing Monroe's work in a larger context.

Rinzler, Ralph. "Bill Monroe—'The Daddy of Blue Grass Music.'" *Sing Out* 13 (February/March, 1963): 5-8. The first work to call for Bill Monroe's recognition as the "Father of Bluegrass."

Rosenberg, Neil V. *Bluegrass: A History.* Urbana: University of Illinois Press, 1985. The definitive work on bluegrass music, written by the leading authority. The best first source for anyone desiring to know more about bluegrass. Contains extensive bibliography as well as discography.

_____. "From Sound to Style: The Emergence of Bluegrass." *Journal of American Folklore* 80 (April, 1967): 143-150. Special emphasis given to the transformation of the Bill Monroe sound into a genre.

Wayne M. Bledsoe

Cross-References

WSM Launches *The Grand Ole Opry* (1925), p. 675; Rodgers Cuts His First Record for RCA Victor (1927), p. 729; Guthrie's Populist Songs Reflect the Depression-Era United States (1930's), p. 810; Hank Williams Performs on *The Grand Ole Opry* (1949), p. 1415; *Wanted: The Outlaws* Revitalizes Country Music (1976), p. 2365.

MARIAN ANDERSON IS BARRED FROM CONSTITUTION HALL

Category of event: Music
Time: January 2, 1939
Locale: Constitution Hall, Washington, D.C.

The Daughters of the American Revolution rejected contralto Marian Anderson for a singing engagement at Constitution Hall, but Anderson rescheduled her appearance outside the Lincoln Memorial

Principal personages:
MARIAN ANDERSON (1902-1993), the first leading African-American singer of classical and operatic roles
ELEANOR ROOSEVELT (1884-1962), a social activist, author, and chair of the United Nations Commission on Human Rights
SOLOMON HUROK (1888-1974), a Russian concert manager
RUDOLF BING (1902-   ), an Austrian impresario who managed New York's Metropolitan Opera until his retirement in 1972

Summary of Event

Even with her rich, warm, evocative contralto, Marian Anderson, the first African American to perform with New York's Metropolitan Opera Company, did not arrive easily at fame and acceptance, particularly among prejudiced whites. The daughter of a poor Philadelphia widow, she got what training she could afford, then evolved an expanded vocal repertoire including material ranging from spirituals to folk songs and grand opera. She developed a significant following among classical music fans. In 1939, after requesting the use of Washington's Constitution Hall from the Daughters of the American Revolution, she was humiliated by a flat rejection.

Marian, the first of three daughters of John and Annie Anderson, was born at her grandmother's house in South Philadelphia on February 17, 1902. Her father, a coal and ice seller, died of brain cancer ten years later, leaving his wife, a schoolteacher, to support the family by taking in laundry and working in Wanamaker's Department Store. Anderson, who progressed from the Union Baptist Church junior choir to public performances of duets and solos, also learned to play the piano and violin. She concentrated on a business curriculum at William Penn High School, then transferred to South Philadelphia High for music training and studied privately under voice coach Mary Patterson.

Public response to Anderson's extensive range and expressive talents brought invitations to a variety of public musical forums and Negro colleges as well as membership in the Philadelphia Choral Society. White philanthropists often donated funds to assist her obviously promising future in music. Despite the beneficence of a few, laws of segregation and local custom required her to travel on separate train cars, ride service elevators, and eat in substandard dining areas maintained for nonwhite patrons. Overnight accommodations in hotels proved so difficult to obtain that she usually stayed in private residences.

In 1921, Anderson received a church-sponsored scholarship for voice lessons with Giuseppe Boghetti, who strengthened her technique and stage presence and taught her operatic roles. With the help of accompanist and manager William "Billy" King, a black pianist, she increased her fee to a hundred dollars per performance. A period of low self-esteem arising from unfavorable reviews deflated her enthusiasm temporarily. The expertise she gained from learning foreign languages to augment her vocal talent, in addition to the backing of her mother, sisters, coach, and manager, restored her to earlier levels of confidence.

In 1925, after defeating three hundred contenders in a local competition, Anderson won the privilege of appearing with the New York Philharmonic at Lewisohn Stadium under the direction of Eugene Ormandy. Good reviews bolstered her competitiveness. As a result, in 1930, on a National Association of Negro Musicians scholarship, she traveled to Europe to study. While sailing on the *Ile de France*, she sang for distinguished passengers. The experience proved beneficial to her career, encouraging her to return to Berlin to immerse herself in the German language. Back in the United States, she demonstrated her cosmopolitan training with a cross-country tour.

It was in the midst of this increasing professional success that Anderson was refused permission by the Daughters of the American Revolution (DAR) to sing at Constitution Hall in Washington, D.C., in 1939. The refusal came solely on account of Anderson's race. At the time of the turndown, Anderson was on tour in California. She met with interviewers to voice her sadness and shame. In characteristic low-key, nonjudgmental style, she refused to affix blame and noted, by way of explanation, that crusading for racial equality was foreign to her nature. She did, however, alter her personal criteria for performance sites and refused to sing where nonwhites were refused admittance.

The refusal to let Anderson sing proved embarrassing to the two hundred thousand members of the DAR, an elite women's historical society founded in 1890 to honor descent from patriots, encourage patriotism and activities related to teaching history, foster genealogical research, honor the American flag and Constitution, found citizenship clubs, award scholarships and medals, assist disabled veterans, and generally further Americanism. To save face in response to press stories about their actions, the group's leaders cited a Washington, D.C., law restricting integrated performances. They insisted that the DAR had in fact challenged bigotry by publicizing the local restrictions that forbade Anderson's performance. This story proved to be false.

Other entertainers and leaders came to Anderson's defense and protested the obvious attempt to hide racial discrimination. As a conciliatory gesture, Eleanor Roosevelt resigned from and broke all ties with the DAR and persuaded Anderson to sing a free Easter concert at the steps of the Lincoln Memorial. The Sunday performance, attended by more than seventy-five thousand people, including government dignitaries, representatives from Howard University, and the secretary of the National Association for the Advancement of Colored People (NAACP), showed Anderson's sincere response to the racist action of an elitist clique. Choked with tears at the sight of so many supporters, Anderson faltered on the words to the national anthem. She drew on her professional training and years of onstage experience to help complete her usual repertoire of hymn tunes, classical arias, and national favorites. She closed with a simple rendition of "America."

Anderson's performance at the Lincoln Memorial became the focal point of her career. To commemorate her public triumph, the Department of the Interior commissioned a mural. Fellow entertainers of all races boycotted future performances scheduled for Constitution Hall. For her self-control and positive attitude, Anderson accepted honors from Eleanor Roosevelt and the king and queen of England. She later entertained at the White House for the inaugural galas of Dwight D. Eisenhower and John F. Kennedy. The policy at Constitution Hall changed in regard to use by nonwhites, and Anderson gave her long-delayed performance.

Impact of Event

The nationwide notoriety resulting from the Washington rejection and its triumphant aftermath brought Anderson a deluge of opportunities to travel, perform, study, and record. Reluctant to release many of her RCA recordings, she reworked studio performances until they reached her high standards. Her most popular disc, a soulful, intense rendering of "Ave Maria," marked by her characteristic vibrato and amplitude, sold a quarter of a million copies.

Twice Anderson toured Denmark, Sweden, Norway, and Finland, impressing Finns by singing in their language. Royalty, local fans, and notable musicians, especially composer Jean Sibelius, escalated her Scandinavian appearances from mere acclaim to "Marian fever." European and Asian audiences, particularly Russians and those in other nations under communist regimes, demanded encores of her spirituals, claiming "Deep River" and "Heaven, Heaven" as their favorites. Konstantin Stanislavsky carried a bouquet of lilacs to entice her to sing *Carmen*.

Returning to America in triumph, Anderson came under the management of Russian impresario Solomon Hurok. Under his direction toward new challenges, she accepted tours in Japan, Africa, and South America and gave standing-room-only concerts at New York City's Town Hall and Carnegie Hall and at the Philadelphia Forum. Far from her original rewards of fifty cents per performance, she earned hefty fees commensurate with her talents. Fans poured out their response to her compassion, which brought them comfort in times of personal crisis. Critics acknowledged her maturing grace, range, control, and musical technique. She performed more than seventy-five concerts per year and had many opportunities she could not accept without overextending her voice and sapping her energies.

Even with increased audience rapport, racism continued to crop up in correspondence, reviews, and public treatment, especially after Anderson was invited to sing before Nazis in the 1940's. Following her reply to their questions about race, Hitler's staff dropped their request for a concert. In the United States, she was presented with the key to Atlantic City, but white hotels refused her requests for a reservation. These unsettling public slurs were somewhat offset by awards and honoraria from fifty universities including Howard, Temple, Smith, Carlisle, Moravian, and Dickinson.

At the age of thirty-seven, Anderson received the Springarn Medal, awarded annually by the NAACP to an African-American achiever. A year later, in 1940, she earned the Bok Award, an annual $10,000 prize accorded a native Philadelphian. She used the money to endow the Marian Anderson Scholarship for students of the arts. To assure unprejudiced administration of the annual award, she placed her sister Alyce in charge.

In 1943, Anderson left the Philadelphia home she shared with her mother and married architect Orpheus Fisher of Wilmington, Delaware, whom she had met during her school years. The couple built Mariana Farm in a rural setting outside Danbury, Connecticut. Often absent from home on tour, she reserved the summer months for domestic pleasures, particularly sewing, cooking, and gardening. Her particular delight was the success of her strawberry patch. By choice, she had no children so that she could avoid the problem of separation from family while she devoted her life to music. To fill the gap left by voluntary childlessness, she immersed herself in the activities of her sisters' children, who were frequent visitors to her home.

In middle age, Marian Anderson continued to achieve renown. At the bidding of German fans, she returned to post-Nazi Berlin to perform. In 1955, New York impresario Rudolf Bing organized her debut as Ulrica, the aged sorceress in Giuseppe Verdi's *Un ballo in maschera* (1857-1858; *The Masked Ball*). This performance at the Metropolitan Opera House was the first ever by an African-American performer. It made extra demands on her limited stage experience, which she met by practicing her acting role and deliberately subduing stage fright. She reprised her part in the opera on tour in Philadelphia, where black fans mobbed the performance. Continuing to refine the role of Ulrica in later appearances, she commented that she felt that perfection of the small character part was an essential part of her training for the operatic stage.

At the age of fifty-four, Anderson wrote her autobiography, *My Lord, What a Morning* (1956), in which she revealed personal reflections on poverty and longing in her childhood, when performing before distinguished audiences lay far outside the grasp of a black singer. Late in her career, having toured Europe and the United States once more, she was named in 1958 as an alternate delegate to the United Nations for her support of human rights. In 1959, two years before formal retirement, she accepted from President Dwight D. Eisenhower the Presidential Medal of Freedom. At the age of seventy-six, she appeared at the Kennedy Center and, as the sole woman among fellow honorees George Balanchine, Arthur Rubinstein, Richard Rodgers, and Fred Astaire, received a national award.

The famed singer returned to the spotlight long after the end of her stage career. At the age of eighty-seven, to raise scholarship funds, Anderson, still regal and gracious, presided over a concert at Danbury's Charles Ives Center. Feted by admirers including Jessye Norman, Isaac Stern, William Warfield, Cicely Tyson, Phylicia Rashad, Connecticut's Governor William A. O'Neil, and President George Bush, she graciously accepted the national acclaim that well-wishers extended. She later became more reclusive but remained a symbol of African-American achievement and grace under pressure.

Bibliography

Anderson, Marian. *My Lord, What a Morning.* New York: Viking Press, 1956. Somewhat dated in style and tone, this autobiography nevertheless contains the most factual information on Anderson's childhood and developing career. Some of the information is sentimentalized, but the author avoids bitterness in recounting prejudicial treatment.

"The Survivors." *Ebony* 46 (November, 1990): 28-33. A brief overview of black achievement during a forty-five-year period. The article helps set Marian Anderson among her black peers. Photographs capture worthy scenes of American entertainment history.

Sweeley, Michael. "The First Lady." *National Review* 41 (September 29, 1989): 65-66. A brief but articulate summary of Anderson's life and career, with particular emphasis on the open-air concert at the Charles Ives Center.

Tedards, Anne. *Marian Anderson.* American Women of Achievement Series. New York: Chelsea House, 1988. A superb illustrated resource for students, from the point of view of African-American achievement. This volume is a must for educators who seek to instruct young people in American history.

"A Tribute to Marian Anderson: Famed Contralto Is Honored at Gala Concert in Connecticut." *Ebony* 45 (November, 1989): 182-185. A photographic tribute to Anderson's concert at the Charles Ives Center. The article fills in information about the singer's retirement and widowhood. Like most accounts of Anderson's career, the article mentions the DAR snub.

Vehanen, Kosti. *Marian Anderson, a Portrait.* Westport, Conn.: Greenwood Press, 1970. An undistinguished biography. The lackluster account of Anderson's life and career bogs down in detail but might prove useful to a researcher or student of music history.

Mary Ellen Snodgrass

Cross-References

Caruso Records for the Gramophone and Typewriter Company (1902), p. 69; Sibelius Conducts the Premiere of His Fourth Symphony (1911), p. 292; Bessie Smith Records "Downhearted Blues" (1923), p. 572; *Hallelujah* Is the First Important Black Musical (1929), p. 772; Billie Holiday Begins Her Recording Career (1933), p. 930; *Stormy Weather* Offers New Film Roles to African Americans (1940's), p. 1159; Mahalia Jackson Begins Her Recording Career (1946), p. 1329.

THE SHERLOCK HOLMES FILM SERIES BEGINS

Category of event: Motion pictures
Time: March 31, 1939
Locale: The United States

Basil Rathbone starred in the first of fourteen films that made him the most popular Sherlock Holmes in cinema history

Principal personages:

BASIL RATHBONE (1892-1967), a successful and respected stage and film actor who achieved his greatest popularity in the film role of Sherlock Holmes

NIGEL BRUCE (1895-1953), the venerable character actor who played Holmes's bumbling sidekick, Dr. Watson

DARRYL F. ZANUCK (1902-1979), the executive producer for Twentieth Century-Fox who signed Rathbone and Bruce for their roles and oversaw the production of the first two films of the series

SIDNEY LANFIELD (1898-1972), the director of *The Hound of the Baskervilles*

MARY GORDON (1882-1963), the character actress who played Holmes's landlady, Mrs. Hudson, throughout the series

Summary of Event

In the spring of 1939, American moviegoers of all ages were familiar with Sherlock Holmes as a film character. First popularized in the late 1880's and early 1890's through the novels and short stories of Sir Arthur Conan Doyle, Sherlock Holmes had been represented on silent film in Europe and America since the turn of the century. After talking pictures were introduced in the late 1920's, a number of Holmes films followed, the most popular being a highly successful five-film series starring British actor Arthur Wontner. By 1939, Sherlock Holmes was still popular in print, had been represented successfully on stage, and had been portrayed in numerous radio versions. Basil Rathbone's portrayal of the Baker Street sleuth was certainly no novelty.

Furthermore, as one of the most popular of the Holmes stories, *The Hound of the Baskervilles* was familiar to many. Sticking fairly closely to its source (unlike later movies in the Rathbone series), this Twentieth Century-Fox film begins with the mysterious death of Sir Charles Baskerville of Baskerville Hall. It is rumored on the Dartmoor marshland that Sir Charles was killed by a supernatural hound that for centuries has been revenging the brutal murder of a young peasant woman by Sir Charles's wicked seventeenth century ancestor Sir Hugo Baskerville. Upon the death of Sir Charles, young Sir Henry Baskerville inherits his uncle's estate, and Holmes is called to investigate the danger that the avenging hound might present to Sir Henry. Holmes eventually discovers that the hound is merely a mortal beast trained by John Stapleton, a neighbor and distant Baskerville relative, who had hoped to kill Sir Henry and claim the estate for himself. After Holmes solves the mystery, young Sir Henry is able to marry Stapleton's stepsister Beryl, presumably to live quietly and happily forever.

Ultimately, the Doyle stories were designed to showcase the deductive powers of Sherlock Holmes and to tantalize the audience with mystery and suspense. By highlighting the vicious canine, however, *The Hound of the Baskervilles* adds a touch of horror and the macabre to the detective mixture. The 1939 film version of Doyle's classic emphasized the horror element. Twentieth Century-Fox advertised the film as "literature's most shocking, spine-chilling mystery story," pitting Holmes "against the giant, unearthly Beast from Hell that roams the fog-swept moor . . . terrorizing the countryside . . . striking horror into the hearts of two young lovers!" As the opening credits roll, the misty Dartmoor setting prepares the audience for what Watson later calls "the dreadful eeriness of this place." Insert titles announce that "in all England there is no district more dismal than that vast expanse of primitive wasteland, the moors of Dartmoor in Devonshire," and the action begins at night on the boggy Grimpen Mire with the terrified Sir Charles fleeing the howling of the hound. Then, when Sir Charles collapses from heart failure, a horrific, wild-eyed man scurries from the bushes to steal Sir Charles's pocket watch. Although filmed entirely at the Twentieth Century-Fox studios, the atmosphere of the moors is genuinely eerie; when the audience finally sees the hound, however, it appears to be of normal size and is not sufficiently frightening.

Twentieth Century-Fox also emphasized the romantic element of Doyle's story. In the end, Sir Henry Baskerville wins the heart of his beautiful neighbor, Miss Beryl Stapleton, and in advertisements for the film, Twentieth Century-Fox gave the lovers as much prominence as Holmes and Watson. Two romantic leads, Richard Greene and Wendy Barrie, were cast to play Sir Henry and Miss Stapleton, and the opening credits gave Greene top billing, followed by Rathbone and Barrie, with Nigel Bruce, as Dr. Watson, receiving secondary billing and separated in the credits from Rathbone. Emphasis on the romantic element was also reflected in Cyril Mockridge's music for the opening credits. The music began by suggesting horror—ominous measures featuring brass instruments—then segued into several bars of sweeping, romantic violins before returning to the opening mood, which continued into the first scene on the moor.

Richard Greene's romantic Sir Henry failed to dominate the screen as Twentieth Century-Fox had presumably anticipated. Instead, it was Rathbone's brisk, electric, intense characterization of Holmes and Bruce's languid, good-natured characterization of Watson that dominated the picture, along with striking portrayals of numerous minor characters. For example, Lionel Atwill, who in *Sherlock Holmes and the Secret Weapon* (1942) would make a very effective Professor Moriarty, here created an effectively mysterious Dr. Mortimer. The slim and gravel-voiced John

Carradine played the Baskervilles' servant with a compelling and taciturn quality, and in a typically brief appearance, Mary Gordon created the role of Mrs. Hudson, which she would play throughout the series. The result was a rich fictive world dominated by the Rathbone/Bruce tandem and especially by the intensity of Rathbone as Holmes.

Five months later, in September, 1939, Twentieth Century-Fox capitalized on the success of Rathbone and Bruce by releasing a second Holmes film, *The Adventures of Sherlock Holmes*, and the two character actors were well on their way to becoming the most popular Holmes and Watson in cinema history. In this and subsequent films of the series, Rathbone and Bruce receive top billing and were featured as the stars; their personal star status was emphasized even more than their roles as Holmes and Watson.

In October, 1939, Rathbone and Bruce began solidifying their new fame by repeating their roles for radio, and they went on to act in more than two hundred radio performances between 1939 and 1946. In September, 1942, Universal Studios purchased the film rights to the Doyle short stories and began a series of twelve more Rathbone/Bruce films, concluding with *Dressed to Kill* in 1946, after which Rathbone quit the series to return to New York and his first love, the stage. Though Rathbone had initially felt challenged by the Holmes role, he eventually tired of it, feeling that he was simply repeating himself rather than growing as an actor. Unfortunately, he had become so identified with the role that his career as an effective character actor was essentially destroyed. Children asking him for his autograph would often not know that Sherlock Holmes was a fictional character and that the man they addressed was really the actor Basil Rathbone, and Rathbone could not appear on screen without reminding audiences of Sherlock Holmes. In the late 1940's in New York, Rathbone worked on stage, radio, and television with some success but without offsetting his typecasting as Holmes, and he even returned to the role in 1953 in a play and a television pilot, both unsuccessful. He did not appear again in film until the middle 1950's, and then with little success. By the early 1960's, he was acting in cheap thrillers for American International Pictures, and he ended his film career by appearing in a pair of obscure films, *Autopsy of a Ghost* (1967) and *Hillbillies in a Haunted House* (1967). Though Rathbone achieved international fame as Sherlock Holmes, his acting career was finally severely limited by that phenomenal success.

Impact of Event

There had been many successful and popular portrayals of Sherlock Holmes before Rathbone's appearance in *The Hound of the Baskervilles* in 1939. William Gillette, H. A. Saintsbury, Eille Norwood, John Barrymore, Clive Brook, Raymond Massey, and Arthur Wontner, among others, had earlier made significant impacts portraying the great detective. Gillette, active until 1935, had played Holmes on stage, in film, and on radio for more than thirteen hundred performances and was considered by many in his heyday to be the definitive Sherlock Holmes, while the British actor Eille Norwood had made forty-seven short silent films in the early 1920's as Holmes. By 1946, though, Rathbone's performance in the series of fourteen Sherlock Holmes films had eclipsed all other portrayals in the public consciousness.

In the decades following Rathbone's departure from the Universal series in 1946, many actors portrayed Holmes; Peter Cushing, Christopher Lee, Douglas Wilmer, Fritz Weaver, John Neville, Stewart Granger, John Wood, Nicol Williamson, Christopher Plummer, Roger Moore, Frank Langella, Ian Richardson, and others played Holmes on film, stage, and television. For forty years, however, no one threatened to dislodge Rathbone as the image of Sherlock Holmes until Jeremy Brett began his long and effective series of Holmes tales for England's Granada Television in the middle 1980's. Thus, for nearly half a century, Rathbone reigned supreme as the popular image of Sherlock Holmes.

Some of Rathbone's popularity in the role must be attributed to his appearance. Tall and slender, with a strong nose, dark hair, piercing eyes, and a slightly receding hairline, Rathbone bore a striking resemblance to the image of Holmes created by the most famous and most influential of Doyle's illustrators, Sidney Paget, who established the initial and most abiding portrait of Holmes in his many drawings for the original publication of Doyle's stories in the *Strand Magazine*. As an excellent and experienced character actor, moreover, Rathbone also brought to the role an intensity coupled with a thoughtful intelligence and an aristocratic manner that perfectly suited the character.

In addition, Rathbone had an advantage over all previous and subsequent screen Sherlocks when he was paired with Nigel Bruce's incomparable Dr. Watson, whose good-natured bumbling served as the perfect foil to Rathbone's characterization. The Watson character has always proved deceptively difficult to play. As a companion and contrast to Holmes, the Watson character tends to be sycophantic, prosaic, even dull, and many actors cannot bring any meaningful liveliness to the role. Bruce, however, managed to create a richly sentimental warmth in Watson along with a genuinely close relationship with Holmes, and in some respects the Watson of Nigel Bruce has proved an even more indelible screen image than the Holmes of Rathbone.

Another factor contributing to Rathbone's enormous popularity was the timing of the series, which coincided with U.S. involvement in World War II. Many of the films in the Universal series exploited the war consciousness, creating un-Doyle-like tales that set Holmes against Nazi spies, and a number of the films in the series ended with uplifting, jingoistic speeches such as the one that caps *Sherlock Holmes in Washington* (1943), in which Holmes quotes Winston Churchill: "In the days to come, the British and American people for their own safety and the good of all will walk together in majesty and justice and in peace." Finally, the timing of the Rathbone series coincided perfectly with the advent of television as a powerful cultural force in the United States. As local stations sought films for their afternoon and late-night movie slots, the Rathbone series proved both useful and popular. Since all the pre-1929 Holmes films were silent and thus not commercially viable, and because most of the pre-Rathbone sound versions were either lost or not readily available, the

Rathbone series enjoyed a virtual monopoly. Consequently, the fourteen Rathbone/ Bruce films became the most popular series of feature films ever shown on American television.

The Rathbone Holmes series is not generally thought of as cinematically innovative or daring, but in one way two of the films are almost shocking for their time. When Doyle created his detective hero at the end of the nineteenth century, he had made Holmes a narcotics addict who injected cocaine, heroin, morphine, and other drugs to combat the monotony of his daily routine. Only when challenged by a particularly difficult case did Holmes find life stimulating enough to make drugs unnecessary. At the end of *The Hound of the Baskervilles*, Holmes has solved all the mysteries, trapped the murderer, and brought peace and justice to Baskerville Hall; he has declared it "a very interesting case for your annals, Watson." Announcing that he has had a strenuous day and will now turn in, Holmes pauses at the door and, turning back to Watson, says, "Oh, Watson, the needle!" This was a startling line, given the conservatism and heavily censored film industry of the 1940's, and Holmes's addiction would not be openly dealt with on film until the mid-1970's, when *The Seven Percent Solution* (1976) unabashedly focused on Holmes's drug use. There is another veiled reference to Holmes's addiction in *Sherlock Holmes and the Secret Weapon* (1942), the second film in the Universal series. Near the end of the film, the evil Professor Moriarty has captured Holmes and has strapped him to an operating table; Moriarty plans to kill Holmes by draining his blood, drop by agonizing drop. Smiling, Moriarty says, "The needle till the end, eh?"

The Sherlock Holmes character, though more than a century old, has remained enormously popular. What can account for such enduring popularity? As for Rathbone, was he simply a fortunate participant in an inexorable trend, or did he serve as a significant stimulus for the continuing popularity of Sherlock Holmes?

Edgar Allan Poe invented the detective genre in the 1840's, and before the century was finished, Sir Arthur Conan Doyle had created in Sherlock Holmes the most compelling of all detective characters. As a kind of popular romantic hero, the detective character entertains audiences by surpassing the limits felt by ordinary people, but the Sherlock Holmes character added a specific appeal for the popular audience because Holmes was a hero of intelligence. Unlike such other heroes as the Western cowboy or the usual police detective, Holmes is extraordinary without resorting to weapons, violence, or physical prowess. He wins with his brain power, specifically the deductive power that permits him to cull meaning from what seem prosaic and meaningless details to everyone else.

Certainly, Rathbone was the perfect actor of his time to portray this quality. His height, intense eyes, angular features, and lack of muscularity all suggested brains rather than brawn, and he brought to his portrayal of Holmes an aristocratic demeanor that had been honed in earlier roles, beginning with his portrayal of the stern Mr. Murdstone in *David Copperfield* (1935) and including a bravura performance as the oily Guy of Gisbourne in *The Adventures of Robin Hood* (1938). Also of no small consequence was Rathbone's precise, deep, and crisp speaking voice, which seemed to capture the very sound of clear thinking. Rathbone's aristocratic manner, so essential to the Sherlock Holmes character, would not be sufficiently recaptured until the advent of Jeremy Brett's Sherlock in the mid-1980's. As Rathbone had become the definitive Sherlock Holmes for movies, Brett promised finally to eclipse him by becoming the definitive Holmes in the next dominant popular media—television and video cassettes.

Bibliography

Davies, David Stuart. *Holmes of the Movies: The Screen Career of Sherlock Holmes.* New York: Bramhall House, 1968. In fourteen chapters and 175 pages, a typical survey of Holmes literature, covering Doyle and the major actors who portrayed Holmes. Three chapters dedicated to Rathbone. Includes photographs and filmography but no index or other useful apparatus. Very readable, literate, and analytical.

Eyles, Allen. *Sherlock Holmes: A Centenary Celebration.* New York: Harper & Row, 1986. A sumptuously illustrated coffee-table book covering Holmes in all popular forms, including radio. One Rathbone chapter and a very useful chapter on recent Holmes figures. Includes index, academically slanted bibliography, chronological list of Doyle stories, and a valuable chronological list of performances. Eleven chapters, 144 pages.

Haydock, Ron. *Deerstalker!: Holmes and Watson on Screen.* Metuchen, N.J.: Scarecrow Press, 1978. Sixteen-chapter survey, with nearly three chapters on Rathbone and Bruce. At 313 pages, longer than most books covering the subject. Written in a very personal, chatty style, Haydock's book includes photographs, an index, and a short, somewhat dated annotated bibliography. The book's main strength is its wealth of detail.

Pohle, Robert W., Jr., and Douglas C. Hart. *Sherlock Holmes on the Screen: The Motion Picture Adventures of the World's Most Popular Detective.* South Brunswick, N.J.: A. S. Barnes, 1977. Though dated, still very useful; unusual thoroughness and specific detail on scores of films. Twenty-seven chapters and 260 pages in oversized format with many photographs, a list of Doyle stories, bibliography, and index. Long chapter on Rathbone series. Careful, accurate, and quotes extensively from original sources.

Rathbone, Basil. *In and Out of Character.* Garden City, N.Y.: Doubleday, 1962. Autobiography of eighteen chapters and 278 pages, in which, amazingly, Rathbone covers the Holmes series in a single ten-page chapter. This chapter, though, is essential reading, as it bristles with deep feeling, includes an incisive analysis of the Sherlock phenomenon, and reveals Rathbone's ultimate disappointment that the series so seriously damaged his acting career.

Steinbrunner, Chris, and Norman Michaels. *The Films of Sherlock Holmes.* Secaucus, N.J.: Citadel Press, 1978. Excellent and long (253 oversized pages) survey; many illustrations and 130 pages dedicated to Rathbone, with a chapter for each Rathbone/Bruce film. The best book of its kind, unusually detailed, informative, analytical, and well written; however, has no index, bibliography, or other scholarly aids.

Terry Nienhuis

Cross-References

The Mysterious Affair at Styles Introduces Hercule Poirot (1920), p. 496; *The Maltese Falcon* Introduces the Hard-Boiled Detective Novel (1929), p. 793; *Little Caesar, Public Enemy,* and *Scarface* Launch the Gangster-Film Genre (1930), p. 839; *The Maltese Falcon* Establishes a New Style for Crime Films (1941), p. 1223; *Dragnet* Is the First Widely Popular Police Show (1951), p. 1531; *The Mousetrap* Begins a Record-Breaking Run (1952), p. 1551.

THE GRAPES OF WRATH PORTRAYS
DEPRESSION-ERA AMERICA

Category of event: Literature
Time: April, 1939
Locale: New York, New York

John Steinbeck's use of journalistic exposé, documentary style, and experimental fiction in The Grapes of Wrath, *a controversial critique of modern inhumanity, produced one of the most controversial novels of the century*

Principal personages:

JOHN STEINBECK (1902-1968), the Pulitzer Prize-winning author of *The Grapes of Wrath*

CAROL HENNING STEINBECK (1906-1983), Steinbeck's wife, an activist in the migrant cause and the typist and editor of the novel

TOM COLLINS (1897?-1961), a government camp worker who acted as Steinbeck's guide and principal resource in the author's observations of migrant farmers in California

PASCAL COVICI (1885-1964), Steinbeck's editor and literary confidant

ED RICKETTS (1896-1948), an amateur biologist and influence on Steinbeck's theories of human behavior

Summary of Event

The man who would come to write the quintessential novel of the American Depression began the 1930's in obscurity and with uneven literary success. John Steinbeck had rejected his middle-class upbringing in Salinas, California, and the pretensions of college (Stanford University) for the life of an itinerant laborer and aspiring writer. His efforts of the early 1930's were regarded by most critics as florid and vague renditions of man's encounter with mystical nature. In *Tortilla Flat* (1935), however, he began to restrain his style and to construct richer, more detailed portraits of the folkways of people on the social margins. With *In Dubious Battle* (1936) and *Of Mice and Men* (1937), he established himself as a sensitive chronicler of America's vanishing rural communities and persistent underclass. These novels also confronted the Great Depression more bluntly than most popular authors dared.

By 1936, waves of destitute farmers ("Okies") were fleeing the Dust Bowl to Salinas and Monterey, where Steinbeck saw them victimized by nature and man. He began researching their plight for a series of journalistic exposés. As the intricacy of the farmers' experience emerged, however, he decided to expand his work into a fictional treatment of the migrant quandary as an emblem for the Depression itself. The situation also invited Steinbeck to make better use of his maturing style and social concerns. His careful attention to regional dialect and folkways, the relationship between political struggle and human need, and the use of innovative narrative techniques all came together in his greatest novel. After several false starts, Steinbeck began serious writing in May, 1938. His wife, Carol, typing and editing throughout, provided the book's title, a line from "The Battle Hymn of the Republic."

The Grapes of Wrath recounts the suffering and human endurance of the Joad family as they abandon their bankrupt farm in Oklahoma for the promise of work in California. Eldest son Tom jumps parole (stemming from a questionable manslaughter conviction) to help lead the family westward. Ma Joad, an intuitive genius of human nature and a noble sufferer, struggles to keep her extended family whole amid despondence. A fallen preacher, Casey, accompanies them as a mouthpiece for the author's folk philosophy and the source of Christian imagery throughout the tale. As the family traverses the legendary Route 66, Steinbeck exposes a litany of American sins: exploitative banks and agribusiness; the xenophobic defensiveness of the middle class; and a socioeconomic order that seems perversely distant from human morality and needs. The Joads and Steinbeck find temporary solace within a "government camp," a utopian model of participatory democracy, altruism, and cooperation. In the end, however, the Joads move on to an exploitative farm camp where Casey is killed (crucified); Tom must flee after he murders again in retaliation.

Steinbeck's migrants are not unambiguous heroes, nor their oppressors simplistic villains. All of his characters' good and bad natures are complicated by circumstance. Material scarcity, social disarray, and an inhuman economic machine cause men to violate their own heartfelt sense of morality. Steinbeck's concept of mankind was deeply influenced by his close friend, amateur biologist Ed Ricketts. Steinbeck developed the quasiscientific notion of the "phalanx"; he believed that individuals in groups were able to locate transcendent elements of human nature, evil, and morality that were not apparent to individuals alone. "Maybe all men got one big soul ever'body's a part of," Casey preaches. Such primal themes pervade the novel, through allusions to Christianity, Jeffersonian agrarianism, American Transcendentalism, and tribal social organization. The thread of hope for American renewal in the face of relentless tragedy courses through Ma and Tom Joad and their ability to locate the common morality of "human spirit." While the literary merits and sophistication of the novel remain controversial, Steinbeck offered his general readers a compelling depiction of modern society as diseased and beyond human control.

Beyond the more apparent social and philosophical messages, Steinbeck wanted to construct a monument to the American "common man." His spare, descriptive writing called attention to the details of human relations rather than to his own literary artistry. Descriptions of physical gestures, dialect and inflection, and quick dialogic exchanges constitute much of the narrative. Such elements were intended to underscore the profundity of common struggles and to suggest the rich meanings within everyday relationships. Steinbeck's most daring literary innovation, however, came in his punctuating of the main plot with numerous "interchapters." These passages wrenched the reader out of the Joads' story and into more general, and often more prosaic, ruminations on the migrants' plight.

Steinbeck intended to disorient and permanently change his readers. Many critics, though, have argued that *The Grapes of Wrath* had a similar effect on its creator. He suddenly became America's most discussed novelist; he was elected to the National Institute of Arts and Letters and was awarded the Pulitzer Prize. His book became a best-seller and produced a firestorm of debate, both political and aesthetic. Critics often dismissed Steinbeck as a mawkish sentimentalist of limited skill. Questions about his place within the literary pantheon were renewed in 1962, when Steinbeck received the Nobel Prize. While he continued to write at a decent pace after 1939, *East of Eden* (1952) was the only subsequent novel that approached his earlier work in its ambition. Steinbeck never again invested in his writing the level of passion, social conscience, and literary experimentation that made *The Grapes of Wrath* a landmark of American cultural history.

Impact of Event

The publication of *The Grapes of Wrath* was among a handful of literary events that reverberated into larger political and social arenas of American culture. Steinbeck anticipated some controversy, and he had the lyrics to the "The Battle Hymn of the Republic" printed on the hardcover edition's endpapers as a sign of his patriotism. The strategy failed; the book has been among the most banned, burned, and censored of modern times. Steinbeck himself was accused variously of instigating worker unrest, of betraying the dignity of the migrants themselves, and simply of being a mediocre writer. Nevertheless, *The Grapes of Wrath* has remained the most widely read work of serious American fiction of the century (fourteen million copies sold) and an influential example of the activist novel.

The political right first attacked the book as inaccurate, biased propaganda, neither fair nor artistic. Steinbeck was called an outright liar and anti-American by some newspapers and many farmowners' organizations around the country. His blistering depictions of brutality by landowners were challenged in all manner of publications. *Collier's* spoke for many when it branded the book subversive propaganda. Still, Steinbeck enjoyed no less a fan than Eleanor Roosevelt, who praised the book's disturbing images of America's underbelly as a call to action. Senator Robert La Follette initiated an official inquiry into the work conditions of California farms. The Supreme Court declared unconstitutional a California law that had been used against migrant workers. The growing momentum for reform faded, however, as World War II provided new opportunities for the itinerant and unemployed.

Controversy over the novel quickly shifted from politics to taste and morality. Most bannings and burnings were responses to the characters' earthy dialogue and occasional mentions of sexuality. Charges of obscenity have maintained the book's dubious place on the list of most-censored works; it has often been removed from school reading lists and libraries. From the time of publication, however, attempts to ban or abridge the novel for reasons of propriety have been challenged as excuses for suppressing its political ideas. Moreover, few authors have enjoyed Steinbeck's broad readership and popular esteem. Though hardly resolved, persistent controversies over who should read *The Grapes of Wrath* often raise deeper questions about the motives and intentions of censorship. Nevertheless, Steinbeck's use of a more frank and naturalistic style may have helped to accustom American readers to the more explicit content of postwar popular fiction.

The deeper cultural impact of *The Grapes of Wrath* was more subtle and enduring than the immediate response in 1939. While the book did not have the same demonstrable social influence as Harriet Beecher Stowe's *Uncle Tom's Cabin* (1852), Edward Bellamy's *Looking Backward: 2000-1887* (1888), or Upton Sinclair's *The Jungle* (1906), controversy generated by the novel foreshadowed persistent arguments about the role of social issues and ideology in an age of mass communications. Even journalists who were sympathetic to Steinbeck's cause at the time pondered the consequences of his blending of reportage with literary license in a popular novel. The question of art's duty to fact and impartiality would become all the more pressing after World War II. As film and television gained authority in American life, the social responsibilities, even politics, of popular artists were more carefully scrutinized; some artists were "blacklisted" for their views. Steinbeck's novel suggested the power of socially committed novelists to redirect political agendas and to influence public opinion. This memory of the radical art of the 1930's certainly informed later attacks on alleged communists in the film and television industries.

To the chagrin of many critics, *The Grapes of Wrath* has been regarded by general readers as one of the great American novels and continues to be a standard text used in secondary English classrooms. Like James T. Farrell, John Dos Passos, and even Charlie Chaplin, Steinbeck strove to engage art in immediate social issues without sacrificing the artist's unique qualities of vision and experimentation. These artists argued that a radically changed modern society required new forms of narrative. Farrell and Dos Passos were more dogged—some say more talented—in their pursuit of this goal. Thus, *The Grapes of Wrath* probably is taught more as history than as literature. Nevertheless, Steinbeck helped to advance the art of the social-issue novel beyond the didacticism of nineteenth century efforts and the often leaden style of much proletarian fiction by the radical left. After World War II, issue-oriented fiction became more the purview of film and television than of literature. *The Grapes of Wrath* suggested a palatable recipe for mixing social activism and fiction. Much of such fiction has humanized social issues, dramatizing the ways in which abstract debates affect common lives. Still, the more provocative blends of literary innovation and social exposé have continued to flourish, especially among African-American novelists such as Ralph Ellison, James Baldwin, Alice Walker, and Toni Morrison. Whatever form the book's legacy has taken, however, the events surrounding *The Grapes of Wrath* have dramatized the ways in which art matters.

Bibliography

Astro, Richard. *John Steinbeck and Edward F. Ricketts: The Shaping of a Novelist.* Minneapolis: University of Minnesota Press, 1973. A detailed chronicle of Steinbeck's relationship with Ed Ricketts. Explores the place of biological science in the author's thought about human behavior and society. Of special importance to

The Grapes of Wrath is a chapter on Steinbeck's "phalanx" theory of society as a biological organism. Photographs of both men are included.

Benson, Jackson J. *The True Adventures of John Steinbeck, Writer.* New York: Viking Press, 1984. A biography of Steinbeck that emphasizes his life over his works.

Bloom, Harold, ed. *John Steinbeck's "The Grapes of Wrath."* New York: Chelsea House, 1988. Anthology of evaluations of the novel by leading Americanists and literary critics, including Harold Bloom, Howard Levant, Donald Pizer, and Frederic I. Carpenter.

Donohue, Agnes McNeill, comp. *A Casebook on "The Grapes of Wrath."* New York: Thomas Y. Crowell, 1968. An anthology of commentary on the novel and Steinbeck. Contemporaneous articles about the book's accuracy, literary quality, and general reception are included from sources throughout American culture. Includes also material on the controversy surrounding Steinbeck's winning of the Nobel Prize in 1962.

Steinbeck, John. *"The Grapes of Wrath": Text and Criticism.* Edited by Peter Lisca. New York: Penguin Books, 1977. This critical edition provides the most reliable version of the original novel and includes selected evaluations of the book from the time of publication into the 1970's. Also includes a selected bibliography of Steinbeck and scholarship on his work.

——————. *Steinbeck: A Life in Letters.* Edited by Elaine Steinbeck and Robert Wallsten. New York: Viking Press, 1975. An indispensable collection of Steinbeck's correspondence. Regarding *The Grapes of Wrath*, there are revealing letters to friends that recount Steinbeck's experiences in migrant farmer camps. Moreover, there are important exchanges with Pascal Covici, Steinbeck's editor, about the novel's form and its controversial ending.

——————. *Working Days: The Journals of "The Grapes of Wrath," 1938-1941.* Edited by Robert DeMott. New York: Viking Press, 1989. An account of Steinbeck's writing of the novel through his own journal entries. DeMott's extensive annotations and supportive material are helpful in establishing the social setting in which the book was created.

Steven Smith

Cross-References

Dreiser's *Sister Carrie* Shatters Literary Taboos (1900), p. 39; Guthrie's Populist Songs Reflect the Depression-Era United States (1930's), p. 810; Socialist Realism Is Mandated in Soviet Literature (1932), p. 908; Rivera's Rockefeller Center Mural Is Destroyed (1934), p. 957; Odets' *Awake and Sing* Becomes a Model for Protest Drama (1935), p. 1006.

NBC LAUNCHES AMERICAN TELEVISION
AT THE WORLD'S FAIR

Category of event: Television and radio
Time: April 30, 1939
Locale: Long Island, New York

David Sarnoff announced the start of regularly scheduled television broadcasting in a prophetic address given at the New York World's Fair

Principal personages:
DAVID SARNOFF (1891-1971), a Russian immigrant who worked for Marconi Radio prior to following his scientific vision and founding his own company
VLADIMIR ZWORYKIN (1889-1982), the inventor of the "iconoscope," or electronic television picture tube
PHILO T. FARNSWORTH (1906-1971), inventor of the "image dissector," a necessary element for television, and founder of Philco, Inc.

Summary of Event

The 1939 New York World's Fair was a technology showcase, but its most significant innovation went largely unnoticed at the time. Television was displayed to the American public for the very first time in the United States on the opening day of the fair. The National Broadcasting Company (NBC) also announced plans to begin regularly scheduled television broadcasting. That afternoon, David Sarnoff, the founder and president of the Radio Corporation of America (RCA, the parent company to NBC), made several truly visionary pronouncements about the industry he was about to launch.

Sarnoff was born in 1891 and moved from Russia to the United States with his family at the age of nine. As a teenager, Sarnoff gained national celebrity working for Marconi Radio: He manned a Morse code receiver for seventy-two hours after the *Titanic* sank, taking down names of its survivors. Sarnoff rose quickly in the Marconi company and eventually struck out on his own in the 1920's, founding RCA. A decade of diligent planning and hard work produced the most successful commercial radio company—manufacturer and broadcaster—of the period. The millions of dollars RCA made with its NBC radio subsidiary (the Red and Blue networks) and its incredible sales of console radios provided the seed money needed to make television a reality.

The term "television" first appeared in a 1907 issue of *Scientific American*; however, experiments in video transmission actually began in the 1880's. Early on, there was a difference of opinion whether mechanical or electronic systems would work best. In the 1920's and early 1930's, Britain's Television, Ltd. developed a cumbersome, clattering contraption that could send a watery image eight miles through the air. Vertically mounted spinning wheels with glass lenses set into their perimeters were used in both the camera and the receiver to transduce light. As the wheels spun, they created a sound similar to a film projector, and the image was likewise displayed on a wall screen. The British Broadcasting Company initially showed a great deal of interest in this system; however, it was never able to send a clear, flicker-free picture, and it eventually was scrapped in favor of the fast-developing electronic television system.

Another Russian immigrant, Vladimir Zworykin, invented the "iconoscope" in 1923. His employer, Westinghouse, showed no interest in the device, so Zworykin sought out his fellow Russian émigré, David Sarnoff. Sarnoff recognized that, crude as it was, the iconoscope represented the basis of an effective electronic television process. The iconoscope used light-sensitive materials to transduce light. Coupled with another new invention, the cathode ray tube (CRT), electronic television was born. During the early 1930's, Zworykin perfected electronic television while Sarnoff went about gathering up all the television-related patents he could get his hands on. In addition to the iconoscope, Zworykin invented the "kinescope," a receiver for iconoscope signals.

Many television components were designed at RCA, but several significant elements were invented by other companies and by independent inventors. Prominent among these inventors was San Francisco-based Philo T. Farnsworth. He created an "image dissector" in 1927. This apparatus was essential to quality electronic television, and RCA initially infringed upon his patent. Farnsworth, in his early twenties and with no formal college-level science training, sued RCA. When the courts finally found in his favor, RCA was forced to pay ongoing royalties to his Philco, Inc. for use of the image dissector.

With an acceptable electronic television system completed, and with all legal questions settled, NBC began experimental television broadcasting from Camden, New Jersey, on July 7, 1936. The initial day's programming consisted of Sarnoff and his senior executives welcoming viewers, of which there were next to none, from his office on the fifty-third floor of Radio City. The broadcast continued with actors from *Tobacco Road* (a Broadway play), a singing act, and dancers from Radio City Music Hall. America was on the air, but she was losing the international race for television.

Both Germany and England already had regularly scheduled television services. Although picture quality was poor, Germany went on the air in 1935, broadcasting daily to eleven public viewing rooms around Berlin. England, having finally settled the issue of electronic versus mechanical television, began its regular service early in 1936. Britain's pioneering efforts in television design had an enormous beneficial side effect, the invention of radar. This technology, closely related to television, proved life-saving to the English during the Battle of Britain in the summer of 1940.

In the United States, Zworykin had estimated that it would cost $100,000 to get television operational, but Sarnoff ended up spending $20 million by 1938. After several years of testing, Zworykin's system was ready. RCA began distribution of its first television set, the TRK 660. This was a $660 console unit that stood four-and-a-half feet tall and had a flip-up, mirrored lid. The picture tube sat vertically, pointing upward inside the cabinet, and the image was reflected and reversed in the mirror so that people sitting around the console could view it. Because of the high price, only about one hundred sets were sold, most of them to RCA and NBC executives, with a few going to New York City bars.

Sarnoff, known to have a flair for the dramatic, chose the World's Fair for his big announcement. The fair opened on April 30, 1939, in Flushing Meadows, Long Island. A gigantic camera tethered to a mobile broadcast van was set up for the opening ceremonies. Franklin D. Roosevelt became America's first "television president" as he described the fair as "a beacon of progress and hope." His speech, along with that of New York Mayor Fiorello La Guardia, was carried by cables to monitors inside the RCA exhibit. It was then relayed to NBC's transmitter for broadcast to monitors in NBC's Radio City headquarters and to the one hundred or more sets around the city. Tens of thousands of people were at the fair that day, but it is estimated that, at most, two thousand people watched these events on television.

NBC broadcast the fair's symbols, including the Trylon and Perisphere, in the background. Its camera swept across the Court of Peace, panned the gathering throng, and captured the arrival of the president's motorcade. Mayor La Guardia recorded the first close-up when he walked up to the camera and stared into it. After televising Roosevelt's initial address, the camera was moved to the RCA Pavilion for Sarnoff's dedication. Fairgoers could step inside and watch the "show" on black-and-white monitors, then step outside to prove to themselves that what they were seeing was indeed real.

Sarnoff, in his speech, promised a new industry for America. NBC began regularly scheduled television broadcasts the same day, and receiving sets began to be made more widely available. Fairgoers also felt a sense of destiny of another sort. Clouds of war were already forming over Europe. Commercial television was interrupted by World War II just as people were learning of its existence, and the war meant a further delay of almost eight years before television sets were in anything but very limited use. That only a few thousand people actually watched the World's Fair on television that day is ironic, because television grew into an industry that prided itself on covering memorable events and broadcasting shared experiences. Still, Sarnoff and NBC were the first to bring America commercial television, an industry for which economic, social, and political effects are still evolving—and being debated—today.

Impact of Event

In retrospect, Sarnoff's presentation was one of the more inconsequential television milestones. Almost nobody saw the broadcast. England and Germany were already "on the air," and the coming world war put American television broadcasting on hold for several more years. The World's Fair broadcast is important because Sarnoff made several indisputably accurate predictions about what television would be like that day. He believed it would bring Americans together as a nation, that it would spawn new industries, and that it would change the American political system. At the time, however, Sarnoff was focusing on a more immediate effect of his announcement.

In the 1930's, the U.S. Federal Communications Commission (FCC) was faced with the task of selecting a national video transmission standard. RCA, Philco, and Dumont each had invested heavily in research on and development of such systems. All were capable of transmitting pictures, but each was totally incompatible with the others. Sarnoff was certain that if he could get his system to market first, a wave of public support (similar to that of early radio listeners) would propel the RCA system to the forefront, forcing the FCC to select it as the national standard. Sarnoff's plan suffered from poor timing. With Americans coming out of the Depression, few had the money to buy a TRK 660. The world war put television development at a standstill, so the great outpouring of support never materialized. Nevertheless, Sarnoff's ploy had the desired effect. The FCC settled on RCA's system, with only minor modifications, as the American video standard in 1941.

Although this rush to market was in RCA's best interest, it has proven less than optimal for American television viewers. The American video standard—the picture seen on American television sets—has lower quality than those of all other major industrial nations. The image is fuzzier and less true to life than television in Britain, France, Germany, and Japan. These nations, with their researchers free from the pressure of private enterprise, took the time to perfect their broadcasting systems before presenting them to the public.

Sarnoff's loftier predictions of things to come were indeed precise. Television has brought viewers together to witness and be a part of all major national events. The first half-century of television history yielded hundreds of common shared experiences, among them John F. Kennedy's assassination, Apollo 11's moon landing, the Vietnam War, the Watergate hearings and the resignation of President Nixon, and the space shuttle *Challenger* disaster. Less notable, but still important in American culture, are the dozens of beauty pageants, Rose Parades, bowl games, and World Series that viewers have watched. As time passed and audiences grew, many of these events were modified to make them easier for television to broadcast.

Sarnoff promised that television would produce many new industries. Prominent among these have been the manufacture of television broadcast and reception equipment as well as the production of programs. There are many parallel and ancillary businesses that owe their existence to television. Radar, satellite communications, and computers all share elements of television technology. Some businesses emerged to support the television industry: the A. C. Nielsen (and other) rating services, cable television, electronic news gathering, and, perhaps most significant, videotape technology and the video rental business.

Sarnoff also believed that showmanship would replace thoughtful expression on the part of politicians once they were exposed to television. It is true that television has had its noteworthy political moments: Ed Murrow's *See It Now* episode that all but brought McCarthyism to an end in 1954, the 1960 Kennedy-Nixon debates, and the combined use of live television and nationwide telephone call-ins that allowed access to the candidates in the 1992 presidential elections. For the most part, it has allowed for one-sided discourse. With only thirty seconds or a minute of commercial time for most messages, and with ideology packaged in an advertiser's format, it became extremely difficult for voters to gauge accurately a candidate's plans, goals, or abilities. Sarnoff was right—the more evocative the picture, the more influenced the voter. Additionally, television matured while its capacity for analysis steadily declined.

Television is a window on the world that did not exist in America, except for limited experiments, before 1939. Sarnoff envisioned greatness for television, yet even he might not have believed that fifty years after television service began in New York City, 98 percent of all American homes would be receiving it. Delivered via direct broadcast, cable, and satellite dish, television reached approximately ninety million American households in 1989, and American households watched an average of seven hours of programming per day. Sociologists and the television networks argue constantly whether the sex and violence beamed into homes is harmful. Educators and parents wonder why television is not used to enlighten and inform rather than to coddle and stupefy. Sarnoff lived into the 1970's, long enough to see his product mature. As a businessman, he understood something that the American public took much longer to realize—that the entertainment programs on television are not what is important; they are just filler between the commercials.

Bibliography

A. C. Nielsen Co. *Nielsen Station Index: U.S. Television Household Estimates (September 1991).* New York: Nielsen Media Research, 1991. This quarterly publication describes how ratings are tabulated and provides the latest audience statistics.

Bilby, Kenneth. *The General: David Sarnoff and the Rise of the Communications Industry.* New York: Harper & Row, 1986. Biography of Sarnoff chronicling his life and the growth of RCA and NBC into the 1980's.

DeFleur, Melvin L., and Everette E. Dennis. *Understanding Mass Communication.* 3d ed. Boston: Houghton Mifflin, 1988. This university text provides both technical and historical information about television's development. Includes pictures and diagrams.

Gordon, George N. *The Communications Revolution: A History of Mass Media in the United States.* New York: Communications Arts Books, 1977. University textbook giving the history of people important to the development of broadcasting in the 1920's and 1930's.

Johnson, Paul. *Modern Times: The World from the Twenties to the Eighties.* New York: Harper & Row, 1983. Looks at the 1939 World's Fair in addition to other events of historical significance in the twentieth century.

Udelson, Joseph H. *The Great Television Race.* University: University of Alabama Press, 1982. Chronicles the people, inventions, and events important to the development of commercial television worldwide.

Winship, Michael. *Television.* New York: Random House, 1988. Covers television from its inception to its current state. Many photographs. Companion to the 1988 *Television* miniseries aired on the Public Broadcasting System.

Thomas C. Breslin

Cross-References

The Art of Radio Develops from Early Broadcast Experience (1920's), p. 469; The British Broadcasting Corporation Is Chartered (1927), p. 712; Radio Programming Dominates Home Leisure (1930's), p. 828; NBC and CBS Launch Commercial Television (1941), p. 1211; NBC Broadcasts the World Series (1947), p. 1367; ABC Begins Its Own Network Television Service (1948), p. 1368.

ROCKEFELLER CENTER IS COMPLETED

Category of event: Architecture
Time: November 1, 1939
Locale: New York, New York

Rockefeller Center, the United States' first planned complex of city office buildings and public spaces, was completed, influencing urban planning and providing a symbolic focus for Depression-era New York City

Principal personages:

JOHN D. ROCKEFELLER, JR. (1874-1960), the financier and developer of the urban complex that would bear his family's name

RAYMOND HOOD (1881-1934), a member of the consortium of architects who designed the center, whose influence dominated the final style of the buildings

NELSON A. ROCKEFELLER (1908-1979), the president of Rockefeller Center, Incorporated, at the time of the center's completion

DAVID SARNOFF (1891-1971), the president of the Radio Corporation of America, whose agreement to become the main tenant in Rockefeller Center spurred its success and tied its identity to popular art and entertainment

Summary of Event

On November 1, 1939, John D. Rockefeller, Jr., drove the last rivet on Rockefeller Center during a ceremony marking the official completion of the New York City commercial and entertainment complex. The building program, which for ten years had symbolized corporate optimism in the face of the Depression, consisted at the time of thirteen structures and the famous plaza. Speaking at the completion ceremony were Nicholas Murray Butler, the president of Columbia University, which held the lucrative land lease on the property; David Sarnoff, the president of the Radio Corporation of America (RCA), which was the anchor tenant in the project's main building; Thomas A. Murray, the president of the Building and Construction Trades Council, who extolled the project as a model of corporate and union cooperation; New York mayor Fiorello H. La Guardia; and Nelson Rockefeller, the president of Rockefeller Center, Incorporated, who served as the master of ceremonies.

Rockefeller Center held both short-term and long-term significance to the institutions and constituencies represented by the speakers. Columbia University saw its income from the land on which the complex was built increase more than tenfold, from $300,000 a year to $3,300,000. RCA received a corporate home of unsurpassed prestige, almost immediate and universal name recognition, and the most modern facilities in which to create and showcase its productions. The ten-year construction period had provided 75,000 jobs at union wages during the height of the Depression, and had created an estimated 150,000 jobs in support industries. The city of New York, in addition to the benefits of employment and tax revenue, found in Rockefeller Center a focal point and landmark that became synonymous with the city itself.

For John D. Rockefeller, Jr., the complex that bore his name would become the most famous and enduring monument and legacy of his career. The son of the oil industrialist John D. Rockefeller, Sr., he had focused his interests on real-estate development and the philanthropic charities that his father had established. At the same time that he was building Rockefeller Center, he was also organizing and financing the restoration of colonial Williamsburg, Virginia. His intentions for Rockefeller Center were impressively fulfilled. He wanted good design, profitable returns on investment, and international tenants who would help to stimulate foreign trade. The center also symbolized his optimism in the nation's future and his belief in civic-minded corporatism.

The completion of Rockefeller Center was the final result of an idea that had originally been relatively traditional and modest. Ten years earlier, the Metropolitan Opera had been looking to build a new theater. Rockefeller became involved and collected rights to the leases on Columbia University's land and neighboring properties in midtown Manhattan, and he helped to implement a plan that would include a new opera house supported by rents from surrounding commercial buildings. He set up the Metropolitan Square Corporation, headed by Arthur Woods, to oversee the property. Todd, Robertson, Todd Engineering was named first as developers and later as managers of the project. L. Andrew Reinhard and Henry Hofmeister were appointed as architects, with Benjamin Morris, Raymond Hood, and Harvey Corbett as consultants. Initially, Rockefeller's involvement was to end with the development of the property and his donation of the public plaza. The stock market crash of October 29, 1929, forced the Metropolitan Opera to withdraw from the project, however, and Rockefeller assumed full financial responsibility.

The overall plan for the center evolved over the next several years. The architectural team of Reinhard and Hofmeister was expanded to include a consortium of firms, including Corbett, Harrison, and MacMurray and Hood, Godley, and Foulihoux, which called itself the Associated Architects. Of this group, Reinhard, Hofmeister, Harrison, and Hood were most active in the design. All the architects had in common a background in the Beaux-Arts tradition of architecture and an interest in and familiarity with modern styles and practices. Their approaches to design and construction might best be described as conservative modernism.

In consideration of the state of the nation's economy, the architects were instructed to maximize the income potential of the land but still to design a complex that would be humane and modern. The central position previously allocated to the Metropolitan Opera House was replaced with a towering skyscraper, the RCA building. Massed around it in an abstract angular composition were other skyscrapers of varying heights that became the corporate centers of such major companies as the Time-Life Corporation, Eastern Airlines, the Associated Press, and the American Rubber

Company. Lower buildings, serving as trade centers for foreign countries, flanked a promenade that funneled pedestrians from Fifth Avenue to the plaza at the center of the complex. By the time Rockefeller drove the last rivet, Rockefeller Center, symbol of the metropolis of the future, occupied more than five million square feet of office space.

While the shape and proportions of the buildings were to a certain extent predetermined by zoning restrictions and tenants' needs, the architect Raymond Hood is credited with dominating the final style of the center. Hood had won the *Chicago Tribune* building design competition in 1922; since then, his skyscraper style had shown an evolving abstraction and simplification of the stepped-back gothic tower popular with architects in the 1920's and 1930's. For Hood and other architects of the period, the setbacks, originally imposed by zoning laws to permit light penetration to the streets, were not merely practical necessities but also design elements that gave skyscrapers upward movement, energy, and visual variety. Hood's incorporation of setbacks to relieve the monolithic nature of the RCA Building thus tied the design of the structure firmly to the more conservative, historically derived forces of early twentieth century architecture, in contrast to the more radical abstract modernism that had developed in Europe by the late 1920's.

Rockefeller Center's unity of design extended beyond related building styles and materials. The interior decoration of the structures was developed according to a theme, the progress of civilization, in order to give the complex spiritual content. Murals and sculptures were sought from the most prominent artists of the day. At times, as in the case of Pablo Picasso, the commissions were refused because artists either were unsympathetic to corporate interests or resistant to dictated content. On one occasion, the management received more than it expected. In 1934, the Mexican painter Diego Rivera's mural "Man at the Crossroads" caused a scandal when Communist iconography was identified in it; Rivera's mural was eventually removed and reconstituted in Mexico City. Throughout the complex, the dominant stylistic influence on the decorative program was Art Deco.

Even before its official completion, Rockefeller Center became a magnet for visitors. Its soaring edifices and open spaces seemed to represent the best that a city could be and encouraged hope in a future of prosperity during the dark years of the Depression.

Impact of Event

Rockefeller Center marked a turning point in urban planning and development in the United States. It was the first time that a complex of stylistically related commercial buildings had been planned in the middle of a city. Its public plaza was unprecedented both for being privately built and supported and for being urban rather than rural or agrarian in design and ambience. The mixture of skyscrapers and low buildings, all visually unified but each one surrounded by light and air, became a benchmark for corporate urbanism and a model for subsequent developments in other cities after World War II. Prior to the construction of Rockefeller Center, the large-scale planning and design of large sections of city property had been the domain of city governments, especially through the "cities beautiful" movement at the turn of the century. Subsequently, it would be the private sector that would lead the way, although frequently with municipal aid and encouragement. Not all of these developments would be as successful as Rockefeller Center, and certain practices, such as the wholesale destruction of older buildings and homes to make way for redevelopment, would become controversial legacies of the Rockefeller program.

Part of Rockefeller Center's success and influence stemmed from its designers' attempts to incorporate features that would relieve the potential for urban congestion inherent in a project of its size. The center featured the first integral garage in an urban commercial building. Underground roadways permitted trucks to make deliveries, and at the completion ceremony, it was noted that eight hundred trucks serviced the center daily without disrupting traffic on neighboring streets. Underground walkways connected the buildings as well. Shops and restaurants helped to service the office workers' practical needs.

Although the primary function of Rockefeller Center was commercial, public use was not only permitted but also encouraged. The famous skating rink in the plaza was added specifically to increase pedestrian traffic in the complex's central area. Visitors were allowed access to terrace and rooftop gardens. Shops and exhibitions invited strolling and browsing. Extravagant displays of flags and seasonal decorations evoked a festive mood. The emphasis on the center as an integrated focal point of the urban fabric of the city, a self-contained community tied to the larger metropolis, reflected the designers' attempt to adapt contemporary European theories of social urban planning to an emphatically capitalistic, profit-motivated enterprise. This integrated approach was to add a new dimension to corporate building in the following decades.

The center's influence was felt not only in the area of corporate urbanism but also in the development of New York City itself. Through its location between Fifth and Sixth avenues, Rockefeller Center anchored and stabilized the shopping district on the first street and helped to revitalize the second. It inaugurated a midtown business district that expanded after World War II as other office towers clustered in its vicinity, borrowing its prestige and, at times, even its designs. Radio City Music Hall became a center of popular entertainment and a main tourist attraction for the area, and the plaza, with its seasonal decorations and ice-skating rink frequently featured in television and movies, became one of the most recognized urban sites in the country.

Bibliography

Balfour, Alan. *Rockefeller Center: Architecture as Theater.* New York: McGraw-Hill, 1978. Descriptive, condensed history of the project. Strength lies in the detailed analysis of the buildings themselves, the architects, and the theoretical and historical influences on the designs. Annotated, but brief and incomplete, bibliography. More than two hundred photographs, including views of the property before construction and later images of the subsequent development in the area. Footnotes and index.

Jordy, William. "Rockefeller Center and Corporate Urbanism." In *The Impact of European Modernism in the Mid-Twentieth Century.* Vol. 4 in *American Buildings and Their Architects.* Garden City, N.Y.: Doubleday, 1972. Informative, considered analysis of the successes and failures of Rockefeller Center's architecture and public spaces. Places the plan within a historical context of urban design and planning, thus explaining its conservative and innovative features. Extensive analysis of the plaza as a public space. Footnotes and photographs. Eighty-five pages.

Kilham, Walter H. *Raymond Hood, Architect: Form Through Function in the American Skyscraper.* New York: Architectural Book Publishing Company, 1974. Subjective, first-person account by a member of Hood's architectural firm. Behind-the-scenes view of architectural practices. Hood's personality and attitudes, and the problems attendant upon various commissions, including fifty-seven pages on Rockefeller Center. Bibliography and index, but no footnotes.

Krinsky, Carol H. *Rockefeller Center.* New York: Oxford University Press, 1978. Comprehensive, contextual history of the project, including later developments through the 1970's. Analysis of impact and influences. Examination of art and decorative program. Includes photographs and illustrations of plans and elevations. Extensive bibliography and index. Scholarly but readable.

Loth, David. *City Within a City.* New York: William Morrow, 1966. Nonscholarly account of Rockefeller Center's history and development. Anecdotal and accessible. Gives background on the principal participants and accounts of colorful episodes. Pleasant reading, but not the first choice for researchers seeking analysis and detailed historical accuracy.

Rockefeller Center, Incorporated. *The Last Rivet: The Story of Rockefeller Center, a City Within a City, as Told at the Ceremony in Which John D. Rockefeller, Jr., Drove the Last Rivet of the Last Building, November 1, 1939.* New York: Columbia University Press, 1940. Essentially a transcript of the ceremony that marked the official completion of Rockefeller Center. Includes texts of speeches describing the history of the property and project. Notably absent are any references to the designers or architects. Statistical information regarding the construction is featured in sidebar labels. Especially interesting for comparative reasons, since certain details of the history recollected in the speeches by major participants have been shown by researchers to be erroneous. Includes photographs of the property before, during, and after construction.

Madeline C. Archer

Cross-References

German Artists Found the Bauhaus (1919), p. 463; A Paris Exhibition Defines Art Deco (1925), p. 654; The Empire State Building Opens as the World's Tallest Building (1931), p. 880; Rivera's Rockefeller Center Mural Is Destroyed (1934), p. 957; NBC Launches American Television at the World's Fair (1939), p. 1143.

GONE WITH THE WIND PREMIERES

Category of event: Motion pictures
Time: December 15, 1939
Locale: Atlanta, Georgia

Following its premiere, Gone with the Wind, *independently produced by David O. Selznick, received a record ten Academy Awards and became the biggest blockbuster in motion-picture history*

Principal personages:

DAVID O. SELZNICK (1902-1965), an independent producer whose perfectionism dominated the film's production

MARGARET MITCHELL (1900-1949), a writer whose 1936 novel was the basis for the film

VIVIEN LEIGH (VIVIAN MARY HARTLEY, 1913-1967), an actress who won an Oscar for her performance as Scarlett O'Hara

CLARK GABLE (1901-1960), a top Hollywood star who portrayed Rhett Butler in the film

OLIVIA DE HAVILLAND (1916-   ), an actress who portrayed Melanie Hamilton in the film

LESLIE HOWARD (LESLIE STAINER, 1893-1943), an actor who portrayed Ashley Wilkes in the film

HATTIE MCDANIEL (1895-1952), an actress who became the first African American to receive an Oscar for her performance in the film

VICTOR FLEMING (1883-1949), a director who received sole screen credit for directing the film

WILLIAM CAMERON MENZIES (1896-1957), the production designer largely responsible for the overall look of the film

Summary of Event

In 1935, David O. Selznick left Metro-Goldwyn-Mayer (MGM), the premiere Hollywood studio of the time, to form Selznick International Pictures. As an independent producer, Selznick made films that were in keeping with his preference for adaptations of classical novels, often with central roles for women. Early in 1936, at the urging of his East Coast story editor Kay Brown, Selznick read a synopsis of an as-yet-unpublished Civil War melodrama by Margaret Mitchell. Worried about the box-office failure of other Civil War stories and the length of the novel, Selznick initially refused to pay the asking price of sixty-five thousand dollars for the book's film rights. Just a week after the book's official publication in July, 1936, Selznick reconsidered and made an offer of fifty thousand dollars, which was accepted. The novel immediately became a runaway best-seller, and the *Gone with the Wind* phenomenon began.

Selznick was obsessive about his role in film production. No detail was too small for his involvement, and no price was too high to achieve the quality he sought. These facts are partially responsible for the cost and length of the production of *Gone with the Wind.* In addition, Selznick had a contract with United Artists to distribute the films he produced through 1938. Popular opinion, however, demanded that Clark Gable, who was under contract to MGM, play the role of Rhett Butler. Louis B. Mayer, the head of MGM, agreed to lend Gable and to provide one-half of the film's financing (estimated then at $2,500,000) in return for world distribution rights and half the total profits. Because he had other films currently in various stages of production and because of his typically extravagant methods, Selznick did not have enough capital to make *Gone with the Wind* on his own. In order to get Gable and financial backing, Selznick eventually accepted Mayer's offer.

In early 1937, Selznick commissioned Sidney Howard, a Pulitzer Prize-winning playwright, to write the screenplay. In six weeks, Howard completed a four-hundred-page script that translated into six hours of screen time. To get the script to a more manageable length, Selznick and Howard worked on three subsequent drafts in early 1938. Still not satisfied with the script, Selznick put it aside while he returned to the unresolved casting problems.

During this time, as a means of focusing public attention on *Gone with the Wind* while stalling production until the contract with United Artists expired, Selznick's publicity director, Russell Birdwell, orchestrated a nationwide "search for Scarlett." Selznick was never convinced that an inexperienced or unknown actress should play the central character, who would be on screen in nearly every shot of the film, but he relished the publicity that the search provided. He considered a number of established Hollywood stars for the role of Scarlett, including Bette Davis, Miriam Hopkins, Paulette Goddard, Norma Shearer, Jean Arthur, Joan Bennett, and Katharine Hepburn, but none was felt to be quite right. Selznick signed with MGM for the use of Gable in August, 1938, and production was scheduled to begin in December, 1938, even though there was still no finished script and the roles of Scarlett and of many of the supporting characters had not yet been cast. The "burning of Atlanta," in which old movie sets on Selznick International's backlot were set ablaze while Rhett and Scarlett doubles fled, initiated the production of the film.

Rewrites on the script continued and employed a number of writers, including Jo Swerling, Oliver H. P. Garrett, Charles MacArthur, F. Scott Fitzgerald, and Ben Hecht. Selznick insisted that the writers use only dialogue from the novel and respect the narrative structure of the original as closely as possible. None of the writers who followed Howard was allowed to work without Selznick's constant interference, and script revisions continued throughout the film's production.

Casting decisions for principal roles were finally announced on January 13, 1939. Olivia de Havilland landed the role of Melanie, which she had actively pursued, and Leslie Howard reluctantly consented to play Ashley as part of a deal that allowed him to produce his next film. Vivien Leigh was chosen to play Scarlett, and though she had been a serious contender for several months, Selznick preferred to have her arrival in Hollywood seem the result of happenstance rather than deliberate planning in order to avoid the wrath of rejected actresses.

On January 26, 1939, production of *Gone with the Wind* began in earnest with George Cukor as director. After only a few weeks of filming, Cukor left the production, in part because of Cukor's refusal to comply with Selznick's demand for approval of every camera setup. In addition, Cukor was widely known as a "woman's director," and Clark Gable felt that his role was being diminished at the expense of the female characters. Victor Fleming, with whom Gable felt comfortable, was chosen to replace Cukor.

The removal of Cukor set the tone of upheaval that was to characterize the remainder of the production. Selznick demonstrated that, with the exception of the stars, all personnel were expendable parts and that he was the dominant creative force of the production. At least five different directors, three cinematographers and countless writers were involved in the production of *Gone with the Wind*—a fact that had surprisingly little effect on the film's look, since it was Selznick, and to a lesser extent William Cameron Menzies, whose vision shaped the film.

Filming officially ended on June 27, 1939, although work on retakes and process shots continued. Postproduction was only slightly less chaotic than the other stages of the film's production, but Selznick showed a four-hour version to MGM executives in late August and received an enthusiastic response. The completion of the music track, intertitles, additional editing, and the largest main title ever designed resulted in a final version running three hours and forty minutes. Two sneak previews in September received an overwhelmingly positive response, although some criticism was leveled at the amount of kissing in the film and at Rhett's final line, "Frankly, my dear, I don't give a damn." The use of any profanity, and specifically the word "damn," was forbidden by the Motion Picture Production Code of 1930. Selznick eventually received permission to use the word, although he was fined five thousand dollars for violating the code.

Gone with the Wind premiered in Atlanta on December 15, 1939, and the occasion delivered all the glamor and spectacle of Hollywood during its heyday. Huge crowds thronged the spotlit theater, women fainted when Clark Gable arrived, and many of the country's most wealthy and powerful people attended. The film went on to garner ten Academy Awards, including the Irving Thalberg Award for outstanding achievement in motion-picture production for Selznick. The first Oscar awarded to an African-American performer went to Hattie McDaniel, who would remain the only black to win an Oscar for another twenty-four years.

Impact of Event

The total production cost of *Gone with the Wind*, including prints and publicity, ran to $4,250,000, more than twice the average for a prestige picture of the time. The length of the film and the inclusion of an intermission were extremely rare practices. *Gone with the Wind*'s production eventually utilized fifty-nine leading and supporting cast members, 2,400 extras, 1,100 horses, 375 pigs, mules, oxen, cows, dogs, and other animals, 450 vehicles, including wagons, ambulances, and gun caissons, 90 sets built using 1,000,000 feet of lumber, 5,500 wardrobe items, and 449,512 feet of film shot in Technicolor, a relatively new process at the time. All of these elements added up to the biggest film spectacle ever produced, and one that many industry insiders predicted would fail to return a profit.

The popularity and profitability of *Gone with the Wind* signaled both the height and the beginning of the end of the Hollywood studio system. The year 1939 was a banner year for Hollywood, which produced such films as *Dark Victory, Stagecoach, The Wizard of Oz, Wuthering Heights*, and *Mr. Smith Goes to Washington*, and profits increased through the war years. Yet the Hollywood system of "vertical integration," in which production, distribution, and exhibition were controlled by the major Hollywood studios, was under attack as a monopolistic practice. In 1948, a court decision put an end to block booking, blind bidding, price fixing, and other unfair business practices, and the major studios were ordered to divest themselves of their theater holdings. The decision effectively put an end to the studio-based production system.

As an independent producer, Selznick already worked outside the studio system, although he relied on the cooperation and financial support of the major studios to produce the top-quality "blockbuster" films that were his goal. The phenomenal success of *Gone with the Wind* marked the arrival of the independent producer as a dominant force in the industry, and Selznick served as a model for the production approach that eventually replaced the studio system in the new Hollywood. Selznick's filmmaking method was not marked by the assembly-line efficiency and economy often equated with the studio system but was both extravagant and painstaking. He believed that the public would pay increased ticket prices to see high-quality film spectaculars, and the reception of *Gone with the Wind* proved him correct.

The marketing strategy employed for the release of *Gone with the Wind* became a model for later blockbuster films. Exhibitors charged seventy cents at the door, two to three times the going rate. Loew's Incorporated, MGM's parent company, charged exhibitors seventy percent of the box-office revenues, twice the usual fee for a top feature, which Loew's then split with Selznick. Initially, the film opened only in large cities in premiere movie theaters; subsequently (nearly two years later, in some cases), it was released to second-run theaters. *Gone with the Wind* was reissued four times by 1948 and continued to reap profits with each new release.

In 1940, Selznick International Pictures had only three films in release, but the company netted $10 million in profits that year. Only MGM, with profits of $8.7 million, was even close, and half its profits came from its distribution of *Gone with the Wind*. The film became the biggest blockbuster in movie history and was not dislodged from its number-one position until 1965 and *The Sound of Music*. Subsequent films have made more money, but none has sold as many tickets as *Gone with the Wind*.

More than a film blockbuster, *Gone with the Wind* also became a cultural phenomenon that still exerts power. The film's world television premiere in 1976 was the highest-rated television program ever presented. The film has inspired stage musicals, merchandising tie-ins, and all manner of spoofs and parodies. A thriving fan network of "Windies" and a number of books devoted entirely to the film attest to its continued popularity. A sequel to the novel, *Scarlett*, was published in 1991, and plans were made for a movie sequel.

Stylistically, *Gone with the Wind* is still notable for its sweeping panorama shots, such as the siege of Atlanta sequence. Because the Technicolor process was relatively new, the film created a spectacular impression simply in terms of its deeply saturated color and beautiful *mise-en-scène*. The melodramatic elements, especially the unhappy ending, are perennially effective, although the treatment of the Civil War and race themes have at times been objectionable to later audiences.

Bibliography

Bridges, Herb, and Terryl C. Boodman. *"Gone with the Wind": The Definitive Illustrated History of the Book, the Movie, and the Legend.* New York: Simon & Schuster, 1989. Published to coincide with the fiftieth anniversary of the film. Contains hundreds of stills, many in color. Brief history of the film, from preproduction to premiere. No index.

Cameron, Judy, and Paul J. Christman. *The Art of "Gone with the Wind": The Making of a Legend.* New York: Prentice Hall, 1989. Introduction by Daniel Mayer Selznick. Another oversized anniversary edition, with full-page photos and more production information than the Bridges book. Includes limited index, original memos, and telegrams related to the film's production.

Flamini, Roland. *Scarlett, Rhett, and a Cast of Thousands.* New York: Macmillan, 1975. Numerous photos from the collection of the author and others. Includes detailed history of the film's production and a good index.

Lambert, Gavin. *GWTW: The Making of "Gone with the Wind."* Boston: Little, Brown, 1973. The author knew Vivien Leigh, George Cukor, and David O. Selznick. Provides interesting information regarding the psychological disposition of the key people involved. Includes bibliography and index.

Schatz, Thomas. *The Genius of the System: Hollywood Filmmaking in the Studio Era.* New York: Pantheon Books, 1988. Explores the Hollywood studio system with close analysis of representative companies, including Selznick International Pictures. Provides insightful historical context for production of *Gone with the Wind.* Includes notes on sources and index.

Toni A. Perrine

Cross-References

The Ten Commandments Establishes Silent-Film Spectacle (1923), p. 567; Hollywood Enters Its Golden Age (1930's), p. 822; The Classic *The Wizard of Oz* Opens (1939), p. 1109; The Hollywood Studio System Is Transformed (1946), p. 1307; *The Civil War* Rivets the Attention of the United States (1990), p. 2657.

STORMY WEATHER OFFERS NEW FILM ROLES TO AFRICAN AMERICANS

Category of event: Motion pictures
Time: The 1940's
Locale: Hollywood, California

Stormy Weather and other big-band musicals created new roles for blacks in Hollywood films, allowing some actors the opportunity to escape older stereotypes and take on more substantive roles

> *Principal personages:*
> LENA HORNE (1917-   ), an actress and singer best known for her performances in the big-band musicals of the 1940's
> WALTER WHITE (1893-1955), the executive secretary of the National Association for the Advancement of Colored People (NAACP) in the 1940's who worked to prompt the film industry to depict blacks as human beings
> WENDELL WILLKIE (1892-1944), a Republican presidential candidate who became a counsel to the film industry and who advocated the equality of blacks in films
> HAZEL SCOTT (1920-1981), a gifted artist and musician who refused to appear before segregated audiences or play roles in films that perpetuated stereotypes
> HATTIE MCDANIEL (1895-1952), the quintessential "mammy" of Hollywood films

Summary of Event

Prior to the 1940's, blacks in Hollywood films were limited to playing a few stereotyped roles such as the mammy, the villain, the jungle dweller, the servant, and the jester. Yet the 1930's gave a hint of what the 1940's would hold for blacks in film. Although black actors in the late 1920's and the 1930's were primarily cast in servant roles, some were shown to be uninhibited entertainers or jesters, as in the films *Hallelujah* (1929) and *Hearts in Dixie* (1929).

The black as entertainer became highly important in the musicals of the 1940's. Dustpans and mops were exchanged for zoot suits and sequined gowns. As Hollywood's black singers, dancers, musicians, and acrobats grew in popularity, a special platform evolved for them to display their talents. Unrelated song-and-dance numbers were injected into some films; black entertainers would pop up and entertain the film audience unhampered by a story line. Frequently, a nightclub scene would be introduced into a film so that performers would have a natural setting in which to entertain. Because such musical numbers were not integrated into the films' scripts, scenes featuring blacks could be cut without spoiling the story should a local or

Southern theater object to such scenes.

Metro-Goldwyn-Mayer (MGM), under the direction of Louis B. Mayer, offered its first long-term contract to a black artist when it signed Lena Horne. The musical *Panama Hattie* (1942) featured Horne, sumptuously gowned, performing a Latin song. For most of her film career, Horne found herself limited to roles as an onstage performer. The studios had not made her into a maid, but they had not made her into much of anything else, either. Horne described herself as "a butterfly pinned to a column" in her films.

All-black musicals were considered a risk, and nearly fourteen years had passed since the last one when MGM decided to proceed with Arthur Freed's production of *Cabin in the Sky* (1943). Yet the film's depiction of blacks resembled that of earlier films. Blacks in the film were depicted as removed from the daily routine of real American life, and the film's characters were placed in remote, idealized worlds. Black stereotypes were played up, and folk culture was still being passed off as the real thing.

In 1943, Twentieth Century-Fox produced a different kind of all-black musical entitled *Stormy Weather*. The songs and dances were integral to the story line, and the film did not revolve around the stereotypes of *Cabin in the Sky*. Although *Stormy Weather* was the story of a black dancer (portrayed by Bill Robinson) who woos Lena Horne and eventually wins her over, the film was, moreover, a revue of black entertainment as seen through the eyes of Robinson. *Stormy Weather* rounded up and displayed the talents of Fats Waller, Cab Calloway, Katherine Dunham, Ada Brown, and the Nicholas Brothers.

In the South, where all-black films were usually shunned, both *Stormy Weather* and *Cabin in the Sky* reached all-black houses, where audiences greeted them with enthusiasm. The films also enjoyed popularity at Army camps and abroad.

The NAACP had been attempting to force change in Hollywood's degrading treatment of blacks for twenty-five years. With the onrush of these 1940's musicals, the NAACP found one of its best weapons. The group's big gun was Lena Horne. NAACP Executive Secretary Walter White assumed personal control over Horne's career; White felt that, since Horne was beautiful and had not yet been typecast, it would be essential for her to establish a different kind of Hollywood image for black women.

Hazel Scott was another black performer who refused to be typecast. She had been a child prodigy, reading by the age of three, learning piano at four. Scott grew into a demanding performer who never attempted to conceal her color or her fiery temperament. She refused to appear before segregated audiences or accept roles in films, because she felt she would have to play stereotyped roles. Instead, she consistently appeared in films as herself, seated at the piano as she would have been in a nightclub. Her specialty was in blending classics and swing music in such films as *I Dood It* (1943), *Broadway Rhythm* (1944), and *Rhapsody in Blue* (1945). She invested her characters with refinement and taste by always sitting upright at the piano, professionally gowned and supremely confident. Unfortunately, her brand of militancy may have dampened her career, and many later blacks viewed her as a woman who was simply trying to prove her worth.

Stormy Weather and the other big-band musicals of the 1940's came at a time of war abroad; it was also a time when the war for racial equality was beginning to erupt on the home front. These 1940's musicals were Hollywood's first attempts, no matter how archaic by later standards, to move beyond black stereotypes. The musicals represented the first time blacks could be seen out of their servant, mammy, or jungle costumes; they had been elevated to the status of acceptable, even glamorous, entertainers. Yet except for small glimpses of real-life characterizations in *Stormy Weather*, blacks were still not portrayed as everyday Americans in everyday situations.

Impact of Event

With the release of *Stormy Weather* and the other big-band musicals of the 1940's, a new front was opening for black artists. The social climate of the country was also beginning to change. Wendell Willkie, the 1940 Republican presidential candidate, had aligned himself with the NAACP and was representing the organization in negotiations with the Hollywood studios. Willkie was giving the NAACP campaign a new clout.

In 1941, President Franklin D. Roosevelt issued an executive order that forbade racial and religious discrimination in employment in war-related industries. Integration was being pushed by the government. Many of the more liberal studios agreed to follow new racial guidelines when depicting black characters and to use black extras whenever possible. New opportunities were beginning to benefit black entertainers while paving the way for the emergence of sympathetic black characters. The studios also strove to integrate more blacks into behind-the-scenes jobs. Even *Variety* announced, "Better Breaks for Negroes in H'Wood."

Black artists themselves were taking different paths with their lives and careers. Lena Horne and Hazel Scott were confident in their mission, although Horne sought to manipulate the system more from within than did Scott. Yet other blacks who had already fought for their niche in the Hollywood system did not want to shake up the status quo.

Horne, especially, was feeling the heat from other blacks who were afraid that she was beginning a large-scale campaign on the part of black actors to raise their status, and in the process, to eliminate jobs held by blacks who excelled at the older, stereotyped roles. One unofficial but influential group of black Hollywood actors protested her close association with the NAACP, saying that she would make it impossible for them to get work, since soon there would be no more "jungle" or "plantation" parts left. Hattie McDaniel, who had been enormously successful playing stereotypical black maids, sympathized with Horne's position but would not support it; McDaniel argued that Horne was not realistic in her approach to working in a white man's world.

When the Disney Studios released *Song of the South* in 1946, the film seemed to signal the demise of the black as entertainer. A throwback to the extreme stereotypes of the 1920's and 1930's, *Song of the South* took place in the pastoral old South, with Hattie McDaniel providing the voice of the family mammy. Although the film made a profit, it was panned by both the white and black press and incited protests from black audiences.

Song of the South, though, did not presage a return to the stereotypes of earlier films. America in the 1940's had confronted fascism in Europe; simultaneously, the nation was being reminded by civil rights groups of the bigotry and racial inequality in American industries and in the armed forces. More forcefully than ever before, America was urged to right its old wrongs.

Sympathetic and real-life black characters began to emerge on the scene along with the 1940's jazz musicals. In *The Ox-Bow Incident* (1943), Leigh Whipper portrayed a somber black preacher who objected to the lynching of suspected cattle-rustlers. In *In This Our Life* (1942), Eric Anderson played an intelligent young law student arrested on hit-and-run charges. Anderson's character was able to maintain his dignity and innocence until the guilty party, played by Bette Davis, stepped forward. In Alfred Hitchcock's *Lifeboat* (1944), a group of Americans confined to a battered lifeboat after their freighter is torpedoed symbolized the elements of American society. An intelligent black steward (Canada Lee) represented America's second-class citizenry. Lee's character was first greeted by Tallulah Bankhead as "Charcoal," but when it was revealed he saved a white woman and child from drowning, he became "Joe."

War films also began diverging from the black caricature. *The Negro Soldier* (1944) was an Army-orientation film directed by Frank Capra that was distributed to the public. Instead of a handkerchief-headed mammy, the film depicted a distinguished black mother who was concerned about and proud of her GI son. The soldier, too, was not portrayed as a superstitious clown but as an intelligent black recruit who qualified for officer training.

During this time of struggle abroad and at home, the stereotyped image of the black American began to crumble. Through the success of *Stormy Weather* and other big-band jazz musicals, Hollywood sought to elevate its servants and mammies to roles as entertainers. With their talents uncovered and with a change in the social climate, blacks began to be offered more sympathetic, realistic, and positive roles. Following the war came further advancements, as blacks pressed on to win other roles more in keeping with their status in and contribution to American life and culture.

Bibliography

Bogle, Donald. *Brown Sugar: Eighty Years of America's Black Female Superstars.* New York: Harmony Books, 1980. An oversized book featuring a fine collection of photographs and personal stories about black female superstars. Covers a span of eighty years and explores these women's personal lives, struggles, and views. The book is divided into sections by decades.

_____. *Toms, Coons, Mulattoes, Mammies, and Bucks: An Interpretive History of Blacks in American Films.* New York: Viking Press, 1973. Maps out a sixty-year span of the cinematic portrayal of blacks, from a 1903 version of *Uncle Tom's Cabin* to the "blaxploitation" films of the early 1970's. Also takes a look at black cinema abroad and compares it to Hollywood.

Buckley, Gail Lumet. *The Hornes: An American Family.* New York: Alfred A. Knopf, 1986. This book, written by Lena Horne's daughter, spans eight generations of the Hornes, a family that often served in the role of black ambassadors to white America. Filled with family pictures and memorabilia and takes a personal look at Lena Horne, framed in the light of a rich heritage and photographed through the eyes of her daughter.

Horne, Lena, and Richard Schickel. *Lena.* New York: Doubleday, 1965. An autobiography of Lena Horne, one of the principal stars of 1940's musicals. Delves into Horne's thirty years on Broadway, in films, in nightclubs, and on television and offers her strong opinions and fresh insights into other black artists of her era.

Leab, Daniel. *From Sambo to Superspade: The Black Experience in Motion Pictures.* Boston: Houghton Mifflin, 1975. Chronicles the portrayal of blacks in films from their earliest days up until 1974. Demonstrates how the black actor has been stereotyped, from "Sambo" portrayals of blacks as irresponsible, loyal, lazy, and humble through the sex-and-violence "superspade" pictures of the 1970's.

Steven C. Kowall

Cross-References

The Harlem Renaissance Celebrates African-American Culture (1920's), p. 480; Armstrong First Records with His Hot Five Group (1925), p. 670; Ellington Begins an Influential Engagement at the Cotton Club (1927), p. 739; *Hallelujah* Is the First Important Black Musical (1929), p. 772; Billie Holiday Begins Her Recording Career (1933), p. 930; Lubitsch's *The Merry Widow* Opens New Vistas for Film Musicals (1934), p. 941; Gershwin's *Porgy and Bess* Opens in New York (1935), p. 1016; Marian Anderson Is Barred from Constitution Hall (1939), p. 1126; *I Spy* Debuts to Controversy (1965), p. 2044; *The Wiz* Brings African-American Talent to Broadway (1975), p. 2334.

KAZAN BRINGS NATURALISM
TO THE STAGE AND SCREEN

Categories of event: Theater and motion pictures
Time: The 1940's and the 1950's
Locale: New York, New York, and Hollywood, California

Director Elia Kazan collaborated with some of the best talent in American theater and film to produce an impressive body of work that emphasized the realistic presentation of scenes and emotions

Principal personages:

ELIA KAZAN (ELIA KAZANJOGLOU, 1909-   ), a Turkish-born director of stage and cinema who broke new ground by introducing naturalism in productions of plays by leading American dramatists

THORNTON WILDER (1897-1975), an American playwright who won a 1938 Pulitzer Prize for *Our Town* and a second Pulitzer in 1943 for *The Skin of Our Teeth*

TENNESSEE WILLIAMS (1911-1983), an American playwright who won Pulitzer Prizes in 1948 for *A Streetcar Named Desire* and in 1955 for *Cat on a Hot Tin Roof*

ARTHUR MILLER (1915-   ), a New York dramatist who won a Pulitzer Prize in 1949 for *Death of a Salesman*

WILLIAM INGE (1913-1973), a Midwestern playwright who won a 1953 Pulitzer Prize for his drama *Picnic*

ROBERT ANDERSON (1917-   ), a successful New York dramatist

JOSEPH MCCARTHY (1908-1957), a rabidly anticommunist U.S. senator who initiated a stringent hunt for citizens whom he considered threats to American democracy

JO MIELZINER (1901-1976), a five-time Tony Award and Academy Award-winning designer who collaborated with Kazan

MARLON BRANDO (1924-   ), a magnetic actor who rose to stardom in Kazan-directed productions

Summary of Event

Famous for his inventive, uncompromisingly emotive stage technique, Elia Kazan became a twentieth century catalyst for the departure from classicism that brought American drama into its golden age. Under the guidance of Lee Strasberg, Harold Clurman, and Cheryl Crawford during his association with the distinguished Group Theatre, the most influential American drama experiment of the 1930's, Kazan received stage training in the gritty, naturalistic Stanislavsky method. In employing this unpredictably emotional type of method acting, actors immersed themselves in the feelings and responses of characters, thereby achieving verisimilitude through their recreation of actual psychological states; such performances were often marked by weeping, shrieks, and other unconventional stage behaviors. Advancing from method acting to a similar style of directing, Kazan earned lasting credit for his work during the 1940's, when he staged Thornton Wilder's *The Skin of Our Teeth* (1942), a bold mix of fantasy and comedy starring Tallulah Bankhead, Montgomery Clift, Florence March, and Florence Reed that opened to rave reviews in the author's hometown of New Haven, Connecticut. For this production, Kazan netted the 1942 New York Drama Critics Circle Award for direction; he followed this success by directing acclaimed productions of *One Touch of Venus* (1943), *Jacobowsky and the Colonel* (1944), and Arthur Miller's *All My Sons* (1947), a gripping post-World War II family drama that won for Kazan a Tony Award and another New York Drama Critics Circle Award.

In 1947, working in conjunction with playwright Tennessee Williams and designer Jo Mielziner, Kazan directed *A Streetcar Named Desire*, a dramatic tour de force set in New Orleans. The production was notable for its stinging, animalistic depictions of Southern decadence, and Kazan earned accolades for his sensitive treatment of the play, one of the most highly regarded and frequently produced dramas of the twentieth century. Kazan followed this productive period with work at the Actors Studio, a teaching institution he founded in 1947 with Lee Strasberg and Cheryl Crawford and where he was brought into contact with such innovative talents as Marlon Brando, who played the role of Stanley Kowalski, the lascivious, semiliterate seducer in *A Streetcar Named Desire*. A year later, Kazan, equal to the challenge of staging the most serious dramatic works of the age, enhanced his stature as the dominant voice in American theater direction with an award-winning production of Arthur Miller's *Death of a Salesman* (1949), which critics proclaimed the prototypical American tragedy. Kazan coaxed powerful performances from stars Lee J. Cobb, Cameron Mitchell, Arthur Kennedy, and Mildred Dunnock, and the play became the dramatic touchstone of its era.

The first of three sons of George and Athena Sismanoglou Kazanjoglou, Kazan was born in Constantinople, Turkey, and emigrated with his family to the United States in 1913. The family settled in a Greek community in New York City and later moved to New Rochelle, New York. As a teenager, Kazan was influenced by a teacher, Anna B. Shank, who encouraged him to forego his family's commercial interests and to follow his intellectual bent. An honors student, he was graduated from New Rochelle High School and attended Williams College, where, in his senior year, he resolved to study drama; he was graduated from Williams in 1930. After two years' work at the Yale University Drama School, Kazan quit what he considered to be worthless, repetitive study, and he allied himself with New York's Group Theatre the following year. There, utilizing the Stanislavsky method, he played roles in Clifford Odets' *Paradise Lost* (1935), *Waiting for Lefty* (1935), *Till the Day I Die* (1935), *Golden Boy* (1936), and *Night Music* (1940), and he also appeared in two Anatole Litvak films, *City for Conquest* (1940) and *Blues in the Night* (1941). A respectable actor, he received favorable notices for his efforts.

After several years' theatrical apprenticeship, Kazan advanced to full-time directing. His early efforts went unnoticed, but in 1942, his production of Thornton Wilder's *The Skin of Our Teeth* brought him serious critical acclaim and opportunities to work with the major American playwrights of the era, including Arthur Miller, William Inge, Robert Anderson, and Tennessee Williams, who would become his closest colleague. For the remainder of the decade, Kazan aspired to greater heights of theatrical creativity in such productions as *A Streetcar Named Desire* and his directorial masterpiece, Miller's *Death of a Salesman*.

Connecting with Tennessee Williams after the playwright saw a performance of *All My Sons* (1947), Kazan formed an unusually cooperative relationship with the writer, who, like Kazan, was a loner and outsider. On opening night of *A Streetcar Named Desire*, the director stood upstage with tears in his eyes, moved by the cooperative effort of writer, cast, and crew. The satisfaction gained from the experience created a lifelong friendship between Kazan and Williams, even though the author received the bulk of the praise for their collaborative achievement.

Although intrigued by the brutal, evocative inner sparrings of *A Streetcar Named Desire*, Kazan admitted that he preferred the humanistic themes of *Death of a Salesman*, particularly as they applied to his own father's commercial career. The popular response to Willy Loman, the play's central character and victim—who has since evolved into an American archetype—became Kazan's pinnacle; the production's resounding success earned the director a reputation as America's most brilliant stage director. The success of Kazan with *Death of a Salesman* stemmed largely from the director's deep respect for the play's verities and his genuine admiration for the character of Willy, a buffoonish loser who never failed to touch the audience's sensibilities.

Impact of Event

Kazan's influence on theatrical realism influenced American stagecraft well into the 1960's, when period drama, Hollywood films, and live television stage plays began to emulate the Actors Studio's insistence on psychological truth. During his heyday, Kazan insisted on an intense stripping of surface niceties; his approach helped to move audiences into a new era of cathartic concentration that spotlighted motivation above spectacle, costuming, and other surface treatment. Actors, many inspired by Brando's inarticulate, boorish stage antics in *A Streetcar Named Desire*, exceeded the bounds of classic theatricality by striving for an exaggerated naturalism, often marked by slovenly dress, nonstandard vocal expression, and working-class realism.

The anticommunist crusades of the Joseph McCarthy era, which for more than ten years deprived notable stage and film talents of opportunities for artistic expression, brought particular public notoriety to Kazan, who in 1952 agreed to testify before the House Committee on Un-American Activities. With unusual candor, Kazan admitted to an involvement with the Communist Party during a two-year period in which he had grown increasingly disenchanted with leftist doctrine. By supplying names, dates, and crucial details, notably about the role of Arthur Miller in leftist activities, Kazan cut himself off from old friends and colleagues, especially from adamant libertarians such as Dalton Trumbo, an eminent and forthright screenwriter who chose to go to prison rather than to accept what he thought was a blatant infringement of his First Amendment rights by the House committee. This turbulent era cost Kazan significant loss of face and caused him to worry that his four children—Nick, Judy, Katherine, and Chris—would suffer for his testimony.

Kazan's career, far from being ended by political scandal, brought him into further collaboration with Tennessee Williams in *Camino Real* (1953), followed by Robert Anderson's *Tea and Sympathy* (1953), Williams' Pulitzer Prize-winning *Cat on a Hot Tin Roof* (1955), William Inge's *Dark at the Top of the Stairs* (1957), and Archibald MacLeish's *J.B.* (1958), a lyric success that Kazan professed not to understand. The amalgamation of such creative talent continued to produce riveting dramas, climaxing in Kazan's last major stage effort, Williams' *Sweet Bird of Youth* (1959), in which Kazan compensated for weak plot development by commissioning Jo Mielziner's multimedia innovations.

In 1962, Kazan left Broadway to become one of the directors of the repertory company at the Lincoln Center for the Performing Arts. Kazan had high hopes for his association with the company, but his first Lincoln Center production, Arthur Miller's *After the Fall* (1962), met with mixed reviews. In 1964, after several badly received productions, Kazan resigned his Lincoln Center post and turned his attention almost exclusively to film direction.

Kazan had begun directing documentary films in 1937; in 1945, he made his first feature, *A Tree Grows in Brooklyn*. That film's popular and critical success led to other Hollywood assignments, including *Sea of Grass* (1947), *Boomerang* (1947), and *Gentleman's Agreement* (1947), for which Kazan won an Oscar as best director. He continued with a series of well-regarded, socially conscious films that included *Pinky* (1949), *Panic in the Streets* (1950), *Viva Zapata!* (1952), and *Man on a Tightrope* (1953). In 1951, Kazan directed the film version of *A Streetcar Named Desire*, in which Brando reprised his role from the Broadway production. Brando's explosive performance in the film made him a major star, and he and Kazan collaborated again in *On the Waterfront* (1954), for which both won Oscars. Many critics viewed *On the Waterfront*, the story of a courageous mobster turned informant, as Kazan's apologia for his testimony at the McCarthy hearings.

In 1955, Kazan enjoyed another major success with *East of Eden*, which brought another intense, brooding actor, James Dean, to stardom. Kazan continued to coax stellar performances from his casts in *Baby Doll* (1956), *A Face in the Crowd* (1957), *Wild River* (1960), and *Splendor in the Grass* (1961). In 1963, Kazan released *America, America*, based on a best-selling novel of the same name that he had published two years before. He published another best-seller, *The Arrangement*, in 1967, but a 1969 film version was a flop. He put out still another popular novel, *The Assassins*, in 1972, but did not translate the story to film. In the 1970's, Kazan largely withdrew from Hollywood, producing instead low-budget "home movies" such as the critically panned *The Visitors* (1972). In 1976, he returned to big-budget filmmaking with an acclaimed production of F. Scott Fitzgerald's 1941 novel *The Last Tycoon*.

In both his film and stage work, Kazan rejected the star system and the use of production gimmicks to create a realism that emphasized the strength of his material. His influence is evident in the work of a wide range of directors; his disciples have included such disparate stage and screen talents as Woody Allen, John Cassavetes, Arthur Penn, Sidney Lumet, and Martin Scorsese. In addition to helping launch the careers of Brando and Dean, Kazan also was instrumental in establishing such stars as Warren Beatty, Julie Harris, Natalie Wood, Eva Marie Saint, Lee Remick, and Carroll Baker. In a career that spanned nearly half a century, Kazan left a major mark on American drama.

Bibliography

Brockett, Oscar G. *History of the Theatre.* Boston: Allyn & Bacon, 1968. A valuable overview of theater history. Gives valuable information about set designers, producers, and music directors who influenced the growth of world theater.

Kazan, Elia. *Elia Kazan: A Life.* New York: Alfred A. Knopf, 1988. A thorough autobiography complete with one hundred photographs and a detailed index. Readers interested in the McCarthy era will find complete information about Kazan's involvement in the Communist Party and his decision to testify before the House Committee on Un-American Activities.

Murphy, Brenda. *Tennessee Williams and Elia Kazan: A Collaboration in the Theatre.* New York: Cambridge University Press, 1992. A thorough study of the collaboration between the playwright and the director on their productions of *A Streetcar Named Desire, Camino Real, Cat on a Hot Tin Roof,* and *Sweet Bird of Youth.* Illustrated, with extensive notes and bibliography.

Pauly, Thomas H. *An American Odyssey: Elia Kazan and American Culture.* Philadelphia: Temple University Press, 1983. A thorough survey of Kazan's career. Illustrated with black-and-white photographs of Kazan's stage productions and stills from his films.

Prideaux, Tom. *World Theatre in Pictures: From Ancient Times to Modern Broadway.* New York: Greenberg, 1953. A remarkable photographic montage of the most significant moments in theater history, featuring original casts and stressing action shots of such Kazan-directed productions as *The Glass Menagerie, A Streetcar Named Desire, The Skin of Our Teeth,* and *Death of a Salesman.*

Mary Ellen Snodgrass

Cross-References

Stanislavsky Helps to Establish the Moscow Art Theater (1897), p. 1; The Group Theatre Flourishes (1931), p. 874; The Federal Theatre Project Promotes Live Theater (1935), p. 989; Odets' *Awake and Sing* Becomes a Model for Protest Drama (1935), p. 1006; Blacklisting Seriously Depletes Hollywood's Talent Pool (1947), p. 1340; *A Streetcar Named Desire* Brings Method Acting to the Screen (1951), p. 1487.

THE NEW CRITICISM HOLDS SWAY

Category of event: Literature
Time: The 1940's and the 1950's
Locale: The United States

More than a generation of writers and teachers emphasized the text itself in literary criticism

Principal personages:

JOHN CROWE RANSOM (1888-1974), a professor at Harvard University and Kenyon College who argued that poetry must be philosophic and that science could not account for the world

T. S. ELIOT (1888-1965), a celebrated writer who argued that poetry was an escape from emotion and that the poem, not the poet, is primary

CLEANTH BROOKS (1906-   ), a scholar whose *Understanding Poetry* (1938) was for many years the basic text used in college classrooms to teach close reading of poetry

I. A. RICHARDS (1893-1979), a Harvard professor whose view of poetry as "emotive language" and "pseudo-statement" helped to shape New Criticism

R. P. BLACKMUR (1904-1965), a professor at Princeton University whose *Language as Gesture* (1952) was a key text of New Criticism

ALLEN TATE (1899-1979), a professor at the University of Minnesota whose poetry and criticism were both regional and metaphysical

Summary of Event

By the end of World War II, a method of literary study (particularly of poems) had gained primacy in American colleges and universities. The method, dubbed "New Criticism," soon triumphed over other ways to interpret literature.

New Criticism was a reaction to and a rejection of previous literary studies that (according to the New Critics) had submerged poetry in historical, philological, cultural, and biographical studies. Spearheaded by early critics such as Thomas E. Hulme (1883-1917) and T. S. Eliot, New Criticism argued that poetry should be interpreted by the reading of individual poems. This may appear to be an obvious truism, but according to Hulme, scholarship in the Romantic age had focused on the poet, whose verbal expressions were seen not so much as poetry as versified statements about the poet's emotional experience. Eliot, in his key critical work *The Sacred Wood* (1920), argued that the poet, rather than seeking to express emotion, should try to escape it by writing a poem, a construction of images, plot, and metaphors that embodies the truth intrinsic to the work itself. The author of a work, Eliot argued, is far less important than the work. Nor are the historical context or moral worldview from which the work comes very important. The New Critics rejected the

Victorian scholar Matthew Arnold's cultural criticism, which had claimed that poetry would replace religion and provide the stability that religion had previously given. New Criticism insisted that poetry is neither religion emotionally stated nor the ornamental prettification of cultural values and hopes. Nor, New Critics argued, is poetry to be valued according to its effect on readers; it is a verbal construct, a thing made—indeed, the word "poetry" comes from the Greek *poieo*, which means "to make." The New Critics thus taught and interpreted the poem as poetry: as a work with various parts and characteristics that were fit together to make an artful whole.

After this initial stage, New Criticism expanded its effect through the work of such other poets and critics as I. A. Richards, R. P. Blackmur, William Empson, Cleanth Brooks, and Allen Tate. In *The New Criticism* (1941), John Crowe Ransom carefully defined the school but lamented its apparent lack of philosophical depth, social awareness, and attention to cultural and moral values. Cleanth Brooks, in *Understanding Poetry* (1938), had provided a text that challenged poets and critics; mostly, however, Brooks's work captivated students by focusing on each individual poem's language, images, narrative, argument, and metaphors and on how these intrinsic qualities worked with and against one another to sustain a tension that was primarily literary and aesthetic.

In a third stage of development, various professors, critics, and poets codified New Criticism into a discernible method of literary criticism that was used to teach poetry to thousands of students between the 1940's and 1960's. Such texts as René Wellek's and Austin Warren's *Theory of Literature* (1949); William K. Wimsatt's *The Verbal Icon: Studies in the Meaning of Poetry* (1954); Murray Krieger's *The New Apologists for Poetry* (1956); Cleanth Brooks and William Wimsatt's *Literary Criticism: A Short History* (1957); Allen Tate's *Essays of Four Decades* (1969), dedicated appropriately to John Crowe Ransom; and Cleanth Brooks's 1956 reprint of *Modern Poetry and the Tradition* (1939) all indicate the formidable authority that New Criticism had achieved.

Several of these men, notably Eliot, Ransom, and Tate, were poets themselves. Their work did not constitute merely an abstract or academic affair but was shaped in the crucible of poetry itself. Thus, the hammer of poetry and the anvil of criticism mutually affected each other and provided a conception of poetry and its effects that was formed in the ongoing process of poetic imagination and critical evaluation.

From these three decades of critical and poetic activity, a remarkable school evolved. While there never was unanimity among the New Critics, their work was largely defined by the following characteristics: a concern for form that meant that poetry was viewed as a structure of events, images, and metaphors; an emphasis on close reading as the method by which texts were to be explicated; the use of structural analysis to determine how the parts of a poem work together to achieve its effect; a deliberate ignoring of the author's life, values, and worldview as well as of the poem's effect on the reader and of the poem's origin in society; an emphasis on semantic studies in which the way words "mean" according to poetic context is used to understand the poem; an insistence that literary criticism must be literary, and not primarily, if at all, moral criticism, social (Marxist) criticism, or psychological or theological criticism; and an understanding that a poem is a vital organic unity—not a mechanical contraption but a living thing that includes everything necessary to, and nothing extraneous to, its meaning. The tenets of the New Criticism exerted a powerful influence on the teaching and interpretation of poetry in the mid-twentieth century.

Impact of Event

Poetry, the New Critics said, is not any other thing; although it is written by human beings about human beings for human beings to human beings, it is not to be mistaken for any other activity, discipline, attitude, object, or value. By maintaining this focus, New Criticism influenced many teachers, readers, writers, and critics; through them, art—not only poetry, but all art objects—gained a new priority in the judgments and views of society. Poetry no longer was merely an ornament for a clergyman's sermon, a politician's platitudes, or a lawyer's case. The new approach invigorated poets and readers, but it also tended to isolate poetry from the lived life of a culture. Yet the theology of T. S. Eliot, the regionalism of John Crowe Ransom, the metaphysics of Allen Tate, and the didactic purposes of Cleanth Brooks prevented poetry from becoming merely "art for art's sake," an artifact that has no origin in culture or influence on society. The effect of a poem was still important, but it was to be construed as a power of the work, lest readers read into the poem and not permit the work to achieve its own proper effect. To use Eliot's metaphor, the poem is an intrinsically valuable "sacred wood"; whatever the wood means must come from the trees, flowers, creatures, and brooks of the wood—that is, from the images, metaphors, characters, setting, and action of the poem.

This view argued for the primacy of each individual reader's right and responsibility to experience poetry, and 1960's culture generally gave full expression to the need for each person to undergo and encounter life in his or her own immediacy. While the New Critics never intended such consequences, their argument that the poem itself is the experience out of which each reader was to cull impressions became part of the larger complex of antecedents and causes of the sensibility of individualism and immediacy that pervaded the era.

Further, the teaching that the message of the poem was not merely contained in the poem but was inseparably embodied in the verbal texture of the text became popularized in the 1960's slogan "The medium is the message." Once one has chosen how one is going to speak, write, or otherwise communicate, one has also chosen, to a large degree, what one will be able to say. In literary terms, this means that the sonnet cannot do what the epic can do, nor can drama achieve what the novel can. Socially, the idea was translated into the view that if one chooses television over newspapers, for example, or propaganda speeches rather than billboards, one will have defined what one might say; sound bites are not lengthy newspaper editorials, nor are press conferences political sermons. New Criticism taught that language and idea, or form and content, are inseparable, that one cannot obtain anywhere else what *Hamlet* or *War and Peace* or *Paradise Lost* says; if this is true aesthetically and academically, it is also the case in the larger social context, although no New Critic would espouse the simplistic platitudes and propaganda of the media or of advertisers.

On a higher and more intellectual level, New Criticism, with its emphasis on the autonomy of the work of art, was criticized for ignoring larger social, moral, and psychological issues and interests out of which poetry was created and about which poetry speaks. Yet two of Eliot's earlier essays were entitled "Tradition and the Individual Talent" and "Religion and Literature"; Ransom spoke of the world's body and the need for an ontology of poetry; Tate was Roman Catholic and Brooks was Episcopalian, and both spoke overtly of their faith and values. Thus, New Criticism was not a reductionism that ignored larger human questions or collapsed literature into questions of merely technical, aesthetic nature; its main point was that word and idea go together, that form and content are inseparable. Thus, the most important and enduring contribution of New Criticism quite probably is its insistence that discovery of truth or wisdom or values comes not from emotion, mysticism, propaganda, or ideology but from carefully wrought verbal statements. Such statements require equally careful examination of their truth and worth, so that no one is victimized by empty platitudes, untrue claims, or the many rhetorical devices by which men and women—from the biblical serpent to the latest soap-box orator or political lobbyist—have seduced or deceived one another. The impact of New Criticism is its proper claim that the question of humanity is a question of language—its truth, its power, and its potential abuse.

Bibliography

Brooks, Cleanth, and Robert Penn Warren, eds. *Understanding Poetry: An Anthology for College Students.* New York: Henry Holt, 1938. A clearly written text that introduces readers to narrative, description, meter, imagery, and theme. Actual poetic texts are analyzed with helpful questions and explanations. An excellent, lucid book for teacher and student alike.

Eliot, Thomas S. *Selected Essays.* New York: Harcourt, Brace, 1950. Written in tight, clear, direct language, these essays are models of analysis and judgment about writers such as Dante Alighieri, William Shakespeare, William Blake, and Alfred, Lord Tennyson. Eliot combines careful scrutiny of the works with ultimate, personal, and even theological verdicts. This book gives the lie to the charge that the New Critics paid no heed to anything but the poem.

Foster, Richard. *The New Romantics.* Port Washington, N.Y.: Kennikat Press, 1973. A reappraisal of New Criticism that shows that its advocates viewed poetry as a vehicle for personal, romantic, and religious views that constitute a new and deep humanism.

Hyman, Stanley Edgar. *The Armed Vision.* New York: Alfred A. Knopf, 1947. Treats many different kinds of critics, placing New Criticism in the larger context. Not for beginners, but an important book about criticism as it was practiced by many.

Krieger, Murray. *The New Apologists for Poetry.* Bloomington: Indiana University Press, 1963. A difficult and complex book; nevertheless, it carefully distinguishes between poet, poem, and reader and shows the difference that is produced by talking about each.

Leitch, Vincent. *American Literary Criticism from the Thirties to the Eighties.* New York: Columbia University Press, 1988. A comprehensive survey that gives a careful description of New Criticism and then places it among other methods. Assumes much previous reading in criticism and literature.

Lentricchia, Frank. *After the New Criticism.* Chicago: University of Chicago Press, 1980. An intellectual argument for the necessity that criticism proceed beyond New Criticism and its progeny. An important work that shows how New Criticism asked all the important questions about the uniqueness of the work of art and yet too easily assumed that each work was available to the reader for interpretation.

Ransom, John Crowe. *The New Criticism.* Reprint. Westport, Conn.: Greenwood Press, 1979. The seminal text that first defined New Criticism and then pointed out that it lacked ultimate, ontological foundations. Does not spell out clearly or finally what poetry, as poetry, really is, or why it is essential. After reading this book, however, one will feel that poetry is both necessary and enriching to the human condition.

Richards, I. A. *Science and Poetry.* New York: W. W. Norton, 1926. The first modern influential text to focus on poetic language, its powers, and its limitations. A subtle, difficult work that shows the demand that thinking about and using language make on humanity.

Wimsatt, W. K., Jr. *The Verbal Icon.* Lexington: The University Press of Kentucky, 1954. A book written for academics; however, its focus on the work of art, as well as its placing of poetry in moral and religious contexts, shows that New Critics did not ignore the place of poetry in the total human situation.

John S. Reist, Jr.

Cross-References

The New Objectivity Movement Is Introduced (1925), p. 631; *Poems* Establishes Auden as a Generational Spokesman (1930), p. 857; The New Novel (*Le Nouveau Roman*) Emerges (1951), p. 1481; Minimalism Emphasizes Objects as Art (1963), p. 1949; Lévi-Strauss Explores Myth as a Key to Enlightenment (1964), p. 1995; Derrida Enunciates the Principles of Deconstruction (1967), p. 2075.

SARTRE AND CAMUS GIVE DRAMATIC VOICE TO EXISTENTIAL PHILOSOPHY

Category of event: Theater
Time: The 1940's and the 1950's
Locale: Paris, France, and New York, New York

Existential philosophy lent itself to dramatization in the plays of Jean-Paul Sartre and Albert Camus, preceding the more interpretive works of the absurdists

Principal personages:
JEAN-PAUL SARTRE (1905-1980), a leading French existentialist philosopher, novelist, and dramatist
ALBERT CAMUS (1913-1960), a French philosopher of the absurd, novelist, and dramatist

Summary of Event

In the late 1940's, the new philosophy of existentialism captured the imagination of Europe and America. Though the roots of existentialism had preceded this period, the movement became a self-conscious philosophy in its own right only after World War II.

Unlike both earlier and later philosophies, existentialism was not a coherent and dogmatic system but a mood, an outlook that contained related themes. It was greatly concerned with existential problems of the human condition. There were atheistic existentialists and religious ones, optimists and pessimists. Moreover, there were many artists and writers who, though not existentialists per se, were influenced by existentialism.

What gave the existentialists a common ground was a similarity of outlook and a common approach to the problems of human existence. Despite the diversity of emphasis among existentialist writers and philosophers, all shared a belief that, as Jean-Paul Sartre asserted in 1947, "existence precedes essence"—that is, the concrete (as opposed to abstract) problems of human existence, as experienced by the unique individual thrown into a problematic world of unique situations, take precedence over abstract, fixed views of life. The human being is a conscious subject in flux rather than an abstract essence or object.

Existentialists approached the whole person as a unity of thought and action and asserted that humans must define their own nature. They emphasized that men and women must courageously define their existence and then take the responsibility for making their own choices. In this view, humans are what they do.

Despite the absence of a fixed view of human nature, the existentialists seemed to agree on the major problems that concerned human beings. These concerns centered on the uniqueness of individuals and their situations, on a preoccupation with anxiety, absurdity, crisis situations, value definition, and choice-making.

It is no coincidence that Jean-Paul Sartre and Albert Camus, the two greatest French existentialists, joined the French Resistance movement during the Nazi occupation of France in World War II. The unprecedented horrors of the war heightened the emphasis on people in extreme situations and raised vital questions about moral commitment to fighting radical evil.

Unlike other philosophies, existentialism lent itself perfectly to literary and dramatic expression. The graphic and powerful imagery and dialogue of the novel and the drama could portray the range of existential problems more effectively than abstract philosophical discourse. Thus, Camus and Sartre became famous chiefly because of their plays. The dramatic voice they gave to the ideas of existentialism and the absurd disseminated those ideas far more effectively than more straightforward treatises could.

Albert Camus became a towering moral philosopher and writer. Born in Algeria in 1913, he settled in Paris and studied philosophy and literature. Before writing his great philosophical works, he began to explore the nature of the absurd in the theater. In 1935, he helped found a theater company in which he acted, wrote, and produced.

Camus' most famous and greatest play, *Caligula*, was written in 1938, when Camus was twenty-five. The play depicted the story of Caligula, a mad Roman emperor who, devastated by the death of his beloved sister, deals with his discovery of absurdity by creating an absurd world, turning his kingdom upside down in an orgy of sex and violence. Caligula grasps for the impossible, but he exceeds all limits, and he is assassinated by a few noble Romans. The play was produced in Paris in 1944 and in the United States to great acclaim.

In his eloquent essay *Le Mythe de Sisyphe* (1942; *The Myth of Sisyphus and Other Stories*, 1955), Camus spelled out his ideas on the absurd. People are strangers, homeless, alienated, condemned to futility, but Camus rejected suicide, aimless pleasure, and empty faith. Instead, one must learn to live with the absurd and to love life. In *L'Homme révolté* (1951; *The Rebel*, 1956), an essay on revolution, Camus asserted that evil and absurdity must be fought, but not at the price of fanaticism and murder. The acceptance of reason and limits and the struggle for individual freedom characterized Camus' outlook.

Caligula was followed by *Le Malentendu* (1944; *The Misunderstanding*, 1948). *The Misunderstanding* deals with a case of mistaken identity: a son who, expecting to be recognized, fails to disclose his identity to his mother and sister, who proceed to rob and murder him. The absurd has triumphed, as the tragic recognition of the misunderstanding results in the death of Martha, the mother. Sincere authenticity (another existentialist value) could have saved the son.

L'État du siège (1948; *State of Siege*, 1958) was an allegorical counterpart to Camus' great novel *La Peste* (1947; *The Plague*, 1948). As the plague threatens to destroy a city, it assumes the face of a malevolent character. "The Plague" is assisted by a cynical bureaucrat, Nada, symbolizing nihilism. Still, some heroic townspeople stand up to evil. Camus' last play, *Les Justes* (1949; *The Just Assassins*, 1958), set in czarist

Russia in 1905 and based on historical incidents, deals with one of Camus' major themes: whether revolutionary ends justify violent means. Idealistic revolutionaries plot the assassination of the grand duke. Some of the the plotters realize they have killed a husband and father in assassinating a symbol of tyranny; Camus lets the spectator deal with the issues.

Jean-Paul Sartre was born in Paris. He began writing plays as a prisoner of war in Germany in 1940. Sartre's dramas differ somewhat in content and emphasis from those of Camus; rather than featuring eloquent characters, Sartre's plays emphasize the depiction of average people in extreme situations and the ways in which those people respond, either by facing up to or by evading their responsibility for making choices. Sartre also turned to Marxism, with a resulting emphasis on social problems. For Sartre, the evocation of great truths was the task of the theater.

Beginning with *Huis-clos* (1944; *No Exit*, 1946), Sartre explored the problems of responsibility, identity, and self-esteem. *No Exit* depicts the mutual torture of three characters who resist change and self-discovery.

Many of Sartre's plays are replete with unusual and violent episodes to portray behavior in extreme situations. In *Les Mouches* (1943; *The Flies*, 1946), based on a Greek myth of revenge, Orestes takes on the responsibility of killing his mother and her lover in defiance of Zeus. *Les Séquestrés d'Altona* (1959; *The Condemned of Altona*, 1960) probes the response to atrocity in the twentieth century. The son of a Nazi industrialist faces up to his father's complicity in the Holocaust. Always the committed existentialist writer, Sartre called attention to the evil of indifference.

Impact of Event

The impact of the existentialist plays of Sartre and Camus manifested itself in a variety of ways. What seemed to appeal to the large audiences in Europe and America as well as to drama critics were the simple plots, the effectiveness of the dialogue and dramatic effects, and the extreme situations, dilemmas, and painful choices confronting the characters of the plays. The unprecedented horrors of World War II and the images of Auschwitz and Hiroshima had wounded much of the older faith in optimism, progress, and moral certainty. These plays were bound to appeal to a generation searching for moral bearings after the upheavals of war.

Many of the plays of Sartre and Camus were performed frequently in France and the United States. They became the ideal vehicle for the presentation of existential ideas; the depiction of extreme dramatic situations and the expression of their ideas became inseparable. Thus, the existentialist dramas of Sartre and Camus were able to reach a far wider and more varied audience than their often difficult philosophical works.

Camus and Sartre directed their plays to their own times, the crisis-ridden twentieth century. *Caligula* is obviously an evocation of the bloody and fanatical dictatorships of Adolf Hitler and Joseph Stalin. Sartre's play *La Putain respectueuse* (1946; *The Respectful Prostitute*, 1947) is set in the American South. The play deals with the problems of racism, political corruption, the exploitation of women, and, above all, the hypocrisy of American life. The play ran for 350 performances in New York but was banned in a number of other American cities. The controversy aroused by the plays of Sartre and Camus, though, simply added to their popularity.

Thus, Sartre and Camus became two of the most popular figures of the cultural avant-garde of Europe. The versatile Sartre continued his prolific creativity and his political and social activism until his death in 1980. Albert Camus received the Nobel Prize in Literature in 1957 at the unprecedented age of forty-four. His death in an automobile accident in 1960 seemed only to add to his stature.

Finally, the plays of Sartre and Camus influenced the mainstream drama of the 1950's and 1960's and set the stage for the innovative works of the theater of the absurd. Outstanding dramatists of the period such as the American playwright Arthur Miller were influenced by the existentialists, particularly their emphasis on moral choice-making in extreme situations.

The theater of the absurd, which began in the 1950's and lasted into the 1970's, featured such notable figures as Samuel Beckett, Eugène Ionesco, Max Frisch, and Harold Pinter. The theater of the absurd took as its point of departure the problems posed by Camus and Sartre. Rather than posing human problems of meaninglessness and anxiety and presenting dramatic and often tragic responses to these issues, as Camus and Sartre did, the dramatists of the absurd simply explored absurd situations for their own sake. The dramas of the absurd tended to eliminate the coherent cause-and-effect of incidents and situations, created passive characters, and sometimes used incoherent language to heighten the atmosphere of meaninglessness and absurdity.

For example, Samuel Beckett's most famous play, *En attendant Godot* (1952; *Waiting for Godot*, 1954), concerned two characters waiting for salvation and providing no real existentialist responses of choice and commitment. The waiting is terrifying and never ends.

The theater of the absurd, however, would not have been possible without the work of Sartre and Camus. The existentialist dramas of Sartre and Camus created and re-created tragic themes in a twentieth century context. In so doing, they created a theater of ideas that remains a permanently influential body of work.

Bibliography

Brosman, Catherine Savage. *Jean-Paul Sartre*. Boston: Twayne, 1983. A well-balanced study with excellent chapters on Sartre's drama. Shows how Sartre's plays emphasize that man's position in the world derives from a collision between the struggle for freedom and the obstacles presented by fate. Characterizes Sartre's plays as dramas of extreme situations and judges Sartre as more pessimistic than Camus.

Camus, Albert. *Caligula and Three Other Plays*. Translated by Stuart Gilbert. New York: Alfred A. Knopf, 1958. Contains *The Misunderstanding*, *State of Siege*, and *The Just Assassins* in addition to *Caligula*. With a revealing 1957 preface by the author.

Cruickshank, John. *Albert Camus and the Literature of Revolt*. New York: Oxford

University Press, 1959. Well-reasoned study showing how Camus evolved from a passive acceptance of the absurd in *The Myth of Sisyphus* to a measured revolt against the absurd in *The Rebel.* Views Camus as a major tragedian of the twentieth century and the characters of his plays as eloquent spokesmen for his "theater of ideas."

Esslin, Martin. *The Theatre of the Absurd.* Rev. ed. Garden City, N.Y.: Anchor Books, 1969. The best single general work on the topic. Surveys the work of twenty-five dramatists in America and Europe, including Eastern Europe. Contains an intelligent evaluation of the influence of Sartre and Camus on the new drama while maintaining that the theater of the absurd departed from existentialism by emphasizing the absurd for its own sake.

Guicharnaud, Jacques. *Modern French Theatre: From Giraudoux to Genet.* Rev. ed. New Haven, Conn.: Yale University Press, 1967. Excellent survey, with fine chapters on Sartre and Camus and good bibliographies. Maintains that Sartre and Camus were in the traditions of the French moralists and both continued and departed from the traditions of classical tragedy. Concludes that Camus and Sartre succeeded admirably in fusing their dramatic talent with their ideas.

Kaufmann, Walter A., ed. *Existentialism from Dostoevsky to Sartre.* Rev. ed. New York: New American Library, 1975. One of the best comprehensive introductions to the existentialists. Contains an excellent introduction and well-chosen excerpts with fine prefaces.

Sartre, Jean-Paul. *"No Exit" and Three Other Plays.* Translated by Stuart Gilbert. New York: Vintage Books, 1956. A useful edition with excellent translations.

_____. *Sartre on Theater.* Edited by Michel Contat and Michel Rybalka. Translated by Frank Jellinek. New York: Pantheon Books, 1976. Invaluable collection of wide-ranging essays, interviews, and comments on his own plays by Sartre. Sartre stresses the importance of theater as a way of distancing the spectator and thus enabling the audience to grasp the truth. Also explores the theater's ability to dramatize basic "myths" (for example, the Hell of *No Exit*) to this end. Sartre argues that theater serves a social function by evoking collective truths.

Leon Stein

Cross-References

Freud Inaugurates a Fascination with the Unconscious (1899), p. 19; Jung Publishes *Psychology of the Unconscious* (1912), p. 309; Sartre's *Being and Nothingness* Expresses Existential Philosophy (1943), p. 1262; Beckett's Trilogy Pushes Against the Frontiers of Fiction (1951), p. 1498; *Waiting for Godot* Expresses the Existential Theme of Absurdity (1953), p. 1573; Ionesco's *Rhinoceros* Receives a Resounding Worldwide Reception (1959), p. 1812; Esslin Publishes *The Theatre of the Absurd* (1961), p. 1871.

GARCÍA LORCA'S *POET IN NEW YORK* IS PUBLISHED

Category of event: Literature
Time: 1940
Locale: Mexico

In Poet in New York, *Federico García Lorca described his feelings of attraction to and repulsion by white urban American civilization from the perspective of an Old World outsider*

Principal personages:
FEDERICO GARCÍA LORCA (1898-1936), a Spanish poet and playwright whose travels to New York City inspired the volume *Poet in New York*
SALVADOR DALÍ (1904-1989), a Surrealist painter and close friend of García Lorca who had a strong personal and artistic impact on the writer
LUIS BUÑUEL (1900-1983), a Spanish Surrealist film director who belonged to García Lorca's circle of close friends
WALT WHITMAN (1819-1892), an American poet whose work influenced the style and content of García Lorca's poetry in general and *Poet in New York* in particular
PEDRO CALDERÓN DE LA BARCA (1600-1681), a Spanish playwright whose work is echoed in *Poet in New York*

Summary of Event

Federico García Lorca is widely regarded as Spain's most distinguished twentieth century writer of poetry and drama. García Lorca was a major participant in the flowering of Spanish literature that occurred in the years between World War I and the Spanish Civil War—an era the richness and diversity of which have been compared to those of the sixteenth and seventeenth century Spanish Golden Age.

Having already published numerous volumes of poetry, in the year 1929, García Lorca found himself at an artistic and personal impasse. Early that year, García Lorca received inquiries regarding the possibility of giving a series of lectures in the United States. At the urging of his family, García Lorca embarked on his first trip outside Spain in the summer of 1929. The trip led him, via France and England, to Columbia University in New York City. The new and completely different surroundings, while essentially stimulating to his literary output, also proved to be overwhelming and shocking to García Lorca.

Written in 1929 and 1930 while the poet was living in New York City and published after García Lorca's death, *Poeta in Nueva York* (1940; *Poet in New York*) belongs to García Lorca's mature period of artistic evolution. It is, in fact, part of a new stage in his development as a poet, both stylistically and thematically. In this volume of poetry, there is a new vision of modern civilization expressed, yet it is a vision that originates from some of the same emotional responses to the world that gave rise to his earlier volumes: *Libro de poemas* (1921; book of poems), *Poema del cante jondo* (1931; *Poem of the Deep Song*, 1987), and *Romancero gitano* (1928; *The Gypsy Ballads of García Lorca*, 1951, 1953). The themes underlying the poems of these early volumes—desire for the unattainable, nostalgia for a lost Eden, and the sterility of self-consciousness—reappear in *Poet in New York*, but with larger social implications. García Lorca's volume also explores the themes of materialism, dehumanization, violence, and racism.

The poet-persona (although the book contains autobiographical elements, the speaker in each of the poems in the volume cannot be identified with the poet) of *Poet in New York* becomes outraged against the empire of office buildings, the river drunk on oil, and the suits of clothing empty of humanity—all of which are the tangible results of humankind's intellectual endeavors. In the midst of this teeming humanity, the speaker of the poems desires a moment of peace and fulfillment (which is unattainable); his nostalgia for childhood grows stronger as Eden grows more inaccessible.

Near the beginning of the volume, García Lorca's persona identifies with a tree that cannot bear fruit because of its self-consciousness. By the end of the volume, however, the speaker identifies with nature, with the blood and human vitality of natural violence. He takes the side of the blacks of Harlem. He experiences all the pain of consciousness, and, rendered passive by the impact of this harsh world upon his suffering sensibility, he can only name the objects of his nightmare vision. Yet in his outrage, when he has sufficient strength to react against this world, he calls for a revolution that will flood the streets with blood and destroy the bloodless suits of Wall Street.

Thus, while some thematic similarities to his earlier poetry exist in *Poet in New York*, the manner in which García Lorca confronts the New World (New York City) differs radically from his manner of expression prior to his departure from Spain (the Old World). García Lorca moves from a state of participation in nature and in his community, manifested in the rhythmical, frequently dramatic poetry of imagery drawn from the natural world of southern Spain, to a state of extreme estrangement and dislocation from his familiar universe. This alienation manifests itself in the dissonant, subjective, and violent imagery drawn from the technological world of New York City. *Poet in New York*, then, reflects García Lorca's experience of depression and alienation in a foreign reality he perceives to be hostile. Yet it is also an account of his psychological journey from alienation and disorientation to reintegration into the natural world.

Poet in New York marks the first appearance in García Lorca's work of poems that seriously address the topic of homosexuality—notably in "Tu infancia en Menton" (your childhood in Menton) and "Oda a Walt Whitman" (ode to Walt Whitman). Under the aegis of the noble American poet Walt Whitman, García Lorca ventures to introduce and defend homosexual love. The poem is an ode not only to Whitman, however, but also to the agonized individuals whose homosexuality brings them only the pain of frustrated love. They are alienated human beings for whom there is no place in the world and who know the anguish of unfulfilled desire.

Transcending the poet's private vision of modern civilization, *Poet in New York* also reflects a metaphysical dimension; modern man recognizes the spiritual waste-land in which he lives. He discovers that he is alone, empty, without roots, and without belief in a divine being. Locked in a prison of subjectivity, he no longer belongs to the world or the cosmos. Now he is conscious, and his vision separates him from the world and his gods; he is fallen. The myth of the Fall expresses both the state of man's alienation from God and nature, resulting from consciousness, and the state of modern civilization's alienation from any unifying reality that might have held society together as a community.

Impact of Event

In the 1920's, Surrealism exploded onto the artistic horizon with the issue of French poet André Breton's *First Manifesto* in 1924 and the publication of the journal *La Révolution surréaliste* (the surrealist revolution). Breton described Surrealism as the poet's surrendering to a state of pure psychic automatism, a state in which the poet could express—by means of the written word—the actual functioning of thought. Poetry, then, was dictated by thought, without any control exercised by reason. Consequently, it was exempt from any aesthetic or moral concerns. García Lorca himself had participated actively in the propagation of the ideas of Surrealism in 1928 by founding and editing *Gallo*, an avant-garde magazine that acknowledged the influence of many prominent Surrealist poets, painters, and musicians of the day.

Because García Lorca's New York poetry was indeed a startling departure from his earlier poetry in its tone of alienation and violent imagery, and because of its surface resemblance to some French Surrealist poetry written by Breton and Paul Éluard, *Poet in New York* was generally labeled as "Surrealist" at the time of its publication. Yet while *Poet in New York* does reflect the influence of Surrealism in both its use of language and imagery, there is a basic difference between Breton's Surrealist poetry and García Lorca's symbolic poetry. García Lorca's New York poetry functions symbolically and metaphorically. The irrational, illogical, surrealistic (but not Surrealist) images, considered together, compose an organic whole expressive of a feeling or idea in the poet's mind; these images come into being by their relation to the subject rather than by their relation to each other. In other words, the notion of automatism or chance, which is at the root of Surrealist creation, is not an active force in García Lorca's New York poetry.

The critical reception of *Poet in New York* has been extremely varied. When the poems started to appear, many Spanish critics, certain that García Lorca was a popular poet, tended to regard the poetry from the New York period as a temporary aberration on his part. It was considered a strange, impenetrable work, apparently Surrealist in origin. To many, the New York poems represented a rejection of the traditional style of his earlier poetry and an embarkation upon a new experiment in poetic creation. García Lorca's "experiment" was regarded by many as a failure: In their opinion the poetry somehow did not measure up to the greatness of his earlier work.

The issue of García Lorca's influence is complex. In Spain, García Lorca's New York poetry did have an effect on his younger contemporaries, but this influence is difficult to isolate from the influence García Lorca himself was receiving. García Lorca certainly influenced the poet Luis Cernuda, a poet of similar but more refined temperament; Cernuda followed García Lorca in the note of rebellion that finally broke out openly in the former's poetry. Other prominent Spanish poets never accepted García Lorca's surrealist manner. They were unable to accept the iconoclastic aspects of his work—both in form and content—specifically those aspects that clashed with Spanish tradition. After the Spanish Civil War of 1936 to 1939, Spanish poets returned to formalism and tranquility, to simple human expression, even to religion, under the varied influence of many poets, such as the modern poet Antonio Machado. Aside from evoking an appreciation of its rebelliousness and prohibited themes, García Lorca's New York poetry had little direct impact on later Spanish poets.

In Latin America, however, the situation proved different. Among the many Latin American poets influenced by García Lorca were Carlos Correa in Chile, Miguel Otero Silva in Venezuela, Jorge Zalamea in Colombia, Claudia Lars in Central America, and Manuel José Lira in Mexico. To them, García Lorca was a spokesman not only for his native Spain but also for the twentieth century Western world. García Lorca's work presented a new spiritual insight. Tormented and mutilated, but still sensually realistic, the New York poems carried a peculiarly important message to the modern age. They were not viewed as the fabrications of a mind that has lost touch with reality, as the outpourings of a Surrealist creating a gruesome antihuman nightmare world. Although they were regarded as García Lorca's most difficult poems—musically discordant, disrupted in meter, poured into arbitrary autonomous form, cascading with the fragments of exploded metaphor—their secret was that a new world of imagery had been created to embody the intense spiritual effort that informs them. The intricate imagistic and metaphorical language of *Poet in New York* proceeds from a vision of the world that, finding no expressive instrument in the traditions of any literary medium, demanded of the poet a new imaginative invention.

Poet in New York, an intensely personal yet strikingly universal work, is an example of modern alienation from self, family, society, and religion. The work has been regarded as an apocalyptic vision of America. On the social level, García Lorca denounces the poverty and exploitation he sees around him, criticizes Wall Street (which was in the midst of the 1929 stock market crash) and its materialism and capitalism, hurls invectives against the pope and much of organized religion, and even looks forward to the day when a cataclysmic upheaval is envisioned as overtaking the city.

Bibliography

Allen, Rupert C. *The Symbolic World of Federico García Lorca.* Albuquerque: University of New Mexico Press, 1972. In this original study of García Lorca's poetic and dramatic use of symbolism, the author discusses *Poet in New York* as a volcanic eruption of symbols of personal as well as social destruction, disease, and disintegration. Contains bibliography.

Barea, Arturo. *Lorca: The Poet and His People*. Translated by Ilsa Barea. London: Faber & Faber, 1954. Although somewhat dated, Barea's study argues that, above all, García Lorca's work is "popular" in the sense that it touched a generation, speaking to the emotional and revolutionary forces that were beginning to take shape. In addition, the author discusses the themes of sex and death in García Lorca's poetry and drama. Includes appendix of Spanish quotations from García Lorca's works.

Cobb, Carl W. *Federico García Lorca*. New York: Twayne, 1967. The aim of this perceptive, well-written work is to give a general overview of some of García Lorca's representative works. Cobb devotes an entire chapter to *Poet in New York* and discusses the prophetically tragic outlook that infuses García Lorca's work with the turbulence, rebellion, and frustration of spirit of the modern age. Chronology, bibliography.

Craige, Betty Jean. *Lorca's "Poet in New York": The Fall into Consciousness*. Lexington: University Press of Kentucky, 1977. This is a brief but scholarly study that focuses upon the "Fall" as the thematic center of *Poet in New York*. The nostalgia for a lost Eden and the sterility of self-consciousness, according to Craige, are the driving forces of the volume. Craige discusses the work in the context of García Lorca's earlier poetry. Contains a brief bibliography.

Londre, Felicia Hardison. *Federico García Lorca*. New York: Frederick Ungar, 1984. This perceptive work discusses the personal and artistic influences in García Lorca's life; his major plays; the musicality of his early poetry; the folk ballads, paintings, and stories; and analyzes the new directions in his more mature poetry. Useful bibliography.

Maurer, Christopher. Introduction to *Poet in New York*. Translated by Greg Simon and Steven F. White. New York: Farrar Straus Giroux, 1988. In this brief but excellent essay, Maurer points out the many reasons why he considers *Poet in New York* to have been a turning point in the poet's work. Also discusses the volume in the context of the poet's life.

Predmore, Richard L. *Lorca's New York Poetry: Social Injustice, Dark Love, Lost Faith*. Durham, N.C.: Duke University Press, 1980. The aim of this original study is to explore and elucidate the poetic symbolism and thematic structure of García Lorca's New York poetry. Predmore measures the poetic language of the work in light of the ambiguous symbolism already developed in earlier works. Contains a brief bibliography.

Genevieve Slomski

Cross-References

The Metamorphosis Anticipates Modern Feelings of Alienation (1915), p. 396;

Pound's *Cantos* Is Published (1917), p. 445; Eliot Publishes *The Waste Land* (1922), p. 539; Surrealism Is Born (1924), p. 604; Buñuel and Dalí Champion Surrealism in *Un Chien andalou* (1928), p. 750; Picasso Paints *Guernica* (1937), p. 1062; Borges' *Ficciones* Transcends Traditional Realism (1944), p. 1268; The "Boom" Captures Worldwide Attention (Late 1950's), p. 1689; García Márquez's *One Hundred Years of Solitude* Is Published (1967), p. 2086.

WRIGHT'S *NATIVE SON* DEPICTS RACISM IN AMERICA

Category of event: Literature
Time: 1940
Locale: Chicago, Illinois

Richard Wright's Native Son *shocked white Americans with its graphic depiction of the rage and violence engendered by racism in the hearts of African Americans*

Principal personage:
RICHARD WRIGHT (1908-1960), an African-American writer whose work depicted racial conditions in American society

Summary of Event

In 1939, Richard Wright completed work on *Native Son*, his second work of fiction and his first full-length novel. The book's publication immediately established Wright as an important author and a spokesman on conditions facing African Americans. Earlier, Wright had published a collection of four long stories entitled *Uncle Tom's Children* (1938), which gained Wright the attention of some literary critics and helped him to win a Guggenheim Fellowship. The fellowship enabled Wright to devote his full time to writing.

Native Son, published by Harper's, was unlike any book by an African-American writer ever published. Speaking of *Uncle Tom's Children*, Wright had said, "I had written a book which even banker's daughters could read and weep over and feel good. I swore to myself that if I ever wrote another book, no one would weep over it; that it would be so hard and deep that they would have to face it without the consolation of tears." *Native Son* was indeed such a book. To avoid the unfocused sympathy of those who wished to avoid the hard realities of life for African Americans, Wright chose as his protagonist a violent young black man in Chicago, Bigger Thomas, who murders two women, one black and one white, and who is then condemned to death that he faces unrepentantly. Bigger and all his friends are resentful, frustrated by racism, and both fearful of the white world and inclined to violence toward it.

Harper's was somewhat concerned about the graphic nature of some of the book, but the publishers insisted on only limited changes. Just before publication, however, the Book-of-the-Month Club expressed interest in *Native Son* if several sexually explicit scenes were removed and if Bigger Thomas did not show such obvious sexual interest in the white character, Mary Dalton. Wright agreed to these changes.

Upon publication in 1940, *Native Son* became an immediate hit. In less than six months, a quarter of a million copies had been sold at five dollars a copy—at a time when the minimum wage was thirty-five cents an hour. The first edition sold out in only three hours. Virtually every major newspaper and magazine in the nation reviewed the book. *Native Son* was on the best-seller list for nearly four months. No other African-American writer had ever achieved such fame and financial success.

Moreover, no other African-American writer had ever focused such attention on the conditions of life in black ghettos before. In the introduction to the first edition, Dorothy Canfield wrote: "*Native Son* is the first report in fiction we have had from those who succumb to . . . crosscurrents of contradictory nerve impulses, from those whose behavior patterns give evidence of the same bewildering, senseless tangle of abnormal nerve-reactions studied in animals in laboratory experiments." For many white Americans, Bigger Thomas became a symbol of the entire black community.

Prior to the publication of *Native Son*, Wright had worked at a variety of jobs to support himself, his invalid mother, a variety of relatives, and a wife. These jobs had included janitorial work, selling burial insurance, employment on the Federal Writers' Project of the Works Progress Administration, and occasional writing for left-wing and Community Party publications. Wright had joined the Communist party in 1935, but he resigned his membership in 1944. With the financial security brought by the success of *Native Son*, Wright could devote himself to literary pursuits, and he spent the rest of his life writing.

The first impact of *Native Son* on Wright's writing was to encourage him to produce an autobiography, *Black Boy* (1945), which described his youth in the South. Wright had been born near Natchez, Mississippi, in 1908, and his parents had taken the family to Memphis, where Wright's father abandoned them. There followed an itinerant existence in Tennessee, Arkansas, and Mississippi that entailed rough and bruising contact with Jim Crow segregation laws and the heavy-handed demands for obsequious behavior made by the racial etiquette of the place and time. *Black Boy* ended with Wright's migration to Chicago and the vaguely expressed hope that life would be better there. This book also became a matter of national debate and helped to establish Wright as a commentator on current racial conditions, not just a writer of fiction. More than four hundred thousand copies of the book were sold within a few weeks.

The financial independence delivered by *Native Son* also allowed Wright to make some personal changes. He divorced his first wife, to whom he had been married for less than a year, and married Ellen Poplar, a Jewish woman, in 1942. The couple had one child, a daughter named Julia.

The African-American community recognized the accomplishment represented by *Native Son* when the National Association for the Advancement of Colored People (NAACP) awarded Wright their prestigious Spingarn Medal in 1940.

Native Son launched Wright's career as a writer. He would go on to produce nineteen major fiction and nonfiction works, screenplays, and stage plays, and he would become the first of the modern generation of African-American writers.

Impact of Event

Since its publication in 1940, Richard Wright's *Native Son* has never been out of print. Orson Welles produced a Broadway play based on the book, and film versions were released in 1950 and 1986. The book and its author have been the subject of numerous scholarly and popular investigations from literary, historical, and sociological perspectives.

Although the author was a Mississippian who set his story in Chicago and wrote it while living in New York, the plot of *Native Son* has continued to be a metaphor for much of the black experience throughout America. The book explores individuals, their environments, and the ways in which environments shape people. In his essay "How Bigger Was Born," Wright wrote of his character:

> He is a product of a dislocated society; he is a dispossessed and disinherited man; he is all of this and he lives amid the greatest possible plenty on earth and he is looking and feeling for a way out. . . . He was an American because he was also a native son; but he was also a Negro nationalist in a vague sense because he was not allowed to live as an American. Such was his way of life and mine; neither Bigger nor I resided fully in either camp.

In 1940, most white Americans were unaware of these feelings on the part of African Americans. There was little contact between the races. In a survey taken in 1942, less than half of all white Americans approved of integrated transportation facilities, and only about one in three approved of integrated schools or neighborhoods. Most whites, however, seemed to feel that blacks were satisfied with existing conditions. The usual white concept of African Americans was bifurcated. On the one hand were the happy-go-lucky "darkies," who were obviously poor and socially unequal but who did not worry about their situation at all. On the other hand were the fearful, down-trodden victims of Southern bigotry. *Native Son* confronted the United States with the fact that the first of these stereotypes was false and that the second was a national, not a regional, problem. The growing urban ghettos of the North and West were not lands of opportunity but were festering wounds in which people lived and died largely without hope. On a broad scale, Wright brought into the open the hatred, fear, and violence that he saw as characterizing American race relations. After *Native Son*, literary critic Irving Howe asserted, "American culture was changed forever." Quaintness and idealized folksiness disappeared from black literature, and the way was opened for later African-American writers to give an emphasis to their own ethnic culture. Later black writers could repudiate white culture and could celebrate black identity and even militancy. Wright's message in *Native Son*, a message whose variations have frequently been played on since, is that African Americans may wish to destroy the symbols of white cultural dominance and control. Trickery, when directed toward the dominant culture, is acceptable, as is militancy. These ideas have become widespread since the publication of *Native Son*.

This does not mean the influence of *Native Son* has been seen as all positive, even by blacks. James Baldwin commented that the book was "the most powerful and celebrated statement we have yet had of what it means to be a Negro in America." Baldwin, however, did not think Wright dealt adequately with the psychological and social conditions of Bigger Thomas' life, and he argued that this failure prevented Wright from conveying any sense of black life as a complex group reality. In a 1949 essay, "Everybody's Protest Novel," Baldwin wrote that *Native Son* was in its own way as simple-minded as Harriet Beecher Stowe's *Uncle Tom's Cabin, Or, Life Among the Lowly* (1851-1852). In "Many Thousands Gone," an essay published in 1951, Baldwin remarked that Wright wrote as if racism were a social problem that could not be cured but that could be checked.

Although Wright's reputation as a writer and as a spokesman for African Americans ebbed during the 1950's, as younger black writers such as Baldwin and Ralph Ellison rejected his naturalistic style of writing as well as the Marxist overtones of *Native Son*, Wright's influence was revived in the 1960's. With the growth of the militant black consciousness movement, there came a resurgence of interest in Wright's work. It is generally agreed that Wright's influence in *Native Son* is not a matter of literary style or technique. His impact, rather, has been on ideas and attitudes, and his work has been a force in the social and intellectual history of the United States in the last half of the twentieth century.

A part of this impact is developed from Wright's work after *Native Son*. Wright described Bigger as "vaguely a Negro nationalist." During the years Wright spent in France, from 1947 to his death in 1960, he spent much of his time supporting nationalist movements in Africa.

Wright wrote with a mixture of fearlessness and brilliance. He said he wanted to move black writing beyond the servile depiction of stereotyped "colored people." In *Native Son*, he accomplished that, while at the same time showing how little black and white Americans really knew about one another.

Bibliography

Abcarian, Richard. *Richard Wright's Native Son: A Critical Handbook.* Belmont, Calif.: Wadsworth, 1970. A good collection of reviews, critical essays, and essays based on topics related to the writings of Richard Wright. Written in the aftermath of the racial unrest of the 1960's, the book contains insights that are worth recalling.

Bakish, David. *Richard Wright.* New York: Frederick Ungar, 1973. A straightforward chronological account of Wright's life. Contains some literary analysis.

Bone, Robert. *Richard Wright.* Minneapolis: University of Minnesota Press, 1969. A short sketch of the life of Wright and, consequently, a good beginning source. While the focus is chronological, there is some analysis.

Fabre, Michael. *The World of Richard Wright.* Jackson: University of Mississippi Press, 1985. Fabre is a major biographer of Richard Wright. This book is a collection of essays written over a period of twenty years. The essays consider many aspects of the art and interests of Wright.

Felgar, Robert. *Richard Wright.* Boston: Twayne, 1980. The Twayne series on major American authors is noted for giving attention to the chronological facts of the lives of its subjects and placing only secondary emphasis on critical analysis. This volume gives a "feel" for Wright's life.

Gayle, Addison. *Richard Wright: Ordeal of a Native Son.* Gloucester, Mass.: Peter Smith, 1983. This biography investigates whether or not Wright was the target of special scrutiny by the U.S. government. Follows traditional chronological lines and gives a good account of Wright's life. Especially good in dealing with his years in France.

Hakutani, Yoshinobu. *Critical Essays on Richard Wright.* Boston: G. K. Hall, 1982. A collection of essays by various writers and critics. Important essays on Wright by James Baldwin and Irving Howe are included.

Michael R. Bradley

Cross-References

The Harlem Renaissance Celebrates African-American Culture (1920's), p. 480; The *Amos 'n' Andy* Radio Show Goes on the Air (1928), p. 755; Gershwin's *Porgy and Bess* Opens in New York (1935), p. 1016; Marian Anderson Is Barred from Constitution Hall (1939), p. 1126; *Stormy Weather* Offers New Film Roles to African Americans (1940's), p. 1159; Ellison's *Invisible Man* Is Published (1952), p. 1541; Baldwin Voices Black Rage in *The Fire Next Time* (1963), p. 1929; Baraka's *Dutchman* Dramatizes Racial Hatred (1964), p. 2000; *The Autobiography of Malcolm X* Is Published (1965), p. 2022; *Roots* Dramatizes the African-American Experience (1977), p. 2397.

HENRY MOORE IS INSPIRED BY SHAPES IN SUBWAY SHELTERS

Category of event: Art
Time: 1940-1941
Locale: London, England

Sculptor Henry Moore accepted a wartime assignment for a series of sketches as a record of England at war after he was inspired by the huddled shapes of Londoners using subway stations as air-raid shelters

Principal personages:
> HENRY MOORE (1898-1986), an artist whose massive surrealist sculptures adorn museums and their grounds around the world
> SIR KENNETH CLARK (1903-1983), a retired director of the London Museum, renowned art historian, and friend of Moore
> HERBERT READ (1893-1968), an art historian, author, and friend and biographer of Moore

Summary of Event

Henry Moore first became known as a sculptor of some repute in 1928. Moore usually is identified as the sculptor of massive stone architectural or landscape figures, of more or less human shape, perforated in their centers and with heads that are often mere protuberances.

Travel in France and Italy in 1925 was a strong catalyst for his art. His *Mother and Child* (1924-1925) shows the influence of Masaccio and a remarkable boldness and austere strength. Cubist works from this period manifest the influence of monumental Mexican Chac Mool statues. Moore's *Seated Woman* (1928), the culmination of his early drawings from life, was the first piece that forecast his lifelong sculptural style. Moore's first major commission was the monumental relief *North Wind* (1928-1929) on the headquarters of the London Transport Board. The first of Moore's characteristic reclining figures, that in Leeds, was done in 1929.

The years from 1929 to 1939 represent Moore's experimental period. Stephen Spender, a poet and friend of Moore, has discussed the prewar meetings of friends at Henry and Irina Moore's studio, where discussions ranged over such topics as abstract art, representationalism, Surrealism, and functionalism. Writing about Moore's drawings, Kenneth Clark noted that from 1932 to 1934 the sketches of reclining figures and mother-and-child groups show Moore moving in the direction of more abstract human shapes and the use of holes. The Moores moved to a new home in Kingston in 1934. It had a field that fulfilled Moore's ideal setting for sculpture as a "monumental art standing freely on the ground, under the sky."

The world of Henry Moore, like that of all Europeans, came apart in 1939 with the intrusion of World War II. The Chelsea School of Art, where he taught, was evacuated from London, and Moore became essentially an unemployed artist. His successive studios were destroyed by bombs. *Recumbent Figure* (1938) was Moore's last large piece before the interruption of war. His next major sculpture would be the Northampton *Madonna and Child* in 1943.

From 1939 to 1943, Moore primarily recorded ideas in notebooks. His drawings, however, were not insignificant, and many later bore sculptural fruit. Kenneth Clark calls *Two Women: Drawing for Sculpture Combining Wood and Metal* (1939) one of Moore's greatest drawings, the colors adding drama and creating space. Similarly, Moore's 1939 lithograph *Spanish Prisoner* first articulated his interest in the perceptual relationship between internal and external form. From this piece evolved his helmet-head sculptures (1939-1940 and early 1950's).

A drawing of 1940 entitled *September 3, 1939* ominously depicted a group of women bathing near Dover, gazing seaward toward France. In the same year came a series of sketches of upright oval "cocoons" within which are inserted abstract "embryos." These were realized in wood *as Internal and External Forms* (1953-1954). Moore referred to them as "a mother and child idea, something young and growing being protected by a shell."

The *Shelter Drawings* of 1940-1941 are without doubt Moore's most famous. Herbert Read identifies two categories of drawings by Moore: those made as rehearsal of ideas for sculpture, including the life drawings of his student days, and drawings done for their own sake, both actual scenes (*Shelter Drawings*) and imaginary scenes such as his most famous drawing, *Crowd Looking at a Tied-up Object* (1942).

The Nazi bombing of London began in earnest in September of 1940 and ended in May of 1941. Moore and his wife were confined in the subway during an air raid. This was Moore's first sight of people lying in an underground station with their blankets, pillows, and necessities. Moore later recalled, "I had never seen so many reclining figures. Even the train tunnels seemed like holes in my sculpture!"

When Kenneth Clark, chairman of the newly formed War Artists' Advisory Committee, saw Moore's sketches of that experience, he persuaded the sculptor to accept a commission. The project had its problems. Rather than intrude on what was left of the privacy of the shelterers, Moore made only quick sketches accompanied by mnemonic notes. He then worked from memory at his Parkhill Road studio and, after it was bombed, at his house at Much Hadham, outside London.

Some of the figures he sketched are seated on benches; some sketches are street scenes of buildings collapsing, such as a *Head Made Up of Devastated Buildings* and *Morning After the Blitz*. The series includes the well-known *Sleeping Child Covered with Blanket* and *Pink and Green Sleepers*, which Moore's friend Stephen Spender favors as Moore's most famous shelter drawing.

Given Moore's penchant for reclining figures, the sight of the huddled and sleeping denizens of the London tube was for him a moving revelation of meaning: the reclining figure as a suffering human being. The drawing *Tube Shelter Perspective* depicts long rows of recliners along the receding length of a subway tunnel.

For many, the shelter drawings appear to be impressionistic studies. Eric Newton, a critic for the London *Sunday Times*, wrote of "Moore's unearthly studies of a white, grub-like race of troglodytes swathed in protective blankets in underground shelters." Moore himself saw them as poetic symbols of the Blitz, comparing them to "the bowels of slave ships from Africa." Herbert Read emphasizes Moore's ability to capture the fear, boredom, and protective love expressed in the bodily attitudes of the people. Clark notes that "the stoicism and dignity of the shelterers" inspired several classical renderings, such as the *Two Seated Figures* that are "like late Roman patricians, awaiting the coming of the barbarians."

As one might expect, in Moore's drawings the human body is given sculptured weight and substance, as if occupying three-dimensional space. When, well after the last raid in May of 1941, Moore revised his exactly recorded drawings into more imaginative finished forms, the results were drawings of monumental power and among the finest graphic works of his career. Moore filled two sketchbooks with groups. Clark has described these sketches as "among the most precious works of art of the present century."

Impact of Event

Wishing to keep Moore under contract, the War Artists' Advisory Committee offered him several unappealing projects. Moore was a son of miners and farmers. When, in 1941, Herbert Read suggested that he make a series of drawings of miners, both Moore and the committee were amenable. Moore decided to work in the Wheldale colliery in his hometown of Castleford, the very mines in which his father had worked. He thus had a great sympathy for the project. In every sense, Moore's *Studies of Miners at Work* was a direct result of his work in the subway shelters. To him, the mines resembled the tube tunnels and the miners recalled the shelter figures "imprisoned in claustrophobic space." This time the drawings were made on the spot, with the coal dust and dimly lit atmosphere producing certain distorting and tenebrist effects that were compatible with the mind of the artist.

When Moore arrived in Castleford, he was given a tour of the tunnels that verified his early memory of the harshness of life and work in the mines. He later recorded his profound impressions of crawling on hands and knees deep into the mine to the actual coalface in "a dense darkness you could touch," the thick coal dust impervious to miners' lamps, under "a mile's weight of rock."

For a week at a time, Moore made sketches by day and refined them in the evening. Finally, his on-site notebook sketches became two sketchbooks and twenty finished drawings in crayon, chalk, watercolor, and india ink. Although Moore was not as emotionally moved by the miners as he had been by the shelterers, his drawings are powerful. Some imbue the miners with an idealized dignity. Moore's studies of miners working on their backs provided him with a rich variety of new ideas for his famous reclining figure sculptures, in particular his *Falling Warrior* (1956-1957) and his *King and Queen* (1952-1953).

Moore was glad to see the end of the miners project in 1942, because it allowed him to return to his first love, sculpture. Although the *Shelter Drawings* were intended as documents of the war and not as studies for generating ideas for sculpture, they nevertheless inspired, by their humanizing force, other drawings of groups of draped figures, often with resultant statues. Moore's work in the 1940's seemed preoccupied with an almost classical concern for human destiny. His drawing of three *Women Winding Wool* suggests the Three Fates; the *Group of Draped Standing Figures* (1942) seem to be characters in a Greek drama, as does the *Crowd Looking at a Tied-up Object*. His drawing *Three Standing Figures* (1947-1948) grew into the stone ladies of Battersea Park, London.

The shelter studies promoted Moore's international fame. Many of them were among the drawings which, with one reclining figure sculpture, composed Moore's first-ever exhibit in the United States, in May of 1943, at Curt Valentin's Buchholz Gallery in New York City. Valentin, who purchased all the pieces himself, disseminated many of them at a profit to major museums such as New York's Museum of Modern Art and Chicago's Art Institute. The exhibit also traveled to Los Angeles.

Moore's commission to make a *Madonna and Child* (1943) for the fiftieth anniversary of St. Matthew's Church in Northampton also resulted from the shelter drawings. Seeking to make the anniversary a magnificent artistic occasion, Walter Hussey, the vicar, commissioned a Benjamin Britten cantata. Hussey was impressed with Moore's work in the war artists' exhibit in London's National Gallery in 1942 and urged the hesitant sculptor to accept the commission. The public reaction to the finished work was either love or hate—nothing in between. Moore became notorious as thousands visited the church just to see what the fuss was all about. The *Madonna and Child* has ceased to raise eyebrows and is considered to be one of Moore's more realistic sculptures.

It is possible to find unarguable echoes of the *Shelter Drawings* in Moore's subsequent output. The year 1950 saw *Helmet Heads No. 1* in lead and bronze and his abstract *Double Standing Figure* for Vassar College (for which Moore made pages of studies in 1948). His bronze *Draped Reclining Figure* and an abstract stone screen adorned the Time-Life Building in London (1952), his *Warrior with Shield* (1953-1954) resides in Toronto, the United Nations Educational, Scientific, and Cultural Organization (UNESCO) Building in Paris commissioned a *Reclining Figure* (1957-1958), and in 1961 the St. Louis airport purchased two bronze figures.

In choosing for his archetypal models the imposing sculptural creations of ancient Egypt and Mexico, Moore asserted his ties to tradition. Although Moore exhibited in Surrealist exhibitions (1933-1939) with Alberto Giacometti, Jean Arp, and Joan Miró, he nevertheless felt apart from that school. He saw roles for both the unconscious, emphasized by the Surrealists, and the conscious. As he explained to Spender, however hard he tried to produce a nonrepresentational piece, even his most abstract work seemed like something real.

Three criteria can be used to judge the greatness of an artist: prolific output, absolute mastery of a medium, and universal representativeness of the art, with relevance for later ages. All three apply to Moore. Moore is representative of the artistic tradition of Western civilization. His work recalls the great art and artists of the past but is modern in its day. In view of his expanding power and clarity of purpose through the years, Moore will doubtless become a model and point of departure for artists of the future.

Bibliography

Berthoud, Roger. *The Life of Henry Moore*. New York: E. P. Dutton, 1987. Lengthy biography filled with detailed anecdotes that seem to have been personally shared by the author. The mind and heart of Henry Moore are intimately presented.

FitzGibbon, Constantine. *The Winter of the Bombs*. New York: W. W. Norton, 1958. Vivid description of the Nazi Blitz of London. Does not go into the work of Henry Moore but is excellent background to his *Shelter Drawings*.

Lichtenstern, Christa. "Henry Moore and Surrealism." Translated by Sally Arnold-Seibert. *The Burlington Magazine* 113 (November, 1981): 645-658. This article intends to demonstrate by a few examples that surrealist impulses shaped Moore's art, particularly from 1930 to 1940 and to a certain extent throughout his career.

Moore, Henry. *Henry Moore Drawings*. New York: Harper & Row, 1974. Affectionate and insightful survey of the development of Moore's art via a study of the relationship between his drawings and his sculpture. Copiously illustrated with 304 plates of Moore's graphic art, 40 in color.

_____. *Shelter Sketch Book*. London: Editions Poetry London, PL, 1940. This small volume contains no text but reproduces beautifully the shelter drawings on eighty-one leaves, in their original colors.

Read, Herbert. *Henry Moore: A Study of His Life and Work*. New York: Praeger, 1965. The most authoritative biography of Moore and a critique of his work, written by a great art historian. Amply illustrated with 245 photographs of Moore's art.

Spender, Stephen. "Realism's Blitz." *Art and Antiques* 9 (January, 1992): 75-77, 97-98. An attractive personal recollection, by a close friend of Henry Moore, of times spent together with other friends and the artistic discussions that took place in the decade before World War II.

Daniel C. Scavone

Cross-References

Kandinsky Publishes His Views on Abstraction in Art (1912), p. 320; New York's Museum of Modern Art Is Founded (1929), p. 782; The Whitney Museum Is Inaugurated in New York (1931), p. 885; The Guggenheim Museum Opens in a Building Designed by Wright (1959), p. 1806; Minimalism Emphasizes Objects as Art (1963), p. 1949.

DISNEY'S *FANTASIA* PREMIERES AND REDEFINES THE BOUNDARIES OF ANIMATION

Category of event: Motion pictures
Time: November 13, 1940
Locale: Broadway (formerly Colony) Theater, New York, New York

Although Fantasia *drew fire from critics and was not a commercial success in its first release, the film advanced the art of animation by freeing it from strict plot and character limits*

Principal personages:

WALT DISNEY (1901-1966), an entrepreneur who turned his production company of cartoon shorts into a multimillion-dollar entertainment colossus

LEOPOLD STOKOWSKI (1882-1977), a British-born American conductor who worked on many Hollywood film scores in the 1930's and who helped to conceive and guide the production of *Fantasia*

DEEMS TAYLOR (1885-1966), an American composer and musicologist who had popularized classical music through radio broadcasts of the New York Philharmonic

Summary of Event

Walt Disney had few naysaying critics left when *Fantasia* appeared in 1940. Less than three years earlier, he had silenced most of those who said that a feature-length cartoon was an absurdity by releasing *Snow White and the Seven Dwarfs* (1937), which was an instant critical and financial success, as was Disney's second animated feature, *Pinocchio* (1940). Even while those two features were being released, however, Disney was working on what would become the most ambitious and controversial animation project of his career: *Fantasia*.

Throughout the 1930's, Walt Disney had been pushing his animators toward continual improvement of their already highly developed painting skills. Many of the Disney artists feared that the goal of such refinement was a photographic, representational realism that would, they felt, take the heart out of animation. There was no lack of grounds for such fears. The 1934 Disney short *The Goddess of Spring* was intended to train animators in realistic animation of human figures; the 1937 short *The Old Mill* was a test run of the multiplane camera, which gave animation a three-dimensional look (a feature that helped to win the short an Academy Award). *Snow White* combined both techniques, and *Pinocchio* improved them, to the extent that reviewers voiced the very fears of the animators: Was Disney headed toward photorealism?

The opening sequence of *Fantasia* removed such fears when the film premiered at

New York's Broadway Theater on November 13, 1940. Unlike the other sequences in the film, this visual interpretation of Johann Sebastian Bach's *Toccata and Fugue in D Minor* developed no story and created no characters. Instead, an abstract movement of line and color grew out of the music. The closest the segment came to any representation was a sequence showing a brief dance of strings and bows, but even this was short-lived. Yet no amount of abstraction in the animation would protect Disney from the charge of music critics such as Dorothy Thompson of the *New York Herald Tribune*, who felt that the pure abstraction of music was tainted by any visualization. From the standpoint of animation, though, Disney had proved that the art could succeed without story or character.

Another anxiety about the premiere of *Fantasia* was the technical innovation the Disney studio called "Fantasound." Decades before the appearance of commercial stereo recording, Disney engineers had pioneered a multitrack recording process, and they envisioned showing *Fantasia* only in studios equipped with the process. The music was recorded on nine sound cameras (through thirty-three microphones) and was played back by an expensive synchronized unit developed by engineers at the Radio Corporation of America (RCA) and installed in the Broadway Theater. Neither Disney nor the Broadway was a stranger to sound technology; Disney himself had developed a technique for synchronizing music with cartoon action in the first sound cartoon, *Steamboat Willie* (1928), which had premiered in the same theater.

The Fantasound unit was itself a source of controversy. Since the unit was a piece of stage equipment, the stage employee's union members argued that they should operate the new toy; since it was electronic, the electrician's union members argued that it should be theirs. By the time a compromise was worked out, allowing both unions a piece of the installation, technicians had to work twenty-four-hour shifts (at overtime rates) to be ready for the premiere. Reviewer Sam Robins of *The New York Times* raved about the sound system. "When the waters hurl Mickey Mouse down a flight of stairs," he enthused, "the music pours out of one corner of the theatre and floods the auditorium."

The sequence Robin referred to was, of course, "The Sorcerer's Apprentice," performed to music by Paul Dukas. Unlike Bach's music, the Dukas piece begs visual and narrative interpretation: It is intended to tell a story (and was in fact based on one by Johann Wolfgang von Goethe). In fact, Disney's treatment of the piece was the kernel around which *Fantasia* grew. In 1938, Disney met Leopold Stokowski at a Hollywood party and mentioned his idea of animating a Mickey Mouse version of "The Sorcerer's Apprentice." Stokowski not only approved but also offered to conduct the piece and suggested expanding it to include other classical works.

In celebrating the ways in which *Fantasia* broke new ground, critics have not always acknowledged the extent to which it grew out of Disney's previous work. From the beginning, Disney's sound cartoons had incorporated music written to augment the action. In 1929, after only six Mickey Mouse sound shorts had been made, Disney and his musical director, Carl Stalling, adapted screen animation to a classical melody, Edvard Grieg's "March of the Dwarfs." To do so, Stalling had to rewrite the music to fit the action, just as Stokowski would do for *Fantasia*. The finished cartoon, *Skeleton Dance*, launched a new series for Disney: He called them "Silly Symphonies." Though the term "symphony" was obvious tongue-in-cheek hyperbole, it indicated that music would dominate these shorts rather than merely punctuate the action, as the music did in the Mickey Mouse shorts. Most of the Silly Symphonies were developed musically, without dialogue. It was as a Silly Symphony, at first, that Disney intended "The Sorcerer's Apprentice"; with Stokowski's collaboration, it became the embryo of *Fantasia*.

Impact of Event

If *Fantasia* can be considered Disney's greatest success, it can also be called his biggest failure. In attempting to bring together the audiences of animated films and classical music, he succeeded, at first, in alienating a goodly percentage of both. Though his studio finally made back its investment after the film was rereleased, Disney never lived to see *Fantasia* find the popular acceptance it finally reached. In an interview conducted for a television special celebrating the fiftieth anniversary of *Fantasia*, Walt's nephew Roy E. Disney recalled that his uncle never got over the popular and critical neglect of what he considered his masterpiece; his audience, he felt, did not understand. "I don't regret it," Disney said in 1961. "But if we had it to do all over again, I don't think we'd do it."

The biggest misunderstanding, perhaps, was Disney's motive. Music critics feared he was trying to turn masterpieces into bits of kitsch; average theatergoers felt he was trying to "elevate" them, and justifiably resented the condescension. "Actually," wrote film critic and historian Neil Sinyard, "nothing was farther from Disney's mind. What he was attempting in *Fantasia* was the same as in his other cartoons— to extend the boundaries of animation."

Extend them he did. Even though *Fantasia*'s box-office doldrums caused Disney to back away both from animating classical music and from purely abstract animation, other animators were inspired by *Fantasia* to expand the art of animation in several directions. Carl Stalling, cocreator of Disney's Silly Symphonies, had left Disney before the *Fantasia* project, yet he began working classical melodies into greater and greater roles in Warner Bros.' "Loony Toons" and "Merrie Melodies" shorts. *A Corny Concerto* (1943) combined music of Johann Strauss and Peter Tchaikovsky in a piano duel; decades later, the Disney studio re-created the scene in *Who Framed Roger Rabbit?* (1989).

Stalling and animator Chuck Jones had Bugs Bunny tackle opera; Gioacchino Rossini's *Barber of Seville* was parodied in *The Rabbit of Seville* (1950), and Richard Wagner's work provided the basis for *What's Opera, Doc?* (1957). Jones, who had animated his first short only two years before the premiere of *Fantasia*, described the segment performed to Tchaikovsky's *Nutcracker Suite* segment as the "happiest, most perfect single sequence ever done in animated cartoons, perhaps in motion pictures." The scenes' influence on Jones's animation is obvious in his work.

Even though the box-office disappointment of *Fantasia* caused Disney to be more cautious in many ways, he and his animators still followed through on two of the artistic implications of *Fantasia*. First, though they never came close to the level of abstraction of the film's opening piece, they did experiment with Surrealism in the "Pink Elephants on Parade" sequence of *Dumbo* (1941); the expressionistic play of light and color in the stag fight scene of *Bambi* (1942) provided further evidence that Disney features were not attempts at photorealism. The entire design of *Alice in Wonderland* (1951) militates against realism, as do the "Never Land" scenes of *Peter Pan* (1953). After the 1950's, any carp about realism became moot, as the new economics of animation forced animators to develop a more linear, stylized approach that would dominate cartoons for two decades, until computer animation and bigger budgets once more made the creation of realistic detail and shading economically feasible.

The second artistic legacy of *Fantasia*, the visualization of music through animation, showed the influence of the film's negative criticism. Several Disney features of the 1940's stitched together musical narratives, but the musical originals this time were more popular. *Make Mine Music* (1946) was a pastiche of ten songs in various styles, their stories told by animation. Stokowski was involved in this film at the outset, though by the time it was in production he was no longer with the project. Similar patchworks were *Fun and Fancy Free* (1947) and *Melody Time* (1948). Furthermore, all Disney cartoon features continued to combine music and action, as the studio's Academy Award nominations for music attested.

Fantasia continued to influence the art of animated film for decades after its release, in part because of its unusual availability after 1969. Disney had established an ingenious cyclical rerelease practice, which kept public interest in the films high, with *Snow White's* second release in 1943. Eventually, the studio settled on a seven-year cycle for most features. *Fantasia's* profits had been so dismal, though, that Disney waited only a little more than three years before rereleasing it in 1944; it was released again only two years later. After three more releases (1953, 1956, 1963), the studio took a chance on leaving prints in permanent circulation beginning in 1969.

The popular reaction was extraordinary, especially among young audiences. The "psychedelic" subculture saw *Fantasia* as mind-expanding and enjoyed watching it again and again, often enhancing the experience with the use of drugs. Many college film series included *Fantasia* on a yearly basis, with no apparent loss in the film's popularity from overexposure. When advanced stereo systems were installed in many theaters in the late 1970's, the multitrack experience of the original 1940 premiere was re-created—though the mistaken belief was current that the stereo version was new; few remembered the elaborate sound system used for the original release.

For the fiftieth anniversary release in 1990, the Disney studio undertook a restoration project for *Fantasia*, cleaning up the negatives frame by frame and releasing the "new" prints for the Christmas season. For the following Christmas, 1991, the Disney studio at last released the film on videotape for home use.

Bibliography

Finch, Christopher. *The Art of Walt Disney.* New York: Harry N. Abrams, 1975. Essentially a picture book. The commentaries on the films are mostly descriptive; what critical comments there are avoid controversy and therefore end up not saying much. The chapter on *Fantasia* is mostly scenario: The closest thing to a critical comment is the noncommittal mention of "great merits and great faults," without elaboration.

Maltin, Leonard. *The Disney Films.* New York: Crown, 1973. A comprehensive guide to all Disney films, by an accomplished film critic. The criticism is some of Maltin's best, revealing his love and admiration for Disney without devolving into blind praise. The section on *Fantasia* is generous in scope and balanced in analysis.

Schickel, Richard. *The Disney Version.* Rev. ed. New York: Simon & Schuster, 1985. The first treatment of Disney as a businessman rather than just an animator, this revisionist history of the man and his studio offers a corrective to the excessive praise of the studio-controlled books that precede it—though it sometimes goes too far in the other direction. The ten-page chapter on *Fantasia* is a good balance of information and excellent film criticism.

Sinyard, Neil. *The Best of Disney.* Greenwich, Conn.: Twin Books, 1988. Though full-color blowups of frames from Disney films are the major attractions of this book, what text Sinyard does give us is insightful commentary from a respected film critic. Sinyard briefly discusses controversies about *Fantasia* not mentioned in the "official" Disney-sponsored sources.

Taylor, Deems. *Walt Disney's "Fantasia."* New York: Simon & Schuster, 1940. Mostly a promotion piece, this profusely illustrated account of the film is nevertheless valuable for Taylor's contemporary comments about the project. Most of the text simply describes the film, though the opening chapter gives interesting behind-the-scenes background.

John R. Holmes

Cross-References

Disney Releases *Snow White and the Seven Dwarfs* (1937), p. 1053; ABC Makes a Landmark Deal with Disney (1954), p. 1612; *The Flintstones* Popularizes Prime-Time Cartoons (1960), p. 1840; Disney Emerges as an Architectural Patron (Early 1990's), p. 2646; *The Simpsons* Debuts, Anchoring the Fledgling Fox Network (1990), p. 2652.

WELLES'S *CITIZEN KANE* BREAKS
WITH TRADITIONAL FILMMAKING

Category of event: Motion pictures
Time: 1941
Locale: Hollywood, California

Orson Welles was invited to Hollywood because he was an outrageous media personality, not an experienced filmmaker, and his first film was a powerful challenge to the studio system

Principal personages:

ORSON WELLES (1915-1985), a radio performer, stage actor, writer, and director who applied all these talents in his innovative film work

WILLIAM RANDOLPH HEARST (1863-1951), a powerful but reclusive media magnate who was, despite Welles's disclaimers, the key model for Charles Foster Kane

BERNARD HERRMANN (1911-1975), a composer and conductor who worked with Welles on radio and wrote the highly evocative music for *Citizen Kane*

JOHN HOUSEMAN (JACQUES HAUSSMANN, 1902-1988), a cofounder with Welles of the Mercury Theater in 1937 and a longtime collaborator with Welles

HERMAN J. MANKIEWICZ (1897-1953), an experienced writer whose exact contribution to the script of *Citizen Kane*, although undoubtedly large, is still disputed

GREGG TOLAND (1904-1948), a pioneer in deep-focus photography whose cinematography helped to give *Citizen Kane* many of its distinctive visual qualities

Summary of Event

Before 1940, Orson Welles was not a filmmaker. Ironically, this fact helped to make it possible for him to make one of the most controversial and influential films of all time. He was an outsider to the Hollywood studio system, a system designed to organize film production like any other industry, efficiently making a "product" that could be marketed at a maximum profit. Yet much of Welles's experience up to that point in his young life—he was only twenty-four when he began work on *Citizen Kane*—prepared him for a career in film, the art that above all others required the combination of visual, verbal, intellectual, dramatic, musical, technical, and organizational skills that he had developed. Since early childhood, Welles acted, directed, and adapted or wrote a variety of plays, and as he gained experience and confidence (although some would say that he never lacked the latter) his projects became increasingly experimental and innovative. For example, he directed an all-black cast in what is sometimes referred to as a "voodoo" *Macbeth* (1936), and his *The Cradle Will Rock* (1937), a radical anticapitalist people's opera by Marc Blitzstein, had to be staged in a completely improvisatory way when bills for costumes, props, and even theater space could not be paid.

At the time, Welles was also extremely active in radio work, partly to help finance his theatrical projects—especially the Mercury Theater, which he and John Houseman formed in 1937—but also partly because the radio offered remarkable challenges and opportunities. Welles could tell stories in new ways, often playing several roles himself, and could reach a mass audience. The stage could make Welles famous, but only a mass medium could make him infamous. Welles could not have predicted the response to the Mercury Theater's radio broadcast of his production of *The War of the Worlds* on October 30, 1938, but when thousands of people took the program to be an authentic report of an alien invasion and panicked, he was undoubtedly thrilled by this tangible proof of the power of art, his dramatic art.

Film companies had earlier expressed interest in Welles before that episode, but now he was an especially hot property, the radio broadcast personality of the year as well as a household name. George J. Schaefer, president of Radio-Keith-Orpheum (RKO), was particularly interested in Welles's high visibility and signed him to a two-picture deal on August 21, 1939. Welles was won over not only by the financial backing that would allow him to keep the Mercury troupe together while making a film but also by a unique clause in the contract guaranteeing him complete creative control over his films once they were approved by the studio.

He went to Hollywood with the intention of making a film of Joseph Conrad's 1902 *Heart of Darkness*, a story he had already presented as a radio play. He was intrigued by Conrad's theme of how greatness of character is inextricably linked with murderous corruption and decay, and he also planned to follow Conrad in making the film, like the story, examine the process of witnessing the rise and fall of a larger-than-life person. Welles soon left this project behind, but he continued to brood over many of Conrad's themes and narrative strategies as he turned to what was to become *Citizen Kane*.

Welles had written a three-hundred-page script entitled *John Citizen, U.S.A.*, which provided a starting point for Herman J. Mankiewicz's radically revised script (worked on also by Welles and Houseman); the revision was initially entitled *American*. The central character in the film, Charles Foster Kane, was obviously modeled on William Randolph Hearst, the head of a powerful newspaper syndicate who was living in luxurious retreat at San Simeon on the California coast. The intention of the film, though, was to use Hearst as a starting point for an analysis of the perils of a particularly twentieth century American style of greatness. Kane is born poor and then has wealth thrust upon him, which both raises and ruins him. The film tells Kane's life through a series of narrators, each of whom knows only part of his story, and even when all the parts are put together to dramatize Kane's many triumphs, mistakes, and inescapable sense of decay and loss, the basic mystery of Kane's life—who is he?—is insoluble. The literal mystery of his dying word, "Rosebud," heard at the beginning of the film, is cleared up at the end, but the audience is still left to wonder whether the image of a sled, a relic of his childhood, is an answer or yet another question.

Even before *Citizen Kane* was released, it caused many problems. Because of his secretive and idiosyncratic working methods and the many delays of the film's release, Welles was ridiculed by some journalists as Hollywood's most well-known director who had not yet made a picture. As *Citizen Kane* neared completion, reports of its allegedly slanderous treatment of Hearst were circulated, and there was great legal and media pressure applied to stop or hinder its release. Offers were made to buy the negative so it could be destroyed; when these offers were refused, the Hearst syndicate did what it could to shun the film and restrict its distribution. *Citizen Kane* finally premiered in 1941 to great critical success, but it was initially a commercial failure and helped earn Welles a reputation as a troublesome, unreliable director. He would never again be granted both solid financial backing and creative control, and although he made other innovative, even brilliant films, he would never again be in a position to make a film such as *Citizen Kane*.

Impact of Event

The legacy of *Citizen Kane* is complex and ambiguous, and what is at stake is much more than Welles's reputation. *Citizen Kane* challenged and expanded the conventional notion of what kind of story a film should tell, how it should tell such a story, and what a film should look like. There had, of course, been earlier Hollywood films showing the corrupt side of powerful people. *Citizen Kane*, however, radically demystified not only one American dreamer but also the basic premises of the American Dream itself: Power is corrupt, love is impossible, friendship is transitory, idealism is a sham, the happy family is an illusion, politics is a stage for liars, and material possessions add up to a pile of junk. In telling this story, moreover, Welles purposely violated many of the conventions of the well-made film. Traditional Hollywood films emphasized continuity and stability of perspective, but Welles aimed for what he called a "prismatic" style, consciously fragmenting Kane's life by reflecting him through various characters, each of whom sees a somewhat different Kane. Welles's themes and narrative style in *Citizen Kane* proved to be influential models for later generations of filmmakers, although it took several decades for this influence to surface, and there is enough in *Citizen Kane* so that highly individualized directors could each gravitate toward something different: forexample, Roman Polanski's *Chinatown* (1974) owes something of its lingering robber-baron ethos and metaphysical and epistemic uncertainty to *Citizen Kane*; Francis Ford Coppola's *Godfather* trilogy (1972, 1974, 1990) is deeply indebted to Welles's epic analysis of a hero who is both captivating and revolting; and even though such films as Robert Altman's *The Long Goodbye* (1973) and *Nashville* (1975) perhaps owe more to later films by Welles, especially *Touch of Evil* (1948) and *The Lady from Shanghai* (1958), their rambling, decentered narrative style also recalls sections of *Citizen Kane*.

Perhaps the deepest ambiguity of the legacy of *Citizen Kane* is that it serves as one of the best illustrations for two apparently contradictory arguments about how films are made. On the one hand, despite Welles's reputation for independence, individuality, and boundless personal creativity, *Citizen Kane* can be regarded as in some ways the triumph of the studio system—perhaps not the conventional Hollywood studio system, but a system of collective enterprise and imagination nevertheless. The script was a collaborative effort involving Welles, Mankiewicz, and Houseman. The actors were primarily members of the Mercury Theater troupe who had worked together for several years, and the film was directed as an ensemble presentation rather than a series of individual performances. Finally, key members of the technical staff were highly skilled, even "star" performers in their own right, but these experts were skillfully blended into the ensemble production. Gregg Toland was an experienced and award-winning cinematographer before he met Welles, but he welcomed the opportunity to work with a new director because it allowed him to experiment. He had used "deep focus" photography before, but never so insistently or adventurously as in *Citizen Kane*; Welles wanted to explore the dynamics of spatial relations in many scenes, and Toland's cinematography allowed him to do that without cutting from one shot to another to maintain focus.

Sound as well as sight was extremely important in the film, and Bernard Herrmann's music plays a particularly important role in conveying the mood of key scenes. Music is not merely incidental in the film, it is central to the plot. Kane's second wife, Susan Alexander, is, by his design, an opera singer, and the music she sings, increasingly strained and hysterical, charts her response to Kane's bullying. The music that surrounds Kane also helps to dramatize his rise and fall, from the buoyant background music as he takes control of his first newspaper to the wailing jazz song that sets the tone for his final argument with Susan. *Citizen Kane* is always identified as "a film by Orson Welles," but this is a shorthand and potentially misleading way of referring to what was unquestionably the product of a skilled group of collaborative artists and technicians.

On the other hand, without denying that the film could not have been made without such collaboration, *Citizen Kane* is often used as an example of how an auteur, an individual director, stamps a distinctive mark even on an ensemble production. Welles was by no means the sole creative force behind the film, but it was primarily his vision that was elaborated and his contributions are everywhere. When one scratches the surface of *Citizen Kane* at any point, one finds Welles's imprint. The myth in the film, its powerful story of the rise and fall of a modern hero, is matched by the myth of the film, its affirmation of the creative force of the independent film auteur working successfully in the midst of a mechanized, bureaucratized, and commodified industry and society. To take only one example of many, this particular aspect of *Citizen Kane* inspired the French New Wave filmmakers, especially François Truffaut and Jean-Luc Godard; to make such a film at so young an age was their dream.

Citizen Kane is consistently ranked as one of the best films of all time; in fact, in polls conducted by *Sight and Sound* magazine, it was twice voted the best film of all time by an international panel of one hundred film directors. Perhaps behind this ranking lies not only respect for the film's technical virtuosity, stylistic variety, and probing analysis of a contemporary crisis, but also astonishment at Welles's audacity and achievement. If *Citizen Kane* is basically a fable about the hollowness at the core of a man of power, it is also an illustration of the world of creative possibilities open to a man of great cinematic imagination.

Sidney Gottlieb

Bibliography

Brady, Frank. *Citizen Welles: A Biography of Orson Welles.* New York: Charles Scribner's Sons, 1989. Comprehensive, illustrated, and fully documented study of Welles's entire life and career. Particularly good on Welles's public and political activities. Contains an extraordinary amount of useful background material and quotations from primary sources, letters, and reviews of Welles's productions.

Carringer, Robert L. *The Making of "Citizen Kane."* Berkeley: University of California Press, 1985. Meticulously researched, carefully argued, balanced examination of the production history of *Citizen Kane.* Details the important contributions of many technicians and artists without denying the role of Welles's talents. Contains many rare illustrations. Particularly interesting sections on art direction, special effects, and *Citizen Kane*'s relation to the *Heart of Darkness* project.

Higham, Charles. *Orson Welles: The Rise and Fall of an American Genius.* New York: St. Martin's Press, 1985. Critical overview of Welles's life and career that repeatedly blames Welles for his exile from Hollywood and failure to live up to his great potential. Useful corrective to the image of Welles as martyred by the Hollywood studio system, but contains many overstated and quirky judgments on Welles. Illustrated.

Kael, Pauline. *The "Citizen Kane" Book.* Boston: Little, Brown, 1971. Contains the shooting script and cutting continuity of *Citizen Kane*, illustrated with many shots from the film, and Kael's long essay "Raising Kane." Disputes Welles's claims of how much of the film was his creation and emphasizes Herman J. Mankiewicz's contributions. Many valuable comments comparing *Citizen Kane* to other films of its time.

Leaming, Barbara. *Orson Welles: A Biography.* New York: Viking, 1985. Personal, sometimes chatty biography based on many interviews with Welles. Focuses much more on his life than his work. Not critically detached, but provides many behind-the-scenes glimpses of Welles, especially during his later years. Illustrated.

Naremore, James. *The Magic World of Orson Welles.* Rev. ed. Dallas: Southern Methodist University Press, 1989. Arguably the best critical book on Welles's entire career. Contains separate chapters on each of his major films, including *Citizen Kane* (chapter 3). Gives recurrent attention to Welles as an illusionist, but balances this with continual analysis of the social and political aspects of his work. Illustrated with shots from his films.

Cross-References

Hollywood Enters Its Golden Age (1930's), p. 822; The Studio System Dominates Hollywood Filmmaking (1930's), p. 833; Renoir Marks the High Point of Prewar Filmmaking (1937), p. 1073; Welles Broadcasts *The War of the Worlds* (1938), p. 1103; The Hollywood Studio System Is Transformed (1946), p. 1307.

1206

MESSIAEN'S *QUARTET FOR THE END OF TIME* PREMIERES

Category of event: Music
Time: January 15, 1941
Locale: Gorlitz, Silesia

Olivier Messiaen's Quartet for the End of Time *was written in a prisoner-of-war camp for the instruments at hand yet serves as an affirmation of the human spirit*

Principal personages:
OLIVIER MESSIAEN (1908-1992), a French composer whose internment during World War II provided him with the rationale for composing the *Quartet for the End of Time*
JEAN LEBOULAIRE, the violinist at the premiere
ÉTIENNE PASQUIER, the cellist at the premiere
HENRI AKOKA, the clarinetist at the premiere

Summary of Event

The circumstances of the composition of *Quatuor pour la fin du temps* (1941; *Quartet for the End of Time*) are remarkable; that the work is one of the key musical masterpieces of the twentieth century makes the story even more amazing. Born in Avignon, France, in 1908, Messiaen joined the French army at the outbreak of World War II and served as a hospital attendant. En route to Nancy following the German invasion of Verdun, he was captured and sent to a prison camp at Gorlitz in Silesia (now in Poland). In Stalag VIIIA, Messiaen protected a precious knapsack containing a variety of miniature scores, including Johann Sebastian Bach's *Brandenburg Concertos* (c. 1721) and Alban Berg's *Lyric Suite* (1925-1926).

When he discovered that his fellow internees included a violinist, cellist, and clarinetist, Messiaen first wrote a short trio that was played in the washroom. Adding a part for himself to be played on the camp's beaten-up piano, Messiaen set to work on the *Quartet for the End of Time* in 1940. The work's first performance on January 15, 1941, joins with the riotous premiere of Igor Stravinsky's *The Rite of Spring* (1913) as one of the great stories in modern music. Messiaen and his three colleagues performed the quartet outdoors, in the dead of winter, before five thousand prisoners. Messiaen later admitted that he had never had such an attentive and appreciative audience as this.

The title has been interpreted as a reference to the static conditions of life in a prison camp, where boredom and frustration were increased by the prisoners' awareness of the frantic activity going on in the rest of Europe, and to the composer's own serene Catholic contemplation of Christian liberty and the illusory nature of time. Were Messiaen not known to be a mystical Catholic, his title might even be understood as a despairing comment about the massive ravages of World War II. Messiaen himself rejected the interpretation that the work was composed as a comment on prison life; instead, he cited the title's literary source, the Revelations of St. John, in which the angel of the Apocalypse tells St. John, "There shall be no more delay; but when the time comes for the seventh angel to sound his trumpet, the hidden purpose of God will have been fulfilled, as he promised to his servants the prophets."

Messiaen's artistic development was influenced by a curious combination of elements, including nature and especially the song of birds, Catholic theology of a particularly mystical nature, and a love of the theater, especially Claude Debussy's opera *Pelléas et Mélisande* (1902). His parents provided him with a rigorously literary upbringing, as his father was an English translator and a Shakespeare scholar while his mother, the poet Cécile Sauvage, wrote a book of poems called *The Flowering Soul* during the composer's gestation. During his musical studies, he developed a fascination with classical Greek rhythms and discovered in a French encyclopedia a complex table of classical Indian rhythms. Messiaen's music is largely concerned with the revelation of God through Christianity, the action of God as shown in human love for others, or the action of God in nature, as illustrated by the songs of birds.

Messiaen's music has been admired for its rhythmic vitality. In a 1958 lecture, the composer said, "Let us not forget that the first, essential element in music is Rhythm, and that Rhythm is first and foremost the change of number and duration." Messiaen had been a pupil of the French composer Paul Dukas, who reportedly urged his students to "rhythmicize your harmonies," which can be interpreted in several ways. In a work that predicts the end of time, Messiaen uses such familiar means as linking the music of eternity with high pitch and slow tempi, as in the "In Paradisum" section of Gabriel Fauré's *Requiem*, which Messiaen is known to have admired. By means of the complicated rhythmic schemes of the various movements, the composer calls attention to rhythmic energy but also to what happens before, after, and between beats in a piece of music.

For Messiaen, rhythm is the key to the depiction of the predicted end of time. The composer uses such techniques as "modes of limited transposition," harmony as a form of timbre (rather than as distinct from it), and extremely slow tempi. The final movement of the *Quartet for the End of Time* is marked "Extremely slow and tender, ecstatic," in the composer's effort to depict the victory of Jesus over time and mortality. It is unusual to find a composer with such a rich and complicated sense of rhythm to be so consistently engaged in the overcoming and denial of time.

Rather contradictorily, Messiaen elsewhere spoke of melody as the supreme element in music. In his book *Technique de mon langage musical* (1944; *Technique of My Musical Language*, 1944-1956), the composer asserts, "Melody is the point of departure. May it remain supreme!" For many listeners, Messiaen's soaring melodies, often underscored by the otherworldly sound of the ondes martenot (an electronic keyboard instrument), are the most captivating element in his music. The fifth and eighth movements of the *Quartet for the End of Time* are distinguished by their slow, regular tempi and their rich melodic lines, played soaringly by the cello over the insistent rhythmic underpinning provided by the piano.

The eight movements of the piece are interrelated in a variety of ways. No. 2 and No. 7 have thematic links, while No. 3 and No. 6 are monodies, unharmonized or unaccompanied. No. 3, "Abîme des oiseaux" ("Abyss of Birds"), is a famous solo for clarinet, while No. 6, "Dance de la fureur, pour les sept trompettes" ("Dance of Fury for the Seven Trumpets"), is played largely in unison by violin, cello, and clarinet. Nos. 2, 6, and 7 are the most vigorous movements, while Nos. 5 and 8, as mentioned above, are the most deliberate and contemplative. The latter two movements also share Messiaen's preferred key of spiritual insight, E major.

Impact of Event

Quartet for the End of Time became one of the most admired and frequently performed pieces of chamber music in the twentieth century. The circumstances of its composition undoubtedly contributed to its appeal, yet the work remains immensely appealing on its own musical terms. Although Messiaen is usually thought of as a composer for the organ and large-scale orchestral forces, the quartet shows his ability to write successfully for small combinations of instruments. Even a chamber group can have the distinctive "Messiaen sound."

One wonders what the captive audience of five thousand at the piece's premiere really made of the quartet, although it is not difficult to imagine the mixed feelings of anxiety, hope, and fear that the composer, his fellow captives, and their guards must have felt in the dark days of 1941. Like Dmitri Shostakovich's Symphony No. 7 ("Leningrad"), Messiaen's *Quartet for the End of Time* became one of the most widely admired compositions to emerge from World War II. Like Shostakovich's Symphony No. 13 ("Babiy Yar") and Krzysztof Penderecki's *Threnody for the Victims of Hiroshima* (1960), it is frequently performed as a disturbing commentary on that war.

When Messiaen was repatriated in 1942, he was appointed professor of harmony at the Paris Conservatoire; this indicates how widely his reputation had extended. Although his name was long linked with the Paris Conservatoire, Messiaen was not officially appointed professor of composition until 1966. His other major works from the war period are *Visions de l'Amen* (1943), for two pianos; *Trois Petites Liturgies de la présence divine* (1944), a controversial work for female choir and orchestra; and *Vingt Regards sur l'Enfant-Jésus* (1945), for solo piano. The religious works were often greeted with incomprehension, often being viewed as shockingly modern by the pious and as sentimental by the modernists.

Before his death on April 28, 1992, Messiaen was arguably the most famous living composer, although he was perhaps more widely admired by musical audiences for his serene faith and as an admirable personality than for his actual musical output. After World War II, Messiaen's reputation gradually grew, throughout the world. Eventually he enjoyed a popularity unusual for a living composer in the twentieth century.

For much of the audience for serious music, Messiaen's reputation rests on the charm of his apparently eccentric titles, which seem to combine overblown baroque Catholic excess with a surrealistic sensuality. Successive movements in the *Turangalîla-*

symphonie (1948) are entitled "Joy of the Blood of the Stars" and "Garden of Love's Sleep" ("Joie du sang des étoiles" and "Jardin du sommeil d'amour"). A trip to Bryce Canyon in Utah inspired *Des Canyons des étoiles* ("Canyon of the Stars," 1971-1974). Messiaen's final large orchestral work, premiered by Zubin Mehta and the New York Philharmonic in the fall of 1992, was entitled *Éclairs sur l' au-delà . . .* (roughly, "Flash Visions of the Beyond"). Not since Aleksandr Scriabin at the beginning of the twentieth century had a composer chosen such bizarre titles for his music.

Messiaen has been accused by his detractors (who are numerous) of mistaking sentimentality for piety and for simply continuing the treacly tradition of sentimental nineteenth century vocal music. To these critics, the contemplative movements of the *Quartet for the End of Time* or the *Turangalîla-symphonie* are uncomfortably close to the sentimental religiosity of the more turgid moments in the operas of Charles Gounod and Jules Massenet. Messiaen himself has insisted that movements such as No. 8 in the quartet, "Louange a l'immortalité de Jésus," in the composer's preferred key for spiritual insight, E major, "are not at all luscious nor sweet; they are simply noble, bare, austere." Detractors, however, insist on finding traces of Massenet and Glenn Miller, and many of these find more saccharin than spirituality. Even an admiring eulogy in *The New York Times* could not resist a patronizing view of the composer's spirituality: "Messiaen's music and the woozy ardor of his Christian devotions are indivisible." This attitude is unfortunately typical of a certain class of academic rationalists who cannot forgive Messiaen for linking a modern, sophisticated musical technique to an unfashionable religious perspective.

Enthusiasts for Messiaen's artistry, however, are more than happy to hear the music of eternity in the composer's mystical contemplations, and they revere Messiaen for his melodic and rhythmic innovations. As the teacher of Pierre Boulez and Karlheinz Stockhausen, Messiaen has been called the "father of recent European avantgarde music," although his own music has never been as chillingly inaccessible as that of many of the composers whose work he has inspired or that was written in reaction against him. Despite his influence, Messiaen's achievement is distinctive and unlikely to be replicated; no other composer is likely to share Messiaen's unusual combination of Catholic spirituality, passion for birdsong, and fascination with classical Indian rhythms. Even his detractors cannot deny the warmth, integrity, and passionate commitment of his music. Not only for the conditions of its composition but for the glowing affirmation of the persistence of the human spirit has the *Quartet for the End of Time* survived as a great musical testament of the twentieth century.

Bibliography

Griffiths, Paul. *Olivier Messiaen and the Music of Time.* Ithaca, N.Y.: Cornell University Press, 1985. Provides a sensitive musical analysis of Messiaen's major works. As the title suggests, it is especially concerned with Messiaen's distinctive attitudes toward rhythm and time.

Holland, Bernard. "An Island of Innocence and Taste." *The New York Times*, May 10,

1992, p. H25(N). Typical of a certain kind of academic attitude toward Messiaen—respectful of his music but condescending toward the deep spirituality that inspired it.

Johnson, Robert Sherlaw. *Messiaen*. Rev. ed. London: Dent, 1989. A fine standard, serious musicological study of Messiaen's compositions. Recently revised to include some of the master's late works, such as his long-awaited opera, *St. François d'Assise* (1975-1983), but not his final major orchestral work, *Éclairs sur l'audelà . . .* , which had its premiere after the composer's death, in the fall of 1992.

Peyser, Joan. *Boulez*. New York: Schirmer, 1976. Admiring study of Messiaen's student, who is indebted to his teacher for his complicated understanding of rhythm. Like many of Messiaen's critics, Peyser cannot resist categorizing him in a condescending way: "church organist, virtuoso pianist, user of Gregorian melodies, specialist in Asiatic rhythms, fanatical follower of bird songs."

Salzman, Eric. *Twentieth-Century Music: An Introduction*. Englewood Cliffs, N.J.: Prentice-Hall, 1967. Identifies the Messiaen of the late 1960's as "the father of recent European avant-garde music" and notes his influence on figures such as Boulez and Stockhausen.

Byron Nelson

Cross-References

Webern's *Six Pieces for Large Orchestra* Premieres in Vienna (1913), p. 367; *The Rite of Spring* Stuns Audiences (1913), p. 373; Stravinsky Completes His Wind Octet (1923), p. 561; Berg's *Wozzeck* Premieres in Berlin (1925), p. 680; Berg's *Lulu* Opens in Zurich (1937), p. 1078; Boulez's *Le Marteau sans maître* Premieres in Baden-Baden (1955), p. 1656.

NBC AND CBS LAUNCH COMMERCIAL TELEVISION

Category of event: Television and radio
Time: July 1, 1941
Locale: New York, New York

Commercial television became a reality when the Federal Communications Commission awarded licenses to broadcasters to offer regular television programming, touching off a ratings war that shaped American broadcasting

Principal personages:

DAVID SARNOFF (1891-1971), the innovative engineer and businessman who built the Radio Corporation of America (RCA) into America's largest communications conglomerate

VLADIMIR ZWORYKIN (1889-1982), the director of electronic research at RCA Laboratories who played a key role in the invention of television

WILLIAM S. PALEY (1901-1990), a brilliant executive and charismatic empire builder who turned a handful of struggling radio stations into the powerful Columbia Broadcasting System (CBS)

FRANK STANTON (1908-   ), a gifted psychologist and pioneer audience researcher who, as Paley's successor, initiated CBS's program of diversification

PETER GOLDMARK (1906-1977), an engineer at CBS Laboratories who developed the first practical color-television system

EDWARD J. NOBLE (1882-1958), a financier who purchased the controlling interest in RCA's old Blue Network, which became the American Broadcasting Company (ABC)

LEONARD HARRY GOLDENSON (1905-   ), the key figure in the history of ABC from 1950 to 1985

Summary of Event

Some are surprised to learn that scientists had worked out in principle the technology needed to transmit pictures and sounds simultaneously by means of electronic impulses long before the Federal Communications Commission (FCC) authorized commercial telecasting in July of 1941. A form of television was invented in Germany in 1884 by Paul Nipkow, an engineer who devised a mechanical "scanning" disk that provided a means of breaking down an image and converting it into electric impulses. In formulating the scanning principle, Nipkow took a giant step toward realizing practical television; all early television systems utilized a version of Nipkow's mechanical scanner. Vladimir Zworykin took another giant step in 1929 when he developed the iconoscope camera tube and the kinescope picture tube, which together formed the first all-electronic television system. Commercial television seemed to be on the verge of becoming a reality; however, funding was a major problem. The history of television is not so much the history of the work of isolated scientists as the history of the large corporations that were able to commit huge sums of money to research and development.

Two corporations undertook such a commitment. One was the Radio Corporation of America (RCA), which was organized by General Electric in 1919 to establish preeminence in radio communication. Arrangements were made for RCA to acquire the assets of the American Marconi Company, and David Sarnoff, who had moved up through the ranks at Marconi, in 1921 became the new company's general manager. In 1929, Sarnoff became executive vice president and general manager of RCA; in 1930, he became president (a position he was to hold until 1947, when he became chairman of the board).

Sarnoff made three far-reaching decisions during his long career in the face of tremendous opposition within and without RCA. First, in 1926, when RCA was the leading manufacturer of radio sets, he insisted on founding the National Broadcasting Company (NBC) as a subsidiary, to ensure that people who bought RCA radios had something to listen to on them. NBC lost money at first, but Sarnoff's faith in the enterprise was eventually justified; during the 1930's, NBC became the nation's most prestigious broadcasting network.

Second, during the 1930's, Sarnoff could see that television would replace radio as the preeminent medium of communication. He channeled huge sums of money into research and development. In November of 1929, Vladimir Zworykin joined RCA as director of its electronic research laboratory. (Zworykin had invented his all-electronic television system at Westinghouse Electric, but his colleagues there had found his work rather impractical.) When Sarnoff asked Zworykin how much it would cost to perfect his system, the latter replied that it would take $100,000. In fact, as Sarnoff frequently pointed out, RCA spent fifty million dollars on television before realizing a penny in profit. The production of television sets was halted during World War II, but beginning in 1947, sales skyrocketed. Again, Sarnoff's faith was justified.

Third, during the 1940's, Sarnoff decided that color television would replace black-and-white television. RCA began to manufacture color sets, and the NBC network transmitted broadcasts in color as often as possible. For several years, NBC found itself alone in this enterprise, and, not surprisingly, RCA lost a considerable amount of money during the period. Again, though, Sarnoff's faith was justified, for during the 1960's color broadcasting became universal.

The history of NBC is inseparable from the history of its parent company, RCA. On November 15, 1926, NBC became the first radio network in the United States, with twenty-five affiliated stations. The following year, NBC split its network into two sections known as the Red and the Blue. NBC entered the television business on April 4, 1928, when it obtained permission from the FCC to operate experimental television station W2XBS (New York), which in 1931 began transmitting from the top of the Empire State Building. NBC introduced television as a regular service in April of 1939, beginning with a broadcast of President Franklin D. Roosevelt's opening speech from the New York World's Fair. The NBC network dated from January 12, 1940, when two stations, WNBC (New York) and WRGB (Schenectady), began broadcasting NBC programs.

The Columbia Broadcasting System (CBS) also committed itself to research and development. This company was founded in 1927 by two talent promoters, George Coats and Arthur Judson. When Sarnoff turned down their request for an exclusive contract to supply performers to the NBC network, Coats and Judson organized their own network, which they called United Independent Broadcasters. Within a year, sixteen stations had become affiliates of United, but the company ran into financial difficulties. The Columbia Phonographic Company invested $163,000 in United, with the proviso that the network be named the Columbia Phonographic Broadcasting System. The name was shortened to the Columbia Broadcasting System when Leon and Isaac Levy took it over in 1928. That year, William Paley bought the controlling interest in the company for $417,000, a sum he raised from his shares in his family's thriving cigar company. On September 16, 1928, two days before his twenty-seventh birthday, Paley became president of CBS. A brilliant executive, Paley turned CBS into the most powerful communications company in the world. Paley quickly signed up forty-nine radio stations, offering them twenty hours of network programs rather than the ten offered by NBC. With the stations in place, he began his search for talent. Initially, he recruited such relatively unknown performers as Bing Crosby, Kate Smith, and the Mills Brothers. Beginning in 1930, Paley balanced the lowbrow soap operas and the thrillers that were staples on radio with regular Saturday afternoon broadcasts from the New York Philharmonic. In 1931, CBS entered television, with regular scheduled programming over W2XAB (New York). Paley's commitment to entertainment was matched by his commitment to news. When newspaper publishers, worried by competition, barred wire services from supplying news to broadcasters, CBS responded by setting up its own news-gathering unit. (During World War II, CBS News established the network—and Edward R. Murrow—as the voice of broadcast journalism.)

Paley surrounded himself with the very best people. Frank Stanton joined CBS in 1935, first as promotions consultant and then as audience researcher. Ohio State University had recently awarded Stanton a doctorate in psychology for his research into audience behavior. For many years, Stanton served as Paley's "point man," turning the latter's creative ideas into realities. Stanton became program analyzer in 1937 and director of research in 1938. During this period, he developed the first recording device that could be placed inside radio sets to record the operations of the sets. In 1945, Stanton became vice president and general manager of CBS, one of the youngest and best-known in the radio industry. By the time he became president in 1965, Stanton had turned his attention to the problem of diversification.

Almost immediately, Paley set up a research unit in anticipation of the shift from radio to television broadcasting. Peter Goldmark joined CBS in 1935. The University of Vienna had recently granted him a doctorate in physics for his pioneering work in the fields of radio and television engineering. Goldmark had tried to find work at RCA, but Sarnoff had found his application unsuitable. Goldmark spent more than three decades at CBS as chief television engineer (until 1944), director of engineering research and development (until 1950), vice president in charge of research and development (until 1954), and president of CBS Laboratories (until he retired in 1971). Goldmark made a number of important contributions in the fields of sight and sound; one of the first practical color-television systems was developed at CBS Laboratories under his direction. (Goldmark liked to point out that his work helped to bring color television to the public a decade faster than it might otherwise have come.) The first color broadcast in history was transmitted in August of 1940 by CBS's experimental transmitter in New York. In addition, Goldmark in 1948 invented the long-playing microgroove phonograph record, which quickly revolutionized the recorded music industry.

Impact of Event

Thanks to Sarnoff's drive, NBC achieved preeminence during the 1930's and the 1940's. During the summer of 1941, NBC signed up its first sponsors, Procter and Gamble, Lever Brothers, Sun Oil, and Bulova. During the summer of 1946, Gillette became the first advertiser to sponsor a television program, the Joe Louis-Billy Conn heavyweight title fight. On October 27, 1946, Bristol-Myers became the first sponsor of a network television series, *Geographically Speaking.* The network introduced coast-to-coast television coverage in 1951 and began broadcasting programs in color in 1954. (By 1966, NBC was broadcasting all its programs in color.) Milton Berle was the most famous name on NBC television during the 1940's and the 1950's. NBC pioneered early-morning programming with *The Today Show*, first seen in 1952, and late-night television with *The Jack Paar Show*, which aired from 1957 to 1962.

Toward the end of the 1940's, however, CBS challenged NBC for preeminence. By offering performers huge sums of money for the rights to their shows, Paley was able to sign such artists as Jack Benny, George Burns and Gracie Allen, and Edgar Bergen. Soon, the majority of the top-rated shows in each broadcast period were CBS shows. It took Paley nineteen years to hire Freeman Gosden and Charles Correll, the two white actors who created and played in *Amos 'n' Andy*, the most popular radio program and the cornerstone of NBC's schedule. In 1948, they signed with CBS, where the show was turned into an equally successful television series. NBC never really recovered from "Paley's Raids," as they were called.

The CBS television network generally dates from 1948. In 1951, CBS began broadcasting the most popular television series of the decade, *I Love Lucy.* In fact, the 1950's may be considered the CBS decade, for during this period CBS introduced some of the most popular soap operas to television, including *Search for Tomorrow* in 1951, *The Guiding Light* in 1952, and *As the World Turns* in 1956. CBS also produced the long-running children's show *Captain Kangaroo*, which ran from 1955 to 1981.

In 1943, Edward Noble, who had built the Life Savers candy company into a multimillion dollar enterprise, acquired NBC's Blue Network of 116 stations for eight million dollars. (Sarnoff was forced to dispose of the network because in 1941 the FCC had ruled that no organization could maintain more than one network.) The name of the network was changed to the American Broadcasting Company (ABC), with Noble as chairman of the board. On April 19, 1948, ABC entered television with its broadcast of *On the Corner*, starring Henry Morgan. ABC ranked as the poor cousin among the networks until 1976, when it surpassed CBS in the ratings. The most popular of the early ABC series was *The Adventures of Ozzie and Harriet*, starring Ozzie and Harriet Nelson, which was first broadcast on October 3, 1952. In 1953, Leonard Goldenson merged his company, United Paramount Theaters (UPT), with ABC. Noble relinquished control but remained with the company as a director. ABC's first major programming success was *Disneyland*, first seen on October 27, 1954. In 1955, Warner Bros. began an exclusive production program with ABC. Three years later, ABC began morning and late-afternoon television broadcasts. The network introduced color programming in 1962, with full color in 1966. ABC's first major attempt at late-night programming was *The Joey Bishop Show*, which appeared from 1967 to 1969.

Bibliography

Campbell, Robert. *The Golden Years of Broadcasting: A Celebration of the First Fifty Years of Television on NBC.* New York: Scribner's, 1976. Resembling a slick annual report, this document gives inside but never intimate details about the people who made NBC the enormous success it is today. Includes more than 250 pictures, a great many in full color. Campbell, though, makes little effort to assess the impact television has had on the United States.

Paley, William S. *As It Happened: A Memoir.* Garden City, N.Y.: Doubleday, 1979. In this memoir, Paley tells his side of the story about the CBS radio and television empire he founded. Readers will be fascinated by his talk of purchasing the foundering network, the heyday of radio and television programming, and the controversies he had with Edward R. Murrow, among others.

Paper, Lewis J. *Empire: William S. Paley and the Making of CBS.* New York: St. Martin's Press, 1987. Moves beyond Paley's autobiography, providing some insight into his leadership style. Paper offers the reader many interesting facts, especially about the history of radio and television broadcasting, but he stuffs them into a difficult chronological framework.

Slater, Robert. *This . . . Is CBS: A Chronicle of Sixty Years.* Englewood Cliffs, N.J.: Prentice-Hall, 1988. This history of CBS explores the development of radio and television from 1928 to the present. Slater's account is firmly linked to the individuals who were involved. Asserts that Paley damaged CBS by clinging to power when he should have been choosing a capable successor.

Slide, Anthony. *The Television Industry: A History Dictionary.* New York: Greenwood Press, 1991. This remarkable book identifies production companies, distributors, and organizations; explains terms widely used in television; and illuminates a wide variety of genres, including children's programming, detective dramas, news, sitcoms, soap operas, and sports. The reader can sift through more than one thousand items. The book concludes with an appendix, which contains page-long essays on Leonard Goldenson, William Paley, and David Sarnoff, key figures in the history of the three networks.

Smith, Sally Bedell. *In All His Glory: William S. Paley, the Legendary Tycoon and His Brilliant Circle.* New York: Simon & Schuster, 1990. This entertaining biography conveys an impressive amount of information about Paley's public and private life. Smith offers a fascinating glimpse into CBS's corporate culture.

Robert M. Seiler

Cross-References

The Art of Radio Develops from Early Broadcast Experience (1920's), p. 469; The British Broadcasting Corporation Is Chartered (1927), p. 712; NBC Launches American Television at the World's Fair (1939), p. 1143; NBC Broadcasts the World Series (1947), p. 1362; ABC Begins Its Own Network Television Service (1948), p. 1368; Television Enters Its Golden Age (1950's), p. 1465; ABC Makes a Landmark Deal with Disney (1954), p. 1612; The Decline of the Big Three Networks Becomes a Fall (Late 1980's), p. 2554; *The Simpsons* Debuts, Anchoring the Fledgling Fox Network (1990), p. 2652.

THE NAZIS BAN NOLDE'S PAINTINGS

Category of event: Art
Time: August 23, 1941
Locale: Berlin, Germany

The banning of Emil Nolde's art as "degenerate" by the Nazis signaled the end of freedom of expression in Germany

Principal personages:
> EMIL NOLDE (EMIL HANSEN, 1867-1956), a German expressionist painter whose Volkish art depicted the beauty of his homeland and its people
> JOSEPH GOEBBELS (1897-1945), the Nazi minister of propaganda who persecuted Nolde and other artists
> ALFRED ROSENBERG (1893-1946), the head of the Combat League for German Culture, who vied with Goebbels for control of the German artistic community
> ADOLF HITLER (1889-1945), the German dictator from 1933 to 1945, who spelled out the standards for German art

Summary of Event

By the early 1930's, Emil Nolde was one of the leading expressionist painters in Germany. His work was highly regarded by other artists as well as art critics, and, according to them, he expressed better than any other painter of his age the forceful, emotional, and intuitive character of expressionism. At times, his paintings appeared violent or grotesque, defeating his stated purpose of moving away from nature while remaining natural; however, his works exhibited an originality that few could match.

Although his name is associated with Die Brücke, a group of expressionist artists to which he belonged in 1906 and 1907, Nolde always remained distanced from the group's members. Nolde was almost a generation older than the rest of Die Brücke's artists, and his art was rooted in nineteenth century traditions, making stylistic and temperamental differences between him and the group unavoidable. Nolde's religiosity, ultra-individualism, and love of the soil contrasted sharply with the intellectual, communal, and humanistic work of Die Brücke, and these differences eventually led to Nolde's withdrawal in 1907.

Following his involvement with Die Brücke, Nolde retreated with his wife, Ada, to the town of Seebüll in his native province of Schleswig-Holstein. During this period, Nolde was briefly involved with the artistic groups New Secession and Der Blaue Reiter. It was also at this time that Nolde focused his attention on the religious, landscape, and flower paintings for which he became most famous. Nolde's religious paintings of the time include *Wise and Foolish Virgins* (1910), *Christ and the Children* (1910), *Pentecost* (1910), and the nine-part *Life of Christ* altar (1912); his landscape and flower paintings are represented by such notable works as *Tugboat on the*

Elbe (1910), *Blue Iris* (1915), *Horses in the Meadow* (1916), and *Nordermühle* (1924).

Nolde especially emphasized the countryside and people of Germany in his paintings. His deep conviction that these subjects needed to be painted encouraged him in his work. Yet Nolde's grotesqueness in portraying some of his subjects and his experimentation with techniques reminiscent of African tribal art placed him on a collision course with the Nazi Party after 1933.

When the Nazis seized power in 1933, the artistic community in Germany was pressured to conform to the new government's art guidelines. In a speech at the Nuremberg Nazi Party rally in 1934, Adolf Hitler outlined his vision for the future form and style of artwork in Germany. According to Hitler, German art henceforth would emphasize only traditional values that corresponded to Nazi doctrine. These guidelines would protect the average citizen from the "degenerate," mind-poisoning art that the Nazis claimed was sweeping Germany. The goal of the new Nazi concept of art was to prevent the perceived moral degeneration of the German people and to announce the ideals of Nazi Germany to the world.

As a result of Nazi policy, many German artists found that they were no longer free to exhibit their works. In particular, the government attacked modern artistic styles such as cubism, Dadaism, Futurism, and expressionism. The Nazis labeled artists who produced works in these styles "saboteurs of art" and accused them of "cultural bolshevism."

Because Adolf Hitler opposed modern art in general and Nolde's work in particular, Nolde faced constant attacks from the government. Nolde's modern tendencies and his use of what Hitler termed "impure" elements from tribal art made him a special target for Nazi repression. Not everyone, however, favored the harsh tactics used against Nolde. Disagreement over Nolde's style created a rift in the Nazi leadership. Nazi repression of Nolde sparked a debate between Alfred Rosenberg, the head of the Combat League for German Culture, and Joseph Goebbels, the president of the Reich Chamber of Culture. Rosenberg attacked Nolde's art and sought to have it banned from all German museums, while Goebbels initially sympathized with those who defended Nolde as an example of "indigenous Nordic art" and the Gothic tendency toward "destruction of form." Soon, however, Goebbels bowed to the will of Hitler and began a crusade against Nolde. By attacking Nolde and other German expressionists such as Ernst Barlach, Goebbels was able to prove to Hitler his ability to manage cultural affairs and to silence rivals, including Rosenberg. Goebbels' success allowed him to consolidate permanently his political power over Nazi Germany's art and culture.

In 1937, in preparation for a "degenerate art" exhibition organized by the Nazis in Munich, Goebbels authorized Professor Adolf Ziegler, the president of the Reich Chamber of Visual Arts, to seize works of art that failed to meet Nazi standards. As a result, a staggering total of 1,052 of Nolde's paintings were confiscated from German museums and art galleries. Twenty-six were exhibited in Munich. Of the roughly sixteen thousand artworks by some fourteen hundred artists confiscated by the Nazis, Nolde's 1,052 constituted the greatest number. He continued to paint, but his art came under close government scrutiny. This was particularly ironic, since Nolde had been a member of the Nazi Party since 1920 and fancied himself a painter of Nordic, Germanic, and Aryan art. In fact, it was probably Nolde's Nazi Party membership that marked him for especially severe treatment; because Nolde's works did not meet the party's guidelines for new art, he was slowly forced underground.

The attacks began by Rosenberg, Goebbels, and Ziegler against modern art increased following the "degenerate art" exhibition in 1937, and by 1940, many German artists had emigrated to other countries. A few, including Nolde, remained to face the wrath of the Nazis. In a letter dated July 2, 1938, Nolde wrote to Goebbels to request the return of his seized paintings and an end to the defamation of his character. Unfortunately, reasoning with the Nazis did not work. Nolde's argument that his work was "German, strong, austere, and sincere" had no effect. His paintings were never returned to him. Finally, on August 23, 1941, the Nazis progressed from repression of Nolde to outright censorship. Nolde was forbidden to paint, his Berlin studio was closed, and all works still in his possession were confiscated by the government.

Impact of Event

Emil Nolde became a victim of the new Nazi policy toward art, along with hundreds of other painters, sculptors, writers, and musicians. The Nazi assault on the arts included not only confiscation of art but also book burnings and censorship of music and film. At first, conditions were tolerable, but any real freedom for artists in Germany was drastically curtailed after 1937.

The Nazis were intent upon implementing their party's policy of making traditional Nordic art the German standard, and any artists who did not meet Hitler's guidelines had their works removed from public view. When the Nazis succeeded in preventing Nolde from painting and exhibiting his work in 1941, they won a great victory in the battle for control of the arts. After 1941, all aspects of art and culture in Germany were controlled by the Nazi regime. A stifling artistic atmosphere developed; mediocre artists' works were exhibited regularly, and talented artists' works were sold, destroyed, or hidden in government storerooms. The disappearance or emigration of the German modern artists attested the regime's ferocity in carrying out its program.

The ban on Nolde's work marked a significant shift in the treatment of the arts in Germany. The already bad conditions for those modern artists who remained worsened progressively after 1941. Forbidden to paint, Nolde worked surreptitiously, using watercolor paints to avoid the telltale odor of oils, which might be detected during the frequent searches conducted by the Gestapo of Nolde's home in Seebüll. These "unpainted pictures"—more than thirteen hundred small watercolor paintings, completed and hidden in the years between 1938 and 1945—show the maturity of Nolde's work and his ability to adapt to changing circumstances. Already in his seventies, Nolde knew that he had little time to waste in completing the paintings that were to be the crowning achievements of his artistic career.

The world artistic community was shocked by the Nazi actions against Nolde and the avant-garde and protested vehemently; however, protest was to no avail. Censorship continued, and Nazi art replaced modern art in museums and galleries. Nazi suppression of modern art occurred quickly and forcefully, until no creative artist was safe from attack. Resistance to the Nazification of art was organized, but Nazi control of the government, the Reich Chamber of Culture, and the Combat League for German Culture gave them a significant advantage in numbers and power over small groups of individual artists. The strength of the Nazi onslaught eventually overwhelmed these isolated groups and succeeded in establishing a Nazi style for the arts. All aspects of culture were regulated, from architecture and painting to literature and film. The Nazis left no area untouched.

The heroism of the artists in the face of these attacks was tremendous, but no amount of sacrifice could stop the determined Nazi oppressors. Many artists remained in Germany and were forced underground at a time when their styles were beginning to mature. This group included Nolde and some Die Brücke artists such as Willi Baumeister, Oskar Schlemmer, Alexey von Jawlensky, Karl Hofer, and Ernst Barlach. Other artists, including Paul Klee, Wassily Kandinsky, Ernst Ludwig Kirchner, Max Beckmann, Oskar Kokoschka, and Hans Hoffmann, were forced to emigrate.

The persecution of German artists changed the face of modern art forever. Emigration spread German art to other countries. Hans Hoffmann became the catalyst for a group of artists who would develop a uniquely American style in New York City; Ernst Ludwig Kirchner exerted an influence over art in Switzerland, and Max Beckmann left his mark in both Holland and the United States. The influence of immigrants from Nazi Germany was even felt at the center of the art world, the École de Paris, where Hans Hartung pushed contemporary painting in new directions.

In addition to causing changes in the world art scene by provoking the emigration of artists, Nazi domination significantly influenced the styles of those artists who stayed in Germany. Artists such as Nolde waged a constant battle to produce and protect their works under Nazi surveillance. The use of smaller canvases, watercolors, and other less traditional artistic styles, begun in order to hide works of art from the Nazis, continued even after the end of World War II and contributed to the changing face of modern art. Nazi repression influenced the development of modern art for years to come.

As a result of his persecution by the Nazis, Emil Nolde gained immense respect in the artistic community after the end of World War II. His resistance to Nazi dictates made him famous. He outlived his persecutors and contributed to the developing art scene of the 1950's. Even at the age of eighty, Nolde produced paintings that were a source of inspiration. He served as an example to other artists that adversity could be overcome and that art could triumph over those who sought to repress it. His irrepressible vigor, his individualism, and his bold style left a lasting mark on modern art.

Bibliography

Bradley, William S. *Emil Nolde and German Expressionism: A Prophet in His Own Land.* Ann Arbor: University of Michigan Research Press, 1986. An interesting but somewhat academic study of Nolde's relationship to the Volkish view of art advocated by the Nazis. Bradley's book discusses the Volkish tendencies in Nolde's work and offers a good general discussion of Nolde's style. Well researched; includes endnotes, bibliography, and index.

Gosebruch, Martin. *Nolde: Watercolors and Drawings.* Translated by E. M. Küstner and J. A. Underwood. New York: Praeger, 1973. Discussion of Nolde's watercolors and drawings. Reprints famous sketches and paintings. Includes a short bibliography of German sources.

Haftmann, Werner. *Emil Nolde: Unpainted Pictures.* Translated by Inge Goodman. New York: Praeger, 1965. A discussion of the watercolor paintings that Nolde completed during World War II. Offers an analysis of Nolde's technique and the changes in his style. Good reproductions of many paintings.

Hinz, Berthold. *Art in the Third Reich.* Translated by Robert Kimber and Rita Kimber. New York: Pantheon Books, 1979. Examines art under the Nazis and the fate of avant-garde artists such as Nolde. Hinz provides a thorough discussion of the political situation in Germany and its effect on the arts. Examples of Nazi-sponsored art are reprinted in black and white. Includes endnotes, bibliography, and index.

Myers, Bernhard S. *The German Expressionists: A Generation in Revolt.* New York: Praeger, 1956. An oversized book featuring a collection of color plates of German expressionist art. Historical background on each artist and his work accompanies the plates. Chapter 17 deals exclusively with Nolde. Includes bibliography and index.

Selz, Peter. *German Expressionist Painting.* Berkeley: University of California Press, 1957. A somewhat dated history of German expressionist artists and movements. Black-and-white and color reproductions of expressionist art. Includes endnotes, extensive bibliography, and index.

Uhr, Horst. *Masterpieces of German Expressionism at the Detroit Institute of Arts.* New York: Hudson Hills Press, 1982. Provides an overview of the major German expressionist artists and samples of their work. Well composed and edited. Includes endnotes, bibliography, and index.

Vogt, Paul. *Expressionism: German Painting, 1905-1920.* Translated by Antony Vivis and Robert Erich Wolf. New York: Harry N. Abrams, 1978. A detailed discussion of the origins of German expressionism, with color plates of early works by expressionist artists. Includes bibliography and index.

Gregory Weeks

Cross-References

The Soviet Union Bans Abstract Art (1922), p. 544; The New Objectivity Movement Is Introduced (1925), p. 631; Socialist Realism Is Mandated in Soviet Literature

THE MALTESE FALCON ESTABLISHES A NEW STYLE FOR CRIME FILMS

Category of event: Motion pictures
Time: October, 1941
Locale: Hollywood, California

Director John Huston's faithful film adaptation of Dashiell Hammett's hard-boiled detective novel became a classic in the film noir *style, influencing filmmakers worldwide*

Principal personages:

JOHN HUSTON (1906-1987), a world-famous director whose first project was the film adaptation of *The Maltese Falcon*

DASHIELL HAMMETT (1894-1961), a leading novelist in the hard-boiled school of mystery writers

HUMPHREY BOGART (1899-1957), an actor who initially specialized in gangster roles but became a superstar after his portrayal of detective Sam Spade

MARY ASTOR (LUCILLE VASCONCELLOS LANGHANKE, 1906-1987), the actress who performed brilliantly in the role of Brigid O'Shaughnessy

SYDNEY GREENSTREET (1879-1954), a veteran stage actor who made his first film appearance in *The Maltese Falcon*

PETER LORRE (LASZLO LÖWENSTEIN, 1904-1964), a famous character actor whose career began in Europe in the early 1930's

Summary of Event

The release of *The Maltese Falcon* in October of 1941 marked a turning point in the careers of three Americans: screenwriter and director John Huston, actor Humphrey Bogart, and novelist Dashiell Hammett. It also greatly boosted the careers of four other actors: Mary Astor, who played the compulsive liar and murderess Brigid O'Shaughnessy; Sydney Greenstreet, who delivered a spectacular performance as the jovial but sinister fat man, Caspar Gutman; Peter Lorre, a veteran film actor who was cast perfectly as the effeminate but dangerous Joel Cairo; and Elisha Cook, Jr., who played "the punk" responsible for the murders of Floyd Thursby and Captain Jacobi.

John Huston, best known up to that time as the son of prominent Hollywood star Walter Huston, had a checkered career before winning the opportunity to direct *The Maltese Falcon.* He had been working as a Hollywood screenwriter, and his experience as a writer proved invaluable to him during the rest of his life. He understood that the most important ingredient of a good film was the story.

Dashiell Hammett's hard-boiled detective novel *The Maltese Falcon* (1929) had been made into motion pictures twice before Huston became involved with it. Hammett's writing appealed to filmmakers for several reasons. He had been a private detective for many years and wrote about crime and detection with authority. He favored a completely objective style of storytelling, describing only what his characters said and did, not what they were thinking or feeling. This objectivity made his novels easily transposable to the screen. Furthermore, Hammett has been called one of the best dialogue writers America has ever produced. The dialogue in the talking films of the 1920's and 1930's had been mostly crude and obvious, and Hollywood was becoming sensitive to this shortcoming now that motion pictures were attracting a more sophisticated audience than had been the case in their infancy.

The earlier film versions of Hammett's novel, one titled *The Maltese Falcon* (1931) and the other *Satan Met a Lady* (1936), had been bowdlerized Hollywood productions. Huston wanted to film the story the way Hammett had written it, retaining its original rapid-fire dialogue and its cynical view of human motivations. Huston shot the film using a script that was little more than a trimmed down version of the novel.

The role of detective Sam Spade went to Humphrey Bogart. Bogart went on to become internationally idolized as a symbol of the modern existential hero who has no illusions about human character but sticks to his principles even though he is doomed to go down in defeat. "Bogie," as the world came to know him, had almost invariably played villains on the screen and had become typecast as a "heavy." One of his most famous roles was that of killer Duke Mantee, who escaped from prison and terrorized a group of innocent people in *The Petrified Forest* (1936).

It was a shock to film audiences to see Bogart playing a hero. As Bogart portrayed him, Sam Spade was a mixture of good and bad, kindness and cruelty, honesty and dishonesty, ugliness and animal sexuality. For Hollywood, this was a revolutionary development. Previously, characterizations were always clearly defined, with heroes and villains in unambiguous roles. There was no mixing of good and bad characteristics.

World War II was changing everyone's perspective. Europe had been embroiled in war for two years, and the United States was being relentlessly dragged into it. People were learning that the world was a brutal place and that good guys could not always act like gentlemen. World War II also saw many of the popular and strikingly handsome male stars of the period going into military service, including James Stewart, Henry Fonda, Tyrone Power, Clark Gable, and Robert Taylor, the biggest names of the time. This created an unusual opportunity for Humphrey Bogart, who was too old for military service.

John Huston joined the Army as a filmmaker and went on to a spectacular career as one of the world's greatest directors. Among his most memorable postwar films were *Key Largo* (1948), *The Treasure of the Sierra Madre* (1948), and *The African Queen* (1951), all starring his friend Humphrey Bogart.

Dashiell Hammett, though he was in his late forties and in poor health when the Japanese bombed Pearl Harbor in 1941, joined the Army and served in the Aleutian Islands. The motion picture versions of his novels *The Maltese Falcon*, *The Glass Key* (1942), and *The Thin Man* (1934) made Hammett one of the most famous writers of his time, with money pouring in from book royalties, radio serials based on his characters, and payments for rights to use his characters Nick and Nora Charles in the many sequels to *The Thin Man* made between 1936 and 1947. Hammett, however, had a serious drinking problem and also ran into trouble with the House Committee on Un-American Activities, which investigated Hollywood artists for Communist affiliations at the inception of the Cold War. The combination of these factors led to Hammett's physical and financial ruin, and he died a pauper. His reputation has grown steadily through the years and he is now regarded as one of America's best writers.

Impact of Event

By 1941, the American public was getting used to the new realities of mid-twentieth century life. It read about the incredible atrocities being committed in Europe and realized how the impact of modern weaponry on warfare threatened to destroy civilization, just as H. G. Wells had predicted in a novel that was made into the chilling British film *Things to Come* (1936). John Huston's film adaptation of Dashiell Hammett's *The Maltese Falcon* might have seemed out of place in the glamorous 1920's or the isolationist 1930's, but it sounded exactly the right note for the beginning of the brutal 1940's, when sons and husbands were being torn from their families by the millions and taught to kill without mercy.

The public's favorable reception of Huston's film naturally inspired imitations. One of the first of these was *This Gun for Hire* (1942), which introduced another famous tough-guy actor, Alan Ladd. Ladd immediately starred in a remake of Dashiell Hammett's *The Glass Key*, in which he took a beating from William Bendix in some of the most brutal scenes ever shown on film up to that time. *The Glass Key* had been filmed in 1935, starring Edward Arnold and George Raft. It is interesting to compare the two film versions of Hammett's novel, because they are textbook examples of the rapid evolution of Hollywood filmmaking in just a few short years. The dark, somber *films noir*, as these cynical, pessimistic films about the underworld came to be known, became a popular style.

The American public's taste for hard-boiled films with dialogue crackling with cynical witticisms led producers to search for stories with similar qualities. They discovered Raymond Chandler and James M. Cain, two other outstanding writers of the hard-boiled school of American crime fiction. Director Billy Wilder, working closely with Raymond Chandler on the adaptation of Cain's novel, created a *film noir* masterpiece with *Double Indemnity* (1944). Wilder went on to make many films in the same realistic genre, notably *The Lost Weekend* (1945) and *Sunset Boulevard* (1950), and James M. Cain had many of his other novels made into memorable films, including *Mildred Pierce* (1945) and *The Postman Always Rings Twice* (1946).

The list of American films influenced by Huston's version of *The Maltese Falcon* is nearly endless, but no discussion of the genre can fail to highlight Raymond Chandler. After Bogart's success as Sam Spade, the actor starred as private eye Philip Marlowe in a 1946 adaptation of Chandler's novel *The Big Sleep* (1939). These two films created a mania for private detective stories that has yet to run its course.

Many of Chandler's novels have been made into successful motion pictures. Probably the best of these after *The Big Sleep* was *Murder, My Sweet* (1944), based on one of Chandler's best novels, *Farewell, My Lovely* (1940). Chandler further influenced Hollywood by working as a scriptwriter, turning out one memorable screenplay for Alan Ladd, *The Blue Dahlia* (1946).

Alfred Hitchcock, one of the most famous directors of all time, was influenced strongly by these and other American films. Hitchcock gave the hard-boiled crime film his own special whimsical flavor in such great films as *Shadow of a Doubt* (1943), *Spellbound* (1945), *Rear Window* (1954), and *Vertigo* (1958). Other classic American *films noir* are *Laura* (1944), *Dead Reckoning* (1947), *Out of the Past* (1947), *Dark Passage* (1947), *Kiss of Death* (1947), *The Naked City* (1948), and Orson Welles's *The Lady from Shanghai* (1948). An outstanding example of the genre, filmed by a British company with an international cast, is *The Third Man* (1949). This is one of the first foreign films to show the growing influence of the American crime film.

France was occupied by the German army during the war and had no contact with Hollywood. After the war, French filmmakers discovered such films as *The Maltese Falcon* and its successors and were captivated by the style, which they dubbed *film noir*. The worldview implicit in these and many other Hollywood films perfectly suited the fatalistic postwar mood of Europeans, who had been devastated by the bloodiest and most destructive war in human history. Many European imitations of Hollywood *films noir* began to appear in the late 1940's and the 1950's. One of the most impressive was director Jean-Luc Godard's *À bout de souffle* (*Breathless*, 1959), which was part of the highly influential "New Wave" of French films. The interest in American crime films led the French to an interest in the hard-boiled American literature from which many of the films were derived; thus, the impact of *The Maltese Falcon* and its successors reached French novelists as well as French filmmakers. Fast-paced, cynical, brooding American and French films went on to influence filmmakers throughout the entire world. That influence remained prominent in many of the motion pictures made throughout the rest of the twentieth century.

Bibliography

Agee, James. *Reviews and Comments.* Vol. 1 in *Agee on Film.* New York: Grosset & Dunlap, 1969. Agee, an admirer of John Huston and author of the screenplay for Huston's *The African Queen*, writes trenchant reviews of Huston's films and an excellent profile of Huston titled "Undirectable Director."

Astor, Mary. *A Life on Film.* New York: Delacorte Press, 1971. Recounts this actress' film career, which lasted from 1922 to 1964. Fully illustrated with photographs. Contains many interesting anecdotes about her experiences working with Bogart, Huston, Greenstreet, and Lorre in *The Maltese Falcon* and *Across the Pacific* (1942).

Benchley, Nathaniel. *Humphrey Bogart.* Boston: Little, Brown, 1975. An insightful and frequently amusing biography of the dedicated but temperamental actor who put his indelible stamp on the role of Sam Spade and whose career skyrocketed after his appearance in *The Maltese Falcon*. Contains many photographs of Bogart at work and at leisure.

Chandler, Raymond. "The Simple Art of Murder." In *The Simple Art of Murder*. Boston: Houghton Mifflin, 1950. This essay is required reading for anyone who wishes to understand the evolution of crime fiction and crime films, in both of which Dashiell Hammett and Raymond Chandler were dominant figures.

Everson, William K. *The Detective in Film*. Secaucus, N.J.: Citadel Press, 1972. This lavishly illustrated overview of detective films in the United States and Great Britain contains an outstanding description and comparison of all three film versions of Hammett's *The Maltese Falcon*, complete with photos from all three films.

Hammett, Dashiell. *The Maltese Falcon*. New York: Alfred A. Knopf, 1930. Any study of the film versions of *The Maltese Falcon* should begin with a reading of Hammett's original novel. This American classic is available in many different editions and has been translated into dozens of foreign languages.

Pratley, Gerald. *The Cinema of John Huston*. Cranbury, N.J.: A. S. Barnes, 1977. This book consists mainly of lengthy interviews with John Huston, supplemented by plot summaries, credits for all of his films up to 1975, and comments by the author. Numerous stills from Huston's films as well as photographs showing what went on behind the camera.

Tuska, Jon. *The Detective in Hollywood*. Garden City, N.Y.: Doubleday, 1978. This excellent historical overview covers the evolution of the American detective film from its beginnings to the making of *Chinatown* (1974). Contains a chapter on Hollywood *films noir*. No bibliography, but many references to the works from which the films derived. Liberally illustrated with stills from famous as well as nearly forgotten Hollywood films.

Bill Delaney

Cross-References

The Mysterious Affair at Styles Introduces Hercule Poirot (1920), p. 496; *The Maltese Falcon* Introduces the Hard-Boiled Detective Novel (1929), p. 793; *Little Caesar, Public Enemy*, and *Scarface* Launch the Gangster-Film Genre (1930), p. 839; The Sherlock Holmes Film Series Begins (1939), p. 1131; *Dragnet* Is the First Widely Popular Police Show (1951), p. 1531; *The Mousetrap* Begins a Record-Breaking Run (1952), p. 1551; Godard's Expressionistic *À bout de souffle* Revolutionizes Film (1960), p. 1845; Coppola Revives Gangster Films with *The Godfather* Trilogy (1972), p. 2265.

THE ITALIAN NEW WAVE GAINS WORLDWIDE ACCLAIM

Category of event: Motion pictures
Time: 1942-1961
Locale: Italy

A series of acclaimed films by innovative directors brought Italy to the forefront of post-World War II international cinema

Principal personages:

ROBERTO ROSSELLINI (1906-1977), a director who initiated neorealism, the first phase of Italian new-wave cinema

LUCHINO VISCONTI (1906-1976), a director whose first film was a landmark in the development of Italian cinema

ANNA MAGNANI (1908-1973), an actress who embodied neorealism's earthiness

VITTORIO DE SICA (1902-1974), a director whose *Ladri di biciclette* (1948; *The Bicycle Thief*) remains a landmark in postwar European humanism

FEDERICO FELLINI (1920-   ), a director whose films were a decisive departure from his artistic origins in neorealism

MICHELANGELO ANTONIONI (1912-   ), a director whose films defined in an Italian context social and psychological conditions peculiar to Cold War Europe

Summary of Event

Together with the postwar French cinema, and in a manner which was at once more cohesive and individualistic, the Italian New Wave created a landmark in the art of the cinema. What is generally known as the new wave of Italian film is a complex phenomenon, however, the terms of reference of which cover a wide range of cultural and artistic ground and the time-span of which is not easy to define. Thus, it may be historically correct to say that Luchino Visconti's *Ossessione* (1942) is the first film indicative of the new mode and outlook of the modern Italian cinema. This film was made, however, three years before the influential *Roma, città aperta* (1945; *Rome, Open City*) of Roberto Rossellini, which is widely regarded as the original exercise in neorealism, a film style that dictated much of the course and development of the Italian New Wave.

On the other hand, it is widely held that one of the major exponents of neorealism was Vittorio De Sica and that *Il giardino dei Finzi-Contini* (1971; *The Garden of the Finzi-Continis*) is De Sica's swansong in that mode. To say, therefore, that the Italian New Wave was of artistic and cultural significance only between the years 1942 and 1961 begs as many questions as it embraces. Nevertheless, in the roughly twenty years of cinema bracketed by these two dates, most of the Italian New Wave had effectively declared itself. Not only had the leading directors of their generation established their careers by the later date, but they had already begun to articulate a critique of the original style and subject matter of postwar Italian cinema. In addition, 1961 saw the premieres of a number of films that may be regarded as distillations of the important emphases of postwar Italian cinema, and may be regarded as the year of neorealism's final eye-catching blooms. Among the films in question are Pier Paolo Pasolini's *Accattone!*, Ermanno Olmi's *Il Posto* (*The Sound of Trumpets*), and De Sica's explicit redaction of neorealist scenarios, *La Ciociara* (1960; *Two Women*).

The range and diversity of the Italian New Wave make it most convenient to survey the movement as a twofold phenomenon. In the first place, the New Wave was a cultural phenomenon of the immediate postwar period. As such, it reflected many of the social concerns of the day, many of which, not surprisingly, revolve around the status of Italy as an invaded and defeated country. The films that appeared during this first phase, which define the period by embodying the neorealist aesthetic, include *Rome, Open City*, *The Bicycle Thief*, Rossellini's *Paisà* (1946; *Paisan*), and *Riso amaro* (1949; *Bitter Rice*) by Giuseppe de Santis. In these films, the emphasis is on the characters' social destiny. The transmission of their innate humanity, which is accomplished by the various means of social exchange proposed by society at large and the more limited means at the characters' disposal, reaches a point of crisis within the humble context of everyday lives.

Yet no sooner was this filmic idiom established than it began to be diversified. For various personal and artistic reasons, directors such as Rossellini and De Sica who had been most directly involved in neorealist film began to modify and develop their interest in it. This departure may be seen as early as De Sica's *Miracolo a Milano* (1950; *Miracle in Milan*), in which a strong element of fantasy is introduced. The broadening of Italian cinema's scope during this period is economically illustrated by the evolving career of Fellini, one of the leading figures in postwar European—and world—cinema.

Fellini began his career as an assistant to Rossellini in both *Rome, Open City* and *Paisan.* Yet in Fellini's *La Strada* (1954), the emphasis is on the human condition rather than on its sociological manifestations. The international appeal of *La Strada* did much to create an audience for subsequent Italian films. The sense of diversity that assisted in the development of the Italian cinematic imagination may also be glimpsed in *Il Gattopardo* (1963; *The Leopard*) and *Rocco e i suoi fratelli* (1960; *Rocco and His Brothers*), both by Visconti. The former is a stately adaptation of one of the most celebrated Italian novels of the nineteenth century, with Burt Lancaster in the lead as the head of the aristocratic household. In contrast, *Rocco and His Brothers* deals with the black-and-white conflicts of characters who are very much at the opposite end of the social spectrum.

The inner lives of the most accomplished films' protagonists form a special area of interest. This emphasis typically portrays the individual as free from society and already in some kind of critical relationship to it. Yet the fluctuating nature of such a relationship, the terms and expectations of which are not conditioned by institutional affiliation or traditional ties, creates a somewhat menacing type of freedom and detachment. Many of the best-known Italian films of the period are extravagant excursions into the semiotics of a hollow and evidently insubstantial world; what might be regarded as the culminating statement on this theme is Michelangelo Antonioni's *Blow Up* (1966).

The nature and quality of such interests and emphases, however, varies widely, from De Sica's study of old age in *Umberto D* (1952) to the lavish representation of various inner states in Fellini's best-known films, *La dolce vita* (1960) and *Otto e mezzo* (1963; *8½*), to the existential romances of Antonioni such as *L'Avventura* (1960), *La Notte* (1961; *The Night*), and *L'Eclisse* (1962; *Eclipse*). It is these films and the early films of Bernardo Bertolucci, in particular *Prima della rivoluzione* (1964; *Before the Revolution*) and *Il conformista* (1970; *The Conformist*), which have created the greatest impact and received the most critical attention outside Italy. In many ways, Bertolucci can be seen as the artistic offspring of the first two phases of the Italian New Wave, combining the social conscience of a De Sica with an equally intense interest in the individual's psychology and sexuality.

Despite the rich, and even provocative, nature of Italian New Wave cinema's range, it is those films that expressed a frankly existential dimension that received the greatest attention. It would clearly be incorrect to suggest that such films' reputation for portraying, in various guises and with a considerable variety of stylistic variation, isolated and alienated modern man at midcentury is unjustified. At the same time, such a critical emphasis, while undoubtedly in keeping with the spirit of the times in which the films in question were released, tends to limit appreciation of their treatment of other, equally rich, thematic material. Regardless of the interpretation and transmission of such themes, however, there remains no doubt that, in terms of vitality, range, technical expertise and imaginative daring, the golden age of Italian cinema remains one of the most impressive cultural phenomena of the postwar period.

Impact of Event

The effect of World War II on European thought and culture may be perceived in terms of a number of disparate but, in hindsight, associated events. The establishment in Paris of the journal *Les Temps modernes* under the editorship of Jean-Paul Sartre is one such event. Another is the organization of writers in West Germany that became known as Group 47. The contribution of the Italian publishing house Einaudi to the renewal of Italian literature is also of related significance. It is in this context that the Italian New Wave must be approached.

On one level, the subject matter of *Rome, Open City* and the other neorealist films of the late 1940's had, by design, an obvious impact. That design, though, was also a reflection of the historical circumstances in which the films came to be made. The use of a mass medium such as the cinema in order to dispel the cultural tone of Fascism received its inspiration from the generally mass character of social life in the immediate postwar period. This character was not confined to Italy; it was reflected in the widespread support received at the ballot box throughout most of liberated Europe for socialist political parties. After the oppressively institutional interwar reigns of the right-wing dictators, it was only to be expected that there would be a cultural and political backlash. The early neorealist Italian cinema is fueled by that backlash's energy.

Therefore, one of the mass medium's most important tasks was to rehabilitate the image of the citizen, the lowest democratic denominator, in reaction to authoritarian leadership. It is for this reason, as well as for practical reasons connected with technical and material filmic resources, that the sets of New Wave films are bleak and sparsely furnished, that such films use a large number of exterior shots, and that the New Wave approach to filmmaking is reminiscent of that of the documentary. In keeping with this approach, the performances aim for depth of expression rather than for breadth of gesture. The overall tendency is to avoid the operatic mode in favor of the limited, the impoverished, the marginal. The ethos of survival pervades these films, and the appeal of such a frankly populist perspective proved undeniable. The portrayal of the new subject, often coupled with the depiction of the hitherto cinematically unacknowledged worlds of rural Italy and the urban poor, is an important rehabilitative gesture.

In a more extended sense, however, the visibility of the peasant or proletarian raised questions about the very process of rehabilitation. Rather than sentimentalize the new figures, the films made them central to a sense of the inadequacy of society either productively to absorb such figures' energy or, failing that, to provide means for that energy to be self-sufficing. The connotation of freedom that the rehabilitation of the image implied was perceived with much ambivalence; it is on this note of ambivalence that the Italian cinema began to focus.

Personal experience was revealed to be not necessarily a source of authenticity. Fellini's elaborate variations of the archetypes of the clown and the innocent, memorably inaugurated in *La Strada*, enact a schematic but surpassingly fluid choreography of hauntings, each denoting the peculiar frailty of the individual. The resonances of Fellini's work, and also of its darker counterparts in Antonioni's, are central to the Western sensibility during the Cold War period and render that sensibility with as much conviction and often with rather more panache than the other notable artistic innovation of the day, the Theater of the Absurd. Fellini and Antonioni were not the first, even in the postwar period, to create a cinema of ideas. At the same time, their films are notable for the rendering of ideas in primarily cinematic terms, providing a balance between image and word, or often insisting on an imbalance between them in such a way as to privilege image.

The work of both these directors with actresses is also a critical feature of their achievement. The installation of the female protagonist, whether it be Antonioni's Monica Vitti or Fellini's Giulietta Masina, is both a gloss on the idea of the new citizen that neorealism emphasized and a reassessment of the function and imaginative possibilities of actresses.

These various innovations, together with the enthusiastic critical reception that they received in the English-speaking world, made a crucial contribution to the artistic liberation of Europe. This liberation was witnessed and its relevance absorbed by a large international film community. The Italian New Wave also extended the flexibility of the medium, both in thematic and technical terms and in the sense of the performer's role in film. The concentration on the innovative place of actresses in the films of the Italian New Wave should not overshadow the role of Marcello Mastroianni as a leading man in many of the productions. In these and other significant ways, such as the emergence of the director as the predominant artistic element in film, the Italian New Wave has proved to be a prototype of the means whereby an international artistic community comes into being and achieves its ends. The creation of such communities is a distinctive feature of postwar Western culture and is one of the continuing signs that the role of the arts remains historically relevant and socially necessary.

Bibliography

Armes, Roy. *Patterns of Realism: A Study of Italian Neo-Realist Cinema.* South Brunswick, N.J.: A. S. Barnes, 1971. A thorough overview of neorealism. Contains both a historical and an aesthetic introduction to the subject, followed by more detailed analyses of neorealism's main works and themes. Concludes with a chronology and a bibliography.

Brunette, Peter. *Roberto Rossellini.* New York: Oxford University Press, 1987. An exemplary study of a path-breaking director. Comprehensive analyses of all Rossellini's films is provided. A detailed filmography is included.

Leprohon, Pierre. *The Italian Cinema.* New York: Praeger, 1972. A survey grounded in a chronological approach. Italian cinema from 1895 to 1969 is covered, with three chapters devoted to the twenty-five years prior to 1969. Contains a biographical dictionary and a select bibliography.

Liehm, Mira. *Passion and Defiance: Film in Italy from 1942 to the Present.* Berkeley: University of California Press, 1984. A detailed study of Italian cinema from 1942 to 1982. All the main phases of filmmaking during the period are covered, with attention being valuably divided between the major works and lesser-known ones. Contains an extensive bibliography.

Solmi, Angelo. *Fellini.* New York: Humanities Press, 1968. The approach to the subject is in two parts. The first takes an intellectual overview; the second examines the director's output on a film-by-film basis. Contains a bibliography and a filmography.

Witcombe, R. T. *The New Italian Cinema.* New York: Oxford University Press, 1982. The survey begins in 1960. Discussion of the later Fellini and Antonioni works is included, but the main emphasis is on the directors who came of age in the 1960's. In particular, the films of Bernardo Bertolucci, Lina Wertmuller and the Taviani brothers receive close critical attention.

Zavattini, Cesare. *Sequences from a Cinematic Life.* Englewood Cliffs, N.J.: Prentice-Hall, 1970. Zavattini scripted such classics as *The Bicycle Thief* and worked closely as a writer with Vittorio De Sica. The work in question is his quirky, informal, imaginative, informative autobiography.

George O'Brien

Cross-References

Westerns Dominate Postwar American Film (1946), p. 1313; Ealing Comedies Mark a High Point in British Film (1949), p. 1427; Kurosawa's *Rashomon* Wins the Grand Prize at Venice (1951), p. 1476; *La Strada* Solidifies Fellini's Renown as a Brilliant Director (1954), p. 1596; The French New Wave Ushers in a New Era of Cinema (1956), p. 1710; Bergman Wins International Fame with *The Seventh Seal* (1957), p. 1742; Godard's Expressionistic *À bout de souffle* Revolutionizes Film (1960), p. 1845.

AGNES DE MILLE CHOREOGRAPHS *RODEO*

Category of event: Dance
Time: October 16, 1942
Locale: Metropolitan Opera House, New York, New York

With Rodeo, *Agnes de Mille secured the legitimacy of American folklore, colloquial gesture, and humor on the ballet stage*

Principal personages:
AGNES DE MILLE (1905-　　　), a pioneer in twentieth century American ballet
AARON COPLAND (1900-1990), the American composer of *Rodeo*
OLIVER SMITH (1918-　　　), the American stage designer who created the decor for *Rodeo*

Summary of Event

In 1942, when Agnes de Mille choreographed *Rodeo*, American ballet was just beginning to separate itself from Russian influence and find an identity of its own. Until the 1930's, there had been few well-trained dancers in America and few choreographers. The public had acquired some awareness and appreciation of ballet with the tours of Russian ballerina Anna Pavlova in the 1920's and the teaching of Diaghilev dancers Mikhail Mordkin, Michel Fokine, and Adolph Bolm and the tours of the Ballet Russe de Monte Carlo in the 1930's. Yet despite the interest they inspired, the Russians inadvertently created a problem: The public came to believe that if ballet was not Russian, it could not be real ballet.

For Agnes de Mille and other major figures in the development of American ballet, though, the days of fairy-tale princesses, Russian exotica, and European character dance were numbered. They were interested in a new ballet that might incorporate into the classical style the emerging forms of modern and jazz dancing, which would revivify gestural content and which would use subject matter reflective of American life and energy.

De Mille, daughter of Broadway writer William de Mille and niece of film magnate Cecil B. DeMille, spent much of her early youth in Southern California. She became familiar with the Southwest and responded deeply to its vast spaces, cloud-swept skies, and pungent herbal aromas and to its people, who matched so distinctively their semidesert surroundings. It was the dynamic movements of the cowboys, the hardiness of the women, and the ebullience of their ethnic dances that she translated into *Rodeo*.

While she was teaching herself her craft, de Mille did not find much support in the United States. She worked abroad between 1929 and 1939, and it was in London that she developed a suite of American dances, one of which was called *Rodeo*. The suite, with an all-female cast, was performed in London in 1938.

In 1942, de Mille, who had returned to New York, was commissioned by the

Ballet Russe de Monte Carlo to do an American ballet. For a composer she requested Aaron Copland, known for his brilliant use of American folk themes in concert music and for several ballet scores, most notably *Billy the Kid* (1938).

Oliver Smith, an unknown twenty-four-year-old designer, was selected to do the decor. Kermit Love designed the costumes.

De Mille decided to re-create, with a mixed cast, the "Americana" dances she had done in London. The story is an uncomplicated tale of a cowgirl who tries to get a man by being "one of the guys," only to discover that she can be much more successful by dressing and behaving like a girl.

De Mille was obliged to choreograph while the Ballet Russe was on tour in the United States. Though the company was a mixture of Russian, English, and American dancers, the training and tone were distinctly that of Russian classical dance. De Mille had to cajole the male dancers into abandoning their usual lightness, to become grounded, walk bowlegged, and execute movements that were a blend of modern and ballet specifically designed to suggest riding horses and roping cattle. She had to convince the female dancers that showing off their virtuoso technique had no place in a piece depicting life in the Old West. The women's movements were either simple or downright rowdy, suggesting the austerity and vitality of ranch life. "If dance gesture means anything," said de Mille, "it means the life behind the movement."

She expressed that life not only by adapting the movement but also by peppering it with colloquial gestures. Her cowboys squatted, squinted, brushed off their trousers and flicked their heads to say, "C'mon, let's go."

De Mille believed that the rhythms of the American West were at the heart of its expression, and she made them the heart of the ballet as well. She incorporated a running square dance performed only to the sounds of clapping and stomping. She created movements conveying the syncopated tread of horses and the repetitive swings of roping. By the use of simple tap steps, she evoked a land in which vast silence is punctuated more by percussive sounds than by talk.

De Mille danced the cowgirl for the opening performance. When it was over, there were twenty-two curtain calls. The ballet's success was a great relief to the Ballet Russe, which was in serious financial difficulty and was looking to de Mille to provide a hit. *Rodeo* also brought de Mille recognition as a leading American choreographer.

Most of her subsequent ballets were done for the Ballet Theatre (later the American Ballet Theatre), the first American ballet company to achieve national stature. In 1948, de Mille created for them her masterpiece, *Fall River Legend*, based on the story of Lizzie Borden. In that work, she brought to its highest fruition her search for movements, gestures, and rhythms that evoked particularly American times, places, and ways of life.

Impact of Event

The impact of de Mille's *Rodeo* must be looked at against the background of classical ballet tradition. Ballet technique has an easily identifiable look, created by the use of a straight spine, a very prescribed use of the arms, an aerial quality and, of course, the pointe shoe.

Agnes de Mille broke all these molds, not single-handedly but in the midst of a ferment of new ideas. Modern dance was already working with a more articulated spine, exploring movement that was more natural to the human body and seeking to bring dance back down to earth. In the beginning, the ballet world was slow to pick up the advances of modern dance, which it thought graceless and earthbound. By her judicious use of modern dance elements in *Rodeo*, de Mille gave ballet a big push in the direction of wider movement possibilities. She used a variety of spinal contractions and replaced balletic arm movements with ones more appropriate to her characters. The "ballerina" in *Rodeo* was a tomboy, her ballet skirt and pointe shoes exchanged for trousers and boots.

De Mille also understood that to create more truth in characterization, it was imperative to go beyond traditional ballet movement. As she explained in the first volume of her autobiography, *Dance to the Piper* (1952), the classical style is interchangeable from one work to the next; classical ballets may differ in arrangement of steps and the interpretation by individual dancers, but not in style. For *Rodeo*, on the other hand, de Mille searched for hours to find the one gesture that was right for a given moment. She had to rehearse the dancers extensively to move them past the automatic responses built in by years of classical training. These efforts (concurrent with those of Antony Tudor at the Ballet Theatre) produced a special breed, the dramatic dancer. Among the foremost of these were Nora Kaye and Sallie Wilson.

In terms of repertoire, the Ballet Russe de Monte Carlo presented Russian classics and new ballets in the Russo-European tradition of Diaghilev's Ballets Russes. The Ballet Russe in America, though dazzling, was in effect an import. Successful works by young American choreographers such as Lew Christensen and Eugene Loring were being presented by Ballet Caravan. *Rodeo*, though, was the first "Americana" ballet successfully performed by Ballet Russe. This meant large audiences, which in turn meant a broadening of the public's receptivity to new forms and styles. It also meant the opening of the Russian company's doors to original American works. In the years following *Rodeo*, the Ballet Russe took into repertoire works by Ruth Page, Todd Bolender, Valerie Bettis, and Ruthanna Boris.

One of the happiest results of *Rodeo*'s success was Richard Rodgers and Oscar Hammerstein II's invitation to de Mille to choreograph their new musical, *Oklahoma!* (1943). By the 1940's, dance in musicals had progressed from the parading beauties and endless kicklines of earlier days, but it was de Mille's choreography for *Oklahoma!* that permanently refocused the function of dance in the Broadway musical.

To begin with, de Mille did not use chorines, who were selected more for face and figure than for dance ability. She chose instead dancers who had been trained in ballet or modern disciplines, hence immediately elevating the quality of dancing. Three of her leading dancers in *Oklahoma!* went on to prominent careers either on Broadway (Bambi Linn and Joan McCracken) or in ballet (Diana Adams).

In *Oklahoma!*, de Mille continued the deft blending of folk movement and ballet begun in *Rodeo*, but it was her dream ballet at the end of act 1 that was strikingly different. Hammerstein had originally wanted a high-energy circus ballet to end the act. De Mille called to his attention the fact that a young girl who was afraid her undesirable suitor might kill the man she loved would more likely have a nightmare. Hammerstein capitulated, and de Mille created a dance in which, by exposing the frightening aspects of the heroine's position, de Mille increased the tension and moved the plot forward. She also took a risk by emphasizing a dark element in the story—not the accepted path for a theater genre meant primarily to entertain. For some time after, there was a plethora of dream ballets on Broadway.

Oklahoma! opened six months after *Rodeo*, and the success of the two works assured de Mille plenty of employment. The best-known of the musicals she subsequently choreographed are *Carousel* (1945), *Brigadoon* (1947), *Gentlemen Prefer Blondes* (1949), and *Paint Your Wagon* (1951).

The decor for *Rodeo*, Oliver Smith's first major work, revealed that he had a special gift for creating American ambiance, rural and urban. Smith became one of the foremost stage designers in the country. Among his ballet credits are Jerome Robbins' *Fancy Free* (1944) and de Mille's *Fall River Legend*. In 1945, he became, with Lucia Chase, codirector of the Ballet Theatre. On Broadway, he designed again for de Mille as well as for hit shows such as *My Fair Lady* (1956), *West Side Story* (1957), and *Hello, Dolly!* (1964), and for the films *Oklahoma!* (1955), *Guys and Dolls* (1955), and *The Sound of Music* (1965).

Agnes de Mille came to be recognized as one of American ballet's most prominent choreographers. As for *Rodeo*, she said of its opening: "If it is possible for all movement, growth and accumulated power to become apparent at one single point, then my hour struck at 9:40, October 16, 1942."

Bibliography

Barnes, Clive. *Inside American Ballet Theatre.* New York: Hawthorn Books, 1977. Pictorial survey of the American Ballet Theatre in the 1970's. Introduction and commentary by *The New York Times'* dance critic Clive Barnes. Has an interesting interview with Agnes de Mille and short essays on Antony Tudor and Jerome Robbins.

Copland, Aaron, and Vivian Perlis. *Copland: 1900 through 1942.* New York: St. Martin's Press, 1984. Copland's autobiography, interspersed with short essays by Vivian Perlis placing Copland in the perspective of the larger musical scene. Reflections on Copland by prominent musicians and composers as well as by dance figures Lincoln Kirstein, Edwin Denby, Eugene Loring, and Agnes de Mille. Index.

De Mille, Agnes. *Dance to the Piper.* Boston: Little, Brown, 1952. De Mille's first autobiographical book, beginning with her earliest days in New York. Contains chapters on Cecil B. DeMille and the film industry in Hollywood, de Mille's work abroad, and the making of *Rodeo* and *Oklahoma!* Wonderful descriptions of the life and major figures of theater and dance from the early 1900's through 1944. Index.

_____. *And Promenade Home.* Boston: Little, Brown, 1956. The second volume of de Mille's autobiography. Covers her courtship and marriage to Walter Prude, overshadowed by World War II, and her 1940's musicals. Interesting discussions on the nature of choreographic work and on women and dance. Center section of selected photographs. Index.

_____. *America Dances.* New York: Macmillan, 1980. A history of dance in America through 1980. Includes sections on ballet, modern dance, Broadway, and films. De Mille writes with wit, humor, and great perception. Many excellent photographs and drawings. Chronology, bibliography, index.

Jackson, Arthur. *The Best Musicals, from "Show Boat" to "A Chorus Line."* New York: Crown, 1972. History of musicals running through early musical comedy, Broadway, the London musical stage, and film musicals. Listings of who's who in show and film music, chronology, song index, plot summaries, bibliography, discography, index.

Mordden, Ethan. *Broadway Babies.* New York: Oxford University Press, 1983. An entertaining and very informative historical analysis of the twentieth century Broadway musical. Chapters on producers, books, scores, choreographers, and superdirectors, among others. One of the few books on the musical with a section devoted solely to dance. Selective discography, index.

Catherine Sim

Cross-References

Boulanger Takes Copland as a Student (1921), p. 508; Tudor's *Jardin aux lilas* Premieres in London (1936), p. 1036; The Ballet Russe de Monte Carlo Finds New Leadership (1938), p. 1088; *Oklahoma!* Opens on Broadway (1943), p. 1256; Robbins' *Fancy Free* Premieres (1944), p. 1274; Graham Debuts *Appalachian Spring* with Copland Score (1944), p. 1284.

PEGGY GUGGENHEIM'S GALLERY PROMOTES NEW AMERICAN ART

Category of event: Art
Time: October 20, 1942
Locale: New York, New York

By promoting the works of avant-garde American artists such as Jackson Pollock, Mark Rothko, and Robert Motherwell, Peggy Guggenheim helped to launch a new school of American art known as abstract expressionism

Principal personages:
PEGGY GUGGENHEIM (1898-1979), a self-educated collector who became a major force in the development of American art
HERBERT READ (1893-1968), an English art critic and modern art enthusiast who guided Guggenheim in the creation of her art collection
MARCEL DUCHAMP (1887-1968), an exponent of cubism and Futurism who introduced Guggenheim to avant-garde trends in European art
MAX ERNST (1891-1976), a Surrealist artist and Guggenheim's husband, who provided the link between Surrealism and abstract expressionism
JACKSON POLLOCK (1912-1956), an abstract expressionist often considered the greatest American artist of the twentieth century

Summary of Event

The 1942 opening of Peggy Guggenheim's Art of This Century Gallery, which showcased part of her remarkable collection of modern art as well as examples of Surrealism seen for the first time in the United States, caused a major stir in New York's embryonic art world. Her "Spring Salon" of 1943 featured the works of avant-garde artists such as William Baziotes, Robert Motherwell, and especially Jackson Pollock, whose works were free of European precedents. Guggenheim was soon established as one of the major promoters of modern art and as a major force in the promotion of abstract expressionism, the first important modern art movement in the United States.

Doing things that were new, different, and controversial had been second nature to Peggy Guggenheim ever since she escaped from the confines of her upper-middle-class background a quarter of a century before to join the American expatriate colony in post-World War I Paris. She had inherited the spirit of adventure from her father, Benjamin Guggenheim, a wealthy entrepreneur who had died in the April, 1912, sinking of the *Titanic.* From her grandfather, Meyer, patriarch of the Guggenheim clan, Peggy inherited business acumen, a willingness to seek and accept advice, and an ability to recognize both talent and value. Although comfortably well-off, Peggy was not rich. Her art collection, which would come to be valued in the tens of millions, was created on a shoestring budget.

Although she mingled with outstanding artists and writers, Guggenheim's life in Paris lacked form and purpose. While she was seeking to recover from an unhappy marriage, a friend in London suggested to her that she open an art gallery there. Fortunately for Guggenheim, Marcel Duchamp, the noted cubist artist, provided the needed advice and helped to assemble the first exhibition for her new gallery, called Guggenheim Jeune, which opened January 24, 1938.

Guggenheim Jeune was one of a handful of galleries featuring modern art in London and became the prototype for Guggenheim's New York gallery. Among the artists exhibited were Wassily Kandinsky (sometimes called the founder of abstract art), the Surrealist Yves Tanguy, and the artist-writer Jean Cocteau. Her most important exhibit was a show of sculpture that included works by Constantin Brancusi, Jean Arp, Alexander Calder, Antoine Pevsner, and Henry Moore. So strong were the prejudice against and the ignorance of modern art that British customs officials at first refused to consider many of the works as art but rather classified them as dressed stone and metal subject to tariffs.

At this time, Guggenheim also gained the services of Herbert Read, a professor of art history, the editor of *Burlington* art magazine, and one of England's most forceful champions of modern art. Read advised her to buy selected works from the art she exhibited in order to build a permanent collection. He provided her with a list of important modern artists whose works were essential to a comprehensive art collection. He also completed the work Duchamp had started of making Guggenheim aware of the movements in modern art and its possible direction.

By 1939, Peggy's collection was of museum quality. She cast about for an appropriate place to exhibit it, but the outbreak of World War II in September changed her plans. With her collection, she left for Paris. In the hectic days preceding the fall of France, Peggy was engaged in one of the most exciting and at the same time most profitable periods in her artistic career—the assembling of the nucleus of her collection. Cash in hand together with Herbert Read's list, she went from studio to gallery collecting first-rate works by artists such as Paul Klee, Georges Braque, Juan Gris, Piet Mondrian, Joan Miró, Giorgio de Chirico, and René Magritte. Guggenheim boasted that the day Adolf Hitler marched into Norway, she bought a major work by Fernan Léger from the artist, a work later worth millions, for a thousand dollars. Guggenheim found the experience exhilarating, oblivious to the danger involved. A Jew, had she fallen into the hands of the Nazis, she might well have died. Her fate in Vichy France, to which she fled shortly before the fall of Paris, was not much more secure.

Guggenheim had approached the Louvre to provide storage for the safekeeping of her collection, but the officials informed her they did not think her collection worth saving. Getting the collection out of Paris with all roads and rail lines clogged with refugees required herculean efforts. She finally reached Grenoble in southeastern France as a way station on a return to the United States via Spain and Portugal.

Leaving France was subject to frustrating delays. In her involuntary stay in Grenoble, Peggy became acquainted with Max Ernst, who was to become a major influence in both her personal and her artistic life. A German who detested his country of origin because of what it was doing to Europe, Ernst not only was an accomplished artist but also possessed a brilliant intellect. Identified with Surrealism, he knew it was the last major European art movement. He also knew that with a barbaric twilight descending over Europe, the further development of modern art must take place elsewhere. Where else but the United States, and specifically New York, its most cosmopolitan city? When, after numerous and frustrating delays, with the famous art collection packed into an old automobile and shipped as "household goods," Guggenheim and Ernst arrived in New York on July 14, 1941, they were ready to sponsor a new direction for modern art—a direction divorced from that of Europe, which many believed had ceased to be an artistic force in Western civilization.

Impact of Event

Immediately upon her arrival in New York, Guggenheim searched for space for a gallery in which to display her collection. She found it above a grocery store on Fifty-seventh Street just west of Fifth Avenue. Trusting to the instinct that had served her in the past, she hired Frederick J. Kiesler, an innovative designer from the Columbia School of Architecture, to mount her collection. Kiesler did his work brilliantly. He divided the space into four separate galleries; he pulled out all the stops to make his staging the real innovation of the gallery's opening. The artwork was displayed without frames, and the dingy loft space became a veritable theme park of gadgets, protrusions, serpentine walls, roaring sounds, and light shows. By consensus, it was Kiesler's mounting, more than Guggenheim's collection, that made the impact when the Art of This Century Gallery opened on October 20, 1942. Fine as it was, Guggenheim's collection of the works of twentieth century European artists duplicated on a smaller scale exhibits that the Museum of Modern Art had been mounting since 1929 and that her uncle Solomon Guggenheim's new museum had started in 1939.

At the opening, Peggy Guggenheim remarked that her undertaking would serve its purpose only if it succeeded in serving the future instead of recording the past. Look to the future she did, eager to advance the careers of unknown American artists. One of the subsections of the Guggenheim display, named appropriately enough the "Daylight Gallery," was dedicated to showing the works of new artists. With authorities such as Alfred Barr and Piet Mondrian to advise her, Guggenheim mounted in May of 1943 an exhibit called the "Spring Salon for Young Artists." It was this exhibit and those related to it that created the real impact of Guggenheim's new gallery, profoundly changing the course of American art.

The stars of the 1943 show were William Baziotes, Robert Motherwell, and, particularly, Jackson Pollock. Pollock, as American as the hills of Wyoming where he was born, had been recommended by Mondrian, who found Pollock's work terrifically exciting. For Pollock, the most important element in the creation of a work of art was the physical act of creation, which in his work revolved around the application of paint. With the canvas on the floor, Pollock energetically, even violently, dripped, swirled, spattered, and daubed paints of various colors in what initially seemed an uncoordinated, irrational manner but that created highly sophisticated works of art. Max Ernst had employed a similar technique, and connections can be made between the works of Surrealists such as Ernst from Surrealism to total abstraction and those of Pollock and his peers. Surrealism, with its contempt for the established, its passion for the new, and its philosophy that any approach to art was valid and that anything could be art, was a logical starting point for Pollock's art. Pollock's style of art became known as "abstract expressionism."

Guggenheim was as enthusiastic over Pollock as Mondrian had been, and she claimed that her greatest achievement—even greater than the assembling of her collection—was her discovery of Pollock's work. She followed up the group show with a one-man show and delighted in the barrage of criticism, even howls of outrage, as she promoted him with almost messianic fervor. Further to encourage his work, she gave Pollock an income so he could paint undisturbed in his Long Island studio.

In retrospect, Pollock was the first painter of his generation of American abstract artists to bring America into the mainstream of the international tradition. During his lifetime, however, it was only with the greatest difficulty that Guggenheim could sell his work. She received his paintings in return for her financial support and often gave them away. It was because of her generosity that many smaller art museums and educational institutions have Pollocks now valued in the millions.

Guggenheim also gave one-man shows to Motherwell, Baziotes, Hans Hofmann, Clyfford Still, Mark Rothko, and David Hare. In other group shows, she included the work of Franz Kline, Willem de Kooning, Adolph Gottlieb, Hedda Sterne, Joseph Cornell, Alexander Calder, Louise Nevelson, Robert de Niro (the actor's father), Richard Pousette-Dart, and Ad Reinhart.

The designation of these artists as "abstract expressionists" proved increasingly uncomfortable, since some, artists such as Willem de Kooning, were not strictly abstract; others, such as Robert Motherwell, were not strictly expressionist. What they did have in common was the vigorous, even athletic manner of creating their art—the idea that the artist grasps authentic being through the act of creating rather than through the finished product. A new name, the Action Painters, was increasingly used for these artists, and as their art became more widely known and appreciated, the group became known as the New York School—the first real American modern art movement divorced from European influence. The movement helped to make New York the world's art capital. No one would dispute that it was Guggenheim's gallery and her tireless, enthusiastic support that was the catalyst in the creation of this school. She could indeed say with conviction that it was in her gallery that abstract expressionism was born.

Bibliography

Ashton, Dore. *The New York School: A Cultural Reckoning.* Berkeley: University of California Press, 1972. The author is a professor of art history at Cooper Union in

New York and has long been interested in the New York School and the artists associated with it. She sets the development of the school in a broader context, attempting to relate it to parallel movements in other arts such as literature and poetry. The prose, though, tends to be dense and the content uncoordinated. Illustrations add to the book's usefulness.

Guggenheim, Peggy. *Confessions of an Art Addict.* New York: Macmillan, 1960. The book is a toned-down version of *Out of This Century*; it is a frank appraisal of Guggenheim's personal and artistic life, especially her unhappy childhood. Guggenheim is always ready to admit her limitations and to give full credit to those who helped her in her career.

_____. *Out of This Century.* New York: Dial Press, 1960. Guggenheim's original assessment of her personal and artistic life reads like a *roman à clef* with personages only thinly disguised. The author is particularly candid about members of her family and those who influenced them, who are often presented in an unflattering light. She is, however, as unkind to herself. The work gives a candid insight into her personality and the reasons for both her fame and unhappiness.

Rudenstine, Angelica Zander, ed. *Peggy Guggenheim Collection.* New York: Harry N. Abrams, 1985. A beautifully produced and illustrated work covering the collection as it is displayed in Venice under the auspices of the Solomon Guggenheim Museum. Pertinent editorial material gives additional information on the works and their relevance to modern art.

Saarinen, Aline B. *The Proud Possessors.* New York: Random House, 1958. A series of essays on famous American collectors. That the author considers Peggy Guggenheim as a collector to be the equal, for example, of Nelson Rockefeller is a tribute to the quality of her collection. One essay's title, "Appassionata of the Avant-Garde," is indicative both of Guggenheim's impassioned approach to life and her love of Italy, where her collection is now housed. The essay is short and readable and is a recommended introduction to the life and career of Peggy Guggenheim.

Weld, Jacqueline Bograd. *Peggy: The Wayward Guggenheim.* New York: E. P. Dutton, 1986. Probably the best single work on Peggy Guggenheim and her collection. The book tends to ramble, but the insights into the characters of people who influenced Guggenheim's life make for interesting reading. The illustrations are numerous and well-chosen. The appendix is also of value, as it lists in chronological order the artists in the various exhibits at both Guggenheim Jeune and the Art of This Century Gallery. Copious footnotes and a valuable index.

Nis Petersen

Cross-References

Kandinsky Publishes His Views on Abstraction in Art (1912), p. 320; Duchamp's "Readymades" Challenge Concepts of Art (1913), p. 349; The Dada Movement Emerges at the Cabaret Voltaire (1916), p. 419; Surrealism Is Born (1924), p. 604;

CASABLANCA MARKS THE ARTISTIC APEX OF 1940'S WAR-THEMED FILMS

Category of event: Motion pictures
Time: November, 1942
Locale: The United States

Combining elements of romance, exotic locale, idealism, and heroic commitment to a cause, Casablanca *quickly became one of the best known and most successful of war-related films*

Principal personages:

MICHAEL CURTIZ (MIHALY KERTÉSZ, 1888-1962), a Hungarian-born film director who won an Academy Award for his work on *Casablanca*

HUMPHREY BOGART (1899-1957), the romantic film star who portrayed Rick Blaine, owner of Rick's Café Americain in Casablanca

CLAUDE RAINS (1889-1967), the wide-ranging British actor who portrayed the Vichy prefect of police, Louis Renault

INGRID BERGMAN (1915-1982), the beautiful and popular actress who played Ilsa Lund, Rick's former paramour

PAUL HENREID (1908-1992), an actor who portrayed Victor Laszlo, Ilsa's husband and leader of the underground

CONRAD VEIDT (1893-1943), an actor who portrayed the film's potent villain, Nazi Major Heinrich Strasser

JULIUS EPSTEIN (1909-   ), a screenwriter assigned by Warner Bros. to produce the film's script

PHILIP EPSTEIN (1909-1952), a screenwriter and twin brother of Julius also assigned to work on *Casablanca*

HOWARD KOCH (1902-   ), the screenwriter called on to finish the adaptation of *Casablanca*

Summary of Event

In 1938, Nazi leader Adolf Hitler seized Austria in a bloodless coup and began demanding that Germany be given the Sudetenland, a province of Czechoslovakia. In the summer of 1938, a New York City high-school teacher and playwright named Murray Burnett and his wife traveled to an apprehension-filled Europe to visit relatives. In Vienna, they observed firsthand the new Nazi regime and the plight of refugees trying to flee Europe. Later, the Burnetts visited a small town in the south of France that was home to a nightclub that featured a black pianist who played for a mixed crowd of French, Nazis, and refugees. Burnett thought at the time that the nightclub would be a marvelous setting for a play.

Back in New York, Burnett and a collaborator wrote a play during the summer of 1940 that used the European refugee problem as its subject. The play was entitled

"Everybody Comes to Rick's" and was set in a fictitious nightclub called Rick's Café Americain in Casablanca, French Morocco, a geographical location that was, in actuality, a key stop along many refugees' escape trails. The unproduced play was submitted to various Hollywood studios for review and possible production.

In late December, 1941, the Warner Bros. studio purchased the play for twenty thousand dollars, commissioned a screenplay to be adapted from the original script, and indicated that the play would be made into a low-budget picture. The studio, however, soon changed its mind. Julius and Philip Epstein were given the assignment to turn the play into a film script, while Hal B. Wallis, the producer of Warner Bros.' major films, cast about for a director. Wallis decided to go with the studio's top director, Michael Curtiz, and *Casablanca*, as the project had been retitled, underwent modification.

At first, it was announced that Ronald Reagan would play the part of Rick Blaine, and Ann Sheridan was slated to play the female lead, an American of sketchy background named Lois Meredith. Reagan and Sheridan, however, went on to other film projects, and as the screenplay evolved, the major parts were filled by other performers. Humphrey Bogart was cast as Rick, and the character named Lois Meredith was replaced by the foreign-born Ilsa Lund, to be played by Ingrid Bergman.

The final version of the film opens with Casablanca swarming with refugees in December of 1941, as the Nazis tighten their grip on Europe. Ugarte (Peter Lorre), a petty crook, has murdered two German couriers and stolen two powerful letters of transit, which can be used by any one of the many who are desperate for exit visas. Ugarte asks Rick (Bogart), the owner of Rick's Café Americain, to keep them until he can sell them, but Captain Renault (Claude Rains), the prefect of police, arrests Ugarte under the approving eye of Nazi official Major Strasser (Conrad Veidt). Rick, unmoved by Ugarte's capture, is shaken by the entrance of Victor Laszlo (Paul Henreid) and his beautiful wife, Ilsa Lund (Bergman).

A flashback reveals that Rick and Ilsa were lovers in Paris and had made plans to leave as the Nazis approached. At the last minute, though, Ilsa stayed in Paris, sending Rick a mysterious note stating that she could never see him again.

In Casablanca, a black marketeer named Ferrari (Sydney Greenstreet) tells Laszlo that Rick probably has the stolen letters of transit. Rick, however, refuses to give them to Laszlo, and Ilsa goes to Rick to beg for help. She admits she has loved Rick all along but that she was married to Laszlo, a European leader of the underground, whom she had thought was dead. She had found out he was still alive the very day she and Rick were to leave Paris, and she could not abandon him.

Rick now agrees to help. He tells Renault to arrest Laszlo when he gives Laszlo the letters. When Renault tries to do so, however, Rick orders Renault to take them all to the airport. Rick puts Ilsa on the plane with Laszlo and the letters and shoots Strasser when he tries to prevent the escape. Instead of arresting Rick, Renault decides to leave Casablanca and join a Free French force with him.

Casablanca was both commercially successful and critically acclaimed when released. It won three Academy Awards in 1943, for best picture, best screenplay, and best direction—giving director Michael Curtiz his only such honor. Though Curtiz directed many major films of the 1930's and 1940's, *Casablanca* became his best-known work.

Curtiz is generally not considered to have been a great visionary or artist. Rather, his forte was the visual side of directing, the use of chiaroscuro lighting, close-ups, and sweeping camera movements. Curtiz, Julius Epstein recalled, "knew just when the cigarette smoke should curl backwards; when to move; when not to move." All these techniques were used to build up to the film's most dramatic moments and to create great emotional power.

Before *Casablanca*, Humphrey Bogart spent several years under contract to Warner Bros., playing mostly tough, ruthless characters. In 1941, he starred in *The Maltese Falcon* and *High Sierra*, which solidified certain aspects of the Bogart character-type that had been tentatively projected in other films. All that was needed to complete the Bogart mystique was a strong romantic element, which *Casablanca* provided. The film established him as a romantic leading man and made him enormously popular. Not long after *Casablanca*, Bogart's new Warner Bros. contract made him the highest-paid actor in the world.

Ingrid Bergman also became an extraordinarily popular star as a result of her performance in *Casablanca*. She went on to star in numerous films, including *For Whom the Bell Tolls* (1943), *Gaslight* (for which she received a 1944 Oscar), *Spellbound* (1945), and *Notorious* (1946).

As for producer Hal Wallis, he had been associated with Bogart on *The Maltese Falcon* along with Peter Lorre and Sydney Greenstreet. Thanks to *Casablanca*, Wallis was presented with his second Irving G. Thalberg Award for the most consistent high-quality production.

Impact of Event

That *Casablanca* made such a tremendous impact on America at the time was the result of several factors. The first was a coincidence of timing; the film's release date had been announced for June, 1943, but in early November, 1942, the Allies landed in North Africa—at Casablanca. Warner Bros. immediately planned to premiere the film in New York on Thanksgiving Day, only eighteen days after the landings. Moreover, the film's general release date, January 23, 1943, came during the Allied summit conferences, also held at Casablanca. It seemed as though President Franklin Roosevelt himself was sanctioning the film.

The second factor accounting for *Casablanca*'s immediate impact was the film's exploration and presentation of an unselfish commitment to ideals. Bogart's portrayal of Rick is *Casablanca*'s moral center and the point around which the plot as well as the other characters revolve. Torn between neutrality and patriotism, cynicism and idealism, independence and romantic involvement, he is the appealing hero who seemed to reflect the mood of wartime America.

It has been said that Rick, at the beginning of the film, represents what isolation looks like—proud, aloof, and attractive on the surface. Perhaps Rick is even a symbol of the American fear of entangling alliances. In the end, though, Rick becomes a visual reminder of the noblest of virtues, personal sacrifice in the face of a crisis. Rick's kind of virtue is what is needed to move any great cause forward. Rick truly wants Ilsa; giving her up is a sacrifice only unselfish idealism could prompt.

Next to Rick, Renault is the most important character. He has the best lines and determines the plot's resolution. In the end, he also represents the most important aspect of the war—how it can be won. Renault is a symbol of the great partnerships that would form between the United States and its foreign allies to defeat the Nazis, just as Rick and Renault team up to defeat Major Strasser. Rick speaks symbolic lines that refer to America as a sleeping giant that, once stirred, will surely crush the impudent and immoral enemy.

A third factor contributing to the film's impact was *Casablanca*'s subtle portrayal of America as a land of promise and greatness, as the ultimate refuge for the war-weary, the persecuted, and the homeless. When Rick lets an unwitting Bulgarian win enough at the roulette wheel to pay for their exit visas, his wife exclaims that Rick is an American and, thus, "America must be a wonderful place." *Casablanca* defined how Americans thought of themselves or, at least, how they wanted to be. *Casablanca* was so influential that Warner Bros. tried to remake it in various guises before the end of World War II; none of the imitations, though, were as popular as *Casablanca*.

Casablanca continued to influence American popular culture long after the war, precisely because it was not a pure war movie at all. Most scholars maintain that the film is either a conventional romance, a morality play adapted to the screen, or a melodrama. The ending of *Casablanca* is like that of many other romantic films; Woody Allen's 1972 takeoff *Play It Again, Sam* shows how easily the war element can be worked around. The title of Allen's film, taken from a famous (and misquoted) line of *Casablanca*'s dialogue, is further testimony to the film's continuing influence.

Casablanca possesses enduring artistic and entertainment value. Audiences keep coming back to it, both to be enraptured by the film and to analyze it. The proliferation of interpretations is testimony to the film's influence on American culture. *Casablanca*, moreover, was largely responsible for the flourishing Bogart cult of the late 1960's and early 1970's.

The superb dialogue of *Casablanca* is among the best remembered in film history, and the film's classic theme song, "As Time Goes By," is synonymous with the film itself. Casablanca, perhaps more than any other Hollywood film, outlines a world view that is characteristically American.

Bibliography

Behlmer, Rudy. "George Raft in *Casablanca*?" In *Behind the Scenes: The Making of . . . .* Hollywood, Calif.: Samuel French, 1990. Written by an acknowledged expert on the history of American films, especially those made by Warner Bros., this book reveals the creative processes that went into the making of fifteen significant films during the period of the Hollywood studio system. The chapter on *Casablanca* is perhaps the clearest and most concise history of the making of the film from start to finish. Puts *Casablanca* in the context of other films made at the time.

Francisco, Charles. *You Must Remember This: The Filming of "Casablanca."* Englewood Cliffs, N.J.: Prentice-Hall, 1980. A film historian tells the detailed behind-the-scenes story of the chaotic fifty-day shooting schedule of *Casablanca.* This work's strength is its discussion of the attitudes, personalities, and contributions of the film's producer, director, writers, and film editor. Also presents examples of the film's impact on American society.

Haver, Ronald. "Finally, The Truth About *Casablanca." American Film* 1 (June, 1976): 10-16. Offers details about the film's ending as well as of the relationships among the production staff. Essentially, the Epsteins came up with the solution to the problem of how the final scene should end and with the film's famous final line, "I think this is the beginning of a beautiful friendship."

Rosenzweig, Sidney. "'A Hill of Beans': *Casablanca."* In *Casablanca and Other Major Films of Michael Curtiz.* Ann Arbor, Mich.: UMI Research Press, 1982. Originally a doctoral dissertation, this book is a volume in the "Studies in Cinema" series. Scholarly in tone, this work provides an excellent synthesis of most of the important analyses and interpretations of *Casablanca.* One large chapter is devoted exclusively to the film. Contains an extensive, useful bibliography.

Schickel, Richard. "Some Nights in Casablanca." In *Favorite Movies: Critics' Choice.* Edited by Philip Nobile. New York: Macmillan, 1973. Contains personal reflections of a noted film critic. The chapter is noteworthy for its analysis of the famous dialogue, characterizations, and symbols in the film. The author assumes that the reader comes to his chapter with some familiarity with films and filmmaking, and his style is not geared to the novice.

Shindler, Colin. *Hollywood Goes to War: Films and American Society, 1939-1952.* London: Routledge & Kegan Paul, 1979. A short volume devoted to the Hollywood war films made between 1939 and 1952. Several pages of carefully selected photographs remind the reader of the films' important scenes.

Andrew C. Skinner

Cross-References

Hollywood Enters Its Golden Age (1930's), p. 822; Renoir Marks the High Point of Prewar Filmmaking (1937), p. 1073; *The Maltese Falcon* Establishes a New Style for Crime Films (1941), p. 1223; Mailer Publishes *The Naked and the Dead* (1948), p. 1373; *Catch-22* Illustrates Antiwar Sentiment (1961), p. 1866.

SINATRA ESTABLISHES HIMSELF
AS A SOLO PERFORMER

Category of event: Music
Time: 1943
Locale: The United States

After selling a million copies of "All or Nothing at All," crooner Frank Sinatra proved that his box-office clout was greater than that of the bandleaders for whom he had fronted

Principal personages:

FRANK SINATRA (1915-   ), a singer, actor, and activist for political and social causes

DOLLY SINATRA (1895-1977), Sinatra's mother, the biggest booster of his early career

HARRY JAMES (1916-1983), a trumpeter and bandleader who gave Sinatra his initial break into the big time and backed Sinatra on "All or Nothing at All"

TOMMY DORSEY (1905-1956), a brilliant trombonist and orchestra leader, a tough taskmaster who provided the key to Sinatra's unique delivery of songs

GEORGE EVANS (1902-1950), a mentor to Sinatra and dynamic press agent who engineered the young singer's rise to stardom by orchestrating press coverage of the antics of Sinatra's fans

Summary of Event

The early 1940's in the United States are remembered as the war years, with the "Free World" fighting against Germany, Italy, and Japan. As zoot suits were traded in for G.I. khaki, citizens sacrificed to buy war bonds and endured rationing. Entertainment, however, also flourished. Pin-up model Betty Grable's legs were insured for a million dollars. Bing Crosby and Bob Hope produced road pictures. Frank Sinatra, the pencil-thin crooner known as "The Voice," added to the culture of these very serious times, causing bobby-soxers to swoon in the aisles at his concert performances.

Frank Sinatra had a very good year in 1943. "All or Nothing at All" sold more than a million copies. Hefty film and radio contracts and sold-out stage and night-club performances attested Sinatra's drawing power. No longer was he a mere vocalist doing refrains or an "extra added attraction" tacked on to some stage show head-lining a big band and its leader. He now performed as a solo artist, earning more than a million dollars a year.

Legend has it that Frank Sinatra was an overnight sensation, but that is not true. Sinatra's career developed slowly before his tremendous success beginning in the early 1940's. During the 1930's, Dolly Sinatra, his tough-minded mother, lined up singing jobs for him at Italian weddings, Irish political rallies, and social clubs around Hoboken, New Jersey. She even bought him a portable public address system and provided money for orchestrations for bands. Sinatra and his mother badgered music companies, song pluggers, local radio stations, musicians, and semiprofessional pickup bands for any chance for him to sing.

In the beginning, Sinatra's voice was not promising. It was high, and some listeners thought it sounded terrible. Neither were his looks an asset. He stood 5'10" tall, weighed 138 pounds, and had a 29-inch waist. This scrawny frame, his protruding ears, and his sharply angular face gave him an emaciated look.

In spite of these handicaps, Sinatra was determined to succeed as a singer. His first important break came when, as a singing waiter at the Rustic Cabin in Jersey Palisades, Harry James heard him. James had formed his own band in 1939 and was looking for a male vocalist. Sinatra signed on and toured with the band, but during their six months together, neither James nor Sinatra made much of a stir in the music world. Their August, 1939, recording of "All or Nothing at All" sold a disappointing eight thousand copies.

Sinatra joined the Tommy Dorsey orchestra in January, 1940. This provided an excellent showcase for the young singer. Not only was he heard on Dorsey records and network radio, he also was seen on the stages of important motion-picture theaters and appeared in several films featuring the Dorsey orchestra, such as *Las Vegas Nights* (1941), which introduced "I'll Never Smile Again."

During this time, Sinatra learned how to play to teenage audiences, making it appear as though he were staring intently into the eyes of each girl in the audience, as if she were his inspiration, and seemingly baring his soul for her alone. He also learned to blend the power and softness of each song's wording, creating an intensity and conviction in what he sang. Most important, Sinatra watched Dorsey's seemingly effortless trombone phrasing, discovering that although Dorsey appeared not to be taking breaths, he actually was, through a tiny opening at the side of the mouth. Sinatra developed a similar technique for his voice, learning to sing six to eight bars of music without a visible breath. Because of his unusual breath control, Sinatra produced flowing, unbroken melodies in which he could slide gently from one note to another. His singing style made him unique—and marketable.

Because of Sinatra's delivery and his growing legion of fans, journalists began to pay more attention to Dorsey's vocalist than to Dorsey as orchestra leader. Budding star Sinatra pressed for greater prominence of his name on billings. Dorsey became displeased, realizing that Sinatra was upstaging the Dorsey orchestra. Sinatra was equally unhappy, wanting to move on as a solo act. After bitter litigation, he finally bought out his contract from the Dorsey organization.

At the time, booking agents were not impressed by ex-band singer Sinatra, now detached from the famous Dorsey orchestra. When Sinatra found work at the Mosque Theater in Newark in 1942, however, he was heard by the manager of the New York Paramount. This led to Sinatra's being engaged as an "extra added attraction" on the bill headed by Benny Goodman. The show opened on December 30, 1942.

George Evans, a master press agent, entered Sinatra's career. Evans happened to be at a performance where an excited girl threw a rose at Sinatra and another moaned. Evans saw the potential of sensationalizing Sinatra. He became responsible for some of the hysteria and bizarre behavior of Sinatra fans at the Paramount Theater, encouraging the establishment of fan clubs and courting press coverage of invented news events about "Sinatramania."

Even Evans could not have foreseen what would happen once he tapped into the fans' fierce adulation and hormonal glands. Fans—dubbed "bobby-soxers" because they wore ankle-length socks with saddle shoes—screamed, stomped, fainted, tore at Sinatra's clothing, overturned cars, and ran under the horses of mounted policemen to get autographs or photos of "The Sigh Guy." They collected his hair clippings, repeatedly watched his films, mobbed train stations when he arrived, and adopted his tastes, from ice cream to prizefighters. They sent hate mail to his critics and picketed vociferously. Shops around theaters sometimes boarded up their windows during his appearances, and the police considered him to be a traffic hazard.

An estimated two thousand fan clubs had sprung up by 1943, including the Bobby Sox Swoonerettes, the Bow-tie-dolizers, and the Hotra Sinatra Club. Some clubs had their own publications, providing advice on writing to Sinatra (who often received more than five thousand fan letters per week), distributing Sinatra buttons, featuring sentimental portraits of Sinatra's family life, listing newly released records and scheduled appearances, and even inventing Sinatra cheers, such as "H and a U and a B, B, A; Hubba, Hubba, Frankie Hey."

Sinatra broke house attendance records wherever he appeared, including the Hollywood Bowl in 1943. The Paramount Theater in New York became "the home of swoon," with Sinatra as the "Sultan of Swoon." He appeared there four years in a row, for a record total of eighteen weeks. His appearance on Columbus Day, 1944, provoked a riot when the girls inside the theater refused to vacate their seats to make room for the next wave of girls. Police officers had to pry them loose.

In 1943, Columbia Records signed Sinatra, wanting him to rerecord "All or Nothing at All," but a musicians' strike prevented the recording. Because Sinatra could not refurbish the song, Columbia rereleased the old Harry James 1939 version. The neglected record that had sold eight thousand copies in 1939 became an instant classic in 1943, selling more than one million copies and establishing Sinatra as a star with clout. Only Bing Crosby before him was able to achieve that kind of power without the backing of a name band.

In 1943, Sinatra signed on to radio's *Lucky Strike Hit Parade*. With Sinatra's arrival, the radio program shifted its longtime emphasis away from brassy bands to the Sinatra sound. Meanwhile, his films, such as *Higher and Higher* (1943) and *Reveille with Beverly* (1943), cleaned up at the box office.

Impact of Event

During the 1930's, male vocalists tried to imitate Bing Crosby's casual style of singing. During the 1940's, they aimed at imitating Sinatra's "natural" vocalizing as well as following Sinatra's lead of breaking away from big-band dominance.

Sinatra's chief competitors, including Perry Como, Bob Eberle, and Dick Haymes, soon became adept at using some of Sinatra's stylizing techniques. For example, they realized that Sinatra achieved an amazing intimacy with his audiences through his expert handling of the microphone, making it an extension of his own vocalization to create suspense and tension or to suggest innocence and sincerity.

Sinatra's competitors also picked up on his breath-control techniques, his ability to handle the legato phraseology seemingly without breathing and seemingly without effort. Moreover, they could duplicate his excellent diction and, to some extent, even his shadings of vocal color, the articulation, rhythm, and nuances of words and music.

No one, however, could duplicate Sinatra's penchant for singing from the heart about his frustrations, disappointments in love, and hangups. As Sinatra sang, he instinctively became engrossed in the lyrics and music. He lived his songs, and audiences could feel his pain or ecstasy.

Sinatra's career as a singer and film star tailed off at the end of the 1940's and during the early 1950's. The bobby-soxers were approaching adulthood. Sinatra's private life hit the scandal sheets, and his voice had deepened. To survive, Sinatra had to change.

Sinatra rededicated himself to his career after winning an Academy Award as Best Supporting Actor in 1954 as the feisty Italian underdog Maggio in *From Here to Eternity* (1953). He moved to Capitol Records, producing his finest works, and he launched successful nightclub appearances, concerts, and television variety-show performances. Critics point out the late 1950's and 1960's as prolific times for Sinatra.

Gradually the smooth, silken voice and the bow-tie image of the young Sinatra gave way to a more "hip," up-tempo, laid-back style. He was among the first to use twelve-inch LP (long-playing) albums, well suited for building moods. He sequenced new bouncy love ballads on such albums as *Swing Easy!* (1954) and *Songs for Swingin' Lovers* (1956).

In an *Ebony* issue in 1958, Sinatra wrote that Billie Holiday had the greatest influence on his singing style during the 1950's. He recalled listening to her vocal renditions in the 1930's and being impressed by her spontaneous sound, the raw, human quality that she brought to her songs, in part sustained melody mingled with unexpected spoken phrases. He also noted the autobiographical nature of her songs, ones associated with her own drug and personal problems. These elements eventually surfaced in Sinatra's own unique style of the 1950's and 1960's.

Sinatra also acknowledged his debt to Mabel Mercer, particularly for her meticulous attention to the shadings of words. Moreover, Sinatra formed a stylistic bond with some of the jazz greats of the 1940's and 1950's, including Count Basie, Peggy Lee, Louis Armstrong, and Ella Fitzgerald. All these kindred spirits interpreted their songs in a seemingly artless fashion, with a natural conversational ease, using slight rhythmic jerks of head and shoulders, finger snapping and hip swaying, bending and teasing the rhythms of words and music. The inimitable Sinatra always found his own style and interpretation, incorporating his animated storytelling powers and the introspective vocalizations associated with the highs and lows of his own personal life.

When Sinatra emerged as the idol of the bobby-soxers, receiving much press coverage for the chaos caused by his young fans, psychologists and sociologists had a field day in interpreting the events for parents and America at large. They offered various explanations for the "Sinatramania" of the early 1940's, including mass sexual hysteria and animal magnetism; wish fulfillment of plain, lonely girls dazzled by Sinatra's celebrity status; Sinatra as surrogate boyfriend while a girl's own boyfriend fought the war overseas; Sinatra as rebel against the establishment; and Sinatra awakening maternal feelings or protectiveness in young girls who warmed to his suggestions of wistfulness, helplessness, or vulnerability. Over the years, such explanations have surfaced and resurfaced, usually when a new popular sensation emerged to threaten traditional values. Academicians feel called upon to trot out the Sinatra phenomenon of the early 1940's as an example, either to reassure that in time the threat will abate or to cast dire warnings about the demise of culture. There is no doubt that teenage idolatry of a pop star will occur again and no doubt that interpreters of popular culture will be ready to explain the phenomenon all over again. What will not occur again, according to critics, is the appearance of a singer and actor of the caliber of Frank Sinatra, one with presence, amazing concentration, sensitivity, and flair. In terms of longevity of career and song styling, Sinatra is a champion. He set the standards as a consummate artist.

Bibliography

Kahn, Ely J., Jr. *The Voice: The Story of an American Phenomenon.* New York: Harper, 1947. A Sinatra profile, appearing in *The New Yorker*, provides valuable data from a Sinatra contemporary on the young singer and on the strange behavior and adoration of his fans during the early 1940's. Funny and revealing.

Kelley, Kitty. *His Way: The Unauthorized Biography of Frank Sinatra.* New York: Bantam Books, 1986. Controversial biography of Sinatra clawing his way up the greased pole of entertainment, emphasizing the lurid and sensational. For balance, read Nancy Sinatra's affectionate examination of her father's life and times.

Pleasants, Henry. *The Great American Popular Singers.* New York: Simon & Schuster, 1974. Although only one essay focuses on Sinatra, the author juxtaposes Sinatra's talents with America's great singers in other essays. Because of Pleasants' expertise in Western classical music, he can technically assess Sinatra's music talents better than most.

Rockwell, John. *Sinatra: An American Classic.* New York: Random House, 1984. Expands and updates Henry Pleasants' assessment of Sinatra as the greatest American pop singer of the twentieth century.

Sinatra, Nancy. *Frank Sinatra, My Father.* Garden City, N.Y.: Doubleday, 1985. Thoughtful commentary from an insider of the Sinatra clan on how her father survived for decades in the brutal music world. The book tells Sinatra's side of controversies surrounding him.

Richard Whitworth

Cross-References

Armstrong First Records with His Hot Five Group (1925), p. 670; Ellington Begins an Influential Engagement at the Cotton Club (1927), p. 739; Goodman Begins His *Let's Dance* Broadcasts (1934), p. 968; Presley Becomes a Rock-and-Roll Sensation (1956), p. 1705; The Beatles Revolutionize Popular Music (1963), p. 1944; *Thriller* Marks Michael Jackson's Musical Coming-of-Age (1982), p. 2512.

OKLAHOMA! OPENS ON BROADWAY

Categories of event: Theater and music
Time: March 31, 1943
Locale: St. James Theatre, New York, New York

Oklahoma!, *the first collaboration between Richard Rodgers and Oscar Hammerstein II, featured an innovative and strongly unified score and production that set new standards for the twentieth century musical*

Principal personages:

RICHARD RODGERS (1902-1979), the composer of *Oklahoma!*, who went on to be one of the most important Broadway musical creators

OSCAR HAMMERSTEIN II (1895-1960), the lyricist and writer for *Oklahoma!*

AGNES DE MILLE (1905-   ), the ballet choreographer who was responsible for the innovative "dance drama" segments in *Oklahoma!*

Summary of Event

Oklahoma! was an immediate and smashing success from the night of its opening at the St. James Theatre on Broadway on March 31, 1943. It ran for five years and a then-record 2,212 performances, greatly advancing the careers of composer Richard Rodgers and librettist and lyricist Oscar Hammerstein II. As a strongly integrated "book" musical (one with a coherent plot and dramatically motivated characters), with a brilliant production directed by Rouben Mamoulian and presented by the prestigious Theatre Guild under its experienced producers Theresa Helburn and Lawrence Langner, *Oklahoma!* set a standard in the American musical theater that stimulated a new seriousness and consciousness of musical theater as an art form. It spurred a generation of writers to create a new type of musical.

The show's tryouts in New Haven, Connecticut, and Boston, Massachusetts, earlier in March, 1943, had met with general acclaim, but its development up to tryouts had been difficult. The Theatre Guild, organized in 1919, had been famous on Broadway as a producing organization in the 1920's and 1930's. The guild had brought distinguished European plays and new American works to the main stages of New York City. Among other playwrights it sponsored, Eugene O'Neill had benefited greatly from the guild's support. The guild had played a role in a milestone in the history of the American musical theater through its production of George Gershwin's *Porgy and Bess*, directed by Rouben Mamoulian, in 1935.

By the early 1940's, the guild had fallen on hard times. Its directors, however, had an idea. Having had some success with an innovative "folk" play, *Green Grow the Lilacs* (1931) by Oklahoman Lynn Riggs, Helburn and Langner tried to sell the idea of converting it into a musical celebrating early twentieth century frontier life. Takers were hard to find. Jerome Kern, composer of an earlier integrated book musical,

Show Boat (1927, with libretto and lyrics by Oscar Hammerstein II), was not interested. Composer Richard Rodgers was.

Unfortunately, Rodgers' longtime collaborator, Lorenz Hart, was seriously ill (he would die in 1943) and in any case skeptical about the suitability of *Green Grow the Lilacs* as material for a musical. Rodgers immediately turned to veteran lyricist Hammerstein, who saw the merits of the idea.

The play was a simple, loosely constructed story about cowboys and farmers living in the Oklahoma Territory at the time of statehood in 1907. The minimal story, ornamented with the singing of genuine folk songs, revolved around the rivalry for the hand of local beauty, Laurey, by a handsome and good-natured cowboy, Curly, and a surly hired man, Jud. In a casual manner, author Riggs brings about the marriage of Curly and Laurey while staging a dance party. When Jud tries to set fire to a haystack on which the newlyweds are standing in order to escape the wedding-night taunts of their friends, Curly leaps down to stop him. Jud draws a knife, and in the ensuing struggle accidentally is stabbed to death himself. As the play ends, Curly is sure of an exoneration and can expect a happy life with Laurey.

Rodgers and Hammerstein took this play and redesigned it while keeping its frontier feel and folk atmosphere. Rodgers did not imitate folk songs, however. His own gift for flowing, melodious music suited this nostalgic view of America's simpler past. His rich harmonies and soaring lines fitted well with a wartime audience needing a reaffirmation of American frontier and heartland values. Rodgers and Hammerstein tightened Riggs's structure by dividing the action into the common two-act format for musicals, by developing a comic but minor love subplot, by focusing the courtship and rivalry over Laurey at an elaborate box social, and by using dance and dance drama to highlight and advance motivation and story.

The show also had an underlying theme: the passing of the rough frontier and the coming of the more stable settlers or farmers, a prelude to statehood and civilization. This theme was present in the play, but Rodgers and Hammerstein extended and reinforced it at every point. In doing this, they created a new sort of musical. All the songs were in character, tied to the plot or situation, and either significantly added to understanding of the theme or advanced the plot conflict. Curly's gentle introduction with the song "Oh, What a Beautiful Mornin' " was an innovation in curtain-raising technique. There were no dancing girls or rousing chorus, just a man sauntering through the corn evoking the landscape, a pastoral vision in song based on Riggs's own prose introduction to the original play.

Rodgers and Hammerstein made perhaps their most brilliant move in deciding to feature dance as a major component of their show. Wanting to keep the folk character of the play but wishing as well not to be too folksy or quaint, they needed to find someone who could combine energetic modern dance techniques with elements of traditional folk dancing. They found Agnes de Mille, who then was commanding attention with her choreography for the ballet *Rodeo* by Aaron Copland. She had researched folk dances for that show, which Rodgers and Hammerstein went to see. It was the kind of combination they were looking for. De Mille created several strikingly original dance sequences for *Oklahoma!*, none more influential and extraordinary than the "dream ballet" that concludes act 1.

The dream ballet, almost a miniature dance drama, combined a medley of tunes previously heard with a pantomime of Laurey's troubled dream about the rivalry of Curly and Jud for her hand. Curly is killed by Jud, and Laurey is won by the animal-like hired man. Using the traditions of ballet as altered to fit the expressive freedom and new movements of modern dance, combined with stylized forms of popular and folk dances, de Mille created a startling musical, dramatic, and dance episode to end the first act.

The second major collaboration of de Mille and the writers is the very opening of act 2, with its "The Farmer and the Cowman" song-and-dance sequence. Again a sort of dance drama, this episode reflects an actual square dance at the site of the box social and also is thematic of the passing of the frontier culture (the cowman) and the rise of the settlers (the farmers). This sequence was more upbeat, crowded, and conventional than was the opening of the first act, but it also segued perfectly from the end of the previous act. The farmers and the cowmen do reconcile, after a brief fight. This dance drama functions as a mediation of values and foreshadows the marriage of Curly and Laurey and the banishment by death of the unruly and uncivilized prestatehood frontier and territory figure of Jud at the very end.

The box social was built upon Riggs's more casual dance episode, so that a more dramatic and symbolic—hence thematic and integrated—scene could point up the shift toward the stable world of marriage and institutional anchoring. Local girls put up their food hampers for the highest bidder, planning to picnic with the young men, flirt, and find beaus. Amid it all, Curly and Jud bid on Laurey's hamper. In a tense exchange of bidding, Curly wins only by selling off his saddle, his horse, and finally his pistol. Jud, the savage figure, loses; Curly sheds his cowboy life-style and agrees to farm, thus winning Laurey's hand. The musical proceeds to its conclusion generally along the lines of the original play.

Rodgers and Hammerstein tightened the play, gave it a sharp thematic focus, softened Curly and Jud, sensed the value of dance for propelling the show along, and crafted songs that have lasted. Lighter numbers such as "The Surrey with the Fringe on Top," "Kansas City," "I Cain't Say No," and "Pore Jud Is Daid" alternate with rich love songs such as "People Will Say We're in Love." The romantic quality of Curly and Laurey's relationship is heightened by contrast to the shenanigans of the comic lovers, Ado Annie and Will Parker. Innovative and indeed startling for its time, *Oklahoma!* is melodious and sweeping. Its tunes are reprised, fragments of them used to underline dialogue and dance. Focusing on frontier life rather than on the artificial "society" of many previous musicals, *Oklahoma!* itself became a piece of Americana.

Impact of Event

Oklahoma! had an influence and impact immediately. An original cast album was made soon after the opening. A first for musicals, this method of diffusing a show became the norm. All later original cast albums from Rodgers and Hammerstein shows had enormous sales and remained vital and entertaining documents decades after the shows opened.

Even during the show's five-year run on Broadway, a touring show was sent out. From 1944 through 1954, it went all over America. An overseas company started up in 1945 to play for soldiers still in the Pacific war zone. Foreign companies had great success as early as the late 1940's. Revivals continued to be frequent in later decades, and the show became a staple of both indoor summer theaters and the vast outdoor stages that dotted America in the South, Midwest, and Southwest. In that sense, *Oklahoma!* returned to its status as a kind of folk play with music.

The 1955 film version opened up the more restricted stage version and made it more realistic and expansive, qualities that the show could handle without becoming too cumbersome. The very successful film, which launched the film career of actress Shirley Jones, helped to cement a new collaboration between Broadway musicals and Hollywood. In particular, the Rodgers and Hammerstein musicals that followed *Oklahoma!* benefited from this collaboration. Rodgers and Hammerstein were astute businessmen and were fully aware of the changes in media and technology that, after the war, allowed saturation marketing and national exposure for the products of Broadway. Their later shows were just as fully thought out and integrated, using successful plays or novels as a base, and were enormously successful on stage and screen. These included *Carousel* (stage 1945, film 1956), *South Pacific* (stage 1949, film 1958), *The King and I* (stage 1951, film 1956), *Flower Drum Song* (stage 1958, film 1961), and *The Sound of Music* (stage 1959, film 1965).

Agnes de Mille worked successfully with Rodgers and Hammerstein in *Carousel* and *The King and I* to create more dance and dance drama sequences that expanded on themes basic to the shows. Songs from the shows became standards almost immediately, even in the era of rock and roll.

Other writers emulated Rodgers and Hammerstein's methods, and the era witnessed a great flowering of classic musicals, among them Cole Porter's *Kiss Me, Kate* (1948), Frank Loesser's *Guys and Dolls* (1950) and *The Most Happy Fella* (1956), Alan Jay Lerner and Frederick Loewe's *My Fair Lady* (1956), and Leonard Bernstein's *West Side Story* (1957). In the 1970's and later, the musicals of Stephen Sondheim built upon and extended the integrated musical as a conscious art form.

Oklahoma! greatly expanded on the idea of an integrated book musical established by *Show Boat*, more fully developing the link between the songs and the plot as well as attaining a higher level of realism in the story line. With these changes to the form of musical theater, the show set new standards for productions that followed and itself remained vital, a model for and a milestone in American popular culture.

Bibliography

Bordman, Gerald. *American Musical Theatre: A Chronicle.* Rev. ed. New York: Oxford University Press, 1986. A massive survey with good summaries of and contexts for major productions. Fully indexed.

Ewen, David. *New Complete Book of the American Musical Theater.* New York: Holt, Rinehart and Winston, 1970. Also a massive survey but with more thorough descriptions and discussions of key musicals. Very good on *Oklahoma!* Indexed.

_____. *Richard Rodgers.* New York: Henry Holt, 1957. Although this is an early study, Ewen's thorough knowledge of the theater serves the book and reader well. Appendices of show data and other compositions; indexed.

Green, Stanley. *The Rodgers and Hammerstein Story.* New York: John Day, 1963. Reprint. New York: Da Capo, 1980. An early, brief treatment benefiting from Green's expertise in musical theater. Illustrated and indexed, with data on shows.

Laufe, Abe. *Broadway's Greatest Musicals.* Rev. ed. New York: Funk & Wagnalls, 1977. A focused study of the best musicals. Full descriptions and some analysis. Chapters on *Show Boat, Oklahoma!, South Pacific,* and *My Fair Lady,* with summary coverage of other shows and the era. Provides good contexts and readably traces the rise of the mature and classic musical. Illustrated, and indexed, with data on shows.

Riggs, Lynn. *Green Grow the Lilacs.* In *Best American Plays, 1918-1958,* edited by John Gassner. New York: Crown Publishers, 1961. The most easily available source of the original play. Very useful to read to see just what Rodgers, Hammerstein, and de Mille had to work with.

Richard Rodgers: Fact Book, with Supplement. New York: Lynn Farnol Group, 1968. Chock full of data on each show: casts, spin-off companies, outlines of the action, song titles, and film and television versions. Indispensable. Reviews of openings and revivals included.

Rodgers, Richard. *Musical Stages: An Autobiography.* New York: Random House, 1975. An inside look paying due attention to techniques, productions, struggles, and successes.

Rodgers, Richard, and Oscar Hammerstein. *Six Plays by Rodgers and Hammerstein.* New York: Random House, 1953. Texts with songs of the key musicals through 1953. The film of *Oklahoma!* uses a new screenplay that, while sticking close to the stage version, does expand and cut. Necessary to reach a better appreciation of the changes made to Riggs's play and of the skillful construction and placing of materials.

Swain, Joseph P. *The Broadway Musical: A Critical and Musical Survey.* New York: Oxford University Press, 1990. As its title suggests, this book is the first serious study of the music of Broadway shows. Although moderately sophisticated technically in its musicological analyses, it can be understood by the lay reader. Interesting insights on Rodgers' music for Hammerstein's lyrics in *Oklahoma!*

Frederick E. Danker

Cross-References

Show Boat Introduces American Musical Theater (1927), p. 745; Gershwin's *Porgy and Bess* Opens in New York (1935), p. 1016; Agnes de Mille Choreographs *Rodeo* (1942), p. 1234; Robbins' *Fancy Free* Premieres (1944), p. 1274; Graham Debuts *Appalachian Spring* with Copland Score (1944), p. 1284; Porter Creates an Integrated Score for *Kiss Me, Kate* (1948), p. 1404.

SARTRE'S *BEING AND NOTHINGNESS* EXPRESSES EXISTENTIAL PHILOSOPHY

Category of event: Literature
Time: June 25, 1943
Locale: Paris, France

Jean-Paul Sartre's Being and Nothingness, *first published while France was occupied by the Germans, became, once the war was over, a generation's key to living authentically*

Principal personages:
JEAN-PAUL SARTRE (1905-1980), an existential philosopher whose positing of freedom as an absolute value chimed with the needs of the time
RAYMOND ARON (1905-1983), a friend of Sartre in his early years who first introduced him to the philosophy of Martin Heidegger, which was to shape Sartre's thought
SIMONE DE BEAUVOIR (1908-1986), Sartre's lifelong friend and lover, who endlessly debated the ideas of his books with him

Summary of Event

Before World War II, Jean-Paul Sartre had devoted much of his time as a writer to literature, composing novels and short stories, while dabbling a little in philosophy. The war, which he thought would be a short one, came as a rude awakening. He saw France quickly fall to the Nazis; was himself interned in a German prison camp; and, when released, found himself living in a Paris under foreign occupation. Beneath the pall of his country's despair, he wrote *L'Être et le néant* (1943; *Being and Nothingness*, 1956), a work of philosophy that emphasized how much freedom the human consciousness intrinsically possessed. The book not only ontologically grounded this freedom but also suggested that liberty weighed heavily on people. Sartre illustrated with psychological thumbnail sketches that awareness of freedom's implications was shamefacedly ignored by most.

In June, 1943, when the book appeared, and while the French were still groaning under their Nazi overlords, its message found little response. As soon as the country was liberated and the war ended, however, Sartre's text was picked up by an immense audience that had been yearning for freedom and now was looking for a break with the immediate, bitter past. With the book's popularity, Sartre, who since 1931 had been supporting himself as an obscure schoolmaster, had to face what few serious philosophers have been bothered with: fame. The French thinker, having already combined the careers of philosopher and fiction writer, took up yet another occupation as a public figure. From then on, to comprehend his literary career it becomes necessary to note his interventions in political and social affairs. Ironically, as Sartre gained more prominence and had more effect on the French nation, his philosophy became more modest in its pretensions for the individual, repeatedly demonstrating how hedged in a single person is by the constraints of environment. Meanwhile, in his fiction, Sartre dwelled on characters who threw away their freedom rather than accept the anxiety and responsibility its acceptance demanded.

The major fictional form Sartre worked with in the postwar years was drama. The most acclaimed of his plays, *Huis-clos* (1944; *In Camera*, 1946; better known as *No Exit*, 1958), followed hard on the heels of *Being and Nothingness.* This tightly constructed drama opens with three strangers finding themselves mysteriously trapped in a locked room and quickly getting on each other's nerves. Gradually they realize they are in hell, where the only—but sufficient—torture is that the doomed are forced to live with people who are maddeningly incompatible. In the work, Sartre wittily created a revised morality in which it was not sin that damned one but rather the refusal of freedom in characters who would not adapt to others. Other works, while continuing to catalog evasions of freedom, fit more with his political concerns. He was afraid that France would be swallowed up by an alliance with the United States and pointed out America's faults. In his play *La Putain respectueuse* (1946; *The Respectful Prostitute*, 1949), for example, he castigated the United States for its racial intolerance and hypocrisy.

Forming a bridge between his philosophy and fiction was Sartre's literary criticism. In *Qu'est-ce que la littérature?* (1947; *What Is Literature?*, 1949), he produced a theory of writing that turned to the more hopeful elements of his first philosophy. Sartre said that human freedom, which is everywhere denied in practice, is at least preserved in good fiction. The honest writer solicits a reader's freedom, asking for an open mind and heart. In return, the author promises to write from his or her freest levels. This was easier said than done, as Sartre was to reveal in major studies of authors such as *Saint-Genet, comédien et martyr* (1952; *Saint Genet: Actor and Martyr*, 1963). In these works, he both explored how writers asserted freedom by making their responses stick in difficult situations and underlined the many obstacles to free expression contained in normal situations.

An important area in French politics after the war was the relationship between the country's large Communist Party, the largest institution on the political left, and liberal and radical intellectuals, who were independent of the party. As one of these independents, Sartre had a close but often tempestuous relation with the Communists, coming to share many of their announced principles, such as their belief that workers should control industry, but constantly upbraiding them for failing to live up to their own ideals. It was his dialogue with the Communists that caused him to scale down his claims for an individual's autonomy as he fit his original concept to a partial acceptance of Marxist determinism.

In his works examining writers, Sartre had attempted to anchor their freedom in choices made in circumstances hampered by the exigencies of class, sex, race, and other factors. In his second major philosophical tome, *Critique de la raison dialectique, I: Théorie des ensembles pratiques* (1960; *Critique of Dialectical Reason I: Theory of Practical Ensembles*, 1976), Sartre abandoned his focus on the individual altogether and tried to locate freedom in group behavior. The direct political precipitant of the text was the war France had become involved in with its colony Algeria. Incensed by his country's leader's misguided attempts to hold on to the remnants of a lost empire and noticing the effectiveness of mass protest, Sartre portrayed the power that rested with the people when they organized into creative, fighting mobs. Drawing his examples from the French Revolution, he revised his concept of freedom, making its bastion leaderless, democratically organized crowds and placing its antithesis in stultified groups such as army units.

The celebrity that the success of *Being and Nothingness* brought to Sartre put the thinker, who was so conscious of moral responsibility, in a position from which he could affect politics. His later writings struggled to be both responses to France's social situations and remoldings and refinements of his opinion of the amount and value of an individual's freedom.

Impact of Event

The end of a war brings joy and relief to the common people, who can hope to avoid the privation, suffering, and devastation that a war entails. The ends of the last great European conflicts also ushered in periods of mass disillusionment. Many of the French who had survived World War II believed that all ideals were hollow—brutality on both sides had made a mockery of them—while their prewar leaders were compromised as bunglers or traitors. The individualistic, down-to-earth message of Jean-Paul Sartre's *Being and Nothingness*, which spoke of abandoning all grand theories and evaluating each moral law as to whether it met the tests of authenticity and freedom, appealed tremendously to those who had come through the recent traumas. It was to the youth, primarily in France but also in other European countries and in the United States, that Sartre's book spoke. It provided them with a new code based on two postulates: The engaged person chose beliefs, recognizing this as a free decision; that person then acted in a committed way to sustain those beliefs. Thus, the position one ultimately took was not as important as one's way of arriving at it and, having arrived at it, of living in a way that proved one's allegiance to it. With the foundations of all ethical systems slipping, Sartre's philosophy grounded morality in the self, which many youths believed was the only thing that was still reliable.

Ethical elements of *Being and Nothingness* made up the message that most of Sartre's young fans took away from the text, but this message did not contain all the essential points of the book. In fact, much of the work consisted of densely argued passages on such philosophical topics as the features of the cogito, which few, except for the philosophically trained, probably waded through. What attracted his large nonacademic following was his basic stance and his way of illustrating it. In the book, he made use of pithy examples to drive home his points. For example—to take a famous case—to show how another person's glance can transfix the viewed in shame and bafflement, Sartre describes a voyeur peering through a hotel keyhole who then looks up and finds that he is being watched. This makes Sartre's philosophical point beautifully palatable. Furthermore, also being a playwright, Sartre could function as his own popularizer, presenting his ideas in simplified form through dramatic situations. This helped make his work accessible. Readers could turn to *Being and Nothingness* after having been prepared for his concepts by watching such relatively lighter fare as *No Exit*. Thus, the philosophical text's popularity was built partially on Sartre's own skill as a propagandist.

Sartre was a leftist, but his book was not appreciated by the largest established leftist group in France, the Communist Party. Attraction to Sartre's philosophy, the Communists believed, turned young people away from the Party and more suitable reading matter such as the works of Karl Marx and V. I. Lenin. Consequently, Communist intellectuals were enlisted to wage war against *Being and Nothingness*. The most famous of the Marxist writers involved was Georg Lukacs, but he merely lambasted Sartre's bourgeois decadence, bringing more rancor than rigor to the debate. More thoughtful was Henri Lefebvre's *L'Existentialisme* (1946), which allowed that Sartre's distaste for conventions was well founded but said that he went overboard in granting so much power in life to individual subjectivity. What is especially interesting about this critique is that later Lefebvre would recant his position, attacking dogmatic Marxism and aligning his own work with Sartre's. In such projects as *Critique de la vie quotidienne* (1947-1962; partially translated as *Everyday Life in the Modern World*, 1971), Lefebvre would abandon the major Marxist categories of labor and production and, following Sartre's emphasis on the everyday, analyze oppression as it is manifested in daily life.

Although Sartre would have liked a French left that was independent, he accepted the fact that the Communists were the dominant group on the left for the foreseeable future. He defended his book against the Party's charges and opened a dialogue with the group that would reach over the years and lead him to write some of his most extraordinary works.

Still, rather than from the Communists, the most trenchant criticism of *Being and Nothingness* came from his friend Maurice Merleau-Ponty. Merleau-Ponty, a fellow existentialist philosopher, took Sartre to task in his major work *Phénoménologie de la perception* (1945; *Phenomenology of Perception*, 1962). Acknowledging the brilliance of much of Sartre's analysis, Merleau-Ponty centered his objection on what he considered to be Sartre's sterile dualizing, his rigid oppositions between self and objects and between self and others. As far as Merleau-Ponty was concerned, the self was not the isolated consciousness Sartre supposed but instead a composite built up of both its own impulses and impulses gathered from the world. To ever properly integrate understanding of one's self with that of the world, Merleau-Ponty argued, one must begin by seeing that these categories are never separate in reality. It should be emphasized, nevertheless, that as different as his view was from Sartre's, it had been formed by a deep meditation on *Being and Nothingness*.

The next generation of French philosophers, the structuralists, who emerged in the 1960's, repudiated Sartre. They believed that overarching structures, such as that of language, are more important determinants of human life than is consciousness. They came to sharpen their positions by attacking Sartre, and in this way they acknowledged the continued influence of his thought. Sartre's *Being and Nothingness* had formed the thought of one era and became the fountainhead of the powerful influence that the next era's thinkers fought to resist.

Bibliography

Flynn, Thomas R. *Sartre and Marxist Existentialism.* Chicago, Ill.: University of Chicago Press, 1984. The book wrestles with the same problem Sartre did, that of integrating his early sense of individual responsibility with his later feeling for the weight of circumstances. Offers a careful and readable treatment of the main philosophical categories of *Being and Nothingness.* With notes, bibliography, and index.

Hayman, Ronald. *Sartre: A Life.* New York: Simon & Schuster, 1987. A fair but far from adulatory biography of Sartre that gets at what distinguished Sartre from other thinkers of his period. Contains notes, photos, bibliography, index, and a chronology that lists the events of Sartre's life alongside a time line of the major historical events of the era.

Jeanson, Francis. *Sartre and the Problem of Morality.* Translated by Robert V. Stone. Bloomington: Indiana University Press, 1980. Sartre recommended this book, originally published in 1947, as a treatment of his early philosophy. The book deals acutely with ethical problems studied by Sartre, at times waxing poetic as the author tries to convey the pleasures of the subject. Contains a foreword by Sartre, a later reconsideration of the material by the author, and an index.

Poster, Mark. *Existential Marxism in Postwar France: From Sartre to Althusser.* Princeton, N.J.: Princeton University Press, 1975. A well-informed account of the political implications of *Being and Nothingness* and how they were interpreted by the right and the left in France. Poster shows how much of Sartre's work was created in a back-and-forth debate with other political thinkers. With index and bibliography.

Sartre, Jean-Paul. *Being and Nothingness.* Translated by Hazel Barnes. New York: Philosophical Library, 1956. In places the book is so densely argued as to become opaque. In such places, it is easy to lose the thread of the argument. Other passages, however, are amazing for their linkage of profound philosophical probing with lucid examples drawn from psychology.

Schilpp, Paul Arthur, ed. *The Philosophy of Jean-Paul Sartre.* LaSalle, Ill.: Open Court, 1981. A good sourcebook that contains an interview with Sartre as well as twenty-eight essays by leading Sartre experts. Of particular interest are the discussion of Sartre's relation to Merleau-Ponty and the analysis of how Sartre embodied some of the ideas of *Being and Nothingness* in drama. With bibliography and index.

James Feast

Cross-References

Bergson's *Creative Evolution* Inspires Artists and Thinkers (1907), p. 161; William

James's *Pragmatism* Is Published (1907), p. 171; Sartre and Camus Give Dramatic Voice to Existential Philosophy (1940's), p. 1174; Beckett's Trilogy Pushes Against the Frontiers of Fiction (1951), p. 1498; *Waiting for Godot* Expresses the Existential Theme of Absurdity (1953), p. 1573.

BORGES' *FICCIONES* TRANSCENDS
TRADITIONAL REALISM

Category of event: Literature
Time: 1944
Locale: Buenos Aires, Argentina

The dazzling short stories in Jorge Luis Borges' Ficciones, 1935-1944 *transformed Latin American fiction, linking it to the European tradition of visionary literature and pointing forward to modernist concerns*

Principal personages:
JORGE LUIS BORGES (1899-1986), an Argentinean writer whose short stories inaugurated a golden age of Latin American literature
CARLOS FUENTES (1928-   ), a Mexican writer and diplomat considered a leading exponent of the Latin American fiction style loosely known as "Magical Realism"
OCTAVIO PAZ (1914-   ), a Nobel Prize-winning Mexican poet and diplomat whose poems echo at times with phrases and paradoxes reminiscent of the works of Borges
UMBERTO ECO (1932-   ), an Italian semiotician and philosopher whose first novel catapulted him to literary fame—and featured Borges, under the alias "Jorge of Burgos," as its villain
MAURITS CORNELIUS ESCHER (1898-1972), a Dutch graphic artist whose paradoxical images offer a close artistic equivalent to the short, paradoxical fictions of Borges in literature

Summary of Event

In 1944, the Argentinean poet, short-story writer, and essayist Jorge Luis Borges published *Ficciones, 1935-1944*, a collection of his short stories. Each story was a pocket universe; each one was built on paradox; each one contained its own infinity.

These were stories unlike any others, and yet they referred constantly to other writings, real and imagined. They were utterly avant-garde yet deeply linked to the European literary tradition. They built from an almost hallucinatory realism of detail to an absolutely hallucinatory sense of reality, a sense that was ominous, nightmare-like, and freighted with omens and destiny. Borges' stories would influence a host of other Latin American writers and—particularly after Borges was awarded the prestigious International Publishers' Prize for 1961—gain a world readership for his work.

In "Pierre Menard, Author of *Don Quixote*," the "realistic" setting is that of a short work of literary criticism, complete with footnotes, citations, stylistic comparisons, and bibliographic listing of previous works, published and unpublished. It is the nature of the book under discussion, however, that gives the piece its hallucinatory quality, for the work Borges critiques is a fragment, textually identical, word for word, with the famous work of Miguel de Cervantes—but the text Borges' story critiques has been written by a twentieth century Frenchman, Pierre Menard.

Borges' fictional author Menard, the reader is told, set himself the task of writing *Don Quixote*, then, not as a seventeenth century Spanish popular novelist but as a Frenchman of the twentieth century, conscious of what has happened in literary history in the intervening centuries (including the publication of Cervantes' work). Though the words and paragraphs of the two versions of *Don Quixote* are identical, Borges assures the reader that the meanings of those words and paragraphs are subtler, more ambiguous, and more self-consciously "literary" in Menard's text than in that of Cervantes.

What Borges reveals here (and his parody of literary criticism is brilliant, hilarious) is the impact that a reader's own culture has on his reading of a work. In the final sentence of the piece, Borges invites the modern reader to consider how the medieval *Imitatio Christi* (c. 1400; *The Imitation of Christ*) would read if it were attributed to James Joyce. Would not a Joycean reading, he asks, renovate (for the contemporary reader) its "tenuous spiritual counsels"? With a vividness that authentic literary criticism must perforce lack, Borges addresses the issue of the reader as true author of the text—an issue that would later loom large in the critical writings of Jacques Lacan and others.

Clearly, Borges is playing a game with literature, and he expects his own readers to be literate, even philosophical. Startlingly modern though "Pierre Menard, Author of *Don Quixote*" is, it is also almost archaic in its reverence for literary history.

In his essay "Narrative Art and Magic," Borges discusses two ways in which cause and effect can be understood—in life as in fiction. According to the naturalistic view, Borges suggests, events are merely "the incessant result of endless, uncontrollable processes," signifying nothing of themselves. A gunshot wound is simply the result of the firing of a gun. It is from this naturalistic perspective that most people view their lives, and naturalism is the philosophical stance of modern, scientific culture. Yet there is also the magical perspective, familiar to us from the anthropological literature, in which "every detail is an omen and a cause." A gunshot wound may be caused, in this magical view, by the breaking of a taboo, by the insertion of a pin into a wax doll—or by the symmetry between one death and another. In this view, all events have meaning, perhaps even multiple meanings, and the world is a text, full of puns, quotations, analogies, correspondences and omens.

For Borges, naturalism in the novel denudes it of the dreamlike, visionary quality that, from Vergil and Dante Alighieri to James Joyce and Franz Kafka, has been its crowning glory. The only possible integrity for the novel, he writes, lies in the magical perspective, and it is that magical perspective that he explores in the short stories that make up *Ficciones*.

Thus, in "The Garden of Forking Paths," Borges has constructed a World War I espionage story the central enigma of which is a novel—written by a retired Chinese scholar—in which each event leads to two or more possible outcomes, which in turn lead to two or more further possibilities, so that time becomes, in both the title of

Borges' story and the novel itself, a garden of forking paths. Life, Borges insists, is a maze of possibilities, and every story has myriad possible endings. In the climax of this version of this story, the characters salute each other as they might have been in other circumstances—in other timelines, in other branches of the same forking tale.

Thus, too, "Death and the Compass" is a detective story in which the detective finds the killer by using cabalistic knowledge. In doing so, the detective walks into a trap. The trap is, literally, a diamond in space-time, formed by four points, each one itself formed of a date and a location on a map. As the detective is about to die, he tells his killer of a similar trap (possible, as it were, on another timeline), this time not diamond-shaped but linear, and the killer replies, "The next time I kill you, I promise you the labyrinth made of the single straight line which is invisible and everlasting."

The stories in *Ficciones*, then, are concerned with infinities, enigmas, mazes and labyrinths, diamonds and mirror images, branchings—in short, with mathematical and logical patterns and paradoxes. Their apparent realism is the device by which Borges contrives to win the reader's sympathetic attention, but it is the logically precise way in which the stories outflank all realistic logic that gives them their peculiar power.

Many of these tales condense a novel-length idea into a short story. Borges' writing in the years that followed would single-mindedly continue this process of compression, generating ever shorter and shorter stories, essays and poems—each one with a diamond paradox at its heart—as his partial blindness approached total eclipse.

Impact of Event

Borges was at once an Argentinean writer and a man of world literary culture, and it was perhaps the supreme irony (and paradox) at the heart of his own life that he should also have been both blind and the national librarian of Argentina. God, Borges writes in his "Poem of the Gifts," "with such splendid irony/ granted me books and blindness at one touch." God and Borges, it would appear, share the same paradoxical and hallucinatorily realistic approach to the act of creation.

Literature, then, not solely Argentinean literature, was the field of Borges' play, his divine tragedy and comedy. In the field of world literature, his spare and haunting *Ficciones* were to create a sensation.

Not all of those who have followed Borges have shared his implacable eye for paradox and mathematical rigor, but many later Latin American writers have approved his juxtaposition of magical elements with realism. Gabriel García Márquez, in his novel *Cien años de soledad* (1967; *One Hundred Years of Solitude*, 1970), betrays the influence of Borges most clearly when the character Ursula Buendia learns of her son's death when the blood flowing from his gun-inflicted wound makes its eerie but unerring way along a street, around two corners, and into her house ("making a wide curve to avoid the living-room table") to form a pool at her feet. García Márquez, moreover, is but the leading representative of a tendency in Latin American writing known as "Magical Realism"—a term that can be applied to the writings of Manuel Puig, Mario Vargas Llosa, and the magisterial Carlos Fuentes; Fuentes' novel *Terra Nostra* (1975) is arguably the great masterwork of the genre.

Terra Nostra is impossible to synopsize; it is a Borgesian nightmare gone to seed, a tangled garden the forking paths of which are overgrown with a tropical riot of times and places, Paris and the New World and Spain, all found in a maze of histories contained in the crazed mind of Philip II of Spain. Borges himself, under the name Pierre Menard, figures in the final chapter of *Terra Nostra*: "Late in life an aged Pierre Menard proposed that all beasts, men, and nations be apportioned a supply of mirrors that would reproduce infinitely their and other figures. . . . Only to a blind man could such a fantasy occur." Borges himself once observed that mirrors were an abomination, since they served to multiply reality.

The short stories of Julio Cortázar, too, show traces of the Borgesian worldview of philosophical enigmas and mirrored realities. "Night Face Up," one of the stories in Cortázar's 1956 collection *Final de juego* (*End of the Game*, 1967), concerns a motorcyclist who, having been in an accident, is hospitalized, etherized, and lying on an operating table—or is he a captive bound down on a sacrificial Aztec altar, his surgeon an Aztec priest with raised obsidian blade? The twin realities mirror one another with nightmarish precision in what Cortázar terms the "infinite lie of the dream."

The Mexican poet Octavio Paz is also at times overtly Borgesian, as in such poems as "Pedestrian," "The Other," "Royal Hunt," and "Apparition," or the brilliant hall-of-mirrors that is his short poem, "Here," which reads in its entirety:

> My steps along this street
> resound
>   in another street
> in which
>   I hear my steps
> passing along this street
> in which
>
> Only the mist is real.

Borges' influence, moreover, extends beyond Latin America. Echoes and reflections of his pristine geometries can be found in the Yugoslavian Milorad Pavić's *Hazarski rečnik* (1988; *Dictionary of the Khazars*, 1988) which is available in two versions ("male" and "female" editions) that mirror each other exactly, with the exception of one paragraph. Borges' influence is also visible in the marvelous tales of the Italians Italo Calvino and Umberto Eco.

In Calvino's *Il castello dei destini incrociati* (1969; *Castle of Crossed Destinies*, 1977), a single spread of the tarot cards can be read as telling the stories of Hamlet, Oedipus, Macbeth, Faust, Lear, Parsifal, and the writer—with each individual card playing a different part in different stories. Umberto Eco's *Il nome della rosa* (1980; *The Name of the Rose*, 1983) concerns a monastic library that is a labyrinth (shades of Borges' "Library of Babel" in *Ficciones*) and features a major character named "Jorge of Burgos" (that is, Jorge Borges), a blind librarian—who is in fact the villain of the piece.

With his characteristic, magically organized interpenetration of history and fiction, Borges reconnected modern world fiction with the epic and visionary currents of Homer and John Milton; blind, as they were, he has restored to his readers' sight the power of the dream. This has been an act of continuity, not rupture; a radical act in both senses of the term—meaning both "revolutionary" and, literally and etymologically, "returning to the roots." It is in this act that he has been followed, not blindly and imitatively but as an exemplar, by so many writers from Cortázar and Fuentes to Calvino and Eco.

Borges brought a characteristic clarity and precision to his worlds of fantasy, and in this he greatly resembled his contemporary, the Dutch graphic artist M. C. Escher, who etched hands drawing hands drawing the hands that drew them, staircases that are subject to a bewildering variety of contradictory gravities, birds whose wings and tails dovetail—the word seems inevitable—with the wings and tails of other birds. His deepest affinity, though, must surely be with James Joyce, who, like Borges, labored constantly to return the sacred logic of the myth to secular fiction, and so to breathe the infinite once again into finite human lives.

Bibliography

Borges, Jorge Luis. *Ficciones.* New York: Grove Press, 1962. The stories collected in *Ficciones* mark a turning point in Borges' writing and the beginning of his characteristic exploration of the magical possibilities of apparently realistic fiction. Brilliantly written, effortlessly entertaining, deeply philosophical short stories by a master of world literature.

Eco, Umberto. *The Name of the Rose.* Translated by William Weaver. New York: Harcourt Brace Jovanovich, 1983. Stunning metaphysical thriller set in a medieval monastery in which a series of murders are committed to protect from profane eyes the books in a very Borgesian library. The villain, Jorge of Burgos, is clearly none other than Borges himself.

Escher, Maurits Cornelius, and J. L. Locher. *The Infinite World of M. C. Escher.* New York: Harry N. Abrams, 1984. A useful compendium of the work of this Dutch artist, whose paradoxical engravings parallel the fictional worlds of Borges' stories. With brief biography and Escher's article "Approaches to Infinity." Visually dazzling virtuosity.

Fuentes, Carlos. *Terra Nostra.* Translated by Margaret Sayers Peden. New York: Farrar, Straus, Giroux, 1976. A novel widely hailed as a masterpiece of Latin American writing. Shows the influence of Borges in its dazzling metaphysical leaps and eccentric handling of time and by providing a cameo appearance of one of Borges' own characters. Enormously long, brilliant, fascinating.

Rodriguez Monegal, Emir. *Jorge Luis Borges.* New York: E. P. Dutton, 1978. Literary biography of Borges by his friend of more than thirty years. Explores the difference between Borges the man and Borges the author of *Ficciones*—a distinction central to Borges' own view of his work. With bibliography and index.

Charles Cameron

Cross-References

Jung Publishes *Psychology of the Unconscious* (1912), p. 309; Surrealism Is Born (1924), p. 604; García Lorca's *Poet in New York* Is Published (1940), p. 1179; The "Boom" Captures Worldwide Attention (Late 1950's), p. 1689; Derrida Enunciates the Principles of Deconstruction (1967), p. 2075; García Márquez's *One Hundred Years of Solitude* Is Published (1967), p. 2086; Pynchon's *Gravity's Rainbow* Is Published (1973), p. 2283.

ROBBINS' *FANCY FREE* PREMIERES

Category of event: Dance
Time: April 18, 1944
Locale: New York, New York

Jerome Robbins' first ballet, Fancy Free, *set to the music of Leonard Bernstein, was a complete success and launched a long and illustrious career*

Principal personages:
JEROME ROBBINS (JEROME RABINOWITZ, 1918-   ), an American dancer and choreographer who found success in his first ballet and went on to become a major figure in American dance
LEONARD BERNSTEIN (1918-1990), an American composer and conductor who made a successful stage debut with *Fancy Free*
OLIVER SMITH (1918-   ), a set designer who contributed the sets for *Fancy Free*, beginning a distinguished Broadway career

Summary of Event

Late in World War II, the New York dance scene was jolted into unexpected recognition of its potential for snappy contemporary commentary and youthful vitality by a new ballet created by a group of remarkable novices. *Fancy Free* was the result of a fruitful collaboration among a youthful group consisting of Jerome Robbins, a dancer-turned-choreographer, Leonard Bernstein, a composer who had recently made the front page of *The New York Times* for his dazzling debut conducting the New York Philharmonic, and Oliver Smith, a gifted set designer. The work marked the beginning of Robbins' long and distinguished career as a choreographer of Broadway shows and ballets and also marked the emergence of Bernstein as an important American composer of serious music who maintained clear links to popular music. In his long association with the New York City Ballet, Robbins came to win the admiration of George Balanchine, the Russian-born dean of the American dance theater; as Lincoln Kirstein noted in *Thirty Years: Lincoln Kirstein's The New York City Ballet* (1978), "Balanchine had long acknowledged Robbins as the native-born choreographer with the strongest structural and musical sense."

Robbins, who was at that time a dancer with the Ballet Theatre, sought out Bernstein at the suggestion of two of the composers with whom he had shared his ideas for a new ballet. Morton Gould and Vincent Persichetti mentioned the name of Bernstein, who was shortly to begin his spectacular rise to musical fame. In October, 1943, while Bernstein was an assistant to Arthur Rodzinski, the director of the New York Philharmonic, he was approached by Robbins about writing a score for Robbins' new ballet. According to Joan Peyser in *Bernstein: A Biography* (1971), Bernstein recalled that he "played a few bars" of music he had been "fooling around with," and Robbins "went wild. 'That's it! That's it!' he screamed. And we were off."

A month later, Bernstein made his spectacular conducting debut with the New York Philharmonic, garnering a front-page rave review from *The New York Times* when he filled in for the indisposed Bruno Walter on short notice. Perhaps on the strength of Bernstein's instant celebrity, the impresario Sol Hurok bought the ballet and offered to produce it for the Ballet Theatre. The ballet was premiered on April 18, 1944, at the old Metropolitan Opera House, with a group of dancers for whom the roles were tailor-made: Harold Lang, John Kriza, and Robbins himself danced the parts of three sailors; Muriel Bentley, Janet Reed, and Shirley Eckl were the three girls in their lives; and Rex Cooper danced the part of the bartender. The ballet was an instant success and was actually danced more than one hundred and sixty times in the first year following its premiere.

Fancy Free takes place in a small neighborhood bar on a hot summer night in New York during wartime. The music begins informally enough, not with an overture or even with music from the pit but with an onstage phonograph recording. "Big Stuff" was written partly in homage to the blues singer Billie Holiday, and it helps to set the tone of loneliness and yearning on a hot summer night; it is rudely interrupted by four brisk big-band drum taps. Three sailors on leave arrive in search of a good time. They are desperate to have some fun during their moment of liberty, and their dancing reveals both their solidarity as a trio and their sense of fun. Thus the first two trick their third companion into paying for their drinks. Then each vies for the attention of the first girl who walks by; they preen and scuffle for her attention, with two sailors knocking down the third and chasing after the girl.

The odd sailor out meets a pretty girl back at the bar, and rather than woo her overtly, he begins to mime his experiences in the war. They conclude a gentle *pas de deux* with a shy kiss. The first two sailors return with their girl, thus setting up the problem of an unequal ratio of sailors to girls. In a kind of latter-day Judgment of Paris, the girls are to judge among the sailors according to their dancing skills. The first offers a show-off routine of as many classic steps as he can muster. The second (now often done by the sailor of the blues duet) offers a subdued, insinuating number. The remaining sailor provides his audience with a slightly satirical, Latin-inflected number.

When it seems that the girls are undecided or possibly indifferent, the dance contest deteriorates into a barroom brawl, from which the sailors emerge to discover that the girls have fled. After reconciling, the sailors sensibly have a second drink, and they begin the whole process again as another beautiful girl walks by. Not closure or fulfillment, but a renewal of the cycle of desire, will be the fate of the sailors.

Fancy Free was remarkable for the happy confluence of new talents that fortuitously collaborated in its creation. The score was Bernstein's first big hit, and it confirmed the instant celebrity he had enjoyed the previous fall for his conducting debut. It remains one of his most persuasive scores, written in the freshest 1940's idiom that remained the hallmark of his best work. Robbins, with a young dancer's enthusiasm, threw every step he knew into the work (most conspicuously in the first sailor's display dance), and he asserted his place in the line of great American choreographers with the ballet. Like Bernstein, Robbins maintained a dual life, both on Broadway and in the classic dance theater, although after *Fiddler on the Roof* (1964) he withdrew from Broadway for a quarter of a century. Robbins' collaboration with Bernstein continued until the latter's death in 1990.

Impact of Event

Although American dance had already claimed a place in the world's dance tradition through the work of such notable choreographers and dancers as Isadora Duncan, Martha Graham, and Agnes de Mille and through the vitality of dancing on the Broadway stage, it was still not prepared for the combination of urban-oriented, jazz-flavored, streetwise dancing of *Fancy Free* in 1944. In a fortuitous pairing of new talents, Robbins found an ideal collaborator in Bernstein, whose sparkling score for the ballet helped to propel him into his long career as a successful Broadway composer. The collaboration of Bernstein, Robbins, and Smith bore further fruit in the successful Broadway musical *On the Town* (1944), which took an alternative view of a day in the life of three sailors on shore leave, and a decade later in the trio's masterpiece, the musical *West Side Story* (1957). The energy of Robbins' choreography and the inventiveness of Bernstein's score set the standard for the American musical in the late 1950's.

Bernstein's biographer, Joan Peyser, claimed to find it odd that audiences would respond in wartime to a lighthearted ballet about sailors on leave, but the image of playful, happy sailors in temporary respite from the rigors of war would seem exactly suited to the public mood in 1944. The eminent American dance critic Walter Terry, in *Ballet Guide* (1977), was more succinct in explaining *Fancy Free*'s direct appeal: "The ballet has remained popular because the theme was projected in movement terms which were fresh, witty, and energetically American." The three collaborators found the ideal idiom for their talents in *Fancy Free* and set the stage for their future Broadway successes, beginning with *On the Town* and underscored by the international success of *West Side Story*.

Rather than recycling any actual material from *Fancy Free*, the musical comedy *On the Town* kept only the idea of the three sailors on twenty-four-hour shore leave. During the summer following the premiere of the ballet, Bernstein and his friends Adolph Green and Betty Comden reconceived the earlier hit as a full-length musical comedy. Now the first sailor (this time given the name Gaby) falls in love with the New York subway system's poster girl, "Miss Turnstiles," and he leads his two colleagues into a frantic quest for a day of happiness. *On the Town* opened on December 26, 1944, and ran for 163 performances; a muted film version appeared in 1949, but it suffered (as did the 1955 film version of *Guys and Dolls*) from the box-office-oriented decision to use Frank Sinatra rather than a Broadway dancer and singer.

Robbins continued his successful collaboration with Bernstein in such further ballet scores as *Facsimile* (1946) and *The Dybbuk* (1974). They may well be best remembered by most of their admirers for *West Side Story* (which opened on September 26, 1957), which again combined the sets of Smith, the music of Bernstein, and the choreography of Robbins. The musical's book was written by the veteran Broadway playwright Arthur Laurents, and the vivid lyrics were contributed by Broadway newcomer Stephen Sondheim, who would go on to write his own music and lyrics for such distinguished shows as *Sweeney Todd* (1979) and *Into the Woods* (1987).

As a Broadway director, Robbins staged *The Pajama Game* (1954), *Bells Are Ringing* (1956), for Judy Holliday, and *Peter Pan* (1954), which was a hit vehicle for Mary Martin on both stage and television in the 1950's, when Martin's spectacular "flying" had to be performed live. As a Broadway choreographer, Robbins devised the dances for such diverse shows as *The King and I* (1951), *Call Me Madam* (1950), for Ethel Merman, *High Button Shoes* (1947), and *Fiddler on the Roof.*

In 1989, *Jerome Robbins' Broadway*, a celebration of Robbins' distinguished contributions to the Broadway stage, opened; somewhat surprisingly, the act of homage also became a long-running hit. As Richard Corliss noted in an admiring review in *Time* (March 6, 1989), Robbins had no one to compete against except his own massive reputation: "He is a man going up against his own legend—as the premier American-born dancemaker, whose works for the ballet and Broadway suavely merged high art with pop culture." *Jerome Robbins' Broadway* may have been the climax of Robbins' long career, but it was not Robbins' farewell to dance in America. *West Side Story* successfully fulfilled the promise, shown by Robbins and Bernstein in their collaboration in *Fancy Free* in 1944, to combine music, dance, and narrative truly descriptive of urban life in mid-twentieth century America.

Bibliography

Corliss, Richard. "Peter Pan Flies Again." *Time* 133 (March 6, 1989): 78-82. Good, efficient survey of Robbins' rich Broadway career, linked with a review of *Jerome Robbins' Broadway*. Corliss notes that the latter cost eight million dollars to mount—a thousand times more than Robbins' first Broadway show, *The Straw Hat Review*, in 1937.

Kirstein, Lincoln. *Thirty Years: Lincoln Kirstein's The New York City Ballet.* New York: Alfred A. Knopf, 1978. Journal-like survey of the fortunes of the dance company most strongly associated with George Balanchine; notes that among younger choreographers, Robbins had the best success in keeping his dances in the repertory of what was essentially Balanchine's company.

Peyser, Joan. *Bernstein: A Biography.* New York: William Morrow, 1987. Designed to shock, this biography of America's most esteemed musician confirmed long-standing suspicions about Bernstein's personal life that were needlessly revealed at the end of the composer's auspicious career. The new details, though, are less disheartening than is the mean-spiritedness of the author's approach.

Schlundt, Christena L., Alexander Ramirez, et al. *Dance in the Musical Theatre: Jerome Robbins and His Peers, 1934-1965: A Guide.* New York: Garland, 1989. Surveys the careers of Robbins and his peers, those choreographers who commuted between Broadway and the formal dance stage.

Terry, Walter. *Ballet Guide.* New York: Dodd, Mead, 1975. Provides an extremely helpful overview of America's serious dance repertory. By the dean of an older generation of dance critics.

Byron Nelson

Cross-References

Agnes de Mille Choreographs *Rodeo* (1942), p. 1234; *Oklahoma!* Opens on Broadway (1943), p. 1256; Graham Debuts *Appalachian Spring* with Copland Score (1944), p. 1284; Balanchine and Kirstein Make New York a World Center for Ballet (1946), p. 1301; Bernstein Joins Symphonic and Jazz Elements in *West Side Story* (1957), p. 1731; Sondheim's *Company* Is Broadway's First "Concept" Musical (1970), p. 2213; Sondheim Uses Operatic Techniques in *Sweeney Todd* (1979), p. 2433.

U.S. HIGHBALL PREMIERES IN NEW YORK

Category of event: Music
Time: April 22, 1944
Locale: New York, New York

Iconoclastic American composer Harry Partch's U.S. Highball *and other works received their New York premiere, calling attention to a composer who invented his own notation and instruments*

Principal personages:
HARRY PARTCH (1901-1974), an innovative American composer who set forth his ideas in his book *Genesis of a Music*
HENRY ALLEN MOE (1894-1975), the secretary general of the Guggenheim Foundation and a supporter of Partch's efforts of the 1940's

Summary of Event

The premiere in the Carnegie Chamber Music Hall of *U.S. Highball* ("highball" is railroad slang for going somewhere in a hurry) as well as some of Harry Partch's other works of the 1940's was the culmination of his Guggenheim Fellowship and the chance for him to expound his theories of music to a wide audience. The program included also *Barstow* (musical settings of graffiti left in a desert town by hitchhikers) and *San Francisco* (settings of the cries of two newsboys); *U.S. Highball*, a musical account of a 1941 hobo trip from San Francisco to Chicago, was the longest work on the program. All these works were scored for a reciting voice (Partch's) and for the instruments that he had invented.

The reviews were mixed: *The New York Times* opined that the value was mostly literary, with the instruments adding atmosphere, whereas the composer Lou Harrison, writing in *Modern Music*, argued that the sounds were often interesting but that the manner in which the instruments were used was too repetitive and that the actual music was negligible. An unsigned review in *The New Yorker*, printed in the magazine's "Talk of the Town" column rather than its "Musical Events" section and written in a somewhat tongue-in-cheek style, was quite laudatory. The concert served to launch Partch on a career as an innovative avant-garde composer who was completely isolated from the musical currents of the twentieth century.

Harry Partch, born in Oakland, California, in 1901, had grown up along the Mexican border, and he claimed Christian hymns, Chinese lullabies (his parents had been missionaries in China), and Yaqui Indian music among his formative influences. Brief stays in the music school at the University of Southern California in 1920 and 1922 alienated Partch from both the concert system and the musical scales and intonation of European art music; in music, he was almost entirely self-taught. After his mother's death in 1920 (his father had died in the preceding year), Partch supported himself in a variety of occupations, mainly as a proofreader but also as a sailor and agricultural worker; for a time, he was even a hobo.

His discovery of the work of Hermann Helmholtz, a nineteenth century German scientist who had studied acoustics, revealed that the tempered scale (the division of the octave into twelve equal semitones) was a relatively recent invention. He also learned that scales based on ratios of a vibrating string discovered in the sixth century B.C. by Pythagoras and elaborated by successive generations of Greek music theorists produced a much purer intonation. Partch set about inventing and even building musical instruments that would reproduce this pure intonation; in later life, he claimed that he was a "philosophic music-man seduced into carpentry."

Partch's system depended upon the ratios of a vibrating string. From the vibrating string, he got the pitches to which he tuned a special reed organ he had built that he called the "chromelodeon." He tuned the chromelodeon not to the tempered chromatic scale of twelve pitches but to his own scale of forty-three pitches. From the chromelodeon, he tuned the other instruments he had devised, chiefly plucked-string instruments or tuned percussion instruments.

Partch's basic-plucked string instrument, the "kithara," was based on an instrument depicted on ancient Greek vases and was built of redwood and fir, with seventy-two strings. His "harmonic canon" was a twin instrument (sometimes called "Castor and Pollux") that resembled the inside of a piano but with movable bridges. Both instruments were played by plucking the strings with a pick.

Partch's tuned percussion instruments were mostly marimbas of various shapes and pitches made from bamboo, oak, or Brazil wood; some were made from such odd materials as light bulbs and liquor bottles. Quite curious, visually as well as audibly, were the "cloud chamber bowls," which were constructed from Pyrex glass bottles suspended by ropes from a rack; the centers of the bottles had been cut out for cloud-chamber atomic experiments. Also visually intriguing were the "gourd tree," a large eucalyptus branch festooned with Indian dharma bells with gourd resonators, and the "spoils of war," a mixture of instruments that included seven brass casings of artillery shells. Partch also constructed adapted guitars and an adapted viola, which he modified by lengthening the necks of the instruments to accommodate his forty-three-note scale.

Partch's final tasks were to devise a musical notation for his new scales, for which he used ratios and colors, and then to teach people to play these new instruments. For the premiere of *U.S. Highball*, he primarily used the kithara (which he played while declaiming the text) and the chromelodeon. For a 1957 recording, he added additional instruments and voices.

Partch later referred to the structure of *U.S. Highball* as a "hobo allegro form" (an allusion to "sonata-allegro form"). He explained that the piece was meant to evoke a fast train trip from San Francisco to Rock Springs, Wyoming; a slow movement of dishwashing while his imagined protagonist is stuck in the town of Green River, Wyoming; and then a rapid trip, punctuated by reprises of first-part material, from Rock Springs to Chicago. The text consisted of meditations by the protagonist, Mac, and the narrator's rendering of graffiti, official signs, humorously distorted state names, and snatches of overheard conversations of hobos and railroad police.

Several other composers had previously experimented with the production of unusual sounds. In the early twentieth century, the Italian Futurists, headed by Luigi Russolo, developed a battery of noisemaking instruments to create a new music for the machine age, but the Futurists' instruments were merely used to accompany rather conventional music. The American Henry Cowell had developed unusual ways of playing the piano, such as using his fist or forearm on the piano keys to produce "tone clusters" or plucking the strings inside the piano, and the Franco-American Edgard Varèse included such noisemakers as fire sirens and lion roars in some of his compositions. Harry Partch, though, outdid them all in developing his new instruments, tunings, and musical notation.

Impact of Event

Though Partch did not have his Guggenheim Fellowship renewed more than twice, he was able to secure a number of temporary university appointments, not as a faculty member but as a research associate. He could thus work on developing new instruments and improving old ones, and the university environment provided him with actors, singers, dancers, and musicians willing to try something new. He changed also his compositional orientation; he stopped writing bardic works such as *U.S. Highball* or *The Letter, A Depression Message from a Hobo Friend* (1943)—a setting for voice and adapted guitar of a letter from one of his hobo friends—and began writing dramatic works. First, however, he completed the statement of his musical ideas and how they could be put into practice: his book *Genesis of a Music*, the first edition of which was published by the University of Wisconsin Press in 1949.

As early as 1934, Partch had discussed a musical setting of Sophocles' *Oedipus Tyrannus* (c. 429 B.C.) with its translator, the poet William Butler Yeats. Yeats, however, died in 1939, long before Partch had completed his setting. The first version of Partch's *Oedipus* was given its premiere in 1952 at Mills College in Oakland, California, and received nationwide reviews. Partch had to rewrite the text, since the agent for Yeats's estate forbade the use of the poet's work in the recording of the production. As a release from composing this tragedy, Partch wrote *Plectra and Percussion Dances* (1952) for an imaginary "satyr-play," after the ancient Greek custom of producing a bawdy theatrical romp after an intensely cathartic tragedy. Included in these dances were a satire on concerts ("Ring Around the Moon") and musical settings of portions of Arthur Rimbaud's *Une Saison en enfer* (1873; *A Season in Hell*, 1932) that included "Happy Birthday to You" arranged as an Afro-Chinese Minuet.

Partch's idea (after the model set by the ancient Greeks) of a total theater that would include dance, mime, declaimed text, and music as equal participants received its best fruition in *The Bewitched*, commissioned by the University of Illinois for its contemporary arts festival in 1957; the piece was filmed for television and performed in New York two years later. A few traditional instruments, especially clarinet, cello, and the Japanese plucked-string koto, were used in addition to Partch's gallery of invented instruments; the traditional instruments were given a colored notation to indicate special lowering or raising of individual pitches.

The work attracted a cult following. Titles of such individual sections as "Visions Fill the Eyes of a Defeated Basketball Team in the Shower Room" and "The Lost Musicians Mix Magic" were to resound a decade later among the "Age of Aquarius" writers of the 1960's, much as Partch's hobo works were to be echoed by the Beat writers of the 1950's. Partch was ahead of his time textually as well as musically. In securing a satisfactory production, however, Partch was at odds with choreographers and stage directors who thought that his music ought to be subordinated to the theatrical productions; Partch wanted his instruments on the stage and their performers to be part of the action.

Partch also discovered film in 1958, recording through overdubbing all the instrumental parts for Madeline Tourtelot's film *Windsong* (1958) for the Brussels World's Fair. She also filmed *U.S. Highball* that year.

In 1962, Partch's appointment as a research associate at the University of Illinois was not renewed. He was unable to secure a faculty appointment there or elsewhere because of his lack of any academic credentials beyond a high school diploma; furthermore, his negative attitude toward the cultivation of European art music antagonized those professors who depended upon traditional Western music as the basis of their instruction. One excuse that was frequently given him was the lack of space for storing his instruments. His last work for Illinois was *Water! Water!* (1962), which included music for a jazz band using Partch's instruments.

Partch returned to California, where he established a studio in an abandoned chicken hatchery in Petaluma. There he wrote *And on the Seventh Day Petals Fell on Petaluma*, which became the prologue to *Delusion of the Fury*, commissioned by the Koussevitzky Foundation and given its premiere performance at the University of California at Los Angeles in 1969. Subsequently, the work was made into a film by Tourtelot. *Delusion of the Fury*, which was influenced by Japanese Nō drama, contained parts for all of Partch's latest, and in some cases most eccentric, instruments.

For reasons of health, Partch left Petaluma for Southern California in 1964. In that year, his friend Danlee Mitchell had been appointed percussion teacher at San Diego State College. Mitchell was to be of invaluable assistance in performing, producing, and conducting Partch's works. Partch was to write one more composition, *The Dreamer That Remains* (1972), for a film, and to update *Genesis of a Music*, which was republished shortly before his death from a heart attack in 1974.

After the 1968 New York premiere of *The Bewitched*, Winthrop Sergeant, music critic for *The New Yorker*, wrote a perceptive review in which he commented on the difficulty of transporting Partch's fragile instruments and ended with the comment that "his art is absolutely unique . . . it will probably die with its creator, never to be heard again." Transfer of the recordings of the 1950's to digital compact discs has brought out the sound of Partch's instruments to the full; the static quality of some of Partch's later work has prefigured both minimalist music and New Age music, and in 1987, thirteen years after the composer's death, his *Revelation in the Court-*

house Park (based on a play by Euripedes) was given a live performance in Philadelphia under the direction of Danlee Mitchell by a new group of musicians who had learned to play Partch's instruments. The legacy of one of America's most original and innovative composers can still be said to continue. His audience, as he would have preferred, includes substantial numbers of listeners without formal training (or prejudices) in art music but open to new musical sonorities and effects.

Bibliography

Bowen, Meirion. "Harry Partch." *Music and Musicians* 17 (May, 1968): 20-25. A highly sympathetic depiction of Partch's life and music for a British audience, with a fine capsule account of *Genesis of a Music.*

Ewen, David. "Harry Partch." In *Composers of Tomorrow.* New York: Dodd, Mead, 1971. Partch is the last composer in this gallery of composers, written for a lay audience, that begins with Charles Ives and Arnold Schoenberg and includes Milton Babbitt and Yannis Xenakis.

"Kitharist." *The New Yorker* 20 (May 27, 1944): 21-22. The most sympathetic and encouraging of the nationally circulated reviews of the New York premiere of *U.S. Highball.*

McGeary, Thomas. *The Music of Harry Partch: A Descriptive Catalog.* Brooklyn: Institute for Studies in American Music, 1991. More than a catalog of Partch's works, this book contains a detailed chronology of his life, facsimiles of his manuscripts, and an extensive bibliography about the composer from 1930 to 1974.

Partch, Harry. *Bitter Music: Collected Journals, Essays, Introductions, and Librettos.* Edited by Thomas McGeary. Urbana: University of Illinois Press, 1991. An extensive collection of Partch's writings, mostly unpublished, including his hobo journal from June, 1935, to February, 1936, with musical notations of speech and the texts of *U.S. Highball.*

──────────. *Genesis of a Music.* Rev. ed. New York: Da Capo Press, 1974. Partch's account of the development of his musical scales and instruments, with the background of six of his major works and a selective bibliography. The photographs of the instruments are supplemented by detailed accounts of their construction.

Schafer, Murray. "U.S. Highball." *Canadian Music Journal* 3 (Winter, 1955): 55-58. Because of the rarity of performances, Partch's music became known chiefly through recordings. This article by one of Canada's leading composers gives a highly sympathetic account of Partch's subsequent musical development.

R. M. Longyear

Cross-References

Yeats Publishes *The Wild Swans at Coole* (1917), p. 440; Cage's *4' 33"* Premieres (1952), p. 1546; Varèse Premieres *Déserts* (1954), p. 1629; The First Successful Synthesizer Is Completed (1959), p. 1785; *Einstein on the Beach* Is a Triumph of Minimalism (1976), p. 2375.

GRAHAM DEBUTS *APPALACHIAN SPRING* WITH COPLAND SCORE

Categories of event: Dance and music
Time: October 30, 1944
Locale: Library of Congress, Washington, D.C.

Martha Graham's choreography of Appalachian Spring *climaxed her exploration of American themes and solidified her stature as a dance artist; the score brought a Pulitzer Prize to Aaron Copland*

Principal personages:
MARTHA GRAHAM (1894-1991), a performer, choreographer, and teacher, the greatest twentieth century artist of modern dance
AARON COPLAND (1900-1990), the Brooklyn-born composer of *Appalachian Spring* who sought to reconcile the idioms of classical and popular music in his expression of American themes
ISAMU NOGUCHI (1904-1988), the Japanese-American sculptor and designer of *Appalachian Spring* who collaborated closely with Graham on her major works
LOUIS HORST (1884-1964), a composer and teacher, Graham's longtime mentor, and the orchestra conductor of *Appalachian Spring*
ERICK HAWKINS (1909-   ), the first male dancer in the Graham company, and later Graham's husband, who performed as the husbandman in *Appalachian Spring*
MERCE CUNNINGHAM (1919-   ), the second male dancer in the Graham company, who performed as the revivalist in *Appalachian Spring*
MAY O'DONNELL (1909-   ), a former member of the Graham company who returned as guest artist to play the pioneer woman in *Appalachian Spring*

Summary of Event

When Martha Graham received a commission from the Elizabeth Sprague Coolidge Foundation in 1944 to create three dances for the Library of Congress, she was already a force in the modern-dance world. Fifteen years previously, she had opened her studio, selected a company, and begun to give annual performances in New York. She was on the staff of the Bennington School of the Dance from 1934 to 1942 and was an artist in residence at its prestigious summer season until 1944. She had received attention for *Heretic* (1929), which introduced her radical dance movements of the contraction and release, and further acclaim for *Primitive Mysteries* (1931), which revealed her powerful individual dance skills. Still, her work was not always understood or appreciated.

With her solo *Frontier* (1935), followed by *American Document* (1938) and *Letter to the World* (1940), Graham began an exploration of American themes. A Pennsylvania-born Presbyterian, she herself was transplanted to California as an adolescent, and the westward movement of the early settlers, as well as their Puritan sensibility, fascinated her.

Frontier presented Graham as a pioneer woman, taming a portion of an infinite land, delighting in the challenge and unafraid of the future. The work marked the first of many successful collaborations with the sculptor Isamu Noguchi; he was a particularly innovative choice as designer, since at the time most designs for dance depended upon the artistry of painters, not sculptors.

American Document was based on events in American history, with recitations of historical texts. The content illustrated Graham's preoccupation with the Puritan sensibility in conflict with sensuality. Erick Hawkins, the first male dancer in the company, made his debut.

The poet Emily Dickinson was the subject of *Letter to the World* (1940). Once more, Graham explored the American past, in particular the talent and passions of a woman confined within a repressive New England household.

These pieces, which combined Graham's interest in American themes with her sensitivity to female psychology, were in a sense preparation for the explosion of creativity that infused *Appalachian Spring* in 1944.

Inspired by a section of Hart Crane's 1930 poem *The Bridge* that tells of an Indian maiden, her lover, and their love of the land, Graham transferred their passions to nineteenth century settlers in the mountains of Pennsylvania. It is spring; there is a sense of new life and rebirth; it is a magical time. A young bride, danced radiantly by Graham, and the husbandman, danced with confidence and strength by Erick Hawkins, take possession of their new house and lands. Her movements reveal the variety of emotions within her inner self: She investigates her new situation tentatively; she presses herself passionately upon the ground in an expression of love for the land; she sits on a bench, tiny fluttering gestures revealing a joy that she is almost afraid to admit.

The husbandman runs his hand over the surface of the house, communicates with his neighbors with decorum, and places a gentle hand protectively on his wife's shoulder. They join in a warm lyrical duet, expressing their hopes for their wedded life.

A community surrounds them; nearby, a stern revivalist, danced in soaring phrases by Merce Cunningham, reminds them fervently of religious obligations and the discipline to which they must submit. His four adoring followers cup their hands to applaud and then pray with him. A pioneer woman (May O'Donnell) conveys support and wisdom in large, muscular gestures, as one who has faced and overcome the obstacles that lie ahead for the newlyweds. At the end, the young couple are welcomed into the community and accept the challenge of the land and their union. *Appalachian Spring* is a celebration not only of wedded life but also of a young country and the spirit that developed it.

Those who collaborated with Graham were equally inspired by the simple tale and the ideas expressed in it. Aaron Copland's score, especially commissioned by

Graham, went beyond appropriate complement to become an independent work of art in itself. Originally scored for thirteen instruments of a chamber orchestra, it was later arranged by the composer as a concert suite for full symphony orchestra. It was fresh, lively, and melodious, with suggestions of American fiddle tunes and country dances, and it concluded effectively with five variations on the Shaker hymn "Tis the Gift to Be Simple," heard against a background of silence and space. The work was awarded the Pulitzer Prize for music in 1944.

Isamu Noguchi designed a spare and economical set with a sculptor's knowledge of three-dimensional form. The frame of a house with a peaked roof, a bench, a six-foot section of fence, a tree stump as a pulpit for the revivalist, and a thin sculpted rocking chair were the few pieces on the stage.

Others contributed their special skills. Jean Rosenthal, Graham's trusted lighting designer for several decades, provided brilliant lighting to enhance the dance movements. Edythe Gilfond created the simple costumes, and Louis Horst conducted the orchestra.

Appalachian Spring was the final offering on the evening of October 30, 1944, at the Library of Congress, and the piece was immediately accepted and enjoyed. The audience, it is reported, left the theater in a state of euphoria. John Martin commented in *The New York Times* that "nothing Miss Graham has done before has had such deep joyousness about it."

Impact of Event

Appalachian Spring has been termed "the greatest national hymn of American dance," a phrase that pays homage to the cultural origin of the work as well as to its celebratory nature. Premiering during the final year of World War II, *Appalachian Spring* was a lyrical reminder to a war-weary audience of the enduring value of family and community and of the pioneering spirit that developed America.

For Martha Graham, now fifty years old, in the prime of her creative powers and a legend in the modern-dance world, the work represented a culmination and a transcendence of her individual, sometimes painful, inquiry into the past and its shadows. It was a turning point, an affirmation of a joyous present. Many years later, she wrote to Aaron Copland, "Appalachian Spring has been one of the pleasures of my life—a kind of keystone and I treasure every note of it and the experience I had to be able to choreograph it."

Aaron Copland was delighted to receive the Pulitzer Prize in music for his score and delighted and surprised to receive also an award for dramatic composition from the Music Critics Circle of New York. Both awards brought him increased public recognition. He noted, however, that it was "Martha's admiration for the music that held the most meaning for me."

The work was remarkable because it was easily accessible to the audience's perceptions. The movements were organic and recognizable. Who could fail to understand the love of the bride and the husbandman, or the warnings of the revivalist? Who could not feel the couple's excitement in their home or their hopes for the future? Who did not identify with a rush of affection with this universal human experience?

Modern dance had conceded little to audience expectations or tastes during its early years. Audiences had struggled to find meaning in the new radical movements, to understand on some level what the dancers were trying to communicate. Meanwhile, the artists themselves had spent much time and energy trying to discredit ballet as they fought to achieve recognition on their own terms, to establish modern dance as not secondary to the music but as a separate art form. They committed themselves to a more honest vocabulary of movement that evolved from natural body rhythms. These movements were not always graceful or aesthetically pleasing, and audiences were often puzzled. Yet the dancers persisted, deliberately eschewing commercial success in preference to artistic integrity.

Dance criticism evolved with modern dance. By 1944, several dance critics sympathized with the goals of the artists and served the art by educating the public through intelligent analysis, praise, and enthusiasm. Edwin Denby spoke of "the mysterious coolness and freshness" of the piece as well as of Graham's "genius"; *Appalachian Spring*, declared Martin, is "a truly beautiful work." For once, the public agreed.

With the enthusiastic reception of the premiere, *Appalachian Spring* thus became one of the staples of Graham's 1944 season, which included the earlier works *Letter to the World*, *Salem Shore* (1943), *Deaths and Entrances* (1943), and *Herodiade* (the second work on the program at the Library of Congress performance). As the years passed, *Appalachian Spring* became one of the most beloved works in the Graham repertoire and was successfully performed all over the world.

The 1944-1945 season was the most successful to date for Martha Graham, not only because the New York public was supportive and appreciative but also, and most important, because the impresario Sol Hurok offered to represent the Graham company on a national tour the following year.

The Hurok organization was a commercial producing company; Sol Hurok was highly regarded as a shrewd businessman. To book a tour nationally with a modern-dance company was a daring move on his part, as well as a marvelous opportunity for the Graham works to travel beyond the college and university audiences into the commercial theater. Most important, a tour represented a major step toward the acceptance of modern dance.

Public resistance and antagonism persisted; the tour the following year was not an unqualified success. Critical comment, though, was far more positive than it had ever been outside New York City, and the way was paved for other artists to follow.

Appalachian Spring influenced the careers and the styles of everyone in the original cast. Merce Cunningham, Erick Hawkins, May O'Donnell, and Pearl Lang later formed companies of their own and choreographed and performed independently. The other three, Nina Fonaroff, Marjorie Mazia, and Yuriko, disseminated the Graham technique to the next generation of students in classes at the Graham Studio and at other schools.

In 1965, the Aspen Institute for Humanistic Studies honored Martha Graham as "the individual anywhere in the world to have made the greatest contribution to the advancement of the humanities." After the speeches and the presentation of the award, the music played was Copland's score of *Appalachian Spring*. The music had become a symbol of the Graham achievement.

The ultimate test of any work of art is its endurance through the years; with a performed piece, the question arises whether one person can assume a role created definitively by another. Biographers note that Graham had great difficulty in relinquishing her roles, although she knew it was necessary. Pearl Lang first inherited the bride's role, performing it many times. On a rare occasion in 1975, another bride, Teresa Capucilli, was joined by Rudolph Nureyev as the preacher and Mikhail Baryshnikov as the husbandman. Thus, *Appalachian Spring* lives on, independent of its creator. It has become a national treasure.

Bibliography

Copland, Aaron, and Vivian Perlis. *Copland: Since 1943*. New York: St. Martin's Press, 1989. A fine autobiography beginning during World War II, with interviews from friends, family, and colleagues from the music and dance world interspersed. Contains an engrossing chapter devoted to the creation and response to *Appalachian Spring*, with anecdotal remarks from Martha Graham, Erick Hawkins, Pearl Lang, and May O'Donnell. Photographs, notes and index.

Denby, Edwin. *Dance Writings*. Edited by Robert Cornfield and William MacKay. New York: Alfred A. Knopf, 1986. A voluminous collection of Denby's critical reviews and essays compiled from the *New York Herald Tribune*, *Dance Magazine*, *Modern Music*, and other writings. Comments relating to Graham's work occur throughout; of interest is Denby's changing perspective and increasing admiration through the decades. Index and sketchy notes.

Jowitt, Deborah. "Group Spirits" and "The Heroines Within." In *Time and the Dancing Image*. New York: William Morrow, 1987. A readable, scholarly history, by a dancer and dance critic, of nearly two hundred years of dance, with perceptive discussions of the evolution of modern dance and of the significance of the Graham works. Photographs, notes, bibliography, and index.

McDonagh, Don. *Martha Graham*. New York: Praeger, 1973. A detailed, thorough biography of Martha Graham, slightly dated. Paints the goddess as temperamental and volatile but human. Also includes a valuable "Choreochronicle" of 155 of Graham's dances, with locations, dates, designers, and cast members. Photographs, index, and bibliography.

Mazo, Joseph H. "Martha Graham: Casta Diva." In *Prime Movers: The Makers of Modern Dance in America*. New York: William Morrow, 1977. An analysis of the work of nine modern dancers from Loie Fuller to Twyla Tharp, with the longest chapter devoted to Martha Graham's works, her technique, and her style. Biographical material is secondary. Photographs, bibliography, and index.

Mellers, Wilfrid. "Skyscraper and Prairie: Aaron Copland and the American Isolation." In *Music in a New Found Land: Themes and Developments in the History of American Music.* New York: Alfred A. Knopf, 1965. Copland continues essential American themes initiated by Charles Ives. The chapter discusses the technical composition of *Appalachian Spring* and other Copland works. Several appendices and a valuable discography are included.

Stodelle, Ernestine. *Deep Song: The Dance Story of Martha Graham.* New York: Schirmer Books, 1984. An elegantly written biography, sensitive and perceptive in description, with excellent word pictures of the major works and extensive photographs of Graham in performance and in private life. A thorough bibliography, index, and chronology of 179 works are included; missing is a cast list.

Joyce E. Henry

Cross-References

The Denishawn School of Dance Opens in Los Angeles (1915), p. 390; Boulanger Takes Copland as a Student (1921), p. 508; Agnes de Mille Choreographs *Rodeo* (1942), p. 1234; *Oklahoma!* Opens on Broadway (1943), p. 1256; Robbins' *Fancy Free* Premieres (1944), p. 1274; Taylor Establishes His Own Dance Company (1954), p. 1602; Cunningham Stages His First Dance "Event" (1964), p. 2011.

ARTS AND ARCHITECTURE MAGAZINE INITIATES THE CASE STUDY PROGRAM

Category of event: Architecture
Time: 1945
Locale: Los Angeles, California

The Case Study Program was an effort to revolutionize postwar American housing in terms of both social meaning and applied technology

Principal personages:
> JOHN ENTENZA (1905-1984), the editor and publisher of *Arts and Architecture* magazine from 1939 to 1962
> CHARLES EAMES (1907-1978), an architect and designer who played a significant role in the editorial policy of the magazine and in the Case Study Program
> PIERRE KOENIG (1925-   ), an architect whose Case Study designs illustrated a mature glass-and-steel style
> RICHARD NEUTRA (1892-1970), an important modern architect who designed two Case Study houses
> GREGORY AIN (1908-   ), the Case Study Program architect most interested in low-cost housing

Summary of Event

John Entenza joined the staff of *California Arts and Architecture* in 1938. The magazine had begun publication in 1911 as a trade journal, *The Pacific Builder*, and had evolved into a regional coffee-table publication, reviewing gardens, houses, and theater performances. During Entenza's tenure as editor and then publisher, the magazine began to focus on modern architecture and culture, and by 1943, as *Arts and Architecture*, it had changed its format and focus.

Entenza's interest in the practice of modern architecture led him to speculate about the nature of postwar housing in the early 1940's. In 1943, the magazine organized "Designs for Modern Living," a competition of designs for modest, modern, family housing cosponsored by twenty-two manufacturers. After publishing the designs of three winners, the magazine highlighted other promising submissions in later issues. In July, 1944, Entenza published a lively and extensive discussion of prefabricated housing by Buckminster Fuller, Eero Saarinen, Charles Eames, and Herbert Mather. The magazine began to build a national and international reputation as a showcase for new talent, and was the first to show the work of such architects as Paul Rudolph and Harry Seidler.

In January of 1945, in an editorial move that cemented the influence and prestige of *Arts and Architecture*, Entenza announced the inauguration of the Case Study Program. His original plan called for the construction of a group of houses, on specific sites, with fixed budgets, undertaken for the magazine. Architects were chosen to begin to study, plan, design, and construct houses that would answer the special needs of life in Southern California. The architects Entenza commissioned represented a cross section of the full spectrum of architects working in a modern idiom in Los Angeles. Richard Neutra and J. R. Davidson were European emigrants whose work represented the ideals of international modernism. A middle generation of modernists included Raphael Soriano and Charles Eames, both of whom had degrees from American schools of architecture and had been in private practice. A younger generation of designers was led by Craig Ellwood, who was twenty-six when he was invited to design for the program, and Pierre Koenig, whose works evidenced a fully developed sense of a style of glass and steel.

Three of the commissions were erected on five acres Entenza purchased for this purpose in Pacific Palisades. One of the houses was designed for Entenza by Eero Saarinen and Charles Eames; Charles and Ray Eames built a Case Study house and studio for themselves on the same parcel. A third Case Study house on the acreage was designed by Richard Neutra. Over time, however, the program's success came to depend on Entenza's matchmaking abilities in finding enlightened clients for the architects he had engaged. By the program's official end in 1966, the series of commissions that resulted had included the construction of twenty-three houses, the presentation of eight experimental projects, and the planning of clustered housing units, two of which were realized.

The Case Study Program was a direct outgrowth of Entenza's progressive agenda. From the start, *Arts and Architecture* published unusually long and informative articles for the interested reader on both basic issues and innovations in a variety of modern art forms including music, film, painting, and design as well as architecture. Entenza saw the postwar years as a fantastic opportunity to refine and redefine American life by exploiting the artistic, social, and technological changes that World War II had generated.

For example, the Case Study Program was based on information and projections of postwar population growth and housing needs. Demographically, the emerging middle class was younger, better educated, and more experienced than its predecessors. Yet the traditional trappings of middle-class domestic life were, at first, unavailable to them because of the need to retool the old war economy. In some important ways, the Case Study houses were to be living research laboratories: both experimental and pragmatic redefinitions of the meaning of home and shelter for "typical" American families and illustrations of the ways in which the latest sociological thinking and newly available war technologies might be put to domestic use. The Case Study Program was motivated by a central democratic ideal shared, to a greater or lesser extent, by Entenza, the architects, participating manufacturers, and clients—a belief that all Americans should be able to live in an affordable, well-designed environment. Ideally, Case Study houses would reflect both the realities and the promise, physical and psychological, of life in America after World War II.

It was a perfect time to be innovative. A second, central Case Study Program goal was to experiment with techniques and materials that had been used in the war effort. Entenza expected that the building process of program houses would take advantage of the sort of rationalization of labor that had enabled the government quickly and efficiently to provide temporary housing for large military and civilian populations. A number of the architects Entenza commissioned for the program, including Charles Eames, had spent the war years experimenting with military applications for materials such as plastics, metal alloys, and molded plywoods, and with new processes, such as cycle-welding, that might now be converted to domestic production and consumption. For example, between 1949 and 1960, the Case Study architects tested the limits of structural steel, a material unavailable for private use during, and immediately after, the war.

Between 1946 and 1966, twenty-four Case Study projects were built in Los Angeles, La Jolla, the San Francisco area, and Phoenix, Arizona. While the first group of houses did not exactly follow Entenza's mandate calling for the use of industrial materials, by the time the Eames and Entenza houses were completed in 1949, a consistent and distinctive style emerged. Case Study houses were characterized by concrete-slab foundations, rectilinear, modular façades and silhouettes, and flat roofs. Case Study buildings made use of standardized, industrial-grade materials such as aluminum siding, stock sheet glass, plywood panels, and concrete blocks. The traditional street façade disappeared, and the house turned inward and toward the privacy of the backyard. Walls of sliding glass doors allowed for the interpretation of the multipurpose interior and outdoor living spaces.

The Case Study Program did not fulfill Entenza's dream of revolutionizing the average American's taste, nor did it have a truly significant impact on the house-building industry. Yet despite criticism that it perpetuated elitist concerns for aesthetics and the single-family detached dwelling, the Case Study Program did have a trickle-down effect on tract housing in the West. The program also provided the prototypes for much of the commercial and industrial building of the 1960's, 1970's, and 1980's, some of it designed by original Case Study Program architects.

Impact of Event

While the Case Study Program did not transform American architectural taste or building practice to the extent that Entenza might have hoped, it did encourage a more widespread acceptance of the compatibility of modern architecture and interiors with the requirements of contemporary American life. Although modernism, as an aesthetic construct and a worldview, dated from the turn of the century, the postwar world was seen as somehow significantly changed, different from prewar society in attitude, ideals, and abilities. Whether all, some, or none of this was actually the case is less important than the resulting sound and fury over the perceived need for change in the smallest details of American life.

Entenza was not the only person interested in future-oriented postwar housing. For example, in 1942, *Architectural Forum* published a group of designs for thirty-three prefabricated projects as part of a piece entitled "The New House of 194X."

As the war began to draw to a close, interior design and women's magazines, including *Woman's Day, House and Garden,* and *American Home,* began to speculate about coming trends and innovations in American domestic design. The Case Study Program itself provoked widespread media coverage that was not confined to the pages of *Arts and Architecture.* Other publications, both trade journals and consumer magazines, including *House and Home, Sunset,* and the *Los Angeles Times* publicized the houses. Public interest was also high. The first six houses, designed, constructed, completed, furnished, and landscaped during the first three years of the program, drew more than 368,000 visitors.

While the forms and façades of the new houses were startlingly untraditional, Americans were quick to clamor for the sorts of amenities that Case Study houses offered: Kitchens were light, efficient, well planned, and equipped with the latest in labor-saving appliances; two bathrooms were the norm; the formal, separate dining room disappeared; and the public and private areas of the house were buffered by patios and transitional spaces.

The Case Study Program did have an influence on mainstream building of the 1950's and early 1960's. The rigor and discipline required of both homebuilder and homeowner in the high style of a Case Study design were gentled and softened into a popularized version that came to be known as "California Modern." This style was a fantasy version of the wonders of life in Hollywood—informal living, ideal weather, and a particular sort of sophistication and glamour—and was not restricted to the geography of the West Coast. Tract homes in this style usually exploited some version of the Case Study architectural vocabulary of overhangs, picture windows, sliding glass doors, and light woods.

Mainstream and tract housing developments of the postwar period did not, however, make use of the signature element of the Case Study Program, structural steel, and so avoided the mass-production component of Entenza's agenda. This was probably for two reasons, each of which offers a hint as to why the program failed to develop widespread appeal. First, Americans were highly resistant to steel as a housing element. Perhaps because of its associations with war production, or perhaps as a result of American architectural history and tradition, steel was unable to overcome industrial connotations that most Americans found offensive in domestic architecture. Second, steel was not as flexible as wood, either physically or aesthetically, particularly for the sort of small, individual units that Americans continued to believe signified "home." It is clear that the Case Study houses did not express the collective American sense of how life should be organized. Both explicitly and implicitly, the needs of "average" American families were being adequately served by tract housing.

Despite the seeming failure of Entenza's manifesto, the Case Study Program is a significant chapter in modern architecture. The importance of the Case Study Program derived from the houses' iconic qualities, whether their designs were realized or not. They were intended as icons of the new American middle class; their meaning stemmed from the images of their intentions, the embodiment of a union of social utopian mythology and the realities of mass production. For those affiliated with the Case Study Program, architecture was a social, as well as functional, art, concerned as much with human problems as with the peculiarities of site and structure.

John Entenza was among the vanguard of Americans interested in affecting the ways the postwar world looked and behaved. In these designs, there is a suggestion that modern existence could involve the personalization and domestication of the same economic impulses that had fueled the war machine. The Case Study Program is particularly American in its optimistic exploration of the expansion of the commercial and social possibilities of industrial production; particularly American in its consistently spatial and technological symbolism. Ironically, the Case Study Program legacy is an international and industrial one. The steel-frame designs of Eames, Koenig, Soriano, and Ellwood had a significant impact on the development of a high-tech style of residential architecture in Great Britain and Europe. The structural and formal innovations of the Case Study Program are most familiar to Americans in industrial and commercial designs of the late 1960's and early 1970's.

The Case Study Program shared the glamorous aura of science, the siren call of the new, and the promise of convenience with its contemporary, the European International style. In the hands of Entenza and his Case Study architects, however, the products of industry were domesticated and brought to an individualized scale. The rational was made to serve the domestic. The Case Study Program offered Americans single-family homes that were aesthetically avant-garde, affordable, and eminently practical. The innovations they introduced were historically significant and internationally influential and made the reputations of a number of important American architects.

Bibliography

Banham, Reyner. "Architecture IV: The Style That Nearly . . ." In *Los Angeles: The Architecture of Four Ecologies.* New York: Harper & Row, 1971. This meditation on urban Los Angeles includes a chapter on Case Study houses as a Southern California architectural style. Eccentric and entertaining. Black-and-white illustrations, bibliography, index.

Goldstein, Barbara, ed. *Arts and Architecture: The Entenza Years.* Cambridge, Mass.: MIT Press, 1990. An anthology of important articles appearing in *Arts and Architecture* between 1943 and 1959. Also includes an essay on Entenza by Esther McCoy. Black-and-white photographs.

McCoy, Esther. *Case Study Houses, 1945-1962.* 2d ed. Los Angeles: Hennessey & Ingalls, 1977. A seminal book by an important historian of California architecture. Black-and-white plates, biographies of participants, bibliography, index.

_____, et al. *Blueprints for Modern Living: History and Legacy of the Case Study Houses.* Los Angeles: Museum of Contemporary Art, 1989. The catalog of an important exhibition and a detailed study of the Case Study Program and its projects. Readable and informative essays by scholars of architectural history and design. Black-and-white photographs, biographies of architects, chronology, bibliography, index, notes.

Pulos, Arthur J. "The Search for Modern Living." In *The American Design Adventure, 1940-1975.* Cambridge, Mass.: Massachusetts Institute of Technology, 1988. Contextualizes the Case Study Program in postwar American housing problems and promises. Black-and-white photographs, comprehensive bibliography, index.

J. R. Donath

Cross-References

The Deutscher Werkbund Combats Conservative Architecture (1907), p. 181; Wright Founds the Taliesin Fellowship (1932), p. 902; Prouvé Pioneers the Prefabrication of Buildings (Late 1930's), p. 1021; Fuller's First Industrial Geodesic Dome Is Erected (1953), p. 1579; Saarinen Designs Kennedy Airport's TWA Terminal (1956), p. 1716; Kahn Blends Architecture and Urban Planning in Dacca (1962), p. 1919.

BRITTEN COMPLETES *PETER GRIMES*

Category of event: Music
Time: June 7, 1945
Locale: Sadler's Wells Theatre, London, England

Peter Grimes, *written and first produced at the end of World War II, revitalized the British operatic tradition and reawakened international interest in English opera*

Principal personages:
BENJAMIN BRITTEN (1913-1976), the British composer whose opera *Peter Grimes* revitalized the moribund British operatic tradition
PETER PEARS (1910-1986), the tenor whose distinctive voice provided Britten with the ideal sound for his stage heroes
MONTAGU SLATER (1902-1956), an English poet and novelist who wrote the libretto for *Peter Grimes*

Summary of Event

Benjamin Britten was a product of the windswept seacoast of Suffolk and retained a lifelong affection for its people and vulnerable landscape. Although he had left England in May, 1939, dreading the onset of World War II and inspired by W. H. Auden's promise of greater artistic freedom in the United States, he eventually returned to England and made his native Suffolk his home. He died in 1976 in Aldeburgh, the village he depicts in his opera *Peter Grimes* (1945). Not counting the operas by the German-born George Handel in the eighteenth century or the light operas of the Victorian team of W. S. Gilbert and Arthur Sullivan, *Peter Grimes* was the first international success by a native English composer since Henry Purcell's *Dido and Aeneas* (1689).

The story of the opera's astonishing success begins and ends in Britten's beloved Aldeburgh. The eighteenth century poet George Crabbe was born and reared in Aldeburgh. Among the portraits in his *The Borough: A Poem in Twenty-four Letters* (1810) is "Peter Grimes," which tells the story of a lonely, unpleasant fisherman who had become an object of local antipathy. Grimes hired three apprentices from the workhouse, each of whom died under mysterious circumstances. The subject is scarcely an instantly appealing one; as Patricia Howard has said of the opera, "its miracle is that a character as unattractive, unapproachable, and undeniably unpleasant as Grimes in the end manages to gain our sympathy."

Britten, who shared with the poet Crabbe a fascination with life along the harsh Suffolk coast, had been impressed in 1934 by his first hearing of Alban Berg's opera, *Wozzeck* (1925), the title character of which is perhaps the ultimate antihero of twentieth century opera. Britten, who had attracted the attention of composer Frank Bridge with his compositional talent, first came to the general attention of English musical audiences in 1934 with his "Simple Symphony." His promise provided consolation to the English audience in the same year that it had lost its three major composers—Gustav Holst, Frederick Delius, and Edward Elgar. Depressed by a combination of factors, specifically his distress as a pacifist at the imminent onset of the war and discomfort with his own homosexuality in a country where this was treated as a punishable offense, Britten moved to the United States in May, 1939, with his companion, Peter Pears.

It was the chance reading in 1941, in California, of an appreciative essay on Crabbe by novelist E. M. Forster that caused Britten to decide to return to England. He was commissioned by conductor Serge Koussevitsky to write an opera, and he called upon a colleague from the Left Theatre, Montagu Slater, to reshape Crabbe's poem into a libretto. The actual composition of the opera took place between January, 1944, and February, 1945, and the first performance was given by the Sadler's Wells opera company in London on June 7, 1945, a month after the collapse of Nazi Germany. Peter Pears sang the title role; Joan Cross (who was also the director of Sadler's Wells) sang the role of Ellen Orford. The director was Eric Crozier, and the conductor was Reginald Goodall.

Britten wrote the opera in a relatively conservative style, rejecting Richard Wagner's goal of "endless melody" in favor of the older operatic practice of providing separate "numbers." Britten later explained, "One of my chief aims is to try and restore to the musical setting of the English language a brilliance, freedom, and vitality that have been curiously rare since the death of [Henry] Purcell." Slater, a prolific poet and scriptwriter, provided Britten with a solid poetic libretto; Britten's vocal writing was strongly influenced by his deep relationship with the tenor Peter Pears, for whom the title role was tailored.

The opera centers on its title character, the lonely Suffolk fisherman. Whereas the Peter Grimes of Crabbe's poem was not accorded any gift for decency or introspection, in Slater's libretto Crabbe's grim fisherman became a character too proud and self-willed to come to terms with society. He is a cranky, stubborn nonconformist and a kind of visionary, as his first-act aria, "Now the Great Bear and Pleiades . . . Are Drawing Up," clearly reveals. He makes the mistake of thinking that he will impress the surly villagers by the acquisition of wealth.

The opera opens, abruptly, with a trial scene, in which Peter is convicted of negligence in the death of his first apprentice. When Ellen Orford, the village widow who genuinely sympathizes with Peter, tries to console him, the music dramatically reveals his inability to communicate: the two sing an unaccompanied duet in different keys. Later, Ellen notices bruises on Peter's newest apprentice; when she inquires about them, Peter brutally strikes her, painfully confirming his reputation as an abusive figure.

As the villagers storm up the hill to Peter's cabin to check on his treatment of the boy, Peter inadvertently pushes the boy over a cliff to his death. This last act of unconscious violence pushes Peter over the brink into madness, allowing Britten to give his hero a familiar staple of romantic opera, the mad scene. Peter's mad recitative sets the pattern of lonely reminiscences of Britten's later deranged or persecuted characters such as Lucretia, Billy Budd, and Aschenbach. In spoken dialogue, Balstrode (Peter's last village friend) tells him to take his boat out to sea and sink it.

Critics have admired the opera for the strength of its choral writing, and it has been compared with other operas in which the community plays an integral role, such as Modest Mussorgsky's *Boris Godunov* (1874) and George Gershwin's *Porgy and Bess* (1935). The opera is filled with great scenes for the chorus, depicting villagers in a variety of social institutions—at Peter's trial, mending fishing nets, in church, and in the village pub. An even stronger case might be made for the orchestra as the true hero. Britten's orchestration skillfully depicts the roaring of the wind, the surging of the waves, and the menace of an ocean storm. The orchestra is called on to provide rousing music for a vivid round, "Old Joe Has Gone Fishing," music for a barn dance, and liturgical music for the church scene. Four of the opera's six orchestral interludes have achieved independent life in the concert hall as the *Four Sea Interludes.*

Stylistically, the opera is notable for its energy and variety. Peter favors the unusual interval of the ninth, a leap suggestive of his idealism. The orchestra initially provides the melody for Peter's aria "Now the Great Bear and Pleiades . . . Are Drawing Up," while the singer holds onto the same note (a favorite device of Giacomo Puccini). The melodies are simple but have piquant twists for a modern listener, such as an unexpected sharp or flat. Britten has the energy and vitality of Giuseppe Verdi and Leoš Janáček's instinct for rendering village activities. Like Dmitri Shostakovich, Britten had the courage to resist serialism and other avant-garde systems, with the result that his music is now admired for its integrity and accessibility to audiences.

Impact of Event

Through the success of the first production of *Peter Grimes* in 1945, Benjamin Britten revived the tradition of English opera. Music critic Henry Davey had once lamented that English opera was "the darkest page in our musical history," noting sadly that no serious English opera either had consistently held the stage outside England or earned the admiration of audiences and critics since *Dido and Aeneas.* The success of *Peter Grimes* proved that there was an audience for an austere opera on a bleak subject at a moment when England was facing the daunting task of repairing the ravages of the war. American literary critic Edmund Wilson was bowled over by the musical and dramatic power of the opera and recognized that it implicitly addressed the issues of the war, specifically "the blind anguish, the hateful rancors and the will to destruction of these horrible years."

The success of the opera revitalized the Sadler's Wells opera company, which had been nearly starved of resources because of wartime austerity, and it helped to reinvigorate England's cultural life in the years between the war's end and the Festival of Britain in 1951. It marked the first operatic collaboration of the creative pair of Britten and his longtime companion, the tenor Peter Pears; their mutual success, as composer and performer, would extend nearly thirty years. Unpromising though it must have seemed in 1945, the story of Peter Grimes set the course of Britten's operatic career, with its main figure a relative innocent who is sacrificed to the will of an inflexible community. This theme would enter the stories of Albert Herring, Billy Budd, and the friends of the prophet Daniel in *The Burning Fiery Furnace* (1966), and it could even be said to describe two other sensitive, tormented figures, Captain Vere in *Billy Budd* (1951) and Aschenbach in *Death in Venice* (1973), as well.

One unspoken subject of *Peter Grimes* and many of Britten's later operas is homosexuality. Britten himself was reluctant to discuss his own sexuality, and until recently even critical works on Britten's life and art were reluctant to raise the subject. The obituary for Britten in *The New York Times* coyly spoke of "the composer and Mr. Pears, both bachelors," yet within a few years critics began aggressively to reinterpret the composer's life and art as a response to his own homosexuality. By these accounts, Peter Grimes's behavior is seen variously as that of an alienated homosexual and potential or actively abusive male, but Britten himself never spoke of the opera in these terms.

Such interpretations are far from Crabbe's original conception of Peter as a man "untouched by pity, unstung by remorse and uncorrected by shame." The character of Peter Grimes is more likely now to be perceived by audiences as lonely, alienated, guilty, and abusive, but as increasingly sympathetic.

The major and unexpected success of *Peter Grimes* at Sadler's Wells led, within three years, to productions throughout Europe and, in America, at the Tanglewood Music Festival and on February 12, 1948, at the Metropolitan Opera. In 1967, the Metropolitan Opera staged a new production with Jon Vickers in the title role, Heather Harper as Ellen, and Colin Davis conducting. Vickers' stern dignity and heavy Wagnerian voice offered a sharp contrast to Pears's distinctive and far lighter tenor voice; since then, Vickers' dark conception of the role is the one that most operatic audiences think of as definitive.

After the first production, Britten proceeded quickly to new operatic projects, both chamber operas on an intimate scale, such as *The Rape of Lucretia* (1946) and *Albert Herring* (1947), and large-scale operas requiring many soloists and a large chorus, such as *Billy Budd* (1951) and *Gloriana* (1953), the latter written to celebrate the coronation of Queen Elizabeth II. *The Little Sweep* (1949) was written as children's entertainment. Britten wrote a trio of "church operas" for semiprofessional performance, *Noye's Fludde* (1957), *The Burning Fiery Furnace* (1966), and *The Prodigal Son* (1968); *Curlew River* (1964) is related to this group. *The Turn of the Screw* (1954) and *A Midsummer Night's Dream* (1960) are based on formidable literary sources. Britten's last opera was *Death in Venice* (1973), based on Thomas Mann's novella; it marked his final operatic collaboration with Peter Pears, for whom so much of his vocal music had been written.

Although the power and invention of *Peter Grimes* are not in dispute, Britten's later operas show increasing sophistication and mastery of technique. Some critics argue for *Billy Budd* as his operatic masterpiece, while others regard *Death in Ven-*

ice as his ripest product, from Britten's golden sunset. If *Peter Grimes* marked the first peak in Britten's reputation as a composer, his *War Requiem* (1962) clearly marks the second. Both works share the composer's mastery of technique and indignation at man's cruelty to man. Like his great predecessor Edward Elgar or his Russian friend and contemporary Dmitri Shostakovich, Britten in his final years produced music that was increasingly austere and melancholy, as well as detached and oblique. Like them, he shared a deeply humanistic compassion for the victims of violence and prejudice.

Bibliography

Brett, Philip, ed. *Benjamin Britten: "Peter Grimes."* Cambridge Opera Handbooks. Cambridge, England: Cambridge University Press, 1983. Useful compendium of essays, including E. M. Forster's positive assessment of Crabbe's poetry that brought the story of Peter Grimes to Britten's attention in 1941. Eager to place the opera in the context of Britten's homosexuality.

Grout, Donald Jay. *A Short History of Opera.* New York: Columbia University Press, 1947. A standard older history of opera, still impressive for its range and conciseness.

Howard, Patricia. *The Operas of Benjamin Britten: An Introduction.* New York: Praeger, 1969. Sensitive but dated study of the operas up to *The Burning Fiery Furnace.*

Kennedy, Michael. *Britten.* Master Musicians Series. London: Dent, 1981. A good chronological study of the composer's works.

Schmidgall, Gary. *Literature as Opera.* New York: Oxford University Press, 1977. Influential study of the interrelationships of operas and their literary sources; features a sensitive chapter on *Death in Venice.*

White, Eric Walter. *Benjamin Britten: His Life and Operas.* 2d ed. Berkeley: University of California Press, 1983. A thorough study, with detailed chapters on each of the operas.

Byron Nelson

Cross-References

Vaughan Williams Composes His Nine Symphonies (1903), p. 90; Elgar's First Symphony Premieres to Acclaim (1908), p. 214; Berg's *Wozzeck* Premieres in Berlin (1925), p. 680; Gershwin's *Porgy and Bess* Opens in New York (1935), p. 1016; Shostakovich's *Lady Macbeth of Mtsensk* Is Condemned (1936), p. 1042.

BALANCHINE AND KIRSTEIN MAKE NEW YORK A WORLD CENTER FOR BALLET

Category of event: Dance
Time: 1946
Locale: New York, New York

George Balanchine and Lincoln Kirstein organized Ballet Society, a performing enterprise that later evolved into America's preeminent ballet company, the New York City Ballet

Principal personages:

GEORGE BALANCHINE (GEORGI MELITONOVITCH BALANCHIVADZE, 1904-1983), the major ballet choreographer of the twentieth century, who with Lincoln Kirstein founded Ballet Society and its offspring, the New York City Ballet

LINCOLN KIRSTEIN (1907-   ), an American writer and manager who championed ballet in the United States with his companies, including Ballet Society and the New York City Ballet

IGOR STRAVINSKY (1882-1971), an unrivaled composer of experimental music in the twentieth century who closely collaborated with Balanchine on the creation of many significant ballets

Summary of Event

The genesis of Lincoln Kirstein's and George Balanchine's Ballet Society in 1946 solidified the status of ballet dance in the United States. This organization, which promoted a radically new admissions policy and presented some radically new efforts in dance, was the forerunner of the unparalleled New York City Ballet. In its two-year existence, Ballet Society nurtured dancers who would become known as among the world's best ballet technicians. Even more significant, this undertaking began to reveal the great depths of Balanchine's genius to increasingly sophisticated dance audiences.

Ballet Society was ambitiously organized as a nonprofit membership organization that would present four evenings of dance each year in various locations around New York City. With the price of membership, theater tickets were provided along with supplementary literature (including *Dance Index*, a magazine edited by Kirstein). An annual yearbook, films, lectures, and phonograph records were also planned as subscription perks. An associate membership cost fifty dollars and was allotted two tickets for each performance; a "participant" paid fifteen dollars and received one seat each night. Modeled loosely after museum membership policies, Kirstein's admissions strategy was meant to elevate ballet to the status of visual art.

Ballet Society's mission was to present new choreography rather than the Franco-Russian revivals that dominated the 1930's. Its elegant twelve-page announcement, distributed in early October, stated that the organization was incorporated "for the encouragement of the lyric theatre by the production of new works" with the goal "to present a completely new repertory, consisting of ballets, ballet-opera and other lyric forms." Kirstein and Balanchine hoped to create an environment conducive to experimentation and collaboration among dancers, choreographers, artists and musicians. They refused to compromise artistic exploration for the sake of large crowds or the pleasure of "the establishment."

Some eight hundred people responded to their initial advertisement. Unable to book a costly theater for a one-night stand, Kirstein and Balanchine chose New York's Central High School of Needle Trades for Ballet Society's debut program on November 20. Despite an ill-equipped auditorium and the company's half-hour delay in starting, the curtain eventually rose on a magical production of *The Spellbound Child*, staged by Balanchine and featuring music composed by Maurice Ravel.

Although the company encountered several technical problems, this was an enchanting beginning for Ballet Society. The evening's main event, however, was the premiere of Balanchine's *The Four Temperaments*. With music commissioned from Paul Hindemith and costumes and scenery by Kurt Seligmann, it was widely hailed as the most exciting Balanchine ballet yet. Both the music and the dance created variations on a theme based upon the four humors of medieval folklore: "Melancholic," "Sanguinic," "Phlegmatic," and "Choleric." The original cast of *The Four Temperaments* included Beatrice Tompkins, José Martinez, Lew Christensen, Francisco Moncion, William Dollar, Mary Ellen Moylan, Todd Bolender, and Tanaquil LeClerq.

Eloquent dance critic Edwin Denby, writing in the December, 1946, issue of *Dance News*, proclaimed that "no choreography was ever more serious, more vigorous, more wide in scope or penetrating in imagination." He did, however, question the ballet's gaudy costumes. Because they obscured the dance, the somewhat notorious outfits were later rejected in favor of black-and-white practice clothes—a look that would soon become a Balanchine trademark.

Ballet Society's next programs were presented at the Hunter College Playhouse, the Ziegfeld Theater, and the City Center of Music and Drama. The group continued to present innovative choreography by Balanchine, younger company dancers, and guest artists. The New York audience, though not enormous, was growing. Primarily composed of balletomanes and dilettantes willing to pay subscription prices, it was repeatedly excited by the premieres of Balanchine's "neoclassical" ballet masterpieces.

For his part, Kirstein startled the public and the press with the idea that sufficient tickets could be sold on a subscription basis rather than individually or at the door. (He even eliminated the sacred press passes; publications had to subscribe to obtain seats for their writers.) Critical acclaim was so overwhelming that the general public clamored to be invited. Kirstein and Balanchine stood firm with their original idea, and subscription sales rose. Ballet Society was a success.

An avid lover of ballet and a prolific writer on art and dance, Kirstein had brought

Balanchine to the United States. Kirstein dreamt of the establishment of a truly "American" ballet, on par with the companies of Europe and Russia and utilizing American-born and American-trained dancers. In 1933, he saw Balanchine's *Les Ballets* performed in London, and he recognized that this was the choreographer who could make his dream possible. Balanchine had choreographed for Sergei Diaghilev's Ballets Russes, and he was at loose ends following the great impresario's death. Kirstein was able to lure Balanchine away from Europe in order to direct a new School of American Ballet. This school would be the training ground for the dancers in Balanchine's subsequent choreography.

Kirstein's and Balanchine's first attempt at beginning a company was in 1934 with the American Ballet, a performing group of students from the school. Although it was the resident ballet company at the Metropolitan Opera House from 1935 to 1938, this group received mixed reviews and had little financial success. Balanchine's innovations exasperated the public, then accustomed to classical ballet technique and subject matter. While he continued to run the school, Balanchine became better known as a choreographer for the René Blum-Sergei Denham and W. de Basil Ballet Russe companies and for Broadway musicals and Hollywood films.

In 1936, Kirstein organized another nationally oriented company, the Ballet Caravan. Balanchine's American Ballet dancers joined Kirstein's group as "American Ballet Caravan" on a tour to South America, but the company was afterward disbanded, its funds depleted. Following service in World War II, Kirstein joined Balanchine in the founding of Ballet Society on the strength of their earlier experiences and undaunted hopes for a new era of innovation in ballet. At this point, their timing and offerings were right. So effective was Ballet Society that the group evolved into an international leader among dance companies: the New York City Ballet.

Impact of Event

The evolution from an exclusive members-only club to a popular civic organization occurred over a two-year span. During that period, Balanchine refined his modern approach to ballet choreography. Kirstein searched in vain for a permanent home for the group and wondered what should be done with all the costumes and sets that had been constructed for one or two performances and then packed away. Ballet Society's popularity mounted, and its founders waited for a benefactor to appear.

While it had a difficult time delivering on all membership promises (particularly the phonograph records), Ballet Society delighted audiences with other artistic endeavors. Gian Carlo Menotti produced his operas *The Medium* (1946), a tragedy, and *The Telephone* (1946), a farce, with the company dancers. These performances were so successful that a run on Broadway followed. Dancer John Taras premiered his *Minotaur* (1947) on the third Ballet Society program; other young choreographers were given chances to experiment as well. Modern dance was also represented in the Ballet Society repertoire; in 1947, Merce Cunningham's first ballet, *The Seasons*, was offered. This piece, with music by John Cage and decor by Isamu Noguchi, marked an auspicious beginning for Cunningham, a young student of Martha Graham.

Works by Balanchine, though, were what audiences most wanted to see. His style was distinctly different from that of earlier choreographers such as Michel Fokine and from contemporaries such as Léonide Massine. Typically emphasizing structure and form over fantasy story or allegory, Balanchine perfected the "plotless" ballet (often referred to as "modern" or "abstract"). He changed the image of the female dancer, in particular, from fragile swan to vital athlete. He captured the daring and playful American spirit in the movements he designed, in essence redefining the classical dancer. Under Balanchine's direction, the craft of choreography—the arrangement of human motion through space—became art rivaling Michelangelo's sculptures and Igor Stravinsky's compositions.

In addition to *The Four Temperaments*, Balanchine created significant works for Ballet Society that remained in the repertory of the New York City Ballet. Among them were *Divertimento* (January, 1947), which allowed the male dancers to show off their skills. Wolfgang Amadeus Mozart's musical counterpoint was skillfully echoed in the choreography of *Symphonie concertante* (November, 1947), which employed more than twenty female dancers and one male. *Symphony in C* (music by Georges Bizet) was hailed as brilliant when it premiered in New York in March, 1948 (it was first created for the Paris Opera in 1947). *Dance News* editor Anatole Chujoy wrote, "If there ever was any doubt that Balanchine was the greatest choreographer of our time, this doubt was dispelled when the curtain came down on his *Symphony in C*."

The premiere of *Orpheus* in April, 1948, signaled a turning point for Ballet Society. Balanchine collaborated meticulously with Noguchi on the decor and with Stravinsky on the music. This powerful ballet treated the mythical tale as a universal theme, weaving a story through the intricate movement to a greater degree than the choreographer's "plotless" ballets. Dancer Maria Tallchief as Eurydice created a furor with her extraordinary technique; other dancers such as Nicholas Magallanes (Orpheus), Beatrice Tompkins, Francisco Moncion, and Tanaquil LeClerq demonstrated the masterful results of Balanchine's coaching. (Eighteen-year-old LeClerq was the first ballerina to be completely a product of the School of American Ballet.)

Public curiosity leading up to *Orpheus* (in the wake of *Symphony in C*'s tremendous success) was so great that Kirstein and Balanchine decided to test Ballet Society's broader appeal. Company funds (typically coming from Kirstein's pockets) were almost exhausted. The organization could not continue to cover its expenses with only four performances a year, the dancers could not survive without a more consistent income, and the repertory was in danger of getting lost after one or two showings. They decided to see if Ballet Society had a future playing longer seasons for the general public. The already scheduled subscriber performance on April 28 occurred as planned, but the evening's program was repeated the following three nights for general admission.

The prestige surrounding these well-received performances attracted the attention of many people, including City Center Chairman Morton Baum. Ballet Society business manager Frances Hawkins had met Baum while leasing the theater for several of the company's previous engagements. In Baum, she recognized a possible solution to the company's imminent fiscal and identity crisis. Although Kirstein was tired of false hopes from would-be sponsors, he went with Hawkins to the City Center office, where Baum made him a decidedly unexpected offer. Ballet Society was invited to take up residence at the City Center and become officially the New York City Ballet. Speechless, Kirstein replied, "If you do that for us I will give you in three years the finest ballet company in America."

The New York City Ballet's opening night in their new City Center home was on October 11, 1948. *Orpheus* was among the ballets featured on that program. While the company was originally engaged as an affiliate of the New York City Opera, three months after its premiere it performed as an independent component of City Center. The company had a permanent home, many of its expenses were supported, and its dancers could count on regular employment. Since then, it has deservedly earned and maintained its reputation as one of the finest ballet companies in the world.

Kirstein stood true to his promise, and in so doing realized his dream of creating an American ballet. While Ballet Society was a private, membership-only venture, the New York City Ballet, with its subsidized ticket prices, became known as the most publicly accessible dance company in the United States. As he trained some of the most technically proficient dancers in history, Balanchine continued to choreograph incredibly diverse and innovative ballets. Unlike other dance companies that emphasized the popular appeal of its stars, the New York City Ballet (like Ballet Society), continued to showcase the choreography itself. Together, Kirstein's ambitious vision and Balanchine's artistic brilliance brought ballet to the forefront of the arts.

Bibliography

Buckle, Richard. *George Balanchine: Ballet Master.* New York: Random House, 1988. Written by a prominent London dance critic, this biography is filled with detail, objective information, and tender remembrances. Chapters entitled "New Beginnings" and "In Search of a Formula" deal specifically with Ballet Society and the New York City Ballet.

Chujoy, Anatole. *The New York City Ballet.* New York: Alfred A. Knopf, 1953. The author, a *Dance News* editor, was witness to the birth and growth of the nation's preeminent dance company. Contains several detailed chapters devoted to Ballet Society. Appendix features a chronological list of repertory and dancers.

Denby, Edwin. *Looking at the Dance.* New York: Horizon Press, 1968. This collection of criticism by one of the most eloquent dance writers in twentieth century America covers much of the history of Ballet Society. Reviews of company choreography as well as commentary about ballet's evolution are offered.

Kirstein, Lincoln. *Thirty Years: Lincoln Kirstein's The New York City Ballet.* New York: Alfred A. Knopf, 1978. The author and founder of Ballet Society provides an interesting account of the history of the New York City Ballet. His original diary entries are offered and then expanded; the book does not attempt to provide a complete record of events but is a significant and accurate volume of memoirs. Appendix includes chronological listing of repertory and dancers.

McDonagh, Don. *George Balanchine.* Boston: Twayne, 1983. A very readable biography that includes both fact and analysis. The ballets performed during Ballet Society's existence are described in detail, as are elements of the choreographer's artistic process. Includes a chronology of Balanchine's life and work and a selective repertoire list.

Reynolds, Nancy. *Repertory in Review: Forty Years of the New York City Ballet.* New York: Dial Press, 1977. Contains introduction by Lincoln Kirstein and essays by Walter Sorell on Balanchine and Nancy Goldner on the School of American Ballet. This volume is the most exhaustive compilation of the ballet company's extensive repertoire. All ballets from 1935 to 1976 are described in detail, along with quotes from the critics; casts, costumes, music, and location are also given. A valuable source of information.

Alecia C. Townsend

Cross-References

Diaghilev's Ballets Russes Astounds Paris (1909), p. 241; *The Rite of Spring* Stuns Audiences (1913), p. 373; Balanchine's *Serenade* Inaugurates American Ballet (1934), p. 974; The Ballet Russe de Monte Carlo Finds New Leadership (1938), p. 1088; *Amahl and the Night Visitors* Premieres on American Television (1951), p. 1536.

THE HOLLYWOOD STUDIO SYSTEM IS TRANSFORMED

Category of event: Motion pictures
Time: 1946-1960
Locale: Hollywood, California, and Washington, D.C.

During the late 1940's and early 1950's, the American film industry was transformed from an all-powerful studio system to a collection of independent producers

Principal personages:
> SPYROS SKOURAS (1893-1971), the head of Twentieth Century-Fox who pioneered CinemaScope
> HOWARD HUGHES (1905-1976), the owner of the Radio-Keith-Orpheum studio
> BARNEY BALABAN (1887-1971), the head of Paramount Pictures who agreed to sell the company's theaters and thus initiate the breakup of the studio system
> HERBERT KALMUS (1881-1963), the inventor of Technicolor who pioneered color films

Summary of Event

During the 1930's and 1940's, eight major studios ruled Hollywood film production, distributing their films throughout the world and even owning the theaters in which most Americans saw their favorite stars on screen. In the decade after World War II, the Hollywood studio system was transformed into a system of independent filmmakers allied with an industry of television series producers. The Hollywood studios did not go away, but their basic functions were altered.

Weekly attendance in movie theaters in the United States crested in 1946, then began to fall steadily to half of what it had been. The cause of this decline generally is believed to be television, but this blame is falsely placed, for it ignores the fact that in most parts of the United States television signals did not become available until long after the decline in moviegoing was well under way. In the late 1940's and early 1950's, only about one-third of the nation had television sets. This was precisely when millions of Americans stopped going to the movies.

More fundamental causes came into play. Millions of returning veterans looked for an ideal life, a new American Dream, taking the money they had saved during the war and spending it on new cars and other big-ticket items that had been unavailable during the war. What postwar Americans wanted most were new homes in the suburbs, free from city congestion and noises, close to good schools. Americans moved in record waves to new suburban subdivisions. Home ownership in the first five years after World War II increased by 50 percent, then by another 50 percent during the following five years.

There were other distractions. Americans filled these new homes with children in record numbers. The birthrate increased to unprecedented levels. Women married at younger ages and had more children. Better-educated people had larger families than in the past. The typical filmgoer of the past (a better-educated, richer, middle-class citizen) was precisely the member of the demographic cohort that most embraced the surburban ideal, including a substantial mortgage and a family with four or five children.

These two factors, suburbanization and the baby boom, dampened moviegoing and would have done so even without the coming of television. The waves of suburbanization took moviegoers far away from downtown movie palaces. Poor public transportation from the suburbs made it difficult to journey downtown routinely. In any case, families had fled the city and its attractions for a new world of Little League and backyard barbecues.

Hollywood had other problems that aggravated the situation. At precisely the same time that suburbanization and the baby boom were fundamentally altering the way Americans lived, the United States Supreme Court forced the Hollywood studios to sell their theaters. An antitrust suit against the eight major studios had begun in July, 1938. After numerous decisions and appeals, the United States Supreme Court ruled in 1949 that the major film studios would have to sell their chains of movie theaters. The Court stated that ownership of both film production facilities and theaters constituted restraint of trade. The Court's decision, however, was by that time almost irrelevant, as declining audiences already were forcing an end to the large theater chains as well as to the huge studios. Howard Hughes had just purchased Radio-Keith-Orpheum (RKO) and embraced the forced sale of theaters. He wanted the cash. Barney Balaban, the chief executive officer of Paramount, also went along; he wanted the proceeds for investment in television. Both these powerful businessmen reasoned that selling theaters might in the long run prove beneficial.

The very basis of film technology changed as well. Hollywood looked to new film technologies to tempt patrons back to the theaters. First the studios embraced color. The best-known name in that field was Technicolor, first used for *The Gulf Between* (1917). Developed by Herbert Kalmus, Technicolor became known through the popularity of such spectacles as *Gone with the Wind* (1939). Through the 1940's, Technicolor was limited to a select group of feature films, principally historical epics and lavish musicals. In 1950, Technicolor lost its legal monopoly. During the early 1950's, giant Eastman Kodak surged into the market.

Suddenly it became inexpensive to shoot color features, and gradually through the 1950's more and more films would be made in color. "New" color systems proliferated. For example, Trucolor was developed by Consolidated Film Laboratories for Republic Pictures, both owned and controlled by Herbert J. Yates. Trucolor never was able to become the dominant system, but its attempted innovation did show that the universal use of color was inevitable.

Hollywood went one step further and made its films "bigger" and thus hopefully even better. In 1952, Cinerama initiated wide-screen movies by melding images from three synchronized projectors. At first business was brisk; *This Is Cinerama* (1952), a travelogue-type film, grossed more than twenty million dollars. The significant additional costs (three full-time projectionists, a new screen, and more) doomed Cinerama.

Other entrepreneurs tried three-dimensional (3-D) films. The process for creating three-dimensional effects had been around since the 1920's, so few were surprised when *Bwana Devil*, a crude African adventure story starring Robert Stack, came out in November of 1952. During 1953 and into 1954, 3-D was hailed as the savior of the American film industry. Warner Bros. issued what was to remain the most successful of the 3-D efforts, *House of Wax*, in April of 1953. By mid-1954, it had become clear that the added expense involved did not lead to greater box-office revenues.

The premiere of the most famous wide-screen process, CinemaScope, came on September 16, 1953. Twentieth Century-Fox's president, Spyros Skouras, praised this technology because it expanded the image while only requiring an anamorphic lens attached both to the camera and to the projector, thus requiring only a small investment. Fox's first film using the technology, *The Robe*, was a spectacular biblical tale costing four million dollars. Its success implied that Skouras had found the answer to bringing back the suburban audience.

The Robe so impressed audiences and other studios that by the final day of 1953 every major studio, except for Paramount with its rival VistaVision process, had jumped on the CinemaScope bandwagon. By November, 1954, it was reported that nearly half the existing theaters in the United States had facilities to show CinemaScope. In the long run, however, equipping theaters proved expensive and limited them to showing only CinemaScope films. Something different was needed. The full impact of the transformation of the studio system would not come until that technical solution was found.

Impact of Event

The technological solution to standardized wide-screen images in color came with the merging of two product offerings: Panavision lenses and Eastman Color film stock. Panavision was a small Hollywood company. Owner Robert Gottschalk had developed innovations that encompassed not only anamorphic attachments, so one could use CinemaScope, but nearly all other needed lens adjustments. By the late 1950's, Panavision attachments became the industry standard. Panavision provided a superior but standardized product for making and showing wide-screen images.

Eastman Color negative and color-print film stock had been introduced by the Rochester photographic equipment giant in 1950 to compete with Technicolor. Eastman Color was easier to handle and seemed to produce colors as vibrant as those of Technicolor. It was cheaper to use, so by the 1950's Eastman Color also had become an industry standard.

Technological concerns settled, the American film industry struggled to deal with suburbanization and the increasingly popular home entertainment medium of television. During the early 1950's, a wave of auto-oriented theaters, or drive-ins, offered a pleasant open space where parked cars filled with families watched triple features on a massive screen. In 1960, the number of drive-ins in the United States crested at five thousand. The peak moviegoing season shifted to summer from fall and winter. The breakup of the theater market caused by the Paramount case meant that the drive-in market was open to independent exhibitors.

Film studios had to find a way to deal with television. At first, the major studios ignored the new medium. Minor studios such as Monogram and Republic jumped in and began producing for television, at first offering Westerns (Gene Autry and Roy Rogers from Republic, for example) and thrill-a-minute serials. Younger television viewers loved these action adventures, but crude production values served to remind longtime film fans of the extraordinary number of treasures still resting comfortably in the vaults of Metro-Goldwyn-Mayer (MGM), Paramount, Twentieth Century-Fox, and Warner Bros.

Billionaire Howard Hughes, then owner of RKO, by late 1953 again was in need of cash. Few were surprised when, in 1954, Hughes agreed to sell RKO's film library to General Tire and Rubber for twenty-five million dollars. General Tire wanted the RKO titles to present on its independent New York television station.

RKO's profit figure on the deal impressed even the most recalcitrant movie moguls. Within the space of the following twenty-four months, all the remaining major companies released their pre-1948 titles to television. Pre-1948 titles were chosen because they were free from paying out residuals to performer and craft unions; post-1948 titles were not. For the first time in the history of film, a national audience was able to confront, at its leisure, a broad cross-section of the best and worst of Hollywood talkies. The concomitant infusion of cash came precisely at a time when Hollywood needed money to support innovation of wide-screen film spectacles.

The television networks, however, wanted to show post-1948 Hollywood features in prime time. This required agreements from the Hollywood craft unions. In a precedent-setting action, the Screen Actors Guild, led by its president, Ronald Reagan, went on strike and won guaranteed residuals for televised airings of post-1948 films. Soon thereafter the National Broadcasting Company (NBC) premiered "Saturday Night at the Movies." Ratings were high, and soon all three television networks were awash with feature films playing in prime time. A zenith was achieved in 1968, when Alfred Hitchcock's *The Birds* (1963) was watched by more than a third of all Americans.

The studios survived, but no longer were there a Big Five and Little Three. The remaining seven major studios (Hughes took RKO out of the game) were equal, distributing films and finding independent producers to make the films. All expanded into television production.

United Artists led the way, showing that a new studio form could succeed by distributing independently made films. United Artists had entered the 1950's so awash with red ink that founders Charlie Chaplin and Mary Pickford agreed to sell. Two New York entertainment lawyers, Arthur Krim and Robert Benjamin, took charge in February, 1951. The new United Artists, within its first year, picked up *High Noon* (1952) and John Huston's *The African Queen* (1951). Krim and Benjamin sought out and attracted the work of such stars as Burt Lancaster, Gregory Peck, and Robert Mitchum and directors such as Billy Wilder, John Sturges, Otto Preminger, William Wyler, and Joseph Mankiewicz.

The audiences for these films differed from those of the "Golden Age" of Hollywood. People over the age of thirty now stayed at home; teens and young adults became the loyal core audience for films shown in theaters. For Hollywood, the good news was that this core audience of young, well-educated people seemed willing to pay more to go out to the movies. It was not until 1956 that the film industry began to exploit this new market. The success of *Rock Around the Clock* (1956) testified that there was money to be made from this new audience.

To recapture filmgoers, Hollywood loosened censorship standards. The strict code of censorship so powerfully self-enforced during the 1930's and 1940's broke down. On May 26, 1952, the United States Supreme Court announced its decision in the case officially known as *Burstyn v. Wilson* and declared that motion pictures should be treated as a significant medium for the communication of ideas. This case led to the eventual end of the Hays Code in 1966. United Artists defied the Hays Code with *The Moon Is Blue* (1955) and *The Man with the Golden Arm* (1955). The first featured a female character flaunting her virginity; the second openly showed drug abuse. A rating system implemented in 1968 classified films by suitability for young audiences rather than prohibiting material that might be unsuitable.

In the end, the Hollywood studios never fully relinquished their core economic power. The major studios continued to be the route to worldwide distribution, thus potentially capturing the largest profits. The major studios still had most of the best films. Thus Hollywood was not broken by the Paramount decision, or by television or suburbanization. Smaller independent companies, however, found niches in the new order that arose. These companies created a wider range of offerings and gave newcomers a chance to enter the film industry.

Bibliography

Balio, Tino, ed. *The American Film Industry.* Rev. ed. Madison: University of Wisconsin Press, 1985. A collection of articles about the history of the American film industry. This should be read in conjunction with Kindem's *The American Movie Industry.* Useful bibliography.

Gomery, Douglas. *The Hollywood Studio System.* New York: St. Martin's Press, 1985. Book-length history of the studio system, with profiles of each studio plus analysis of the gestation and transformation of the system. Useful bibliography. Aimed at a general audience.

——————. *Shared Pleasures.* Madison: University of Wisconsin Press, 1992. A history of how Americans watched films, from the nickelodeon to the videocassette recorder. Covers in detail the changing nature of the audiences for films in the United States during the late 1940's and early 1950's.

Kindem, Gorham, ed. *The American Movie Industry.* Carbondale: Southern Illinois University Press, 1982. A collection of articles about the history of the American film industry. Should be read in conjunction with Balio's *The American Film Industry.* Contains an essential bibliography.

Mast, Gerald, ed. *The Movies in Our Midst.* Chicago: University of Chicago Press, 1982. A collection of documents and essays about the changing social impact of the American film. Covers all phases of the impact of the changing studio system. Massive bibliography.

Douglas Gomery

Cross-References

Sound Technology Revolutionizes the Motion-Picture Industry (1928), p. 761; The First Academy Awards Honor Film Achievement (1929), p. 799; Hollywood Enters Its Golden Age (1930's), p. 822; *Gone with the Wind* Premieres (1939), p. 1154; Blacklisting Seriously Depletes Hollywood's Talent Pool (1947), p. 1346.

WESTERNS DOMINATE POSTWAR AMERICAN FILM

Category of event: Motion pictures
Time: 1946-1962
Locale: The United States

The classic Western films produced during the postwar era reflected major concerns of the time while revealing significant American cultural values

Principal personages:

JOHN FORD (SEAN ALOYSIUS O'FEENEY, 1895-1973), a filmmaker whose career spanned half a century and whose work created and defined the form of the Western

HOWARD HAWKS (1896-1977), a tough-minded, efficiently professional filmmaker who placed stoic, isolated protagonists in his Westerns

ANTHONY MANN (EMIL ANTON BUNDMANN, 1906-1967), a less prominent but still important filmmaker whose work in the 1950's offered a darker, firmly moralistic perspective on the West

JOHN WAYNE (MARION MICHAEL MORRISON, 1907-1979), the dominant actor of American Western films, whose presentation of character became an archetype for the American action hero

Summary of Event

From the earliest days of the American film industry, the Western has been an important genre. In his first year as a director in 1917, John Ford, the great master of the classic Western, directed silents titled *Cheyenne's Pal* and *Straight Shooting*, among other films. After some initial enthusiasm, the genre began to decline during the Depression and was largely ignored during World War II. Then, in the late 1940's, a Western revival began.

Aside from the Western's capacity for rendering and examining essential elements in American cultural life, there were several crucial contributing factors in this resurgence. First, the uncertainty, angst, and anomie generated by the Cold War; the revelation of an almost unfathomable evil spawned by the Nazis; and the uneasiness caused by the threat of nuclear destruction, international tension, and internal paranoia left many people groping for some basic values in the fabric of an older, more tradition-bound time in American history. In addition, the rise of urban centers on the Pacific shore marked the closing of the frontier and thrust the vision of a frontier into the mythic plane of artistic imagination. Finally, technological advances provided an opportunity for a wide-screen transportation into a realm of adventure where justice often triumphed after a thrilling and frequently deadly struggle.

None of these conditions would have been sufficient for a revival of Westerns without the presence of men like John Ford. Aside from his skill as a filmmaker, his vision of a stable community of interesting, eccentric, and basically decent people fit perfectly the Western mold of an isolated settlement surrounded by hostile forces. His belief in the necessity of a strong man to lead the citizenry with courage, modesty, and principle corresponded to the Western ideal. Other directors modified or challenged some of Ford's ideas, but they knew how important his work was. No one escaped his influence, either as a positive force or as an ideological or stylistic presence to be reckoned with.

The era of the classic Western begins with Ford's first postwar film, *My Darling Clementine* (1946), in which Wyatt Earp (Henry Fonda), much like many soldiers returning from combat, marries and begins a family following his defeat of the evil Clanton gang. The end of the era is marked by *The Man Who Shot Liberty Valance* (1962), in which, in a retrospective and rueful but admiring look at the entire epoch of Western history, Ford depicts the open West of Tom Doniphon (John Wayne) giving way to the Eastern ideas (schools, rules, fences, roads, and government) of the greenhorn lawyer Rance Stoddard (Jimmy Stewart).

Between these two films, Ford made his noted cavalry trilogy (*Fort Apache*, 1948; *She Wore a Yellow Ribbon*, 1949; and *Rio Grande*, 1950), which describes and celebrates service to one's country as valorous and satisfying for a man while showing the military as a kind of mobile utopian society. In the same year that he completed the trilogy, he also made *Wagonmaster*, in which two young, directionless cowhands join a Mormon wagon train and become involved in the responsibilities of the group. Then, after a period of five years in which his vision of the West perceptively darkened, Ford made *The Searchers* (1956), a highly acclaimed, complex psychological adventure story in which Ethan Edwards (John Wayne) is involved in a relentless, obsessive pursuit of the Indians who have abducted his niece. Ford returned to the mode of the cavalry Western with *The Horse Soldiers* (1959), transposing the setting to the Civil War in a return to the style of his earlier, more authoritative depictions of the necessity of resisting evil. He concluded his contribution to the classic Western with two films that anticipated the elegiac, almost tragic mood of *The Man Who Shot Liberty Valance. Sergeant Rutledge* (1960) was a tentative consideration of the trials of the African-American Westerner, while *Two Rode Together* (1961) contrasted Jim Gary's (Richard Widmark) idealistic sense of moral action with Guthrie McCabe's (Jimmy Stewart) somewhat more worldly and self-protective position.

Even during his most pessimistic moments, Ford rarely moved into the almost *film noir* realm of Anthony Mann's West. The prolific Mann cast Jimmy Stewart against his boyish image in five Westerns made consecutively, *Winchester '73* (1950), *Bend of the River* (1952), *The Naked Spur* (1953), *The Far Country* (1955), and *The Man from Laramie* (1955), in which the protagonist is presented as a man possessed of obsessions, self-doubt, and emotional eccentricity. The reluctant hero eventually is moved to correct human violence against a natural moral order, but his decision always is difficult and his actions rarely completely conclusive. On the other hand, while Howard Hawks conceived of a Western hero who was much more isolated than Stewart in Mann's films, he also suggested in *Red River* (1948), *The Big Sky* (1952), and *Rio Bravo* (1959) that a certain completeness and mature dignity was possible.

The comic element in his work extends and humanizes the protagonist.

No other director of the era brought the cinematic competence of Ford, Mann, and Hawks to more than a few films, although Budd Boetticher developed a distinct style and outlook in a group of lesser-known B-films. Many directors whose primary achievements were in other genres made noteworthy Westerns during the period. Among the most prominent were George Stevens, perhaps best known for his serious social dramas, who made *Shane* in 1953; Fred Zinnemann, a versatile and politically astute director who made *High Noon* in 1952; William Wyler, whose work ranged from the epic *Ben Hur* (1959) to the feathery *Roman Holiday* (1953), who made *The Big Country* in 1958; Arthur Penn, who went on to make the revisionist *Little Big Man* (1970) but began his career with *The Left-Handed Gun* in 1958; and Samuel Fuller, an inventive maverick with a singular style who ventured twice into Western territory with *I Shot Jesse James* (1949) and the idiosyncratic but prophetic *Forty Guns* (1957). In a demonstration of the relevance and flexibility of the genre, lesser-known directors also found the Western congenial ground for some of their better work. Among them are Delmer Davis with *3:10 to Yuma* (1957), Henry King with *The Gunfighter* (1950), and Robert Aldrich with *Apache* (1954) and *Vera Cruz* (1954). John Sturges united serious character study with superb action sequences in *Bad Day at Black Rock* (1955), *Gunfight at the O.K. Corral* (1957), and his worthy adaptation of Akira Kurosawa's masterpiece *The Seven Samurai* (1954) rendered as *The Magnificent Seven* (1960).

Impact of Event

One of the primary reasons that the classic Western has had such an impressive impact on American cultural life is that the original West identified America as it existed in the minds of Europeans. That West was a dream of space, freedom, wilderness, and plenty, represented in earlier times by William Shakespeare's appeal to a "brave, new world" and in the early twentieth century by F. Scott Fitzgerald's typically lyric evocation of the promise of "a fresh, green breast of the new world," as he put it on the last page of *The Great Gatsby* (1925). At its most inviting, the myth of the West is the equivalent of the myth of America itself, and from the beginning, the Western film has reflected the aspirations of people attempting to build a new society on a huge, open continent and has expressed the desires of people determined to escape the influence of "kings and priests," the powermongers Thomas Jefferson warned against.

During the 1950's, Western films gave this vision its most vivid and complete expression; the devastating disappointments of the late 1960's were still a part of an unforeseen future. In its most optimistic form, *Shane* offered Alan Ladd riding out of a pure mountain mist, dressed in golden deerskin perfectly tailored to his lithe and powerful physique, arriving in time to rescue the decent, humble farmers from the corporate villainy of the corrupt cattle barons. Before killing the reptilian Wilson (Jack Palance), Shane is a perfect brother to Van Heflin, ideal lover for Jean Arthur, and athlete/hero for Brandon deWilde. Their life on the farm appeals to him, but like most Westerners, he is defined ultimately by the necessary use of his gun, and he knows that he cannot settle down. The resonance in the story enabled Clint Eastwood to repeat its basic structure in *Pale Rider* (1985) without much alteration.

Shane and the earlier Ford films were made with such skill and conviction that their somewhat unrealistic conceptions of frontier life created a fantasy West that overwhelmed historical fact. An audience ready to accept the legendary configuration matched the filmmakers' conception, and even later Westerns of the 1960's such as Sam Peckinpah's *The Wild Bunch* (1969), which undercut many of Ford's (and Stevens') assumptions, still had to respond to such archetypal motifs as the grandeur of the landscape and the personal honor of the heroic participants.

In *Shane*, one of the conflicts is between North and South, with Wilson the gunfighter described as a "Yankee" and Shane, like many cowboys, as a displaced Southerner seeking a new start after the Civil War. The ridiculous and inaccurate idea of the "showdown" on Main Street, with its bizarre chivalric concept of not drawing first, stems from the idea of honor. In a larger sense, one of the most enduring aspects of the Western involves a man's (heroes were almost exclusively male) attempt to define himself and live by a code he has developed and must follow to maintain personal integrity.

High Noon, for example, pitted a lawman (Gary Cooper) against an outside menace to his town, in which people were too complacent or frightened to assist him. The film has been perceived as allegory to Communism and McCarthyist red-baiting. Carl Foreman, the blacklisted writer of the screenplay, maintained that it was written as just such an allegory. At the core of the conflict, the sheriff must balance his individual responsibilities with his social obligations. John Wayne disliked the film because he thought it betrayed the "frontier spirit." The theme of a man "torn 'twixt love and duty" suffering the internal debate of a troubled conscience was also a part of Mann's films with Stewart and was epitomized by Peckinpah's *Ride the High Country* (1962), another film from the conclusion of the Western era, ending that era on a note of nostalgia as the Western code was recalled one last time by two old friends. The value of the code also was stressed by Henry King in his presentation in *The Bravados* (1958) of an aging gunfighter, Jimmy Ringo (Gregory Peck), who has outgrown his wild days but cannot find an escape from the destiny he has previously created. In each case, a hero must sacrifice personal safety in order to act properly.

Similarly, somewhat offbeat films such as Arthur Penn's *The Left-Handed Gun*, which told the story of Billy the Kid (Paul Newman) from an almost existentialist perspective; Samuel Fuller's *Forty Guns*, which anticipated television's *The Big Valley* by placing Barbara Stanwyck at the head of a line of riders; or Sturges' *Bad Day at Black Rock*, which put a handicapped stranger (Spencer Tracy) amid the stupid bigotry of a small town, depended upon the implicit acknowledgment by the filmmaker and audience of a series of shared values and moral principles. Being out of step with a limited society did not make the protagonist unsympathetic but instead made him (or her) a version of the antihero whose rejection by a flawed social order contributed to an admirable posture of singular strength. Even Howard Hawks, who shared Wayne's dislike for *High Noon*, used humor when the conventions of the Old West began to seem strained for a modern audience, gently undercutting the most rigid formulations as well as casting for contrast by pairing the sensitive, introspective Montgomery Clift with John Wayne in *Red River* (1948) and teen idol Ricky Nelson with Wayne in *Rio Bravo* (1959).

Both its range of possibility and its potential for political parallels with the present were significant reasons for the predominance of the Western in the postwar era, but the paucity of other useful forms, with the exception of the *film noir*, was also a factor. The rise of the New Wave in Europe, the revisionism inevitable in the turmoil of the 1960's, and the maturing of American films were all aspects of changes after 1962 that took the focus away from Westerns.

Bibliography

Bogdanovich, Peter. *John Ford.* Berkeley: University of California Press, 1978. An affectionate and knowledgeable tribute by an accomplished filmmaker, combining anecdotes and factual material with interviews and analysis.

Fenin, George, and William K. Everson. *The Western.* New York: Grossman, 1973. A comprehensive history of the genre. Detailed and thorough, with intelligent commentary and many illustrations.

French, Philip. *Westerns.* New York: Viking Press, 1974. One of the first studies to consider the Western in a totally political and sociological perspective. French is a creative stylist, and his opinions are sometimes quite speculative, but the book is always interesting and engaging.

Kitses, Jim. *Horizons West.* Bloomington: University of Indiana Press, 1969. Intellectually provocative and lucidly explained, Kitses' theories tend toward rigid categorizations that are useful in developing an overview of the genre.

Lenihan, John. *Showdown: Confronting Modern America in the Western Film.* Chicago: University of Illinois Press, 1979. Contains a strong chapter on the 1950's as well as a list of Westerns from 1939 to 1978, a bibliographical guide to collections, and a lengthy bibliography.

Tusca, Jon. *The American West in Film.* Westport, Conn.: Greenwood Press, 1985. A very solid study, with critical and analytical commentary on films, plentiful inside data on directors, many interesting photographs, notes, an extensive bibliography, and an index with film dates.

Leon Lewis

Cross-References

Grey's *Riders of the Purple Sage* Launches the Western Genre (1912), p. 304; Ford Defines the Western in *Stagecoach* (1939), p. 1115; *Gunsmoke* Debuts, Launching a Popular Television Genre (1955), p. 1668; Seven of the Top Ten Television Series Are Westerns (1958), p. 1768; *Bonanza* Becomes an American Television Classic (1959), p. 1800; Leone Renovates the Western Genre (1964), p. 1984.

PARKER'S PLAYING EPITOMIZES BEBOP

Category of event: Music
Time: March 28, 1946
Locale: Los Angeles, California

Charlie Parker's first 1946 recording session for Dial Records produced some of the finest recordings of the bebop era

Principal personages:
CHARLES CHRISTOPHER "BIRD" PARKER (1920-1955), an alto saxophonist, composer, bandleader, and stylistic innovator
JOHN BIRKS "DIZZY" GILLESPIE (1917-1993), a trumpeter, composer, and bandleader
MILES DEWEY DAVIS (1926-1991), a trumpeter, composer, and bandleader

Summary of Event

There was nothing in the early life of Charlie Parker to indicate the remarkable achievements that were to come. Born in Kansas City, Kansas, he began his musical career by playing the baritone horn in high school. He gained some musical knowledge playing the horn, but he had another instrument in mind. When he was fifteen years old, he asked his mother to buy him an alto saxophone. Fortunately for the history of jazz, she did so. From then on, Parker neglected school to concentrate on playing music, but initially his efforts bore little fruit.

Parker was fortunate in being able to play professionally early on, and he gained valuable experience both on the bandstand and by asking questions of the more experienced musicians with whom he worked. After having played for only one year, he joined the band of Lawrence Keyes (bassist Gene Ramey later recalled that Parker was the worst player in the band), and later he played frequently with alto saxophonist Buster Smith, who became his mentor.

In 1937, Parker spent the summer playing with a band in the Ozarks. He spent all of his free time that summer practicing the saxophone and studying the records of the Count Basie band, a Kansas City mainstay. Lester Young (known as "Prez," or the "President"), the featured tenor saxophonist in the Basie band, was one of his favorite musicians, and he memorized all of Young's recorded solos. When Parker came back to Kansas City, he was a changed musician. He played with a new confidence, an improved technique, and a greater understanding of music than he had had only a few months earlier.

From that point on, Charlie Parker's musical ability increased rapidly and dramatically. He played in various bands, including that of Jay McShann, and traveled to Chicago and New York. All the while, he worked to increase his knowledge and understanding of music. His relentless desire to become a better musician stood him in good stead; he demonstrated in his playing a discipline that was lacking in his personal life. Like many musicians of his era, he fell victim at an early age to drug and alcohol abuse. This proclivity to indulge himself to excess ultimately contributed to his early death, but his fierce determination enabled him to achieve musical greatness.

In 1943, in New York, Parker joined the band of pianist Earl Hines. He met a number of other fine young musicians who were, like him, open to experimentation. These musicians, who included trumpeter Dizzy Gillespie, trombonist Benny Harris, and singer and bandleader Billy Eckstine, were tired of playing the same old music and wanted to find a new way to play. They, and other musicians, were experimenting with new harmonies, new rhythmic patterns, and new approaches of all kinds. Parker became particularly close to Gillespie, who was as restless an innovator as himself. In 1944, Gillespie, Parker, and a host of superb young musicians joined the newly formed Billy Eckstine band, which became a kind of incubator for the music that came to be called bebop (the word is derived from a rhythmic pattern that occurred frequently in the music).

Charlie Parker and Dizzy Gillespie, along with such musicians as pianists Thelonious Monk and Bud Powell, pianist and arranger Tadd Dameron, and drummer Kenny Clarke, revolutionized the world of jazz. The style that they developed featured harmonies more complex than those that had previously been heard in popular music, a tendency to rework standard songs to create entirely new musical entities, and a new approach to drumming that rejected the usual straightforward four-to-the-bar approach in favor of less regular accents. In addition, they often played this complex music at fast tempos that intimidated all but the very best players. Within a relatively short period, these players were lionized by many young musicians. They were also reviled by many others, particularly those who could neither understand nor play their music. Both attitudes served to increase the notoriety of the music.

After he left the Eckstine band, Parker played and recorded in New York in a small band with Dizzy Gillespie, after which he organized a band of his own that included the young trumpeter Miles Davis, who received the schooling of his life trying to keep up with Parker's blazing tempos. It was partly the experience of trying (and being unable) to play as cleanly and rapidly as the virtuosic Parker and Dizzy Gillespie that led Davis to develop the style that made him famous, which involved playing only what he considered the essential notes—the fewer the better.

Parker was involved in a number of recording sessions in 1946 that yielded classic jazz recordings, but one of the finest took place in Los Angeles, where Parker had traveled with Dizzy Gillespie's band. Although their music, which was quite popular in New York, was not well received in Los Angeles, and although Parker struggled financially there and had difficulty procuring the heroin and other drugs he required, he remained in Los Angeles when the rest of the Gillespie band returned to New York.

Parker's recording date for Dial Records, a company that had just been founded by Ross Russell, previously a record-shop owner, began inauspiciously. Pianist Joe Albany and bassist Red Callender left Parker's band just before the session. Replacements were found at the last minute, however, and the session, which took place on March 28, 1946, included Miles Davis on trumpet, Lucky Thompson on tenor sax, Dodo Marmarosa on piano, Arv Garrison on guitar, Vic McMillan on bass, and Roy Porter on drums.

The four pieces recorded for Dial on March 28 included two tunes by Parker, "Moose the Mooche" (named for Parker's local drug pusher) and "Yardbird Suite"; one by Dizzy Gillespie, "A Night in Tunisia"; and a piece by Benny Harris, "Ornithology," which was derived from a solo Parker had played with Jay McShann. Parker's playing throughout the session was superb, and all the recordings made that day are still studied and appreciated by jazz musicians and aficionados, but some of the recordings were truly remarkable. His four-bar solo on the first take of "A Night in Tunisia" is an astounding example of bebop playing that jazz critic Gary Giddins has called a "break of baroque complexity and numbing speed" and Ira Gitler has described as "a miniature history of modern jazz." Unfortunately, the rest of the band had difficulty with the piece, and the take was unsuccessful and incomplete. The solo was so remarkable, however, that Dial released it in incomplete form as "Famous Alto Break." The three recorded versions (there were four, but the second was lost) of "Ornithology" are also excellent, and the final (and fastest) version contains a solo by Parker that stands as one of the finest of his career. The two versions of "Yardbird Suite" are notable for the "cool" style of Parker's playing (as opposed to his frequent "fiery" style), and the three takes of "Moose the Mooche" contain some fine playing by Miles Davis on trumpet as well as excellent playing by Parker.

Parker signed over half of his proceeds from the session to Moose the Mooche to cover his drug debts; not long after, as a result of drug abuse, lack of money and acceptance, and stress, he wound up in a mental institution in Camarillo, California. After six months in the hospital, however, he emerged healthy and ready to play, and he went on to make many more classic recordings before his premature death in 1955.

Impact of Event

Parker's March 28, 1946, recording date for Dial Records was significant because it produced recordings that were among those considered essential by musicians, critics, and fans. The body of Parker's best work was important because his music, more than that of any other artist, defined bebop. The influence of bebop changed popular music in general, and jazz in particular, forever.

One indication of the influence of bebop is the fact that certain aspects of the music that shocked at least some listeners in the 1940's sound perfectly normal to modern ears. The innovations of Charlie Parker, Dizzy Gillespie, Thelonious Monk, and many others are now heard commonly not only in jazz but also in rock and pop music, film and television scores, and even in Muzak.

One of the most important influences of bebop had to do with its use of harmonic structures that were more complex than those that had been used in earlier jazz. It was common practice in jazz playing to use the harmonic structure of a recognizable song as a jumping-off point for improvisation, but a bebop player would play, when a particular chord was called for, notes that were different from those that a swing player would use. For example, when a swing player was improvising over a piece of music that called for a C dominant seventh (C7) chord, he or she would be likely to play the notes that are actually used in that chord: C, E, G, and B-flat. A bebop player, however, would be likely to play the notes D, F-sharp, and A over the same chord, actually playing a thirteenth chord instead of a seventh chord. This practice is known as playing the extensions of the chords that are specified. One does not need to have musical training to understand that playing completely different notes over a particular chord gives the music an entirely different sound. It was this sound that beboppers enjoyed and certain other players and listeners despised.

Another area in which bebop differed from earlier forms of jazz was that of drumming. During the swing era, it was common for drummers to play the bass drum on every beat, or every other beat, of the bar, which tended to give the music a predictable sound. Bebop drummers such as Kenny Clarke and Max Roach, however, began to keep time on the cymbals, reserving the bass drum for punctuation at irregular intervals. Using the bass drum in this way was called "dropping bombs." In addition, bebop drummers tended to play in a somewhat softer, more "legato" style that made it possible to use a wider range of sounds and play more flexibly. In contrast, swing drummers were required to adhere more rigidly to the specific role of keeping the beat. Although bebop drummers also kept the beat, they tended to imply it rather than to state it directly.

It was not only bebop drummers who took a new approach to rhythm. Saxophonists, trumpeters, trombonists, pianists, and bassists also experimented with new ways of accenting notes and phrases, and they sought to use in their solos and compositions rhythmic patterns that had not been commonly used up to that time. Parker was a master of rhythmic phrasing, as even the most cursory exposure to his music will demonstrate. Many well-known swing musicians had difficulty learning to "feel" this new rhythmic approach. One common practice in bebop (it had also been used by earlier musicians) was that of soloists playing in such a way that they seemed to be slightly behind (slower than) the rhythm section. This practice gave the music a particular kind of swing feeling that is difficult to define but easy to hear.

Another important contribution of beboppers was that they raised the standards of musicianship. Musicians such as Parker and Dizzy Gillespie were so technically skilled that they could play music that many established musicians simply could not play. One feature of bebop was that it was frequently played at incredibly fast tempos, which meant that in order to play the music effectively, a musician had to have achieved a high level of technical ability. It often happened that, when musicians who were not completely grounded in bop asked to sit in and play with beboppers, they found that they simply could not keep up. The high level of musicianship exhibited by the beboppers performed a tremendous service to jazz, because it gave young musicians an extremely high level of skill to which to aspire.

Parker's Dial Records recording session of March 28, 1946, provides a superb example of the features of bebop playing. In addition, it should be noted that Parker's playing here, as elsewhere, demonstrates an extremely unusual combination of tremendous creativity, passionate emotional intensity, and remarkable technical skill. Many musicians exhibit one or two of these qualities, but only the greatest possess all three. Charlie Parker was certainly one of the finest musicians in the history of jazz, and his music continues to inspire players and listeners.

Bibliography

Feather, Leonard. *Inside Jazz*. Reprint. New York: Da Capo Press, 1977. Originally published in 1949 as *Inside Bebop*, when bebop was at its peak, this is perhaps the finest book available on the subject. The book is divided into three parts. Part 1, "When," includes separate chapters on Charlie Parker and Dizzy Gillespie. Part 2, "How," which discusses bebop in musical terms, is essential reading for musically literate persons who are interested in bebop. Part 3, "Who," is a set of brief biographies of musicians who were involved in playing bebop or influenced those who did. An extremely important and influential book.

Giddins, Gary. *Celebrating Bird: The Triumph of Charlie Parker*. New York: Beech Tree Books, 1987. An excellent study of Parker's life and music by a fine contemporary jazz critic. Particularly interesting for its examination of Parker's early years, based on the reminiscences of Rebecca Parker Davis, Parker's first wife. Includes a selected bibliography and many fine black-and-white photographs.

Gitler, Ira. "Charlie Parker and the Alto and Baritone Saxophonists." In *Jazz Masters of the Forties*. New York: Collier, 1974. This chapter provides a relatively brief but surprisingly comprehensive study of Parker's life, music, and influence. This would be an excellent place to begin a study of Parker. The rest of the book examines other bebop innovators, such as Dizzy Gillespie and Kenny Clarke.

Koch, Lawrence O. *Yardbird Suite: A Compendium of the Music and Life of Charlie Parker*. Bowling Green, Ohio: Bowling Green State University Popular Press, 1988. This fine volume focuses on Parker's music, analyzing his recordings session by session. Musically knowledgeable individuals will find it particularly useful, but it can be read profitably by those who do not have a strong background in music. Includes an "analysis section" that is particularly useful. Also includes numerical and alphabetical listings of Parker's recordings. Highly recommended.

Reisner, Robert George. *Bird: The Legend of Charlie Parker*. Reprint. New York: Da Capo Press, 1977. A sourcebook made up of reminiscences about Parker by those who knew him: musicians, friends, and relatives. The stories, which are often fascinating, show many of the aspects of the personality of this complex man. Includes a chronological chart of Parker's life and a useful discography.

Russell, Ross. *Bird Lives! The High Life and Hard Times of Charlie (Yardbird) Parker*. New York: Charterhouse, 1973. This fascinating and informative book was written by the owner of Dial Records, who knew Parker well. This is a useful source, although it should not be viewed as accurate in every detail. Russell was involved in many of the events described in his book, and he has been accused by some writers of altering the truth for dramatic effect. Best used in combination with other sources. Includes an index and a discography.

Shawn Woodyard

Cross-References

Billie Holiday Begins Her Recording Career (1933), p. 930; Goodman Begins His *Let's Dance* Broadcasts (1934), p. 968; Davis' *Birth of the Cool* Recordings Spawn 1950's Cool Jazz (1949), p. 1438; The First Newport Jazz Festival Is Held (1954), p. 1617; Davis' *Bitches Brew* Vitalizes Jazz-Rock Fusion (1969), p. 2153.

THE BIKINI SWIMSUIT IS INTRODUCED

Category of event: Fashion and design
Time: July 5, 1946
Locale: Paris, France

The most meager bathing suit yet, the bikini, was exhibited for the first time by a French fashion model at a Parisian poolside fashion show, but the European fashion would not be popular on American beaches for at least a decade

Principal personages:
　LOUIS RÉARD (1897-1984), a French mechanical engineer and swimsuit designer who dubbed the diminutive swimsuit the "bikini"
　JACQUES HEIM (1899-1967), a French couturier who designed a tiny two-piece swimsuit to be sold in his beach shop in Cannes
　MICHELINE BERNARDINI, a French striptease artist hired to model the first bikini

Summary of Event

Separately, but nearly simultaneously, two daring French fashion designers released the twentieth century version of the tiny two-piece bathing suit that would become known as the bikini. During the summer of 1946, Jacques Heim, a couturier, designed a style of swimwear to be sold in his beach shop in Cannes. He called his new style the "Atome" because of its minuscule size and advertised it with a skywriting plane that spelled out his slogan "Atome—the world's smallest bathing suit" in the sky over the crowded beaches in the south of France. Although this daring new beach attire began as a very localized phenomenon, it was not destined to remain that way for long.

Just three weeks later, Louis Réard, a mechanical engineer turned swimwear designer, hired his own skywriting aircraft in order to advertise his newest creation to sun worshipers basking along the same stretch of French Riviera. With Réard's slogan, "Bikini—smaller than the smallest bathing suit in the world," the tiny swimsuit was given the name by which it would soon be known throughout the world.

Although two-piece swimwear that exposed a little bit of the midriff was nothing new and had been seen on the beaches and in Hollywood since the mid-1930's, nothing had come close to revealing as much female flesh as Réard's bikini. Seen for the first time at a poolside fashion show at the Piscine Molitor in Paris on July 5, 1946, the bikini caused a shock wave, especially among the American reporters who covered the fashion show for *The International Herald Tribune.* That paper alone ran nine bylined stories on the bikini, thus introducing the concept of the tiny bathing suit to the American public with a definite undertone of amused disapproval. The lead story was written by bureau chief Tex O'Reilly, who reported that "all of a sudden, a blonde named Micheline Bernardini ambles out in what any dern fool could see was the smallest bathing suit in the world."

When arranging for his bikini to be displayed in the fashion show, Réard had difficulty finding someone willing to exhibit his creation. Not one of the traditional French fashion models would consent to wear this first navel-, back-, and upper-thigh-exposing bikini, so Micheline Bernardini, a blonde striptease dancer, was hired to parade around the pool in the skimpiest swimwear to date.

The *Herald Tribune* correspondents did not take the bikini seriously, and neither would their readers for some time to come. The 1940's American fashion writers would not soon come to accept the navel-exposing bikini and considered the fashion to be particularly suited to naughty European beach goers rather than to their conservative American counterparts. For more than a decade, bikinis were strongly discouraged from American public beaches and banished from most private clubs. Only in the privacy of one's own backyard could an American woman dare to wear the fashion that was being worn openly on beaches in France, Italy, and Spain as well as in Brazil.

Réard never made public his reasons for calling the tiny swimwear creation a bikini; however, world events provide bikini enthusiasts with a likely theory as to the origin and popularity of the name. During the summer of 1946, the United States conducted a series of nuclear tests on a tiny atoll in the Pacific Ocean. These were the first nuclear bombs to be detonated since the devastation at Hiroshima and Nagasaki that ended World War II and shocked the world. The rumors of these postwar nuclear tests caused a panic among some Parisians, who speculated that the tests might go out of control and cause a chain reaction that would destroy the world. When the bombs were set off, such fears proved to be unfounded, but one of the tiny, uninhabited islands, Bikini, gained a considerable notoriety as it was smashed by the explosions. Related theories abound that the label "bikini" became popular because of the devastating effects the fashion had on anyone who saw a woman wearing it. The bikini was a fashion bombshell, so to speak.

Although the bikini is thought of as a twentieth century phenomenon, it appears that such swimwear attire was merely reinvented during the twentieth century. In fact, Minoan wall paintings dating from 1600 B.C. are the earliest known evidence of women wearing bikini-type coverings. Other depictions of early bikini wearers were later found in 1952 by an Italian archaeologist excavating a luxurious fourth century A.D. Roman villa on the island of Sicily. In the villa's gymnasium, a mosaic depicting eight female gymnasts, each wearing a diaper-like pantie and a strapless bandeau, proved that bikinis were invented long before the 1946 Parisian poolside fashion show.

Impact of Event

The bikini received plenty of media attention and stirred up enormous controversy in the fashion world, yet it remained a swimwear stepchild throughout the decade following its invention. In the United States, the bikini was initially little more than a symbol of the contrast between American conservatism and European liberalism.

In the late 1950's, however, the bikini became a catalyst for the liberalization of American beaches. The bikini did not make a sudden and dramatic entrance into popular culture, but it certainly was a means for the public and the media to test the likely degree of acceptance of such a challenge to American conservatism. Clues abound as to the bikini's subtle incursion; a 1958 issue of *Newsweek* magazine reported that this variety of beachwear "had a record of bans and secret sales second only to *Lady Chatterly's Lover.*"

Boutique owners and major department stores stocked the two-piece bathing suit despite its risqué reputation, and much to their surprise, the bikinis sold each season and so were reordered again for the next summer season. Against the predictions of the outraged swimsuit designers, the bikini did sell to the American populace, although it was not commonly seen in public swimming and sunning venues. At least two factors seem to have sustained the bikini throughout one of the more conservative periods in American history. First of all, there was a dramatic increase in the number of private swimming pools in the United States; the number rose from approximately twenty-five hundred in 1949 to more than eighty-seven thousand ten years later. Women may not have been wearing their bikinis on the beaches, but they were wearing them in the privacy of their own backyards. The second factor that may have sustained the bikini in the American market was the notable increase in international travel. As evidenced by the increase in the number of U.S. passport holders—from fewer than 25,000 in 1946 to more than 675,000 during the 1950's—Americans were clearly enjoying their postwar prosperity. As international airlines flourished, more formerly landlocked Americans began to travel to the European beaches from which the bikini had emerged, and there they were exposed to the revealing fashion.

In the late 1950's, a small but significant stamp of approval came when *Harper's Bazaar* and *Esquire* published color photographs of America's first supermodel, Suzy Parker, wearing a bikini. By 1960, wearing a bikini was akin to making a cultural statement. Diane Vreeland, the fashion editor at *Harper's Bazaar*, began advocating the demise of the one-piece and the success of the skimpy two-piece, equating fashion choice to attitude. "Bikini says to me the best things in life are free," she wrote. "The world of the Bikini is the normal world, a world completely consumed by the elements. It makes me think of boats, of a lonely South African beach, of the pride Mediterranean folk have in their bodies. We city people forget that the elements take up more space than people, thank God."

The summer of 1960 was a watershed one in the bikini's acceptance. Although American designers leaned slightly toward more modest designs than the Europeans, the new decade provided the final impetus to dramatically break the monopoly of the one-piece swimsuit, and the bikini was seen for the first time as a popular choice. In July, 1963, *Newsweek* asserted that "the bikini, long the scarlet woman of the $200 million-a-year U.S. swimwear industry, is unmistakably moving toward respectability."

Teenagers, whose figures were generally best suited to the minute fashion, created the largest demand for the bikini in the United States. The designers knew that these youths were still under the fashion thumb of their conservative parents and were quite innovative in creating the "convertible" or "modified" bikini. These two-piece novelties had drawstrings or bows on the sides of the bottoms and in the middle of the tops. If a teenage daughter wanted to appear modest when saying goodbye to her parents before her day at the beach, she could simply adjust the amount of skin exposed to a quite demure level. Once at the beach and out of sight of disapproving parents, she could readjust and display as much skin as she dared.

Largely because of Hollywood's influence, during the 1960's the bikini became a major cultural symbol of America's youth. In 1960, the pop song "Itsy Bitsy Teenie Weenie Yellow Polkadot Bikini" made the charts, and *Where the Boys Are*, a film about college students on the beaches of Fort Lauderdale, Florida, inaugurated a wave of beach films that would help to entrench the bikini as the summer uniform of the teenaged girl.

Ever since the late nineteenth century, swimwear fashions have continually vacillated. Therefore, it is no surprise that each year since the success of the bikini, some designers have predicted that the fad, at last, is over, that women do not want to have that much skin exposed, that revealing less is more provocative. Others have predicted that topless suits would become the fashion staple. Some seasons models have paraded down the fashion runways in suits with skirts that have been added to bikini bottoms for more modesty, while other years so-called dental-floss bathing suits that reveal virtually all have been seen on the most fashionable beaches. Nevertheless, when Réard died in 1984 at the age of eighty-seven, the bikini was responsible for nearly twenty percent of all American swimsuit sales—far more than any other model.

Bibliography

Leerhsen, Charles, Meggan Dissly, Elizabeth Bradburn, and Mac Margolis. "A Brief History of the Bikini: Women Are Observing Its Birthday by Covering Up." *Newsweek* 108 (July 7, 1986): 50. A concise, fact-filled tribute to the then forty-year-old bikini. Explores the social impact of the bikini through a discussion of music and films that it inspired. Documents the firm initial resistance American women had to the fashion and notes that the commitment to the bikini has continued to waver as prominent designers have continued to promote one-piece styles.

Lenček, Lena, and Gideon Bosker. *Making Waves: Swimsuits and the Undressing of America.* San Francisco: Chronicle Books, 1989. An oversized volume that studies the design and manufacture of swimwear, chronicles the evolution of swimsuits from the nineteenth century through the 1980's, and explores the psychological and social roots of swimsuit styles and their appeal. Has hundreds of photographs, lithographs, and drawings of swimwear worn by Hollywood stars and *Sports Illustrated* models.

Martin, Richard, and Harold Koda. *Splash! A History of Swimwear.* New York: Rizzoli, 1990. An oversized book printed on high-quality paper. Features a fine collection of photographs of men's and women's swimsuits, including the first bikini. An excellent study in style that discusses fashion icons, designers, and photographers. Lacks a bibliography, but all photos have excellent references and are cross-referenced in the index of illustrations.

Panati, Charles. "Bathing Suit: Mid-19th Century, Europe." *Extraordinary Origins of Everyday Things.* New York: Harper & Row, 1987. A well-written, concise history of the evolution of bathing suits into swimming suits, then into the shockingly small bikini. Ties in the beginning of the nuclear age with the explosive impact of the bikini. Contains an illustration of a prototype bikini as depicted in a fourth-century Roman mosaic.

Probert, Christina. *Swimwear in Vogue Since 1910.* New York: Abbeville Press, 1981. A fully illustrated book covering seven decades of primarily American swimwear fashions as represented in *Vogue* magazine. Gives a chronological portrayal of swimwear fashion development from the 1920's through the 1970's. Of particular interest is the discussion of the beginning of midriff-exposure swimwear, the predecessor to the bikini.

Jeremy K. Pearl

Cross-References

Poiret's "Hobble Skirts" Become the Rage (1910), p. 263; Jantzen Popularizes the One-Piece Bathing Suit (1920), p. 491; Dior's "New Look" Sweeps Europe and America (1947), p. 1346; Quant Introduces the Miniskirt (Early 1960's), p. 1824; Madonna Revolutionizes Popular Fashion (1980's), p. 2454.

MAHALIA JACKSON BEGINS HER RECORDING CAREER

Category of event: Music
Time: October 3, 1946
Locale: New York, New York

Mahalia Jackson launched a recording career that included a contract with Columbia Records and popularity that transcended racial lines, bringing black gospel music into the mainstream

Principal personages:

MAHALIA JACKSON (1911–1972), a gospel singer who brought the emerging music of the black folk church to worldwide recognition

THOMAS A. DORSEY (1899–1993), a gospel song composer who teamed up with Jackson to promote gospel music

MARTIN LUTHER KING, JR. (1929–1968), the inspirational preacher and civil rights leader, who became a close friend of Jackson and for whom she did much to support

STUDS TERKEL (1912–   ), the Chicago-based radio personality and writer of oral histories who put Jackson on his radio show and helped make her famous

JOHN HAMMOND (1910–1987), the record producer and talent scout who helped to get Jackson on Columbia Records and who promoted the indigenous music of America

Summary of Event

On October 3, 1946, Mahalia Jackson made her first gospel recordings for the New York label Apollo. Her first two singles for the label did not sell well, but in 1947 she recorded a song that went on to sell a million copies. "Move on Up a Little Higher" covered both sides of the record. It had been written by the Reverend W. Herbert Brewster, a well-known Memphis preacher and songwriter. The song put Jackson on her way to national prominence.

Other Apollo recordings in the next eight years sold well, and Jackson became in demand nationwide as a leading exponent of the newer gospel songs. She became the official soloist of the National Baptist Convention, a black church, and was a popular figure on Studs Terkel's radio program in Chicago, where she lived. Terkel had always had an ear for folk, blues, and gospel music and found Jackson to be one of the finest singers and interpreters, with her rich and strong contralto voice. Her outgoing personality and deep knowledge of black culture and musical roots made her a local favorite when she appeared on Terkel's television show in the early 1950's. In the segregated America of that time, her artistry still was confined mainly to African-American audiences. In the huge ghettos of Chicago's South Side, New York's Harlem, and Los Angeles' Watts, she began to reign supreme.

Jackson was born poor in New Orleans in 1911. She grew up listening to the blues recordings of singers such as Bessie Smith and Ma Rainey but gravitated more to the religious songs of the Baptist church. Nevertheless, she thought that the more passionate singing in the Sanctified and Holiness churches, where instruments were allowed, matched better with the feelings she wanted to express. Hearing the local jazz musicians and their improvising bands also inspired her at an early age. After moving to Chicago's South Side ghetto in 1927, she began to sing in church choirs and joined a small gospel group committed to the newer up-tempo gospel songs she admired. Singing at storefront churches and around the Chicago area, she started to develop the ecstatic and freely embellished style of handling spirituals and hymns that became her trademark.

Through the 1930's, Jackson survived by singing and by running a series of small businesses including a florist shop, a hairdresser's shop, and even a house-to-house homemade cosmetics sales operation. She also met Thomas A. Dorsey, a central figure in the creation of modern black gospel song.

Dorsey had by this time turned away from his earlier blues performing, recording, and songwriting to turn to the writing of the gospel blues. These religious songs with blues tonalities soon caught on among the new migrants to Chicago from the Deep South who had grown up with the older African-American religious song styles. Dorsey recaptured much of that style in his songs and slowly won over the more staid mainline church choirs and pastors—as well as their congregations—to the new impassioned singing of the good news (the gospel). Teaming up with Jackson, he toured the Chicago area and the South, selling his songs on sheet music and playing piano behind Jackson's interpretations of his songs. Jackson and he thus helped expose Northern African Americans to their folk-derived music.

Jackson and Dorsey came to a parting of ways over her freedom with the printed music he wrote. She had developed her own style of decorating, embellishing, slowing down, or speeding up spirituals, hymns, and even the new songs, so that each performance was different. She had brought the old oral tradition, stemming from Africa, to the North. Her singing became a testimony-in-song to joy and faith, to suffering and loss, as she shouted and moaned or pushed her contralto into falsetto. The musical assimilation of the mainline churches, with formal music reading and stolidness, was not for her.

Jackson did make a record for Decca in 1937, but it went nowhere. That song was recorded with a combination of piano and organ that she came to prefer for live performances throughout her career. Undaunted, she kept on touring to whatever church wanted her, communicating with audiences through inviting them to respond with hand clapping and sung responses in the traditional call-and-response style. Piano playing was most often in the hands of Mildred Falls, who came to understand Jackson's style and simply provided backing triplets or a percussive touch to Jackson's improvisatory handling of lines and phrases. The organ, likewise, played its role by sustaining notes and chords while Jackson "worried" words and phrases and frequently sang in a free rhythm over the accompaniment. Using melisma (a group of notes sung to the same syllable), she freely altered melodies, repeated phrases, and marvelously reshaped old spirituals and new songs in her own style. She was on her way.

Impact of Event

Jackson's success with the Apollo label from 1946 through 1954 made hers a household name among African Americans. She had a half-hour radio show in 1954 and 1955 and even broadened her repertoire to include pieces such as Brahms's *Lullaby* and *Silent Night*. Network television seemed afraid of her in this segregated era. Even on radio and local Chicago television, she found pressures that bothered her and that she would encounter for the rest of her career.

Jackson never sang a song the same way twice. As she moved into the world of recordings, radio and television broadcasts, and the mass media, she found producers, directors, and musicians who did not know black culture or religious music and who pressured her to limit the length of her performances to fit into time slots or the limits of singles recordings. Studio musicians and orchestras worked from written parts and scores; she was used to improvising and establishing her own pulse with Mildred Falls. This difference created conflicts in her recording career. Later in her career, strings, horns, guitars, drums, and large choirs were added to her recordings—sometimes overdubbed—and she thought that this sometimes compromised her music. As she became more mainstream, some of her roots in folk traditions were lost.

A major turning point in her career came in 1951, when she appeared at the Music Inn in Lenox, Massachusetts. Singing her songs and explaining their roots before an audience of jazz experts and musicologists, Jackson was surprised to find a fan in John Hammond, a famous talent scout and record producer. He soon worked to get her a contract with Columbia Records, a mainstream label that had earlier, under Hammond's guidance, recorded such important artists as Bessie Smith, Billie Holiday, Benny Goodman, and Count Basie. Hammond had organized the famous 1938 and 1939 Spirituals to Swing concerts in New York and would later in his career help to get Bob Dylan and Bruce Springsteen signed to Columbia. He had a great ear for traditional and indigenous American music. In Jackson, he saw an important American talent with folk roots.

From 1954 until her death from heart failure in 1972, Jackson recorded for Columbia. She recorded many albums of spirituals, hymns, and gospel songs. Although producers urged her to appeal to pop audiences by recording pallid inspirational songs and Christmas carols, she largely resisted. Some recordings were overproduced with orchestral accompaniment, but she now had the opportunity to record her songs without restrictive time limits. Most of her recordings were albums; some featured live performances such as those at the prestigious Newport Jazz Festival and on foreign tours. Two singles reached the pop charts: "He's Got the Whole World in His Hands" in 1958 and "Silent Night, Holy Night" in 1962.

In the late 1950's and through the 1960's her fame spread across the world. She was acclaimed in Germany, France, Sweden, England, Japan, and India, among other countries. She met presidents and royalty and sang at John F. Kennedy's inaugural. Utilizing the William Morris booking agency, she appeared at better venues, from Carnegie Hall to Constitution Hall. In the 1960's, she also became a favorite guest on network television shows including those of Dinah Shore, Ed Sullivan, and Steve Allen. Church benefits and one-night stands continued, but Jackson now had a wider choice.

One of the most important aspects of her life was her deep and lasting friendship for and active support of Martin Luther King, Jr. She shared with him the Christian message of love and tolerance and a sharp sense of the injustices that they and all African Americans had to endure. After meeting King in 1955, Jackson immediately took to singing for his rallies. Risking her safety, she journeyed to Montgomery, Alabama, in 1956 to sing gospel songs for the civil rights demonstrators. She walked with King and thousands of others through the violent streets of Chicago in 1966 in a demand for open housing. As a preacher, King shared with Jackson a love of spirituals and gospel song. For him, she sang the spiritual "I Been 'Buked and I Been Scorned" before thousands in front of the Lincoln Memorial at the great March on Washington in August, 1963, just before he delivered his famous "I Have a Dream" speech. Most poignantly, she sang his favorite gospel song at his funeral in April, 1968: Dorsey's "Take My Hand, Precious Lord."

This same song was sung at Jackson's funeral in 1972 by Aretha Franklin, perhaps her best-known disciple. Franklin sang in her father's Detroit church as a child and knew Jackson at that time. The Reverend C. L. Franklin was a famous preacher and singer in the old improvised or oral style of sermonizing, in which chanted lines were built into song, with responses from the congregation. Another figure associated with this style was James Cleveland, who, like the Reverend Franklin, made many recordings of songs and his own brand of song-testimony with choral response. These black church traditions were basic in Jackson's approach to song. In this tradition, Aretha Franklin carried on much of Jackson's work, even when she branched off into soul music in the 1970's. She continued to sing gospel music as well.

Jackson refused to sing blues or work in nightclubs. Thus, she would never have sung soul music, the deeply gospel-inspired music that became popular in her later years. Franklin became one of its best exponents, as did similarly gospel-inspired singers such as James Brown and Ray Charles. Soul music was too secular for Jackson. White gospel music stems from a different tradition than does black gospel and was easier to put into the mainstream market. Jackson's example of finding a mass audience for religious music ran parallel to the popularity of white singers such as Tennessee Ernie Ford, whose network television show in the 1950's and 1960's featured his singing of gospel songs. His best-selling spiritual albums also brought the old spirituals, hymns, and new gospel songs to a mainstream audience. Because a considerable overlap exists between the repertoires of white and black religious song, Ford's efforts added further to the acceptance of the gospel in song. Singers such as Elvis Presley and Johnny Cash also fostered a mass acceptance of religious songs. It was Presley who sang Dorsey's "Peace in the Valley" on Ed Sullivan's television show in January, 1957, and then saw his recording of it become a pop hit. In 1971, Jackson sang the classic folk spiritual "Amazing Grace" on Johnny Cash's network television show. Jackson set an example of service to her music and her people. Her influence crossed racial lines and helped immeasurably to ensure the emergence of one of America's great musical forms.

Bibliography

Cusic, Don. *The Sound of Light: A History of Gospel Music.* Bowling Green, Ohio: Bowling Green State University Popular Press, 1990. A good general survey of the history and roots of religious music in America, both black and white. A chapter discusses Mahalia Jackson and Sam Cooke together. Good bibliography. Indexed fully.

Goreau, Laurraine. *Just Mahalia, Baby: The Mahalia Jackson Story.* Gretna, La.: Pelican, 1984. The most comprehensive biography to date. Goreau, a friend and intimate in later years, offers an enormous six-hundred-page anecdotal coverage of Jackson's professional and personal life. The writing is often awkward. No notes as such. Many photos and an index. Valuable for its insights and sense of the milieu and the tensions of Jackson's life.

Harris, Michael W. *The Rise of Gospel Blues: The Music of Thomas Andrew Dorsey in the Urban Church.* New York: Oxford University Press, 1992. A fine and detailed study not only of Dorsey's career but also of the whole Chicago scene in the 1930's, with reference to the new gospel style of singing. Dorsey's work with Jackson is discussed. Good and comprehensible (for a general readership) musical analysis. Notes and index.

Heilbut, Tony. *The Gospel Sound: Good News and Bad Times.* New York: Simon & Schuster, 1971. The best popular history of black gospel music. Well written and engaging. Includes a chapter on Jackson. Illustrated. Indexed by names and songs, with discography.

Jackson, Mahalia, with Evan McLeod Wylie. *Movin' On Up.* New York: Hawthorn Books, 1966. A short autobiography, but useful and insightful, especially concerning Jackson's feelings about civil rights and Martin Luther King, Jr. Complements Goreau in capturing the strongly held views Jackson had but kept somewhat private.

Lovell, John. *Black Song: The Forge and the Flame, the Story of How the Afro-American Spiritual Was Hammered Out.* New York: Macmillan, 1972. The long subtitle captures the focus of this long book. A fully comprehensive overview. Indexed thoroughly, with good source notes.

Schwerin, Jules. *Got to Tell It: Mahalia Jackson, Queen of Gospel.* New York: Oxford University Press, 1992. A short anecdotal memoir by a documentary filmmaker who worked with Jackson. Illustrated, discography, no index.

Frederick E. Danker

Cross-References

Bessie Smith Records "Downhearted Blues" (1923), p. 572; Guthrie's Populist Songs Reflect the Depression-Era United States (1930's), p. 810; Billie Holiday Begins Her Recording Career (1933), p. 930; Marian Anderson Is Barred from Constitution Hall (1939), p. 1126; Presley Becomes a Rock-and-Roll Sensation (1956), p. 1705.

CAPRA RELEASES *IT'S A WONDERFUL LIFE*

Category of event: Motion pictures
Time: December 20, 1946
Locale: The United States

Frank Capra's It's a Wonderful Life *was released to somewhat mixed reviews, only later to emerge as one of the most enduringly popular films of all time*

Principal personages:
FRANK CAPRA (1897-1991), an award-winning but independent-minded Hollywood producer and director
JIMMY STEWART (1908-   ), a well-known film star recently returned from service in the U.S. Army Air Corps who was cast in the lead role of George Bailey
DONNA REED (DONNA BELLE MULLENGER, 1921-1986), a relatively unknown young actress cast as George Bailey's wife, Mary
LIONEL BARRYMORE (1878-1954), a veteran stage and screen actor cast somewhat against type as the stingy banker H. C. Potter

Summary of Event

Having built his reputation during the 1930's with such populist films as *Mr. Deeds Goes to Town* (1936) and *Mr. Smith Goes to Washington* (1939), as well as with adaptations of popular novels (including 1937's *Lost Horizon*) and Broadway plays (such as 1938's *You Can't Take It with You*), Frank Capra had discontinued the making of feature films for the duration of World War II, producing instead for the U.S. War Department an acclaimed series of documentaries collectively entitled *Why We Fight.* At war's end, Capra was more than ready to return to commercial filmmaking, albeit on his own terms; together with fellow directors George Stevens and William Wyler, Capra had by early 1946 founded Liberty Films. He had already acquired rights to the material that he would fashion into *It's a Wonderful Life* and had also chosen Jimmy Stewart to play the film's lead role.

In its original form, the film's material was a very short story, "The Greatest Gift," prepared by the writer-publicist Philip Van Doren Stern as a Christmas card to be sent to his friends. By the time Capra bought the rights to the story for ten thousand dollars, "The Greatest Gift" was already second-hand and somewhat shopworn; acquired by Radio-Keith-Orpheum (RKO) Pictures at the request of screen star Cary Grant, the story had undergone several attempts at adaptation for the screen by accomplished scenarists and dramatists that included Marc Connelly and Clifford Odets.

It is likely that Capra, his presumed optimism somewhat tempered by the experience of war and its aftermath, was less deterred than his predecessors by the curious mixture of life and death, light and darkness, that lurks just beneath the surface of

Van Doren Stern's tale, in which George Bailey, an apparently successful business-man, husband, and father, is rescued from a sudden impulse toward suicide by an angelic presence who shows him what the world might be like had he never been born. From the start, Capra envisioned Stewart in the role of George, on the basis of the actor's range of performance in previous Capra films; the rest of the casting was left more or less to chance, with a number of supporting actors appearing in roles other than those for which Capra originally considered them. Jean Arthur, Cap-ra's—and apparently Stewart's—first choice to play George's wife, Mary, was then committed to another production, so Capra decided to "borrow" the much younger Donna Reed—an inspired if unexpected choice—from the studio that held her con-tract.

Planned and promoted as a major Hollywood production, *It's a Wonderful Life* nevertheless fell somewhat short of the rousing initial success that Capra had quite justifiably predicted for it. With filming completed in July, 1946, editing continued through the fall, and release was projected for the late winter of 1946 or early spring of 1947. No sooner was editing completed, however, than Capra was pressured by his partners and colleagues to release the film in time for Christmas, replacing other productions that were slow to reach completion. Despite the film's time-framing device of Christmas Eve and Christmas, Capra had never envisioned *It's a Wonder-ful Life* as a "Christmas film" but rather as the portrayal of one man's life in context, in all seasons. Rushed into release, promoted as a "Christmas comedy" before au-diences that recalled only the lighter side of Capra's prewar films, *It's a Wonderful Life* presented a dark side—implicit in George's death wish and the nightmarish vision of what his town would have been like without him—that kept the film's earliest audiences somewhat off-balance, uncertain whether to laugh or to cry.

Superstitious observers might well have found a negative omen in the fact that commercial printing of the film began on Friday, December 13, 1946, one week to the day before the first prints were shown before audiences in selected markets such as New York City. In New York and other parts of the northeastern United States, a record snowfall kept many potential viewers at home; those few brave souls who did venture out to see the new film could hardly have been impressed with the new technique, developed at Capra's request, for simulating snow and ice on film. Al-though *It's a Wonderful Life* won none of the Academy Awards for which it was nominated during 1947, members of Capra's "snow team" would in fact win a special-effects Oscar for 1948, the year in which the film would have been eligible for com-petition had it been released during 1947 as originally planned.

Nationwide, the general release of *It's a Wonderful Life* proceeded on schedule late in January, 1947, and was followed by a promotional visit by Capra and Stewart to the "representative" American town of Beaumont, Texas, shortly before the Acad-emy Awards ceremony in which the film failed to win, place, or show. Not long thereafter, *It's a Wonderful Life* was released in Great Britain to decidedly negative reviews, whereupon Capra began to lose faith in the film of which he had expected so much. Despite decent performance at the box office, more than returning the initial investment of three million dollars, the film tended to be dismissed as a relative failure both by Capra and by the film establishment at large. It was soon made available for late showing on the new medium of television, where it would proceed to reach a new, unforeseen, and largely invisible audience, particularly during the season between Thanksgiving and Christmas.

Impact of Event

As Capra would later recall, it was the television audience, unforeseen at the time of the film's release, that would keep *It's a Wonderful Life* "alive" throughout the succeeding decades, generating from the 1950's onward a steady flow of correspondence that Capra took pains to answer personally. Spectators would ask, for example, where Capra had found the footage depicting Harry Bailey's combat experience, or why the dastardly Potter, portrayed by Lionel Barrymore in a most memorable performance, remains apparently unpunished for the theft of eight thousand dollars. By the early 1970's, the film had truly acquired a "wonderful life" of its own, sustained largely by word of mouth.

Nevertheless, most of the film's lasting values remained locked in spectators' minds until some time after 1974, when no one in charge bothered to renew the commercial copyright of *It's a Wonderful Life* at the end of twenty-eight years. The film then passed into the public domain, available free of charge to television and other video markets. Before long, *It's a Wonderful Life* was appearing at all hours of day and night on public and private television throughout the Christmas season, attracting audiences unborn at the time of its release and emerging as a true Christmas classic.

During the early years of its rediscovery in the mid-1970's, *It's a Wonderful Life* was seen primarily as an inspirational, sentimental Christmas film, having accumulated with age the value of nostalgia for a lost small-town America which, like that of the illustrator Norman Rockwell, might never have existed at all. Sentiment alone, however, could hardly account for the film's continuing hold upon its viewers, especially those who considered themselves educated beyond the Norman Rockwell level. In the meantime, intertextual references to *It's a Wonderful Life* had begun to surface throughout American popular and middlebrow culture, from the mention of "plastics" as the way to success in Mike Nichols' *The Graduate* (1967) (an echo of the words and deeds of George Bailey's friend Sam Wainwright) to the naming of the most popular Muppets on the children's television show *Sesame Street:* In the film, Bert and Ernie, respectively played by Ward Bond and Frank Faylen, are the police officer and cabdriver who grow up with George Bailey and who almost witness his suicide. By the middle 1980's, at least one novel had been published featuring the film's characters in later life, and professional critics had begun to examine the film in depth seeking the source of its perennial appeal even to those who "ought to know better."

To be sure, close analysis of *It's a Wonderful Life* reveals somewhat more depth and complexity than are to be found in most films from the heyday of Hollywood. George Bailey's impulse toward suicide, although immediately triggered by the eight-thousand-dollar shortfall engineered by Potter, is in fact deeply rooted in George's personal history of self-sacrifice and thwarted dreams. Running parallel to George's life, and often intersecting with it, is a credible chronicle of American social history: Born around 1907, a year or so earlier than the actor who played him, George grows to manhood during the Roaring Twenties only to get sidetracked from his dreams by the Great Depression and its aftermath. Others, such as George's younger brother Harry (whom George rescues from drowning after a daredevil trick on thin ice in 1919) and their friend Sam Wainwright, grow rich or famous, leaving George behind in Bedford Falls to tend the home fires or hold the bag, as need be. Disqualified from military service during World War II by a hearing impairment he had suffered when he rescued Harry, George fights "the battle of Bedford Falls" as an air-raid warden, once again denied the chance to leave the town and test his "wings."

Two images predominate throughout the film: those of George's "bad ear," into which good news is always whispered, and of wings, both those on Harry's plane and those sought by the second-class angel Clarence Odbody when he plunges into the river, confident that George will dive in to save him as he did Harry. Complementary to the images of hearing and flight is that of George "lassoing the moon" to court and please Mary; like the moon, George's life has both a bright and a dark side. Conceivably, it was the dark side of George's life, and nature, that helped to keep at bay postwar audiences that sought only to be entertained; conversely, the same dark side has ensured the film's longevity. Perhaps without knowing quite why, the audience that discovered *It's a Wonderful Life* through the medium of television identified with George Bailey's death wish.

Viewed in retrospect, George Bailey's recovery is truly ambiguous; even as he recovers from his sudden urge toward suicide, George is "recovered," taken back and covered over, by the same small-town society that had pushed him toward the bridge, and the brink. At the same time, the interlude with Clarence has caused him to discover, as if for the first time, the small wonders of participation in life, of give and take. Potter, George's perennial antagonist and possibly his mirror image, the dark side, remains invulnerable to such recovery, having never learned to give.

Significantly, Bedford Falls without George's birth, interaction, and intervention has become "Pottersville," a town of honky-tonks and cheap thrills totally controlled by Potter, who knows how to release—and to profit from—those same human instincts that he has long suppressed in himself. The film's nightmare sequence, in which the anonymous George roams Pottersville with Clarence at his side, might well have served, visually and conceptually, as a model for some of the crime movies that would soon follow and that would be honored and imitated by the French as *le film noir*, or "dark movie."

Toward the end of Capra's long life, critics began a serious assessment of his contribution to the vocabulary and history of film, finding in his work a progression and coherence equal, if not superior, to that of many European filmmakers already immortalized for their art. For a number of critics, *It's a Wonderful Life* emerges, despite its popular appeal, as Capra's most complex and aesthetically sophisticated film, completing the cinematic statement begun with his originally better-known films of the 1930's. Ironically, the limited initial success of *It's a Wonderful Life* led not only to the eventual buyout of Liberty Films but also to a scaling-down of Capra's filmmaking ambitions; with the possible exception of *State of the Union* (1948), he would produce no truly significant films during the years to follow. Capra would, however, live to the ripe age of ninety-four, long enough to appreciate the recognition of his work in general and of *It's a Wonderful Life* in particular.

Bibliography

Basinger, Jeanine. *The "It's a Wonderful Life" Book*. New York: Alfred A. Knopf, 1986. Includes full texts of the final shooting script and the Van Doren Stern short story, together with interviews with Jimmy Stewart and cinematographer Joseph Biroc by film critic Leonard Maltin. Basinger's long, illustrated introductory essay, entitled "The Many Lives of *It's a Wonderful Life*," is informative, balanced, and perceptive.

Capra, Frank. *The Name Above the Title*. New York: Macmillan, 1971. Capra's autobiography, well-written if anecdotal, with useful information on *It's a Wonderful Life*. Perceived errors of fact are discussed in the introductory essay to Basinger's book.

Carney, Raymond. *American Vision: The Films of Frank Capra*. Cambridge, England: Cambridge University Press, 1986. Carney's exhaustive scholarly analysis seeks to situate Capra's films within the context of American art and literature from the nineteenth century onward. Carney, well-versed in structuralist, post-structuralist, and psychoanalytical theory, reveals codes and structures in *It's a Wonderful Life* that show it to be the most complete expression of Capra's developing vision.

Glatzer, Richard, and John Raeburn, eds. *Frank Capra: The Man and His Films*. Ann Arbor: University of Michigan Press, 1975. Deceptively titled, Glatzer and Raeburn's volume is little more than a compendium of reviews interspersed with occasional essays. Useful for reconstructing Capra's checkered career; well-illustrated with stills from major films, including *It's a Wonderful Life*. Includes negative review by noted author James Agee.

Poague, Leland. *The Cinema of Frank Capra*. South Brunswick, N.J.: A. S. Barnes, 1975. Historical in aim and scope, Poague's study traces Capra's career from his earliest work in films. Includes one of the first full-scale analyses of *It's a Wonderful Life*.

David B. Parsell

Cross-References

Hollywood Enters Its Golden Age (1930's), p. 822; The Classic *The Wizard of Oz* Opens (1939), p. 1109; The Hollywood Studio System Is Transformed (1946), p. 1307; *Amahl and the Night Visitors* Premieres on American Television (1951), p. 1536; *The Sound of Music* Captivates Audiences (1965), p. 2033.

BLACKLISTING SERIOUSLY DEPLETES HOLLYWOOD'S TALENT POOL

Category of event: Motion pictures
Time: 1947-1951
Locale: Hollywood, California, and Washington, D.C.

The Hollywood blacklist, a ban on employment of alleged Communists, hurt both individual careers and the morale of the film community as a whole

Principal personages:

J. PARNELL THOMAS (1895-1970), the chairman of the House Committee on Un-American Activities (HUAC), 1947-1949, who interrogated the Hollywood Ten

JOHN S. WOOD (1885-1968), a chairman of HUAC who began a second probe of Hollywood Communism

DALTON TRUMBO (1905-1976), a scriptwriter, one of the Hollywood Ten who defied HUAC in 1947

RING LARDNER, JR. (1915-   ), a scriptwriter, one of the Hollywood Ten who defied HUAC in 1947

ELIA KAZAN (ELIA KAZANJOGLOU, 1909-   ), a stage and motion-picture director who cooperated with HUAC in 1952

CARL FOREMAN (1914-1984), a motion-picture scenarist and blacklist victim

Summary of Event

During World War II, the Soviet Union and the United States were allies against Nazi Germany. When the war ended in 1945, a rapid worsening of Soviet-American relations turned the American Communist Party, advocating the Soviet model of socialism, from a tolerated political sect into a band of persecuted political outcasts. As Soviet dictator Joseph Stalin installed puppet governments in one Eastern European country after another, blockaded Berlin, and acquired the atomic bomb, American Communists came to be seen as actual or potential traitors who, for the safety of the country, needed to be purged from trade-union leadership, government employment, the teaching profession, and even the entertainment industry. American anxiety about domestic Communists later was heightened by the Korean War.

The American Communist Party had been more popular in the 1930's, when massive unemployment at home contrasted with apparently full employment in Stalin's Soviet Union, and when Stalin opposed German expansion and helped the Spanish Republic battle fascist rebels. The party's respectability, diminished by the German-Soviet Pact of August, 1939, was restored when Germany invaded the Soviet Union in June, 1941.

Communism had special appeal for writers, who found Hollywood to be an oasis of good pay in the economic desert of Depression-era America. After talking pictures were introduced, journalists, playwrights involved in New York City's struggling left-wing theater, short-story writers, and even some who had never written before found scriptwriting jobs in the film industry. Many of them joined the Hollywood branch of the Communist Party, which helped organize the Screen Writers Guild. The industry's profit orientation, however, left Communist writers little chance, except during World War II, to give films an ideological slant.

The House Committee on Un-American Activities (HUAC) was created in 1938. In 1947, Committee Chairman J. Parnell Thomas demanded that individuals in the film industry answer questions about their own and their colleagues' past or present Communist affiliations. That October, ten of those subpoenaed—the so-called Hollywood Ten—refused to answer questions, basing their refusal not on the Fifth Amendment's guarantee against self-incrimination but on the First Amendment's protection of freedom of speech and association. Five of the Hollywood Ten— Lester Cole, Ring Lardner, Jr., Dalton Trumbo, Edward Dmytryk, and Adrian Scott— were then under contract to major studios. The House of Representatives voted the Hollywood Ten to be in contempt of Congress.

When the rude behavior of some of the Hollywood Ten at the hearings turned public opinion against them, the heads of the major studios became frightened. In November, 1947, the Motion Picture Association of America announced that the Hollywood Ten would be dismissed·from their jobs at the various studios and that no known Communist would be hired in the future. This ban on employment, the blacklist, later was extended to all who refused to cooperate with HUAC, whether they were proven to be Communists or not. The American Legion exerted pressure on motion-picture studios to maintain the blacklist; other private organizations and individuals smoked out Communists, publishing lists of supposedly subversive entertainers and writers. Liberal actors and directors who once had vocally opposed the HUAC investigation now stopped doing so, fearing for their careers. The president of the Screen Actors Guild, a young actor named Ronald Reagan, cooperated with the blacklisters. On April 10, 1950, the U.S. Supreme Court, after a long legal battle, upheld the Hollywood Ten's lower court conviction on contempt charges; in June, nine of them went to prison. Adrian Scott was sentenced in September.

In 1951, HUAC, with John S. Wood of Georgia now its chairman, resumed its investigation of Hollywood Communism. This probe continued through 1951. Some of those summoned refused to cooperate, citing the Fifth Amendment; others, including stage and motion-picture director Elia Kazan, cooperated willingly, naming past associates who had been Communists. Either because of eagerness to leave prison and resume his career or because of a genuine change of heart, Dmytryk publicly renounced Communism, giving the names of past associates who were Communists. He was the only one of the Hollywood Ten to do so.

In the late 1950's, HUAC suffered some setbacks, and its investigatory zeal began to flag. In 1958, Arthur Miller, a gifted playwright whose entry into film work had been blocked by his reputation as a leftist, rejected the HUAC demand that he name past associates who were Communists. Miller's conviction on contempt of Congress charges in 1957 was overturned by a higher court decision in 1958. In 1956, Carl Foreman, who had been blacklisted for refusing to cooperate with HUAC, finally offered, in a closed session with Chairman Francis Walter, to cooperate. This time, however, the chairman did not ask Foreman to name names. Foreman's name was removed from the blacklist. In 1975, after public tolerance toward dissent had been enlarged considerably by the turmoil over civil rights and the Vietnam War, HUAC was abolished.

In 1960, director Otto Preminger announced that Dalton Trumbo had written the script for *Exodus* (1960). Actor and producer Kirk Douglas stated that Trumbo had written the script for *Spartacus* (1960). Neither film's box-office success was hurt seriously by airing Trumbo's contribution. Trumbo, in fact, won an Academy Award for Best Original Story for *The Brave One* (1956), writing as Robert Rich. His award went unclaimed until 1975. Frank Sinatra in 1960 reneged, under pressure, on a promise to hire Albert Maltz, another of the Hollywood Ten. Not until the late 1960's, when Ring Lardner, Jr., was hired to write the screenplay for the antiwar black comedy *M*A*S*H* (1970), did the blacklist era really end.

Impact of Event

The effects of the blacklist, and of the era of suspicion that it exemplified, were many. The blacklist is estimated to have claimed about three hundred victims. It certainly harmed individual careers, although not all blacklistees were hurt equally. Scriptwriters could keep working in several ways: by leaving the United States and working for foreign film studios; by arranging to have someone else, a "front," pretend to be the author of scripts that they had written, while letting the true author get at least some of the monetary reward; or by writing under a pseudonym. Some blacklisted scriptwriters ultimately regained their careers in the American film industry, but many did not.

Actors and actresses who refused to cooperate with HUAC, or who were revealed by informers or professional Communist-hunters as guilty of past association with Communist causes, usually saw their livelihoods ruined. Working under a pseudonym was impossible, as their faces would appear on screen. The film industry shunned them; the nascent television industry, dependent on corporate sponsors for advertising revenue, was even more determined to steer clear of politically trained performers. One actor committed suicide, possibly because of problems caused by the blacklist. Left-leaning African-American singer and actor Paul Robeson was stripped of his passport and was shunned even by black civil rights leaders.

Playwrights, such as Lillian Hellman (who had written Hollywood scripts in the 1930's and 1940's) and Arthur Miller, did not suffer as much financially from their refusal to cooperate with HUAC as did other creative types. Playwrights had an outlet for their written output on Broadway, which the blacklist never affected as completely as it did the cinema and television.

The damage done to the film industry by the blacklist was ameliorated by the extent to which the blacklist could be circumvented. The practice of writing under a pseudonym not only allowed some blacklisted screenwriters to keep writing; it also allowed motion-picture companies to take advantage of the blacklistees' skills at reduced rates of pay. The Hollywood studios sometimes were permanently deprived of the services of blacklisted writers who found employment in foreign film industries; Joseph Losey, who carved out a career for himself in Great Britain, is an example. The stigmatization of playwrights Arthur Miller and Lillian Hellman as Communist sympathizers meant that Hollywood studios, but not Broadway, deprived themselves of the talents of two first-rate dramatists. The banishment of actors and actresses for past political actions did cost the film industry some talent. In an industry with a surplus of fresh new faces always eager to break in, however, the loss was small.

One effect of the blacklist, one that is sometimes neglected, was the loss of foreign-born talent. Some of the German refugees who had been living and working in Hollywood during World War II went back to Europe to escape harassment for their political views. These included dramatist Bertolt Brecht, who had coauthored a screenplay; novelist Thomas Mann; and composer Hanns Eisler. Charlie Chaplin, the once-beloved British-born film comedian, was hounded out of America for a while because of revulsion against both his allegedly left-wing political views and his supposed moral peccadilloes.

Not only the employees but also the bosses of the Hollywood film empire were frightened by the specter of anti-Communist vigilantism. The type of films produced, therefore, was to some extent affected. The trend toward daring films of social realism that had been evident in the late 1940's was halted, at least for a while. There was a spate of pointedly anti-Communist films, all of them of poor artistic quality and almost all box-office failures. They probably were produced to appease congressional investigators and anti-Communist vigilante organizations. Examples include *The Red Menace* (1949), *I Married a Communist* (1950), *I Was a Communist for the FBI* (1951), and *My Son John* (1952).

The first Hollywood films to discuss the blacklist explicitly, *The Way We Were* (1973) and *The Front* (1976), were released after the era was safely over. Two films made during the blacklist era, however, dealt in a disguised form with the issues involved in the blacklist and the anti-Communist witchhunt. *High Noon* (1952), the story of a Western marshal who is forced to face a band of outlaws alone without the aid of the townsmen, is often regarded by film critics as a veiled criticism of Hollywood's timidity in the face of congressional investigating committees. Carl Foreman wrote the script shortly before he was blacklisted for his noncooperative stand at a HUAC hearing and was forced to seek work in Great Britain. Elia Kazan's *On the Waterfront* (1954), in which a longshoreman works up the courage to inform on corrupt union bosses, is often seen as a veiled justification for Kazan's decision, during the HUAC hearings of 1952, to inform on past Communist associates from his days in the New York City theater in the 1930's.

The decision of some Hollywood figures to cooperate with congressional investigators by naming names, thereby exposing others to the blacklist and perhaps even destroying such people's careers, created rifts in the Hollywood community, and in the entertainment world in general, that lasted for years. Elia Kazan, for example, was still defending his 1952 decision in his 1988 autobiography, *Elia Kazan: A Life.*

Bibliography

Ceplair, Larry, and Steven Englund. *The Inquisition in Hollywood: Politics in the Film Community, 1930-1960.* Garden City, N.Y.: Anchor Press/Doubleday, 1980. An exhaustive study of the Hollywood Ten, the investigation of 1951-1952, and the fate of the blacklistees. Especially informative on the pre-1947 Hollywood Communist subculture. The authors view Hollywood's Communists with a mixture of criticism and admiration. Bibliography, endnotes, index, and photographs. Relies heavily on interviews. For scholars.

Cole, Lester. *Hollywood Red: The Autobiography of Lester Cole.* Palo Alto, Calif.: Ramparts Press, 1981. The life story of a screenwriter who never beat the blacklist and who never recanted his faith in Communism. Although obviously biased, it provides a good victim's-eye view of the post-World War II purge of the film world. Filmography, photographs, and index. For the general reader.

Kanfer, Stefan. *A Journal of the Plague Years.* New York: Atheneum, 1973. A film critic's chronicle of blacklisting from 1947 to 1958, showing its effects on radio, television, and Broadway as well as Hollywood. Especially informative on the private individuals and organizations that helped HUAC by ferreting out show-business Communists. Sympathetic to blacklistees. Photographs, annotated bibliography, index, no notes.

Kazan, Elia. *Elia Kazan: A Life.* New York: Alfred A. Knopf, 1988. In this lengthy but briskly written autobiography, covering everything from childhood to professional life to love life, Kazan vigorously defends his decision to cooperate with HUAC in 1952. Provides some insights into Communism in the 1930's New York City theater. Photographs and index. For the general reader.

Navasky, Victor S. *Naming Names.* New York: Viking Press, 1980. A journalist examines the ethical dilemma faced by those who named names for HUAC, thus avoiding their own blacklisting but causing others to be blacklisted. Excellent chapter, based on interviews, on informers' motives. Rejects anti-Communism as a morally valid rationale for naming names. Endnotes, list of interviewees, index. For the general reader.

Schwartz, Nancy Lynn. *The Hollywood Writers' Wars.* New York: Alfred A. Knopf, 1982. A history of the Hollywood Communist screenwriters' subculture during the 1930's and 1940's. The author expresses nearly undiluted admiration for that subculture. Supplements but does not supplant the book by Ceplair and Englund. Endnotes, photographs, index, and filmographies of more than thirty blacklisted and investigated actors and writers. For scholars.

Vaughn, Robert. *Only Victims: A Study of Show Business Blacklisting.* New York: Putnam, 1972. A television actor's warmed-over political science thesis chronicles, in plodding prose, the jousting between HUAC and the entertainment industry from 1947 to 1958. Contains extensive quotations from the HUAC hearings. Based on the public record, supplemented by a questionnaire sent to blacklistees in 1969 and 1970. Chapter notes, bibliography, and index. For scholars.

Whitfield, Stephen J. *The Culture of the Cold War.* Baltimore: The Johns Hopkins University Press, 1991. The author, a cultural historian, views the blacklist as part of a general trend toward conformity in America during the 1940's and 1950's. Especially useful is his examination of how blacklist-era anxieties affected the kind of films made. Excellent bibliographical essay. Index; no notes.

Paul D. Mageli

Cross-References

Hollywood Enters Its Golden Age (1930's), p. 822; The Group Theatre Flourishes (1931), p. 874; The Federal Theatre Project Promotes Live Theater (1935), p. 989; Odets' *Awake and Sing* Becomes a Model for Protest Drama (1935), p. 1006; Kazan Brings Naturalism to the Stage and Screen (1940's), p. 1164; The Hollywood Studio System Is Transformed (1946), p. 1307; *A Streetcar Named Desire* Brings Method Acting to the Screen (1951), p. 1487.

DIOR'S "NEW LOOK" SWEEPS EUROPE AND AMERICA

Category of event: Fashion and design
Time: Spring, 1947
Locale: Paris, France

Christian Dior's "New Look" heralded the end of the austerity imposed by World War II and started a fashion revolution

Principal personages:

CHRISTIAN DIOR (1905-1957), a French fashion designer whose styles dominated postwar European and American women's wear

ROBERT PIGUET (1901-1953), a designer who gave Dior his first job in haute couture

LUCIEN LELONG (1889-1958), a prominent French designer who played an important part in maintaining France's prominence in the fashion world during World War II

PIERRE BALMAIN (1914-1982), a friend and neighbor who taught Dior the financial ins and outs of the couture business

Summary of Event

Born in 1905 to a comfortably well-off family, Christian Dior always remembered his mother as a woman of great elegance. His father liked things English and dressed little Christian in sailor suits. He had governesses and tutors until age eleven, when he was sent to school at Gerson, France. During his teen years, Dior excelled at dressing up for costume events and suggesting ensembles for schoolmates who took part in amateur theatrical productions. Intended by his father for a career in politics, Dior attended the École des Sciences Politiques, where he earned his degree in 1926. He then went on to complete his military service.

Politics did not suit Dior; nor did he want to enter the family fertilizer manufacturing business. Dior did not want to abandon the artistic interests he had forged during his teenage years. In his first foray into the art world, Dior formed a partnership with Jacques Bonjean to open an art gallery. Their gallery featured young artists; Dior and Bonjean were among the first to exhibit works by Georges Braque, Giorgio de Chirico, Raoul Dufy, Maurice Utrillo, Fernand Léger, and Pablo Picasso. Of them all, perhaps only Utrillo, with his gentle cityscapes, eventually influenced Dior's designs. Dior learned fashion drawing from his friend Jean Ozenne and for a time supported himself as a fashion illustrator. Another friend, Max Kenna, taught him about color and balance.

Soon, Dior began to sell his designs to established fashion houses. By designing the costumes for productions of several plays, he kept his interest in theater alive. Robert Piguet employed Dior as a designer in 1938. With Piguet, Dior learned the exacting standards of haute couture. Women's fashion leaned toward romanticism then; the major Paris designers decreed the use of soft, flowing lines and frilly decorations. Dior, though, credited Piguet with teaching him the virtue of simplicity.

Fashion does not exist in a vacuum; world events shape even the width of a hem. Adolf Hitler's march to power and program of world conquest exerted enormous influence on the fashion world. When German forces occupied France in World War II, the Germans rationed clothes. The wives of German officers wanted Paris fashions, however, so the Germans excluded haute couture from rationing. Paris did not suffer from the bombing raids that the Germans inflicted on much of Europe, so the business of fashion went on almost as usual. Of course, not many fabrics could be obtained, and the war influenced design. Square shoulders, to-the-knee skirts, and a sort of military look dominated the fashion scene.

When Germany invaded France, Dior again found himself in the army. France surrendered, the army disbanded, and Dior finally had to accept a job on a farm. In 1941, though, he joined the design house of Lucien Lelong and once again worked in the job that he loved.

When the war ended, Parisians turned their attention back to fashion. Fashion critics, though, contended that the fashions designed during the postwar years did not meet their critical standards. Many called them vulgar and even ugly. In this fashion climate, in 1946, Dior opened his own salon. His largely female staff adored him and devotedly worked long hours. The exquisite fit needed for the clothes he designed required long hours from both his expert fitters and his clients. Even the most simple style needed at least two hundred hours of hand-finishing.

Dior wanted to make a name for himself; he thus looked for something different, something special. Going back to the softer silhouette of the 1930's, Dior made some essential changes. His spring, 1947, collection drew rave reviews. The fashion writers dubbed it the "New Look."

In Dior's new designs, shoulders rounded gently. Ladylike sleeves fitted neatly into narrow armholes. Waists followed natural lines, and skirts stopped just above the ankle. Dior chose gentle, subdued colors for his innovative collection. He used sumptuous fabrics, including thick velvets, fine wool, and sinuous silk. Evening gowns featured strapless bodices, meticulously hand-beaded embroidery, and extravagantly flowing skirts. (Although the New Look was terrifically popular, an anecdote of the day recounted that one man complained that he had difficulty telling his Dior-clad dance partner apart from a bird cage.)

Dior's seemingly simple silhouette relied on clever seaming and complicated darts. Boning, stiffening, waist cinchers, hip padding, and tailoring contributed to the garments' "hanger appeal," meaning that the clothes looked almost as good on the hanger as they did on a woman.

By 1948, versions of the New Look could be found in stores on both sides of the Atlantic. Women's magazines gave hints on how to buy an original Dior: Stay at only the best hotels, they said. Drive up in a Rolls-Royce; if a woman did not have one, they advised, then she should rent one. Last but not least, a prospective buyer was advised to bring pockets full of money, because an original Dior did not come cheaply.

Impact of Event

British and European teenagers immediately tried to make the New Look their own. Shortages of fabric, and even thread, made these girls invent ingenious new ways to use the mend-and-make-do techniques they had learned during the war to achieve the look. At one and the same time, they began to forge their independence and to reject their parents' generation.

The British government appealed to women's patriotic impulses when asking them not to adopt the New Look during a time of shortages and rebuilding. Princess Elizabeth (later Queen Elizabeth II), however, wore the New Look on her state visit to France. Her sister, Princess Margaret, chose Dior to make the gown she wore to her twenty-first-birthday ball; afterward, nothing could stop British women from embracing the Dior fashion rage.

Not everyone liked the New Look. Women in the work force found it difficult to wear. It took time to achieve the look, moreover; a woman had to don a push-up bra, a waist cincher, several stiffened petticoats, and very high heels. A small flowered hat with a veil and pristine white gloves topped off the New Look. Women in the legal and medical professions grumbled, saying they found the fashions almost impossible to wear. Secretaries could not fit the style's voluminous skirts into their chairs. Women in the upper echelons of the business world, too, felt that they did not look serious in Dior-inspired designs.

During the war, women had joined the work force in large numbers, making a vital contribution as they kept factories turning out weapons and civilian necessities. When the war ended, most were expected to give up their jobs and go back to hearth and home; many women, however, did not want to do that. In the context of the time, therefore, many women protested that the New Look turned women into decorative stereotypes and hindered them from keeping their positions in the workplace.

Some who disliked the New Look formed "Just a Little Below the Knee" clubs and vowed not to wear the look. Club members picketed Dior's hotel room in Chicago, bearing signs urging others to join them in the fight for freedom in manner of dress.

Dior, however, pursued his own vision of women. He saw them as flowers, and he thought that their legs should be shrouded in mystery. Dior retained his prewar sense of life and hence of style; some critics claimed that he imagined a carefree and happy life that never really existed. Moreover, Dior expected women to shape their bodies to his clothes. He "packaged" women for male consumption and subscribed to the old-fashioned religious view of women as temptresses.

Designer Coco Chanel thought that Dior's New Look embodied all the worst aspects of clothes designed for women by men. She disliked Dior's fashions so much that she reentered the fashion business, and critics agree that she produced her best work during this period.

Chanel's actions raised an interesting question: Should men be the final, if not the sole, arbiters of what should be created for women to wear? Before the advent of the nineteenth century English dressmaker Charles Frederick Worth, women designed for women. The Industrial Revolution, however, revolutionized the fashion industry, and what had before been made by hand now came out of a machine. Worth gained fame as a couturier during this transitional period; some say he created haute couture single-handedly. He insisted that he could dress women more elegantly than anyone else could. Soon, men took over the couture industry. In time, women did the handwork but did not contribute much to the designs.

In practical terms, the debate over fashion designers' gender revolves around the fact that men do not wear the garments they design; women, though, design within the parameters of their own bodies. Feminist critic Naomi Wolf raises other compelling objections. Wolf contends that the multibillion-dollar fashion and beauty industry keeps women out of the mainstream of both the business and the political arenas. Women must meet ever-changing beauty ideals created by men. Unable to meet these ideals, women learn to hate themselves.

The question of whether or not men can design beautiful yet functional clothes for women still has not been resolved to everyone's satisfaction. Both sides of the question have merit.

That argument notwithstanding, as the world scene changed, so did the fashion scene. The 1960's spawned an atmosphere of questioning. No one seemed to be satisfied with the status quo anymore. Women began to exercise, and they wanted clothes that would display sleek, toned physiques. In London, Mary Quant introduced a saucy look that seized the imagination, and the pocketbooks, of young women on both sides of the Atlantic. The Italians and the Japanese both entered the fashion arena with a vengeance. No longer did Paris dictate what everyone would wear.

From the New Look onward, Dior influenced the designers that give modern women their choice and their chic. Dior developed separates, "little girl" day dresses, tight sheaths, cocktail and dinner suits, and cotton as a fashionable fabric. Though Dior died in 1957, in a very real sense, his New Look and the House of Dior live on.

Bibliography

De Marly, Diana. *Christian Dior.* New York: Holmes & Meir, 1990. A very readable biography, liberally sprinkled with Dior's fashion sketches and pictures of his designs.

Giroud, Françoise. *Dior: Christian Dior, 1905-1957.* Translated by Stewart Spencer. New York: Rizzoli, 1987. A biography filled with sumptuous pictures of Dior's homes, his workrooms, and his clothes. An absolutely must-see book.

Robinson, Julian. *Fashion in the Forties.* New York: St. Martin's Press, 1976. A detailed account of French, British, and American fashion, especially during World War II, that helps one understand the evolution of Dior's New Look.

Steele, Valerie. *Paris Fashion: A Cultural History.* New York: Oxford University Press, 1988. A look at the fashion industry through the eyes of a sociologist and historian.

Wolf, Naomi. *The Beauty Myth: How Images of Beauty Are Used Against Women.* New York: William Morrow, 1991. A cogent study of the fashion and beauty industry from a feminist's point of view. Whether fashion aficionados or not, readers will find this book provocative and instructive.

Maxine S. Theodoulou

Cross-References

Poiret's "Hobble Skirts" Become the Rage (1910), p. 263; Chanel Defines Modern Women's Fashion (1920's), p. 474; Jantzen Popularizes the One-Piece Bathing Suit (1920), p. 491; The Bikini Swimsuit Is Introduced (1946), p. 1324; Quant Introduces the Miniskirt (Early 1960's), p. 1824; Punk's Antifashion Style First Appears (1974), p. 2299; Madonna Revolutionizes Popular Fashion (1980's), p. 2449.

THE GREAT BOOKS FOUNDATION IS ESTABLISHED

Category of event: Literature
Time: July, 1947
Locale: Chicago, Illinois

Creation of the Great Books Foundation brought to fruition the lifelong goal of a number of academicians that the classic books of Western civilization be made readily available to anyone with a desire to learn

Principal personages:

JOHN ERSKINE (1879-1951), a professor of English literature who first expressed the great books concept during World War I

MORTIMER J. ADLER (1902-   ), an early student of Erskine who became an outspoken and ardent supporter of the great books idea

ROBERT MAYNARD HUTCHINS (1899-1977), the president and chancellor of the University of Chicago whose commitment to the great books program led to the establishment of the Great Books Foundation

Summary of Event

In July, 1947, the Great Books Foundation, under the chairmanship of Robert Maynard Hutchins, opened its offices in Chicago. Its purpose was to expand the great books course beyond the University of Chicago, bringing to all of the United States the knowledge of the classic books of Western civilization. These books, representing more than two thousand years of European knowledge and philosophical thinking, ranged from the works of the Bible and Homer, through Aristotle, Dante Alighieri, and William Shakespeare, to Charles Darwin and Fyodor Dostoevski. For John Erskine, of Columbia College, a great book was simply "one that has meaning, and continues to have meaning, for a variety of people over a long period of time." The establishment of the foundation and the expansion of its programs represented a giant step forward in adult education in the United States. In a sense, however, the creation of the foundation was merely a new phase in a thirty-year-long dream.

As early as 1917, a small but influential group of college professors, led by John Erskine, expressed concern about the nature and quality of liberal-arts education in the United States. Erskine believed that, in order for all people to have common ground for intellectual discussions, every person should be exposed to the classic books of Western civilization. Erskine was a professor of English literature with no background in the Greek and Latin literature, theology, or political philosophy. Nevertheless, he proposed to teach a curriculum of approximately sixty books in those areas of study, as well as English literature, to be read and discussed at the rate of one per week over two academic years. The General Honors course, as it was originally called, was offered to Columbia juniors in 1921, and it differed dramatically from any course of study previously offered at any American university.

The course was to be taught, or more appropriately, led, by professors who were not necessarily experts in the fields covered by the books. The books were to be read in chronological order, in English rather than in their original languages. The intense course of study—each book to be discussed at one two-hour class meeting per week—left little room for in-depth examination of the material. No written test was given; grades were based upon participation in the discussion group and an oral examination.

Erskine had tried out his idea while serving with the United States Army in France and Germany after World War I. He led discussion groups of ordinary American soldiers, many of whom had no formal education beyond grade school, and he determined that one could appreciate and benefit from reading the classic books without any background in or intense study of the material. Upon returning to Columbia, Erskine convinced the college to adopt the General Honors course.

For Erskine and his students, it was not only the material that was being studied but the manner in which it was studied that was important. The noted philosopher Mortimer Adler, who studied under Erskine in the first General Honors course from 1921 to 1923, later became a leading advocate of the great books program. For him, the experience of studying the great books under Erskine was perhaps the most fortunate circumstance of his life. Adler said that the discussion groups were "conducted in the manner of highly civil conversations about important themes and in a spirit of inquiry." In 1923, when new sections of General Honors were formed, they had two instructors per class, each from a different department of the school, who could supplement each other's knowledge in some subject areas. This discussion method, utilizing two discussion leaders, has been retained by the Great Books Foundation in the groups it assists in establishing.

Adler remained at Columbia as a graduate student and instructor, and, at the age of twenty-one, he was himself leading a General Honors section. Several years later, he met Robert Maynard Hutchins, who was at the time the dean of the Yale University Law School. Adler moved to Yale, where he and Hutchins worked together on several projects relating to legal philosophy. Adler's enthusiasm for the great books curriculum was contagious, and Hutchins was soon convinced of the importance of the course. When Hutchins was named president of the University of Chicago in 1930, at the age of thirty-one, he invited Adler to join him and to implement the great books curriculum at that school.

Hutchins created a stir at Chicago when he himself began teaching the great books curriculum to college freshmen. He did it, he said, because Adler had convinced him that his education was lacking and because he would learn twice: first by reading the books and then by leading discussions of them. More important, he saw the great books program in a larger context, as being the fount of Western democratic ideals. The curriculum, in a somewhat different form from that used at Columbia, soon became required for all University of Chicago undergraduate students. The curriculum was also adopted by Amherst College and by St. John's College in Annapolis, Maryland.

Hutchins and Adler took the great books curriculum two steps further, ultimately completing the circle that Erskine had begun drawing thirty years before. First, in 1933, they began leading great books discussions with students at University High School, which was affiliated with the University of Chicago. Perhaps never before had the president of such a prestigious institution found himself teaching high school students—and learning so much from and with them.

Second, and more important, the university, with the cooperation of the Chicago Public Library, began offering the great books reading and discussion program to working adults through extension courses in the Chicago area. They trained discussion leaders for more than thirty groups. Although adult-education programs had existed for some time, this was probably the first that was not vocation-related, recreational, or part of a high school equivalency program. One group, which was moderated by Hutchins and Adler themselves, came to be known as the "Fat Man's Class" because of the affluence of the participants, who were among the business and industrial elite of the city.

Ultimately, operating the adult great books programs became too burdensome for the university. In addition, Hutchins wanted to expand the programs beyond Chicago. By 1946, there were more than five thousand participants throughout the United States. Walter Paepcke, a member of the "Fat Man's Class," was approached by Hutchins to assist in creating a foundation that would more properly run and expand the great books courses. By July, 1947, the Great Books Foundation, with the assistance of the Old Dominion Foundation and the Ford Foundation's Fund for Adult Education, was up and running.

Besides establishing and operating adult great books discussion groups, including the training of discussion-group leaders, the foundation had a second goal: to make inexpensive, uniform editions of the books available to all group participants. Fortunately, Hutchins and the University of Chicago had a ready and willing partner, the Encyclopaedia Britannica.

In 1943, William Benton, a longtime friend of Hutchins and also a member of the "Fat Man's Class," became part-owner of Britannica. After finding it extremely difficult to locate all the necessary great books in the book shops of Chicago, Benton proposed that Britannica publish the entire set of great books for use by participants. At the same time, Adler offered to compile a cross-reference of "great ideas," an index of the great books, which he called a "Synopticon." Hutchins served as general editor, Erskine on the advisory board of editors. The project took more than eight years.

Over the years since its creation, the Great Books Foundation has seen an ebb and flow of participants, who have at times numbered fifty thousand. The program was also expanded to reach ever-younger students. High school great books groups, utilizing the same materials as the adults, were organized in the late 1950's and early 1960's.

Impact of Event

Although participants in programs sponsored by the Great Books Foundation are not as numerous as in the foundation's heyday, the great books idea has had a substantial and continuing effect on American education. More people than ever before have read the great books. Many are read and discussed in adult-education programs unrelated to the foundation as well as in elementary and high schools. One may find the ideas of the great books in speeches of politicians, editorial pages, and popular books. Thus, the "Great Conversation," as Hutchins called the continuing exchange of important ideas, continues unabated.

For John Erskine, the great books were essential for intelligent discourse. Adler regarded them with reverence, delighting in new nuances of meaning with every reading of one of the books. Hutchins had loftier goals in mind. An advocate of a world constitution, he felt that the great books would serve as the basis for, and the culture of, a new world order. In general, the program gave new insights and expanded the intellectual horizons of its participants, both college students and working adults.

The program, however, was not without its critics. At Columbia, two major objections were raised. First, it was claimed that the students would never be able to handle the volume of material. Erskine responded that deep insight was not to be expected; rather, stimulation of the mind was the desired effect. In addition, it would give students a common basis on which to have intelligent conversations.

Second, the instructors of Greek and Latin, along with their fellows in the French and German departments, felt that students would lose the primary benefit of reading the works of Homer, Vergil, Voltaire, Immanuel Kant, and others if they read them in English translation. The poetry and nuance of the writers would be lost. Erskine felt that, on the contrary, by being exposed to the ideas of these writers, students might then wish to read them in the original languages. Besides, it was the ideas that were important; no one, for example, claimed that a person unable to read ancient Hebrew would not benefit from reading the Old Testament in English.

A more lasting and problematic criticism of great books programs is that they are elitist. The belief that the books may be accessible or meaningful to only the upper classes originates in the idea that the elite alone have the education, time, and money to read and study the great books. Hutchins discussed this issue at length in his introductory essay to the great books series. It was exactly this notion that Erskine, Adler, and, more directly, Hutchins, wished to dispel. The whole idea was to demonstrate that any person who knew how to read was sufficiently educated to glean at least some meaning from the books.

More important, reading the great books and discussing them with others not only would be an education in itself but also would stimulate a desire for further education. To Hutchins, this was to be the great books' most important contribution to education. He felt that loss of the urge to learn was a sign of spiritual decay. As for time, anyone who had the time to watch a baseball game or quiz show on television, or to read a romance or mystery novel, had sufficient time to read great books. Finally, the cost of the great books was tremendously reduced by the use of inexpensive paperbacks and by printing them in sets for use in discussion groups.

A final criticism, prevalent in the 1980's and 1990's, was that the great books program was Eurocentric and sexist and reflected almost exclusively the views of Western European men. While this was essentially true, it was also the point of the program in the first place—to present the ideas of Western civilization, which developed over a long period of time when, unfortunately, women and minority group members were marginalized.

At the same time, said the critics, it should be recognized that many ideas in Western, especially American, culture derived from other sources, African and Asian. Thus, the writings of black Americans such as W. E. B. Du Bois and the teachings of Buddhism and Hinduism should be included. Although the reading list of the Great Books Foundation has been amended to respond to these criticisms, particularly in its junior programs, the charge is still often heard.

Even in the criticism, however, one can see that the great books idea is fulfilling one of its goals—to stimulate intelligent discussion. In addition, many ethnic and religious organizations in the United States have developed their own great books lists and discussion groups, in order to learn more about themselves and how they fit in to the larger fabric of world civilization. This fulfills a second goal of the great books idea—education for its own sake.

Hutchins felt that, ultimately, the great books are the bulwark of a liberal-arts education and must continue to be read if modern people wish to remain or become free. The great books, to a large extent, are expressions of the yearning for freedom, political and intellectual, that may be found in virtually any person who has considered the issue. In the view of the proponents of the movement, as long as the great books are studied, the idea and the ideal of freedom will not die.

Bibliography

Adler, Mortimer J. *Philosopher at Large: An Intellectual Autobiography.* New York: Macmillan, 1977. Adler's personal story of intellectual growth, the development of ideas, rather than a recitation of events. Of particular relevance are the chapters titled "General Honors," "Book Lists Without End," and "The Great Ideas." Includes a description of the problems of indexing *The Great Books of the Western World.* Contains a complete bibliography of Adler's works through 1976, as well as Erskine's and the Great Books Foundation's original lists of authors.

Ashmore, Harry S. *Unseasonable Truths: The Life of Robert Maynard Hutchins.* Boston: Little, Brown, 1989. A lengthy biography by a close colleague. Details Hutchins' struggle to implement the great books program at the University of Chicago as well as his work with Encyclopaedia Britannica and the Great Books Foundation.

Erskine, John. *My Life as a Teacher.* Philadelphia: J. B. Lippincott, 1948. The autobiography of the professor who originally conceived the great books program. Published shortly after the establishment of the Great Books Foundation, it predates publication of *The Great Books of the Western World.* A chapter is devoted to the development of the Columbia great books program.

Fitzpatrick, Edward Augustus. *Great Books: Panacea or What?* Milwaukee: Bruce Publishing, 1952. Fitzpatrick defends the great books concept in detail. In one chapter, he coyly parodies Socratic dialogue to illustrate his point. Good for the ardent fan of the great books philosophy.

Hutchins, Robert M. *Great Books: The Foundation of a Liberal Education.* New York: Simon & Schuster, 1954. This lengthy essay, 115 pages, lays out the philosophy behind the great books program and its importance to general education. Hardly dated, Hutchins seems prescient in his discussion of the influences and misuses of electronic mass media.

Richard A. Flom

Cross-References

Melville Is Rediscovered as a Major American Novelist (1920), p. 502; Wallace Founds *Reader's Digest* (1922), p. 549; Luce Founds *Time* Magazine (1923), p. 577; The Book-of-the-Month Club and the Literary Guild Are Founded (1926), p. 686; Dickinson's Poems Are Published in Full for the First Time (1955), p. 1662.

GERMAN WRITERS FORM GROUP 47

Category of event: Literature
Time: September, 1947
Locale: Bannwaldsee, Germany

Many important German writers joined Group 47 to confront the Nazi past and provide a forum for mutual support and criticism following World War II

Principal personages:

HANS WERNER RICHTER (1908-   ), a former German prisoner of war and free-lance writer who became known as the "father of Group 47"

ALFRED ANDERSCH (1914-1980), the cofounder of Group 47 with Richter

HEINRICH BÖLL (1917-1985), a German author and the 1972 winner of the Nobel Prize in Literature, who participated in the meetings of Group 47

GÜNTER GRASS (1927-   ), a German author who participated in Group 47

Summary of Event

At the beginning of September, 1947, a group of fifteen German authors met at the home of Ilse Schneider-Lengyel in Bannwaldsee, near Füssen in the German province of Allgäu. The group provided a forum for the discussion of the serious problems facing German writers in the post-World War II era. Among those present at the meeting, in addition to Schneider-Lengyel, were Hans Werner Richter, Walter Kolbenhoff, Walter M. Guggenheimer, Friedrich Minssen, Wolfgang Bächler, Nicolaus Sombart, Heinz Friedrich, Heinz Ulrich, and Wolfdietrich Schnurre. They had no awareness at the time that their small group would become the nucleus of one of the greatest literary movements in German history, Group 47, named after the year in which the first meeting took place.

The idea for Group 47 originated in the mind of Hans Werner Richter while he was interned as a prisoner of war in the United States. At the beginning of 1945, the United States government began moving prisoners of war with antifascist records to Fort Kearney and Fort Getty on the Atlantic coast, where they attended courses to prepare them as future administrators for the new democracy that would be founded in Germany after the Allied Powers—France, Great Britain, the United States, and the Soviet Union—reunited the various occupation zones and phased out military government. Because of his writing experience and journalism background, Richter was moved to the Atlantic coast and appointed editor-in-chief of a German newspaper, *Der Ruf* (*The Call*), by the U.S. camp authorities. With the assistance of Alfred Andersch and Walter Kolbenhoff, Richter's newspaper became the most liberal and widely distributed German camp newspaper in the United States in 1945 and 1946.

After his release as a prisoner of war, Richter's request that *Der Ruf* be printed and distributed in Germany was granted, and the newspaper was published there from August, 1946, until April, 1947. Both the American and German editions of *Der Ruf* dealt with topical issues, including German collective guilt for the Nazi past and the future of German government. Publication of the German edition was halted by U.S. military authorities after only sixteen issues, however, perhaps at the prompting of the Soviet Union, which did not fare well on the editorial pages of the paper. Richter had hoped to continue the work of *Der Ruf* in the form of a satirical periodical, but the military government was no longer willing to grant him a license. In response, Richter organized the meeting of friends and writers at the home of Schneider-Lengyel. The meeting was the first of a series that lasted from 1947 until 1967.

The moral support and mutual understanding that Group 47 offered were invaluable in helping to overcome the psychological effects of years of Nazi brutality and oppression. As a forum for free thinkers, Group 47 gave everyone the opportunity to express an opinion. In general, however, the group was homogeneous. Its members shared certain beliefs and opinions: They all leaned to the left of center politically, were strongly concerned about the future of German language and literature, and were suspicious of complex writing and complicated grammar.

Although Group 47 was not primarily a political group, its members were often involved with political causes and discussed and debated current issues. This is hardly surprising, given the atmosphere in which Group 47 was formed. The postwar era in Germany was a time of political upheaval and political change, and Group 47 was not immune from variations in the German national political scene.

In general, Group 47 was distrustful of political institutions, politicians, and government agencies. There was a fear that youthful vigor and naïveté could be misused, as it had been under the rule of Adolf Hitler, if a warning was not issued. Many of the works by authors involved with Group 47 centered on this theme.

No previous generation had warned the members of Group 47 of the dangers of politics in causing war. The German authors of the 1920's had spent some time discussing the devastating consequences of World War I, but the question of how to avoid a repetition of the tragedy did not play a major part in most of their works. Erich Maria Remarque's *Im Westen nichts Neues* (1929; *All Quiet on the Western Front*, 1929) was a notable exception, but its main focus was to discuss the horrors of war, not how to avoid them. Group 47 examined the political scene rather than the front lines. In this sense, it did much more than the post-World War I literary groups had done to attack the establishment—from common citizens to high-ranking politicians—and to prevent further war in Europe.

In contrast to the literary groups that emerged in the wake of World War I, notably the Spartacus movement (1918-1919), Group 47 was not born out of the fires of war in Germany; the movement came rather from the prisoner-of-war camps of America and was transplanted to Germany. Group 47 was the third and most important force pushing German literature forward after World War II. The other two groups, the émigré writers and the writers who had remained behind to resist the Nazis, did little to move the German literary scene toward new horizons. Group 47 provided the impetus for new, groundbreaking literary developments.

Impact of Event

From 1947 to 1959, a number of German writers made forceful and significant attempts to come to terms with the legacy of the Nazi dictatorship. The German *Trümmerliteratur* (literature of ruins) that appeared immediately after the end of World War II sought confrontation with the past as a means of assuring that a Nazi dictatorship would never again occur. Authors such as Günter Grass and Heinrich Böll, later participants in the meetings of Group 47, addressed Germany's Nazi past in their novels and short stories.

For instance, Grass's novel *Die Blechtrommel* (1959; *The Tin Drum*, 1961) dealt with the problems of guilt and answerability for the events of the war. By blurring the lines between right and wrong, good and evil, Grass forced his readers to think about the events of the Hitler era. This distortion was at times humorous but was more often serious, showing how difficult it was to answer the questions raised by mass executions, gas chambers, and concentration camps.

In a similar way, Böll addressed Germany's Nazi past in his novel *Billard um halbzehn* (1959; *Billiards at Half Past Nine*, 1961). Böll focused on a single family and its experiences before and after the war, creating a fictional picture that closely resembled reality. Like Grass, Böll forced his readers to think about the events of the recent past and to ask themselves questions.

Both Grass and Böll returned to German literary traditions, reviving the techniques of the twentieth century German literary giant Thomas Mann while initiating new techniques. Böll and Grass were keenly aware that a return to traditional styles of writing was one method of avoiding the distortion of the German language that had taken place under Nazi rule. No matter how much these two authors fell back on earlier literary tradition, however, the beauty of their prose was always secondary to their main purpose: the search for truth through their writing.

Group 47 not only had a great deal to do with the topics that Grass and Böll chose but also had a great deal to do with the topics that appeared in all postwar German literature. The topics that Group 47 discussed became the topics of German literature for the next twenty years. More than half of the German authors who achieved international fame between 1947 and 1967 were advanced by Group 47. Almost every major German author of the postwar period participated in the meetings of Group 47 at one time or another. Famous writers such as Ingeborg Bachmann, Paul Celan, Peter Handke, Siegfried Lenz, Peter Weiss, Erich Kästner, Marie Luise Kaschnitz, Ernst Bloch, Luise Rinser, Walter Jens, and Uwe Johnson all took part in the meetings of Group 47 as readers, critics, or guests. Works by those associated with Group 47 would shape modern German literature to an extent that no other literary movement ever had.

Group 47 strengthened the German literary community and brought together writers of different backgrounds and varying experience. The older writers acted as mentors to the younger writers, helping both young and old to achieve their full potential. The comments made by Group 47 members about works at their meetings often helped authors work out details before manuscripts were sent to publishers.

In 1949, two years after the founding of Group 47, the Federal Republic of Germany was established. Almost immediately, works by the group's members were recognized as an important part of the new nation's culture. Despite its original antiestablishment crusade, Group 47 was slowly becoming the establishment. Authors who participated in Group 47 usually had little trouble getting their works published, and many new writers saw participation in Group 47 as a way to gain recognition in the literary community.

By 1959, Group 47 was firmly ensconced as the German literary establishment. Written works by members of Group 47 during this period, some of them masterpieces of German poetry and prose, were numerous, yet the decline of Group 47 was already beginning. Because it had been a loose association of authors even from the beginning, the group finally found that some of its participants resented the restraints that attachment to an organization imposed. They wanted to pursue their own literary destinies. Others felt that they no longer needed Group 47's moral support because of the stabilization of German society. The major problem for Group 47, though, was that it gradually lost sight of its original goals in the years between 1959 and 1967. Maintaining their reputations at the expense of Group 47 and controlling the literary climate of the Federal Republic of Germany became more important to some members of the group than working for the good of the German people and producing quality writing. As authors began to use the group primarily as a stepping-stone to success, the movement began to fall apart. The miraculous economic recovery of Germany during the 1950's and 1960's improved life for the German people, but the quest for money in German society often meant that ethical principles were replaced by greed among Group 47's members. Better writers distanced themselves from the movement because of its weaknesses, and the quality of the writing discussed at the group's meetings began to decline. In the end, Group 47's members lost their idealism.

Group 47 had become the literary establishment in Germany without effort; in order to hold that position, however, it needed to serve the purpose for which it had originally been founded: the provision of mutual aid and moral support among writers seeking to restore and advance German literature after the debacle of the Nazi era. When Group 47's members no longer supported one another and resorted to political infighting to determine their course, the group began to collapse. The founders of Group 47 had always feared the dangers of large political organizations; however, student protests at the last meeting of the group in Pulvermühle, Germany, made them painfully aware that they were now considered just such an organization. Only when student protesters disrupted the meeting with chants and shouts did those associated with Group 47 realize the magnitude of the problems that had developed in their association.

The power of Group 47 eventually led to its downfall. Those seeking to use the group to further their own interests destroyed it. Still, Group 47 maintained its position as the driving force in German writing for nearly twenty years and claimed some of the greatest German writers of the twentieth century as participants. As a result of the accomplishments of its members and the strong influence that it maintained over writing in Germany, Group 47 reserved a secure place for itself in literary history.

Bibliography

Bangerter, Lowell A. *German Writing Since 1945: A Critical Survey.* New York: Continuum, 1988. A comprehensive survey of the authors, works, literary movements, and directions of German writing in the postwar era. A good general reference book. Includes bibliography and index.

Bettex, Albert. "Modern Literature (1885 to the Present)." In *German Literature: A Critical Survey*, edited by Bruno Boesch. Translated by Ronald Taylor. London: Methuen, 1971. Covers the main trends and movements in German literature from before World War I to the 1970's. Emphasis is given to exile writing during the Third Reich and the skepticism that developed among German writers following World War II. Includes a general bibliography and index.

Demetz, Peter. *Postwar German Literature: A Critical Introduction.* New York: Western Publishing, 1970. Deals with the profound social and intellectual transformations in German literature since 1945. Portraits of the authors, poets, and playwrights who have shaped German postwar literature make up the body of the work. Includes suggestions for further reading and index.

Reed, Donna K. *The Novel and the Nazi Past.* American University Studies, 1st series, Germanic Languages and Literature, vol. 28. New York: Peter Lang, 1985. A nicely organized, interdisciplinary account of post World War II German literature and its handling of twelve years of Nazi dictatorship. Focuses on the works of Günter Grass, Heinrich Böll, and Alfred Andersch. Includes footnotes, bibliography, and index.

Robertson, John George, et al. *A History of German Literature.* 6th ed. Elmsford, N.Y.: London House & Maxwell, 1970. A general history of German literature from its beginnings to the present. The sections on National Socialism and the postwar era in Germany are useful. Includes chronological table, endnotes, bibliography, and index.

Gregory Weeks

Cross-References

Mann's *The Magic Mountain* Reflects European Crisis (1924), p. 588; *All Quiet on the Western Front* Stresses the Futility of War (1929), p. 767; Hitler Organizes an Exhibition Denouncing Modern Art (1937), p. 1083; The Nazis Ban Nolde's Paintings (1941), p. 1217; Wiesel's *Night* Recalls the Holocaust (1956), p. 1700; Grass Publishes *The Tin Drum* (1959), p. 1780; Celan's Influential *Atemwende* Is Published (1967), p. 2070.

NBC BROADCASTS THE WORLD SERIES

Category of event: Television and radio
Time: September-October, 1947
Locale: New York, New York

Television coverage of the 1947 World Series helped create a boom in the sale of television sets and establish a lasting linkage between television and professional sports

Principal personages:

DAVID SARNOFF (1891-1971), the guiding force at the Radio Corporation of America (RCA) and in its development of television

FRANK FOLSOM (1894-1970), the RCA executive who worked for the expansion of commercial television in the late 1940's

JOE DIMAGGIO (1914-   ), the New York Yankees outfielder who became a symbol of excellence

AL GIONFRIDDO (1922-   ), a diminutive reserve outfielder for the Brooklyn Dodgers whose remarkable catch in the 1947 World Series gave him a place in baseball lore

DIZZY DEAN (1911-1974), a flamboyant star pitcher of the 1930's who became an equally flamboyant star broadcaster of the 1950's

Summary of Event

In the early fall of 1947, the hectic pace of life slowed in New York City, as baseball became the chief preoccupation of its usually bustling citizenry. The upstart Dodgers of Brooklyn won the championship of the National League, and the powerful Yankees returned to their pre-World War II mastery of the American League. The two were to clash in a rematch of the 1941 World Series (won by the Yankees) in a city where only a fraction of the eight million residents could attend the best-of-seven-games series. Brooklyn's Ebbets Field held only thirty-four thousand seats, and even massive Yankee Stadium could accommodate only seventy-four thousand fans. Sensing the presence of an avid potential audience, David Sarnoff, the president of the Radio Corporation of America (RCA), decided to expand RCA's rudimentary television system to cover the 1947 World Series. This decision brought together for the first time two of the giants in the entertainment industry: big league baseball—for several decades the nation's most popular professional sport—and television, which would soon leap from the electronic laboratory to dominate mass communications.

Sarnoff and RCA faced a basic problem in their plans to promote a profit-making television broadcasting system: There were only eight thousand television sets in the possession of consumers in 1947. Potential viewers would purchase a television receiver (which was a very expensive item in 1947) only if they were convinced that it could present to them programs of compelling interest. Yet RCA's television operation, a new division of the National Broadcasting Company (or NBC), did not have the experience to produce television programs with mass-audience appeal. Without a large audience, NBC could not sell advertising time to sponsors—the essential factor in generating income. One solution was the coverage of athletic events, which NBC had already begun as early as 1944 with the *Gillette Cavalcade of Sports.* The Gillette Safety Razor Company was satisfied with its sponsorship of the earlier program and agreed to purchase advertising time on the broadcast of the 1947 World Series. Therefore, NBC's coverage of the 1947 World Series was an experiment that pulled together for the first time crucial ingredients for success in commercial broadcasting: a program with innate mass appeal, a limited but potentially huge viewing audience, and a corporation willing to pay for air time to advertise a product.

NBC's decision to cover the 1947 World Series was not simply the product of postwar economics but also the outgrowth of RCA's work with television technology, which had begun in the late 1920's. David Sarnoff had spent considerable money to support technical experiments and to purchase patents. He had also weathered rugged competition from inventors such as Philo Farnsworth and corporate challengers such as Philco. Sarnoff's 1939 decision to push for the expansion of commercial broadcasting led to a flurry of activity that included television coverage of a college baseball game between Princeton University and Columbia University on May 17, 1939. World War II soon intervened, however, and commercial television temporarily lost its impetus.

Sarnoff had an imperial presence in the boardrooms of RCA and NBC, but one of his able lieutenants, Frank Folsom, played an important part in the decision to emphasize popular sports in the early days of television. Sarnoff was a Russian émigré with aristocratic tastes and an obsessive interest in technology; Folsom was a pragmatic marketing expert who had earned his corporate reputation at Montgomery Ward. The two men seemed to bring together a vigorous combination of technical innovation and inventive marketing that contributed to NBC's success with the 1947 World Series.

Most of the nation's television sets were concentrated in the New York area, where the 1947 World Series had a special appeal, but these seven games offered an unusual display of player virtuosity and fan excitement. In the fourth game, the Yankees' Bill Bevens needed only one more out to complete the first no-hit game in World Series history when Cookie Lavagetto, the Dodgers' second-string third baseman, slammed a double off the Ebbets Field outfield wall that not only broke up the no-hitter but also gave Brooklyn a victory. The legendary Joe DiMaggio hit two home runs in the series, but he was deprived of a third home run in the sixth game by a seemingly impossible running catch made some four hundred and fifteen feet from home plate by the fast-footed Al Gionfriddo. Had Gionfriddo not made the catch, DiMaggio's drive would have put the Yankees ahead in the sixth game and could have decided the outcome of the series. Gionfriddo's feat astonished the seventy-four thousand spectators, twenty-five Yankees, and the television audience. In spite of the remarkable efforts of Gionfriddo and Lavagetto, the Dodgers fell to the Yankees, whose relief pitcher, Joe Page, turned in a stellar performance in the seventh and decisive game.

The excitement of television coverage of a dramatic World Series created widespread public interest, but there were problems for the broadcast medium. *The New York Times* commented that the television camera in Yankee Stadium could not handle the sharp contrast between sections of the field bathed in bright sunlight and the shadows cast on the infield by the stands behind home plate. The cameras also had difficulty in following the rapid movement of a batted ball and in covering the simultaneous actions of runners and fielders. Nevertheless, NBC's broadcast of the World Series achieved its purpose of stimulating public interest in television and stimulating the sale of television sets. Many sports fans' initial experience with television came in viewing the 1947 World Series in the confines of a neighborhood bar, where the cost was limited to the price of a beer.

Impact of Event

The broadcast of the 1947 World Series spread out through a primitive network that reached four cities: New York, Philadelphia, Schenectady, and Washington, D.C. Although there were other factors involved in promoting the sale of television sets, the broadcast must be considered a major contribution to the cultivation of public fascination with the medium. In particular, the adult male sports fan was, in a still male-dominated society, generally the primary wage earner in a family. His response to television coverage of the World Series and to peer pressure within America's sports-oriented culture was a crucial factor in his decision to purchase a television set. After the fall of 1947, the consumer demand for television sets grew rapidly. Households with television rose from eight thousand in 1946 to three hundred thousand in 1948 to four million by 1950. Sarnoff and Folsom presided over the growth of NBC television into a nationwide network with huge advertising revenues.

Baseball and television became inextricably, if at times unhappily, linked after 1947. The problems in telecasting day games declined with improvements in camera capability in the 1950's, but the complexity and rapidity of crucial plays continued to defy even the most skilled director. These brief moments of intense excitement were spread out over a two-to-three-hour period in which ruminative pitchers and dawdling hitters could slow the pace of the game to a veritable standstill. Announcers searched for interesting commentary, and television viewers left for the kitchen. Former St. Louis Cardinals pitcher Dizzy Dean provided a solution on the Columbia Broadcasting System (CBS) *Game of the Week* in the mid-1950's with his neverending stream of anecdotes, corn-pone humor, and—when all else failed—a fullvoiced rendition of the folk-pop song "The Wabash Cannonball." In his disarming, country-bumpkin style, Dean pioneered color commentary and linked it to a sanitized version of sports humor that later broadcasters could only mimic or praise.

Baseball soon found a formidable competitor in the television sports arena— professional football. Encouraged by the commercial success of baseball on television, the networks moved cautiously into the fall season's Sunday afternoon games in the 1950's. Professional football was at the time a marginal operation that occasionally grabbed the headlines with the presence of a few ex-college all-Americans. The game itself, however, was better suited than baseball for the technology of television. The center of action was the line of scrimmage, which moved across a measured and carefully lined one-hundred-yard field. The sideline camera could follow most of the action with ease. The forward pass introduced an element of uncertainty, but a long (or wide) camera angle usually was sufficient to capture the play. The breakthrough season for televised football was probably 1958, when the Baltimore Colts defeated the New York Giants in a sudden-death overtime game for the National Football League (NFL) championship. The television viewers, much better than the fans in the stadium, saw the full impact of Baltimore fullback Alan Ameche's decisive plunge into the end zone and sports mythology. The tension, explosiveness, and violence of this championship game formed the prototype for television football of the future.

The relationship between television and sports intensified as broadcasts drew larger audiences and, therefore, larger advertising revenue. For both baseball and football, television came to mean a substantial increase in team owners' profits and players' salaries. By the 1970's, football commissioner Pete Rozelle and baseball commissioner Bowie Kuhn worked more as heads of multimillion-dollar corporate entities than as coordinators of sports associations. Both Kuhn and Rozelle saw large television contracts as crucial to the health of their respective organizations.

Professional football's golden era in the 1970's and 1980's glittered all the more because of improvements in television technology, especially the magnetic-tape video recorder, which made the slow-motion replay possible. Baseball also eventually benefited from this and other changes. The videotape replay, along with new camera lenses and higher-quality pictures, made baseball a much more photogenic subject. The outfield camera, usually located just behind and above the left-center-field fence, provided a close study of the micro-war over home plate involving the pitcher and the catcher pitted against the hitter. Slow-motion replay and multiple camera angles made it possible to review the details of quick double plays and stolen bases and the trajectories of towering home runs, deceptive curveballs, and floating knuckleballs.

The symbiotic relationship between television and professional sports created a bonanza in income for both, but in the process also created a new, and not entirely admirable, dimension in the culture of sports in the United States. In its first two decades, television conveyed feats of prowess and courage that helped to build the heroic personas of baseball's Joe DiMaggio, Ted Williams, and Willie Mays and football's Johnny Unitas and Jim Brown. By the 1970's, though, television's contribution to mythic image-making diminished. The flood of advertising income made sports stars into millionaires at the same time that journalism exposed some wealthy stars in all of their lust for money, female companionship, and media attention. Yet the improvements in video technology and corresponding adjustments by directors, announcers, and analysts presented in unprecedented detail the continuation of the decades-old drama of confrontation and the humorous mixture of playful exaltation and sly sarcasm that carries professional sports beyond its darker side of meanness and greed.

Bibliography

Abramson, Albert. *The History of Television, 1880 to 1941.* Jefferson, N.C.: McFarland, 1987. A detailed account of the scientific experiments and engineering innovations that resulted in workable television broadcast systems before World War II. Based on research in United States and European technical journals and archives.

Barnouw, Erik. *Tube of Plenty: The Evolution of American Television.* New York: Oxford University Press, 1975. Broad survey of the history of television, with emphasis on entertainment and news programs. Little attention to televised sports, but thorough examination of general trends in the industry.

Lasch, Christopher. *The Culture of Narcissism.* New York: Warner Books, 1979. A wide-ranging critique of American culture. Chapter 5, "The Degradation of Sport," is an indictment of the impact of television on athletics, especially football.

Lyons, Eugene. *David Sarnoff.* New York: Harper & Row, 1966. A sympathetic biography of the founder of RCA. Lyons stresses Sarnoff's insights into technological advancement and his organizational skills but underplays RCA's internal squabbling.

Morgan, Edward P. "Fifty-Mile Bleachers." *Collier's* 120 (September 27, 1947): 128-132. Interesting description of the arrival of televised sports to bars in the weeks before the 1947 World Series. Includes discussions of the growth of television and the use of different types of television sets.

Rader, Benjamin. *In Its Own Image: How Television Has Transformed American Sports.* New York: Free Press, 1984. Provocative study of the impact of television on sports. Rader emphasizes the 1950's and 1960's, when sports became a major part of television broadcasting. He also contrasts the attitudes and actions of players in the age of big-budget television with the heroic images of players from earlier decades, laments the triumph of high salaries and selfishness over discipline and teamwork, and connects the transformation to larger changes in politics and culture.

Smith, Curt. *America's Dizzy Dean.* St. Louis: Bethany, 1978. A thoughtful biography of the hard-throwing pitcher for the St. Louis Cardinals' "Gas House Gang" of the 1930's. Smith traces Dean's career from his halcyon days as a big-league star to his comeback as a popular baseball broadcaster.

Sobel, Robert. *RCA.* New York: Stein & Day, 1986. A critical history of the corporation from the 1920's to the early 1980's, with Sarnoff as the central character. Discusses many of RCA's internal struggles as well as its bitter competition with other communications companies. Chapters 6 to 8 set the context of the decision to broadcast the 1947 World Series.

Voigt, David Quentin. *American Baseball: From Postwar Expansion to the Electronic Age.* University Park: Pennsylvania State University Press, 1983. History of baseball from 1945 to 1982 that combines interesting detail with measured generalizations and provides solid background on the emergence of televised baseball.

John A. Britton

Cross-References

NBC Launches American Television at the World's Fair (1939), p. 1143; NBC and CBS Launch Commercial Television (1941), p. 1211; ABC Begins Its Own Network Television Service (1948), p. 1368; Television Enters Its Golden Age (1950's), p. 1465; ABC Makes a Landmark Deal with Disney (1954), p. 1612; The Decline of the Big Three Networks Becomes a Fall (Late 1980's), p. 2554.

ABC BEGINS ITS OWN NETWORK TELEVISION SERVICE

Category of event: Television and radio
Time: 1948
Locale: New York, New York, and Hollywood, California

Leonard Harry Goldenson created one of the "Big Three" television networks by raising cash from the sale of theaters; a deal with Walt Disney secured a future for ABC-TV

Principal personages:

LEONARD HARRY GOLDENSON (1905-   ), the man who built ABC television into one of the three dominant networks in the United States, in part based on his dealings with Disney

ROBERT E. KINTNER (1909-1980), the man who helped Goldenson in the early years and then in 1956 resigned to begin a second career at NBC-TV

WALT DISNEY (1901-1966), the creative head of a small Hollywood studio, who with his brother Roy Disney linked filmmaking with television and built a popular culture empire

Summary of Event

ABC-TV is the youngest of the three early surviving over-the-air television networks, and for much of its history it was the weakest. It was begun not by creative entrepreneurship but by government order. The first government-forced action took place in 1943, when the National Broadcasting Company (NBC) was ordered to give up one of its two radio networks. Edward J. Noble, famous as the father of Life Savers candy, purchased NBC Blue, the weaker of NBC's networks, for $8,000,000. In 1945, he formally changed the name to the American Broadcasting Company, or ABC.

From this radio base came the ABC television network. The flagship station in New York went on the air in 1948. Nobel and his aides scrambled to pick up affiliates in cities where NBC and the Columbia Broadcasting System (CBS) already had lined up the strongest television stations. Having fewer affiliates than NBC and CBS, ABC-TV started from a base of smaller audiences and thus was at a disadvantage in the new television world. As television began to expand, the best-known radio, popular musical, and film stars naturally gravitated to CBS or NBC. Program packagers developed shows for NBC and CBS, rarely risking investments on the third-place ABC-TV.

The ABC television network was further crippled by a delay by the Federal Communications Commission (FCC) that froze television license allocations. From 1949 through 1952, no new television stations were permitted to go on the air, while the FCC decided how to proceed. During the freeze, there were many major cities with only one or two television stations, leaving ABC without an affiliation. Lucky television pioneer stations took only the top shows on NBC and CBS, shutting out ABC-TV. Even when the FCC freeze ended in April, 1952, ABC-TV was forced to accept affiliation with weaker ultrahigh frequency (UHF) stations at a time when most television sets did not have the proper tuning mechanism for UHF signals.

Through the late 1940's and early 1950's, ABC-TV made do with low-cost programming such as roller derby and professional wrestling. In the 1951-1952 television season, as CBS pioneered with *I Love Lucy*, ABC-TV was forced to run *Wrestling from Columbia Park*, starring announcer Dennis James. Against Ed Sullivan's popular *Toast of the Town* variety show, ABC-TV gave the time back to local affiliates.

As late as 1954, ABC had affiliations with only forty of the more than three hundred television stations on the air. This shortfall was reflected in advertising. In 1954, ABC-TV had one-tenth of the network billings, while NBC and CBS split the rest. ABC-TV had to make do with such prime-time fare as *The Chicago Symphony Chamber Orchestra*, *Industries for America*, and *Harness Racing*.

ABC-TV might have gone the way of the DuMont network had it not been for Leonard Goldenson and his United Paramount Theaters. By a 1948 Supreme Court ruling, Hollywood's Paramount Pictures had to sell its chain of movie theaters. Goldenson took charge of the new theater company and merged it with ABC.

United Paramount Theaters used the money from selling movie theaters to buy ABC for $25 million. ABC got not only an infusion of cash but also a set of experienced show-business managers, led by the former head of Paramount's one-thousand-theater chain, Leonard Goldenson, and his assistant Robert Kintner. Goldenson and Kintner would shepherd ABC through those tough times with skill that perhaps deserves more credit than that given to their more famous rivals, David Sarnoff of NBC and William S. Paley of CBS.

Goldenson relied on techniques he learned at Paramount: find a niche audience not served by larger rivals, then specialize. Thus ABC-TV, seeing the baby boomers abandoned by advertisers, NBC, and CBS, sought out the youth market with programs such as *American Bandstand*, *Maverick*, and in the most fortuitous deal the company made, *Disneyland* (and the shows that evolved from it) and *The Mickey Mouse Club*. ABC stars included Edd "Kookie" Byrnes of *77 Sunset Strip* and Ricky Nelson, among other teen heartthrobs. Critics attacked *The Untouchables* for its violence, but that simply got ABC-TV publicity it could not afford through normal means. ABC-TV aimed at the bottom line, appealing to the mass of television viewers with a variety of offerings rather than aiming programming at the elite.

The rise of ABC was remarkable. At the time of the ABC-United Paramount merger in February, 1953, the company owned only two television stations in major markets and shared a third. In 1952, ABC had lost more than $140,000 and had $12 million of debt on its books. Despite continual innovations, Goldenson and Kintner daily battled to raise ad sales, boost affiliate relations, and not follow DuMont out of business.

ABC-TV slowly built up. As more stations went on the air after the FCC freeze was lifted, they had no choice but to affiliate with ABC-TV. These new stations tended to be weaker UHF stations, so even as ABC-TV's coverage grew it could not match that of NBC or CBS through the 1950's.

Goldenson countered with new talent. If there was a turning point, it came in 1953, when Danny Thomas' *I Love Lucy* knockoff, *Make Room for Daddy*, went on the air. It soon proved that the network could create a prime-time hit. Deals with Walt Disney and Warner Bros., however, were what carried ABC-TV over the financial hump.

In April, 1954, Walt Disney and ABC-TV announced plans for a *Disneyland* television series. Network television was a means to an end for Disney. Sensing a new audience in the baby boom and a new means of access through the widespread sale of automobiles, Disney wanted to build a new type of theme park for families in the suburbs. Roy Disney had approached banks but could not convince conservative officers that Disney would build something more than another Coney Island. The conservative financial institutions turned Roy Disney down; they wanted no part of the proposed Disneyland.

Walt and Roy Disney tried to interest a television network. David Sarnoff at NBC-TV and William Paley at CBS-TV were not interested. The Disney brothers then turned to Goldenson, who agreed to back Disneyland if the Disney company would produce a one-hour television series for ABC.

The Disney television show went on the air on Wednesday nights on ABC-TV beginning in October, 1954. It moved to Friday night in 1958 and then Sunday night in 1960, and it would remain a Sunday-night fixture for more than two decades. ABC-TV had its first top twenty ratings hit, seeing the Disney show finish sixth overall in the ratings for the television season that ran from September, 1954, through May, 1955.

This pioneering television series was designed to kindle interest in the Disneyland theme park that opened in July, 1955. ABC-TV took a one-third financial interest in the park as well as all profits from food concessions for the first ten years in exchange for providing financing. Disneyland and the *Disneyland* show proved to be instant hits, forever transforming ABC-TV.

A new segment of the Disney television effort on ABC-TV surpassed all expectations. The December, 1954, "Davy Crockett, Indian Fighter" episode, shown during "Frontierland," created a national obsession of enormous proportions. By mid-1955, "The Ballad of Davy Crockett" had become a pop music hit, coonskin caps were atop nearly all baby-boom children, and Fess Parker had become one of television's first true stars. In the process, television set owners scrambled to tune in ABC-TV.

With the Disney success, Goldenson was able to convince Warner Bros. to produce television shows. *Cheyenne, 77 Sunset Strip, Surfside 6*, and *Maverick* enabled ABC to begin making a profit. Soon after came *Hawaiian Eye* and *The Roaring Twenties*. ABC was not only surviving but was looking forward to thriving.

Impact of Event

It was not until the mid-1970's that ABC-TV would finally rank with NBC and

CBS. Goldenson's pioneering efforts through the 1950's, however, should be seen as revolutionizing American television. His greatest achievement was to unite television with Hollywood. Prior to the ABC deals with Disney and Warner Bros., Hollywood had tried to take over television. ABC proved that a "marriage of convenience" was the best, in the long run, for all.

ABC-TV survived on expedient moves and the exploitation of fads until the mid-1950's, when Goldenson was able to sign Disney and then Warner Bros. to produce shows. This proved to be a turning point in the rise of ABC-TV, ensuring that the fledgling third network would remain a permanent part of the American television broadcasting scene. ABC-TV's bold action also brought Hollywood into the television business and ensured that Hollywood would remain at the center of television production thereafter.

In the years immediately following the success of the *Disneyland* show and the Warner Bros. entries, the other major Hollywood studios followed. By 1960, television production was primarily a Hollywood effort. The days of live television drama broadcast from New York City were over. Disney and ABC made Hollywood the center of television production and the major Hollywood studios the locus of that production.

ABC-TV skillfully copied its larger rivals. When CBS pioneered with *I Love Lucy*, ABC found its low-cost versions produced by independent companies headed by Ozzie Nelson and Danny Thomas. In time, *The Adventures of Ozzie and Harriet* would run 435 episodes on ABC, *Make Room for Daddy* 336 episodes, and *The Donna Reed Show* 274 episodes.

Goldenson should be praised for his skilled experiments. He ran news on Sunday nights against Ed Sullivan's highly popular *Toast of the Town*, anticipating the genre of investigative news shows such as *60 Minutes.* He was bold enough to telecast—live—the Army-McCarthy hearings.

With ABC's growing profits, Goldenson purchased television stations in Detroit and San Francisco so that ABC would have a base of operations in the major American cities to match CBS and NBC. The ABC-owned-and-operated stations were all on channel 7 because in the early years of television many broadcasters believed that "high band" channels (those beginning with channel 7) were inferior to the original allocations on the part of the spectrum space labeled channels 2 through 6. The technical distinction proved not to matter, and in time ABC's owned stations became a reliable source of financial support for the ABC-TV network.

In time, ABC-TV would join NBC and CBS, with stature as one of the three dominant networks in American television. Popular programming included coverage of the Olympics, an expensive but high-profile venture. There were hit shows such as *Happy Days* in the mid-1970's. By 1976, with its rise to the position of top-rated network, ABC-TV had ceased to be thought of as a stepchild, as had been true in the early days. It continued to be at the defining core of production and dissemination of news and entertainment within the cultural and social fabric of the United States.

Bibliography

Barnouw, Erik. *The Image Empire.* Vol. 3 in *A History of Broadcasting in the United States.* New York: Oxford University Press, 1970. This is the final volume of the Barnouw trilogy covering the basic history of radio and television.

Castleman, Harry, and Walter J. Podrazik. *Watching TV: Four Decades of American Television.* New York: McGraw-Hill, 1982. Presents a remarkable amount of basic information on the early history of television. The rise of ABC as a television power is treated in some detail throughout.

Goldenson, Leonard H. *Beating the Odds.* New York: Charles Scribner's Sons, 1991. A candid autobiography by the man who created ABC-TV. The deal with Disney is described in some detail, as is the impact on ABC-TV in particular and on the television industry in general. This should be read in conjunction with *Inside ABC* by Quinlin.

Grover, Ron. *The Disney Touch.* Homewood, Ill.: Business One Irwin, 1991. This well-written book offers a business portrait of the fascinating history of the Disney company, from its founding to the late 1980's. This is no corporate puff piece but a serious analysis of why the Walt Disney Company succeeded.

MacDonald, J. Fred. *One Nation Under Television: The Rise and Decline of Network Television.* New York: Pantheon Books, 1990. Offers a basic survey history of television and includes a great deal of information on ABC. This is a comprehensive and well-documented study.

Quinlin, Sterling. *Inside ABC: American Broadcasting Company's Rise to Power.* New York: Hastings House, 1979. Should be read as a serious history, tendered by a former vice-president of the company. Quinlin offers significant detail on the rise of ABC-TV and its dealings with Hollywood. Should be read in conjunction with *Beating the Odds* by Goldenson.

Williams, Huntington. *Beyond Control: ABC and the Fate of the Networks.* New York: Atheneum, 1989. Principally a history of ABC during the 1970's and 1980's, but contains a useful survey of the rise of ABC. Williams worked on the public relations staff of Leonard Goldenson.

Douglas Gomery

Cross-References

NBC Launches American Television at the World's Fair (1939), p. 1143; NBC and CBS Launch Commercial Television (1941), p. 1211; NBC Broadcasts the World Series (1947), p. 1362; Television Enters Its Golden Age (1950's), p. 1465; ABC Makes a Landmark Deal with Disney (1954), p. 1612; The Decline of the Big Three Networks Becomes a Fall (Late 1980's), p. 2554.

MAILER PUBLISHES *THE NAKED AND THE DEAD*

Category of event: Literature
Time: 1948
Locale: New York, New York

Norman Mailer's publication of The Naked and the Dead *launched the career of a dominant personality in American literature in the second half of the twentieth century*

Principal personages:
 NORMAN MAILER (1923-   ), an American novelist who became a voice
  for a generation
 JAMES JONES (1921-1977), a writer whose *From Here to Eternity* (1951)
  rivaled *The Naked and the Dead*

Summary of Event

In 1948, Norman Mailer's *The Naked and the Dead* was published. The book was an immediate commercial success; it topped *The New York Times'* best-seller list for eleven weeks and sold 197,185 copies its first year.

Within a year after he had been graduated from Harvard University with a degree in engineering sciences, Mailer had enlisted in the U.S. Army, and during World War II he served in the Philippines. Mailer used his personal military experience and individual artistic vision to transcend the genre of the war novel. Critics agreed that his 721-page book was the finest novel to come out of World War II. Mailer suddenly was considered the best literary mind of the war generation.

Yet although critics praised *The Naked and the Dead*, many underestimated the depth and artistry of Mailer's book and focused instead on the effective verisimilitude of the novel. Most critics at the time did not recognize the allegorical implications of the characters and the metaphoric nature of the plot.

Critics eventually discovered, however, that *The Naked and the Dead* was far more than a realistic novel of men at war. Mailer had written a rich parable of power, a novel of character, a novel to take its place with classic, symbolic American literature. As Mailer was to say, he had written a symbolic book concerned basically with characters.

Critics commented on Mailer's technical prowess and his ability for recording reality, but it took a while for most to recognize Mailer's full accomplishment. From the first, though, it was clear that, in Mailer, a new sensibility had been born.

The Naked and the Dead is a novel about war on a small island in the Pacific, but it is a metaphor for much larger concerns—the human condition and man's struggle to retain some humanity amid the savagery of war. The totalitarianism of the Army generally proves too strong for the book's individuals; if it does not, fate does.

The Naked and the Dead is about the invasion of the mythical Japanese-held island of Anopopei and the challenge of Mount Anaka on the island. The commander of the division that invades Anopopei is General Cummings, an egotistical fascist. His adversary is the liberal Hearn, who holds on to style as substance slips away from him. Also pivotal are aggressive, sadistic Sergeant Croft, who finds war is his natural element and who shares the will and vision of Cummings, and Croft's adversary, Red Valsen.

The long patrol of a single platoon to Mount Anaka brings a resolution to their hopes and illusions. At the end, Hearn is dead, Cummings has not gotten credit for the victory, Croft has failed to conquer or even understand his mountain, and Valsen is a submissive survivor. The man who by accident gets credit for the victory is a mediocre, banal major with foolish ideas.

The Naked and the Dead was a controversial novel because of its language and sex. In the novel, the soldiers speak crudely, and the book's first potential publisher, Little, Brown, and Company, refused to use the profanity. Mailer took the book to Rinehart and Company, which was also reluctant but less intransigent. Mailer agreed to cut down his profanity and to use the euphemistic "fug" in place of the more offensive term.

The Naked and the Dead looked at the moral and philosophical questions raised by war as no novel ever had. Mailer was compared favorably to Ernest Hemingway, John Dos Passos, and Joseph Conrad, and his novel was mentioned as worthy of comparison with *The Red Badge of Courage* (1895) and *War and Peace* (1865-1869).

Mailer burst on the scene with his first major full-length publication, but he had written other novels. At the age of nineteen at Harvard, he wrote a short novel called *A Calculus at Heaven* that was the genesis of *The Naked and the Dead*. It was one of fifty-one works by promising writers published in a 1944 anthology. In the months after his graduation, Mailer wrote a six-hundred-page novel about mental illness, *A Transit to Narcissus*, which went unpublished.

When *The Naked and the Dead* was published, Mailer was living in Paris with his first wife. He came back to the United States a famous writer. In 1951, James Jones published *From Here to Eternity*, a war novel in many ways similar to Mailer's, to considerable praise, but Mailer did not envy him; Mailer had already gained renown.

After the publication of *The Naked and the Dead*, playwright Lillian Hellman tried to adapt the book into a play, with Mailer's blessing, but she was unsuccessful. In 1958, *The Naked and the Dead* was made into a film starring Cliff Robertson and Raymond Massey; Mailer told the journal *Film Heritage* that the result was one of the worst films ever made.

Despite such difficulties, *The Naked and the Dead* made Mailer a major literary figure. Harvard-educated and from a middle-class Jewish Brooklyn background, Mailer had risen above his esoteric heritage to become the voice of a new generation. Mailer saw the power of authority in both the Army and society, and he saw the loss of individual possibility and faith. In *The Naked and the Dead*, Mailer issued a provocative alert to the postwar world.

Impact of Event

The publication of *The Naked and the Dead* launched Mailer as a major artist and personality. He rivaled Ernest Hemingway in the stories told about his personal life and became recognized as a major twentieth century literary persona. *The Naked and the Dead* gave him his platform, and he did not relinquish it.

The Naked and the Dead was revolutionary in its treatment of obscenity and sex. No novelist had used obscenities as Mailer did. At the time, obscenity charges could be brought against a publisher, so Mailer's frankness was dangerous. Critic Bernard DeVoto was sent Mailer's manuscript by publisher Little, Brown, and DeVoto criticized the manuscript for its profanity and obscenity and did not support the book's publication. Even in the watered-down form published by Rinehart and Company, the book was a milestone of explicit language and a harbinger of frankness to come.

When the novel came out, many critics saw Mailer as influenced by John Dos Passos. Later, others tried to define *The Naked and the Dead* by what Mailer subsequently wrote and tried to find evidence of his existentialism and political liberalism in the novel. Those that saw the novel as a parable of power were most successful. Mailer himself said that the source of the novel was Herman Melville's *Moby Dick: Or, The Whale* (1851); like the whale in Melville's novel, the mountain in Mailer's book was a symbol of obsession and defeat.

In *The Naked and the Dead*, Mailer portrayed the arena of war with new insight. His book showed war and society as creating a new totalitarianism that threatened the soul of man and society. In *The Naked and the Dead*, the characters experienced a loss of faith that Mailer suggested an entire society faced.

Mailer's subsequent work was not so well received critically. His subsequent novels, including *Barbary Shore* (1951), *The Deer Park* (1955), *An American Dream* (1965), *Why Are We in Vietnam?* (1967), *Ancient Evenings* (1983), *Tough Guys Don't Dance* (1984), and *Harlot's Ghost* (1991), have had uneven, sometimes hostile, receptions. Mailer was perhaps more successful in composing nonfiction and in mixing elements of nonfiction and fiction. He received critical affirmation as well as Pulitzer Prizes for both *The Armies of the Night* (1968) and *The Executioner's Song* (1979); the latter was released as "A True Life Novel." Mailer also tried his hand at directing films, but with desultory results. *Marilyn: A Biography* (1973) and *The Prisoner of Sex* (1971) were two nonfiction books that gave Mailer more visibility.

With *The Naked and the Dead*, Mailer embarked on a career that was a personal, cultural, and artistic quest for identity. Mailer was on a raw and relentless search for the meaning of life in the twentieth century; he was a twentieth century Ishmael, hunter and hunted.

One of the enduring effects of his quest is the myth of Mailer. He has called himself "a psychic outlaw." Mailer became a large personality, his image fueled by his public actions. He had a lengthy feud with Gore Vidal, who once called him "a fake"; in turn, Mailer insulted Vidal on television and once threw a drink on Vidal at a party. Mailer earned additional notoriety for stabbing one of his wives with a penknife and for campaigning unsuccessfully to become mayor of New York City. For Mailer, success was secondary to trying.

The Naked and the Dead was a milestone because it captured the sensibility of an era. It was derivative yet individual—both a bridge into postwar fiction and a beacon on America's changing values and loss of values because of the war. Mailer wrote about the meaning of power, its deceptions, limits, and corruption. *The Naked and the Dead* was very much about the American Dream and loss of faith.

Ernest Hemingway and T. S. Eliot depicted the Western world's loss of values after World War I; Mailer showed the loss of values that came with World War II, and he predicted a dismal fate for America. In the failure of *The Naked and the Dead's* four major characters—Hearn is dead, and the others are left disengaged and disillusioned—Mailer leaves readers with a vision of a world of irony and ineffectuality.

With *The Naked and the Dead*, Norman Mailer began his quest as a cultural warrior, besieged by friends and foes and by a diminishing world, trying to redeem moral power. His body of work constitutes a participation in postwar America and shows how he lived and evaluated the experience of a changing America. Mailer has been a man in search of himself, charting his personal Mount Anaka, in search of heroism in a world of many icons but few if any heroes.

Bibliography

Lucid, Robert F., ed. *Norman Mailer: The Man and His Work.* Boston: Little, Brown, 1971. This collection of critical essays, seventeen pieces mostly by major critics (all originally published elsewhere), shows Mailer's controversial reputation. Effective introduction by Lucid. Included are Richard Foster's notable lengthy study and a classic essay by Diana Trilling.

Marcus, Steven. "Interview with Norman Mailer." In *Writers at Work, Third Series.* New York: Viking Press, 1967. This *Paris Review* interview reveals some of Mailer's techniques and intentions. Mailer discusses his influences, his method of working, and the writing of *The Naked and the Dead.*

Merrill, Robert. *Norman Mailer.* Boston: Twayne, 1978. A thought-provoking interpretation of *The Naked and the Dead* emphasizing that the book is a novel of character. Defends Mailer's ending and argues against others' rejection of it on the grounds that they were looking for something Mailer was not trying to do.

Mills, Hilary. *Mailer.* New York: McGraw-Hill, 1982. The first full-length biography of Norman Mailer. Mills presents a view of Mailer in his totality; there is an effective balance between Mailer the artist and Mailer the man. Mills leans a little in the way of gossip, but she has much solid factual information about Mailer's publication history, his wives, and his personal and public experiences.

Poirier, Richard. *Norman Mailer.* New York: Viking Press, 1972. Poirier ranks Mailer alongside F. Scott Fitzgerald, Ernest Hemingway, and William Faulkner and analyzes Mailer's literary transformation as a writer as well as performer. Poirier recognizes Mailer's mastery of language, but he suggests that Mailer has created a system that may have confined him.

Tony Macklin

Cross-References

Hašek's *The Good Soldier Švejk* Reflects Postwar Disillusionment (1921), p. 523; Hemingway's *The Sun Also Rises* Speaks for the Lost Generation (1926), p. 696; *All Quiet on the Western Front* Stresses the Futility of War (1929), p. 767; Grass Publishes *The Tin Drum* (1959), p. 1780; *Catch-22* Illustrates Antiwar Sentiment (1961), p. 1866; *Dog Soldiers* Portrays Vietnam in Fiction (1974), p. 2315; *Platoon* Explores the Vietnam Experience (1986), p. 2576.

OLIVIER'S *HAMLET* IS RELEASED
TO ACCLAIM AND CONTROVERSY

Category of event: Motion pictures
Time: 1948
Locale: Great Britain and the United States

The second of Laurence Olivier's major Shakespearean films, Hamlet, *although controversial, was a milestone in the presentation of William Shakespeare's plays on film and influenced many later film versions*

Principal personages:
    LAURENCE OLIVIER (1907-1989), the producer, director, and star actor of
        Hamlet
    ALAN DENT (1905-1978), the film's script editor
    WILLIAM WALTON (1902-1983), the composer who wrote the film's music
    ROGER K. FURSE (1903-1972), the film's designer
    BASIL SYDNEY (1894-1968), the actor who played King Claudius
    EILEEN HERLIE (1920-   ), the actress who played Queen Gertrude
    JEAN SIMMONS (1929-   ), the actress who played Ophelia
    FELIX AYLMER (1889-1979), the actor who played Polonius
    TERENCE MORGAN (1921-   ), the actor who played Laertes
    PETER CUSHING (1913-   ), the actor who played Osric

Summary of Event

By the time he decided to make a film of *Hamlet*, Laurence Olivier had been acclaimed as the leading Shakespearean actor of the century on both stage and screen and had also established himself as a Shakespearean director. Since his first leading Shakespearean role, as Romeo in 1935, Olivier had appeared on stage as Macbeth, Henry V, Coriolanus, Iago, Sir Toby Belch, Hotspur, and King Lear, and had in 1937 twice played the part of Hamlet (once at London's Old Vic Theatre and once in Elsinore, Denmark).

Olivier had also become the leading exponent of Shakespeare on film. This aspect of his career had not had an auspicious start. His first role was as Orlando in a 1936 film version of *As You Like It* directed by Paul Czinner, but the film was not a success either with critics or at the box office. At the time, Olivier himself believed that Shakespeare's plays could not effectively be translated into the medium of film, and he confessed that he was "frightfully snobbish about films." His attitude changed, however, after he had some successful movie roles (notably as Heathcliff in 1939's *Wuthering Heights* and as Lord Nelson in 1941's *Lady Hamilton*). He then took on the task of making a film version of Shakespeare's *Henry V.* The film, which Olivier directed and in which he also played the title role, was a resounding critical and popular success upon its release in 1944.

In tackling the far greater challenge of making a film version of *Hamlet*, Olivier was at first reluctant to play the part of Hamlet himself. He later remembered that he thought his style of acting was more suited to "stronger character roles, such as Hotspur and Henry V, rather than to the lyrical, poetical role of Hamlet." Also, Olivier did not want the audience to link his film Hamlet with his earlier portrayal of Henry V; this was one reason he dyed his hair blond for his role as *Hamlet.* (Another reason was to make himself conspicuous in long shots.)

The basic idea for the film came to Olivier with a visualization of the film's final shot, of Hamlet's funeral bier on the battlements of the castle. After that glimpse, Olivier saw how the whole film could be built up. He decided to film in black and white rather than in color, in part because that would enable him to use deep-focus photography, which ensured that figures in the background could be seen with great clarity. The technique also enabled the production team to shoot unusually long scenes.

"The core of Hamlet," Olivier wrote in 1986, "is his loneliness and desolation after the death of his father, and his feeling of alienation from the new court." Olivier regarded Hamlet as "a nearly great man—damned by lack of resolution." This interpretation was made explicit at the beginning of the film, when Olivier speaks as a voiceover nine lines of Hamlet's speech from act 1, scene 4 of the play; the lines concern how a man can be overthrown by "the stamp of one defect" in his character. The words also appear on the screen. This speech is immediately followed by Olivier's own capsule summary of the theme of the film: "This is the tragedy of a man who could not make up his mind."

Hamlet's desolation, his restlessness, and his inability to find a stable point of reference in his world is conveyed by the seemingly endless movement of the camera. As it peers down passages and tracks across large empty rooms, the camera seems to become emblematic of Hamlet's own searching consciousness. The austere and abstract settings added to this effect. "Olivier wanted a dream-like, cavernous place as the setting for a drama which is centered in shadowy regions of the hero's mind," wrote Roger Furse, the film's designer.

The shadowy regions of Hamlet's mind are also emphasized by Olivier's acceptance of the Freudian theory, applied to *Hamlet* by the psychoanalyst Ernest Jones, of the Oedipus complex. The Oedipal view postulates that Hamlet has a subconscious desire to kill his father and engage in sexual relations with his mother; he thus finds it almost impossible to kill Claudius, because his uncle embodies this buried aspect of his own personality, and so Hamlet identifies with him. This interpretation is emphasized in the film by lingering close-up shots of the marriage bed and by a display of emotions between mother and son that go beyond what might be considered normal.

One major problem Olivier had to face was how to cut the text of the play, which runs for more than four hours, in order to produce a two-and-a-half-hour film. The editing principle he adopted with Alan Dent was based, Olivier wrote, on "making a new but integral pattern from the original, larger pattern of the play itself." According to Dent, the result "must be utterly respectful to the spirit of Shakespeare and to the audience's consciousness of Hamlet. . . . One has to choose between making the meaning clear to 20,000,000 cinemagoers and causing 2,000 Shakespearean experts to wince." Yet because of the drastic nature of the cuts (half of Shakespeare's text was discarded), Olivier thought that the film should be regarded as an "Essay in Hamlet" rather than as a direct interpretation of Shakespeare's play. The characters of Rosencrantz, Guildenstern, Fortinbras, Reynaldo, and the second gravedigger were eliminated from the film version. The omission of Fortinbras virtually eliminated the political aspects of the play (including the conflict between Denmark and Norway) and left Horatio to assume the Danish throne at the film's end. Two of Hamlet's soliloquies, "O what a rogue and peasant slave am I" and "How all occasions do inform against me," were omitted, as was most of Shakespeare's play-within-the-play. The omission of the second soliloquy meant that one plausible reason for Hamlet's hesitation—he fears the ghost of his father that has appeared may have been a devil—is never mentioned.

Twenty-five words that Olivier believed would be unfamiliar to a film audience were modernized. (For example, Claudius' line "For like the hectic in my blood he rages" was changed to "For like the fever in my blood he rages," and Ophelia's words to Laertes, "recks not his own rede," became "minds not his own creed.") Another Olivier innovation was to illustrate events that in Shakespeare's play are merely described—such as Ophelia's description of Hamlet's coming to her closet, a sea fight involving Hamlet and pirates, and Ophelia's death—while retaining Shakespeare's description as a voiceover.

Impact of Event

Hamlet was made at a time when many Shakespeare purists, in spite of the success of Olivier's *Henry V* film, still doubted whether Shakespeare's greatest plays could be adequately conveyed on the screen. Olivier's *Hamlet* seemed to settle the issue once and for all, and it is probably no coincidence that the film marked the beginning of a great flowering of cinematic versions of Shakespeare. Eight films of Shakespearean plays were made in the nine years immediately following *Hamlet*, including Olivier's own *Richard III* (1955). Moreover, for millions of filmgoers, many of whom had probably never seen a stage production of Shakespeare's play, *Hamlet* forever became, thanks to Olivier, "the tragedy of a man who could not make up his mind." The influence of the film was so great that one college professor complained that he was tired of hearing his students, year after year, insist that Gertrude knowingly drank the poisoned wine in the play's final scene. The students had all seen Olivier's film, in which Gertrude guesses the treachery of the king in advance and drinks the wine in an act of self-sacrifice and atonement. This, however, is not even hinted at in Shakespeare's play, and critics of Olivier's film pointed out that such an interpretation attributes a strength of character to Gertrude that is out of keeping with her behavior in the play as a whole.

Olivier's *Hamlet* was highly acclaimed in the film industry. It received five Oscars, including one for Olivier as best actor, and also won an award at the Venice Film

Festival. In addition, many reviewers were enthusiastic about Olivier's achievement. James Agee, for example, wrote in *Time* magazine that *Hamlet* was "a sternly beautiful job, densely and delicately worked," and concluded that "a man who can do what Laurence Olivier is doing for Shakespeare is certainly among the more valuable men of his time." In *The New Yorker*, John McCarten shared Agee's positive view, praising the "fine acting, remarkable sets, superb music" as well as Olivier's paring of Shakespeare's text. McCarten added that "it will be a presumptuous movie director indeed who attempts to improve upon the effort Olivier has made." Yet critical reception of the film was not unanimously favorable. In the *Kenyon Review*, for example, Parker Tyler, though acknowledging the "superior intelligence" that went into the production, asserted that *Hamlet* was a "bad movie simply because it is far more conscious of being traditional cinema than of being traditional theater . . . and on the whole, it is poorly acted, especially by Olivier, whose face is revealed by the intimate camera as less expressive than one might have hoped." Tyler also argued that by accepting the Oedipal interpretation of *Hamlet*, Olivier "utterly relieved himself of the obligation of a personal interpretation." In *Life and Letters*, R. Herring complained that the film failed because Olivier's "use of the medium is not, fundamentally, cinematic." Had Olivier chosen to utilize the full resources of film, Herring argued, he would have created a film with more striking visual images.

Olivier's film nevertheless had a marked influence on subsequent film treatments of the play. The versions directed by Franz Wirth (1960) and Tony Richardson (1970) both used abstract settings that recall those in the Olivier film. Olivier's use of the voiceover for the Hamlet's "to be or not to be" soliloquy—which, he said, seemed to be the most natural way in the world of conveying it—was also used by the Russian director Gregori Kozinstev in his 1964 film version. Franco Zeffirelli's 1990 version also shows traces of Olivier's influence. Like Olivier, Zeffirelli placed Hamlet's "to be or not to be" soliloquy immediately after the nunnery scene, rather than, as in Shakespeare's text, immediately before it. The effect is to give a much more intelligible reason for Hamlet's distraught state of mind. Zeffirelli also followed Olivier in accepting the Oedipal complex as an explanation of Hamlet's character; also like Olivier, he eliminated the character of Fortinbras, so emphasizing the familial and psychological dimensions of the drama at the expense of the social and political elements.

Bibliography

Agee, James. *Agee on Film.* New York: Grosset & Dunlap, 1969. Appreciative review by one of America's leading film critics. Argues that the film manages to strike a balance between the screen, the stage, and literature. Olivier's performance is one of the most beautiful ever put on film, although a few crucial passages are disappointing.

Barbarow, George. "Hamlet Through a Telescope." *Hudson Review* 2 (Spring, 1949): 98-104. One of the more harshly critical views of the film. Argues that the cutting of the text weakens the main element of the drama, the conflict between Hamlet and Claudius, since Claudius is made too weak. Also criticizes the moving camera, which fragments the action and confuses the viewer, and the presentation of soliloquies.

Cross, Brenda. *The Film "Hamlet": A Record of Its Production.* London: Saturn Press, 1948. Contains Olivier's own comments on the film ("An Essay in Hamlet") and articles by those involved in all aspects of its making: casting, camera and lighting, design and costumes, music, script editing. Actors Harcourt Williams (the Player King,) Stanley Holloway (the gravedigger), and Jean Simmons (Ophelia) also contribute short pieces. Includes more than thirty photographs.

Eckert, Charles, ed. *Focus on Shakespearean Films.* Englewood Cliffs, N.J.: Prentice-Hall, 1972. Contains two articles about *Hamlet.* Mary McCarthy ("A Prince of Shreds and Patches") regrets the omission of Fortinbras and also comments that Olivier sees Hamlet as an immature boy; as a result, she argues, the drama becomes a kind of initiation ceremony. Peter Alexander ("From School in Wittenberg") sees a tension in the film caused by the differences between popular and scholarly approaches.

Jorgens, Jack J. *Shakespeare on Film.* Bloomington: Indiana University Press, 1977. The chapter on *Hamlet* is the fullest critical discussion of the film to appear. Argues, among other things, that the Freudian interpretation does not narrow the character of Hamlet as much as has sometimes been said and that the film effectively captures the inner Hamlet. Jorgens, though, criticizes the simplification of the ending, which gives a sense of fulfillment rather than the mixture of triumph and defeat that Shakespeare's play conveys. Compares Olivier's film to the 1964 *Hamlet* of the Russian film director Gregori Kozintsev.

Manvell, Roger. *Shakespeare and the Film.* New York: Praeger, 1971. Argues that of the three Shakespearean films directed by Olivier, *Hamlet,* in spite of its faults (too drastic cutting of the text, excessive camera movement), is the one that most rewards detailed examination. Cites sets, photography, acting, music.

Olivier, Laurence. *On Acting.* London: Weidenfeld and Nicolson, 1986. Olivier emphasizes the importance of deep-focus photography, praises the performances of his fellow actors, and explains the principles behind the editing of the film, including his practice—criticized by some—of providing visual images to accompany passages of descriptive verse (such as the drowning of Ophelia).

Bryan Aubrey

Cross-References

Freud Inaugurates a Fascination with the Unconscious (1899), p. 19; Welles's *Citizen Kane* Breaks with Traditional Filmmaking (1941), p. 1200; Kurosawa's *Rashomon* Wins the Grand Prize at Venice (1951), p. 1476; The Royal Shakespeare Company Adopts a New Name and Focus (1961), p. 1888; Great Britain Establishes the Royal National Theatre (1962), p. 1924; The Theatres Act Ends Censorship of English Drama (1968), p. 2131.

VARIETY SHOWS DOMINATE
TELEVISION PROGRAMMING

Category of event: Television and radio
Time: 1948-1957
Locale: The United States

Early television producers transferred vaudeville acts to American television screens, in the process producing a number of the most popular variety programs

Principal personages:

ARTHUR GODFREY (1903-1983), a former radio performer who turned his variety-show empire into a CBS franchise during the 1950's

LEONARD HARRY GOLDENSON (1905-   ), the man who built ABC into one of the three dominant American networks

WILLIAM S. PALEY (1901-1990), the man who built CBS radio and then CBS television

DAVID SARNOFF (1891-1971), the man who built NBC radio and then NBC television

ED SULLIVAN (1902-1974), the former newspaper columnist who created one of the first television variety shows and developed it into an American Sunday-night institution

Summary of Event

Television variety shows, vaudeville-inspired mixtures of comedy, song, and any entertainment fad of the day, evolved both from live vaudeville and from radio. Radio's first professional variety show came in October, 1929, as the Fleischmann Yeast program, hosted by crooner Rudy Vallee and featuring guest stars from the vaudeville world. The almost unvarying formula for the variety show included a popular star as host, guests from all reaches of the world of show business, and a band.

Popular from the start, radio variety shows included everything from *The National Barn Dance* and *The Grand Ole Opry* to newspaperman host Ed Sullivan presenting new talent in the manner of impresario Florenz Ziegfeld of Broadway. Comics, beginning with Eddie Cantor, seemed to develop the variety shows with the highest ratings through the 1930's and 1940's. Radio added innovations that would be carried over—along with the basics of the formula—to television. For example, Ed Wynn's radio variety program introduced studio audiences that would provide live reactions over the air.

Such was the state of affairs in the late 1940's, as the new medium of television required hours of programs to fill air time. Television network heads—David Sarnoff of the National Broadcasting Company (NBC), William S. Paley of the Columbia Broadcasting System (CBS), and Leonard Harry Goldenson of the American Broadcasting Company (ABC)—all were familiar with variety shows from their experiences in radio. They knew that there were empty theaters in New York City and talent that would jump at a chance to work in television. As a consequence, variety programs and sports broadcasts were the most abundant forms of programming on early network television in prime time.

No variety show was more popular in the late 1940's than Milton Berle's *Texaco Star Theater*, which began in June of 1948 on NBC. The influential trade paper *Variety* noted that Milton Berle had created a new style of performance with his shouting one-liners, constant leering, clowning, simple-minded mugging, and camp appeal. *Texaco Star Theater* had been on radio since the fall of 1938 but with other hosts, including Fred Allen, Alan Young, Gordon MacRae, and Ken Murray. Berle in fact rotated as host of the television show for several months before being selected as permanent host.

American viewers seemed to fall in love with Milton Berle making fools of himself and his guests. Berle delivered familiar one-liners and topical jokes, employed weird costumes and settings, and booked famous guest stars. Berle had had little success on radio, but his visual style worked on television. Berle delivered a cleaned-up version of his nightclub routine, then introduced a series of singers, with Pearl Bailey as the star of the first show. Berle became famous for never letting his show lag, dashing on stage at slow moments to ham it up.

Soon, early television—on Tuesday nights—belonged to Milton Berle's variety hour on NBC. It was not unexpected when, in 1948, William S. Paley's CBS unveiled its own television vaudeville show, *Toast of the Town*, hosted by Ed Sullivan. *Toast of the Town* quickly became a regular Sunday-night fixture, just behind *Texaco Star Theater* in the variety show ratings race.

Sullivan's *Toast of the Town* was calm compared to Berle's hectic hour of antics. Sullivan sought to offer something for everyone and let his crafty choice of acts carry the day. In the long run, the staid Sullivan outlasted the antics of Berle and survived on television as other variety shows that appeared in the late 1940's and early 1950's died. Sullivan was on the air until the end of the 1970-1971 television season.

Sullivan knew talent. On his first television variety show he featured the then-unknown Dean Martin and Jerry Lewis along with a classical pianist and an interview with a noted boxing referee. Sullivan's tribute shows (to Oscar Hammerstein II, Helen Hayes, and Cole Porter, among others) drew some of television's highest ratings. Sullivan's mixtures of high culture, popular culture, the exotic, and the sensational became a variety hallmark. This mixture revised the formula for television variety shows. Sullivan presented jugglers, dancing bears, and plate spinners as well as performances by dancer Margot Fonteyn, singer Maria Callas, and the Beatles.

Berle and Sullivan's popularity meant that the new television medium would be flooded with imitators. Bandleader Russ Morgan hosted *Welcome Aboard*. The DuMont television network launched *Cavalcade of Stars* with comic Jack Carter as emcee. NBC launched *Saturday Night Revue*.

All these shows failed within several years, but they fostered continual experimentation that led to such highly innovative shows as *Your Show of Shows* with Sid Caesar, sidemen Howard Morris and Carl Reiner, and writers Neil Simon and Mel Brooks. When CBS's *The Ed Wynn Show* was produced in Los Angeles on film, it set a trend that would remake the television industry and ironically cripple New York City as a center of variety-show production. Ed Wynn, seeking to differentiate his program, moved west to be able to book guests from Hollywood. Buster Keaton and Lucille Ball both made their television debuts on *The Ed Wynn Show.*

Of all the early imitators, none proved more important than former radio host Arthur Godfrey. Conducting two weekly prime-time variety series on CBS-TV as well as a daily radio show, Godfrey proved that variety shows could make money. By the mid-1950's, Godfrey was reported to be responsible for more than $100 million worth of advertising flowing to CBS.

It seemed simple. Godfrey's first television venture, *Arthur Godfrey's Talent Scouts,* was a variation of the old amateur hour. Godfrey brought young professionals looking for a break to New York City to perform before a live audience that voted on the acts through an "applause meter." *Arthur Godfrey and His Friends,* at first an hour-long variety show, had a stable cast including singer Julius LaRosa. Godfrey's style was low-key. Guests came on, engaged in mild conversation, and sang a song or two. Godfrey was so valuable because he was the ultimate pitchman, hawking products he truly seemed to believe in, attracting advertisers in record numbers.

Paley liked the profits associated with Godfrey, and therefore CBS pioneered the long-running *The Red Skelton Show.* Sarnoff's NBC countered with *The Perry Como Show.* Garry Moore began a daytime variety show in 1950 and by the early 1960's was making stars out of performers including Carol Burnett.

Impact of Event

Along with the successes, there were numerous failures. Ole Olsen and Chick Johnson had had a popular run in vaudeville, but their humor fell flat in television's *Fireball Fun-for-All.* Their spontaneity, with cornball jokes and custard pies in the face, worked best unscripted. Their variety show was shot in long takes and thus seemed distant on television. In contrast, Milton Berle, Ed Sullivan, and Arthur Godfrey worked in highly scripted routines and exploited the intimacy of the close-up. Joe E. Brown's *The Buick Circus Hour* lasted less than a year. Red Buttons had to change the format of his show several times in its less than three years. Clearly, even though variety shows dominated the top programming, not even stars had guaranteed success in the genre.

Through the late 1950's there were few variety shows more popular than *The George Gobel Show.* Symbolically, soon after CBS positioned the Hollywood western *Gunsmoke* opposite Gobel, the folksy variety show went off the air. This was one of the signals of the changing tastes of American television viewers.

In the 1960's, the apex of the variety show was reached, probably the night the Beatles appeared on Ed Sullivan's show early in 1964. The master of the variety show had been late in picking up on rock-and-roll acts, but even Sullivan knew he needed to revitalize his ratings. By the time Sullivan introduced the Beatles on February 9, 1964, they were the top musical group among teenage listeners. Two of three American homes had Sullivan on that night, as the Beatles opened and closed *The Ed Sullivan Show*. No one anticipated the reaction shots of teenage girls weeping, screaming, and even fainting.

Momentarily, the variety show seemed revitalized. Hosts Dean Martin, Andy Williams, and Flip Wilson sought to revive the form, but they could not. By the mid-1970's, the variety show genre in its pure form had disappeared from television. Carol Burnett made a valiant attempt to revive it on CBS. *The Carol Burnett Show*, with regulars Harvey Korman, Vicki Lawrence, Lyle Waggoner, and Tim Conway, almost made it until the 1980's from its beginning in 1967. This, in part, resulted from her experiments, such as opening the show by answering questions directly from the audience. Burnett was skilled at spoofing not only films but also television series. Even Carol Burnett, however, could not keep the pure variety show on the air, and the form died as the 1980's commenced. Variations, however, survived and thrived.

Morning shows offered variations on the variety show. Modern shows including *Good Morning America* are descendants of Dave Garroway's *Today*, which premiered in 1952. They offer variety elements in addition to news and weather. The late-night counterpart proved even more vital. *The Tonight Show* added casual talk with performers to variety performances. Interview shows with interspersed performances became staples of late-night television, with hosts such as Arsenio Hall, Merv Griffin, and David Letterman.

Prime-time variety shows were popular as long as Hollywood was not involved in the making of television shows. That commenced in 1951, with *I Love Lucy*, which would define the situation comedy genre. The setup was a combination familiar to the radio fans of Jack Benny or Ozzie and Harriet, with professional lives and home life delicately combined. This meant music and comedy, as Desi Arnaz played Ricky Ricardo, a Cuban bandleader who worked in a New York nightclub. This scenario let Arnaz play himself while Lucy took on the comic broadsides. Within four months of its October, 1951, debut, *I Love Lucy* had deposed Milton Berle's *Texaco Star Theater* as the top-rated show on television. Although its premise involved some use of musical numbers, *I Love Lucy* clearly moved out of the variety format and heralded a change in popular tastes.

Bibliography

Barnouw, Erik. *The Golden Web*. Vol. 2 in *A History of Broadcasting in the United States*. New York: Oxford University Press, 1968. The second of an important trilogy of books about the history of radio and television in the United States. The rise of the television variety show receives treatment in this volume.

Berle, Milton, and Haskel Frankel. *Milton Berle: An Autobiography*. New York: Dell, 1974. This is the life story of the founder of the variety format. Somewhat informative as biography and important as the only Berle biography as of the early 1990's.

Bilby, Kenneth. *The General: David Sarnoff and the Rise of the Communications Industry.* New York: Harper & Row, 1986. The complete biography of David Sarnoff, the founder and longtime head of NBC. No decision at the NBC radio or television network before the mid-1960's was made unless Sarnoff approved. This biography serves as a substitute for a network history.

Bowles, Jerry. *A Thousand Sundays: The Story of the Ed Sullivan Show.* New York: Putnam, 1982. Chronicles twenty-three years of Sullivan's show. Mostly descriptive, with little analysis.

Castleman, Harry, and Walter J. Podrazik. *Watching TV: Four Decades of American Television.* New York: McGraw-Hill, 1982. Although at first glance resembling a picture book, this source contains a remarkable amount of basic information, season by television season. The rise and fall of the variety show is treated in some detail.

MacDonald, J. Fred. *One Nation Under Television: The Rise and Decline of Network Television.* New York: Pantheon Books, 1990. A history of television in the United States. MacDonald offers a comprehensive and well-documented study.

Smith, Sally Bedell. *In All His Glory: The Life of William S. Paley.* New York: Simon & Schuster, 1990. The complete biography of William S. Paley, the founder and longtime head of CBS. No decision at the network before the 1980's was made unless Paley approved. *In All His Glory* serves as a second-best substitute for a badly needed network history.

Douglas Gomery

Cross-References

"Mr. Television," Milton Berle, Has the Top-Rated Show (1948), p. 1394; Television Enters Its Golden Age (1950's), p. 1465; *The Red Skelton Show* Becomes a Landmark on Network Television (1951), p. 1520; *The Tonight Show* Becomes an American Institution (1954), p. 1623; *Rowan and Martin's Laugh-In* Is the Top Show on Television (1968), p. 2115; *The Sonny and Cher Comedy Hour* Brings Glitz to Television (1971), p. 2244; *Saturday Night Live* Is First Broadcast (1975), p. 2355.

ZHDANOV DENOUNCES "FORMALISM" IN MUSIC

Category of event: Music
Time: February 10, 1948
Locale: Moscow, Union of Soviet Socialist Republics

The Central Committee of the Communist Party of the Soviet Union published a decree opposing "antidemocratic formalism" in the music of the country's leading composers

Principal personages:

ANDREI ZHDANOV (1896-1948), Stalin's heir apparent, who presided over the humiliation of the Soviet composers

JOSEPH STALIN (JOSEPH VISSARIONOVICH DZHUGASHVILI, 1879-1953), the premier of the Soviet Union

SERGEI PROKOFIEV (1891-1953), the leading Soviet composer, whose works did not escape criticism

DMITRI SHOSTAKOVICH (1906-1975), a major Soviet composer and target of many attacks

ARAM ILICH KHACHATURIAN (1903-1978), a Soviet composer of Armenian descent whose colorfully orchestrated works incorporated echoes of Oriental folk music

NIKOLAI MIASKOVSKI (1881-1950), a senior Soviet composer whose music was denounced

TIKHON KHRENNIKOV (1913-   ), the president of the Union of Soviet Composers and chief accuser of his musical colleagues

VANO MURADELI (1908-1970), a Georgian composer whose opera *Great Friendship* was the immediate cause of the attacks on postwar Soviet music

Summary of Event

On February 10, 1948, the newspapers of the Soviet Union published a decree on music by the Central Committee of the Communist Party of the Soviet Union. The decree was preceded by a three-day conference presided over by Andrei Zhdanov, Joseph Stalin's heir apparent, even though both his health and power were in decline. At that conference, the works of internationally famous Soviet composers—Sergei Prokofiev, Dmitri Shostakovich, Aram Ilich Khachaturian, and Nikolai Miaskovski in particular—were denounced and musical modernism or formalism was condemned explicitly.

The Soviet Union emerged from World War II considerably enlarged in territory but suffering from the immense destruction of four years of intense, total war with Nazi Germany and its allies. Attempts to subvert the governments of neighboring countries to increase Soviet dominance led to a reaction by the Western countries, in particular the Truman Doctrine (1947) to prevent further Soviet expansion through subversion in Turkey and Greece and the formation of the North Atlantic Treaty Organization in 1949. Western reaction against Soviet expansionism, poor harvests in the devastated western parts of the Soviet Union, and fear of popular disaffection resulted in an intensification of dictatorial controls after an initial relaxation of wartime stringencies. Stalin cut the Soviet Union and its client states off from contact with the West, encouraged Russian nationalism, and proclaimed hostility to all foreign influences.

Stalin's actions usually took place behind the scenes and were revealed only obliquely by others, whose role was to take public initiatives in denouncing trends to which Stalin was hostile. Andrei Zhdanov was assigned to this role. The period of control over the arts, sciences, and philosophy between 1946 and 1948 has been called the Zhdanovshchina, or Zhdanov's purge. Zhdanov at this time was engaged in a power struggle with Georgi Malenkov, minister for heavy industry, and Lavrenti Beria, head of the secret police, to succeed Stalin, who was in his late sixties.

Music actually was one of the last areas to be placed under tight state control. By early 1948, Zhdanov was in poor health, with a heart condition exacerbated by years of heavy drinking. His political influence had waned; his chief claim to influence was the marriage of his son to Stalin's daughter. The Soviet people, however, did not know about Zhdanov's eclipse, and his very appearance before the Union of Soviet Composers as a senior member of the governing Politburo signaled official government sanction of his decrees.

Zhdanov's speech opening the general assembly of Soviet composers in January, 1948, began, as did the attack by the Central Committee, with denunciation of the opera *Great Friendship* by Vano Muradeli, a Georgian composer of limited gifts, for its lack of melody, misuse of the orchestra, dissonant harmonies, and lack of folk music to characterize the North Georgian peoples. He compared portions of the work to "noise on a building lot, at the moment when excavators, stone crushers and cement mixers go into action."

Zhdanov did not attack any other composers by name. This was left to Tikhon Khrennikov, the new president of the Union of Soviet Composers. He referred to an article in *Pravda* in 1936 condemning Shostakovich's excesses and attacked the "formalistic distortions and anti-democratic tendencies" in the postwar music of the leading Soviet composers, whose works were well known and popular in the West as well—Prokofiev, Khachaturian, Shostakovich, and others. He also denounced the overemphasis on abstract music at the expense of program music on subjects of Soviet life, and the "anti-realistic decadent influences . . . peculiar to the bourgeois movement of the era of imperialism." His speech closed with attacks on Igor Stravinsky, Paul Hindemith, Arnold Schoenberg, Olivier Messiaen, and such younger composers as Benjamin Britten and Gian Carlo Menotti.

One composer of popular music asked whether the workers in factories and on collective farms loved the symphonies of Shostakovich and Prokofiev. Others attacked the ultraindividualist conception of life, derived from bourgeois idealism, artistic snobbishness, neoclassicism as musical escapism, a desire to startle with spicy and scratchy harmonies, and a cult of form and technique, the latter described by many as "bourgeois formalism."

Examination of individual works criticized reveals the grounds for these criticisms. Prokofiev's Sixth Symphony (1945-1947) is not an optimistic and accessible work like the wartime Fifth Symphony; it is grim, with moments of horror in the first two movements and with a barely concealed menace in the seemingly lighthearted finale, which ends with the sad theme of the first movement. The symphony seems to be not a celebration of victory but a portrait of the horrors of war. Shostakovich's symphonies of the 1940's displayed even sharper contrasts. The Seventh ("Leningrad") Symphony of 1941 is a textbook example of Socialist Realism (although denounced in 1948 as doing a better job of depicting the advancing Nazis than of showing the resistance of the Soviets), whereas his Eighth Symphony of 1943 is a gloomy, austere work with inner movements that almost graphically depict the terrors of war. The Ninth Symphony of 1945, lightheartedly neoclassical in tone, was criticized three years later as frivolously mocking the victory of the Soviet people (there are amusing parodies of military march idioms in the other movements), though the second movement did receive praise for its lyricism.

Prokofiev, Shostakovich, Muradeli, Khachaturian, and the other composers made dutiful obeisance in published statements in which they repented their errors. The congress summed up its work in a letter to Stalin in which its members acknowledged the justness of the Party's criticism of Soviet music and apologized for forgetting the traditions of Russian musical realism.

Impact of Event

For two months in 1948, none of the music of any of the denounced composers was performed publicly in Moscow, a most effective way of showing what government control could mean to composers suspected of the slightest dissidence. Prokofiev's first wife (Spanish by birth) was even arrested as a spy and sentenced to eight years in the labor camps of the gulag.

A few of Prokofiev's works subsequently were performed that year. He devoted most of his time, limited because of his declining health, to writing vocal works on topics fitting the Communist Party line, such as his oratorio *On Guard for Peace* (1950). The main work of his final period is a reworking of an earlier cello concerto as the *Sinfonia Concerto for Cello and Orchestra* (1950-1952), written for the young Russian cellist Mstislav Rostropovich. Prokofiev's death from a cerebral hemorrhage on March 5, 1953, ironically was on the same day as Stalin's death.

Miaskovski turned to a simpler style in his last piano sonatas, teaching pieces for children, and his twenty-seventh and last symphony. Khachaturian continued to compose, but none of his subsequent works achieved the popularity of his colorful scores of the 1940's such as the piano and violin concertos of the *Gayaneh* ballet, from which the "Saber Dance" remains his most popular composition.

Shostakovich, after a duly submissive letter to Stalin, composed film music and

Party-line works such as the oratorio *Song of the Forests* and extremely simple and accessible works such as the Fourth String Quartet, very placid in contrast to the grotesqueries of the preceding quartet. He was sent to the United States in 1949 as part of a peace delegation but withheld his Tenth Symphony from performance until after Stalin's death. The tone of this work is darkly brooding, with a sense of forced gaiety in the finale. One frightening portion is said to be a musical portrait of Stalin.

The thaw of the Nikita Khrushchev years permitted Shostakovich to rewrite his earlier controversial opera that had gotten him into trouble with Stalin in 1936, *Lady MacBeth of the Mtsensk District*, as *Katerina Izmailova*. His two epic symphonies on the genesis of the Communist revolution, the Eleventh ("The Year 1905") and Twelfth ("The Year 1917"), were followed by the controversial Thirteenth, which includes a setting of Yevgeny Yevtushenko's poem "Babiy Yar," in which the poet condemned not only the Nazis but their local accomplices as well. Such a condemnation angered the Leonid Brezhnev regime, and the poet was compelled to change the text. The Fourteenth Symphony is a chamber symphony with solo voices; the Fifteenth, one of the composer's farewell works, contains quotations from Gioacchino Rossini's *William Tell Overture* and the "Fate" motive from Richard Wagner's *Die Walküre* (1856; the Valkyrie).

Shostakovich's greatest postwar works are his string quartets. Only two of these were written before 1945. The most frequently performed is the Eighth, written during a visit to Dresden (in what was then the German Democratic Republic); the sight of the ruins left by the Allied bombardments in 1945 provoked the composer to dedicate the quartet to the victims of war and Fascism. The quartet includes citations from several of his earlier works, including the First and Fifth symphonies, the Violin Concerto, and the E Minor Piano Trio, which Shostakovich wrote in 1944 after reading about the atrocities in the Majdanek extermination camp. Its opening movement and especially the last two movements have been compared to a lunar landscape, whereas the second movement is an intensely terrifying war piece (like the third movement of the Eighth Symphony) and the third is a nightmare waltz. Other important quartets include the Twelfth, with its experimentation with serial techniques, and the last, the Fifteenth, composed of six slow movements with no fast movement to relieve the prevailingly gloomy atmosphere.

The decree on music from the Central Committee was not rescinded until 1958. Stalin, and secondarily Malenkov and Beria, were blamed for the 1948 resolution, with its harsh judgments examples of the negative traits that marked the period of the cult of personality, a code phrase for Stalinism. The composers once condemned were officially rehabilitated.

Khrennikov continued to serve as president of the Union of Soviet Composers, surviving under the regimes from Joseph Stalin through Mikhail Gorbachev and able to tell composers what and how they had to write if they wanted their music played. Many of the younger composers emigrated as a result. In 1992, after the breakup of the Soviet Union, the Union of Soviet Composers was dissolved. Khrennikov reportedly found a position teaching composition part-time at the Moscow Conservatory.

The decree of 1948 did much damage to Soviet music and also to the reputation of the Soviet Union abroad. Although the Red Army had stopped Adolf Hitler and contributed markedly to his eventual defeat, the following crackdowns on literature, art, science (especially genetics), philosophy, and finally music repelled many intellectuals in the West who originally had been grateful to the Soviets for the defeat of Fascism and were attracted to Communism for its alleged support of the arts, as opposed to the commercial orientation of the West.

Bibliography

Hahn, Werner G. *Postwar Soviet Politics: The Fall of Zhdanov and the Defeat of Moderation, 1946-1953.* Ithaca, N.Y.: Cornell University Press, 1982. The author advances the thesis that Zhdanov was a moderate, locked in a power struggle with such hard-liners as Malenkov and Beria, and that the attack on music came after Zhdanov had been stripped of most of his influence.

MacDonald, Ian. *The New Shostakovich.* Boston: Northeastern University Press, 1990. Emphasizes Shostakovich as a dissident who used a covert musical language of dissent against Communism.

Moor, Paul. "A Reply to Tikhon Khrennikov." *High Fidelity/Musical America* 36 (August, 1986): 52-54, 79. Shows the control that Khrennikov continued to exercise over Soviet music even into the years of Gorbachev's *glasnost.*

Norris, Christopher. "Shostakovich: Politics and Musical Language." In *Shostakovich: The Man and His Music.* Boston: Marion Boyars, 1982. The author suggests that a new form of artistic biography is necessary for this composer, wherein the central themes are impulse and commitment.

Robinson, Harlow. *Sergei Prokofiev: A Biography.* New York: Viking Press, 1987. A discussion of the composer's life more than of his music, this very readable biography places him in the Soviet context during the various changes of government.

Schwarz, Boris. *Music and Musical Life in Soviet Russia, 1917-1970.* New York: W. W. Norton, 1972. An excellent study that shows the impact of Zhdanov's purges in all areas of Soviet musical life.

Slonimsky, Nicolas. *Music Since 1900.* 4th ed. New York: Charles Scribner's Sons, 1971. Contains the texts of the resolutions, speeches, and letters of Soviet musical policy in 1948 and the document of rescission in 1958.

Volkov, Solomon. *Testimony: The Memoirs of Dmitri Shostakovich.* New York: Harper & Row, 1979. These memoirs have been attacked as an ideological anti-Communist tract, but many passages give a strong feeling of the paranoia of the Soviet Union in 1948. Prokofiev, Muradeli, and other composers are assailed.

Werth, Alexander. *Musical Uproar in Moscow.* London: Turnstile Press, 1949. Contains a valuable discussion of Zhdanov by the Moscow correspondent of *The New Statesman* and the speeches of attack and defense made at the January, 1948, meeting preceding Zhdanov's denunciation.

R. M. Longyear

Cross-References

The Soviet Union Bans Abstract Art (1922), p. 544; Stravinsky Completes His Wind Octet (1923), p. 561; Socialist Realism Is Mandated in Soviet Literature (1932), p. 908; Stalin Restricts Soviet Composers (1932), p. 914; Shostakovich's *Lady Macbeth of Mtsensk* Is Condemned (1936), p. 1042; Hitler Organizes an Exhibition Denouncing Modern Art (1937), p. 1083; The Nazis Ban Nolde's Paintings (1941), p. 1217; Blacklisting Seriously Depletes Hollywood's Talent Pool (1947), p. 1340.

"MR. TELEVISION," MILTON BERLE, HAS THE TOP-RATED SHOW

Category of event: Television and radio
Time: June 8, 1948-Spring, 1951
Locale: The United States

As host of Texaco Star Theater, *the most popular variety show in the history of television, Milton Berle earned the sobriquet of "Mr. Television"*

Principal personages:

MILTON BERLE (MILTON BERLINGER, 1908-   ), the host of the *Texaco Star Theater*, credited with popularizing television for the general public

SID STONE (1903-1986), the pitchman and commercial announcer for Berle from 1948 to 1951

RUTH GILBERT (1899-   ), the actress who played Max, Berle's secretary, as a regular on the show from 1952 to 1955

FATSO MARCO, a regular on the *Texaco Star Theater* from 1948 to 1952

ARNOLD STANG (1925-   ), a character actor who appeared regularly on the show from 1953 to 1955

Summary of Event

During the early years of television, the most popular hour of the week arguably was Tuesday night from 8:00 to 9:00 P.M. It was during that hour that *Texaco Star Theater*, starring Milton Berle, was broadcast by the National Broadcasting Company (NBC).

Early television was a medium dominated by humor. In 1952, for example, nearly half of network programming was comedy based, either situation comedies or comedy-variety shows. Much of the comedy was heavily influenced by the styles and formats of vaudeville. The perception of those watching the small screen was that they were observing a theatrical performance.

Beginning in the early days of radio, most programming involved production by single sponsors or advertising agencies. In 1948, Texaco, a leading oil company, was interested in sponsoring a show. Myron Kirk of Madison Avenue's Kudner Agency contacted Milton Berle on Texaco's behalf. The result was the *Texaco Star Theater*, which aired on Wednesday nights on American Broadcasting Company (ABC) radio.

Berle already had his eye on television. Berle had spent most of his life as an entertainer, starting at the age of five, and he saw the potential in television as a medium of entertainment. He had been among the first to perform on television, having appeared in experimental broadcasts as early as 1929. Berle pushed for a television show, and Texaco agreed to sponsor one.

The program as originally envisioned by the sponsor was to be a seven-act vaudeville show performed on television. Hosts would rotate weekly until a permanent headliner was chosen. Berle hosted the first show, on June 8, 1948. Programs were performed before a studio audience. During the early years, cameras were mounted on portable platforms, and the studio audience often could not even see the stage. It was not until 1952 that the studio audience was provided with monitors.

The first show was aired on NBC's flagship station in New York, WNBT, and the seven station affiliates on the East Coast. Other performers who hosted the show, on a rotating basis, during the summer of 1948 included Morey Amsterdam, Jack Carter, Peter Donald, Georgie Price, Harry Richman, and Henny Youngman. Clearly, however, Berle was the most popular. By September, Berle had become the permanent host.

During the first year of the show, Berle hosted thirty-nine Tuesday night shows for NBC in addition to thirty-nine shows for ABC radio on Wednesday nights. The basic format for the show varied little from week to week and mimicked the old vaudeville style. Generally, a half dozen or so guests appeared each week. They might be comedians, singers, or acrobats. Each show began with the four "Texaco Service Men" singing the Texaco jingle. Berle would then come onstage, usually dressed in an outlandish costume of some sort.

Berle's performances were the highlights of the show. With his rubbery face and broad slapstick humor, Berle instinctively brought to the new medium what was needed to increase its popularity: innovation. One week he would be a Mexican bandit, the next a cancan dancer or Carmen Miranda's sister. He wore elaborate evening gowns, accompanied by layers of makeup. Pies were thrown in his face. He was a master at pratfalls. He sang with his guests, danced with his guests, and once even ate the fruit from Carmen Miranda's headpiece during her act.

Berle's joke file was said to contain between fifty thousand and two million bits of material, much of it in the form of outlandish puns. Since not all of it was original, Berle also earned the title of "Thief of Badgags."

The show was aired live and was not infrequently the victim of faulty props or defective plots. Once, when playing the part of a June bride, Berle's bridal train was caught on the backdrop as it rolled up. Fatso Marco, playing the groom, was left speechless, so Berle ad-libbed his way through the scene. During another show, on which the guests included an elephant act, the animals did what animals often do after a meal. The elephant show was followed by a dancing act, in which the performers slid their way through their performance.

The finale of the program generally ran about sixteen minutes. During this period, the guests would sing, play the piano, or carry out some other performance. The show would then conclude with Berle singing his theme song, "Near You." During an ad-lib at the conclusion of one show, Berle referred to himself as "Uncle Miltie," another sobriquet with which he would be associated.

From 1948 to 1952, the format of the show changed little. More emphasis was placed on Berle and his gags, but since the show earned top ratings in its first three seasons, there seemed little reason for the format to be altered. By 1951, however, other shows and performers had entered the medium, and ratings began to drop.

Arthur Godfrey's Talent Scouts became the top-rated program of the 1951-1952 season. In the fall season of 1952, Berle changed the form of the show. Fewer guests appeared, and each show was built around a central comedy plot. In 1953, Texaco dropped its sponsorship, and the show became the *Buick-Berle Show.* From 1954 to 1956, the title was simply *The Milton Berle Show.* It alternated with various other programs in its time slot. By 1956, the show was dropped from the Tuesday night lineup, as the interests of the viewing public moved into other areas.

Impact of Event

When Milton Berle made his debut as host of *Texaco Star Theater* in 1948, television was an entertainment medium primarily for the rich. Mass marketing of sets was still in its infancy. Fewer than 190,000 televisions were believed to be owned by the general public, and programming offered little variety.

This all changed with the weekly appearance of Berle. Viewers who saw his program in bars or on displays in stores decided that they too should own a set. At least one magazine reported that during the years of Berle's show more than twenty-one million sets were purchased by the general public. It was estimated that at the show's peak, more than 80 percent of television sets in use while the show was on were turned to *Texaco Star Theater.* It became clear that television was an entertainment source in its own right, one that could compete effectively with films or other means of relaxation. One could justifiably argue that the American national obsession with television began with Milton Berle.

The *Texaco Star Theater* was only the first of a long line of comedy and variety shows. Other networks and other sponsors, observing the success of Berle's form of slapstick, developed show formats that bore a striking similarity to that developed by Berle. Among the most successful of these shows, also on NBC, was *Your Show of Shows*, featuring stars such as Sid Caesar, Imogene Coca, and Carl Reiner and young writers such as Mel Brooks, Neil Simon, and Woody Allen. All would later make a significant impact in the entertainment industry. In a sense, the presence of comedy-variety shows on NBC was the continuation of a tradition, since the most popular comedy-variety shows on radio had also been found on NBC.

The Columbia Broadcasting System (CBS) was to offer its own version of comedy-variety show, initially titled *Toast of the Town.* First broadcast in 1948, it became *The Ed Sullivan Show* in 1955. With his stiff gestures and no-nonsense approach, Sullivan by no means imitated the visual comedy associated with Berle, but the variety format represented a continuation of that initiated by the comedian.

Other successful comedy-variety shows first shown on CBS included those hosted by Ed Wynn, Red Skelton, and Jackie Gleason. Although the presence of these shows was in part a response to Berle, it was also only natural that the style and format associated with decades of stage or vaudeville entertainment be carried over to television.

For a variety of reasons, mostly economic, both CBS and the newer ABC network evolved toward situation comedies in response to the success of NBC. The late 1940's and early 1950's saw the first appearance on television of shows such as *The Gold-bergs*, *The George Burns and Gracie Allen Show*, and *I Love Lucy* on CBS and *The Adventures of Ozzie and Harriet* and *Make Room for Daddy* on ABC.

The situation comedies, or "sitcoms," differed in significant ways from the comedy-variety form of entertainment. Each sitcom episode was based on a recurring theme, such as a home, workplace, or family. The same characters appeared each week, and the comedy was based on the interactions between the stars. Guest stars played a secondary role to the main characters.

Situation comedies were generally produced on film rather than broadcast live. Since most sitcoms involved a package of thirty-nine episodes each season, they could be shown as repeats during the summer break or sold to other television market areas. It was some years before variety shows such as Berle's were filmed, and most of these early shows are forever lost.

One cannot ignore the impact of success on Berle himself. Berle had been a moderately successful vaudeville, movie, and nightclub entertainer for thirty-five years when he began his radio program for Texaco. Once he began hosting *Texaco Star Theater*, however, his became a household name. Among the items marketed under the Berle name or face were comic books, T-shirts, and chewing gum. His appearance on other programs cost the sponsor up to $1,000 per minute.

In 1951, NBC signed Berle to an exclusive thirty-year contract. Under the terms of the contract, NBC had the exclusive rights to Berle's acting, producing, directing, and writing. In return, Berle was guaranteed an annual income of $200,000, whether or not he worked. The contract actually was the result of a compromise. Berle had hoped to have his shows filmed, allowing for later telecasting of the reruns, with appropriate residuals for its host. The network refused, but the thirty-year contract assured Berle of the financial security he desired. The downside, not initially apparent, was that when NBC decided not to use Berle, he could not work elsewhere.

Berle continued with his show on NBC, under different names and different formats, until 1969. Texaco continued its sponsorship until the end of the 1952-1953 season, when it dropped Berle's show in favor of one starring Jimmy Durante and Donald O'Connor on alternate weeks. Buick became the sponsor of Berle's show. For the 1955-1956 season, *The Milton Berle Show* moved its operation from New York to Hollywood, becoming one of the first color variety shows being broadcast from California. RCA Whirlpool and Sunbeam signed on as sponsors. Among the guest stars appearing on the show was a new singer named Elvis Presley.

Berle's popularity had peaked by 1956. He continued on NBC for several more years, hosting *The Milton Berle Show* until 1959, *Milton Berle Starring in the Kraft Music Hall* (1958-1959), and an unsuccessful *Jackpot Bowling Starring Milton Berle* (1960-1961).

Clearly, Berle's future was at an impasse with NBC. In 1965, he renegotiated his contract with NBC, reducing its yearly payments to him to $120,000. In return, Berle had the right to appear on other networks. In addition to appearing in a number of dramatic roles, eliminating any fear of being typecast, Berle hosted several variety shows during the next decade. In 1978, he received a special Emmy for lifetime achievement, in recognition for his work in ensuring the success of the television medium. It is easy to forget that the success of television was by no means assured in its early years. The *Texaco Star Theater* was an experiment. Its success came about because the visual comedy of the host meshed so perfectly with the vaudeville concept of the program. The modern variety show was probably inevitable and would no doubt have evolved even in the absence of Milton Berle, but there can be no doubt that its appearance was significantly hastened as a result of Berle and that his success on television speeded the acceptance of television as entertainment.

Bibliography

Brooks, Tim, and Earle Marsh. *The Complete Directory to Prime Time Network TV Shows, 1946-Present.* 5th ed. New York: Ballantine Books, 1992. Contains descriptions of all prime-time shows from the inception of television. An excellent description of *Texaco Star Theater* is provided, including a list of major entertainers associated with Berle's shows.

Fireman, Judy, ed. *TV Book.* New York: Workman, 1977. An entertaining book that consists of discussions on the history of television and reminiscences of scores of stars. Milton Berle provides a number of anecdotes associated with *Texaco Star Theater.* Numerous photographs.

Lyman, Darryl. *Great Jews on Stage and Screen.* Middle Village, N.Y.: Jonathan David, 1987. A collection of biographies, including that of Berle. Contains a succinct description of Berle's show business career, including a list of major stage, screen, and television performances.

McCrohan, Donna. *Prime Time, Our Time.* Rocklin, Calif.: Prima, 1990. Provides a decade by decade description of the development of television programming. Much of the book is presented as social history. Highly readable.

MacDonald, J. Fred. *One Nation Under Television.* New York: Pantheon Books, 1990. An excellent history of the medium, particularly of the early years. An entire section is devoted to the history of early vaudeville-type shows and the evolution of the situation comedy. Much space is devoted to a description of Berle's impact.

McNeil, Alex. *Total Television.* New York: Penguin Books, 1991. Provides a thorough yet succinct description of all major television programs from 1948 on.

Rose, Brian G., ed. *TV Genres: A Handbook and Reference Guide.* Westport, Conn.: Greenwood Press, 1985. Describes various television genres, such as police shows and Westerns. A thorough discussion is provided on the historical development of each area of programming. Bibliographical surveys and videographies.

Richard Adler

Cross-References

Variety Shows Dominate Television Programming (1948), p. 1383; Television Enters Its Golden Age (1950's), p. 1465; *The Red Skelton Show* Becomes a Landmark on Network Television (1951), p. 1520; *The Tonight Show* Becomes an American Institution (1954), p. 1623; *Rowan and Martin's Laugh-In* Is the Top Show on Television (1968), p. 2115; *The Sonny and Cher Comedy Hour* Brings Glitz to Television (1971), p. 2244 *Saturday Night Live* Is First Broadcast (1975), p. 2355.

KUKLA, FRAN, AND OLLIE PIONEERS CHILDREN'S TELEVISION PROGRAMMING

Category of event: Television and radio
Time: November 29, 1948-August 31, 1957
Locale: Chicago, Illinois

One of television's earliest and most endearing shows, Kukla, Fran, and Ollie *made the gentle banter of puppets with one human performer the unlikely formula for an early hit television show*

Principal personages:
> FRAN ALLISON (1924-   ), the show's hostess and confidante of the puppets (indeed, the only nonpuppet on camera)
> BURR TILLSTROM (1917-1985), the puppeteer who operated Kukla and the other "Kuklapolitan Players"

Summary of Event

If by the end of World War II Chicago had declined as a radio broadcasting center, within a few years it had become a thriving source of some of television's earliest hit shows. While *Garroway at Large*, with Dave Garroway, and *Stud's Place*, with Studs Terkel, provided the intimacy of good conversation, *Kukla, Fran, and Ollie* provided a company of puppet players in gentle conversation with one on-camera human performer, the actress Fran Allison. Almost entirely improvised, the low-budget show was fresh and lifelike, and it offered the promise of good conversation among a likable set of friends.

Burr Tillstrom, the show's puppeteer and the voice of all the puppets, created the character of Kukla in 1936. Tillstrom gradually added an entire troupe of puppets to fill out his repertory company. The gentle Kukla, who consisted of little more than a tennis ball head and a smaller red ball for a nose, was the show's stable center of low-keyed good sense (*Kukla* simply means "doll" in Russian). Kukla found an ideal complement in the boisterous extrovert Oliver J. Dragon, who clearly relied on the soft-spoken Kukla to restrain his imaginative and aggressive nature. With his single floppy and occasionally threatening snaggle tooth, Ollie would often swat Kukla with his beak or bite Kukla's tempting nose in exasperation, but the bonding between the two unlikely friends was deep and enduring.

The third pillar of the company, Fran Allison, would often introduce the topic of conversation and guide the debate on moral or topical problems between the two puppets. Originally a schoolteacher and radio singer in Iowa, she portrayed the obstreperous "Aunt Fannie" on *Don McNeill's Breakfast Club* on Chicago radio in the mornings before joining the puppets for the evening's television show.

Although the show was occasionally criticized for its lack of development and action, the critics were generally as enthusiastic as the public, which consisted equally of children enjoying the puppets' antics and adults, who found the compatibility and intelligence of the conversation among Fran and the puppets soothing. In 1949, a reviewer for *The New York Times* celebrated the show's upbeat tone: "The puppets, manipulated by Burr Tillstrom, are astonishingly lifelike and informal in their bantering with Miss Allison, who has a knack for treating them as humans yet always keeping her tongue in cheek."

The show's 1948-1957 run almost exactly coincided with the period in which television captured the hearts and living rooms of the American public; in this time, televisions were installed in two-thirds of all American homes and became the primary source of home entertainment. Among the earliest and more naïve hopes for television were that it would renew family life by keeping family members at home and that it would unite the family after the dislocations of the Depression and World War II. In this period, the primary site of spectator amusement moved from the motion-picture theater to the home, and television was welcomed as the best approximation of live entertainment.

The theater was very much the model for early television shows, and while the legitimate theater clearly inspired early anthology drama showcases such as *Kraft Television Theatre* and *Playhouse 90*, vaudeville was the model for variety shows such as *The Texaco Star Theater* with Milton Berle and *Your Show of Shows* with Sid Caesar. Jack Benny spoke for many when he said that television was an extension of the stage. *Kukla, Fran, and Ollie* accepted the theatrical convention by clearly placing the puppets within a miniature proscenium arch puppet stage, with Fran Allison always standing outside the stage to the left of the puppets. When she occasionally sang, the puppets would remain onstage to watch her and applaud her performance; Ollie would fall over backward in an amusingly erotic swoon. Burr Tillstrom appeared at the show's end to take a bow with the puppets.

The show embraced the theatrical metaphor by supplying an entire troupe of puppets to support Kukla and Ollie. Cecil Bill, the company manager, spoke a sweet but unintelligible language of his own, while Colonel Crackie, the troupe's emcee, was florid and long-winded in the manner of a stereotypical Southern senator. Madame Oglepuss was the company's haughty opera singer; for some years, the puppets did a stylized annual version of *The Mikado*, with Kukla as Nanki Poo.

Others of the puppets implied a domestic life for the group. Fletcher Rabbit was a harried mailman who always promised to have his ears starched so as not to fall over his eyes. Dolores Dragon, Ollie's niece, was a smaller version of Ollie with curly hair, and Beulah the Witch provided an occasional note of menace. Yet the troupe left the general impression of a large, boisterous but affectionate family. With modesty unthinkable in today's media, Tillstrom never developed his puppets into commercial properties, despite the enormous sales that Ollie puppets or Kukla games might have generated.

Impact of Event

It is possible for someone growing up with television to remember with great affection the form of *Kukla, Fran, and Ollie* without remembering much of anything of its content. The puppets bickered and occasionally even resorted to violence, as when Ollie attacked Kukla's nose or when Beulah appeared with her broomstick; but viewers mostly recall the gentleness and the affection among the puppets and their human companion. The show, in its remarkably low-keyed way, demonstrated the potential of television for generating affection for its characters, even for relatively crudely realized puppets like Kukla and Ollie. The show was always done live, and the idea of filming the show for later use would have been as repugnant to its creators as writing out the scripts would have been.

As the novelty of the medium wore off and as audiences in the early 1950's increasingly demanded more realism and sophistication from the shows, *Kukla, Fran, and Ollie* survived the complaints that gradually eliminated the variety shows. Audiences began to demand that such shows provide greater unity than that afforded by the vaudeville show formula and insisted that situation comedies provide more realistic characters.

The puppets may not have looked particularly lifelike or realistic, but they clearly served as a positive family model, though without the oppressive wholesomeness that made so many early television families later seem cloying and unwatchable. Usually shown at 7:00 P.M. Eastern time, *Kukla, Fran, and Ollie* did help to unite families around the television set during the dinner hour and provided a model of a diverse, occasionally squabbling and unruly, and affectionate family. In an age when television tapped a white, middle-class image and when minorities were either invisible or treated as comic stereotypes, *Kukla, Fran, and Ollie* implied both racial and social complexities. Despite his essentially benign nature, the rambunctious Ollie was, after all, a dragon, and his presence hinted at a world of aliens and "others."

Tillstrom wore out several versions of Ollie during the show's run and actually cobbled them together from unlikely scraps of fabric, including a bit of Imogene Coca's mink coat for the puppet's neck. If Ollie's race was unclear, his phallic appearance was enough to make any Freudian viewer happy; Tillstrom brilliantly manipulated the puppet's one loose dragon's tooth and could open Ollie's beak into a cheerfully barbaric yawp.

The relationship between Kukla and Ollie was roughly analogous to that of Pogo the Possum and Albert the Alligator in Walt Kelly's comic strip *Pogo*, although the television show was less politically inclined and lacked the darker, satiric tone of the comic strip. The influence of *Kukla, Fran, and Ollie* would be felt years later on the public television children's show *Misterogers' Neighborhood*, on which King Friday's castle shared the television screen with the human performers as Kukla's proscenium arch served as a contrasting space for Fran Allison. The influence was even clearer on *The Muppet Show*, which borrowed the motif of the harried theater company trying to put on a show from the Kuklapolitan Players; the long-suffering Kermit the Frog served as a crutch on which the boisterous and overbearing Miss Piggy could lean, just as Ollie had come to depend on Kukla. *The Muppet Show*'s weekly guest stars served the role Fran Allison so cleverly originated; by contrast, *Kukla, Fran, and Ollie* never featured guest stars.

Unlike *The Muppet Show*, with its opulent mid-1980's budget, *Kukla, Fran, and Ollie* brilliantly displayed the potential of television with a single set and a single human performer, in live broadcasts (of either fifteen minutes or a half hour) with improvised scripts. Tillstrom explained in 1950, "If I ever plotted exactly what I was going to say or do, Kukla and Ollie wouldn't work for me. . . . After all, you don't need a script when you're talking to your friends."

Through the charm of several appealing puppets and Fran Allison, *Kukla, Fran, and Ollie* helped to wean the American public from radio to television. As radio comedian Fred Allen, commented, "When you see Kukla, Fran and Ollie come alive on that little screen, you realize you don't need great big things as we had in radio." Without the glitz or big budgets of the variety shows and the dramatic anthologies of early television, *Kukla, Fran, and Ollie* realized the full potential of television to attract audiences by warm relationships and good-natured improvisational play.

Bibliography

Brooks, Tim, and Earle Marsh. *The Complete Directory to Prime Time Network TV Shows, 1946-Present.* 4th ed. New York: Ballantine Books, 1988. Provides a full list of the "Kuklapolitan Players," including such rarely seen figures as Ollie's mother, Olivia, who doubled Ollie's number of teeth.

McNeil, Alex. *Total Television.* 2d ed. New York: Penguin, 1991. Commends *Kukla, Fran, and Ollie* show for making a great achievement on a minimum of resources.

Sigler, Lynn. *Make Room for TV: Television and the Family in Postwar America.* Chicago: University of Chicago Press, 1992. Without mentioning *Kukla, Fran, and Ollie*, discusses the transitional period from 1948 to 1955, when television changed from a futuristic possibility to the dominant mode of home entertainment.

Sternberg, Joel. "Television Town." *Chicago History* (Summer, 1975): 108-117. Notes Chicago's role in the explosion of television programming in the late 1940's with shows such as *Garroway at Large* and *Kukla, Fran, and Ollie*.

Weiner, Ed, et al. *The TV Guide TV Book.* New York: HarperCollins, 1992. Commends *Kukla, Fran, and Ollie* for its candor, warmth, and spontaneity.

Byron Nelson

Cross-References

Television Enters Its Golden Age (1950's), p. 1465; *Captain Kangaroo* Debuts (1955), p. 1678; *The Flintstones* Popularizes Prime-Time Cartoons (1960), p. 1840; *Sesame Street* Revolutionizes Children's Programming (1969), p. 2185; *The Simpsons* Debuts, Anchoring the Fledgling Fox Network (1990), p. 2652.

PORTER CREATES AN INTEGRATED SCORE
FOR *KISS ME, KATE*

Categories of event: Music and theater
Time: December 30, 1948
Locale: New York, New York

For the highly crafted theater piece Kiss Me, Kate, *Cole Porter wrote a song score that was his first to belong to the characters and story line*

Principal personages:
> COLE PORTER (1891-1964), a composer and lyricist who was known for his witty rhymes
> SAMUEL SPEWACK (1899-1971), a playwright who created, primarily, light comedies and libretti for musicals
> BELLA SPEWACK (1899-1990), Samuel Spewack's wife and partner
> WILLIAM SHAKESPEARE (1564-1616), an Elizabethan dramatist whose *The Taming of the Shrew* formed the basis for *Kiss Me, Kate*

Summary of Event

By 1948, the idea of combining the work of William Shakespeare with music was not a particularly novel concept. There were, after all, several operas and ballets in the standard repertoire, and Shakespeare himself often had added music to his plays. Indeed, Lehman Engel, a noted musical theater conductor and scholar, suggested that the structure Shakespeare employed in his plays lent itself to musical theater libretti. Engel concluded that if Shakespeare were writing in the twentieth century, he would be writing musical comedies.

In fact, in a way, he already had. In 1938, Richard Rodgers (composer), Lorenz Hart (lyricist), and George Abbott (producer, director, and librettist) sent *The Boys from Syracuse* to Broadway. That musical was based on one of Shakespeare's earliest plays, *The Comedy of Errors* (pr. c. 1592-1594). The score included "This Can't Be Love," "Falling in Love with Love," and "Sing for Your Supper." Some critics believed that the songs improved Shakespeare's work.

Composer/lyricist Cole Porter was not very enthusiastic when playwright Bella Spewack approached him with an idea to turn Shakespeare's *The Taming of the Shrew* (pr. c. 1593-1594) into a Broadway musical. Spewack had thought it was a bad idea when she first heard about it as well. The idea originated with a stage manager, Arnold Saint Subber, and a costume designer, Lemuel Ayers. Ayers and Saint Subber wanted to be producers and decided that a musical version of *The Taming of the Shrew* would be their first project. When the idea was suggested to Bella Spewack, her reaction was negative. She thought that adding music to Shakespeare was "high school" and not worthy of her talents. She was interested in Broadway-quality work.

She knew that field. Bella and Samuel Spewack were a married writing team that had numerous Broadway successes. Their collaboration started when they were quite young. Both were journalists with different organizations in New York. Bella also wrote numerous short stories. During a series of long walks, she suggested to Samuel that they become partners. She meant professionally, but Samuel assumed that it was a proposal of marriage. Both partnerships were long-lasting and rewarding. In 1932, they opened *Clear All Wires.* In 1938, this was turned into the musical *Leave It to Me!* The score was by Cole Porter, Gene Kelly was in the chorus, and one of the highlights was Mary Martin singing "My Heart Belongs to Daddy." Other plays included *Spring Song, Boy Meets Girl, Miss Swan Expects,* and, several years following *Kiss Me, Kate, My Three Angels.* They were also involved in the writing of such screenplays as *My Favorite Wife* (1940) and *Weekend at the Waldorf* (1945).

With this experience, the Spewacks were not interested in simply adding music to Shakespeare. Six weeks after Saint Subber approached her with the idea, however, Bella had formed her own conception of the project. There was, surprisingly, some disagreement about the selection of a composer. The producers suggested Burton Lane, but he was busy. They then attempted to sign an untried talent, but the Spewacks were not interested in that.

The Spewacks were interested in Cole Porter. The producers were hesitant because Porter, though a great talent, had not had a hit in three years. The Spewacks were determined, however, and became even more determined when Porter initially turned them down. He told them that he did not believe that he could create the proper score, but privately he thought the project was too highbrow for Broadway. In addition, he was very interested in another project that involved a musical about Miss America pageants. This was proposed by Elaine Carrington, a writer who wanted to move from soap operas to the Broadway stage.

The Spewacks were persistent. When Porter objected that the plot was too complicated for the average audience member, the writers broke it down for him as a rather basic boy-loves-girl story. When Porter complained that he just did not understand the script, Bella Spewack arrived to read sections to him. Porter, a highly intelligent man, was using these measures largely as delaying tactics. Finally, several events occurred that turned Porter's attention to *Kiss Me, Kate.* Porter realized that the Miss America project was not going to work. Health and tax problems continued to annoy Porter, and he knew that work—specifically, a new show—was the best therapy. Bella Spewack continued her campaign, and in February, 1948, Cole Porter agreed to create the music and lyrics for *Kiss Me, Kate.*

Porter set to work, and most of the score was finished by May. This did not solve all the problems, however. Money had to be raised for the production, and investors were cautious. To begin with, the Spewacks were known primarily for nonmusicals, and Porter's recent record did not instill confidence. The director, John Wilson, was known as a producer. One of the producers was a designer, and the other producer was a stage manager. Finally, the prevailing opinion at the time was that Shakespeare never worked on Broadway. After what seemed an endless number of backers' auditions, the $180,000 needed to produce the show was raised. It was clear, however, that few people had much faith in *Kiss Me, Kate.*

Fortunately, during this trying time, the Spewacks and Cole Porter continued their work. After his early hesitation, Porter devoted himself to the project. He praised the book as the best ever written for a musical, and he composed so many songs that the Spewacks begged him to stop. Their entreaty fell on deaf ears, which was fortunate since Porter then wrote "Brush Up Your Shakespeare," one of the great comedy songs in musical theater.

As the writing progressed, the issue of performers soon became crucial. From the beginning, everyone had agreed that Alfred Drake was the perfect choice for the male lead. Drake had established himself as the lead in *Babes in Arms* (1937) and had made history as Curly in the first production of *Oklahoma!* (1943). He had experience in Shakespeare, which made him ideally suited for the role. A female lead was more difficult. Porter first approached an opera diva, Jarmila Novotna, but she did not want to attempt the Broadway stage. Mary Martin also was considered. Negotiations fell apart through bad communications, and Richard Rodgers and Oscar Hammerstein II were able to lure her away with a project that became *South Pacific.* John Wilson, the director, first approached Lily Pons, but her health was not up to the demands of a Broadway show. Finally, he came across a young movie actress named Patricia Morison. Porter was impressed with her and worked on her singing until he was convinced that she could play the role.

The rest of the company included Lisa Kirk and Harold Lang. Hanya Holm was the choreographer, Pembroke Davenport was the musical director, Robert Russell Bennett created the arrangements, and Lemuel Ayers doubled as producer and designer of sets and costumes. Conflicts eventually arose between Porter and the Spewacks during rehearsals, but they were not serious enough to disrupt the project.

The show premiered out of town in Philadelphia on December 2, 1948. The production team was confident, but others surrounding the show were convinced that it would be a flop. This led to a great deal of last-minute shuffling of shares in the production. Usually, out-of-town tryouts led to drastic cuts and changes. It was decided in the case of *Kiss Me, Kate* that no changes were needed. In fact, the only changes Bella Spewack admitted to were some cuts of verses in the songs, the elimination of several songs (from a very rich score), and the return to the original draft in some scenes. In the chaos that usually precedes the New York opening of a musical, this sort of calm was very rare.

As it turned out, it was well-founded. The show came into New York on December 30, 1948, under budget. The reviews were not universally glowing (Harold Clurman found the music weak), but the majority were raves. *Kiss Me, Kate* continued for 1,077 performances in New York and toured for three years. The London production was not greeted as warmly, yet it ran for four hundred performances. It also won several major awards, including the Tony.

It is interesting that the show toured so successfully, because, besides the foundation in Shakespeare, a touring show is essential to the plot of *Kiss Me, Kate.* From the beginning, with the song "Another Opening, Another Show," the audience is watching a show about a show. A struggling company is attempting to stage a musical production of *The Taming of the Shrew*, Shakespeare's classic version of the battle of the sexes. Katharina is the headstrong woman who is being pursued by the pompous Petruchio. Katharina's sister, Bianca, is pursued by Gremio, Hortensio, and Lucentio. Katharina's attitude toward all of this pursuit is best summed up in the song "I Hate Men." True love is resolved and the battle of the sexes, though not finished, reaches a happy truce.

Meanwhile, there is another, more pitched, battle of the sexes being fought in the wings. Fred Graham, the director, producer, and star, is the former husband of Lili Vanessi, his leading lady. Sparks still fly between them, some romantic and some violent. Fred has been involved with Lois (the company's Bianca), who is in love with Bill (Lucentio). Bill is involved with gamblers, who come backstage to collect on debts and who demonstrate a greater appreciation for Shakespeare than anyone would have imagined. The musical moves between the onstage action, created by Shakespeare, and the offstage affairs of the actors.

A film version, *Kiss Me Kate*, featuring the dancing of Ann Miller and Bob Fosse, was released in 1953. The show was translated into more than a dozen foreign languages and was the first American musical to be presented in Germany, Italy, and Vienna, the home of the European operetta.

Impact of Event

It would be easy to claim that *Kiss Me, Kate* was a wonderful success story in the history of musical theater and leave it at that. A composer who had charmed audiences and the social elite alike since the 1920's and had made a real mark on the Broadway stage in the 1930's came back with his best work and his biggest hit just when everyone assumed that his career was over. That story itself sounds like a good plot for a Cole Porter musical, but there was more to reality, especially for Porter. While there was still plenty of glow in *Kiss Me, Kate*, Rodgers and Hammerstein opened *South Pacific* (with Mary Martin) and stole some of the luster. There also were a few more Cole Porter scores following *Kiss Me, Kate*. He wrote scores for the musicals *Can-Can* (1953) and *Silk Stockings* (1955) and for the film *High Society* (1956).

The real importance of *Kiss Me, Kate* is what it demonstrated about Cole Porter, the artist. Porter's place in musical theater history is clear. The 1930's were his era. He shared them, of course, with Rodgers and Hart, but there is significance to that. The shows of Rodgers and Hart and the shows of Cole Porter (indeed, most of the musicals of the 1930's) are remembered primarily for the strength of the score. The story line was of little concern and had little effect on the song selection. One exception to this might be *Pal Joey* (1940) by Rodgers and Hart. Much of it is set in a nightclub, which lends itself to all sorts of possibilities for numbers.

One of Porter's great successes, *Anything Goes* (1934), was given a new plot structure shortly before it opened because the original structure too closely resembled a current event. In recent revivals, several songs have been dropped from the score of

Anything Goes and other, more popular Porter tunes (from other shows) have been put in their place. This indicates several things. First, Porter was capable of creating memorable songs even when the books were less than memorable. It also indicates that songs were lifted easily from Porter scores, showing that the songs were not closely tied to character. "I've Got You Under My Skin," for example, is a song written for a lover. Many musicals have many lovers, and that song would fit in many situations.

In the 1940's, the musical began to change. Hammerstein's work on *Show Boat* (1927) anticipated these changes but did not cause a trend at that time. Most historians point to *Oklahoma!* by Rodgers and Hammerstein as the watershed. Characters, plot, songs, and dances were all fully integrated, and it was very difficult to separate one from the other. No one would consider taking "Oh! What a Beautiful Mornin'" from Curly and giving it to the King of Siam. Alan Jay Lerner and Frederick Loewe followed the trend with *Brigadoon* (1948).

Cole Porter worked on songs, composing both the music and the lyrics. Very few have been successful at this in the musical theater. Frank Loesser and Meredith Willson are early examples, with Stephen Sondheim coming later. Porter was caught in a transition. He was asked to go from creating wonderful, witty, danceable tunes that could slide in and out of a plot to creating a score that was integrated with and, indeed, helped to further the plot. He had to do all of this while maintaining the Porter standards of wit, heart, humor, passion, charm, and some of the most ingenious rhymes this side of W. S. Gilbert and Sir Arthur Sullivan.

The world discovered, with *Kiss Me, Kate*, that he was able to do this. His rhymes are still a surprise, for example, the rhyme of Padua with "cad you are." The brooding passion of "So in Love" reminds the listener that it is by the same musician/poet who created "Night and Day." The difference was that any lonely lover could sing "Night and Day"; "So in Love" belongs to a specific situation and a specific show. Though *South Pacific* soon overshadowed the accomplishment of *Kiss Me, Kate*, it was not lost on Cole Porter that he had accomplished, with words and music, what it took the team of Rodgers and Hammerstein to do.

Bibliography

Eells, George. *Cole Porter: The Life That Late He Led.* New York: G. P. Putnam's Sons, 1967. A thorough biography of Cole Porter. It is well written and well researched, and there are good pictures. Presents Porter's personality; not as much detail is given to his work as an artist. This is a book for the layperson. Very good detail in the interview with Bella Spewack.

Engel, Lehman. *Words with Music.* New York: Macmillan, 1972. A serious look at the needs and problems of the libretto in the musical theater. Engel's background as a conductor and theorist of the musical makes his opinions especially important. His study of structure is quite good. An essential book for the serious study of the musical.

Green, Stanley. *The World of Musical Comedy.* New York: Grosset & Dunlap, 1960.

One of the basic sources. Although not particularly current, it provides an excellent source for the earlier days. Especially good are the pictures, which give a real sense of another time in the theater.

Porter, Cole. *The Complete Lyrics of Cole Porter.* Edited by Robert Kimball. New York: Alfred A. Knopf, 1983. An impressive coffee-table book. Helpful for research. One could wish for a bit more information on the shows.

Richards, Stanley, ed. *Ten Great Musicals of the American Theatre.* Radnor, Pa.: Chilton Book Company, 1973. Part of a marvelous and valuable series of anthologies of musical theater libretti. Includes some helpful background notes. It is best, however, as primary research. Good for the scholar studying structure or the producer looking for future shows.

William B. Kennedy

Cross-References

Show Boat Introduces American Musical Theater (1927), p. 745; *Oklahoma!* Opens on Broadway (1943), p. 1256; Bernstein Joins Symphonic and Jazz Elements in *West Side Story* (1957), p. 1731; Willson's *The Music Man* Presents Musical Americana (1957), p. 1752; Sondheim's *Company* Is Broadway's First "Concept" Musical (1970), p. 2213.

BRECHT FOUNDS THE BERLINER ENSEMBLE

Category of event: Theater
Time: 1949
Locale: East Berlin, East Germany

Under Bertolt Brecht's direction, the productions of the Berliner Ensemble pro-
vided theater audiences with opportunities to challenge the "dramatic" theater by
participating in "epic" theater

Principal personages:

BERTOLT BRECHT (1898-1956), a director and playwright who built upon
the epic theories of Erwin Piscator

ERWIN PISCATOR (1893-1966), a theorist who invented epic drama in the
1920's and pioneered what later became known as "documentary theater"

HELENE WEIGEL (1900-1971), an actress and director who was Brecht's
wife and worked with him to perfect epic theater with the Berliner
Ensemble

ALFRED JARRY (1873-1907), a playwright who wrote the first epic drama,
Ubu roi, in 1888

ERICH ENGEL (1891-1966), the director who first staged *The Threepenny*
Opera

Summary of Event

Bertolt Brecht explored the didactic nature of the theater. It was Brecht's belief
that the purpose of theater is to teach people how to survive in a world of absurdity.
He did not want his audience simply to feel empathy with the situation of the characters. Instead, Brecht's goal was to cause people to think about what was taking place
and to look for ways to change the world. Brecht was convinced that audiences must
be made to realize that plays suggested the need to find answers to sociopolitical and
economic problems outside the theater. In Brecht's theater, people do not escape
their problems; instead, they are made to recognize the problems and seek ways to
solve them.

Realism was the dominant form of theater up to the 1950's. Major influences on
the theater included Charles Darwin's theories in science, Karl Marx's theories of
politics and economics, and Sigmund Freud's theories of psychology. These influences are apparent in epic theater, wherein the world is viewed as dynamic and ever-
changing and needs must be met actively by people.

To achieve his dramatic goal, Brecht followed the lead of Erwin Piscator in developing and using the techniques of epic theater. Brecht was influenced strongly by the
work of Max Reinhardt. Reinhardt sought to fuse the actor and the audience through
the use of light, color, music, and mass movements on the stage. The major tech-

niques of epic theater include use of episodic dramatic structure. Brecht also used music. He would have characters break the action and cross over the imaginary "fourth wall" at the front of the stage to sing a song to the audience. Often the character's song would be in direct contrast to the nature of the character as shown in the plot. Musicians were placed on the stage in full view of the audience. Another technique would have the lighting instruments hanging so that the audience was aware of them being used. Brecht would have the scenery changed without the curtain being brought down so that the audience would observe scenery changes taking place as the plot developed. Further, he used scenery that was nonrealistic.

Additionally, Brecht employed the technique of "alienation." In his work, Brecht sought to have the audience take an active role in the dramatic production. Alienation was a process of making the dramatic action and the characters seem strange to the viewer through a variety of theatrical devices. In this way, the audience members could be sufficiently distanced from the play to allow them to watch it critically without empathy for the characters. Brecht was not concerned with having the audience identify with the individual psyche of a character; instead, he wanted the audience to react to the sociopolitical and economic forces affecting the characters in the play.

Another technique Brecht used was "historification." Brecht attempted to create a sense of past. This involved a process of emphasizing the history of an event so that the audience could evaluate the events of the dramatic action of the plot. He wanted the viewers to recognize changes that have occurred throughout history. By seeing change, Brecht hoped, his audience would realize that events in their lives could be changed for the better.

Epic theater is a drama form and production style intended to provoke spectators into a heightened sociopolitical awareness rather than emotionally involving them in realistic situations. Its ultimate goal is change. This form was not limited to unity of time, place, and action. Usually, episodic plots were revealed early in the dramatic action, without use of exposition. Works usually covered long periods of time— weeks, months, or even years. The dramatic action was contained in many short, fragmented scenes, with alternation between shorter and longer ones. Often the plot unfolded across an entire city or country rather than in one house or a single room. Action usually involved large numbers of characters, up to several dozen. Brecht would juxtapose serious and comic scenes in an effort to alienate the viewer. Generally there were several lines of action contained in the play's plot. Characters often served the narrative function of a Greek chorus; Brecht sometimes used a narrator to speak or sing directly to the audience.

Brecht was essentially an anarchist, questioning all societal restraints. In 1926, Brecht embraced the socioeconomic theories of Karl Marx. Brecht believed in the Marxist theory that society evolved as a result of economic forces, not through the activities of any given individual. He supported the principle of economic determinism. It was Brecht's opinion that only powerful and well-connected individuals truly benefited from the existing sociopolitical and economic structures of society.

He became a member of the Communist Party in 1928. What Brecht wanted was for people to be made to think and be moved to social action. Epic theater was moralistic in asserting that personal destiny is controlled by sociopolitical factors. It intended to study and make visible the conditions in society in an effort to bring positive change to people's lives.

Brecht rejected the prevailing practice in Western theater of seeking to make a production a synthesis of the arts, with each reinforcing the other for a unified whole. He was convinced that Oriental drama was superior to the majority of Western theater. He wanted to employ various Oriental techniques as an antidote to realism.

In an effort to develop and formalize his thinking concerning epic theater, Brecht founded the Berliner Ensemble. The Berliner Ensemble opened in 1949 at the Deutches Theatre. It remained there until 1954, when it moved to Theater-am-Schiffbauerdamm. The ensemble's first production was Brecht's own *Mutter Courage und ihre Kinder* (*Mother Courage and Her Children*). This play is the epitomizing example of epic theater.

In his productions with the Berliner Ensemble, Brecht employed a strategy of long and careful rehearsals, sometimes lasting as long as six months. He was meticulous in every detail of production. His style was highly dictatorial and matter-of-fact. Brecht was almost fanatical in his attempts to make sure that each production achieved his goals.

Impact of Event

Important productions by Brecht's ensemble include *Mother Courage and Her Children*, *Der gute Mensch von Sezuan* (written 1938-1940; *The Good Woman of Sezuan*, 1948), *Der kaukasische Kreidekreis* (written 1944-1945; first produced in English, as *The Caucasian Chalk Circle*, 1948), *Die Dreigroschenoper* (1928; *The Threepenny Opera*, 1949), and *Leben des Galilei* (first version written 1938-1939; *Life of Galileo*, 1947). In these productions, Brecht was able to implement his theoretical concepts of epic theater, with its alienation and historification. The work of the Berliner Ensemble was received with considerable enthusiasm. Under Brecht, the Berliner Ensemble was the height of cultural and artistic achievement.

From 1949 through 1956, the staging techniques used by Brecht were highly influential on the world of drama. As playwright and director with the Berliner Ensemble, Brecht was the dramatic leader of his generation. The Berliner Ensemble served as the culmination and realization of Brecht's epic theories. His involvement allowed the ensemble to enter new realms of dramatic expression.

Brecht sought to confront and challenge his audiences through the work of the Berliner Ensemble. Much of what he did as artistic director has been assimilated by contemporary theater. For example, he abandoned the use of the front curtain. In addition, he did not attempt to hide scenery changes and instead had them completed in full view of the audience. As a result of Brecht's influence, lighting instruments and musicians are now often in full view.

Other elements of epic theater as demonstrated by the Berliner Ensemble continue to influence dramatists and theater practitioners. Among these are a more presentational acting style. Although most theater companies use the more representational style advocated by Konstantin Stanislavsky, there are directors and dramatists who use the presentational style, which employs the breaking of the fourth wall of the theater. Neil Simon's *Brighton Beach Memoirs* (1983) is often staged in a presentational manner. The episodic structure can be seen in a number of plays, including *Other People's Money* (1989) by Jerry Sterner. Additionally, this play can be produced using projections to establish the location of action.

Brecht's techniques of achieving estrangement and displacement, the ultimate goals of epic theater, perhaps unfortunately have been absorbed by mainstream theater. Audiences now view his plays like any others and therefore are less likely to experience the sense of need to seek social change in the world after leaving the theater.

Like George Bernard Shaw, Brecht was a social dramatist. Brecht's style, however, was unlike Shaw's. Brecht's plays, like parables, intended to instruct the audience. Perhaps a problem resulted from Brecht's approach because he combined pleasure and learning through his epic theater. Ultimately, the plays seem to entertain as much as they instruct, and his messages might have come across more forcefully if he had used a more direct approach.

An irony in what Brecht hoped to accomplish, along with his communist associates, is that his left-wing political beliefs may have alienated his audiences too well. With the collapse of the Soviet communist bloc in the late twentieth century, some people questioned Brecht's obvious support of socialistic changes.

The combined effect of the Berliner Ensemble, Brecht, and epic drama on the theater is likely the broadest of any movement in recent theater history. The Berliner Ensemble performed some of the most far-reaching experiments in modern theater. In the 1954-1955 season, the Berliner Ensemble received the award for the best production at the Theater des Nations conducted with the support of the United Nations in Paris, France. The ensemble extended the influence of Brecht and his epic drama to cities and countries throughout Europe. It also extended the influence of actors, designers, and directors trained in its school of dramatic production. This troupe has had the most influence on production techniques of any group in the modern theater.

Bibliography

Barnet, Sylvan, Morton Berman, and William Burto. *Types of Drama: Plays and Essays.* Boston: Little, Brown, 1972. The sections on the nature of drama, the language of drama, and tragicomedy are useful to the student of absurdism in understanding the movement.

Brecht, Bertolt. *Brecht on Theatre: The Development of an Aesthetic.* Edited and translated by John Willett. New York: Hill & Wang, 1964. Sections dealing with the modern nature of epic theater, theater for pleasure or instruction, and experimental theater are particularly informative concerning Brecht's views on theater.

Brockett, Oscar G. *The Essential Theatre.* 5th ed. Fort Worth, Tex.: Holt, Rinehart and Winston, 1992. Provides a complete introduction to the basics of drama and the theater. Chapters 9 and 10 are particularly valuable in that they inform the reader about the absurdist and ethnic theater movements.

_____. *History of Theatre.* 6th ed. Boston: Allyn & Bacon, 1991. This comprehensive study of the theater is required reading for serious students of the theater. Brockett provides a thorough look at trends and movements affecting the evolution of the epic theater movement.

_____. *The Theatre: An Introduction.* New York: Holt, Rinehart and Winston, 1979. In chapters 11 through 13, Brockett offers an excellent overview of historical trends in the theater from 1915 through 1975.

Hall, James B., and Barry Ulanov. *Modern Culture and the Arts.* New York: McGraw-Hill, 1967. Hall and Ulanov provide information on cultural heritage that is stimulating and enlightening. This book is a good source on which to build a foundational knowledge of the arts.

Hartnoll, Phyllis. *The Concise History of Theatre.* New York: Harry N. Abrams, 1968. The author gives a synoptic view of major movements in the theater.

Klaus, Carl H., Miriam Gilbert, and Bradford S. Field, Jr., comps. *Stages of Drama: Classical to Contemporary Masterpieces of the Theater.* 2d ed. New York: St. Martin's Press, 1991. This collection with notes contains excellent production photographs.

Roose-Evans, James. *Experimental Theatre: From Stanislavsky to Today.* New York: Universe Books, 1970. Roose-Evans provides the reader with a clear and concise description of major movements in the theater. Gives a unified view of what has led to much of contemporary practice in modern theater.

Wilson, Edwin. *The Theater Experience.* 4th ed. New York: McGraw-Hill, 1988. The author examines numerous aspects of the theater in a discussion that highlights various developments in staging, acting, directing, and play writing. The book contains an excellent set of five appendices, including "Major Theatrical Forms and Movements" and "Historical Outline."

Willis M. Watt

Cross-References

Stanislavsky Helps to Establish the Moscow Art Theater (1897), p. 1; Freud Inaugurates a Fascination with the Unconscious (1899), p. 19; Reinhardt Becomes Director of the Deutsches Theater (1905), p. 145; *The Ghost Sonata* Influences Modern Theater and Drama (1908), p. 199; Brecht and Weill Collaborate on *Mahagonny Songspiel* (1927), p. 724; Sartre and Camus Give Dramatic Voice to Existential Philosophy (1940's), p. 1174; *Waiting for Godot* Expresses the Existential Theme of Absurdity (1953), p. 1573.

HANK WILLIAMS PERFORMS ON
THE GRAND OLE OPRY

Category of event: Music
Time: 1949
Locale: Nashville, Tennessee

Hank Williams' 1949 recording of "Lovesick Blues" and his performance on The Grand Ole Opry *marked the emergence of country music as a national force in popular music*

> *Principal personages:*
> HANK WILLIAMS (1923-1953), a singer and songwriter from southern Alabama who set the pattern for modern hard, or "honky-tonk," country music both as a songwriter and as a vocal stylist
> FRED ROSE (1897-1954), a songwriter and Nashville publisher who helped Williams throughout his career
> AUDREY SHEPPARD WILLIAMS (1923-1975), Hank Williams' first wife, who was instrumental in advancing his career and whose marital difficulties with him seemed to have inspired some of his songs

Summary of Event

Little did Hank Williams know when he recorded the old Tin Pan Alley song "Lovesick Blues" in December, 1948, that he would soon become the most popular star in country music and a regular member of the prestigious show *The Grand Ole Opry.* The song, written by Cliff Friend, had been recorded before, and Williams probably learned it from his fellow Alabamian Rex Griffin. Williams had already been singing "Lovesick Blues" in live performances, and he finally persuaded his song publisher and record producer, Fred Rose, to let him record it.

Released in early February, 1949, Williams' version of "Lovesick Blues" shot up the country charts and became Williams' first number-one song. His bluesy, subtly inflected vocal, highlighted by a distinctive mini-yodel, effectively turned a standard into a country lament. Williams' propulsive singing rode over a driving band and handled well the song's middle section with its minor progressions. The recording was different from the usual country fare of the time, which tended to feature rather four-square rhythm-chord patterns. The song stayed on the country charts for forty-two weeks, sixteen at number one, and even made the pop charts in twenty-fourth position. From March through the end of 1949, "Lovesick Blues" was the country song of the year.

Between 1947 and 1949, Williams had already had hits on the new Metro-Goldwyn-Mayer (MGM) label: "Move It on Over" had been a number-four hit, "I'm a Long Gone Daddy" had reached number six, and "Honky-Tonkin'" had made number fourteen; all were Williams' own compositions. Already a star on the new *Louisiana Hayride*, broadcast from Shreveport, Louisiana, Williams was ambitious. The *Hay-*

ride, like *The Grand Ole Opry*, was a radio barn show with a live audience, and came to be regarded as a sort of farm team for the *Opry* in Nashville. With his new hit rising on the charts, officials of the *Opry* visited the *Hayride* and decided that Williams belonged on their show, even though he had a reputation in the music business for drinking and carousing. Tested since 1937 on radio and the honky-tonk circuit, he was a dynamic interpreter of his own songs, and he combined the influences of country stars Roy Acuff and Ernest Tubb into a haunting new synthesis of plaintive vocalizing and energetic, committed presentation.

When Williams appeared on the Saturday night *Opry* broadcast of June 11, 1949, to sing "Lovesick Blues" and had to do six encores, the *Opry* knew it had found a new sensation who would broadcast a tough style of hard, honky-tonk country across the United States and enhance its growing dominance of the country airwaves. From then through the time of his firing from the *Opry* in August, 1952, Williams had hit after hit, mostly from his own pen. Nearly all his records stayed in the top-ten country charts for weeks, and seven reached number one. A phenomenon in sales and in live performances across the nation, Williams quickly put together a top-flight road band, the Drifting Cowboys, that helped set the norm for modern country bands with its driving, jazz-and-blues-influenced style. Combining fiddle, steel guitar, lead electric guitar, and slap acoustic bass, the Drifting Cowboys became a band hard to beat either on the road or in the studio.

As Williams penned and sang his songs of heartbreak, despair, and loneliness leavened with paeans to good times in the honky-tonks and celebrations of a working-class and Southern-rooted culture, he seemed unbeatable. His "overnight" success, though, had been hard won. He had paid his dues for years playing one-night stands, writing his songs, and refining his style. Born into rural poverty in 1923 near Mount Olive, Alabama, in the pine woods of the deep South, he had early on learned from local musicians, including the black itinerant Rufus Payne. On Montgomery radio as early as 1937, Williams had traveled the small-time circuit for years before joining the Louisiana Hayride in 1948.

After he married Audrey Sheppard in 1944, his career took a more ambitious turn. An ambitious woman herself, Audrey spurred Williams to get his songs published by a major firm. She was lucky in bringing Williams to Nashville in 1946. That trip became the key to his future and stardom; Fred Rose was there.

A longtime pop songwriter who had also written for cowboy film star Gene Autry in Hollywood, Rose turned to country music and came to Nashville in the early 1940's to help set up the city's first country music publishing company, Acuff-Rose. Founded in 1942 by Rose and country star Roy Acuff, the firm came to symbolize the growing importance of the city as the center of the country music industry springing up around *The Grand Ole Opry.* The *Opry*, founded in the 1920's, had come to dominate the airwaves and the barn-dance format with its cast of singing stars, instrumentalists, and dancers. The *Opry* was a dominant broadcast show on a clear-channel, fifty-thousand-watt station, and the program's live venue, the cavernous Ryman Auditorium in downtown Nashville, provided rural fans with a real show-business event for several hours each Saturday night.

Another factor in the growing power of country music was the formation of Broadcast Music, Incorporated (BMI) in 1939 as a rival to the older American Society of Composers, Authors, and Publishers (ASCAP). The older performing-rights organization (which acted to collect payments on live performances of songwriters' and publishers' copyrighted material) had run into a snag when proposing higher licensing fees on broadcasters in the late 1930's. To counter ASCAP, some radio executives formed BMI, temporarily banned ASCAP songs (largely drawn from New York's Tin Pan Alley stable), and set out to find new writing talent. What BMI collared were white country and black rhythm-and-blues and blues talents. Thus, a new catalog of more indigenous music was formed, and until-then neglected music began to pay its creators. Acuff-Rose was part of this movement. Interested in signing up raw talent, Fred Rose was duly impressed when Audrey Williams brought Hank to him in 1946.

Signing Williams to a writing contract, Rose soon pitched Williams' songs to country singers and managed to get Hank onto the small New York Sterling label in 1946. Though his first few records did little in sales, his debut on the new West Coast MGM label brought results from 1947 on, leading inexorably to that June 11, 1949, debut on *The Grand Ole Opry.*

Impact of Event

Williams' success from the time of his *Opry* debut until his death on January 1, 1953, can be attributed to several factors. Williams' greatest long-term influence beyond the world of country music stemmed from his songwriting skills. Though Fred Rose seems to have done some touching up of words and carefully supervised Williams' recording sessions—sometimes adding his own piano to the mix—Williams was the creative genius who knew all the idioms of country song. Whether writing songs of unrequited love or songs celebrating honky-tonking and general good times, he crafted lyrics filled with telling images, laconic phrases, and sprightly repartee. His lyrics etched the highs and lows of rural and working-class life and were put across on recordings and in live performances with an emotional sincerity and true-to-life conviction that was the root of country music's appeal and staying power. Songs such as "Mansion on the Hill," "Honky-Tonkin'," "I'm So Lonesome I Could Cry," "The Blues Come Around (When the Sun Goes Down)," "Hey, Good Lookin'," and "Jambalaya" became standards of country music. Train and prison songs such as "Pan American" and "Lonesome Whistle" (cowritten by Jimmie Davis) evoke landscapes and rural life in a way that may never have been equaled.

Although some of Williams' early songs "crossed over" into the pop field when they were covered by mainstream singers, it was only with songs such as "Cold, Cold Heart," "Half as Much," "I Can't Help It," "Your Cheating Heart," and "You Win Again," recorded from 1951 on, that Williams and Rose saw major pop music success. Williams himself rarely had any pop chart action; he was just too rural sounding. When Tony Bennett covered "Cold, Cold Heart" in 1951 and saw it become a number-one pop hit and sell a million copies, however, things started to change. They would never be the same again, either for Williams' song catalog or for the country music industry. Country music could now consistently cross over and into the pop charts, and country songs done by pop artists could bring great financial profit to country publishers. Acuff-Rose became a symbol of what could be done in spreading rural music to a wider public. In years to come, Nashville would find itself the envy of the older music centers.

Williams' songs soon were being covered by the likes of Rosemary Clooney, Jo Stafford, Joni James, and Frankie Laine, all major pop singers of the era. Such crossover success helped spur the Nashville music industry in the late 1950's and beyond to tailor its own recordings to a pop market by cutting out fiddles and steel guitars and mixing in strings, horns, and choruses, hallmarks of pop arranging. The famous "Nashville Sound," which sprang from the desire to beat pop record makers at their own game, helped make Nashville an even more important music center from the 1960's onward.

Within the country music field itself, Williams' other talents proved influential. His vocal style—alternately harsh and tender—was a classic country voice, nasal but quite flexible, with a range extending from quick falsetto leaps to low rasps and variable, melismatic ornamental flourishes. He could croon and shout, "worry" a word or phrase for expressive purposes, moan and semi-yodel, harden and soften his voice in and between phrases. Moreover, Williams sang mostly his own songs, which were in many cases rather thinly disguised voicings of the turbulence and emotional highs and lows of his own life, especially with regard to his tension-fraught marriage with Audrey. Thus, for his audiences, both on record and live, he sang about the life he lived.

Williams' band was also a key factor in his success and influence. The Drifting Cowboys combined Western swing, jazz, and blues influences. Steel guitarist Don Helms and fiddler Jerry Rivers did outstanding "take-off breaks" between Williams' verses (as in jazz, this kind of break does not stick closely to the melody line but spins off into improvisational flights). Williams used several electric lead-guitar players in the studio and on the road, and all were successful in working out new single-string lead solos. Zeke Turner and Sammy Pruett, in particular, developed a "dead-string" method of using wrist action to dampen strings to provide a percussive effect. Combined with Williams' bass players' acoustic slap bass, the resultant sound, especially in uptempo numbers, was a precursor of the work of rockabilly guitarists such as Carl Perkins and was a sign of the increasingly rhythmic feel of country music in the 1950's.

Sadly, Williams' career declined rapidly in 1952. Afflicted by then with chronic alcoholism and recurring back problems, he began to take various drugs prescribed to ease his pain. While being chauffeured to a New Year's Day show in Ohio, Williams died of heart failure on January 1, 1953.

Late in December, 1952, while visiting his family home in the pine woods of southern Alabama, Williams casually recorded "The Log Train," a song with just his own guitar accompaniment. The song is a narrative about Williams' father, Lon, who had once been a driver for a logging company locomotive. Williams evokes those days of a "long time ago" in memorializing his father's daily life, but he also captures, in his hoarse voice and laconic images of the Deep South, the fact that the 1920's were for himself also a long time ago. He had traveled and had seen success. He had created, and he had stumbled into despair and regular drunkenness. There had been miles of smiles—and miles of loneliness.

His style of singing and performing as well as his too-short life became legends. The artist who dies young with unfulfilled promise is an icon of music and literature, and after his death, Williams came to be regarded as a virtual patron saint of country music. Such is one part of Hank Williams' legacy.

The other part endures in the songs he wrote, which represent the largest single catalog of continually performed and recorded country songs. This legacy—and much of his life—epitomizes a folk heritage and a "white blues" tradition. Like his black counterpart from neighboring Mississippi, Robert Johnson, who also burned himself out and died young, Williams stands as a towering influence on countless subsequent singers and songwriters who created from their roots and their hearts.

Bibliography

Caress, Jay. *Hank Williams: Country Music's Tragic King*. New York: Stein & Day, 1979. A good general biography with some attention to the music scene and songs. Index, illustrations, and general discography.

Flippo, Chet. *Your Cheatin' Heart: A Biography of Hank Williams*. New York: Simon & Schuster, 1981. A more gritty life and legend approach, but with Flippo's creation of imaginary dialogues one is on dangerous ground. Revels too much in the unsavory side of things. Interesting as a supplementary account, but Flippo is really an outsider to the cultural contexts. Illustrated and indexed, but no discography.

Koon, George William. *Hank Williams: A Bio-Bibliography*. Westport, Conn.: Greenwood Press, 1983. An excellent study of man and music. A balanced and informed biography, a good understanding of the country music idiom, and thoughtful discussion of the songs. A few illustrations, index, and a good and comprehensive general discography.

Pleasants, Henry. *The Great American Popular Singers*. New York: Simon & Schuster, 1974. Has a chapter on Williams as well as others on country singers Jimmie Rodgers, Johnny Cash, and Elvis Presley. Sets Williams in an informative context. Good on vocal styles. Index, illustrations.

Williams, Roger M. *Sing a Sad Song: The Life of Hank Williams*. 2d ed. Urbana: University of Illinois Press, 1981. Perhaps the best study overall, although Koon's rivals it. Full biography, well researched, music and songs covered. No illustrations, but indexed. Good discography by premier country music discographer Bob Pinson.

Frederick E. Danker

Cross-References

Handy Ushers in the Commercial Blues Era (1910's), p. 252; ASCAP Is Founded to Protect Musicians' Rights (1914), p. 379; WSM Launches *The Grand Ole Opry* (1925), p. 675; Rodgers Cuts His First Record for RCA Victor (1927), p. 729; Guthrie's Populist Songs Reflect the Depression-Era United States (1930's), p. 810; Bill Monroe and the Blue Grass Boys Define Bluegrass Music (1939), p. 1121; Presley Becomes a Rock-and-Roll Sensation (1956), p. 1705; *Wanted: The Outlaws* Revitalizes Country Music (1976), p. 2365.

NINETEEN EIGHTY-FOUR PORTRAYS TOTALITARIANISM AND MIND CONTROL

Category of event: Literature
Time: 1949
Locale: Great Britain and the United States

George Orwell's most powerful warning against totalitarianism in any form fulfilled his stated desire to make political writing into an art and also celebrate his belief in the strength of the human spirit

Principal personages:
GEORGE ORWELL (ERIC ARTHUR BLAIR, 1903-1950), a writer whose somber vision was informed by his steadfast belief in the essential decency of the common man
FREDRIC WARBURG (1898-1981), Orwell's friend and director of Martin Secker & Warburg, the only British publisher willing to publish Orwell's most politically controversial works

Summary of Event

When *Nineteen Eighty-Four* was published in June, 1949, George Orwell had entered the last phase of his chronic illness. Despite his persistent stubborn hopes of a full recovery from the respiratory problems and tuberculosis that plagued his adult life, he must also have felt a strong sense of urgency. The speed of planning and writing of the book, completed in two years, exceeded even his usual astoundingly short periods of composition, especially considering that his work on the book was interrupted constantly by periods of hospitalization. As Michael Shelden recounts in his 1991 biography of Orwell, the book was to be Orwell's self-described most important work. It was impelled by his cumulative disappointment in socialism as an effective deterrent to fascism and perhaps by a subconscious realization of his own precarious mortality. Orwell wanted *Nineteen Eighty-Four* to be his best creative work, a distillation of language, style, and ideas that would convey most compellingly his desire (as he wrote) to make political writing into an art, as James Joyce had transformed fiction writing. It was also to be the strongest expression of the moral vision that shaped both Orwell's life and his writing.

Orwell's commitment to the idea that the individual must struggle constantly for freedom from tyranny of any kind—physical, political, or spiritual—began early in his adult life. Having failed to win entrance to the University of Oxford following his largely mediocre and unhappy school career, he more or less stumbled into joining the Indian Imperial Police in Burma. His maternal grandmother still lived there, and his father, a lifelong minor functionary in the Indian Civil Service, believed that Orwell could follow a similar secure, respectable, and patriotic career. Although he did his conscientious duty in his lonely five-year tenure (1922-1927), Orwell hated the Imperial Police. He came to loathe the values that had fueled British empire building, especially the paternalistic concept of "the white man's burden," and to understand with a mixture of sympathy and fear the extent of the hatred that the Burmese felt toward their British rulers. "Shooting an Elephant" (1936), one of the many penetrating, luminously written autobiographical essays that Orwell was to produce, powerfully portrays the dilemma of authority in which a British civil servant with a lively conscience could find himself anywhere in the sprawling British Empire.

The forging of Orwell's social consciousness in Burma continued through his sojourns in London and Paris between 1927 and 1929. Periodically, and by choice, he lived as a tramp and menial laborer on the fringes of these two great cities, endangering his already precarious health and threatening his personal autonomy.

Orwell's first, strongly autobiographical, book, *Down and Out in Paris and London* (1933), chronicles these experiences. Its generally good reviews marked the permanent adoption of his pen name George Orwell and gave him the opportunity to complete *Burmese Days* (1934), a very personal and vivid novel based on his Imperial Police experience. Its mixed success gave Orwell the means to abandon a wretched job to write full-time, marry, and move to the Hertfordshire countryside, where he and his wife, Eileen, ran a small country store. *A Clergyman's Daughter* (1935) and *Keep the Aspidistra Flying* (1936) were the resulting two novels in which he explored both the writing of pure fiction (largely a failure) and more memorably the lives of two alienated, emotionally starved individuals stifled by the rigid morality of middle-class England. In these novels' central protagonists are the seeds of Winston Smith's character and lonely struggle for personal fulfillment.

The rise of fascism in Europe during the 1930's stirred Orwell's interest in socialism, which, he declared in his next nonfiction work, *The Road to Wigan Pier* (1937), was the only ideological and political movement that could stand in opposition to fascism. In 1936, Orwell went to Spain, eventually joining the International Brigade, to fight the fascists led by Francisco Franco. He recounted his difficult sojourn in Spain in *Homage to Catalonia* (1938), in which his disillusionment with internal party politics and his political idealism are expressed in some of his best writing to that time. In typical fashion, he understated his own dedication and heroism in that struggle.

Recovering slowly from a bullet wound to the throat, an exhausted Orwell conceived and wrote his next novel, *Coming Up for Air* (1939), during a "rest cure" in Morocco. Its lyrical depiction of the South English countryside (later echoed in *Nineteen Eighty-Four*'s Edenic Golden Country) is undercut by a strong sense of doom, soon given credibility by the Luftwaffe's devastation of England's major cities and much of its southern landscape during World War II.

Orwell devoted himself courageously to the civil defense of England throughout the war. His writing during this period was confined to a series of more and more confident and incisive essays and reviews, in which he polished both his prose and his insightful political commentary into brilliance. In 1945, he published *Animal Farm*, the political fable that was finally to bring him enormous popular fame. This satirical indictment of the Russian Revolution's worst aspects appealed to the public imagination in Great Britain and North America just as the Cold War was beginning. *Animal Farm* paved the way for *Nineteen Eighty-Four* and elucidated Orwell's opinion that socialism itself was not the danger: the Soviet model and its power-hungry leaders were.

Impact of Event

George Orwell died in January, 1950, so he certainly was aware of the huge popular success of *Nineteen Eighty-Four* and its critical acclaim, but he could not have envisioned its lasting domination in the literary firmament. "Orwellian" is an adjective now popularly used (and abused) to describe repression or diabolical ideology of any kind; the widespread recognition (if not reading) of at least Orwell's last two fictional works is testimony to their impact.

Nineteen Eighty-Four was the work toward which his vision, through almost all of his other fiction and nonfiction, had developed. At its center is Orwell's perception that power and its abuse are the essential evils against which the individual spirit must always pit itself. Under the all-seeing, paternalistic eye of Big Brother, Winston Smith (embodying in his given name the fierce spirit of Winston Churchill and in his surname, common man) struggles to preserve his memory, emotions, identity, and above all his hope against the forceful repressiveness of the sterile totalitarian society in which he exists. The principles of INGSOC (English Socialism), summarized in a trio of paradoxical slogans, provide the regime's overtly simple public ideology. The welfare of the state is not the real *raison d'être* of INGSOC; it is instead the complete subjugation of its people to the power of a tiny elite. Control of daily life is pervasive and absolute. Although Smith recognizes this truth intellectually, he clings stubbornly to the hope that one day the mass of the "proles" will rise up and overthrow the tyrants. Even his recognition of the proles' apathy and debasement does not quench either his optimism or a will to survive that he perceives as endemic to humans. "DOWN WITH BIG BROTHER," writes Smith repeatedly in his illicit diary. His personal crusade for freedom also includes an emotionally fulfilling but forbidden love affair with the cheerfully defiant Julia.

Smith eventually is subjugated to the Party's power through torture inflicted physically, mentally, and then emotionally. The torture is carried out meticulously and with leisurely certainty by O'Brien, Big Brother's Mephistophelian spokesman and a man in whom Smith mistakenly had sensed an ally. Despite the explication of the Party's overwhelming control that O'Brien unfolds, Smith clings with all of his assaulted strength to his own belief: "I *know* that you will fail. There is something in the universe—I don't know, some spirit, some principle—that you will never overcome." The novel's closing sentence—"He loved Big Brother"—seems to signify Smith's defeat, yet enough ambiguity accompanies the final scene to leave the door open a crack, for hope.

The novel's projected title was *The Last Man in Europe*. On January 25, 1949, Orwell and his publisher, Fredric Warburg, agreed on *Nineteen Eighty-Four* as a more suitable title, arrived at simply by reversing the last two digits of the novel's year of completion. The former title does embody much of the novel's central vision. Smith indeed can be seen as Europe's "last man," the articulator of humankind's desire to be free, the representative of what Orwell called elsewhere in a poem "the crystal spirit." As well, the word "Europe" in the novel's first title conjures the specter of thousands of years of history (however bloody at times), civility, and culture crushed under tyranny's heel. Whatever its title, the novel makes vividly clear Orwell's main intention: to warn against totalitarianism in general, whether Right or Left in the political spectrum. That he makes his political point so well in a book that also succeeds as a work of fiction is a tribute to Orwell's formidable powers as a writer.

Critical acclaim for *Nineteen Eighty-Four* in both Great Britain and the United States was even more positive and widespread than it had been for *Animal Farm*, with respected writers such as V. S. Pritchett, Lionel Trilling, and Aldous Huxley weighing in with praise. Any criticism from socialists that the novel was an attack on socialism in particular Orwell denied swiftly and firmly in letters and articles he wrote in response. He reaffirmed his support of socialism as an ideology, though he continued to criticize its abuses.

A general fear of Joseph Stalin's continued power, underscored by acceleration of the Cold War and the rise of McCarthyism in the United States, made Orwell's reading public especially vulnerable to fears of the future and the loss of personal freedom. Interestingly, 1949 also saw the production of Arthur Miller's *Death of a Salesman*, which celebrates so poignantly the spiritual triumph of that inveterate dreamer, lover of the pastoral, and "little" man, salesman Willie Loman, over his stifling urban life and his total failure to "measure up."

Right up to his premature death, Orwell displayed his own "crystal spirit," hopeful to the end that he would get well, burning as usual to get on with other writing projects. His legacy to humanity has been his clear-eyed vision and sharp, luminous prose, urging readers over and over again to fight for individual and spiritual freedom.

Bibliography

Calder, Jenni. *"Animal Farm" and "Nineteen Eighty-Four."* Philadelphia, Pa.: Open University Press, 1987. Part of a series of short introductory books about major writers, texts, and literary concepts. Seven chapters link common thematic, stylistic, and political aspects of the two novels. "Suggestions for Further Reading" is geared to student work on Orwell's principal novels. Helpful and straightforward.

George Orwell and "Nineteen Eighty-Four." Trivandrum: Institute of English, University of Kerala, 1985. The papers of conference speakers who represent the cream of Orwell scholars. The novel is examined under four topics: "The Test," "The Man," "The Book," and "Its Meaning Today." A comprehensive, annotated bibliography follows. Invaluable for in-depth study of the novel.

Hammond, J. R. *A George Orwell Companion: A Guide to the Novels, Documentaries, and Essays.* London: Macmillan, 1982. Clear, uncluttered, chronological discussion of Orwell's work in four parts: "Life and Literary Achievements," "Novels and Documentaries," "Essays," and "Key to Characters and Locations," an alphabetically arranged, annotated dictionary of characters and places in Orwell's work. Not overly scholarly; accessible to students.

Howe, Irving, ed. *Orwell's Nineteen Eighty-Four: Text, Sources, Criticism.* 2d ed. New York: Harcourt Brace Jovanovich, 1982. This essential compendium consists of the text of the novel and eight more parts comprising short, succinct selections by and about Orwell and his works; criticism by such luminaries as Aldous Huxley, Bertrand Russell, and Lionel Trilling; reviews of the novel; analyses of totalitarianism; and recent views.

Meyers, Jeffery, ed. *George Orwell: The Critical Heritage.* London: Routledge & Kegan Paul, 1975. An enormously rich collection of critical writing, mainly book reviews in whole or in part, on all of Orwell's fiction and nonfiction, including posthumous. Essential study compiled by the preeminent Orwell expert.

_____. *A Reader's Guide to George Orwell.* London: Thames and Hudson, 1975. In clear, straightforward, chapters, Meyers guides readers through the Orwell canon. Chapter 8 is a particularly interesting theory of the novel's sources of inspiration. Bibliography and index included.

Reilly, Patrick. *Nineteen Eighty-Four: Past, Present, and Future.* Twayne's Masterwork Studies 30. Boston: Twayne, 1989. A scholarly work in two sections. The first discusses historical context, the novel's importance, and its critical reception; the second is a series of four interpretations, quite idiosyncratic, of the novel's several themes. Very thorough bibliography and index.

Shelden, Michael. *Orwell: The Authorized Biography.* New York: HarperCollins, 1991. An exhaustively researched chronicle of Orwell's life, inspiration, and works, written in lucid prose. Includes photos, bibliographies of primary and secondary sources, comprehensive source notes, and an excellent, thorough, useful index. The viewpoint is somewhat biased in places, but fact and commentary are generally well balanced. Absorbing and essential.

Thomas, Edward M. *Orwell.* Writers and Critics Series. Edinburgh, Scotland: Oliver & Boyd, 1965. Eight straightforward, readable chapters chronicling the parallel development of Orwell's life, political convictions, and writings. Includes a thorough bibliography of primary and secondary sources. Uncluttered style and information.

Woodcock, George. *Orwell's Message: 1984 and the Present.* Madeira Park, British Columbia: Harbour, 1984. Woodcock was Orwell's friend and a respected critic who perhaps knew Orwell and his writings most intimately. He presents a reassessment of the novel in four thorough, informative chapters. Index.

Jill Rollins

Cross-References

The Soviet Union Bans Abstract Art (1922), p. 544; Huxley's *Brave New World*

EALING COMEDIES MARK A HIGH POINT IN BRITISH FILM

Category of event: Motion pictures
Time: 1949-1951
Locale: London, England

Michael Balcon's Ealing Studios produced a series of well-written, carefully crafted social comedies that pitted "the little man" against the social institutions of postwar Great Britain

Principal personages:

MICHAEL BALCON (1896-1977), the head of production at Ealing Studios from 1938 until its demise in 1959

CHARLES CRICHTON (1910-   ), a prolific director whose long career at Ealing included *Hue and Cry* (1947) and *The Lavender Hill Mob* (1951)

HENRY CORNELIUS (1913-1958), the director of perhaps the best known of all the Ealing comedies, *Passport to Pimlico* (1949)

ROBERT HAMER (1911-1963), the director of *Kind Hearts and Coronets* (1949), the most critically acclaimed of the Ealing comedies

ALEXANDER MACKENDRICK (1912-   ), the director of *Whiskey Galore* (1949) and *The Man in the White Suit* (1951)

T. E. B. CLARKE (1907-   ), the most prolific writer at Ealing, whose credits include *Passport to Pimlico* and *The Lavender Hill Mob*

ALEC GUINNESS (1914-   ), the actor most intimately associated with the Ealing comedies

Summary of Event

Under Michael Balcon, London's Ealing Studios was known for promoting a co-operative, family-like atmosphere; on one of the studio's walls was painted the slogan "the studio with the team spirit." For this reason, Ealing received remarkable loyalty from its directors and writers, many of whom stayed until the studio disbanded. Although the studio's principal personnel had various abilities and degrees of talent, it is possible to identify certain features that the studio's famous comedies share. These films are not lavish spectacles but carefully crafted, wittily written satires on authority. They depict ordinary people attempting to break free from the numerous constraints of postwar British society and its rigid, conventional morality. In the films, the world is turned upside down and the government, industry or class system challenged—but this is done gently, with a degree of respect for what is being derided.

The films known as "Ealing comedies" constitute only a small number of the films made at Ealing, just west of London. Films were being produced there from the early years of the twentieth century. In 1930, Basil Dean's Associated Talking

Pictures took over the site, and Dean remained at Ealing until Balcon's arrival in 1938, when the facility became known as Ealing Studios. Balcon remained in charge until the release of the last Ealing film in 1959. The British Broadcasting Corporation (BBC) had purchased the studios in 1955, however, and the last seven films to bear the Ealing name were produced elsewhere. Throughout this period, Ealing turned out films in many genres, although comedies were always prominent. The term "Ealing comedies" commonly refers only to a small group of films made in the last years of the 1940's and the early 1950's. It is on these that the enduring fame of the Ealing name rests; and film scholars generally agree that the major films of this group are *Passport to Pimlico, Whiskey Galore*, and *Kind Hearts and Coronets*, all released in 1949, and *The Lavender Hill Mob* and *The Man in the White Suit*, both from 1951.

These films were preceded in 1947 by *Hue and Cry*. Directed by one of the Ealing stalwarts, Charles Crichton, from a script by T. E. B. Clarke, the film is the story of a group of children who defeat a gang of villains who are communicating via a comic strip. *Hue and Cry* lacks the lightness of touch that marks the later films, but its use of the bomb-site locations that scarred postwar London prefigures the world of Miramont Place, the setting of Henry Cornelius' *Passport to Pimlico*. In that film, children playing near the site of London's last unexploded bomb accidentally roll a tire onto it. The ensuing explosion uncovers a cave containing both treasure and an old manuscript. The manuscript reveals that the street in Pimlico where it was found is a part of the old French Dukedom of Burgundy and thus is not subject to the laws of Great Britain. The residents of Miramont Place are thus freed from the rationing system—limiting the quantities of food, clothing, and other items that might be purchased—that was in full force in postwar Great Britain. At first, the residents welcome the change and strike out for independence; they band together in a spirit of cooperation, seemingly nostalgic for the wartime experience of unity and purpose. Shortages of water and food and the invasion of the area's borders by black marketeers, however, eventually lead to a reconciliation with the British authorities.

Alexander Mackendrick's *Whiskey Galore* again presents a community uniting in the face of unreasonable official regulations. When a ship carrying whiskey runs aground just offshore, the inhabitants of Todday, deprived by the war of their favorite drink, are determined to rescue as much of its cargo as possible. The Scottish islanders are opposed by Captain Waggett, an upper-class English Home Guard commander (played by Basil Radford, an Ealing regular, who portrayed a similarly stuffy government official in *Passport to Pimlico*). The island setting of *Whiskey Galore* gives it at times an almost documentary feel, an impression that is enhanced by the ensemble acting it shares with *Passport to Pimlico*. The remaining three major films, however, all feature Alec Guinness. In Robert Hamer's *Kind Hearts and Coronets*, Guinness plays all the members of the d'Ascoyne family, who are killed off one by one by a dispossessed poor relation, Louis Mazzini (Dennis Price), as he successfully murders his way to the family inheritance and its dukedom. This is the wittiest and most acclaimed of all the Ealing films, its black comedy and wry humor pointing up the class divisions and social inequities of British society with cruel wit and dazzling power. *Kind Hearts and Coronets* thus completed a trio of films that established Ealing's reputation for comedy. Unlike the other films, though, *Kind Hearts and Coronets* had no obvious successors and remains, many critics believe, an isolated tour de force.

The Lavender Hill Mob, directed by Charles Crichton from a T. E. B. Clarke script, again stars Guinness, this time as a meek bank employee who robs the gold bullion van that he rides from mint to bank every Friday. In Mackendrick's *The Man in the White Suit,* Guinness is a naïve scientist who believes he has created a fabric that will not get dirty or wear out—and which he turns into the brilliant white suit that he dons for the last third of the movie. His efforts are opposed both by textile mill owners and workers; eventually, after he has encountered his poor landlady, who chastises him for trying to take from her the income she gets from doing others' washing, the white suit starts to disintegrate of its own accord. Mackendrick's last work for Ealing, *The Ladykillers* (1955), another movie plotted around the exploits of a criminal gang, is the best of the later comedies.

Impact of Event

All the major Ealing comedies except *Passport to Pimlico* use the voice of a narrator to frame the action of the film, and the use of this device allows the films to present a rather more ambiguous final message than they otherwise might. At the end of *The Lavender Hill Mob,* viewers discover that Holland, the Alec Guinness character who has been narrating the story of his crime from an elegant nightclub, is actually handcuffed to the man who has been listening to him. The reversals in the other films are more morally ambiguous: In *Kind Hearts and Coronets,* Louis Mazzini, writing his memoirs from jail, provides the narrative impulse for the film. When he is freed, he forgets the memoirs, which may mean that he will hang after all. In the Mackendrick films, the narrators are not the central characters. The islanders of Todday are represented by the voice-over of an unseen narrator who, at the end of the film, says that the whiskey soon ran out again and that the islanders, other than those who did not drink, lived unhappily ever after. At the end of *The Man in the White Suit,* in which the narrator is a textile mill owner and the chief antagonist of the hero, Sidney (Alec Guinness) walks away defeated—but accompanied by the sound of a bubbling that has come during the film to signify his thoughts and that suggests that he may not be finished yet. Thus Ealing's reputation for quaint, comfortable, respectful, and nostalgic versions of British stereotypes is not warranted by the best of its comedies, even if it is by such later films as *The Titfield Thunderbolt* (1953) and *Barnacle Bill* (1957).

When the BBC took over at Ealing, a plaque went up to commemorate the studio. The words, chosen by Balcon, read: "[h]ere during a quarter of a century were made many films projecting Britain and the British character." Certainly, Ealing succeeded in developing an image for British comedy to the extent that, as Ian Green and others have pointed out, certain films, of which Henry Cornelius' *Genevieve* (1953) is the most notable, seem to many to be Ealing comedies, even though they were not made by the studio. The popular series of *Carry On* films, which began in 1958 with the release of *Carry on Sergeant* and continued until 1980, seems at first glance to be very different from the Ealing comedies. The *Carry On* films depict and challenge the repressed sexuality of British society in a coarse, ribald fashion, but they share with the more respecting and respectable Ealing films an antagonism to the institutions and regulations that support privilege and a strict morality.

Like many of the Ealing films, the *Carry On* series depends on a familiar ensemble of actors, but if the series has a face, it must surely be the creased smile of Sid James, who had appeared opposite Alec Guinness in *The Lavender Hill Mob.* Guinness himself emerged as a star from the great comedies and has remained both popularly and critically acclaimed ever since, appearing in a wide variety of roles both in the cinema and on British television.

It is perhaps appropriate that the home of Ealing's comedies was taken over by a television company. It has long been accepted that in Great Britain, unlike in the United States, television has been responsible for more interesting work than the cinema, and this is as true in the realm of comedy as elsewhere. Many British situation comedies have been characterized by the gentle satire associated with Ealing. The long-running *Dad's Army,* for example, featured a wartime Home Guard unit run by pompous, rule-following Captain Mainwaring (Arthur Lowe), the town's bank manager, a character who owes much to Basil Radford's Captain Waggett in *Whiskey Galore.* The assault on institutions, regulations, and taboos, but without the comforting nostalgia of such series as *Dad's Army,* is also evident in the work of Great Britain's most famous comedy team, Monty Python. In 1988, two major strains of British comedy met when the seventy-eight-year-old Charles Crichton directed two Monty Python members, John Cleese and Michael Palin, in *A Fish Called Wanda,* a film that did indeed offer something between Ealing's wit and Monty Python's anarchy.

The history of British cinema has been erratic, and it is not easy to trace influences over long periods. Perhaps the best testimony to the power of the Ealing comedies, however, is that they are still seen as so typically British. Balcon's policy as studio head was never to attempt to conquer the American market by producing epic films designed to sell elsewhere; such attempts led to the failure of many other British studios. Balcon aimed at creating a distinctly British product, and when the films themselves are able to critique the nature of that Britishness, as do *Kind Hearts and Coronets* and *Whiskey Galore,* they remain fresh and exciting. "We always were English, we always will be English and it's just because we are English that we're sticking up for our rights to be Burgundian" shouts a woman in *Passport to Pimlico.* It is this spirit of gentle mockery that pervades the Ealing films and determines both their pleasures and their limitations.

Bibliography

Armes, Roy. "Balcon at Ealing." In *A Critical History of the British Cinema.* New

York: Oxford University Press, 1978. The best general survey of British cinema history up to the early 1970's. Chapter on Ealing concentrates on the comedies. Argues that Mackendrick and Hamer are much the best of the Ealing directors and sees *Kind Hearts and Coronets* as one of British cinema's few masterpieces.

Barr, Charles. *Ealing Studios.* Woodstock, N.Y.: Overlook Press, 1980. Concentrates heavily on the comedies, devoting complete chapters to those Barr believes to be the best: *Whiskey Galore, Kind Hearts and Coronets,* and *The Man in the White Suit.* Intelligent, comprehensive analysis, many stills, filmography, and biographical notes make Barr's book the best single text on Ealing.

Green, Ian. "Ealing: In the Comedy Frame." In *British Cinema History,* edited by James Curran and Vincent Porter. London: Weidenfeld and Nicolson, 1983. Discusses how comedy may overcome censorship and how the framing devices that characterize so many of the Ealing films allow a delicate balance between fantasy and realism to be presented.

Landy, Marcia. "Film Comedies." In *British Genres: Cinema and Society, 1930-1960.* Princeton, N.J.: Princeton University Press, 1991. Sets the Ealing films in the context of comedy as a genre within the British cinema and in the context of postwar British society; includes brief, but perceptive, accounts of the narratives and implications of the major films. A highly readable and thoroughly researched introductory account.

Perry, George. *Forever Ealing: A Celebration of the Great British Film Studio.* London: Pavilion Books, 1981. Entertaining history of the studio from its inception until 1959. Especially useful in providing a comparison between the earlier comedies and the postwar examples by which the studio earned its fame. An excellent supplement to Barr's more detailed account of the major films. Many stills, comprehensive filmography.

Wilson, David, ed. *Projecting Britain: Ealing Studios Film Posters.* London: British Film Institute, 1982. Full-color collection of the advertising posters for the Ealing films.

Chris Lippard

Cross-References

Sennett Defines the Slapstick Comedy Genre (1909), p. 230; Chaplin Produces His Masterpiece *The Gold Rush* (1925), p. 659; Keaton's *The General* Is Released (1926), p. 691; The Classic Screwball Comedy Reaches Its Height in Popularity (1934), p. 951; *Monty Python's Flying Circus* Captures Audiences Worldwide (1969), p. 2174.

KELLY FORGES NEW DIRECTIONS
IN CINEMATIC DANCE

Category of event: Dance
Time: 1949-1952
Locale: Hollywood, California

During the heyday of the Metro-Goldwyn-Mayer musical, Gene Kelly developed an eclectic style of cinematic dance drawing on ballet, tap, and folk elements

Principal personages:
GENE KELLY (1912-   ), a celebrated American screen dancer, director, and choreographer
FRED ASTAIRE (FREDERICK AUSTERLITZ, 1899-1987), the most elegant of cinema's dancers, who provided the paradigm against which Kelly defined his own persona
BUSBY BERKELEY (WILLIAM BERKELEY ENOS, 1895-1976), the first important cinema choreographer
STANLEY DONEN (1924-   ), an esteemed director of many Metro-Goldwyn-Mayer musicals
ARTHUR FREED (ARTHUR GROSSMAN, 1894-1973), a respected film producer whose fabled Freed Unit at Metro-Goldwyn-Mayer produced most of Kelly's important musicals during the 1940's and 1950's
VINCENTE MINNELLI (1910-1986), a noted director of film musicals who collaborated with Kelly

Summary of Event

In the late 1940's and early 1950's, the American musical film reached its apex of creative and popular success in the Metro-Goldwyn-Mayer (MGM) releases starring the exuberant Gene Kelly. Although best known to the public for his screen persona as a genial yet rugged individual whose characters' romantic and artistic quests were expressed in muscular yet lyrical dances, Kelly also made significant contributions, as a choreographer and director, to the development of the musical.

Kelly's filmography is impressive. From his first film for MGM, *For Me and My Gal* (1942), to *That's Entertainment* (1974) and *That's Entertainment, Part 2* (1976), Kelly's credits for that studio include such glittering classics as *Anchors Aweigh* (1945), *Ziegfeld Follies* (1946), *The Pirate* (1948), *On the Town* (1949), *An American in Paris* (1951), *Singin' in the Rain* (1952), *Brigadoon* (1954), *It's Always Fair Weather* (1955), and *Invitation to the Dance* (1957).

Kelly's specific contributions fall into two broad realms, conceptual and practical. First is the career-long concern with working out a theoretical framework for cinematic dance; for Kelly, that framework started with the concept of the integrated musical, an ideal fusing of story and dance into a seamlessly interconnected and unified dramatic whole. Second is Kelly's work, his musicals for MGM in which theory was transformed into practice, with each film's particular narrative and musical elements contoured to fit the paradigm of the integrated musical. In that process, Kelly helped create a uniquely American form of dance with an emphasis on American music and American character types. It was a form well suited to Kelly's own brash personality and athletic grace, as well as to his eclectic borrowings from the highbrow world of classical ballet, avant-garde modern dance, the show business heritage of tap and soft shoe, and various vernacular and ethnic dance traditions.

It is also important to note that Kelly was fascinated with the film medium itself, its technology as well as its capacity for telling stories through music and dance. Therefore, though Kelly is usually thought of as a dancer who happened to be a star, he also should be regarded as a serious filmmaker, a director and choreographer whose comprehensive knowledge of and concern with the cinematic world make him a far more complex and complete cineaste than his two worthy predecessors, Busby Berkeley and Fred Astaire.

When Kelly arrived in Hollywood in 1941, he had a list of impressive Broadway credits, including the Cole Porter musical *Leave It to Me* (1938), William Saroyan's Pulitzer Prize-winning *The Time of Your Life* (1939), and the Richard Rodgers and Lorenz Hart musical hit *Pal Joey* (1940). Playing the demanding title role of *Pal Joey*, the caddish nightclub entertainer Joey Evans, Kelly proved himself an able actor as well as a virtuoso dancer. He also choreographed his dance numbers, an opportunity he used to exploit his athletic dancing style in order to help create and mold his character. *Pal Joey*, while making Kelly a star, also enabled him to make important if tentative steps toward realizing his goal of the integrated musical. The role also allowed him to develop means for creating a more complex character who could both outrage and charm audiences. "Joey was a meaty character," Kelly recalled in one interview. "After some scenes I could feel the wave of hate coming from the audience. Then I'd smile at them and dance and it would relax them. It was interesting to be able to use the character to manipulate the audience." Clearly, this was the voice of a director-to-be, as well as that of an actor, dancer, and choreographer.

At first, MGM was tentative as to how best to use Kelly. Although he debuted opposite Judy Garland under Busby Berkeley in *For Me and My Gal*, the studio assigned him straight acting roles for the 1943 war dramas *Pilot No. 5* and *The Cross of Lorraine*. MGM then loaned him to Columbia Pictures for *Cover Girl* (1944), an impressive musical with Rita Hayworth. Kelly was given choreographic carte blanche, which he used to great effect. The public was impressed; so were Hollywood and MGM, which thereafter gave Kelly the freedom to experiment and create under the aegis of producer Arthur Freed. World War II was to intervene, but before joining the United States Naval Air Service in late 1944, Kelly appeared on film in two classic routines, the innovative dance-fantasy "The King Who Couldn't Dance" with an animated Tom and Jerry in *Anchors Aweigh*, and the *pas de deux* with Fred Astaire, "The Babbitt and the Bromide," from *Ziegfeld Follies*.

When Kelly was discharged from the Navy in 1946, it was with two years of experience as a writer and director of documentaries for the War Department's photographic section, an experience that furthered his interest and expertise in film technique. Back at MGM, and with Arthur Freed's backing and the support of the studio's talent-laden musical production team, Kelly's star was poised to light up the postwar cinematic firmament with a string of extraordinary musicals that stand as landmarks of the American musical film.

Impact of Event

Kelly is in many ways a crowning figure in the history of the American musical. He brought the concept of the integrated musical to full realization by recognizing that he not only had to dance but also choreograph and direct. Consequently, in works such as *On the Town, An American in Paris*, and *Singin' in the Rain*—arguably his most consistently satisfying and significant films—dance, story, setting, and song swirl together. Kelly's synergetic meldings evoke composer Richard Wagner's idealized notions of universal artwork, in which the elements of the music drama—music, lyrics, settings, and *mises en scène*—work harmoniously to serve the transcendent needs of the overall drama.

As a dancer and director, Kelly was aware of the challenges of transferring the three-dimensional dance medium to the two-dimensional motion picture. In order to emulate the kind of kinetic energy that Kelly believed spectators sensed when watching dance in a theater, he choreographed his camera and dancers so that the sensation of dancers moving toward the camera—and, therefore, psychologically toward the film audience—was emphasized. Conversely, in order to ease transitions at the end of production numbers from dance back into dialogue, Kelly often reversed the process, as in the title number from *Singin' in the Rain*, when Kelly's Don Lockwood walks away from the camera as it booms up and into a fade-out. Kelly also heightened the sensation of movement by placing vertical props in the foreground or background of shots using a panning camera, a strategy that created its own vectors of momentum and speed.

Kelly also was adept at using cinema's unique resources for manipulating space and time. The "New York, New York" routine from *On the Town*, for example, is a "dance" that was created in the editing room with jump cuts that whisk three sailors (Kelly, Frank Sinatra, and Jules Munshin) around Manhattan, thus compressing what would have taken several hours into a three-minute whirlwind tour. Whether shooting on location or in the studio, Kelly took full advantage of the spatial dimensions of his sets. Instead of confining the dance to an implied proscenium arch, as Astaire was mostly content to do, Kelly moved his dancers through as much space as his sets allowed. For "Good Morning," from *Singin' in the Rain*, Kelly had himself, Debbie Reynolds, and Donald O'Connor move from one room to the next, a ploy that added another force field to those already generated by the music, lyrics, dance, and camera movements.

Kelly's stylistic eclecticism is another hallmark. Instead of using one dominant approach to the dance, Kelly plotted each film's choreography on the basis of the particular characters and dramatic situations. Thus in *American in Paris*, Kelly called on the resources of ballet to express his protagonist's dreamlike reflections on art and the quixotic nature of romance. Set to George Gershwin's classic 1928 tone poem, the seventeen-minute "American in Paris" ballet is perhaps Kelly's culminating achievement. It also is an example of Kelly's dedication to American music or, as he has said, the synthesis of old dance forms with new rhythms.

In contrast to the elegant, even aristocratic figure portrayed by Fred Astaire, Kelly's persona was that of an earnest and hardworking though wisecracking and sometimes deceitful protagonist who comes clean in the end. It's a persona fleshed out through Kelly's muscular athleticism, an aspect of his raw physicality first displayed in the gyms and playing fields of his native Pittsburgh, Pennsylvania. It also is a persona carefully developed in a series of portrayals of "everyman" characters who were essentially just plain, regular guys—a sailor in *On the Town* and an ex-soldier and struggling painter in *An American in Paris*. Even in *Singin' in the Rain*, although Kelly plays a silent film star, the character has an engagingly common touch, a sense of decency and fair play, and a resourceful practicality reinforced by the revelation of the character's rough childhood and struggle to make it to the top. Audiences could identify and associate with Gabey (*On the Town*), Jerry Mulligan (*An American in Paris*), and Don Lockwood (*Singin' in the Rain*), three likable fellows whom anyone would be pleased to call "friend." Kelly was a star in part because of his substantial yet often underrated acting skills as well as his universally recognized talents as a great dancer and choreographer.

Although Kelly has deprecated his own singing skills, like Fred Astaire he helped put over many a song with his raspy voice, sincerity, and winning smile. For example, when he intoned "You Were Meant for Me" to Debbie Reynolds' Kathy Selden in *Singin' in the Rain*, viewers believed him—and so did she.

By the mid-1950's, Kelly, like the film industry itself, was increasingly buffeted by the competition for America's leisure time from the "free" programming of network television. Hollywood, provoked further by the Supreme Court's decision in the Paramount case mandating that the major studios divest themselves of their theater chains, was in turmoil. Like the other studios, MGM under mogul Nicholas Schenck ordered downsizings in production costs, salaries, and personnel. For Kelly and the Freed Unit, the most immediate impact was MGM's decision virtually to eliminate all original musicals. In place of the innovative and written-for-the-screen *On the Town*, *An American in Paris*, or *Singin' in the Rain*, MGM opted for glossy adaptations of Broadway blockbusters such as *The Band Wagon* (1953), *Brigadoon* (1954), *Guys and Dolls* (1955), and *Silk Stockings* (1957). There were also comparatively easy-to-make biographies such as *Love Me or Leave Me* (1955), with Doris Day as Ruth Etting. The postwar teen market was another factor, especially with hits such as Elvis Presley's *Jailhouse Rock* (1957). Coupled with the box-office failure of Kelly's most ambitious project, the experimental all-dance, no-dialogue *Invitation to the Dance*, and the disappointing *Les Girls* (1957)—Kelly's eighteenth and last MGM musical appearance until his hosting chores for the studio's *That's Entertainment* projects of 1974 and 1976—it was clear that the heyday of the original musical had passed.

Kelly went on to direct *The Tunnel of Love* (1958), *A Guide for the Married Man* (1967), and *Hello, Dolly!* (1969). There also were acting opportunities, such as the role of newspaperman E. K. Hornbeck in Stanley Kramer's production of *Inherit the Wind* (1960), as well as various television and theater projects. Although Kelly acquitted himself with his usual professionalism, he never again reached the heights he had attained with Freed's MGM musical unit.

Kelly's legacy is nevertheless secure. His MGM musicals continue to shine. They also have continued to influence dance talents as varied as Bob Fosse and music video superstar Michael Jackson. Among Kelly's many honors is a special Oscar he received in 1951 from the Academy of Motion Picture Arts and Sciences "in appreciation of his versatility as actor, singer, director and dancer, and especially for his brilliant achievements in the art of choreography on film."

Bibliography

Altman, Rick. *The American Film Musical.* Bloomington: Indiana University Press, 1987. An important scholarly treatment of the musical, with emphasis on genre theory and narratology as well as the musical's historical evolution. Frequent citations of Kelly and his films. Illustrated.

Delamater, Jerome. *Dance in the Hollywood Musical.* Ann Arbor, Mich.: UMI Research Press, 1981. The most authoritative study of dance in the Hollywood musical, with comprehensive chapters on the contributions of Kelly, Busby Berkeley, Fred Astaire, and Ginger Rogers, among others. Includes an informative interview with Kelly by Paddy Whannel plus a useful bibliography.

Fordin, Hugh. *The World of Entertainment! Hollywood's Greatest Musicals.* New York: Doubleday, 1975. A detailed chronicle of the two decades of films produced by MGM's musical unit under Arthur Freed's supervision. Includes detailed filmography. Illustrated.

Hirschhorn, Clive. *Gene Kelly: A Biography.* Chicago: Henry Regnery, 1974. Hirschhorn's lively book provides a well-drawn account of the evolution of Kelly's dance style as well as useful information on the Freed Unit at MGM and each of Kelly's films.

Thomas, Tony. *The Films of Gene Kelly: Song and Dance Man.* Secaucus, N.J.: Citadel Press, 1974. An incisive account of each of Kelly's films, with credits and publicity stills. Thomas' introductory chapter, "The Loneliness of the Long-Distance Dancer," is a brief but especially good overview of Kelly's background, unique persona, and accomplishments. Includes Fred Astaire's appreciative "Foreword." Copiously illustrated.

Charles Merrell Berg

Cross-References

Berkeley's *42nd Street* Revolutionizes Film Musicals (1933), p. 925; *Top Hat* Establishes the Astaire-Rogers Dance Team (1935), p. 984; *Stormy Weather* Offers New Film Roles to African Americans (1940's), p. 1159; *The Sound of Music* Captivates Audiences (1965), p. 2033; *Saturday Night Fever* Epitomizes the Disco Craze (1977), p. 2386; *Thriller* Marks Michael Jackson's Musical Coming-of-Age (1982), p. 2512.

DAVIS' *BIRTH OF THE COOL* RECORDINGS
SPAWN 1950'S COOL JAZZ

Category of event: Music
Time: January 21 and April 22, 1949; March 9, 1950
Locale: New York, New York

The landmark Birth of the Cool *recordings by the Miles Davis Nonet had an incalculable influence on the course of modern jazz*

Principal personages:

MILES DAVIS (1926-1991), the trumpeter and leader of the *Birth of the Cool* sessions, who went on to uncover fresh talent and dominate new jazz developments for the next twenty-five years

GERRY MULLIGAN (1927-), a *Birth of the Cool* baritone saxophonist and composer-arranger who formed an influential pianoless quartet in the 1950's

JOHN LEWIS (1920-), a *Birth of the Cool* pianist and composer-arranger who founded the Modern Jazz Quartet, the paramount small jazz group for more than three decades

LEE KONITZ (1927-), the *Birth of the Cool* alto saxophonist, a disciple of cool pianist Lennie Tristano

Summary of Event

During the late 1940's, a small group of jazz musicians working together closely made a conscious effort to go beyond the "bop" style of jazz then popular and create a new kind of jazz. The features that characterized their work—emphasis on smooth lines rather than on harmonies or rhythm, soft dynamics, and a light, spare sound—gave their music an emotional pitch lower than that of bop, and the new style came to be known as "cool" jazz.

Instrumental in the evolution of cool jazz was the Miles Davis Nonet, which in 1949 began making a series of influential recordings for Capitol Records. The band's fresh and distinctive sound, which would have an important influence in the 1950's, stemmed in part from pioneering work done during the previous decade by pianist, composer, arranger, and bandleader Claude Thornhill and arranger Gil Evans. Other important ingredients were alto saxophonist Lee Konitz's cool lines, which were inspired by pianist Lennie Tristano, and Konitz's light, dry, almost vibratoless sound. The Capitol recording sessions also included Gerry Mulligan, a baritone saxophonist who also had a light, dry tone and who had played and arranged for Thornhill. Davis' nine-piece band was unusual in that it did not include either a guitar or a tenor saxophone; the instrumentation was filled out by trombone, French horn, tuba, and rhythm section.

Drawing some of its members from the Thornhill Orchestra and others from several of the bop groups active in New York City, the Miles Davis Nonet, after extensive rehearsals, consolidated the influences of Thornhill, Evans, and Tristano in three high-quality Capitol recording sessions. Two of these sessions were held shortly after the recording ban was lifted in January and April of 1949, with a third following almost a year later in March of 1950. Each session produced four tunes. The bulk of the arrangements were penned by Gerry Mulligan ("Godchild," "Jeru," "Venus de Milo," "Rocker," "Darn That Dream") and John Lewis ("Move," "Budo," "Rouge"). Gil Evans contributed two arrangements ("Boplicity" and "Moon Dreams"), and Davis and John Carisi one arrangement apiece ("Deception" and "Israel").

Originally released in the era's 78-rpm format, these performances were later issued by Capitol on a long-playing record entitled *Birth of the Cool.* Of all the late 1940's recordings made by groups employing "cool" concepts, the Davis Nonet recordings are remembered and cited the most. The recordings mark the first of many instances in which Davis was closely involved with major innovations in jazz.

In its music, the Nonet tried to realize a number of interrelated goals. Foremost among these was the development of an approach to ensemble writing that combined the immediacy and freshness of improvised music—in which were fused elements from bop, especially from Charlie Parker's music—with a light, vibratoless tonality and a more subtle approach to rhythm than that of the boppers. The band also made an effort to achieve the broadened textural and coloristic palette of a large orchestra while using a relatively small number of instruments. A corollary goal was the production of a more seamless, balanced integration between the music's improvised and written elements than was characteristic of bop. The arrangement, in effect, would lead and anchor the soloist, who was expected to resolve the improvisation in reference to the written segment that followed.

An emphasis on arrangements was not common in bop, and the Nonet's arrangements gave bop tunes distinctive twists. Most bop groups assigned the melody to the horns, which played in unison before and after a series of long, improvised solos; the Davis Nonet replaced that approach with a scheme that wove short improvised solos into written arrangements, much as Duke Ellington had done. Some arrangements also placed attractive melodic figures underneath some of the solos. Orchestral textures were occasionally altered, always gracefully, within a single arrangement.

The dry, mellow textures achieved by the Nonet's unique instrumentation and the subdued feeling that Davis, Konitz, and Mulligan brought to their solos created a truly delicate, cool sound. The band was not brassy, loud, or massive-sounding. Its music was light and sophisticated and, at times, resembled classical chamber music. Recordings of the same period by groups led by pianist Lennie Tristano also achieved this effect.

Some have argued that these 1949 recordings of Tristano—made with a group of followers that included guitarist Billy Bauer and saxophonists Lee Konitz and Warne Marsh—may have had more to do with the development of cool jazz than the Miles Davis sides did. Influenced as much as his studies in European concert forms as by the jazz tradition, Tristano put aside easy musical excitement and focused on linear invention. His music was deliberately unemotional—some proclaimed it cold-blooded—and his rhythm sections were reduced to playing the role of timekeepers. Yet outside of acquiring a small in-group reputation, these recordings, reluctantly released by Capitol, had no immediate influence on jazz developments of the day.

Initial sales of the *Birth of the Cool* recordings must have disappointed Capitol officials, and the poor sales probably account for the lengthy gap between the second and third sessions. Jazz audiences of the late 1940's were seemingly indifferent to the music of the Nonet, and did not support its New York club dates. Nevertheless, the *Birth of the Cool* recordings received favorable critical reaction and caught on quickly among fellow musicians, who recognized not only the beauty and creative audacity of the music but also the quietly revolutionary approach of the Nonet. The Nonet sides remain a milestone in the discography of jazz.

Impact of Event

In the wake of the *Birth of the Cool* sessions, a number of small jazz combos could be found sporting a cool sound. One example is the fleet, subdued interplay of the George Shearing Quintet, which made several best-selling records. The Red Norvo Trio was also definitely of the cool persuasion. Perhaps the most versatile and, beyond question, the most durable of all the small combos to emerge in the cool tradition was the Modern Jazz Quartet, led by pianist, composer, and theorist John Lewis. Skilled in both classical music and jazz, Lewis imposed his quiet but unbending will on his responsive cohorts to achieve a unique blend of piano, vibraharp, bass, and drums, with all four instruments playing equal, rather than dominant or supportive, roles. Though the group showed a meticulous concern with structure, it never lost touch with the lifeblood of improvisation. Both Lewis and the Modern Jazz Quartet's supreme soloist, vibraharpist Milt Jackson, came out of the Charlie Parker combos and the Dizzy Gillespie big band of the 1940's, another instance of cool jazz's debt to bop.

The *Birth of the Cool* sessions spawned a working alliance of Los Angeles-based musicians—the West Coast School—that nearly cornered the jazz market in the early 1950's. With hindsight, it can be seen why certain traits of cool jazz would appeal to this group. Many of these musicians were casualties of the breakup of one or another of the big bands of the 1940's; almost all were alumni of those bands. They were drawn to Southern California by the congenial climate and, given their technical and arranging skills, the possibility of securing lucrative jobs in the motion-picture and recording studios. For the most part, these musicians, most of whom were white, had received more formal musical training than had their black counterparts. Not surprisingly, the theoretical and disciplined approach of the Miles Davis Nonet appealed to them. When they in turn began recording, they reflected a similar approach in their performances.

The cool style of the West Coast employed lightweight, bright-colored tones that had dry, soft textures. Although it incorporated the harmonic and melodic advances of bop, the West Coast style, with its restrained and understated approach, had a smoother, more tune-like sound than bop improvisation. In contrast to the intensity of bop, this music often projected a relaxed feeling. Drummers in this style played quietly and less interactively than did bop drummers. Though the West Coast was the primary center for such music, the cool style of jazz was not the only one played on the West Coast in the 1950's, and the cool style could be heard on the East Coast as well.

One important West Coast stylist was Gerry Mulligan, the baritone saxophonist and composer-arranger in the Miles Davis Nonet. Mulligan moved to California in 1952 and began a series of pianoless quartets consisting of himself on baritone saxophone accompanied by another horn player, a bass player, and a drummer. The pianoless quartets of Mulligan, who had a dry, light-colored tone and an unhurried and subdued approach to improvisation, had a lighter, clearer, simpler sound texture than quartets using a piano. In 1953, Mulligan led a ten-piece band that included a French horn and tuba. His writing also played a significant role in his East Coast-based Concert Jazz Band, which featured a light, dry sound and simple, relaxed playing.

California pianist-composer Dave Brubeck led a series of small bands during the late 1940's that employed approaches similar to those of the Miles Davis Nonet. From 1951 to 1967, Brubeck led a quartet—probably the best-known jazz combo of the period—with alto saxophonist Paul Desmond. Though Desmond's light, dry tone resembled that of Lee Konitz, his approach to improvisation was his own. His playing was extremely economical, quite melodic, and very cool.

A saxophonist-clarinetist who composed for the Woody Herman band, Jimmy Giuffre, wrote much West Coast-style music. Based on the West Coast from 1946 to 1960, he produced original compositions and jazz improvisations that were the essence of cool jazz. He played with a soft, diffuse sound, his lines understated and melodic; he ranks with Miles Davis in his mastery of silence and economical attitude in constructing solos. A trio he led in 1958 and 1959 with trombonist Bob Brookmeyer and guitarist Jim Hall produced light and lyrical jazz and featured close, three-way cooperation in the creation of gentle, contrapuntal improvisations.

Another prominent figure associated with the West Coast style was trumpeter-composer-arranger Shorty Rogers, who wrote for Woody Herman. Rogers led jazz quintets and produced music that was similar to that of the 1940-1950 Miles Davis Nonet and the 1953 Mulligan ten-piece band.

During the 1950's, Miles Davis collaborated again with arranger Gil Evans on some notably successful examples of orchestral jazz. Their music surpassed the soloist-with-strings approach by integrating the solos with the arrangements on such albums as *Porgy and Bess* (1958) and *Sketches of Spain* (1959). The latter album, which explored a Latin theme with great sensitivity, was a commercial success and made Davis' name virtually synonymous with modern jazz.

In the early 1950's, many found cool jazz a disciplined, lucid, quietly audacious music bringing to jazz a refreshing new musical sensibility. By the middle of the decade, however, the cool style was suffering from over-arranging, bland solos, and lifeless rhythm sections. Suddenly, black musicians, mainly working in the East, launched a musical-ideological revolt that brought down the polite, cerebral sound of cool jazz almost overnight. Disdaining cool as "white man's music" that had wandered far afield from the soul and down-home, body-based impulse of black music, they mounted a self-conscious revival of the black gospel and funky blues roots of jazz, resulting in a new style of jazz known as "hard bop." Ironically, Miles Davis, a founding father of the cool style, was among the first to drive a nail in its coffin with a 1954 recording of "Walkin," a twelve-bar blues characterized by straight-ahead funkiness. By decade's end, Davis was seen as an innovator once again, this time as a founding father of the hard-bop school of modern jazz.

Bibliography

Berendt, Joachim. *The Jazz Book: From Ragtime to Fusion and Beyond.* Rev. ed. Westport, Conn.: Lawrence Hill, 1987. Translated by Helmut Bredigkeit, Barbara Bredigkeit, and Dan Morgenstern. In a concise discussion of jazz developments in the 1950's, Berendt finds hard bop, which eventually undercut the cool style, creating something new without sacrificing vitality.

Carr, Ian. *Miles Davis: A Critical Biography.* New York: William Morrow, 1982. Highly recommended. Provides a detailed examination of Davis' life and musical development. Sees Davis as responsible for many innovative approaches to jazz, one of the first being the *Birth of the Cool* sessions.

Cole, Bill. *Miles Davis: A Musical Biography.* New York: William Morrow, 1974. Contains a good discussion of the *Birth of the Cool* sessions, which, according to Cole, more than anything else established Davis as a leader.

Davis, Miles, with Quincy Troupe. *Miles: The Autobiography.* New York: Simon & Schuster, 1989. Davis insists that *Birth of the Cool* came from black musical roots, but he acknowledges that cool jazz was, unlike bop, a style of jazz that white listeners could understand and appreciate.

Tirro, Frank. *Jazz: A History.* New York: W. W. Norton, 1977. Especially helpful is chapter 11, "The Fifties—A Proliferation of Styles," which relates cool jazz to other jazz styles developed during the period.

L. Moody Simms, Jr.

Cross-References

Joplin Popularizes the Ragtime Style (1899), p. 13; Armstrong First Records with His Hot Five Group (1925), p. 670; Ellington Begins an Influential Engagement at the Cotton Club (1927), p. 739; Goodman Begins His *Let's Dance* Broadcasts (1934), p. 968; Parker's Playing Epitomizes Bebop (1946), p. 1318; Cage's *4' 33"* Premieres (1952), p. 1546; The First Newport Jazz Festival Is Held (1954), p. 1617; Davis' *Bitches Brew* Vitalizes Jazz-Rock Fusion (1969), p. 2153; Wynton Marsalis Revives Acoustic Jazz (1980's), p. 2454.

POUND WINS THE BOLLINGEN PRIZE

Category of event: Literature
Time: February 20, 1949
Locale: Washington, D.C.

A controversy concerning the relationship between an artist's life and his work erupted when the first Bollingen Prize for poetic achievement was awarded to Ezra Pound's The Pisan Cantos

Principal personages:

EZRA POUND (1885-1972), a poetic innovator and self-taught classical scholar whose influence in American literature has not been diminished by his political stupidity

T. S. ELIOT (1888-1965), an Anglo-American poet who reigned as the leading arbiter of modernist thought through the first half of the twentieth century

JAMES LAUGHLIN (1914-), a visionary publisher and lyric poet whose New Directions Press was instrumental in introducing and supporting many of the most original American writers of the twentieth century

ARCHIBALD MACLEISH (1892-1982), an American man of letters whose positions in the government permitted him to work toward a humane and generous conception of an artistic community

KARL SHAPIRO (1913-), an American poet and literary critic perhaps best known for his essay collection *In Defense of Ignorance*

ALLEN TATE (1899-1979), a poet and a leading proponent of the New Criticism

E. E. CUMMINGS (1894-1962), a maverick poetic stylist and iconoclast whose political perspective made him sympathetic to Pound's predicament

JULIEN CORNELL (1910-), a Quaker, a pacifist, and an active member of the American Civil Liberties Union (ACLU) who defended Pound

HAYDEN CARRUTH (1921-), a poet, essayist, and anthologist

Summary of Event

On July 26, 1943, a District of Columbia grand jury delivered an indictment of treason against Ezra Pound and seven other Americans who were broadcasting under the auspices of the Axis Powers. Pound was living in Italy then, and when he was eventually apprehended by Italian partisans in May, 1945, he was interned by the U.S. Army in Pisa. During the time he was held there—at first in a semi-outdoor barbed-wire stockade and, later, in a medical compound—Pound composed the poems that came to be known as *The Pisan Cantos*. On November 17, 1945, Pound was flown to the United States; in December, he was placed in the criminal and lunatic ward of St. Elizabeths Hospital in Washington, D.C., after a jury found him not competent to stand trial for treason. From the moment of Pound's incarceration, friends in the literary community (including T. S. Eliot and Ernest Hemingway) began to plan a strategy to win his release. Pound, though, was held in St. Elizabeths until April, 1958, in spite of the continuing efforts to free him. One of the reasons for his lengthy incarceration was the tremendous controversy surrounding the 1949 Bollingen Prize presentation, which, according to Pound scholar Harry Meacham, "made cowards of us all."

Many of Pound's old friends in America, including William Carlos Williams, Louis Zukovsky, Marianne Moore, and E. E. Cummings, came to visit Pound, and after he had adjusted to the conditions of the ward life, he began to read and write with something like his old energy. In 1947, James Laughlin, who had been urged to begin New Directions Press by Pound in the late 1930's, published Pound's Confucian translations as *The Unwobbling Pivot and the Great Digest*; meanwhile journals such as *Poetry, The Sewanee Review*, and *The Quarterly Review* (which devoted an issue to assessing Pound's reputation in 1948) presented a number of his most recent poems. Laughlin was prepared to publish *The Pisan Cantos* in one volume, but he held back, fearing an adverse reaction. After a meeting between Laughlin, Archibald MacLeish, W. H. Auden, Cummings, and Allen Tate, a plan was conceived that had as its key the award of the first national prize for poetry to Pound. The award, the group reasoned, would place the Department of Justice in an "awkward if not untenable position" that would hasten Pound's release.

The Bollingen Foundation had been established by Paul Mellon, a financier and patron of the arts, to publish the collected works of the Swiss psychiatrist Carl Jung (the foundation took its name from the name of Jung's home). In 1943, Allen Tate, then the poetry consultant to the Library of Congress, had proposed that a committee of fellows in American literature meet to award an annual prize for the best book of each year, and the Bollingen Foundation was approached as a possible source of funds. The foundation's trustees agreed to take part, but the details were not worked out until 1948. Léonie Adams, the foundation's poetry consultant, served as chairman, and the remainder of the judges were made up of accomplished writers and prominent socialites who knew Pound either by reputation or personal acquaintance. The judges included younger poets such as Robert Lowell, Louise Bogan, and Karl Shapiro, transoceanic celebrities such as Auden and Eliot, respected critics and poets such as Tate and Conrad Aiken, and Katherine Garrison Chapin (the wife of former Attorney General Francis Biddle, who had prepared the original indictment against Pound). The committee met for the first time on November 18, 1948, and Tate remarked that a nomination for Pound's *Cantos* (not necessarily only *The Pisan Cantos*) seemed probable. On the following day, though, three other nominations were offered to the committee. The only challenge to Pound's work was William Carlos Williams' 1948 volume *Paterson, Book Two*; on the first ballot, eight judges voted for *The Pisan Cantos*, three voted for *Paterson, Book Two*, and two abstained. The three judges supporting Williams' book were Shapiro, Aiken, and Chapin, although Tate urged Shapiro to support the Pound nomination, saying that such a vote from the only Jewish member of the panel would "give anti-Semitism a telling blow." Shapiro, however, felt uneasy about anti-Semitic comments made by Pound in some of his wartime radio broadcasts and in some of his earlier writings and considered resigning from the committee. A debate continued, and a decision was made to have a postal ballot taken in February.

Eliot's stature in the literary community made his strong support for Pound hard to resist, and Williams himself remarked that he thought Pound should be awarded the prize. Adams wrote to Julien Cornell, Pound's lawyer, wondering if the publicity surrounding the deliberations would be harmful to Pound as his case was about to be reviewed; Cornell replied that he doubted that the award would hurt Pound (a miscalculation) and that it might cheer him up. When the postal ballot was taken, Aiken also voted for Pound, a position consistent with the support he had shown for Pound when Random House had attempted to remove Pound's poems from its *Anthology of Famous English and American Poetry* in 1946. Lowell, who admired Williams, nevertheless continued to support Pound, in part because of his own incarceration as a conscientious objector during World War II. Shapiro did not support Pound, explaining that "I am a Jew and cannot honor antisemites"; in addition, Shapiro stated, he believed that "the poet's political and moral philosophy ultimately vitiates his poetry and lowers its standards as literary work." Katherine Chapin remained displeased that Pound was even considered for the award, and her husband wrote to the foundation's librarian, Luther H. Evans, that he "recommended strongly against the decision." Tate, on the other hand, had written to Evans a month before the announcement saying that it would be "cowardly" to choose *Paterson, Book Two* or not to make the award at all, since *The Pisan Cantos* "had been universally acclaimed" as the most significant book of the year.

Huntington Cairns, a senior officer of the Smithsonian Institution who had helped establish the Bollingen award, visited Pound on the weekend before the official announcement and reported that Pound knew about the award and was "obviously excited." According to Cairns, Pound had prepared a typically wry statement for the media, "No comment from the Bug House," but had decided against releasing it. The award carried an honorarium of $1,000, which Pound accepted. He observed to Cairns that the committee's action was "Bollingen's bid for immortality" and often called the award the "Bubble-Gum Prize." Since Pound had had expectations of winning the Nobel Prize in Literature for *The Pisan Cantos*, anything less had to be a disappointment.

Impact of Event

The public reaction to the award was even more agitated than the committee anticipated. *The New York Times*, in an uncharacteristically tabloid-like headline, announced that "POUND, IN MENTAL CLINIC, WINS PRIZE FOR POETRY

PENNED IN TREASON CELL." Some of Pound's severest critics, including Albert Deutsch and William Barrett, condemned the prize committee. Deutsch wrote in the leftist journal *PM* that Pound was like Benedict Arnold and that those who had supported him were turncoats. Radio Moscow, seizing the opportunity to attack capitalism, observed that the quality of poetry in the United States had to be very low if "even the insane and verified ravings of a confessed madman could win a literary prize." Among the more measured responses, Shapiro explained his position in *Partisan Review*, contrasting his views with the official statement of the prize committee, which he called "evasive, historically untrue, and illogical." In the same *Partisan Review* symposium (May, 1949), other prominent writers and cultural commentators offered opinions that ranged across a spectrum of considered philosophical and aesthetic positions.

W. H. Auden directly confronted the question of anti-Semitism, widening the debate to reflect the devastating revelations of the Holocaust, which had just begun to be assimilated by the Allied countries after World War II. "Anti-Semitism, is, unfortunately, not only a feeling which all gentiles at times feel," he wrote, "but also, and this is what matters, a feeling of which the majority of them are not ashamed." George Orwell called Pound's broadcasts "disgusting" and said that after reading the written transcripts, he had the impression that the broadcasts were not "the work of a lunatic." Neither man addressed the quality of Pound's poetry. The art historian Clement Greenberg attempted to tangle with the difficult question of suppression of any artist's work, saying, "I am not against the publication of *The Pisan Cantos*, even though they offend me," arguing from a classic First Amendment position that his "fear of censorship" outweighed his "sensitivity as a Jew." Greenberg also commented that he was prepared to "swallow" the consequence of his position but that he wished that the Bollingen committee "had been, or shown themselves, more aware of the additional consequence when they awarded their Bollingen Prize." The critic Robert Gorham Davis also argued for publication of *The Pisan Cantos* but stated that "they deserve no prize."

The most severe and sustained attack by a serious literary critic was Robert Hillyer's two-part essay (June 11 and June 18, 1949) in *The Saturday Review of Literature*. Hayden Carruth, a man of liberal sensibilities who frequently wrote for the progressive journal *The Nation*, regarded Hillyer's attack as scurrilous and edited an issue of *Poetry* entitled *The Case Against the Saturday Review of Literature*. The *Poetry* issue contained statements by Tate, Adams, and Evans (who "stood like a rock during the Pound trauma"), reprints of reviews by MacLeish and Mark Van Doren, and letters from well-known critics Yvor Winters and Cleanth Brooks and from the poet John Berryman. Berryman charged that "under the pretense of attacking the award of the Bollingen Prize to Ezra Pound" *The Saturday Review of Literature* had "sanctioned and guided a prepared attack on modern poetry and criticism." Seventy-three signatures were appended to Berryman's letter. Carruth himself wrote an editorial in which he said that "whatever is the outcome of the Ezra Pound case, the enemies of poetry must not be allowed to damage the process of our art through their untoward anger." He went on to explain that "many generations will pass before a young poet can overlook the work of Ezra Pound"—a prophetic insight—and contended that "truth and experience" would provide a necessary perspective to judge poetry of even the most damaging sentiments. For his contribution to the debate, Carruth was fired by the trustees of the magazine. Their action reflected the fear and alarm that ran through the cultural community. While individual artists often acted on principle and with courage, the social patrons who were involved in financing and supporting publications were frightened by actions like those taken by Senator Jacob Javits of New York, who demanded an investigation of the award. The Library of Congress bowed to the pressure to the extent that it was decided that Yale University would assume responsibility for administering the award in the future.

Pound himself was already convinced that the government of the United States was misguided in its policies, and the controversy over the award did nothing to alter his opinion. He showed Cairns a box of clippings and letters concerning the prize on April 2, indicating his awareness of the public furor in spite of his presentation of a façade of indifference. He was probably amused by a telegram he received from Cummings that said, somewhat sardonically, "Hearty congratulations to Capitalist system and to Andrew Mellon in particular." Although Pound was too close to death to appreciate the historical parallel, the Bollingen affair was repeated in 1972, when Pound was nominated for and then denied the Emerson-Thoreau Medal. The debate that ensued recapitulated the one that had taken place in 1949, and came no closer to resolving the question of how a man who was such a poetic genius could have also been such a political imbecile.

Bibliography

Carpenter, Humphrey. *A Serious Character: The Life of Ezra Pound.* Boston: Houghton Mifflin, 1988. An extremely detailed and lively biography that thoroughly covers the Bollingen controversy. Effectively uses the minutes of the Bollingen prize committee in the Library of Congress.

Heymann, C. David. *Ezra Pound: The Last Rower.* New York: Viking Press, 1976. Described as a "political profile," Heymann's work contains extensive quotations by participants in the Bollingen controversy but is biased by the author's dislike for Pound.

Norman, Charles. *The Case of Ezra Pound.* New York: Funk & Wagnalls, 1968. A close examination of the actual case brought by the government, with lengthy quotes from transcripts, useful annotations, comments from supporters, and other documentation. See also Harry Meacham's *The Caged Panther* (New York: Twayne, 1967), which provides the text of many letters from and to Pound during the time he was at St. Elizabeths.

Stock, Noel. *The Life of Ezra Pound.* New York: Random House, 1970. Draws on Pound's family papers; Stock had the approval of Pound's wife Dorothy in the project. A somewhat limited but accurate factual account.

Tytell, John. *Ezra Pound: The Solitary Volcano.* New York: Doubleday, 1987. An incisive, stylish biography that offers balanced judgment and a useful bibliography. Written with a perceptive sense of Pound's accomplishments as a poet.

Leon Lewis

Cross-References

Harriet Monroe Founds *Poetry* Magazine (1912), p. 314; The Imagist Movement Shakes Up Poetry (1912), p. 326; Yeats Publishes *The Wild Swans at Coole* (1917), p. 440; Eliot Publishes *The Waste Land* (1922), p. 539; Crane Publishes *The Bridge* (1930), p. 851; *Poems* Establishes Auden as a Generational Spokesman (1930), p. 857.

BEAUVOIR'S *THE SECOND SEX* ANTICIPATES
THE WOMEN'S MOVEMENT

Category of event: Literature
Time: June and November, 1949
Locale: Paris, France

The Second Sex *became a seminal work and astonished Europe and the United States with its historical, comprehensive, and frank portrayal of women as unequal, second-class citizens of the world*

Principal personages:
SIMONE DE BEAUVOIR (1908-1986), a philosopher and novelist
JEAN-PAUL SARTRE (1905-1980), a world-renowned existentialist philosopher whose life was linked with Simone de Beauvoir
NELSON ALGREN (NELSON AHLGREN ABRAHAM, 1909-1981), an American writer, friend and lover of Simone de Beauvoir
COLETTE AUDRY (1906-   ), a colleague and lifelong friend of Simone de Beauvoir, involved in education, politics, and literature

Summary of Event

The Second Sex is a carefully researched and highly intellectual work. Book 1 of *Le Deuxième Sexe* was published in Paris, France, in June of 1949, with book 2 following in November. The English translation appeared in 1952. The book became extraordinarily influential, shaping the women's movement as it began to gain power in the 1960's. It is considered to be a classic in women's literature. Using all the resources available to her both in the Bibliothèque Nationale in Paris and in the United States, Simone de Beauvoir in this book delves into anthropology, biology, philosophy, psychology, psychoanalysis, politics, sociology, and literature. Book 1 includes topics ranging from the destiny of women to their history and myths. Book 2 covers the formative years of women through their old age as well as the justifications for women's attitudes, concluding with an array of ideas that she insists lead toward the liberation of women.

Essentially, the seven hundred pages of analysis of women as the "second sex" rely heavily on a framework of philosophy, particularly that of existentialism as exemplified by Jean-Paul Sartre, Beauvoir's lifelong companion, in his *L'Être et le néant* (1943; *Being and Nothingness*, 1956). The idea for Beauvoir's book originated with Colette Audry, a fellow philosophy teacher and colleague of Beauvoir at the Rouen Lycée. Audry's influence on Beauvoir is apparent, as Beauvoir eventually recognized the inequalities in the status of men and women. Beauvoir never married and received a first-rate education at the Sorbonne, so never felt the full brunt of male power. Her friend Audry chafed because Frenchwomen were not given suffrage until 1947; eventually, she succeeded in convincing Beauvoir of the limitations women faced as a powerless gender. Beauvoir's book was titled *The Second Sex* because men are the first sex, with women distinctly second in importance. Homosexuals are often dubbed the "third sex."

The Second Sex, using the idea of women as "the Other," is grounded in Marxist socialism and in Sartrean existentialism, which recognizes existence before essence and stresses the concept of the responsibility of choice and freedom. This set of beliefs often elicits fear and anxiety. Beauvoir refers to one's ontology, or what it is to be a human being at a fundamental level. One of the earliest voices for feminism she cites is that of the seventeenth century Frenchman Poulain de la Barre, whose *On the Equality of Both Sexes* was published in France in 1673. He wrote, "All that has been written about women by men should be suspect, for the men are at once judge and party to the lawsuit." Deirdre Bair, in *Simone de Beauvoir* (1990), wrote that this statement sets the parameters for Beauvoir's research and methodology.

Beauvoir, in *The Second Sex*, examined the sexuality and socialization of women, believing that they are programmed to be unequal and inferior from birth. Therefore, they are subjected to inordinate pressures to prepare for marriage, which is a woman's best hope of survival, economically and socially. This emphasis on marriage limits women to the roles of wife, mother, and housekeeper, essentially powerless roles that reflect a subordination to men. A woman is, because of her role as re-producer, unless independently wealthy, at the mercy of men for economic and so-cial survival. This double standard of the sexes imprisons women in a monotonous repetition of unpaid labor. Beauvoir used the term "transcendent" to indicate the role of men as they aspire to higher realms in occupations utilizing their imagina-tion, resourcefulness, and risk-taking skills, as compared with women, whose work in the home limits them to a treadmill existence, which she called "immanence." Even love is not possible, claimed Beauvoir, unless men and women experience equality.

Beauvoir's main thesis urges women to work outside the household for personal and economic betterment. She was unalterably opposed to housewifery as the sole option for women. Men and women must share the responsibilities of housework and child rearing. Ultimately, Beauvoir was opposed to marriage, which often forces women into unpaid sex with husbands and which creates a climate that impairs, if not destroys, romance. She warned that children's development and outlook will be limited severely if they are reared by women who remain at home. A main and repetitive thread in *The Second Sex* is the hope that women can be made conscious of their inferior status and subsequently be urged to take steps to upgrade this status.

By the time that Beauvoir published *The Second Sex* in 1949, she had already pub-lished (in French) several novels, *The Ethics of Ambiguity* (1948), and *America Day by Day* (1952), a travel book. Her fifteen-year intermittent love affair with the American writer Nelson Algren became doubly significant, since Algren introduced her to an array of American novels and writers, including Richard Wright. This liaison, it is universally acknowledged, contributed an American tone to *The Second Sex*, which when published created a sensation throughout France. The book was particularly excoriated by the Catholic church, which Beauvoir indicted as a bastion of archconservatism toward women, and by an angry French bourgeoisie. Despite this initial outpouring of vicious opposition, through this book Beauvoir gained a considerable reputation of her own, never again to experience recognition only through her relationship with Sartre as his friend, companion, critic, and editor.

Impact of Event

Within ten years after its publication, *The Second Sex*, with its compendious analysis of literature and documentation of histories, autobiographies, essays, and psychoanalysis, no longer created a furor. When the vitriol subsided, the respect for the book and for Beauvoir began, as women and many men around the world cited their debt to her as spokeswoman and supporter of women's rights. Although the book continued to be attacked by male chauvinists and by antifeminists such as Phyllis Schlafly, commentators and critics generally agreed that *The Second Sex* is engagingly informative, unique, reasonable, and witty.

The Second Sex created a permanent impact on culture and society. It attacked Freudian psychoanalysis insofar as this theory denies choice and, therefore, is considered deterministic. Woman, Beauvoir insisted, is not constrained by sexual determinism. She vehemently disagreed with Freud that biology is destiny. She believed that women should assume their condition, not accept it. Transcendence occurs when women assert themselves, rather than locking themselves into immanence.

Beauvoir frontally attacked figures such as St. Paul, Pierre Joseph Proudhon, D. H. Lawrence, and Henri Rousseau, who consigned women to immanence. She reiterated belief in options, as did Virginia Woolf, and condemned "bad faith," the term Sartre used to mean abdication of the human self.

Because of Beauvoir's intimate association with Sartre (although after an initial sexual liaison they became a platonic "professional couple") and her fiercely independent spirit, Beauvoir was mocked by those who called her "La Grande Sartreuse" and "Notre Dame de Sartre." By the 1960's, when the women's movement in the United States reached a crest, these snide remarks had become passé as *The Second Sex* assumed a reinvigorated life. It became required reading in women's studies programs, discussed in seminars and at conventions. The Modern Language Association, a society of academics and scholars, offered panels on the book in the areas of literature, psychology, history, anthropology, and feminism. Carolyn Heilbrun, a professor of literature at Columbia University, declared the book to have had an extraordinary and profound, although delayed, influence on not only women's studies but also the raising of women's consciousness. Betty Friedan, often dubbed the grandmother of feminism in the United States, was so emotionally affected by *The Second Sex* that she took to her bed. Although Friedan did not accept the "either/or" assertions of Beauvoir's polemic, she, like other well-known feminists including Gloria Steinem, Kate Millett, and Marilyn French, paid homage to this book and its pervasive influence around the world. The book has caused women to rethink the position that they have been socialized into, opening them to other options. A remark about Beauvoir by the feminist and writer Elisabeth Badinter is a telling one:

"Women, you owe everything to her!"

Beauvoir's book inspired the formation of an international Simone de Beauvoir Society. Television stations vied for interviews, and magazines hounded her for contributions. French television filmed four 52-minute segments about Beauvoir, her life, her books, and her ideas about feminism. American television initially banned the series because of explicit references to clitoridectomy of Arab girls, but eventually some public television channels offered the film in censored form.

Whenever and wherever women's liberation is discussed, *The Second Sex* commands attention and respect. Some scholars have referred to it as the most significant and forceful vindication of the rights of women published in the twentieth century. Many women in the United States took Beauvoir as their guide and guru. Militant feminists in the 1960's and the 1970's lamented that *The Second Sex* was not militant enough, yet it was considered "radical" in its day. Despite disparate views on this quintessentially influential book, most women familiar with her work assert that Beauvoir is a heroine who lit the torch of the women's movement in the twentieth century.

The resulting fame from the publication of *The Second Sex* placed Beauvoir squarely in the limelight. Invitations to speak poured in from around the world. Beauvoir encouraged and financially supported centers for aid to battered women, encouraged the dissemination of information on birth control, and marched with the Mouvement de Libération des Femmes (MLF) in Paris in November, 1971, calling for free contraception and abortion on demand. Beauvoir's fame lent weight to all these causes. *The Second Sex* already had become a powerful lever.

Betty Friedan, famous and powerful for *The Feminine Mystique* (1963), joined hundreds who traveled to Paris for interviews freely given by Beauvoir. Friedan recounts, especially in *It Changed My Life: Writings on the Women's Movement* (1976), her interviews with Beauvoir, with whom she often disagreed but to whom she paid homage for introducing her to reality and political responsibility concerning women. Scores of other books have expressed gratitude for the impact of Beauvoir's *The Second Sex* on their authors' own writings, including the well-known *The Dialectic of Sex: The Case for Feminist Revolution* (1970) by Shulamith Firestone, *The Female Eunuch* (1970) by Germaine Greer, and *Sexual Politics* (1970) by Kate Millett.

Four years after Beauvoir's death, Deirdre Bair's *Simone de Beauvoir* was published. This work scrutinizes all phases of Beauvoir's life. The reader becomes aware that, although Beauvoir's book explores the environment of the bourgeoisie during her lifetime and carefully annotates the stages leading to the research and writing of *The Second Sex*, there is no specific plan for militancy and little theory from which to construct innovations for feminine behavior, an omission some feminists deplore. Beauvoir's book nevertheless had a significant impact, inspiring the founding of women's organizations, women's magazines, and even banks for women. Beauvoir appeared to be the only woman in contemporary literature to be integrally associated with the causes, events, and actions of her age. Her analysis of women's immanence and her attempts to use ideology to encourage women toward transcendence are grounds for a canonization of Beauvoir according to many feminists.

The Second Sex, which initially ignited consternation, shock, and hatred as well as admiration and devotion, came to be considered a temperate exposition of women's rights. Given the progression of women's struggle and notable changes in morality, many young women are unaware of the influence of this book on the acceptance of women into medical and law schools and into the armed services. They remain similarly unaware of Beauvoir's influence in achieving the improved climate for women in business, the media, and other professions. The influence, whether recognized or not, is there. *The Second Sex* is a classic book, required reading for those concerned with feminism and its history.

Bibliography

Bair, Deirdre. *Simone de Beauvoir*. New York: Summit Books, 1990. This exhaustive, well-annotated biography is largely the result of five years of interviews with Beauvoir. It is well written and complete, particularly in the sections dealing with Beauvoir's association with Sartre and her romance with Nelson Algren. End notes are thorough and complete.

Beauvoir, Simone de. *The Second Sex*. Translated and edited by H. M. Parshley. New York: Vintage Books, 1989. Covers the history of women from the perspectives of biology, mythology, psychology, psychoanalysis, literature, and sociology. Beauvoir discusses the different stages and ages of women, love, mysticism, and liberation.

Cottrell, Robert D. *Simone de Beauvoir*. New York: Frederick Ungar, 1975. A compact presentation of Beauvoir's life and work, discussing her bourgeois family, her interest in ethics, and her novels. Might be considered as an introductory work.

Keefe, Terry. *Simone de Beauvoir: A Study of Her Writings*. New York: Barnes & Noble Books, 1983. Keefe focuses on Beauvoir's entire set of works, not centering on feminism or Sartre. Particularly absorbing are chapters on *The Second Sex* and Beauvoir's most successful novel, *The Mandarins* (1956).

Winegarten, Renee. *Simone de Beauvoir: A Critical View*. New York: St. Martin's Press, 1988. Deals with Beauvoir's association with Sartre, her rebellious spirit, politics, feminism, and the metaphysical novel. A chronology at the end of the book is clearly presented. Bibliography.

Julia B. Boken

Cross-References

Cather's *My Ántonia* Promotes Regional Literature (1918), p. 452; Woolf's *Mrs. Dalloway* Explores Women's Consciousness (1925), p. 637; Sartre and Camus Give Dramatic Voice to Existential Philosophy (1940's), p. 1174; Sartre's *Being and Nothingness* Expresses Existential Philosophy (1943), p. 1262; Plath's *The Colossus* Voices Women's Experience (1960), p. 1850; Lévi-Strauss Explores Myth as a Key to Enlightenment (1964), p. 1995; Derrida Enunciates the Principles of Deconstruction (1967), p. 2075.

"ANGRY YOUNG MEN" EXPRESS
WORKING-CLASS VIEWS

Categories of event: Literature and theater
Time: The 1950's
Locale: London, England

Novels and plays by new, mostly working-class writers termed by journalists the "Angry Young Men" expressed widespread alienation and social discontent in mid-1950's Great Britain

Principal personages:

KINGSLEY AMIS (1922-   ), a novelist whose first book, *Lucky Jim*, featured an irreverent, antiestablishment, deliberately subversive lecturer at a provincial university

JOHN ARDEN (1930-   ), a playwright whose *Serjeant Musgrave's Dance* was an intense antiwar "unhistorical parable"

JOHN BRAINE (1922-1986), a novelist whose *Room at the Top* and *Life at the Top* portrayed both its protagonist's aspirations and his disillusionment

JOHN OSBORNE (1929-   ), a playwright whose *Look Back in Anger* was the first offering of the English Stage Company at the Royal Court Theatre

HAROLD PINTER (1930-   ), a playwright whose seemingly oblique "comedies of menace" perplexed theatergoers with ominous silences and unexplained events

ALAN SILLITOE (1928-   ), a novelist whose *Saturday Night and Sunday Morning* and *The Loneliness of the Long-Distance Runner* featured unabashedly working-class protagonists who disdain middle-class respectability

DAVID STOREY (1933-   ), a former professional athlete whose first novel, *This Sporting Life*, offered an unidealized first-person account of the public and private life of a rugby-league football player

JOHN WAIN (1925-   ), a novelist whose first book, *Hurry on Down*, was a picaresque account of a man who rejects his lower-middle-class background

KEITH WATERHOUSE (1929-   ), a novelist whose *Billy Liar* captured the alienation of an adolescent in a provincial English town

Summary of Event

Although the "Angry Young Men" who emerged during the mid-1950's and early 1960's are often referred to as a "movement," these novelists and playwrights were never part of a coordinated literary group. Although their political orientation was generally left of center and certainly opposed to the status quo, they adhered to no specific doctrine or ideology. The term, which appears to have been inspired by the title of the novel *Angry Young Man* (1951) by the Irish writer Leslie Paul, became a journalistic catchphrase used to describe a number of writers, many of whom were of working-class origin and were from the English provinces rather than London, the traditional center of English literary culture. The fact that their iconoclastic attitudes, stylistic vigor, raucous humor, and working-class characters and settings were similar has often caused these authors' individuality and distinct differences to be overlooked.

Many novels from the period feature protagonists who, like their creators, were young, irreverent, brash, and profane; they celebrate individuality, berate conformity, defy conventional behavior, and delight in subverting traditional institutions. Some, including the narrators of Brendan Behan's autobiographical *Borstal Boy* (1958) and Alan Sillitoe's *The Loneliness of the Long-Distance Runner* (1959), are teenaged inmates of a borstal (reform school); others, like the protagonist of *Saturday Night and Sunday Morning* (1958), feel hardly less confined in the factories where they are employed. Similarly, the narrator of David Storey's *This Sporting Life* (1960) finds that life as a member of a professional sports team turns play into work; in Kingsley Amis' *Lucky Jim* (1954), the title character comically subverts the conventions of university life. With brash disregard for stolid middle-class morality, including (especially) its sexual constraints, these protagonists were also unabashedly sexual and often far from monogamous. The title character of Bill Naughton's *Alfie* (1966) shamelessly seduces numerous girlfriends, married and unmarried alike, while making commitments to none; Arthur Seaton of *Saturday Night and Sunday Morning* enjoys illicit sex not only with a coworker's wife but also, separately, her sister. The novels in which they appear are often episodically structured and follow various adventures of their antiheroic protagonists, modern-day counterparts of the picaresque heroes of earlier literature.

Although their attitudes toward women now seem callously chauvinistic and were often exploitative, these characters' vitality, physicality, and defiance of conventional norms made them the male "sex symbols" of their day—a reputation that was enhanced when commercially successful, critically acclaimed films were based on the novels, including *Lucky Jim* (1957), *Room at the Top* (1958), *Saturday Night and Sunday Morning* (1960), *The Loneliness of the Long-Distance Runner* (1962), and *This Sporting Life* (1963).

In the theater, simultaneously, a number of "angry young playwrights" were establishing themselves in what admirers later termed English drama's "Second Elizabethan Age." Two theater companies were at the forefront of theatrical innovation: the English Stage Company, founded by George Devine at the Royal Court Theatre in 1956, and Joan Littlewood's Theatre Workshop at the Theatre Royal, Stratford East, London. The 1956 premiere of John Osborne's *Look Back in Anger*, the English Stage Company's initial production, inaugurated a new age in contemporary theater and startled theatergoers as alienated young Jimmy Porter, the play's protagonist, harangued both the other characters in the play and the audience itself. In contrast to the standard commercial star vehicles that predominated in London's West End theater district, the English Stage Company was, from the outset, self-proclaimedly a writer's theater. Though constantly financially imperiled, it offered the first productions of many of the then-controversial playwrights who were to become recognized as the most important dramatists of postwar Britain, including Harold Pinter, John Arden, Arnold Wesker, David Storey, and Edward Bond. Littlewood's Theatre Workshop, influenced by the theories of German playwright Bertolt Brecht, emphasized collaborative repertory theater and lengthy rehearsal periods; the workshop also established directors as creative cocreators with the playwrights, the most prominent of whom was Brendan Behan.

Because these playwrights were controversial, their defenders performed a particularly important function. Among the foremost of the group's defenders were Kenneth Tynan of *The Observer* and the writers for *Encore* magazine, the self-proclaimed "voice of vital theatre" that was the most ardent and exhortative (sometimes literally the only) defender of the theater's most daring and innovative new forms. Disdaining "moribund" West End commercialism, the new playwrights sought a new audience that would, in Lindsay Anderson's words, come to the theater "not with the passive expectation of 'entertainment,' nor just with mouths wide open for another slab of minority culture, but themselves prepared to give something, to work, with minds open and alert, themselves creative.

Impact of Event

The foremost achievement of the "Angry Young Men" is the uncondescending incorporation of authentic working-class voices, characters, and issues into the English literary tradition, from which they had been conspicuously absent. These writers' virile, defiant, iconoclastic protagonists (often described as muscular or physically big) stand in marked contrast to long-familiar caricatures of the working class in English literature—the clownish artisans in William Shakespeare's *A Midsummer Night's Dream* (1595-1596), the drunken porter in *Macbeth* (1606), the genially shiftless Alfred Doolittle in George Bernard Shaw's *Pygmalion* (1913), the ever-indolent comic-strip character Andy Capp, and countless one-dimensional, more or less competent servants who, if they perform their jobs well, go virtually unnoticed by or subordinate themselves to their social "betters" (even when such betters are as fatuous as Bertie Wooster and his friends in P. G. Wodehouse's numerous stories of the perfect butler, Jeeves).

The few major protagonists in pre-1950 fiction who are of working-class origins— Pip in Charles Dickens' *Great Expectations* (1860-1861) and Paul Morel in D. H. Lawrence's *Sons and Lovers* (1913) for example—typically, if wrongly, regard their class background as something to be escaped and perceive themselves as both apart from and better than "common" people. The post-1950 writers are more divided on such issues; Sillitoe's characters express no desire whatsoever to leave the working class, while Braine's Joe Lampton is successful in marrying his way out of it but ultimately becomes disillusioned. Many of Storey's characters rise into the professional classes through education but find themselves in a social limbo, at home neither in their new class nor in their old one.

Notwithstanding such diversity, the Angry Young Men also gave voice to a wide-spread alienation and discontentment in Great Britain, particularly among the working-class young who came of age during the decade of postwar shortages, reduced expectations, and painful readjustment following the dismantling of the Empire. Significantly, most of the protagonists of these plays and novels are or recently were adolescents; as such, like the characters portrayed by the American actor James Dean, they are "rebels without a cause," railing against the status quo but doing little or nothing to effect meaningful change, remaining ultimately unempowered. Accordingly, they enjoy engaging in secret subversions of middle-class propriety, acts of defiance with a value more symbolic than real. For almost all of these characters, the ultimate authoritarian enemy is the modern urban social institution, whether a prison, factory, sports team, or school, which embodies and enforces life-stifling constraint, conformity, and regimentation. Against the threat of such dehumanization, the body and its pleasures provide the principal refuge—a respite from workaday monotony and the dreariness of life in a class-ridden world. Accordingly, the much-vaunted "anger" manifested itself more in talk, rowdiness, and violation of sexual strictures than in meaningful action toward social reform. Characters such as Sillitoe's Arthur Seaton may occasionally fantasize about blowing up the factory but will never take such radical action, primarily because they are having too much fun otherwise.

The novelists' straightforwardly realistic prose style stood in clear contrast to the oblique, self-consciously literary experimentation of such writers from the previous generation as James Joyce, Virginia Woolf, and Joseph Conrad. The playwrights, on the other hand, tended to be more innovative and challenging, willing to risk seeming inaccessible in order to experiment with untraditional forms. While the number of plays set in dingy working-class flats earned the genre the nickname "kitchen-sink realism" (a description applied to *Look Back in Anger* and Pinter's 1957 *The Room* and 1960 *The Caretaker*), others, like John Arden's *Serjeant Musgrave's Dance* (1959) and Behan's *The Hostage* (1958), were influenced by the antirealistic theories of the German playwright Bertolt Brecht, whose overtly didactic plays blended history, comedy, and song. Pinter's "comedies of menace" puzzled audiences by combining naturalistic events, ominous silences, unexplained motivation, and the philosophical premises of the Theatre of the Absurd. David Storey's "poetic naturalism" in *The Contractor* (1970) and *The Changing Room* (1972) presented ostensibly plotless plays with a Chekhovian mastery of subtext.

Although the then-shocking anger of the Angry Young Men now seems pale in comparison to the rage of more militant writers and literal revolutionaries in the later 1960's, the literary contribution made by these groundbreaking novelists and playwrights is of permanent value. They vigorously expressed attitudes that had been excluded from serious literature and expanded literature's subject matter by including the experience of working-class people whose culture had been marginalized and whose voices had been long suppressed. The autobiographical writings of Alan Sillitoe in *Raw Material* (1972) and John Wain in *Sprightly Running* (1962) are particularly noteworthy personal explorations of a now-lost way of life among earlier generations of the working class.

Bibliography

Doty, Gresdna A., and Billy J. Harbin, eds. *Inside the Royal Court Theatre, 1956-1981: Artists Talk.* Baton Rouge: Louisiana State University Press, 1990. Based on the proceedings of a conference celebrating twenty-five years of the English Stage Company, this book transcribes discussions among its artistic directors, playwrights, directors, managers, designers, and critics. The remarkably distinguished list of participants includes all but one of the living past and present artistic directors of the company. Photographs, index, bibliography.

Findlater, Richard, ed. *At the Royal Court: Twenty-Five Years of the English Stage Company.* New York: Grove Press, 1981. This collection of reminiscences about the history of the English Stage Company at the Royal Court Theatre contains not only memoirs by many of the major playwrights and directors who worked there but also numerous photographs, charts of production details, financial tables, and cast lists for every play produced there between 1956 and 1980. Index.

Gray, Nigel. *The Silent Majority: A Study of the Working Class in Post-War British Fiction.* New York: Barnes & Noble, 1973. Focuses on adolescence and manhood in Barry Hines's *Kes* (1976), Waterhouse's *Billy Liar* (1959), Behan's *Borstal Boy*, Sillitoe's *Saturday Night and Sunday Morning*, Storey's *This Sporting Life*, and Naughton's *Alfie.* Useful, although the assessment of Sillitoe seems unduly harsh. Frequent lengthy quotations from the novels are included; index.

Machsler, Tom, ed. *Declaration.* London: MacGibbon & Kee, 1957. This collection of essays by many of the foremost young writers of the mid-1950's, including many of the Angry Young Men, embodies their diverse aesthetic and political principles. Contributors to the volume are Lindsay Anderson, Stuart Holroyd, Bill Hopkins, Doris Lessing, John Osborne, Kenneth Tynan, John Wain, and Colin Wilson. Photographs.

Marowitz, Charles, Tom Milne, and Owen Hale. *Theatre Voices of the Fifties and Sixties: Selections from Encore Magazine, 1956-1963.* Introduction by Michael Billington. London: Eyre Methuen, 1981. As London's self-proclaimed "voice of vital theatre," *Encore* magazine was consistently the foremost—and sometimes virtually the sole—advocate for and defender of such new dramatists as Pinter, Osborne, Arden, and others. This collection offers a representative, if regrettably brief, selection of witty, iconoclastic, aggressively opinionated, and occasionally vituperative reviews.

Rabinovitz, Rubin. *The Reaction Against Experiment in the English Novel, 1950-1960.* New York: Columbia University Press, 1967. Following a chapter-length survey of novelists of the 1950's, Rabinovitz examines in detail the works of Kingsley

Amis, Angus Wilson, and C. P. Snow. Useful comprehensive bibliography on the individual authors plus a more general list of secondary sources. Notes, index.

Roberts, Peter, ed. *1953-1968.* Vol. 1 in *The Best of "Plays and Players."* London: Methuen, 1988. The monthly issues of *Plays and Players* magazine offer the most comprehensive (and best-illustrated) coverage of English theater's "second Elizabethan age." More eclectic and less partisan than *Encore*, which it subsumed in 1965, its often insightful reviews, interviews, and feature articles provide candid insights. Roberts' selections are representative and judiciously chosen. Photographs.

Taylor, John Russell. *Anger and After: A Guide to the New British Drama.* Rev. ed. London: Eyre Methuen, 1969. This is the most comprehensive single-volume overview of the dramatists of the 1950's, offering succinct assessments of major and minor writers; such breadth, though, necessarily precludes much in-depth analysis. Photographs; index.

_____. *The Second Wave: British Drama of the Sixties.* Rev. ed. London: Methuen, 1978. This sequel to *Anger and After* profiles the so-called second generation of "angry" playwrights, including Edward Bond, Joe Orton, David Storey, Howard Brenton, and David Hare.

William Hutchings

Cross-References

The Beat Movement Rejects Mainstream Values (1950's), p. 1460; Dean Becomes a Legend in *Rebel Without a Cause* (1955), p. 1640; Presley Becomes a Rock-and-Roll Sensation (1956), p. 1705; Osborne's *Look Back in Anger* Opens in London (1956), p. 1721; Behan's *The Hostage* Is Presented by the Theatre Workshop (1958), p. 1757; Pinter's *The Caretaker* Opens in London (1960), p. 1861.

THE BEAT MOVEMENT REJECTS MAINSTREAM VALUES

Category of event: Literature
Time: The 1950's
Locale: Principally New York, New York, and San Francisco, California

The Beat generation rejected the conventional and academic in literature, and the force of its outlaw art and pronouncements helped to energize the antinomian movements of the 1960's

Principal personages:
> ALLEN GINSBERG (1926-   ), author of the epochal poem *Howl* and arguably the movement's best artist
> JACK KEROUAC (1922-1969), the Beat novelist who wrote *On the Road* and *The Dharma Bums*
> GREGORY CORSO (1930-   ), a New York-born poet who wrote *The Vestal Lady of Brattle, and Other Poems*
> WILLIAM S. BURROUGHS (1914-   ), a novelist who wrote *Junkie* (as William Lee) and *Naked Lunch*
> LAWRENCE FERLINGHETTI (1919-   ), a poet who founded San Francisco's influential City Lights Bookshop
> GARY SNYDER (1930-   ), a poet, scholar, and aficionado of Zen Buddhism

Summary of Event

The writers of the Beat generation were almost exclusively white males, but they nevertheless represented an impressive variety of experiences and accomplishments. They were generally literate and well-read (Lawrence Ferlinghetti earned a doctorate in art history from the Sorbonne, and Gary Snyder became a knowledgeable student of Zen Buddhism); some were lovers of jazz music; William S. Burroughs and Allen Ginsberg were determined experimenters with drugs; several who were homosexual were quite open about it; and several Beat writers included petty criminals among their friends and even had their own rap sheets. Collectively, they constituted a talented bohemia. The writers of this loose confederacy of cultural rebels emerged as a vital force in the early 1950's (the term "Beat Generation" was used by John Clellon Holmes to describe Jack Kerouac and his companion Neal Cassady in Holmes's 1952 novel *Go*), with 1955 being perhaps the most significant date. In that year, Ginsberg and Snyder met at the University of California at Berkeley, and Ginsberg launched the San Francisco Poetry Renaissance with a reading of "Howl" at San Francisco's Six Gallery on October 7.

Ginsberg described the Six Gallery as "a run down secondrate experimental art gallery in the Negro section of San Francisco." The program that famous evening of October 7, 1955, began with readings by Philip Lamantia, Michael McClure, and

Philip Whalen; Ginsberg came on about 11:00 P.M. The audience was stunned by Ginsberg's power and the intensity of his own feelings and began chanting "Go! Go! Go!" McClure remembered it this way: "In all of our memories no one had been so outspoken in poetry before—we had gone beyond the point of no return—and we were ready for it, for a point of no return. None of us wanted to go back to the gray, chill, militaristic silence, to the intellectual void—to the land without poetry—to the spiritual drabness." Gary Snyder followed Ginsberg with a much-appreciated reading of his own, but Ginsberg had begun an era in American cultural and literary history.

In 1956, Lawrence Ferlinghetti published Ginsberg's *Howl and Other Poems,* and in June, 1957, was arrested for selling obscene literature. The American Civil Liberties Union provided bail, and the case came before Judge Clayton Horn in municipal court three months later. Of the expert witnesses called, Professor Mark Schorer proved most influential in Ferlinghetti's defense. The publication and sale of *Howl* was approved by Judge Horn, who provided this summation of the work:

> The first part of *Howl* presents a picture of a nightmare world; the second part is an indictment of those elements in modern society destructive of the best qualities of human nature; such elements are predominantly identified as materialism, conformity, and mechanization leading toward war. The third part presents a picture of an individual who is a specific representation of what the author conceives as a general condition.

Just a few weeks before Judge Horn's ruling, another significant Beat work was published: Jack Kerouac's novel *On the Road.* Kerouac was from Lowell, Massachusetts, and had played football at Columbia University. Kerouac invented a character named Sal Paradise to tell his story, and his real-life friend Neal Cassady was transformed into Sal Paradise's fictional sidekick Dean Moriarty. *On the Road* is a heedless epic journey of male companionship, a search for self in the midst of national diversity, and a celebration of Dionysian submission to impulse. *On the Road* became widely popular and found its way onto college reading lists as the major representation of Beat fiction.

Lawrence Ferlinghetti opened City Lights Bookshop in 1953, and the store immediately became a center of left-wing cultural activity. In 1955, he began publishing his *Pocket Poets* series, which eventually included the work of poets Denise Levertov, Gregory Corso, Frank O'Hara, Robert Duncan, Kenneth Patchen, and Ginsberg. These achievements made Ferlinghetti a powerful force in mid-twentieth century American literature.

Ferlinghetti's own writing, too, is noteworthy, especially the poems collected in *A Coney Island of the Mind* (1958). Most evident in Ferlinghetti's work is the depiction of American culture as materialistic, hypocritical, and susceptible to bouts of mindless patriotism. His hatred for these elements in American life culminated in *Tyrannus Nix?* (1969), a ranting demonization of President Richard Nixon. If there was little aesthetic merit in Ferlinghetti's political screeds, they nevertheless spoke for a considerable number of less articulate people who shared his rage at what they saw as an oppressive establishment.

After Ginsberg, the two most talented of the Beat poets were Gary Snyder and Gregory Corso. Snyder studied Asian languages, Zen Buddhism, and anthropology and combined these interests with a vigorous outdoor life—logging, working for the U.S. Forest Service, going to sea—to create a fresh voice. His best work can be found in the "Cold Mountain Poems," *Riprap* (1959), and *Myths and Texts* (1960). Corso's milieu complemented Synder's in many ways. Whereas Snyder studied at Berkeley and Indiana University, the orphaned Corso was educated on the streets of New York City and endured his first prison detention when he was twelve. What Zen meant to Snyder, the poet Percy Bysshe Shelley represented to Corso, whose hope and idealism emerge in the titles of *Long Live Man* (1962) and *Herald of the Autochthonic Spirit* (1981). Corso's quick wit and love of words are at their best in his much-anthologized poem "Marriage."

Impact of Event

The Beats' reputation—and their identity as a group—had grown enough by 1957 that Kenneth Rexroth could say in "Disengagement: The Art of the Beat Generation" that "as an old war horse of the revolution of the word, things have never looked better from where I sit." Rexroth compared Ferlinghetti, Ginsberg, Snyder, and other Beat writers to the avant-garde poets Robert Creeley, Denise Levertov, Charles Olson, and Robert Duncan, and he praised them all for having made poetry "an actual social force." Rexroth contrasted the work of such poets with that of T. S. Eliot, John Crowe Ransom, Allen Tate, and Randall Jarrell, whom he condemned as having inspired academic "policemen" who had "produced dull academic poets." Rexroth's remarks were prescient; the Eliot-Ransom-Tate school had to make way in the academy for some loud voices, and the East Coast had to surrender part of its cultural hegemony to the West.

John P. Sisk, writing in *Commonweal* (April 17, 1959), put the Beats in an American tradition as old as Roger Williams and Anne Hutchinson, "that antinomian daughter of the inner light who today might be quite at home in a San Francisco pad." The Transcendentalists were more recent forebears, especially the figure of Walt Whitman, who was a major influence on Ginsberg. Sisk stressed the importance of a subversive bohemia engaged in dialectic with a society sometimes seen as hostile to its creativity: "Each is with respect to the other a control . . . against potentially destructive excesses."

If for Sisk bohemians were essential figures in American public life, for Norman Podhoretz they were "The Know-Nothing Bohemians," as he entitled a telling attack on Beat values in the *Partisan Review* in the spring of 1958. Podhoretz argued that an audience bored by the respectability of postwar poetry helped to create the Beats, and he wrote of suburbs "filled to overflowing with men and women who uneasily think of themselves as conformists and of Bohemianism as the heroic road." The free spirits in Kerouac's *On the Road* who hitchhiked around the country smoking marijuana, listening to jazz, and living hand-to-mouth were living out suburban myths, in Podhoretz's understanding of the Beats' appeal.

Podhoretz cited Kerouac's romantic depiction of a Nebraska farmer ("It was the spirit of the West sitting right next to me") as an example of "a kind of know-nothing populist sentiment." Middle-class workers, chained to their daily rounds, suffered from spiritual death in the Beats' vision, which resembled Henry David Thoreau's view that "the mass of men lead lives of quiet desperation." Despite Thoreau, Podhoretz found the Beats unique: "This tremendous emphasis on emotional intensity, this notion that to be hopped-up is the most desirable of all human conditions, lies at the heart of the Beat Generation ethos and distinguishes it radically from the Bohemianism of the past." Thus Podhoretz rejected Sisk's identification of the Beats with a subversive tradition in American letters, and he perhaps overstated his case. In addition to their ties to Thoreau, and to Whitman and his "barbaric yawp," the Beats had affinities with other American writers; John Steinbeck's characters in *Sweet Thursday* (1954) and *Cannery Row* (1945) in some ways resemble Kerouac's drifters, as do the outcasts of Bret Harte's Poker Flats.

For Podhoretz, though, American bohemianism of the Greenwich Village variety in the 1920's and 1930's was imbued with lofty—and civilized—ideals. Writers of the 1920's rebelled against the suffocation of American society, and the radical writers of the 1930's had humanitarian political goals. Podhoretz may have been correct in these observations, but the figures he cited—F. Scott Fitzgerald, Ernest Hemingway, T. S. Eliot, Ezra Pound, and Sinclair Lewis—would not likely suggest bohemianism to most readers. In sum, the Beats were not the Lost Generation, but they were not without roots, either.

The poet and critic John Ciardi, writing in *Saturday Review*, February 6, 1960, shared some of Podhoretz's scorn for the Beats' reliance on the intuitive: "I hope the next time the young go out for an intellectual rebellion, they will think to try the library. It's still the most subversive building in town, and it's still human headquarters." Ciardi, though, was much more generous and not without fine literary discriminations. He identified Ginsberg and Burroughs (now safely domesticated with seats in the American Academy of Arts and Letters) as the most talented, a judgment that seems to become sounder year by year. Although Ciardi did not think Burroughs was a true Beat, he praised *Naked Lunch* for its passion, which he viewed as having been "suffered rather than theorized."

The Beats' legacy is considerable. Although they are now no more threatening than Anne Hutchinson and Walt Whitman, their rowdy voices invigorated the cultural chorus—at least one section of it—and spoke for many who, though alienated from the academy and traditional literary modes, were nevertheless vitally interested in poetry and fiction. Decades after their beginning, the Beats lived on to an extent in the ideals of the Naropa Institute, a colony established in Boulder, Colorado, in 1973 by the Tibetan lama Chogyam Trungpa. Ginsberg and Anne Waldman, a poet and director of the St. Mark's Poetry Project in Greenwich Village, organized the Jack Kerouac School of Disembodied Poetics at Naropa in 1975. In 1982, the Naropa

Institute marked a high point with an enthusiastic celebration of the twenty-fifth anniversary of the publication of *On the Road*.

Bibliography

Charters, Ann, ed. *The Beats: Literary Bohemians in Postwar America*. Detroit: Gale, 1983. This is an exceptional bibliography both of the Beats—sixty-eight individuals are discussed—and of works about them. Critical essays treat individual writers, and Jennie Skerl has compiled a chronology of twenty-five years of Beat history. An invaluable resource.

Foster, Edward Halsey. *Understanding the Beats*. Columbia: University of South Carolina Press, 1992. Foster studies Kerouac, Burroughs, Ginsberg, and Corso, stressing their rebellion against conformity and materialism. They were also genuine writers for whom language and aesthetics were of paramount concern, and Foster examines their influence on other writers.

French, Warren. *The San Francisco Poetry Renaissance, 1955-1960*. Boston: Twayne, 1991. An admiring and perceptive study that is good on the Beat sensibility, the women in the movement, Beats and the American tradition, and the people on the fringes. The annotated bibliography will point the beginner to everything important, including two Kerouac newsletters.

Parkinson, Thomas, ed. *A Casebook on the Beat*. New York: Thomas Y. Crowell, 1961. An excellent anthology of Beat writing and some of the very best of the early critical commentary. Besides essays by Kenneth Rexroth, John Sisk, Norman Podhoretz, and John Ciardi, there are pieces by Dorothy Van Ghent, Warren Tallman, Henry Miller, Paul O'Neil, Herbert Gold, Carolyn Gaiser, and Lawrence Lipton. Parkinson contributes a fine summary essay.

Stephenson, Gregory. *The Daybreak Boys: Essays on the Literature of the Beat Generation*. Carbondale: Southern Illinois University Press, 1990. Major essays on Kerouac, Ginsberg, Burroughs, Corso, John Clellon Holmes, Michael McClure, and "The Literary Legend of Neal Cassady."

Frank Day

Cross-References

The Dada Movement Emerges at the Cabaret Voltaire (1916), p. 419; Eliot Publishes *The Waste Land* (1922), p. 539; Surrealism Is Born (1924), p. 604; "Angry Young Men" Express Working-Class Views (1950's), p. 1454; Warhol's *The Chelsea Girls* Becomes a Commercial Success (1966), p. 2053.

TELEVISION ENTERS ITS GOLDEN AGE

Category of event: Television and radio
Time: The 1950's
Locale: New York, New York

Between 1950 and 1959, television went from reaching a small slice of a relatively affluent group of Americans to an audience including 90 percent of all American households

Principal personages:
EZEKIAL GATHING (1903-1979), a United States congressman, chairman of the House Committee on Un-American Activities
FRANK STANTON (1908-　　), the president of the Columbia Broadcasting System, 1946-1971
SYLESTER "PAT" WEAVER (1908-　　), the president and chairman of the National Broadcasting Company, 1949 to 1956
NEWTON MINOW (1926-　　), the chairman of the Federal Communications Commission, 1961 to 1962

Summary of Event

The first public demonstration of television took place at the World's Fair in New York City in 1939. Before the new industry could get under way, World War II intervened and America's attention was directed elsewhere. It was not long after the war, however, before the television industry was reborn and, starting in the early 1950's, began to enter the American mainstream.

Television's impact started slowly but soon made rapid headway. At the outset of the 1950's, television sets remained a fairly expensive luxury item, owned by less than 10 percent of the American population. By 1955, television had entered half of America's homes, and by 1959 it had reached 90 percent. Most of America was watching what many critics consider to be the most innovative programming in television history.

The "Golden Age of Television" refers as much to America's warm embrace of the new invention as to the critically acclaimed live programs that aired during this period. Much heralded were the live, intellectually stimulating weekly dramatic plays, which ran the gamut from classics such as Henrik Ibsen's *A Doll's House* (1880) to works by contemporary playwrights such as Arthur Miller, Rod Serling, and Gore Vidal. Also included among these weekly performances was television's first ninety-minute live dramatic anthology program, *Playhouse 90*, voted the greatest network series of all times in a 1970 *Variety* poll. Also lauded were the live variety shows and comedy routines of the period. The live format constantly tested the quick-witted skills of such performers as Jack Benny, Red Skelton, Arthur Godfrey, Jackie Gleason, Martha Raye, George Burns, Gracie Allen, Sid Caesar, and "Mr. Television" himself, Milton Berle.

There are two reasons for this Golden Age, reasons that also foreshadowed the end of the Golden Age. The first was the rapid expansion of programming to meet the seemingly insatiable demand of the public. Programming steadily increased during the 1950's. In 1950, the four networks combined produced ninety hours of programming a week; by the end of the decade each of the three remaining networks (DuMont folded in 1955) was producing this much programming weekly. This constant pressure to produce more and more would cut into the creative juices of the writers and force network executives to turn from the emphasis on quality noticed in the first half of the decade to the emphasis on quantity that surfaced later. Ultimately, the live format of such top-rated shows as *Texaco Star Theatre* and *Colgate Comedy Hour* would give way to Hollywood-set shows that took up considerably less of the network's time and studio personnel. This move away from quality was also a result of the public's moral sensibilities, which, according to Ezekial Gathing's congressional investigation in 1952 and 1953, were upset because of the moral issues raised by live dramatic performances of works such as *A Streetcar Named Desire* (1947) and the routines of many comedians, whose uncensored remarks and caustic comments sometimes went beyond the bounds of what some considered decent.

The second reason for television's Golden Age rests with the rise of the networks, which initially encouraged creativity and spontaneity on television. During the second half of the 1940's, the networks had little control over programming. What was on television rested largely with the sponsors, or, more specifically, with the advertising agencies that handled the sponsors. These agencies and sponsors were notoriously dictatorial; they had little to no interest in the programs other than how they conveyed an image of the sponsor. The sponsors' rules were simple: Never offend a single viewer. The networks set out in 1950 to destroy the sponsors' heavy-handed, self-serving policies.

The networks' war with the sponsors was made clear in policies formulated by Frank Stanton, who headed the Columbia Broadcasting System (CBS), and Pat Weaver, network chief at the National Broadcasting Company (NBC). CBS and NBC were the two dominant networks at the opening of the decade. Weaver, in particular, led the charge by assembling some of the best talent available and producing, in the mid-1950's, big-budget, network-produced, specially scheduled live programs that had no other motives behind them but to build an audience by entertaining the public. The concern of the network shifted, from "Will the public like the product that brings it the show?" to "Will the public enjoy the show?" Of these two approaches, the latter certainly was less dictatorial, freeing program content to tackle more challenging issues and themes.

The Golden Age of Television coincides with the decline in sponsor-dominated shows during the 1951-1952 season and stretched into the 1956-1957 season, which saw the launch of the last major live dramatic program, *Playhouse 90*. The enthusiasm and experimentation with various formats that marked the early 1950's was already waning by mid-decade. The shift away from quality programs was given impetus by Congressman Gathing's moralistic crusade, which would result in thematic self-censorship not only by the networks but by the book and film industries as well. The shift to quantity over quality was prompted further by the demands of the public, which turned away from NBC and CBS's live formats to the canned, staged-set shows that the rival American Broadcasting Company (ABC) began to offer in the 1955-1956 season with a new Western series produced in Hollywood, *Cheyenne.* The success of this show soon led to a host of imitators, including seven of the top ten shows in the 1958-1959 season: *Gunsmoke, Wagon Train, Have Gun Will Travel, The Rifleman, Maverick, Tales of Wells Fargo,* and *Wyatt Earp.* These and similar staid shows led Federal Communications Commission chairman Newton Minow in 1961 to dub television a "vast wasteland." The Golden Age of live, provocative, socially relevant plays and comedic satire was officially pronounced dead.

Impact of Event

In the postwar 1940's, radio was the primary pastime of Americans, followed closely by attendance at film theaters, which reached an all-time high during this period. As Americans turned increasingly to television in the early 1950's, spending an average of twenty-five hours per week in front of their sets, their time had to come from somewhere. It came from other leisure-time pursuits and dramatically affected the other forms of pretelevision entertainment, as well as just about every other aspect of American life.

Radio was the parent of television. Both NBC and CBS had invested heavily in radio and even used some of their radio profits to finance the final stages of television development. Television shows themselves at first were little more than radio shows with pictures; *Amos 'n' Andy* and *Burns and Allen* simply transferred their skits to a visual format. Soon the television child was outshining its radio parent. Sponsors, reluctant to leave radio at first, saw the child grow to adulthood and shifted their advertising dollars to television, cutting radio's revenue in half almost overnight. Having nothing to play on the air that was not on television and needing revenue, radio appeared to have little future. It was rescued by a new musical format, rock and roll, from which television shied away because the new music was too raw and too untamed. Radio itself initially was reluctant to be associated with this scurrilous music for fear of losing listeners and sponsors, but deserted by its primary adult listeners, radio found the teenage market through rock and roll. The dramatically changed format gave radio a comfortable spot alongside television.

Like radio, films had been an American obsession almost from their inception. Films remained strong through the Depression and the war years, having some of their best years immediately following World War II. Movie moguls initially ignored television as nonthreatening because of the small picture screen. They soon discovered their error, as audiences deserted film theaters throughout the 1950's. To stay competitive, the film industry tried all kinds of technological gimmicks: 3-D, Panavision and Cinemascope, and Circle-Vision. The last of these survived for decades at Disney theme parks around the globe. Other strategies also were employed.

Lower-quality films ("B movies"), particularly Westerns, had been coopted by television. Hollywood abandoned this segment and tried to make a big impact with multimillion-dollar blockbusters. Additionally, Hollywood films all went to color, and more pictures were filmed on location, leaving the large studio lots looking like deserted ghost towns of the Old West. The days of the film studio appeared numbered. Studios managed to survive by changing their condescending attitude toward television in the mid-1950's, by freeing their stars from the prohibition against appearing on television and by selling old films to the networks, giving birth to the Sunday night movie. Studios also began using their production talent and stage and sound lots to begin making films designed for the networks.

Unlike radio and films, newspapers were not affected immediately by television, largely because programming was limited in the early 1950's to the time between 8:00 P.M. and 11:00 P.M. There was still time to read the morning and evening newspapers before turning one's attention to television. Television began to expand its programming in the mid-1950's to "fringe hours" (just before prime time) and introduced fifteen-minute news programs. Formats were extended even further during the late 1950's to include daytime hours and talk shows, which were peppered with news items. This expanded programming cut into newspaper readership, especially after 1963, when NBC and CBS debuted the first thirty-minute news segments. Expanded programming and the move into news are considered to be major reasons for the demise of the evening newspaper across America, though they did not affect morning editions dramatically. Nor did television affect the number of books published, since the less faithful book readers had earlier gone over to radio and films. Television did affect library circulation, which plummeted in the 1950's, most noticeably for fiction. It thus directly affected the type of books published. A move toward nonfiction titles is one of the most prominent trends since the introduction of television.

During the 1950's, television accounted for one-third of all leisure-time activity, dramatically affecting other forms of leisure. It affected, directly or indirectly, just about every other nuance of life as well. Little remained untouched by television. Family dining shifted, turning many dining rooms into places used solely to entertain guests. Television gave rise to TV dinners and the TV tray. Crime has been found in some studies to be related to television, because television makes people more aware of what they could, but do not, have, as well as showing crime as an everyday event. Television has been found to increase knowledge of the world and its events, curiosity, interest in sex, and verbal ability. It also has been found to increase consumer demand and to stimulate desire for immediate gratification, aggressive behavior, and ethnic stereotyping, while decreasing physical activity, creativity, and attention span. Whether for better or for worse, television has become part of everyday life around much of the globe.

Bibliography

Barnouw, Erik. *Tube of Plenty: The Evolution of American Television.* 2d rev. ed.

New York: Oxford University Press, 1990. An outstanding in-depth study of television as it passed through its growth stages. Of special interest because of its discussion of the development and impact of certain shows on television, such as Edward R. Murrow's confrontation with Senator Joe McCarthy. Pictures.

Boddy, William. *Fifties Television: The Industry and Its Critics.* Urbana: University of Illinois Press, 1990. One of the most detailed accounts of television in the 1950's. Boddy challenges the popular critical notion of television's Golden Age and sees the period less from the standpoint of high cultural, live programming than as a time of trial-and-error experimentation in order to discover viewers' program preferences.

Comstock, George. *The Evolution of American Television.* Newbury Park, Calif.: Sage Publications, 1989. The dean of television analyzes the medium's roots in economic and social consideration of the 1940's and 1950's as key to understanding the specific form and content of television programming for the next three decades. He appraises the new medium as less revolutionary than evolutionary.

Harris, Jay, comp. and ed. *TV Guide: The First Twenty-five Years.* New York: New American Library, 1980. Articles and schedules from *TV Guide* from the time of its birth in April, 1953. The sixteen-page color section depicting personalities who have graced the cover of *TV Guide* is itself an illustrated history of television. Numerous pictures.

Steinberg, Cobbett. *TV Facts.* New York: Facts on File, 1980. A detailed breakdown of prime-time shows on all networks, including DuMont, from 1950 to 1980. The information is presented in six parts: programs, viewers, ratings, advertisers, awards and polls, and networks and stations. Replete with easy-to-read charts and graphs.

John Markert

Cross-References

NBC Launches American Television at the World's Fair (1939), p. 1143; NBC and CBS Launch Commercial Television (1941), p. 1211; NBC Broadcasts the World Series (1947), p. 1362; ABC Begins Its Own Network Television Service (1948), p. 1368; Variety Shows Dominate Television Programming (1948), p. 1383; "Mr. Television," Milton Berle, Has the Top-Rated Show (1948), p. 1394; *Kukla, Fran, and Ollie* Pioneers Children's Television Programming (1948), p. 1400; *The Red Skelton Show* Becomes a Landmark on Network Television (1951), p. 1520; *I Love Lucy* Dominates Television Comedy (1951), p. 1525; *Dragnet* Is the First Widely Popular Police Show (1951), p. 1531; *Amahl and the Night Visitors* Premieres on American Television (1951), p. 1536; ABC Makes a Landmark Deal with Disney (1954), p. 1612; *The Tonight Show* Becomes an American Institution (1954), p. 1623; *Gunsmoke* Debuts, Launching a Popular Television Genre (1955), p. 1668; *The Honeymooners* Enchants Audiences of All Ages (1955), p. 1673.

TELEVISION FAMILY COMEDY BECOMES EXTREMELY POPULAR

Category of event: Television and radio
Time: The 1950's
Locale: The United States

Post-World War II parents found the baby-boom culture they were creating mirrored in family oriented television comedies that played up the humor of family life and played down the stresses and difficulty

Principal personages:

OZZIE NELSON (1907-1975), the producer, director, head writer, and star of *The Adventures of Ozzie and Harriet*, who turned his real-life family into a prototype of the 1950's television family

DONNA REED (DONNA BELLE MULLENGER, 1921-1986), an actress who epitomized the television mom and suburban housewife yet who began to break out of the stereotype in the final seasons of her starring vehicle *The Donna Reed Show*

ROBERT YOUNG (1907-), a film and radio actor who made the transition to television as the archetypal omniscient and moralizing father in *Father Knows Best*

DANNY THOMAS (AMOS JACOBS, 1914-1991), the producer and star of *Make Room for Daddy* (later called *The Danny Thomas Show*)

JACKIE GLEASON (1916-1987), the actor who portrayed Ralph Kramden in *The Honeymooners* and Chester Riley in *The Life of Riley*

WILLIAM BENDIX (1906-1964), an actor who re-created the role Jackie Gleason had established four years earlier in a successful revival of *The Life of Riley*

JERRY MATHERS (1948-), one of television's most memorable "cute kids," the star of *Leave It to Beaver*

Summary of Event

The post-World War II advent of commercial television programming in the United States coincided with the return of millions of American servicemen with two clear goals: starting a family and forgetting the war. Thus, an ideal format for comedy in the first decade of the television era was family-oriented escapism. Though the production of such shows was a perfect fit for the young television industry, it later proved to be a major source of criticism, leveled at 1950's television. Beginning in the 1970's, critics complained that early family comedies had been too escapist, had not dealt with important issues, had made Dad too omniscient, Mom too submissive, and the kids too well-behaved. Such shows, critics complained, were not "real."

There is some truth to such complaints, though only a partial truth. It is true that the image of the family represented by early television sitcoms was idealized; by definition, the ideal is not the real. Yet the idealized Dad was not always omniscient; there was a second character type, the bumbling father, who was much more common in the 1950's. The archetypes of the omniscient father, *Father Knows Best*'s Jim Anderson (played by Robert Young) and *Leave It to Beaver*'s Ward Cleaver (Hugh Beaumont) were later arrivals who made their debuts in 1954 and 1957, respectively. The first television entry in the bumbling father school was *The Life of Riley*'s Chester Riley (Jackie Gleason), which premiered in 1949.

The prototype for the bumbling father, though, was Ozzie Nelson, who played himself in the radio series *The Adventures of Ozzie and Harriet*, beginning in 1944. The creation of the type was to some extent a fluke: Nelson did not set out to typify the American father, but rather tried to use a gentle form of self-deprecating humor to offset the fact that he was placing himself on center stage. In 1952, *The Adventures of Ozzie and Harriet* began a twelve-year television run that made Nelson the epitome of the bumbling father. If anything, the television Ozzie was the direct opposite of the real-life Nelson: ineffectual and wishy-washy on television, Nelson was by all accounts a firm and demanding director and father. Furthermore, Nelson's real-life accomplishments were tremendous; he was, at various times, the starting quarterback for Rutgers University's football team, a law-school graduate, a composer, a musician, and a big-band leader in the heyday of swing bands. The only thing "unreal" about the on-screen Nelson was that he wrote his character smaller than life, not larger.

Yet there was something about the pathos of the bumbling father image Ozzie created that appealed to radio and television audiences. Whether Americans saw themselves—or their own fathers or husbands—in the character, or whether the type's ridiculousness made viewers feel superior, audiences loved the character. In American television, success spawns imitation.

On October 4, 1949, Jackie Gleason made his television debut in *The Life of Riley*. The Chester Riley character he created was even more hapless than the on-screen Ozzie Nelson. Nelson may have been klutzy, stammering, and ineffectual, but his life-style was clearly that of the upper-middle class. In fact, the often-asked question "What did Ozzie do for a living?" indicated a leisure unknown to Chester Riley, a working stiff who worked hard and yet who barely managed to support himself and his wife, Peg (Rosemary DeCamp). When William Bendix took over the role in 1953 (and Marjorie Reynolds took over the role of Peg), the character became if anything even more pathetic. In the same year, Stu Irwin created another bumbling father in *The Trouble with Father*.

The kind of television wife exemplified by Peg Riley was not universal, but represented one of the limited female types in early television. Another was the "supermom" type, usually married to the "omniscient dad"; supportive, domestic, yet glamorous, supermom cooked and cleaned in pumps and pearls. The quintessential supermom was Donna Reed; on her show, she, not her television husband Alex Stone (Carl Betz), was the star. The show's title sequence, and the way it changed over the course of eight seasons, told the tale. In the early years, Reed was shown getting her children (Paul Petersen and Shelley Fabares) ready for school and her husband ready for work. In the last two seasons, with her children grown and women's roles changing, Reed herself is seen leaving with a briefcase—though not until after she has taken care of her family. June Cleaver (Barbara Billingsley) of *Leave It to Beaver,* Margaret Anderson (Jane Wyatt) of *Father Knows Best,* and Harriet Nelson of *The Adventures of Ozzie and Harriet* were other examples of the supermom type; it was Reed, though, who made the character the star.

Similarly, Theodore ("The Beaver") Cleaver (played by Jerry Mathers) made the "cute kid" character the star of *Leave It to Beaver.* His predecessors were Ricky Nelson of *The Adventures of Ozzie and Harriet,* Bud Anderson (Billy Gray) of *Father Knows Best,* and Rusty Williams (Rusty Hamer) of *Make Room for Daddy.* Beaver typically disturbed the idyll of the American family dream by his penchant for getting into trouble, but the trouble was usually mild and was always corrected by wise and stern counsel from omniscient dad Ward Cleaver (Hugh Beaumont).

These character types—dad, either bumbling or omniscient; wife, either supermom or shrew; kids, cute but slowly growing into mature copies of mom and dad—dominated television family comedies for almost two decades. Yet the types, and the family comedies that presented them, would not survive the 1960's.

Impact of Event

If one had to pick a year to mark the end of the first family sitcom era, 1966 would be a good candidate. The year marked the end of two archetypal series: *The Adventures of Ozzie and Harriet,* with its classic bumbling father, and *The Donna Reed Show,* with its classic supermom. It was also the year *Family Affair* appeared, but even that show's advent demonstrated the change in the idealized American family. The traditional nuclear family, while still the norm, was shown to be less than universal. *Family Affair*'s cute kids Buffy and Jody (Anissa Jones and Johnnie Whitaker) and teenager Sissy (Kathy Garver) were orphaned and were reared by their Uncle Bill (Brian Keith); the genteel butler Mister French (Sebastian Cabot) became a surprising source of the maternal element. *Family Affair* was the first step in the mutation of the television nuclear family from 1966 to 1984, when Bill Cosby brought the archetype back to life.

The idea of a bachelor uncle playing an omniscient father type was not unique to *Family Affair.* John Forsythe played a similar role in *Bachelor Father* from 1957 to 1962, though without the cute kids; he reared a teenage niece. Bob Cummings, in *Love That Bob* (1955-1959), came close to the formula; the program showed him living with his widowed sister and her teenage son, to whom Cummings was a father figure. The fragmentation of these nuclear families, however, was always the result of an earlier death (divorce was never mentioned), and such fragmentation was always remedied before the series began—with the "bachelor father" solution or with remarriage, as in *Make Room for Daddy, The Brady Bunch* (1969-1974), or *Eight Is Enough* (1977-1982). The unique and drastic solution of writing out the children turned Doris Day from a widowed mother of two boys to a career single in the last season of *The Doris Day Show* (1968-1972).

By the mid-1970's, however, it was time for television to admit that divorce existed. Norman Lear, whose antitype of the 1950's family sitcom, *All In the Family* (1969-1978), had heralded the end of the genre, introduced the first divorced mother in situation comedy on *One Day at a Time* (1975-1984). The following season saw the emergence of *Alice* (1976-1985), a show with virtually the same premise.

The change from escapism to what Lear's eulogists called "dealing with the issues" in family comedy was apparently irreversible. When the family shows that had not survived 1966 attempted comebacks or "reunions," the families had changed. Danny Thomas fared worse as grandparent than parent in *Make Room for Granddaddy* (1970-1971). The "generation gap," which did not exist for Rick and Dave Nelson in *The Adventures of Ozzie and Harriet*, surfaced in Ozzie's abortive comeback *Ozzie's Girls* (1972-1973), in which two college women (including the only African-American regular on Ozzie's shows) rented the boys' room. *The Father Knows Best Reunion* (1977), a made-for-television film, presented an Anderson family beset by all the problems that did not exist on screen in the 1950's—including divorce, infidelity, and marital strife. A television film reuniting the *Leave It to Beaver* cast, *Still the Beaver* (1984), which led to a short-lived cable-television show, depicted a middle-aged Beaver still turning to his mother for advice after being divorced and losing his job. The initial offering of a short-lived 1988 comeback for *The Brady Bunch* dealt with the alcoholism of one of the now-grown Brady children.

Although the family comedy genre was represented only by such failed revivals in the 1970's, it returned in substantially its original form in the 1980's behind the success of *The Cosby Show* (1984-1992). Though many critics praised Cosby for breaking the 1950's mold of the omniscient father, a more accurate analysis may be that he revived the bumbling father character without making him an incompetent. Cosby's character Cliff Huxtable was an obstetrician, and his wife, Claire (Phylicia Rashad), was a lawyer. The focus of the show was clearly the family, and except for a few segments "dealing with issues," the plots and conflicts were surprisingly like those of the 1950's—revolving around dating, duties, and discipline.

The Cosby Show was not alone in reviving the family comedy. The same year, 1984, saw *Family Ties* rise to fifth place in the ratings, with *The Cosby Show* third. In the two following seasons, *Family Ties* held second place in the ratings behind *The Cosby Show*, which remained television's top-rated show until 1989 (and in the top five until it's voluntary retirement in 1992). *Family Ties* had a premise that bridged the gap between the "innocent" 1950's and the "relevant" 1970's. The show's parents, who had been committed to the counterculture of the 1960's and 1970's, found themselves as the "establishment" of the 1980's, with children as alienated from their values as they had been from those of their own parents.

A third entry in the family comedy renaissance, *Growing Pains*, was stigmatized as a white version of *The Cosby Show* or, at best, a blatant imitation of *The Cosby Show*'s successful formula. Since *Growing Pains* appeared a year after *The Cosby*

Show's premiere and followed a similar pattern, with a medical father (psychiatrist this time) and professional mother (a reporter), such criticism was understandable. Considering the patterns of the early television sitcoms, however, it may be more accurate simply to say that *Growing Pains*, like *The Cosby Show* and *Family Ties*, brought the 1950's television family into the 1990's. Though the 1990's also brought the popularity of situation comedies such as *Roseanne, Married . . . with Children*, and *The Simpsons* that satirized the genre, the success of the family-comedy format in the 1980's was a clear legacy of the shows of the 1950's and 1960's.

Bibliography

Eliot, Marc. *American Television: The Official Art of the Artificial.* Garden City, N.Y.: Doubleday, 1981. Highly subjective criticism of virtually every prime-time television show before 1981. Evaluates all the shows mentioned above. The criticism tends to be revisionist, debunking many myths about 1950's television; the book thus serves as a contrast to the Ozzie Nelson and Danny Thomas autobiographies listed below.

Hough, Arthur. "Trials and Tribulations—Thirty Years of Sitcom." In *Understanding Television*, edited by Richard Adler. New York: Praeger, 1981. While this article only mentions in passing the television shows discussed above, it provides a comprehensive overview of the genre of television situation comedy from 1950 to 1980 and places the family comedy in a wider context.

Nelson, Ozzie. *Ozzie.* Englewood Cliffs, N.J.: Prentice-Hall, 1973. Autobiography of the creator of *The Adventures of Ozzie and Harriet.* This book offers an insider's look at one of the prototypical family comedies of early television. Written shortly before Nelson's death, and before the future of family comedy was clear, the book demonstrates no awareness of the changes that took place in the genre in the 1960's and 1970's.

Newcomb, Horace. *TV: The Most Popular Art.* Garden City, N.Y.: Anchor Press, 1974. Of interest mostly for its second chapter, "Situation and Domestic Comedies," this book, though by a leading academic authority on television, is written in a popular style. The chapter studies the family comedy in general rather than specific shows.

Thomas, Danny, with Bill Davidson. *Make Room for Danny.* New York: Putnam, 1991. Published just before Thomas' death, this autobiography offers many behind-the-scenes glimpses of the family comedy *Make Room for Daddy.* Though the early portion of the book concerns Thomas' film and radio career, a good portion is devoted to his television show.

John R. Holmes

Cross-References

Television Enters Its Golden Age (1950's), p. 1465; *I Love Lucy* Dominates Television Comedy (1951), p. 1525; *The Honeymooners* Enchants Audiences of All Ages

(1955), p. 1673; Situation Comedies Dominate Television Programming (1960's), p. 1835; *The Flintstones* Popularizes Prime-Time Cartoons (1960), p. 1840; *The Dick Van Dyke Show* Popularizes Situation Comedy (1961), p. 1908; *All in the Family* Introduces a New Style of Television Comedy (1971), p. 2234; *The Jeffersons* Signals Success of Black Situation Comedies (1975), p. 2339; *The Cosby Show* Makes Television History (1984), p. 2532; *The Simpsons* Debuts, Anchoring the Fledgling Fox Network (1990), p. 2652.

KUROSAWA'S *RASHOMON* WINS THE GRAND PRIZE AT VENICE

Category of event: Motion pictures
Time: 1951
Locale: Venice, Italy

The unexpected victory of Rashomon *at the Venice Film Festival established Kurosawa's international reputation and brought Japanese cinema to the attention of the West*

Principal personages:
AKIRA KUROSAWA (1910-   ), Japan's best-known film director, famous for his epic productions and humanist values
TOSHIRO MIFUNE (1920-   ), the greatest actor of the Japanese cinema and the star of many of Kurosawa's movies
RYŪNOSUKE AKUTAGAWA (1892-1927), the writer of the short stories upon which Kurosawa based *Rashomon*

Summary of Event

When *Rashomon* was entered in the 1951 Venice Film Festival at the prompting of Italian producer Guilliana Stramigioli, who had seen and liked it upon release the previous year, nobody in the Japanese film industry expected the film to do well. After all, this was a peculiarly Japanese film set in the medieval Heian period, which seemed unlikely to be of interest to a Western audience. Certainly, its director, Akira Kurosawa, had not made *Rashomon* with an international audience in mind, but Venice loved it. The Venice prize was, at the time, the biggest honor in world cinema; its award to *Rashomon* hinted at the riches of an until then almost-unknown cinema and established the reputation of Kurosawa as its most internationally powerful practitioner.

Kurosawa had begun work as an assistant editor in 1936 under Kajiro Yamamoto, the man he credited with being his only teacher. In 1941, Kurosawa directed part of Yamamoto's patriotic *Uma* (*Horses*), and in 1943 he made *Sugata Sanshirō* (*Sanshiro Sugata*), a martial-arts movie. In 1948, Kurosawa's eighth film as a director, *Yoidore tenshi* (*Drunken Angel*) starred Toshiro Mifune, whom Kurosawa had recently discovered, as a cruel young gangster dying from tuberculosis. Mifune played opposite Takashi Shimura—who had worked on most of Kurosawa's previous films—and these two remained the director's major stars for many years, the central elements of an ensemble of talented actors who reappeared from film to film. At this point, Kurosawa temporarily left Tokyo to work at the other center of Japanese film production, the ancient capital of Kyoto, where many period films were made. There, in 1950, after making three more films all starring Mifune and Shimura, he directed *Rashomon*.

Rashomon is a film about the subjective nature of reality and the ways in which one's sense of oneself—one's egotism—determines the way one sees and understands events. The film opens in the shadow of the ancient and massive ruined gate of Rashomon, outside Kyoto. A woodcutter (Shimura) and a priest (Minoru Chiaki), sheltering there from the pouring rain, describe to a passing peasant (Kichijiro Ueda) four versions of the rape of a woman and the death of her husband, events that happened three days before and that they have heard recounted at a police inquiry. After the woodcutter, who claims to have witnessed the events, has described how he came to be in the forest dell where the events took place, the story is told first by the bandit and rapist, Tajomaru (Mifune), then by the wife (Machiko Kyo), then— relayed through a medium—by the dead husband (Masayuki Mori), and finally by the woodcutter himself. Each succeeding version of the "truth" denies the previous one, and the film offers no obvious way of determining which story or combination of stories is most reliable. The priest and the woodcutter seem much more horrified by the conflicting evidence than by the nature of the crime. At the end of the film, the three men hear the cry of a baby that they discover abandoned in a corner. The peasant takes an amulet from the child's arm and goes off, proclaiming that all men are selfish and dishonest and need to be so in order to survive. The woodcutter, however, declares that he will rear the child with his own family. This gesture, the priest says, allows him to retain his faltering faith in the goodness of man. *Rashomon*'s source lies in two classic stories by Ryūnosuke Akutagawa, derived in their turn from a twelfth century collection of Japanese tales. Kurosawa sticks fairly closely to the Akutagawa tales, but the finding, robbing, and caretaking of the baby is his addition, one in which many critics have seen a hope and compassion for humanity that would otherwise be missing from *Rashomon* and that is characteristic of Kurosawa's philosophy.

Rashomon's exploration of individual motivations and multiple points of view is reminiscent of Orson Welles's *Citizen Kane* (1941)—which Kurosawa had not seen— but offers no equivalent to the final clue to Kane's motivations presented in the American film. Like *Citizen Kane*, however, *Rashomon* is important—and was rewarded in Venice—as much for its cinematic qualities as for its moral or message. *Rashomon* is typical of Kurosawa's films in its use of weather and landscape to comment on the action. The scenes in the forest where the rape and murder take place are played out in brilliant sunshine and amid the shifting shadows of the trees. The rain at the gate provides a striking contrast, symbolic of the anguish and obscurity against which the characters are struggling. At the end, as the woodcutter leaves with the child, the sun is shown beginning to break through. The scene also illustrates another characteristic of *Rashomon*: the "180-degree cut," in which the camera is positioned first looking in one direction and then the opposite. Thus, the woodcutter is first shown from behind with the stationary priest in the foreground; the scene is then presented from the other side, so that the priest is in the background. Kurosawa also used "hard-edged wipes," a technique in which a scene is changed by one shot "pushing" the preceding image off the screen, as if a line were passing across it. Western audiences were not used to such abrupt changes, which, like the complex series of flashbacks that constitute the narrative, tend to draw attention to the construction of the film. The deliberate emphasis on the film's construction was an obvious connection to the worldwide modernist movement in the arts that flourished in the first half of the twentieth century.

Impact of Event

With *Rashomon*'s success in Venice, the Japanese film industry in general and Kurosawa in particular became objects of interest to filmmakers and filmgoers everywhere. Rarely has a national cinema been so abruptly brought to world attention. Kurosawa gradually came to be seen as the representative of a group of humanists working in the Japanese cinema. His films that followed *Rashomon* typically concerned integrity to self and the attainment of peace through suffering. In contrast to Japanese traditions of feudalism and strict obedience to others, Kurosawa's work emphasized individuals coming to terms with themselves. If this can be achieved, his work often suggests, then there is hope for humanity even in the bleak world of *Rashomon*—or of the atomic bomb, which haunts the background of his 1991 release *Rhapsody in August*, set in contemporary Nagasaki.

Despite his success with *Rashomon* and such brilliant follow-ups as *Ikiru* (1952) and *Shichinin no samurai* (1954; *The Seven Samurai*), Kurosawa's desire to make epic films with expensive sets, his use of three cameras to shoot many scenes, his high shooting ratio (a measure of the amount of film shot relative to the amount used in the final film), and his attention to detail often made it hard for him to get financing for films. For this reason and because of his success abroad, Kurosawa, despite his often very Japanese concerns, became one of cinema's earliest international directors. In 1975, he made *Dersu Uzala* in the Soviet Union, and in 1980, *Kagemusha* (*Kagemusha: The Shadow Warrior*) was financed partly with American money under the auspices of George Lucas and Francis Ford Coppola. Both films won major film festival awards.

Kurosawa has great respect for and has clearly been influenced by the Western movies of John Ford, and Kurosawa, in his turn, has influenced the American cinema. Thus George Lucas' extraordinarily successful *Star Wars* (1977) is based on Kurosawa's *The Hidden Fortress* (1958), which, in its use of landscape and characterization, is reminiscent of Ford. *The Seven Samurai* and *Yojimbo* (1961), another samurai film, have been remade in the West as, respectively, *The Magnificent Seven* (directed by John Sturges in 1960) and *A Fistful of Dollars* (Sergio Leone, 1964). Kurosawa's influence is evident, too, in "revisionist" Westerns, such as those made by Sam Peckinpah, that question Hollywood's Western stereotypes. Meanwhile, the modernist traits of *Rashomon* and other complexly narrated Kurosawa movies such as *Ikiru* have influenced such avant-garde films as Alain Resnais and Alain Robbe-Grillet's *L'Année dernière à Marienbad* (1961; *Last Year at Marienbad*), in which the viewer can never be sure what has happened and in which the nature of storytelling, and thus filmmaking, is the primary concern.

In Japan, Kurosawa has had few imitators, although the work of Masaki Kobayashi, whose best-known film is the extremely long three-part *Ningen no Joken* (1959-1961; *The Human Condition*), a meditation on the immorality of war, shares many of his concerns. While Kobayashi was struggling to make his masterpiece, a "new wave" was breaking in Japanese cinema just as it was—in the work of François Truffaut and Jean-Luc Godard—in France. The leading figure in Japan, Nagisa Oshima, and his contemporaries in this movement had little time for Kurosawa's humanist philosophy and psychologically motivated characters, preferring a radical break with such "realist" traditions in cinema. Nevertheless, a movie such as Oshima's *The Man Who Left His Will on Film*, which is concerned with the unknowability of events and which presents several different versions of a film a dead man may have shot prior to his murder or suicide, evidently replays many of the themes and questions of *Rashomon*. Oshima has followed Kurosawa in finding international sources of funding for his films; *In the Realm of the Senses* (1976), his most widely known film in the West, was largely French-financed.

Many of Kurosawa's films take as their theme the master-disciple relationship that develops between two, almost always male, characters. Toshiro Mifune, who played the disciple role in the early films, progressed to that of the master in later films, and it is perhaps Mifune, rather than any director, upon whom Kurosawa's influence has been greatest. Although recognized around the world primarily for his portrayal of warring samurai in such films as *The Seven Samurai*, *Yojimbo*, and *Sanjuro* (1962), Mifune played many very different roles for Kurosawa, from the dying gangster of *Drunken Angel* to the benevolent industrialist of *Tengoku to Jigoku* (1963; *High and Low*). Mifune has credited Kurosawa for his development as an actor and for bringing him to notice both in Japan and elsewhere. He has praised him as an artist of extraordinary power and depth.

Kurosawa's victory in Venice not only influenced future production but also led to greater interest in older Japanese directors, of whom Yazujiro Ozu and Kenji Mizoguchi are the most prominent. Their films are perhaps slightly less accessible to Western audiences and more steeped in typically Japanese concerns and aesthetics than are most of Kurosawa's, but together they represent the best of the formidable achievement of the Japanese cinema.

Bibliography

Bock, Audie. *Japanese Film Directors.* New York: Kodansha International, 1978. Discusses ten major directors, including Kurosawa. Bock sees Kurosawa as a humanist who makes films about individual integrity that have become increasingly universal in their appeal. Filmography to 1975.

Burch, Noel. "Kurosawa Akira." In *To the Distant Observer: Form and Meaning in the Japanese Cinema*, edited by Annette Michelson. Berkeley: University of California Press, 1979. The best account of the history of Japanese cinema, Burch's book discusses Japanese culture and is theoretically sophisticated. Sees postwar Japanese cinema, with its closer relation to the Hollywood model, as inferior to that of the "golden age" between 1930 and 1945. Kurosawa's work, however, is viewed as an exception. Many stills.

Desser, David. *Eros Plus Massacre.* Bloomington: Indiana University Press, 1988. Excellent survey of films by the Japanese new-wave directors such as Oshima, whose work both develops and reacts against Kurosawa's.

Erens, Patricia. *Akira Kurosawa: A Guide to References and Resources.* Boston: G. K. Hall, 1979. Lists articles on Kurosawa, sources for his films, and distributors of his work in the United States. Filmography to 1977.

Kurosawa, Akira. *Something Like an Autobiography.* Translated by Audie E. Bock. New York: Alfred A. Knopf, 1982. Kurosawa's own, very accessible, account of his early influences and filmmaking up to *Rashomon*'s success at Venice. Intriguing insights into the making of the early films.

McDonald, Keiko. *Cinema East: A Critical Study of Major Japanese Films.* Rutherford, N.J.: Fairleigh Dickinson University Press, 1983. Detailed accounts of various Japanese films from the 1950's and 1960's, including *Rashomon*, which is analyzed through its symbolism of light and dark as a masterly account of human pride and egotism.

Richie, Donald. *The Films of Akira Kurosawa.* Berkeley: University of California Press, 1965. Film-by-film account of Kurosawa's work up to *Akahige* (1965; *Red Beard*). Sees Kurosawa as a philosopher working in film whose central message is one of hope against the odds in a cruel world. Many stills, excellent filmography to 1965.

_____. *Japanese Cinema.* Garden City, N.Y.: Doubleday, 1971. Includes much material on Kurosawa, who is depicted as the star of the postwar flowering of Japanese cinema and is ranked with the much more traditional Ozu as Japan's greatest directors. Richie considers *The Seven Samurai* the best Japanese film ever made. Some Kurosawa material repeats information in the earlier book.

_____, ed. *Focus on "Rashomon."* Englewood Cliffs, N.J.: Prentice-Hall, 1972. Collection of essays on *Rashomon* and its success at Venice.

Sato, Tadao. *Currents in Japanese Cinema.* Translated by Gregory Barrett. New York: Kodansha International, 1982. Collection of writings by Japan's leading film critic ties films to social and cultural movements, includes perceptive comments on Kurosawa's major themes, and provides a Japanese perspective on Japanese cinema. Highly readable and entertaining. Excellent chronology of the main events in Japanese film history.

Chris Lippard

Cross-References

Ford Defines the Western in *Stagecoach* (1939), p. 1115; Welles's *Citizen Kane* Breaks with Traditional Filmmaking (1941), p. 1200; Westerns Dominate Postwar American Film (1946), p. 1313; Leone Renovates the Western Genre (1964), p. 1984; Kawabata Wins the Nobel Prize in Literature (1968), p. 2147.

THE NEW NOVEL (*LE NOUVEAU ROMAN*) EMERGES

Category of event: Literature
Time: 1951
Locale: France

The "antinovel" content and styles of their works reflected the fact that traditional novel form could not express the New Novelists' views of the world or preoccupations with the role of writing

Principal personages:

MICHEL BUTOR (1926-   ), a novelist, playwright, poet, and critic who expressed his views on literary form and the writer's role

ALAIN ROBBE-GRILLET (1922-   ), a novelist and filmmaker who in *For a New Novel* (1963) gave a formal statement of the New Novelists' preoccupations and goals

NATHALIE SARRAUTE (1900-   ), a French novelist of Russian birth who in *The Age of Suspicion* (1956) was among the first to state her opinions on the possibility of truth in literary representation

MARGUERITE DURAS (1914-   ), a novelist, playwright, and filmmaker whose worldview is profoundly and sensuously interpreted in semi-autobiographical narratives relating human rapports and social abuses

Summary of Event

Although works by Nathalie Sarraute (*Tropismes*, 1938, 1957; *Tropisms*, 1963), Claude Simon (*Le Tricheur*, 1945), and Marguerite Duras (*Les Impudents*, 1943) had appeared years earlier, the birth of the New Novel movement has been situated in 1951 with the publication of Samuel Beckett's *Molloy*. Since the interwar period in France, writers had been expressing various aspects of their dissatisfaction with the style of the traditional novel. The antinovel style and content of *Molloy* made a jolting statement of the impossibility of communication in an incomprehensible and uncaring world. In a sense, this placed Beckett in a leader's role, but unlike previous literary trends, this movement never constituted a homogeneous group from the point of view of either style or content of the works. The unifying factor was instead the preoccupation of all of its writers with the problems of literature and of reading. That is, beginning with Sarraute's *L'Ère du soupçon* (1956; *The Age of Suspicion*, 1963) and continuing in the writings of both Alain Robbe-Grillet (*Pour un nouveau roman*, 1963; *For a New Novel*, 1965) and Michel Butor (*Répertoire I*, 1960; *Répertoire II*, 1964; *Répertoire III*, 1968), these and other writers of their times expressed their doubts about the validity of writing when the author must suspect the words of his own characters. They believed that writing became an impossibility because the writer no longer believed in his or her characters, and so the reader would not. Thus Beckett's universe of alienation and silence was the inheritance of the New Novelists. The style of the New Novel is typified in two ways. The first is the "death of the character," that is, presenting beings in their ultimate honesty, stripped of subjective descriptive qualities that would classify them traditionally as personae. Second is obsession with ambiguity and doubt in thematic development rather than chronological development of a plot from beginning to end.

Jean-Paul Sartre's essay "What Is Literature?" (1947) expressed the ideas of the French avant-garde at the time and opened the way for the continued discussion of the disenchantment with literary forms that stifled rather than expanded the ability to express the life of the new age. The sense of dissatisfaction both with society and with the means of expressing that feeling arose with the existentialists but became more all-encompassing with those who immediately followed. Eugène Ionesco, Arthur Adamov, and Samuel Beckett, all of whom had matured in the influence of Dadaism, Surrealism, James Joyce, and the general literary aestheticism of Paris since the interwar years, gave voice to this angry feeling of alienation. They differed from the existentialists in believing that there was no possibility of personally bringing about change or of communicating. Thus it was with the "voices of silence," the combined cacophony of the surrounding world and the absence of voice or communication, that the New Novelists wrote to their public. The alienation of the hero seen in the existential novel continued as a thread in the New Novel, but the philosophy did not prevail. There is no exit, no salvation, for the character of the New Novel. The world is beyond his or her reach, and though some characters in the New Novel world strive for understanding of this world or for participation in it, it remains separated from them and continues its relentless grind.

What, then, was the purpose of writing or of reading? This question is the grist of the New Novel mill. All of those who wrote in the New Novel style were writing about style. They were analyzing for their public, who often remained mystified, the essence of writing as a process of communication and of reading as a means of reception. New Novel creations are often conglomerates of styles, including narrative, dialogue, music, encapsulated objects, and blank space. In this sense, they show a descent from Stéphane Mallarmé, the Symbolist poets, the Surrealist writers, and artists such as Marcel Duchamp, whose artworks contain various objects and bits of writing yet are presented as paintings on a canvas. Writers of the New Novel movement sought the participation of the reader in the act of creativity. Each writer in his or her own way involved the reader and used the reader's personal knowledge and experiences to broaden the content and effect of a work. Novels, plays, films, and musical works such as Butor's opera, *Votre Faust: Fantaisie variable genre Ópera* (1962) were given alternative sequences or alternative endings from which an audience or a reader could choose or draw conclusions. Some works essentially erased and rewrote themselves as they grew on paper.

The public's reception of the New Novel was not immediately positive. Many readers found the New Novel incomprehensible or boring because there was no plot or action to follow in the traditional sense. Others found exhilarating the stimulation of the joint activity of reading and participating in the work's creation. The movement continued to develop and to pose its questions to the reading and viewing public, with more works appearing in cinematic as well as book form.

The New Novel's appearance formalized the fact that these writers were making statements about the form and reception of literature that needed to be heard and deserved to be considered. It is generally agreed that the movement became recognized as such in the early 1950's. Its writers were sometimes called "le groupe de Minuit" (the Midnight Novelists) after the Paris firm Les Éditions de Minuit, whose owner, Jérôme Lindon, took the risk of publishing their works.

Impact of Event

In receiving the New Novel, the public split into two groups that saw the content of these works quite differently. Because the works did not describe characters or background or follow chronological sequencing, the public considered them difficult to read. Because of their desire to break with traditional form and identify their literature with their times, the writers treated subjects and created works that were not enthusiastically received in literary circles either. Although they became well established as literary figures, these writers and their works were considered worthless or scandalous by those upholding the standards of literature. A quarter of a century passed before a public developed for the New Novel. Though never easy reading, the subject matter and forms became the norm of twentieth century literary production, and through the influence of these writers the public gained an awareness of the need for a literature that expressed the social, political, and very personal complications that constituted their world.

Michel Butor's novel *La Modification* (1957; *A Change of Heart*, 1959) received the Prix Théophraste-Renaudot in 1957 and is esteemed for the precision of its narrative structure. His narrative reflects the earlier twentieth century masters Marcel Proust, André Gide, and Jean-Paul Sartre in its attention to stylistic detail. His novels and essays on the art of writing demonstrate a profound level of erudition and the sincere desire that humanity share the pleasure of the creative experience. His early works *Passage de Milan* (1954), *L'Emploi du temps* (1956; *Passing Time*, 1959), and *Degrés* (1960; *Degrees*, 1963) share many of the technical aspects of Robbe-Grillet's works of the same period. Later works such as *Mobile: Étude pour une représentation des États-Unis* (1962; *Mobile: Study for a Representation of the United States*, 1963), *Matière de rêves* (1975), and *Boomerang* (1978) illustrate the many-leveled thought and dream times of storytelling that echo the Surrealists' attempts at automatic writing. Butor's technique, however, tries to lead the reader into parallel exploration of his or her own consciousness and experiences and thus to fuller appreciation through participation in the creativity of reading.

Alain Robbe-Grillet achieved a level of general appreciation by the public as a result of his brilliant spokesmanship for the movement and his filmmaking. His work *L'Année dernière à Marienbad* (*Last Year at Marienbad*), filmed with director Alain Resnais, received the grand prize at the 1961 Venice Film Festival. Robbe-Grillet became the unifying force that fused into one school a great variety of writers who stood in agreement on what they were against in literary style. He founded two prizes (the Prix des Critiques and the Prix Médicis) to promote new literary talent, was for years a principal reader for Les Éditions de Minuit, and gave his time and support to younger writers in their efforts to publish.

Nathalie Sarraute perhaps did the most to change the way readers were to look at characters in a story. Her fiction, such as *Tropisms, Le Planétarium* (1959; *The Planetarium*, 1960), and *Les Fruits d'or* (1963; *The Golden Fruits*, 1964) reports the unconscious mannerisms, attractions, aversions, and even perversions of human beings in social contact. Her behavioral studies show that, like plants, humans have tropisms that reveal their true feelings. Her special aptitude is that, like Marcel Proust, she makes relevant statements about love, affection, hypocrisy, and the failings of bourgeois society's standards. In *The Age of Suspicion*, she was the first to state what the new literature was to be about. It was time to renew the idea of writing because the character had become suspect. The reader would no longer believe in the traditional character because the literary lie no longer applied to the new age. The effect that Robbe-Grillet later termed *nouveau roman-homme nouveau* (new novel-new man) had already made its appearance.

Marguerite Duras expresses deep anger at social abuses past and present, yet all the personal stories she tells become universal through her technique of detached-voice story relation. The "voices" of Duras speak softly and monotonously in the background of her scenes. As though these speakers have seen and experienced all in some distant time or place, they soothe the pain or horror of the reality being enacted. Thus it becomes bearable to read or to view the indescribable abuses human beings inflict upon each other. It is also through this detachment that the reader is moved beyond the level of sensual experience to know the depth of human love and becomes aware of the infinite possibilities for good that Duras finds at the core of a person's being. In the novels *Moderato Cantabile* (1958; English translation, 1960) and *Le Vice-consul* (1966; *The Vice-Consul*, 1968), the screenplay and film *Hiroshima mon amour* (1960), and the prose-play-film *India Song* (1973), Duras tells her life's story in both real and fictionalized representations. The stark truth she tells about herself creates an intimacy and a universality that enable her to express the feelings of abused womankind and abused humanity.

An emphasis on language and the need to express every aspect in its minutest detail, seen particularly in the works of Robbe-Grillet and Butor, are elements of all the New Novelists' works. The obsession with the description of things has been called an escape from reality, but Robbe-Grillet states that the things are just a means of proving that there is no objective reality. The minutiae of his descriptions in *Last Year at Marienbad* and *La Jalousie* (1957; *Jealousy*, 1959), for example, prove that each person makes his or her own reality and that the will to choose happiness can be the source of hope for the new age.

Bibliography

Fletcher, John, and John Calder, eds. *The Nouveau Roman Reader.* London: John

Calder, 1986. Calder writes comprehensive and perceptive introductions to the postmodern situation, the New Novel, and the eight authors whose works are featured. Partial bibliography of each author's works (English and French versions) and selected critical bibliography. The introduction on postmodernism is for readers with thorough knowledge of literary history and criticism; the remainder is for general readers.

Heath, Stephen. *The Nouveau Roman: A Study in the Practice of Writing.* Philadelphia, Pa.: Temple University Press, 1972. Describes the importance of the practice of writing for the novelists and critics of the New Novel era. Each of four authors is treated in detail. Select bibliography of authors' works, books and special numbers of periodicals dealing with the New Novel, and New Criticism on writing. For readers with knowledge of and interest in the development of the novelists' techniques and literary criticism related to writing technique in the postmodern era. Index of proper names and titles.

Le Sage, Laurent. *The French New Novel: An Introduction and a Sampler.* University Park: Pennsylvania State University Press, 1962. General résumé of the history and development of the movement. Discusses psychology, characterization, narrative structure, device, and style. Gives general bibliographical references for discussions of the New Novel. General introduction for each author and selection. A good introductory work.

Mercier, Vivian. *The New Novel from Queneau to Pinget.* New York: Farrar, Straus & Giroux, 1971. Introduction describes foundations of and people involved in the New Novel, then discusses precursors and finally achievements of the movement. In-depth discussion of the style and content of each author's work, with ample examples given. Selective bibliography of each author's works (English and French versions) and of criticism for each author. Index of proper names and titles.

Rahv, Betty T. *From Sartre to the New Novel.* National University Publications Series in Literary Criticism. Port Washington, N.Y.: Kennikat Press, 1974. Brief introduction to the New Novel, centered on the idea of narrative perspective. Chapters treat the Sartrian fictive mask, manipulation of person and time in Sartre, Albert Camus, Sarraute, Robbe-Grillet, and Butor. Select bibliography of general articles on the New Novel, special periodical issues dealing with the New Novel, and works on Sartre, Camus, and Robbe-Grillet.

Sturrock, John. *The French New Novel: Claude Simon, Michel Butor, Alain Robbe-Grillet.* New York: Oxford University Press, 1969. Factual and practical introduction to the meaning of the New Novel. Sturrock explains where and when the term originated and what its writers stood for and against. Simon's, Butor's, and Robbe-Grillet's concepts, works, and successes are explained clearly. Select bibliography of philosophical and literary background for the movement, with most entries in French. Bibliography of full-length studies and special periodical issues treating the New Novel, all in French. Bibliography of authors' works and select criticism for each author, all in French.

Patricia A. Struebig

Cross-References

Proust's *Remembrance of Things Past* Is Published (1913), p. 355; *The Metamorphosis* Anticipates Modern Feelings of Alienation (1915), p. 396; Joyce's *Ulysses* Epitomizes Modernism in Fiction (1922), p. 555; Celine's *Journey to the End of the Night* Is Published (1932), p. 890; Sartre's *Being and Nothingness* Expresses Existential Philosophy (1943), p. 1262; Beckett's Trilogy Pushes Against the Frontiers of Fiction (1951), p. 1498.

A STREETCAR NAMED DESIRE
BRINGS METHOD ACTING TO THE SCREEN

Category of event: Motion pictures
Time: 1951
Locale: The United States

When Elia Kazan and Marlon Brando collaborated on A Streetcar Named Desire, *they created a landmark film that influenced directorial and acting techniques in the ensuing four decades*

Principal personages:

ELIA KAZAN (ELIA KAZANIOGLOU, 1909-   ), a stage and film director, actor, writer, and producer who introduced method acting to the movies

MARLON BRANDO (1924-   ), an actor who brought his naturalistic stage performance as Stanley Kowalski to the film and significantly changed movie acting styles

VIVIEN LEIGH (VIVIAN MARY HARTLEY, 1913-1967), a British stage and screen actress who won an Academy Award for her role in *A Streetcar Named Desire*

TENNESSEE WILLIAMS (1911-1983), a dramatist, short-story writer, poet, and novelist who wrote the play and screen versions of *A Streetcar Named Desire*

Summary of Event

On September 20, 1951, the film version of Tennessee Williams' Pulitzer Prize-winning drama *A Streetcar Named Desire* opened at New York's Warner Theater. This landmark film was created by the combined talents of Tennessee Williams, who wrote the screenplay; the director Elia Kazan, who also had directed the original Broadway production in 1947; the actors, Marlon Brando, Vivien Leigh, Karl Malden, and Kim Hunter, the last three of whom won Academy Awards; and finally, the art director Richard Day and set designer George James Hopkins, who also won Academy Awards.

Kazan had been an actor-producer-director for the Group Theatre in the 1930's, and in 1947 he, along with Lee Strasberg and Cheryl Crawford, organized the Actors Studio, which taught the method acting techniques pioneered by the Russian actor and director Konstantin Stanislavsky, cofounder of the Moscow Art Theater. Brando, a stellar graduate of the Actors Studio, first played the story's protagonist, Stanley Kowalski, in the original Broadway production, and after making his screen debut as an embittered paraplegic in *The Men* (1950), he electrified the public and gained stardom with his revolutionary performance in the 1951 film. Kazan employed almost the same Broadway cast, replacing Jessica Tandy with Vivien Leigh, who had played the female lead, Blanche DuBois, in a London production directed by her husband Laurence Olivier. Twelve years after her role as the headstrong Southern belle Scarlett O'Hara in *Gone with the Wind* (1939), Leigh played the sensitive and doomed Southern dreamer who is raped and driven to insanity by the twentieth century ape-man Kowalski.

A Streetcar Named Desire is a landmark film for three related reasons: its blending of theatrical and naturalistic elements; the method acting of Brando; and finally, the complexity of its characters and the uncompromising nature of its mature themes and subject matter. Kazan blended Williams' characteristic lyricism and realism into a highly theatrical, symbolic, and naturalistic production that captured the essence of the conflict between Blanche and Stanley. Kazan artfully balanced scenes of poetic sensibility with brutal confrontations. For example, Blanche's mesmerizing reconstruction of her haunted past, filmed on a pier fronting a dance hall made spectral by swirling fog and a shimmering lake, is followed by her abortive birthday party, during which Stanley disgustingly licks his fingers and then smashes plates against the wall as he attacks Blanche's checkered past. Williams' artistic magic found its ideal presenter in Kazan, who explained that it was "a beautiful play that I shot without softening or deepening . . . because there was nothing to change."

Leigh and Brando established their characters through their different acting styles. Blanche is slight, sensitive, sultry, and confused. In the beginning of the film, she steps through the steam at the train station into vision like a sleepwalker. At Stella's apartment, Blanche is always bathing, as she tries to cleanse herself of her sordid past. Stanley is stubbornly hostile, sweating in his stained T-shirt, unregenerate in his earthiness, and determined to rip apart her life.

His rape of Blanche is consummated on the night Stella has given birth, and the attack is signified by the cracked mirror and the washing of the dirty street the next morning. Stanley has won the intense cat-and-mouse game with the pathetic Blanche, and although Stella is appalled at what has happened to her sister, it is obvious that after a period of anger she will return to the arms of her barbaric husband, because they need each other. Kazan, Brando, Leigh, Malden, and Hunter captured the essence of Williams' unflinching vision of "the ravishment of the tender, the sensitive, the delicate, by the savage and brutal forces of modern society."

At the end of the film, as Blanche is led away by two nameless and ominous representatives of the institutional world, a poker game, the round of bestial life, goes on, with Stanley as its leader. Brando translated the brutal, domineering psychology of Kowalski into an unpredictable, menacing, and explosive presence. Leigh invested Blanche with a ghostly, spiritual aura. The sneering Kowalski pursues her relentlessly in the close and tawdry confines of their Elysian Fields flat; they engage in a dance of death to the accompaniment of Alex North's sensual and raw jazz score. Although the actual rape is not presented, the film serves as a milestone in the depiction of sexual relationships. For, in a sense, the entire film is an intense assault inflicted by Stanley's insistent physicality and brutal psychological need to strip Blanche of her pretensions.

Three years after the appearance of *A Streetcar Named Desire*, Kazan and Brando collaborated again to create another major film, *On the Waterfront* (1954), for which they both won the Oscars that had eluded them in 1951. In addition, Eva Marie Saint won the best supporting actress award, Budd Schulberg the Oscar for best writing, Boris Kaufman the best cinematography Oscar, and Richard Day, the art director for *A Streetcar Named Desire*, the award for best art direction. In this exposé of waterfront gangsterism, Brando played Terry Malloy, a tough longshoreman with a Kowalski-like philosophy of life, who, unlike Stanley, undergoes a process of moral regeneration through the love of Edie Doyle. In the guise of the reformed Terry Malloy, Stanley Kowalski passed into the mainstream of American film as the sensitive brute with a capacity for violence, honesty, and regeneration.

Impact of Event

A major tenet of method acting is that the director and actor become so closely involved that they serve as mirrors of each other's creativity. Elia Kazan and Marlon Brando achieved this kind of productive involvement in their films. Kazan's background in the Group Theatre and Actors Studio gave him a respect for the written script and method acting, which he defined as psychology turned into behavior. Kazan made poetry out of the common elements of life and invested acting with a naturalism that conveyed the psychological conflicts of the characters.

After *A Streetcar Named Desire* and *Viva Zapata!* (1952), Kazan and Brando next teamed together for *On the Waterfront*, in which Terry Malloy informs on his father-figure, waterfront gangster Johnny Friendly. As a sanctified informer, Terry is an idealized validation of Kazan's testifying against friends before the House Un-American Activities Committee in 1952. After he was attacked for "naming names," Kazan transformed his personal tensions into notable films, including, in addition to *On the Waterfront, East of Eden* (1955), *Baby Doll* (1956; written by Tennessee Williams), and *America, America* (1963). Kazan's films exerted an important influence on Sidney Lumet, who in 1959 directed the *Fugitive Kind*, which starred Brando and which was based on Williams' *Orpheus Descending;* on Arthur Penn, who in *The Left-Handed Gun* (1958), *Mickey One* (1965), and *Bonnie and Clyde* (1967) used Paul Newman and Warren Beatty as disaffected heroes; and, finally, on John Cassavetes, whose improvisational techniques and exploration of blue-collar angst in *Shadows* (1960), *Faces* (1968), *Husbands* (1970), and *Woman Under the Influence* (1974) made him Kazan's closest heir.

Marlon Brando initiated a revolution in American acting with his role as Stanley Kowalski, for which he employed method acting techniques as a new means of naturalistic self-expression. Brando embodied the voices of angry young men who were both brutish and sensitive but who hid their vulnerability under grunting exteriors. As Richard Schickel has remarked: "This untutored, unspoken sensitivity informed all of Brando's early roles, and the suspense in all of them revolved around whether or not he would acknowledge his best self, articulate his aspirations and his pain." Brando's great accomplishment was to make self-consciousness and self-doubting visible.

In *A Streetcar Named Desire*, Kazan and Brando prepared the way for some of the most exciting actors and directors of the next four decades. Although the method acting approach was derided by some critics as the "grunt and groan" school of acting, its techniques provided the impetus for a naturalistic style of American performing that also influenced the "angry young men" of England, such as Richard Burton in *Look Back in Anger* (1958), Albert Finney in *Saturday Night and Sunday Morning* (1960), and Richard Harris in *This Sporting Life* (1963). It is no coincidence that many of Brando's acting heirs had roles as athletes, usually boxers, whose competitive viciousness must be disavowed in order for them to develop into decent human beings.

In 1955, James Dean appeared in two movies, Nicholas Ray's *Rebel Without a Cause* and Kazan's *East of Eden*, in which he played sensitive, troubled, and unpredictable heroes who desire to discover who they are. Dean did not have the bullying presence of Brando, but he did convey a similar yearning for authenticity, which he transmitted by idiosyncratic physical and verbal gestures.

In two roles as a brutish strongman and fading heavyweight boxer, Anthony Quinn followed Brando's style. As Zampano in Federico Fellini's *La Strada* (1954), he played a cruel circus strongman who abuses and deserts his mute consort Gesolmina. After her death, he feels remorse and recognizes the magnitude of his resulting solitude. As the victimized heavyweight boxer Mountain Rivera in *Requiem for a Heavyweight* (1962), he tries to find a new life after fourteen years of boxing beatings, but he is thwarted by his exploitative manager and becomes a clownish wrestler. Quinn's groping and gruff attempts to find respectability make him a tragic figure of unrealized worth.

Paul Newman, as Rocky Graziano in Robert Wise's *Somebody Up There Likes Me* (1956), rises to the top of the middleweight ranks after he learns to leave behind his loutish, tough-guy persona. Newman mimics Graziano's New York accent and his bouncy walk to achieve a winning style. In 1976, a second cinematic Rocky, played by Sylvester Stallone, also achieved greatness inside and outside the ring. Earlier in his acting career, Stallone had expressed the desire to play Kowalski; in *Rocky*, Stallone's character is a blend of Kowalski and Malloy who works as a waterfront enforcer and a part-time club fighter. He is a never-was who gets a second chance and overcomes all odds to save himself and his shy girlfriend.

As Jake La Motta, Robert De Niro played another troubled boxer-bum in Martin Scorsese's *Raging Bull* (1980). In *Mean Streets* (1973), *Taxi Driver* (1976), *New York, New York* (1977), *The King of Comedy* (1982), and *GoodFellas* (1990), Scorsese and De Niro established a reciprocal artistic relationship similar to that enjoyed by Kazan and Brando. In *Raging Bull*, De Niro fulfilled method acting's injunction to inhabit the role from the inside out by gaining sixty pounds to play the bloated La Motta, who brutalized himself, his family, and his opponents. After his traumatic arrest and disgrace, Jake begins a comeback as a comic actor who practices Terry Malloy's celebrated "I could have been somebody" speech in front of a mirror.

Although some critics have attacked the excesses of Kazan and Brando's respective styles, when these artists collaborated on *A Streetcar Named Desire*, they created a milestone film that influenced future directors and actors and expanded the psychological and sexual boundaries of the cinema. Through the intelligence and intensity of their involvement, they asserted that films have moral, social, political, and psychological importance.

Bibliography

Kazan, Elia. *Elia Kazan: A Life.* New York: Alfred A. Knopf, 1988. An 850-page reconstruction of Kazan's eventful life. Kazan discusses his fruitful personal and artistic relationships with Tennessee Williams and Marlon Brando. He also provides fine insights into the many decisions he had to make to satisfy the conflicting artistic and moral forces involved in the filming of *A Streetcar Named Desire.*

Manvell, Roger. *"A Streetcar Named Desire."* In *Theater and Film.* Rutherford, N.J.: Fairleigh Dickinson University Press, 1979. Manvell clearly identifies the elements that made the play great and then explains how the movie developed from the play and at the same time diverged from it to establish its own effectiveness. Contains a dated bibliography on film and theater and an appendix listing dramatists whose plays have been filmed.

Murphy, Brenda. *Tennessee Williams and Elia Kazan: A Collaboration in the Theatre.* Cambridge, England: Cambridge University Press, 1992. Murphy provides an excellent discussion of Kazan's work with the Group Theatre and Actors Studio and then shows how he brought these methods to the stage version of *A Streetcar Named Desire.* Murphy details the complexities of the relationship between Kazan and Williams, as these two artists merged their respective talents into a writing and directing partnership. Contains an extensive bibliography on Williams and Kazan.

Phillips, Gene. *"*Elia Kazan: *A Streetcar Named Desire* and *Baby Doll.*"* In *The Films of Tennessee Williams.* London and Toronto: Associated University Presses, 1980. Phillips' discussion of the film version of *A Streetcar Named Desire* provides important insights into the ways Kazan and the Breen Office conflicted over its mature aspects: homosexuality, carnality, and the rape of Blanche. Phillips astutely describes the symbolic ways Kazan managed to convey these themes without directly presenting them. Contains selected bibliography and filmography up to 1980.

Schickel, Richard. *Brando: A Life in Our Times.* New York: Atheneum, 1991. Schickel provides not only an account of Brando's life and career but also an assessment of what his stage and film roles have meant to his art and audiences. Schickel traces the dimensions and significance of Brando's various roles as Stanley Kowalski, Terry Malloy, Fletcher Christian, and Don Corleone and shows how his performance as the lonely and embittered Paul in *Last Tango in Paris* (1972) is the culmination of the first two decades of his career. Contains many pictures and a short bibliography and filmography.

Frank Ardolino

Cross-References

Stanislavsky Helps to Establish the Moscow Art Theater (1897), p. 1; The Group Theatre Flourishes (1931), p. 874; Kazan Brings Naturalism to the Stage and Screen (1940's), p. 1164; Blacklisting Seriously Depletes Hollywood's Talent Pool (1947), p. 1340; *La Strada* Solidifies Fellini's Renown as a Brilliant Director (1954), p. 1596.

YOUNG READERS EMBRACE *THE CATCHER IN THE RYE*

Category of event: Literature
Time: 1951
Locale: Boston, Massachusetts

J. D. Salinger's The Catcher in the Rye *popularized the rebellious but sensitive young protagonist, providing a different kind of role model for the disillusioned youth of the 1950's*

Principal personage:
> J. D. SALINGER (1919-   ), a college dropout, soldier, recluse, and writer who published only one novel

Summary of Event

The Catcher in the Rye was published on July 16, 1951. Reviewing it on the day of publication, *The New York Times* called it "an unusually brilliant first novel." The *Saturday Review* praised it as remarkable, and the *Chicago Tribune* found it "engaging and believable." Although not all reviews were so favorable, the book climbed to number four on *The New York Times* best-seller list and stayed on the list for almost thirty weeks.

The literary impact of J. D. Salinger's first (and only) novel was not immediately predictable. Not until the mid-1950's did *The Catcher in the Rye* become a talisman for disaffected adolescents on college campuses across America. Since then, it alternately has enjoyed the dubious distinction of being the book most often banned in schools as well as being required reading in freshman English classes. Innumerable essays have analyzed and psychoanalyzed the personality of the protagonist, Holden Caulfield, but despite any conclusions drawn by literary critics or Parent-Teacher Associations, *The Catcher in the Rye* continues to reach out and affect adolescents going through the turmoil of growing up.

The Catcher in the Rye was published when J. D. Salinger was thirty-two years old. Although he began to write at the age of fifteen and had short stories published in magazines when he was twenty-one, this was his only novel. Prior to its appearance, Salinger had twenty-one short stories published in such popular magazines as *Collier's, Esquire, The Saturday Evening Post,* and *The New Yorker.*

These stories can be classed in three categories. "The Young Folks" (1940) and several other early works deal with social mores, family ties, artistic frustrations, and loss of innocence. The second group of stories derives from Salinger's experiences in World War II. In 1942, Salinger was drafted and trained as a special security agent in the Army Counter-Intelligence Corps. He landed in Normandy on D day and took part in five campaigns in the European theater. His stories about the war range from one-pagers with surprise endings to explorations of the effects of the war on families. In "Last Day of the Last Furlough" (1944), Holden Caulfield makes his first appearance as a missing soldier. Holden's character continues in the postwar stories "I'm Crazy" (1945) and "Slight Rebellion Off Madison" (1946). In 1946, Salinger submitted a ninety-page novella about Holden Caulfield that he later withdrew. Although Holden appeared in seven stories, it was not until 1951 that Salinger thought that his novel about this sensitive, disturbed sixteen-year-old was ready for public scrutiny.

With *The Catcher in the Rye*, Salinger became a household name. He was not well equipped to handle fame. Just before *The Catcher in the Rye* was published, he escaped to Britain to avoid the public's reception of his work. He made his publisher promise not to send him any reviews and was annoyed that the original issue had his photograph on the back cover.

When he returned from Britain, Salinger dealt with his newfound celebrity status as best he could. He moved to an apartment in New York City and attempted to fit in with the literary crowd. In March, 1952, he went on a trip to Florida and Mexico. Upon his return, he decided to abandon New York for a cottage in the small town of Cornish, New Hampshire. He moved in on his thirty-fourth birthday and lived there in as much seclusion as possible.

Salinger did not publish for two years after the success of *The Catcher in the Rye*. On January 31, 1953, *The New Yorker* magazine printed "Teddy," a story that reflected Salinger's growing interest in Eastern philosophy and the teachings of the Hindu mystic Sri Ramakrishna. Between 1953 and 1965, Salinger wrote stories exclusively for *The New Yorker*. These were later published in the collections *Nine Stories (1953)*, *Franny and Zooey* (1961), and *Raise High the Roof Beam, Carpenters and Seymour: An Introduction* (1963). Salinger's only post-1953 story not to be included in a collection was the last: "Hapworth 16, 1924" (June, 1965). The stories that followed *The Catcher in the Rye* predominantly involve various members of the Glass family, which Salinger had introduced in earlier stories. There is no further mention of Holden Caulfield.

Salinger did not write anything for publication after 1965. His attempts to elude public attention were thwarted several times. In 1974, an unauthorized edition of previously uncollected stories was printed by unidentified parties. Salinger brought suit against the San Francisco booksellers who were distributing the pirated material and finally won in 1986. Also in 1986, Ian Hamilton, a British writer, attempted to publish an unauthorized biography containing private material. Salinger obtained a restraining order. Two federal courts upheld his case, which was finalized when the U.S. Supreme Court refused to review these previous verdicts. A permanent injunction was issued, but this did not prevent Hamilton and his publishers from releasing a redrafted book entitled *In Search of J. D. Salinger* (1988).

Another disturbing invasion of Salinger's privacy came in 1988. John Lennon's assassin, Mark David Chapman, identified with Holden Caulfield and quoted from *The Catcher in the Rye* at his trial. The novel's influence on the murderer was dramatized in *The Man Who Shot John Lennon*, a documentary broadcast on British television and the American Public Broadcasting Service *Frontline* program.

Since 1965, it would seem that the impact of Salinger's *The Catcher in the Rye* has been overshadowed by the aura of mystery surrounding the author himself. Occasionally, a journalist will claim to have been granted an interview. Most of these "scoops" are brief and uninformative; one actually was a hoax that earned the writer a lawsuit. In W. P. Kinsella's novel *Shoeless Joe* (1982), J. D. Salinger was written in as a character who is kidnapped and taken to a baseball game. In this fantasy, Salinger speaks openly of his life and work. Perhaps this is Kinsella's way of compensating for the curiosity about the secretive man who wrote one of the most cherished and controversial novels of post-World War II literature.

Impact of Event

The theme of man against society is a common one. Literature and drama abound with heroes who put their individuality above the structured dictates of a rigid society, sometimes at the cost of their freedom or life. From Cyrano de Bergerac to Captain Ahab to Huck Finn, these protagonists stimulate rebellious natures, compelling action based on an instinct of what is the right, as opposed to the socially acceptable, thing to do. Salinger provided the youth of the 1950's and subsequent decades with just such a protagonist in the person of Holden Caulfield, hero of *The Catcher in the Rye.*

Caulfield is a sixteen-year-old who has just been expelled from his third prep school. Rather than return home to his parents' wrath, he decides to take a brief vacation in New York. Freed from the demands of school, classmates, and family, Caulfield roams the city for forty-eight hours. The reader, as his constant companion, shares his every thought and adventure. Caulfield is intensely sensitive and profoundly disturbed by just about everything. He feels sorry for people but cannot seem to get along with anyone other than his ten-year-old sister, Phoebe. Tormented by the angst of adolescence, he imagines himself being a "catcher in the rye," preventing innocent children playing in a field from falling off a cliff. In Caulfield's mind, this will keep them safe from the danger of growing up into a world of corrupted "phonies."

Tragically, Caulfield's rebellion is ineffectual. Life is not static. He cannot hold back change. His strike for independence and a sense of meaning is negated by his youth, inexperience, and overprotective upbringing. He does not have a personal quest or goal, merely an intense disgust for things as they are. All of his actions are thus in vain, resulting in more harm (usually to himself) than accomplishment.

In the aftermath of World War II, the Cold War and increasing materialism contributed to a dearth of spirituality and morality. In 1950, David Riesman published *The Lonely Crowd: A Study of the Changing American Character*, a sociological study of the alienated individual torn between existential autonomy and the comfort of conformity. Holden Caulfield personified this struggle.

By the mid-1950's, the teenage revolution was in full swing. Movies such as *Rebel Without a Cause* (1955) and *The Wild One* (1954) turned James Dean and Marlon Brando into idols. For teenagers in the working class, leather jackets and motorcycles became essential symbols of the rebellion. On university campuses, however, *The Catcher in the Rye* was being rediscovered after a hiatus in popularity. Holden Caulfield's futile search for honesty and "something noble to die for" reached out to the middle-class students who saw themselves as disillusioned intellectuals. Holden was elevated to the top of "best loved" student polls. Salinger gained the reputation as spokesperson for the young and was sought after as a guest speaker, much to his dismay.

The popularity of *The Catcher in the Rye* has not diminished with the decades. Although a product of the late 1940's, Holden Caulfield continues as a symbol of youthful rebellion against conformity. Scholars have contended that the Civil Rights movement and the Vietnam War gave purpose to Holden's passive nihilism, providing a motive for his anger. Readers associated Holden with antiwar antiheroes John Yossarian in Joseph Heller's *Catch-22* (1961) and Billy Pilgrim in Kurt Vonnegut's *Slaughterhouse-Five: Or, The Children's Crusade, a Duty-Dance with Death* (1969). These books provided intellectual arguments supporting the protest movements of the 1960's and 1970's.

The intensely emotional soul searching of adolescents seeking to define themselves in an adult world is universal and timeless. *The Catcher in the Rye* has gained worldwide recognition as a post-World War II classic and is required reading in many high schools and colleges. Holden Caulfield's popularity, however, has always gone hand in hand with notoriety. Vulgar language and sexual content have caused *The Catcher in the Rye* to be banned so often that the *American School Board Journal* of 1973 called it "the most widely censored book in the U.S." Educators, parents, and literary critics label it as obscene, profane, and scandalous, removing it from library shelves and reading lists. Teachers who have assigned the book have been reprimanded or fired. Although the banning of *The Catcher in the Rye* appears to be on the wane as sensibilities change with the times, this same censorial scrutiny began in the 1980's and 1990's to be directed toward art exhibits and rap music lyrics. The conflict between freedom of speech and the protection of children from harmful material warrants discussion in the home, classroom, and court of law.

Some critics believe that exposure to controversial material is not as critical as the way in which it is presented by the teacher. Context is as vital as content. Misinterpretations can have dire consequences, as in the case of John Lennon's assassin, Mark David Chapman. Chapman identified strongly with Holden Caulfield. He believed that he was protecting the innocence of Lennon, who was about to be corrupted by commercialism. Chapman did not understand that this rationale contradicts Holden's conclusion at the end of the book, which is that "if they (children) fall off, they fall off."

The Catcher in the Rye is perhaps the most popular and the most censored novel of post-World War II America. It has been labeled "great," "true," "perverse," and "immoral." Holden Caulfield has been called "the new American hero," "a sorry little worm," and "a very normal specimen of his age." This broad spectrum of opinion dictates that readers judge for themselves.

Bibliography

Belcher, William F., and James W. Lee, eds. *J. D. Salinger and the Critics.* Belmont, Calif.: Wadsworth, 1962. Essays written within a decade of the publication of *The Catcher in the Rye.* Interesting because they are dated, these studies critique the novel and Salinger's stories up to *Franny and Zooey.* Contains an amusing section called "Suggestions for Study and Writing" that probably was relied upon heavily by teachers of the 1960's. Incomplete bibliography and extensive list of "Critical Studies."

French, Warren. *J. D. Salinger, Revisited.* Boston: Twayne, 1988. Intelligent look at Salinger's work by a retired university professor who published his first book on Salinger in 1963. Brief and nonintrusive biography followed by thoughtful critiques. Chronology, references, and selected bibliography.

Hamilton, Ian. *In Search of J. D. Salinger.* New York: Random House, 1988. Salinger biography by a self-indulgent writer. This is the "authorized" version of the biography that Salinger took to court as an invasion of privacy. The last section describes the legal action in great detail; one can almost hear the author whining as the Supreme Court refused to reopen the case. References.

Salzman, Jack, ed. *New Essays on "The Catcher in the Rye."* New York: Cambridge University Press, 1991. Five essays presenting distinct viewpoints on specific aspects of the novel. Interesting introduction covers trends in Salinger criticism over the forty years after publication of *The Catcher in the Rye.* Written for students of American literature. References and selected bibliography.

Wenke, John. *J. D. Salinger: A Study of the Short Fiction.* Boston: Twayne, 1991. Part 1 is Wenke's exploration of Salinger's short stories; part 2 contains "Biographical Reflections on J. D. Salinger"; part 3 is a selection of critical excerpts discussing the later stories. Chronology and selected bibliography.

Susan Frischer

Cross-References

Hemingway's *The Sun Also Rises* Speaks for the Lost Generation (1926), p. 696; "Angry Young Men" Express Working-Class Views (1950's), p. 1454; The Beat Movement Rejects Mainstream Values (1950's), p. 1460; Dean Becomes a Legend in *Rebel Without a Cause* (1955), p. 1640; *Catch-22* Illustrates Antiwar Sentiment (1961), p. 1866; Vonnegut's *Cat's Cradle* Expresses 1960's Alienation (1963), p. 1939.

BECKETT'S TRILOGY PUSHES AGAINST
THE FRONTIERS OF FICTION

Category of event: Literature
Time: 1951-1953
Locale: Paris, France

Writing originally in French, the Irish-born Samuel Beckett published three thematically linked prose narratives that questioned and redefined the nature and intended functions of the novel

Principal personages:
SAMUEL BECKETT (1906-1989), a previously obscure Irish poet and novelist also interested in writing for the theater
JÉRÔME LINDON (1925-   ), a neophyte French publisher

Summary of Event

Samuel Beckett was graduated from Dublin's Trinity College in 1927, and he embarked tentatively upon a career in the teaching and scholarship of French literature. Awarded a lectureship at the prestigious École Normale Supérieure in Paris for two academic years beginning in 1928, Beckett soon joined the circle of Irish expatriate writers surrounding James Joyce. Joyce, already acclaimed—and controversial—as the author of *Ulysses* (1922), was then at work on his second high-modernist magnum opus, *Finnegans Wake* (1939). Along with certain other Joyce disciples, Beckett published occasional poetry and prose to some favorable notice, and he was commissioned by the Paris-based Hours Press to prepare an English-language monograph on the French novelist Marcel Proust, acknowledged along with Joyce as one of the masters of high modernism in prose fiction.

Returning in 1930 to teach at Trinity College, Beckett soon grew bored with his job and nostalgic for life on the Continent. After some fifteen months on the job, fearing for his physical and mental health, Beckett fled during the Christmas holiday to visit relatives in Germany, resigning his position by mail. From 1932 to 1937, Beckett maintained a marginal existence divided among Dublin, London, and the Continent, largely dependent upon handouts from his family as he sought to establish himself as a writer. After forty-two rejections, Beckett's second attempted novel, *Murphy* (1938), was accepted for publication at the end of 1937. Beckett had just settled in Paris, where he felt most at home; he would remain there, except during the disruptions of World War II, for the rest of his long life.

Resolutely apolitical, Beckett nevertheless participated actively in espionage activities for the French Resistance after the fall of France in 1940, primarily out of allegiance to his Jewish friends. In 1942, threatened with imminent arrest by the Nazis, Beckett and his future wife, Suzanne, fled on foot toward the South of France. In the small town of Roussillon, Beckett earned his keep with farm work, writing to stave off boredom whenever he was not working. The result was the novel *Watt* (1953), the last of Beckett's longer works to be written in English. After the war, returned to his old apartment in Paris, with Suzanne to look after his needs and protect his privacy, Beckett embarked on the most productive phase of his literary career. He began composing his works first in French to achieve an affectless style, incidentally freeing himself from the Joycean influence that had marked, and somewhat marred, his earlier writings in English. Between 1947 and 1949, Beckett composed the prose narratives *Molloy* (1951; English translation, 1955) and *Malone meurt* (1951; *Malone Dies*, 1956) as well as the play *En attendant Godot* (1952; *Waiting for Godot*, 1954). To Beckett's surprise, a publisher was soon found, albeit a financially strapped one; Jérôme Lindon, who had spent the war years with General Charles de Gaulle's Free French forces in England, had recently purchased the formerly clandestine publishing house Les Éditions de Minuit. Lindon's goal was to parlay Minuit's reputation for patriotic subversion into an equally strong reputation for the innovative and daringly avant-garde. Beckett's oddly solipsistic texts, questioning not only the use of first-person narrative but also the functions of language itself, struck Lindon as precisely the sort of creative experiment that Minuit ought to publish, even at the risk of losing money.

Divided into two separate, approximately equal parts (which, according to some critics, demand to be read in inverse order), *Molloy* begins with the title character, of uncertain age, in his mother's room for more than a year, unable to account for where his mother is or how he came to be there. His job is to write pages of prose, which are collected once a week. He recalls strange scenes of wandering and violence that turn out to be circular; his narrative ends much as it began. The second part, narrated by a detective of sorts named Jacques Moran, chronicles his assigned search for Molloy, during which he loses his poise, authority, and, in time, most of his faculties, in fact "becoming" the aging, crippled Molloy. Read "backwards," starting with Moran, the narrative suggests that Moran and Molloy are one and the same—and that nothing is as it seems.

"Malone is what I am called now," says the narrator at the start of *Malone Dies*, implying that Moran, Molloy, and others, including Murphy from Beckett's earlier fiction, are manifestations of the same narrative "urge," voice, or consciousness, manifestations to be invoked, abandoned, or "killed off" at will. Well past eighty years of age, Malone is a compulsive spinner of tall tales, recalling or inventing the misadventures of a father and son called Saposcat, at least one of whom will later resurface as Macmann ("son of man"). Alone in a room with the figments or products of his imagination (or are some of them, in fact, "real" memories?), the aging invalid laments the impossibility of recording his own impending death, "murdering" characters at will as his mind ranges farther afield, and darkly hinting that he might, at least once, have committed actual murder. The narrative voice simply trails off at the end of the novel, only to reemerge from silence and darkness at the start of *L'Innommable* (1953; *The Unnamable*, 1958), originally unplanned and in fact not composed until 1949, after *Waiting for Godot*. As critic Richard Coe has observed,

"The dramatic crisis in the *Trilogy* occurs in the blank space between *Malone Dies* and *The Unnamable*; for, in that space, Malone/Macmann *does* die . . . and his death solves precisely nothing." Indeed, it is the perceived need (or possibility) of a "solution" that keeps the narrative voice somehow "alive" beyond death, although now without hands to transform speaking into writing. The narrator, sometimes known as Mahood, describes himself as an armless, legless remnant stuffed into a jar as though he were a potted plant, the jar's opening just flush with his mouth. Perhaps, indeed, Mahood and his predicaments are still further inventions of the postmortem Malone; at all events, the narrator is quite familiar with all the Murphys, Molloys, and Morans that have preceded him. As in the case of *Malone Dies*, no solution is ever found; the narrative ends with the sentence, "I can't go on, I'll go on."

Taken together, Beckett's first novels to be composed originally in French broke new ground in prose fiction, questioning the functions of the writer, the reader, and language itself insofar as it relates to consciousness. Although somewhat different in form and intent from the "New Novel" that would emerge in France just a few years later, Beckett's thoughtful, unorthodox fiction nevertheless helped to prepare a receptive climate for the work of such unabashedly experimental practitioners as Michel Butor, Alain Robbe-Grillet, Robert Pinget, and Claude Simon—all of whom, incidentally, would choose (or be chosen by) Éditions de Minuit.

Impact of Event

With the publication of *Molloy* late in the spring of 1951, Beckett's fiction began for the first time to attract both critical attention and favorable reviews; the release of *Malone Dies* just a short time later brought even more positive comment, stimulating sales of *Molloy* as well. Although reputedly difficult to read (or understand) and pessimistic in their outlook, Beckett's novels, with their provocative blend of challenging thought and innovative style, appealed to the informed postwar French readership. The favorable reception of Beckett's novels helped also to prepare a receptive climate for *Waiting for Godot*, to which Lindon held publication rights pending production of the play.

Thanks to a grant obtained through the good offices of Georges Neveux, a playwright and screenwriter then serving with the Ministry of Arts and Culture in Paris, *Waiting for Godot* was accepted for production early in 1952. The play opened almost exactly one year later, to initially mixed but soon quite positive reviews. If the success of Beckett's novels had encouraged him to seek production for the play, it would soon be the play that drew attention to his fiction. (Ironically, it is likely that Neveux, a dramatist to the core, had never read the novels when he perceived the merits of the play submitted to him.) Other Beckett champions, meanwhile, encouraged his new audience to read his novels.

Despite a similarity of concerns linking his fiction to his plays, Beckett, whether he liked it or not, would continue to attract a wider audience on the stage than in print, in part as a result of the immediacy of the theater. The pattern of reception established in Paris would repeat itself worldwide; the runaway success of *Waiting for*

Godot during the 1950's, before such unlikely audiences as the inmates of San Quentin Prison in California (after a generally unsuccessful run on Broadway), would soon draw critical attention to Beckett's novels as well.

By the early 1960's, Beckett had become something of an international literary celebrity, even as he shunned publicity of all sorts. Josephine Jacobsen and William Mueller, addressing themselves to an informed if general audience early in 1964, lamented that "the disparity between Beckett's prestige, his influence, and even the vehemence of his detractors, and the number of readers truly familiar with the body of his work is extraordinary." Arguably, Beckett's work remained more often discussed than read, except by professional critics in search of publication. Notably exceptional were the plays, as loosely linked to the Theater of the Absurd as was Beckett's fiction to the so-called New Novel.

Working (or sometimes, not working) in obscurity for the first half of his eighty-three years, Beckett achieved worldwide fame as both a novelist and a playwright. He started out, however, as a poet, albeit a rather derivative one. Jacobsen and Mueller were among the first critics to recognize that Beckett's gifts remained those of a poet, no longer derivative, who had simply translated his talents into prose, both onstage and off. Humanity's innate desire to know, to make sense, and above all to speak, write, or somehow to communicate, remain alive in Beckett's work in both genres, even after the death of Malone.

During the 1960's, in the heyday of his fame, it was fashionable to claim Beckett's plays and narratives as influential. In fact, his work now seems to remain in a class by itself, difficult, if not impossible, to imitate or follow except through internal reflection. No doubt Beckett's harrowing inquiries, internalized by readers or spectators with creative aspirations, have brought forth a progeny of sorts, but one in which his influence is hard to trace. Perhaps his greatest influence, shared with that of the New Novelists, has been upon what is now called postmodern criticism, in which the boundary traditionally separating creative from critical writing is frequently blurred and the nature and function of language subjected to numerous questions.

Bibliography

Bair, Deirdre. *Samuel Beckett: A Biography.* New York: Harcourt Brace Jovanovich, 1978. Prepared without Beckett's "help or hindrance," Bair's study is useful for tracing the genesis and evolution of the trilogy, as well as for insights into Beckett's creative process.

Barnard, Guy C. *Samuel Beckett: A New Approach.* New York: Dodd, Mead, 1970. Barnard's "new approach" is that of psychoanalysis, particularly with regard to schizophrenia. The approach seems a bit strained when applied to the plays, yet offers useful, still valid interpretations of the trilogy.

Ben-Zvi, Linda. *Samuel Beckett.* Boston: Twayne, 1986. A good guide for the general reader, Ben-Zvi's study is especially valuable for its situation of Beckett's prose within the narrative tradition.

Coe, Richard N. *Samuel Beckett.* New York: Grove Press, 1970. Among the best earlier monographs on Beckett, Coe's study is especially useful for its reconstruction and interpretation of Beckett's "universe" as expressed both on the stage and on the page.

Fletcher, John. *The Novels of Samuel Beckett.* New York: Barnes & Noble Books, 1964. Still authoritative both as criticism and as literary history, Fletcher's is perhaps the strongest study dealing only with Beckett's narrative prose.

Jacobsen, Josephine, and William R. Mueller. *The Testament of Samuel Beckett.* New York: Hill & Wang, 1964. Addressing themselves to the general reader and spectator, Jacobsen and Mueller were among the first critics to explore the poetic dimensions of Beckett's drama and fiction; their study is notable also for its analysis of Beckett as critical phenomenon.

Kenner, Hugh. *Samuel Beckett: A Critical Study.* New York: Grove Press, 1961. Subsequently revised and often reprinted, Kenner's pioneering study of Beckett's narrative and dramatic art remains among the most entertaining and informative. See also Kenner's *A Reader's Guide to Samuel Beckett* (1973).

David B. Parsell

Cross-References

Joyce's *Ulysses* Epitomizes Modernism in Fiction (1922), p. 555; Sartre and Camus Give Dramatic Voice to Existential Philosophy (1940's), p. 1174; Sartre's *Being and Nothingness* Expresses Existential Philosophy (1943), p. 1262; The New Novel (*Le Nouveau Roman*) Emerges (1951), p. 1481; *Waiting for Godot* Expresses the Existential Theme of Absurdity (1953), p. 1573.

LE CORBUSIER DESIGNS AND BUILDS CHANDIGARH

Category of event: Architecture
Time: 1951-1963
Locale: Paris, France, and Chandigarh, Punjab, India

Acknowledged as one of the world's greatest architects, Le Corbusier designed his most visionary, monumental, and complete urban plan in a harsh, underdeveloped region

Principal personages:

LE CORBUSIER (CHARLES-ÉDOUARD JEANNERET, 1887-1965), one of the twentieth century's most influential architects and the chief designer of Chandigarh

PIERRE JEANNERET (1896-1968), a cousin of Le Corbusier, his longtime administrator, and the chief architect and planner of Punjab

MAXWELL FRY (1899-   ), a British architect who developed housing types for Chandigarh

JANE DREW (1911-   ), a British architect and Fry's collaborator on Chandigarh housing design

WALTER GROPIUS (1883-1969), one of the twentieth century's most distinguished functionalist architects and an early influence on Le Corbusier

JAWAHARLAL NEHRU (1889-1964), an Indian prime minister who supported Le Corbusier

Summary of Event

Approached by two Indian officials who proposed in November, 1950, that he design the new capital city of the Punjab, Chandigarh, Le Corbusier agreed, several months later, to undertake what would prove to be his first complete urban plan. Earlier, a New York architectural firm had drafted a master plan for Chandigarh in line with other ambitious urban projects exalting newly won Indian independence, but Le Corbusier assumed overall responsibility for the city's design with the presumption that significant changes were inevitable. His principal caveats about Chandigarh were that little money was available for the project, that construction logistics were primitive, and that the site itself was a forbidding one: a scorched level plain, with the Himalayas as a backdrop, subject not only to extreme heat but also to earthquakes, wind, and sandstorms.

Famed for his radical, usually controversial single structures—the Villa Savoye, Stein, and Shodan, the Pessac housing settlement, the LaRoche and Jaoul houses, the Ronchamp Chapel and La Tourette monastery, and the Swiss and Brazilian pavilions for Paris' University City—he had actively sought to design or redesign substantial sectors of existing cities. Among the many of his writings in which he had vigorously expressed this desire was *La Ville radieuse* (1933; *The Radiant City*, 1967). In this characteristically rhetorical and polemical work, he aimed to spread the doctrine that modern man's life-styles and values dictated that urbanism assume the fundamental role in machine-age civilization—and he lent his words substance. In years before and after this publication, Le Corbusier drafted many detailed proposals, accompanied by his building models, for the design, variously, of a "Contemporary City" in 1922 and for the redesign of Paris (his "Voisin Plan" of 1925), of Algiers (seven plans after 1930), of Stockholm, Moscow, Buenos Aires, Rio de Janeiro, and—representative of his larger scheme for Marseille—of the Marseille Block of apartments (1945-1952).

Le Corbusier's lifetime of spinning variations of his grand urban theories—all complementary to his artistic and social philosophy—would probably have yielded few physical manifestations without the opportunities presented by Chandigarh. Either because his political views proved untimely or uncongenial to authorities, or because his early Purist and later Brutalist architectural styles offended the tastes of decision-makers, none of his urban schemes—except for occasional buildings—had won general approval. In contrast, India, exuberantly independent in 1950 and anxious to demonstrate its capacities for modernity, was warmly receptive to the radical and comprehensive architectural statement Le Corbusier offered. Equally important, Mahatma Gandhi's spiritual heir, the already legendary Prime Minister Jawaharlal Nehru, befriended and supported Le Corbusier and all that Chandigarh symbolized aesthetically and politically.

Based mainly in Paris, Le Corbusier assigned on-site supervision of the project's execution to his cousin, friend, and collaborator, Pierre Jeanneret, while housing, markets, furnishings, and other details of the urban fabric were the responsibilities of two British architects, Maxwell Fry and Jane Drew. Le Corbusier himself concentrated primarily upon Chandigarh's capitol complex and on designing the new city's monumental architecture. Yet the city's overall design was his too. To it, he applied his carefully articulated traffic system, which was future-oriented in the underdeveloped Punjab, and in terms of urban scaling, he invoked the well-tested principles of the "golden rectangle" (which called for the major attractions to be separated by distances of from 800 to 1,200 meters, a plan similar to that used in the design of Paris, for example) along with his own patented "Modulor" system to ensure retention of human dimensions amid monumentality.

Within the symbolically vital capitol sector, Le Corbusier focused upon the provincial government's center, located in open land on the city's northern extreme. There, the design of four structures preoccupied him: the High Court, the Legislative Assembly, the Secretariat, and the Governor's Palace. Each building, in accord with Le Corbusier's predilections, was constructed of rough, reinforced concrete (*béton brut*) conveying its own architectural statement. The Secretariat, the Assembly, and the High Court were framed against the distant Himalayas and were both spaced and mirrored by reflecting pools. Reportedly, architect Jane Drew further encouraged Le Corbusier to reaffirm his philosophy by constructing a series of additional monuments built within the capitol's pedestrian area: a Museum of Knowledge, a Modulor and Harmonic Spiral, a Tower of Shade, and, as if to put his signature upon the whole, a Monument of the Open Hand.

Always the complete artist, Le Corbusier left his detailed imprimatur everywhere: in his sun breaks (*brise-soleil*), in his horn and open-hand motifs, in his bold use of pastel paints on the buildings, in his ingenious ventilating systems drawn from his Mediterranean experience, in his sometimes whimsical use of the Modulor, and in his personal design of interior tapestries, paintings, reliefs, and sculptures.

By 1963, two years before Le Corbusier's death, Chandigarh had essentially assumed its planned urban form. Major structures and monuments of the capitol complex upon which Le Corbusier had concentrated were complete, as were their ancillary pedestrian ways, arterials, pools, and parks. So, too, was the low-rise central business district (all under four stories except for the post and telegraph building) and the variously stylized fabric of shops and housing that had been left to Pierre Jeanneret, Fry, and Drew.

Impact of Event

Within two years of Chandigarh's substantial completion, both Le Corbusier and Nehru were dead. Since then, architects, architectural historians, critics, informed laypersons, and, most important, large numbers of the Indian public—for whom the Punjab capital has become as important an aesthetic focus as the Taj Mahal—agree that Le Corbusier's city, its failings acknowledged, stands as one of the world's great architectural and philosophical landmarks. Built from scratch in a forbidding landscape, the monumental structures of its capitol complex achieve a uniqueness and a harmony that makes their geometric cubes, pillars, sunbreaks, parasol roofs, and rough yet colorful concrete surfaces appear to be carved from wind and water. Inspiration—that of Le Corbusier and many others—integrated the functional and symbolic roles of these buildings and monuments with a designed urban fabric for a city of nearly half a million people.

Intellectually and artistically, the creation of Chandigarh had its most immediate impact upon Le Corbusier himself. If the city was eventually to become his masterpiece, its evocation was also the supreme challenge to his lifetime of urban theorizing and the keenest test of his ability to extrapolate lessons gleaned from his extraordinary knowledge, experience, and imagination. As the author of more than fifty books expounding and clarifying his perceptions, Le Corbusier was articulate about the grand problems presented by Chandigarh. He was not obliged, he explained, to transform or redesign a traditional walled Indian city of kings, princes, and nobles. Rather, he was faced with occupying a plain; he was confronted by a geometrical event and constrained to battle space. While he believed that, in time, geometric designs and modern materials would prevail in architecture, he conceded that a reliance upon sensation would have to precede employment of the almost Cartesian logic and rationalism that had been hallmarks of his architecture and writings. By implication, such explanations underscore the fact that Le Corbusier intensively immersed himself only in the formulation of Chandigarh's grand design and monumental aspects. As well-disposed critics have noted, he devoted little attention to understanding local cultural conditions and left it to the genius and skill of others to flesh out and join the city's more mundane business center, shops, and housing to the sturdy skeleton that he provided.

Because of what he judged to be his inability to harmonize humanity and modern society even at Chandigarh, Le Corbusier regarded the city, by that criterion, a personal failure, though this reaction was in consonance with his consistently tragic view of the human condition. The international architectural community, however, despite reservations, evinced more positive reactions. It was favorably impressed generally by the modified, less harsh, and more "natural" Brutalism that Le Corbusier employed there. A number of architects and architectural critics, such as Peter Blake, found words inadequate to describe the power of Chandigarh's appearance and message, and many of Blake's professional colleagues pronounced it one of the most stunning achievements of twentieth century building. For them, Le Corbusier, brilliantly and effectively, had treated Chandigarh's monumental structures as primordial sculptures displayed against a neutral background. Architectural historians such as Norma Evenson have further noted that professionals perceived the massive plasticity of form and bold exposures of rough concrete that were among Le Corbusier's hallmarks at Chandigarh as one of the seminal influences in liberating postwar architecture from restrictions of the then-regnant International Style.

Nearly all qualified observers read in the city's principal buildings and monuments, moreover, a remarkable synthesis of Le Corbusier's aesthetics with the additions attributed to him in architecture's semantic vocabulary: *pilotis*, *brise-soleil*, *ondulatories*, pie-shaped assembly, endless museum, *béton brut*, hyperbolic shells, parasol roofs, inexpressible space, undulating glass walls, Modulor designs, and so on. Critics also recognized that because Le Corbusier had long been such an enormous influence over his profession, much of the architectural vocabulary employed at Chandigarh was, by the 1950's, already clichéd. There was likewise a general recognition that the masterpiece of spirit and structure at Chandigarh would preclude the construction of similar projects in the future. Le Corbusier's Chandigarh, in company with the masterworks of Ludwig Mies van der Rohe and Frank Lloyd Wright, had brought the heroic age of urban theorists and designers, and thus the modern architecture of which these men were the acknowledged masters, to an end.

Even Le Corbusier's most ardent admirers drew lessons from his failures at Chandigarh. Some felt the rigorous Western theory applied to the Indian city's development, in the process ignoring the vitality and visual interest of native life, was strikingly unimaginative and shockingly insensitive. A few felt that the whole scheme represented a misplaced "Garden City" project, although Le Corbusier decades earlier had repudiated such concepts. Some observers simply found the concentration of attention upon the capitol complex's widely spaced monuments to be monotonous and regretted the lack of compaction. Other critics complained that government buildings were too dispersed—too far apart for their personnel either to appreciate the other monuments around them or to communicate by walking, or even cycling, as was customary in the underdeveloped Punjab. Serious criticisms fell upon the city's housing and residential sectors, with which Le Corbusier was scarcely involved. Criticisms of specific buildings, the stuff of professional architecture, were numerous: too much compaction in one area, failure to achieve a democratic ambience in another, contrasts that were too violent elsewhere, and impractical design and faulty workmanship in many spots.

Both the praise and criticism of Le Corbusier's Chandigarh comprehended the fact that Le Corbusier, in closing an era of urban monumentalism, still had helped to provide a functional and structural framework for future cities, meanwhile giving humanity stirring buildings upon which to look.

Bibliography

Blake, Peter. *The Master Builders.* New York: Alfred A. Knopf, 1960. A splendid work for placing Le Corbusier in context with Mies van der Rohe and Frank Lloyd Wright, the twentieth century's other two architectural giants. Blake, a respected architect and architectural writer, skillfully emphasizes Le Corbusier's philosophy and principles in this readable, objective account. Numerous photos highlight the evolution of Le Corbusier's work. No notes or bibliography, but a useful index. An authoritative synthesis and introduction to great architects.

Choay, Françoise. *Le Corbusier.* New York: George Braziller, 1960. A brief, incisive, readable introduction to Le Corbusier's ideas and career by a noted French author who is an admiring critic of "Corbu." Eighty-seven excellent plates, a useful summary chronology, select bibliography, and index.

Evenson, Norma. *Le Corbusier: The Machine and the Grand Design.* New York: George Braziller, 1969. By a noted architectural historian and University of California professor. Evenson's doctoral dissertation on Chandigarh was the first such study on Le Corbusier's major works. Admiring but critical. Good chapter on Chandigarh, but deserves full reading. Plates, notes, bibliography, index.

Gardiner, Stephen. *Le Corbusier.* New York: Viking Press, 1974. A chronological sketch of the development of Le Corbusier's major themes and ideas. Good, if brief, material on Chandigarh. Twenty-three interesting plates, a biographical note, select bibliography, and useful index. Useful as an introductory background to Le Corbusier. Should be supplemented by Blake, Choay, Evenson, or Jencks.

Jencks, Charles. *Le Corbusier and the Tragic View of Architecture.* Cambridge, Mass.: Harvard University Press, 1973. Scholarly, authoritative, and readable. The author's chronological approach places Le Corbusier in meaningful artistic and intellectual contexts while tracing his philosophical development. Scores of illuminating photos, sketches, and building plans. Informative notes and an excellent triple-columned index. An insightful analysis.

Le Corbusier. *The Radiant City.* New York: The Orion Press, 1967. The English translation of the 1933 French publication, this is an interesting insight into what proved to be Le Corbusier's lifelong dreams about urbanism and urban design.

Despite sometimes peculiar grammar, gives a sense of the grandeur of his ideas. Few aids for readers, but Le Corbusier's view was that life was a losing struggle.

Serenyi, Peter, ed. *Le Corbusier in Perspective.* Englewood Cliffs, N.J.: Prentice-Hall, 1975. Twenty-six fine essays by twenty-two architects, urban planners, architectural historians, authors, and critics from the United States, Great Britain, and Europe. Excellent reading. Good scope in the entire collection. Thirty-two plates, a fine bibliography, biographical data, notes, and a useful index.

Clifton K. Yearley

Cross-References

Gaudí Completes the Casa Milá Apartment House in Barcelona (1910), p. 257; German Artists Found the Bauhaus (1919), p. 463; Le Corbusier's Villa Savoye Redefines Architecture (1931), p. 869; Wright Founds the Taliesin Fellowship (1932), p. 902; Saarinen Designs Kennedy Airport's TWA Terminal (1956), p. 1716; Kahn Blends Architecture and Urban Planning in Dacca (1962), p. 1919.

POWELL PUBLISHES THE EPIC
A DANCE TO THE MUSIC OF TIME

Category of event: Literature
Time: 1951-1975
Locale: Great Britain

By completing the A Dance to the Music of Time *series, Anthony Powell concluded one of the most ambitious, complex, and dazzling literary projects of all time*

Principal personage:
   ANTHONY POWELL (1905-   ), an English editor and writer, almost entirely known for the series *A Dance to the Music of Time*

Summary of Event

The first forty-five years of Anthony Powell's life gave little hint that he would produce anything like *A Dance to the Music of Time.* The son of a regular army officer with a Welsh aristocratic lineage, he did inherit major expectations. Education at Eton and Balliol College, Oxford, reinforced these. He left the University of Oxford with a third-class degree in history and started work at the publishing firm of Duckworth. The position was secure but lacked distinction. Born into the generation that matured after World War I, in the era that ushered in both the Jazz Age and the Great Depression, Powell became one of the Victorian aristocrats who discovered that ancestral privilege provided few groceries in times of economic failure. Everything, it appeared, was falling apart; failure was built into the structure of things. Powell's first fiction centered on these perceptions. When he was in his mid-twenties, his own firm started publishing his novels. Shortly afterward, he was married. By the age of thirty, he was well on his way to becoming one of the leading English novelists, although his novels did not provide an independent income. He became a scriptwriter for Warner Bros. in England and continued writing novels for awhile, but World War II intervened.

For seven years, Powell served in the military, first in the infantry, then in intelligence. At the end of the war, Powell did not return immediately to fiction. Instead, he worked on a biography of John Aubrey, a seventeenth century English antiquarian and memoirist. In Aubrey he found a kindred spirit, a writer who both memorialized his age and re-created its spirit, so that it gained a higher reality through him. Powell decided that this was what he wanted to do. Visiting the Wallace collection in London, which housed *A Dance to the Music of Time*, the painting by seventeenth century French painter Nicolas Poussin, also helped. By combining Aubrey's kind of writing with the thrust of the painting, Powell found his literary focus, theme, and pattern. In his *A Dance to the Music of Time*, he would design a fictional universe reflecting the period of his life and its social and cultural changes.

The painting presents a conventional Renaissance allegory of the passage of time. Four gowned and garlanded maidens dance sedately in a garden while a seated, winged god, aged but muscular, strums a harp. One of two cherubs plays a pipe, and the other stares at an hourglass. A statue of a two-headed god stands to one side. The god is Father Time, and the goddesses are his daughters, Memory and the Seasons. The daughters dance to the unheard music of time, measuring out the processes of history. The theme of the work coincided with Powell's mature reflections on fiction. Recognizing that most novelists work from their own lives and experiences, repeating their characters, plots, and themes, he decided to build a massive *roman-fleuve*, a chronicle, usually in many volumes, of several generations. Furthermore, he would use himself and his acquaintances as a foundation. Thus he could create a universe free of conventional constraints—that is, of the common demands of plot and character—and therefore be free to reproduce the writer's view of his experiences.

The plot could simply follow the flow of time, limited only by its current; the characters would dance along its stream, joined both by it and by their own efforts. The same forces that guide life would direct the fiction; fate would rule both, and patterns would emerge only in retrospect. Powell limited himself to his own milieu, the upper and upper-middle classes, which at the beginning of the twentieth century constituted the elite but lost status in an increasingly egalitarian century. The cast of characters is vast and diversified, and their lives intersect in unexpected and unpredictable ways. The apparently random connections reveal subtle patterns when viewed from a distance. Up close, the movements of the dancers look spontaneous and improvised. From afar, the dance becomes a figure. Powell's fiction reflects the intelligibility of life; he creates the fictional equivalent of chaos theory, the concept that a reproducible order underlies even apparently random fluctuation.

Powell published the first volume in the series, *A Question of Upbringing* (1951), when he was forty-five years old, setting himself a formidable challenge. A twelve-volume series, at fifty thousand words per volume, would amount to six hundred thousand words. To produce one volume every other year, reasonable even for a stylist like Powell, would mean consigning himself to a twenty-four-year contract, running until he would be nearly seventy years old. Powell stuck largely to this schedule. Remarkably, the pace of the series is even, and the patterns that emerge almost imperceptibly do seem to mirror the patterns of wisdom acquired by experience. Upon completion in 1975, the series was recognized as a rarity, a work of art that truly imitates life.

Impact of Event

While Powell was composing *A Dance to the Music of Time*, critics paid little attention to the developing architecture and judged the novels as single entities. In 1964, for example, when he brought out the seventh volume, *The Valley of Bones*, commentators noted that he was concluding more than half of a program that already had consumed fifteen years; at that rate, they calculated correctly, he would not be finished until he reached the age of seventy. When he finished the series, a common first reaction was to congratulate him solely for the effort, for the literary record teems with incomplete projects. The physical feat of completion, however, pales before the subtle revelations that multiply as readers finish the sequence. The title of the twelfth volume, *Hearing Secret Harmonies* (1975), sums up the effect, which duplicates the experience of the author in fashioning the narrative.

Powell wrote these stories very much as they are read, as gradually accumulating cells of experience originally lived through as single, separate units. Powell intended his narrative to duplicate the process of living. To accomplish this, he had to avoid predetermining outcomes or allowing completed volumes to affect the one in hand. This also makes some of the units quite unlike conventional novels. In dividing the narrative, Powell sometimes arbitrarily determined starting and stopping points, just as the calendar defines where months begin and end. Each book is concerned primarily with capturing a period in life rather than in following a conventional plot with conventional characters. Thus some of the outcomes are indefinite and ambiguous; sometimes the significances are vague and imprecise. This corresponds with life, which often does not reveal what an episode was about until long after it is over. Powell accomplishes this restraint with great integrity; parallels and correspondences emerge on their own rather than through the manipulations of the author.

Powell's achievement generally has been hailed as one of the most important works of the twentieth century. He has suffered some detraction, especially in England, where his writing has been less well received than it has been in the United States. Acceptance of his work seems to be connected closely to social level and choice of subject, particularly because Powell memorializes a superseded class and a rejected way of life. He has undergone the reevaluation experienced by his friend Evelyn Waugh, also now demoted from the eminence he once enjoyed. When questions about the world he represents—really an extraliterary consideration—are ignored, however, Powell's triumph is regularly admitted. Even his detractors note that Powell wrote the epitaph of the elite class, documenting its demise. He obviously was aware of its deficiencies.

Powell's achievement lies partly in his fidelity to the perception that the privileged classes determined the character of English life in the first half of the twentieth century. Powell focuses on the way the upper class presided over the disintegration of the very imperial system that raised it to prominence and made it necesssary; that is, the elite voluntarily relinquished their power. Furthermore, they also rose to the occasion during World War II, which could not have been waged without their direction. Powell bids farewell to past glory.

Powell's vision is subtle, penetrating, and detailed. He focuses on behavior, especially on the nuances of social interaction, the choices and actions that betray character. His presentation is detached and objective, almost photographic: characters appear frontally, their actions and words speaking for them. Since many reappear at later stages, the reader sees certain traits persist over time and control personality. Character manifests itself early and remains substantially intact.

The novels group themselves into sets of three. Their reissue as a quartet of trilogies reflects organization. The first triple deals with youth and early adulthood. It begins with *A Question of Upbringing*, which underpins the entire sequence, establishing the central character opposition and suggesting how character developed in youth directs behavior throughout life. The source of intelligence is the main figure, Nicholas Jenkins, who tells his story as if his life were incidental. He chronicles the vicissitudes and follies around him with gentle irony, but without judging, acting throughout with decency, integrity, and loyalty, supposedly the values of the upper classes, though these values are often violated. Set against him is Kenneth Widmerpool, the first and most persistent of a set of ambitious power brokers, ruthless in pursuit of position. They encounter each other repeatedly. The second trilogy deals with the period of marriage and family rearing, establishing careers, and forming social groups. The third presents World War II, the high point of this generation. The fourth deals with the decline of the upper classes following the war. It is difficult to imagine a more complete depiction of the character of this class and this civilization than that presented by Powell. In his close attention to character, he has chronicled the end of an era as well as offering a monumental epic.

Bibliography

McEwan, Neil. *Anthony Powell.* Modern Novelists. New York: St. Martin's Press, 1991. A small book (147 pages), but full of useful information. It has much more material about Powell's writings than about his life. Analyzes *A Dance to the Music of Time* from three different points of view, as narrative, myth, and artwork. Notes, select bibliography, and index.

_____. *The Survival of the Novel: British Fiction in the Later Twentieth Century.* London: Macmillan, 1981. The chapter on Powell is the best brief introduction available to *A Dance to the Music of Time.* Places Powell's work in relation to twentieth century fiction in general. McEwan is less partial in his judgments than are most commentators. Index and bibliography.

Powell, Anthony. *To Keep the Ball Rolling: The Memoirs of Anthony Powell.* 4 vols. New York: Holt, Rinehart and Winston, 1976-1982. Powell's memoirs are almost as entertaining and just as well written as his fiction. Since the fiction is based on his life and times, the memoirs provide a number of illuminating parallels. They will not clear up all the questions, for reticence and refusal to judge characterize the memoirist as well as the novelist.

Powell, Violet, ed. *The Album of Anthony Powell's "Dance to the Music of Time."* London: Thames and Hudson, 1987. This collection of photographs and illustrations related to the novel sequence is an indispensable companion for a fan embarking on a rereading. Much of the sequence is concerned with the function of the memory in making sense of one's life experiences; this work aids the process.

Spurling, Hilary. *Invitation to the Dance: A Guide to Anthony Powell's "Dance to the Music of Time."* Boston: Little, Brown, 1977. The most complete guide to the sequence, its characters, the real-life parallels and analogues, the motifs and patterns, and the recurrent themes. It is full of charts and lists and features several types of cross-referencing and indexing.

James Livingston

Cross-References

Heart of Darkness Reveals the Consequences of Imperialism (1902), p. 51; Proust's *Remembrance of Things Past* Is Published (1913), p. 355; Mann's *The Magic Mountain* Reflects European Crisis (1924), p. 588; *Nineteen Eighty-Four* Portrays Totalitarianism and Mind Control (1949), p. 1421; "Angry Young Men" Express Working-Class Views (1950's), p. 1454; García Márquez's *One Hundred Years of Solitude* Is Published (1967), p. 2086; *The Forsyte Saga* Is a Hit on Public Television (1969), p. 2168.

STRAVINSKY'S *THE RAKE'S PROGRESS* PREMIERES IN VENICE

Category of event: Music
Time: September 11, 1951
Locale: La Fenice Theater, Venice, Italy

Inspired by a series of satirical paintings by William Hogarth, an eighteenth century English artist, Igor Stravinsky collaborated with W. H. Auden to produce a brilliant pastiche of neoclassical opera

Principal personages:
 IGOR STRAVINSKY (1882-1971), a Russian-born composer who was among the outstanding innovators in twentieth century music
 ALDOUS HUXLEY (1894-1963), an English-born essayist, memoirist, and novelist, Stravinsky's neighbor
 W. H. AUDEN (1907-1973), an English poet, essayist, librettist, screenwriter, editor, and playwright, one of the outstanding writers of the century
 CHESTER KALLMAN (1921-1975), an American poet and scriptwriter, Auden's collaborator and companion after 1946

Summary of Event

In 1940, Igor Stravinksy, having fled Europe at the outbreak of World War II, arrived in America, which he had already triumphantly toured three times. He was fifty-eight; his wife and his mother had both died earlier that year. Ready to choose his final home, he settled in Hollywood, California, where he had been enticed partly by the promise of lucrative contracts but probably even more by the challenge of succeeding in a musical medium that he had not yet attempted: film scoring. Some younger colleagues—Sergei Prokofiev, Dmitri Shostakovich, William Walton, and Aaron Copland—were celebrated in the press for their Hollywood triumphs, and Stravinsky disliked being superseded. Other composers—Miklos Rozsa, Dmitri Tiomkin, and Bernard Hermann—had graduated directly from European conservatories to the studios, ignoring concert halls for "the medium of the future." Stravinsky was not ready to join the past.

For the next seven years, Stravinsky worked on film scores but failed to place one. He salvaged his pride somehow, and he salvaged his music by recasting it in other forms, which were uniformly successful. Besides, he had found in George Balanchine the perfect choreographer for the dance music he was born to write. Still, he had failed at film music. He thought he knew why.

Motion pictures depended on continuity and flow. They blended with music that underscored those qualities—the lush, gorgeous billows of late Romanticism or the filmy draperies of Impressionism. Stravinsky had reacted against this; he was rhythm incarnate, punctuation, discontinuity—music for dancing, not swooning. His music suited only certain kinds of stories. The trouble Stravinsky had adapting his music to film pointed up a more serious omission from his musical achievement: Now nearly sixty-five, he had written no major opera. To meet the challenge, he had to find the right narrative and the right text.

In 1947, Stravinsky attended an exhibit of paintings by the seventeenth century English artist William Hogarth at the Chicago Art Institute. Hogarth was famous for having invented an early kind of comic strip. He depicted a conventional moral narrative in a series of paintings that, like the novels of Daniel Defoe, combined steamy scenes with pious platitudes, thus attracting both lewd and religious. Hogarth's series included paintings entitled "The Harlot's Progress" and "The Rake's Progress." The technique intrigued Stravinsky. This kind of narrative was discontinuous, a succession of distinct scenes. The abstractions and character types of a cautionary tale would also cause displacement. Unlike cinema, such a narrative would not depend on luring a viewer in, but on making the viewer an eavesdropper.

Opera history provided strong precedent for such material. The story of the wastrel heir had immediately reminded Stravinsky of *Don Giovanni* (1787), the Wolfgang Amadeus Mozart-Lorenzo Da Ponte fable that exposed the moral ambiguity of conventional behavior. Mozart had perfected a scenic approach to opera, proceeding through a series of set pieces and ensembles stitched together by recitative narrative lines. The combination had worked because Da Ponte's lyrics and lines perfectly matched Mozart's music in bite, wit, and irony. This fusion is both fragile and dangerous. For example, in *Così fan tutte* (1790), another collaboration, the plot shows two pairs of lovers who, despite oaths to the contrary, prove quite willing to betray their partners for romantic adventures, provided they can get away with their misdeeds; the audience is then informed that everyone is like that. To entertain by insult takes a subtle hand.

Stravinsky had his material; he now needed a partner. For help, he turned to his neighbor Aldous Huxley, himself a respected writer. Huxley made the perfect choice. He suggested Stravinsky contact W. H. Auden, then forty, ironic, witty, and a master of forms. Stravinsky wrote; Auden responded; before long they were conferring in California. Their talents jelled so well that their failure to continue collaborating remains a puzzle. Auden granted Stravinsky full control over the main directions of story line and characters, contenting himself with making suggestions; in his view, librettist followed composer. He did talk Stravinsky into accepting a cocollaborator, the relatively unknown Chester Kallman, who had become Auden's confidant. Unexpectedly, Kallman proved a gifted composer and versifier.

The fusion, though, was not easy or immediate. Stravinsky set the text exactly as he received it, requesting only the reprise of one chorus. The text looks relatively straightforward, but it conceals a struggle. The writers had had to make a living character out of Tom Rakewell, the "rake," who is essentially a puppet in Hogarth's painting, and they had to create a continuing context in which he could be defined.

They solved the first problem by making the hero struggle against temptation rather than merely succumb to it passively. They solved the second by creating two characters, Nick Shadow and Ann Truelove, not even hinted at in Hogarth's work. They combined the two with the fairy-tale strategy of giving Tom Rakewell three wishes.

Text in hand, Stravinsky set to work, completing one act in each of the following three years. His task was quite different from that of the librettists. He had deliberately taken on the challenge of rivaling Mozart, whose music for the theater is generally considered formally impeccable and emotionally compelling, perfectly matched to the words yet constantly propelling and pacing the action. Furthermore, even if Stravinsky succeeded, critics could easily say that he had succeeded only by imitating the master. The consensus seemed to be that the opera was a jewel and a triumph but that the parts, unlike those of Mozart's works, did not lend themselves to extracts.

The Rake's Progress remains Stravinsky's largest and largest-scored work. Its premiere was eagerly awaited. Different venues bid for the honor, which was won by the La Fenice Theater in Venice; attempts by fervent Stravinskyites to buy blocks of tickets drove prices up and caused a shortage of tickets. Although the performance was not flawless, the work was acclaimed brilliant, and no fewer than twenty companies performed it before 1951 was out.

Impact of Event

The production of *The Rake's Progress* certainly marked a culmination and a turning point in Stravinsky's career. It closed the so-called neoclassical period of his work, characterized by his resuscitation of structural patterns and techniques of the eighteenth century and earlier. Stravinsky had demonstrated repeatedly that new wine could be poured out of old bottles, and that the new vintage could transcend the old. The mixture of familiar or near-familiar forms with new musical language made these compositions some of his most approachable, so that they would continue to be staples of the standard repertoire. Many of his most popular works, from *Pulcinella* (1920) and *Petrushka* (1911) to *Oedipus Rex* (1927) and *The Rake's Progress*, belonged to his neoclassical period. In the wake of *The Rake's Progress*, however, he turned exclusively to a more abstract music that was based on the contrapuntal serialism of Arnold Schoenberg and his circle. In 1953, Stravinsky did envision another opera—apparently quite different from *The Rake's Progress*—with the Welsh poet Dylan Thomas as librettist and focusing on the unlikely theme of the aftermath of a nuclear holocaust. The project had entered the planning stage when it was cut short by the poet's death.

The opera closed the period in Stravinsky's career in which he was preoccupied with demonstrating how the musical resources of the past could continue to be developed and remolded. For decades, he had seemed compelled to show that the past had not been exhausted, that it still had something to give to the present. This characteristic linked Stravinsky's work with parallel developments in other arts. In 1914, for example, the British critic T. E. Hulme had called for English literature to return to the qualities and modes practiced before the Romantic "distortion" had set in; similarly, the post-World War I period revived interest in the once-moribund Metaphysical poets of the seventeenth century at the expense of the Romantics and Victorians. Fashions in art, too, focused on primitive and pre-Renaissance works— which had not been infected with the "diseases" of rational perspective and representation. These movements resonated with elements in Stravinsky's soul. In *The Rake's Progress*, Stravinsky showed off, demonstrating that he could write classical opera as well as Mozart had. He also, however, realized that his success raised the uncomfortable question of what he could do on his own. He proceeded to answer such concerns with the rest of the music he composed, now suddenly not based on existing models.

The significance of *The Rake's Progress* as far as musical history is concerned is more difficult to assess. Its premiere was a blockbuster event, and its success continued. *The Rake's Progress* has been produced more often by far than any other twentieth century opera. Its success, however, stems at least in part from its approachability; yet it is approachable because it deliberately and self-consciously imitates the manner and technique of Mozart and Da Ponte. In that respect, the opera arrives at a kind of cultural dead end. It points out no new directions. Other composers can hardly use *The Rake's Progress* as a model; such an attempt would doubtless make the resulting work merely imitative and derivative. *The Rake's Progress* thus asks, awkwardly, where does opera go from here? It provides little in the way of answer, perhaps because Stravinsky recognized that imitation could only go so far and that the resources of the past were limited.

Such problems, however, may have more to do with the function of opera in the twentieth century than with *The Rake's Progress*. Along other lines, the success of the Stravinsky-Auden alliance has been marked. Shortly after the premiere of *The Rake's Progress*, a team composed principally of Leonard Bernstein, Lillian Hellman, and Richard Wilbur produced the operetta *Candide* (1952), which resembled the opera in uncanny ways: It was based on an eighteenth century work, had a literary inspiration, and was satirical in focus and scenic in construction; it also depended on wit and irony for its effects. Thereafter, Stephen Sondheim, a consultant on *Candide*, went on to pioneer new directions in musical theater. Sondheim has made a career out of musicals that are literate, witty, ironic, and partly based on the past, including *Company* (1970), *A Little Night Music* (1973), and *Sunday in the Park with George* (1984). Andrew Lloyd Webber's successes *Cats* (1981) and *Phantom of the Opera* (1987) seem to come, in part at least, out of the same mold. The influence of *The Rake's Progress* can also be detected in Peter Shaffer's 1979 play and 1984 film *Amadeus*, which made Mozart himself the vehicle of a connection between the eighteenth and twentieth centuries. Although *The Rake's Progress* has had little direct influence on formal opera, it has certainly spun off into other forms of musical theater.

In another respect, the opera's influence on culture has been profound. Just as Richard Wagner's operas stand as symbols of the profoundest art of their culture,

The Rake's Progress represents the state of the imagination at midcentury. The simple moral fable at its center betrays the secret and unacknowledged anxieties of the time. Rakewell discloses the fear that prosperity will erode moral character, that good times will provide nothing to replace the soul-shaping of adversity. That he gets what he wishes for, but always in a form that invalidates his desire, merely underscores the same point. Even the moral principle at the center is ambiguous: Rakewell evades death but loses his mind; and even though the practice of love seems to be vindicated in the character of Truelove, she chooses to love a degenerate whom she cannot rehabilitate and who would apparently have few scruples about ruining her. This kind of ambiguity provides a fertile seedbed for irony and wit; it welcomes the raking glance of intelligence.

Prosperity was a fact at midcentury; but so were vague, ominous fears that it was too good to last, that it had no substantial foundation. *The Rake's Progress* captured and reflected this unease.

Bibliography

Boucourechliev, Andre. *Stravinsky*. Translated by Martin Cooper. New York: Holmes & Meier, 1987. A readable general biography, accessible to the general reader but technical enough for the sophisticated. Boucourechliev is excellent in relating Stravinsky's works to his life and his developing art. Worklist, calendar, bibliography, and indexes.

Craft, Robert. *Stravinsky: Chronicle of a Friendship, 1948-1971.* New York: Alfred A. Knopf, 1972. Craft was the friend, constant companion, and business and personal manager of the composer during the period covered by the book. He provides fascinating anecdotes about Stravinsky's personal and professional lives. His stories about the development of the opera furnish interesting sidelights. Thoroughly indexed.

Druskin, M. S. *Igor Stravinsky: His Life, Works, and Views.* Translated by Martin Cooper. Cambridge, England: Cambridge University Press, 1983. The standard scholarly biography. Collects more detail on every aspect of Stravinsky's life and art than any other source. Cogent and thorough; provides balanced coverage of pertinent sources and critical positions. Calendar, worklist, bibliography, and indexes.

Griffiths, Paul. *Igor Stravinsky: The Rake's Progress.* New York: Cambridge University Press, 1982. The definitive study of the opera. Griffiths gathers an astounding array of information and presents it effectively; even a casual fan of the work can profit from browsing here. Extensive lists, bibliography, and index.

Stravinsky, Igor. *Igor Stravinsky: An Autobiography.* New York: M. & J. Steuer, 1958. Although not always factually reliable, Stravinsky's own accounts of the genesis and development of his own works are insightful—he was a keen observer, of himself as well as of others.

Walsh, Stephen. *The Music of Stravinsky.* New York: Routledge, 1988. Despite its title, this is as much a biography as it is an account of the music; furthermore, it is largely intended for the general reader. Yet it is considerably more than simply an introduction or armchair companion, since Walsh generally provides learned discussions of the works in chronological order. Fully annotated.

James Livingston

Cross-References

The Rite of Spring Stuns Audiences (1913), p. 373; Stravinsky Completes His Wind Octet (1923), p. 561; Berg's *Wozzeck* Premieres in Berlin (1925), p. 680; *Poems* Establishes Auden as a Generational Spokesman (1930), p. 857; Berg's *Lulu* Opens in Zurich (1937), p. 1078; Britten Completes *Peter Grimes* (1945), p. 1296; *Amahl and the Night Visitors* Premieres on American Television (1951), p. 1536.

THE RED SKELTON SHOW BECOMES A LANDMARK ON NETWORK TELEVISION

Category of event: Television and radio
Time: September 30, 1951-August 29, 1971
Locale: The United States

A top-rated show for much of its twenty-year run, The Red Skelton Show *was the most enduring comedy-variety show in television history*

Principal personage:
RED SKELTON (1913-   ), the producer and star of *The Red Skelton Show* from 1951 to 1971

Summary of Event

When *The Red Skelton Show* premiered on the National Broadcasting Company (NBC) on Sunday evening, September 30, 1951, the audience, and Skelton himself, had been prepared for several years. As early as 1940, Skelton's film contract included an unusual clause ensuring his availability for a regular television show. An overwhelming success on radio, Skelton had been lionized by critics who lamented that his talent for mime and physical comedy was wasted on the sightless medium of radio, and many fans yearned for his appearance on the video screen. Of course, Skelton had appeared in films for more than a decade; his film debut had been made in *Having a Wonderful Time* (1938), and his 1940 screen test for Metro-Goldwyn-Mayer (MGM) became an underground success in its own right. Nevertheless, what his film appearances lacked was what made Skelton a star: the spontaneity that came with working before an audience, a condition that live television offered.

The intense anticipation of Red Skelton's television debut did not totally work in his favor. As fellow comedian and television pioneer Steve Allen pointed out thirty years later, the idealized imaginary picture of the splash Skelton would make was built up so much by anticipation that no one could live up to it. In 1982, Allen wrote that "Red was so good on the radio, so funny in films . . . that most of us could hardly wait to see him on TV. When we finally did we had oversold ourselves."

Yet several elements conspired to overcome the liability of a premature buildup and give Skelton one of the most successful first seasons in television history. The first two factors working in his favor were technical, and totally coincidental: the development of coaxial cable for carrying television signals, and NBC's success in convincing Skelton to perform the show live. In the first few years of network television, shows were carried live only on the East Coast, because regular telephone lines could not carry the complex television signal on a coast-to-coast hookup. Kinescopes (films taken off a television screen in the days before videotape) of these live shows were then broadcast a night later west of the Mississippi. The advent of coaxial cable, which could carry the complex signal television required, meant that shows could be beamed live coast to coast—and cable became available just when Skelton was ready to begin his show.

Another factor in the overwhelming success of Skelton's first season was his almost thirty years of experience in vaudeville and stand-up comedy. Much of the visually oriented material he had been performing since his youth, and perfecting before live audiences, had no place on radio or film, so Skelton had a cache of rich material already tested by the same type of audience he would face on television. This asset had a hitch, however: In television, a performer has much the same audience every week. Television performers cannot reuse old material, as is possible in a nightclub, where each night brings a new audience. "In my first year on TV," Skelton later recalled, "I used up a hundred and sixty-five routines. Some of it was stuff I'd spent years putting together."

The opening show was an even mix of new and old material. It began with an animated graphic combining Skelton's head and a box of Tide laundry detergent— the show's sponsor. As a female chorus sang "Tide presents Red Skelton!" the picture cut to Skelton entering before a curtain, wearing a tuxedo for his debut. (His tailored gray three-piece suits, which became standard for the next twenty years, first appeared the following week.)

The opening monologue, of course, was necessarily new material, as it consisted of topical comments on the day's news stories. One new bit of physical comedy that shocked and delighted Skelton's first television audience became standard in the next few weeks: At the end of the monologue, without warning, a pair of hands reached out from under the curtain, grabbed Skelton's legs, and pulled him offstage. The routine was highly effective, but it had to be abandoned after Skelton sustained serious internal injuries in such falls. Another new bit featured Skelton's country-bumpkin character, Clem Kadiddlehopper, as an Irish tenor singing a fully orchestrated classical piece with the Dave Rose Orchestra. The anomaly of hearing such a beautiful voice emerge from such a comic face created a delightful conflict in the audience, which anticipated something similar to Frank Fontaine's "Crazy Guggenheim" sketches on *The Jackie Gleason Show*.

If the first show opened with new material, it closed with some of Skelton's oldest—his serious, even sentimental disclaimer. Though it endeared Skelton to his audience, many critics felt the disclaimer took the edge off his comedy, that too much sweetness spoiled the pathos of such characters as his clown-tramp Freddy the Freeloader or his drunk Willie Lump-Lump. At the end of the show, Skelton's smile would turn somber and, as Steve Allen once noted, his voice would modulate to "something almost like baby talk." Skelton would say, "Ladies and gentlemen, I want to thank you for putting up with my nonsense. I sincerely hope I haven't said or done anything to offend anyone. If I have, I didn't mean it."

If anyone was offended, it did not affect the show, which was an immediate popular and critical success. The program shot to the top of the ratings—unusual, even in 1951, for a new show—and finished its first season in the number-four spot. At the Emmy Awards ceremony on February 18, 1952, *The Red Skelton Show* won the Emmy for best comedy show of 1951, and Skelton won another Emmy as the year's best television comedian.

Impact of Event

The sheer longevity of *The Red Skelton Show* assured it a lasting influence on the history of television, for by stretching for more than two decades, the program was seen by the first two generations of television audiences. By the early 1990's, however, the show had been off the air longer than it had been on. Unlike situation comedies and adventure shows, comedy-variety shows rarely work in syndication, and so Red Skelton reruns were not syndicated.

Part of the reason for *The Red Skelton Show*'s demise may in fact be generational. The incredible success of *The Smothers Brothers Comedy Hour* (1967-1969) on the Columbia Broadcasting System (CBS) and *Rowan and Martin's Laugh-In* (1967-1973) on NBC made network executives insist on a youth appeal that those shows had and that the aging Skelton could not offer. The contrast became readily apparent in 1970, when CBS, which had taken over production of the show from NBC in 1953, dropped Skelton as part of an image makeover. NBC picked up his show for the following season; back on NBC, the Skelton show, pared to a half-hour, became a lead-in for *Rowan and Martin's Laugh-In* at 7:30 Monday nights. Skelton's polished schtick looked dated next to the frenetic, rapid-fire pace of *Rowan and Martin's Laugh-In*, with its youthful ensemble cast of fresh new comedians. No single comedian, not even one of Skelton's stature, could compete.

Cancellation had been a threat from the beginning, as is the nature of network television. After the unusual critical and ratings triumph of *The Red Skelton Show*'s rookie year, ratings plummeted, and the critical accolades stopped. Skelton had seen the same phenomenon in Milton Berle's television career. The first great comedian in the new medium, Berle became so associated with it he became known as "Mister Television." When Skelton won the Emmy as best comedian of 1951, he was ending a streak of Emmies for Berle, who in 1948 had won the first ever given. Only three years later, Berle had not even been nominated. Yet toppling the top comic was uncomfortably like regicide: It sent the message that all leaders, including the conquerors, can themselves be conquered. Skelton may not have been thinking in such terms, but the press did; the *Hollywood Reporter* review of his opening show proclaimed, "Move over Mr. Berle—Mr. Skelton has arrived."

Weathering three seasons of relatively bad ratings, however, Skelton emerged in 1955 at number fourteen, breaking in and out of the top ten for the next fifteen years. Skelton's show had its highest ranking in the mid-1960's, just before network executives began demanding youth-oriented shows. Yet even in the show's best season ranking, when it was the number-two program on television, it brought only a little more than a quarter of the audience share; it is audience share, and not position, that buys sponsors.

Perhaps the demands of "youth appeal" by networks were premature: in 1979, Skelton was a hit on the college comedy circuit, and in the 1980's, the Home Box

Office (HBO) cable network showcased him in comedy specials usually targeted at college and young-professional audiences. In 1987, Skelton appeared in the Fox network's *Television Academy Hall of Fame* show, and two years later, he reappeared as an inductee to that prestigious body. The Screen Actors Guild awarded Skelton its achievement award in 1987, and in 1989 he appeared on the American Broadcasting Company (ABC) network's *Third Annual Comedy Awards.*

These periodic appearances twenty years after his show's cancellation are not the only testimony to the enduring impact of *The Red Skelton Show.* One of the greatest legacies of the show is a collection of some of television's most enduring characters, some of which have become part of the show-business lexicon: the "Mean Widdle Kid," the country bumpkin Clem Kadiddlehopper, the tramp Freddy the Freeloader, the drunk Willie Lump-Lump, the boxer Cauliflower McPugg, the cowboy Sheriff Deadeye, the corrupt politician San Fernando Red, and Professor J. Newton Numbskull. In fact, two of Skelton's most popular characters, the two seagulls Gertrude and Heathcliffe, appeared only in his monologue. A book (illustrated by Skelton, an accomplished painter in oils) called *Red Skelton's Gertrude and Heathcliffe* appeared in 1971. The show's cancellation that year did not harm sales, and the book was reprinted in 1974.

Steve Allen wrote in 1982 that, despite Skelton's seminal place in the history of television comedy, discussions of the genre rarely brought up his name any longer. Yet that same year, Michigan newspaper reporter Mary Achterhoff put the question directly to Skelton: A decade after his show's cancellation, did people still recognize him? Skelton drew himself up in dignity and responded, "Honey, do you have a mall around here?" When Achterhoff said yes, he replied, "Take me there!" The story Achterhoff printed the next day described the instant recognition and adulation Red Skelton received by mall shoppers young and old. The influence of Red Skelton did not end with *The Red Skelton Show.*

Bibliography

Allen, Steve. *The Funny Men.* New York: Simon & Schuster, 1956. Written when Skelton's television show was still relatively new, this book is a good picture of the world of comedy at the time the show began. The section on Skelton is penetrating and eloquent.

_____. *More Funny People.* New York: Stein & Day, 1982. The section on Skelton in this book is more than just an update of the one in Allen's previous book; it is a fresh and analytical look at the nature of Skelton's comedy. Deals with the television show only peripherally in a general study of Skelton's style.

Davidson, Bill. "I'm Nuts and I Know It." *Saturday Evening Post* 240 (June 17, 1967): 66-76. A personality sketch written at the height of the television show's popularity, this article implies but does not explore too deeply the manic undercurrent in Skelton's comedy. A good source of contemporary comments on the show, with twelve color photos (including the cover).

Marc, David, and Robert J. Thompson. *Prime Time, Prime Movers.* Boston: Little,

Brown, 1991. A compartmentalized study of prime-time television. Begins with a chapter on "Performer Authorship" in the early days of television that offers several pages of analysis on the rise and fall of Skelton's show.

Marx, Arthur. *Red Skelton: An Unauthorized Biography.* New York: E. P. Dutton, 1979. The most complete study of Skelton available, this book is also one of the most balanced. Because Marx's book is "unauthorized," it can cover some of the more controversial areas of Skelton's life and works; yet it does so with sensitivity and without sensationalism. A comedy writer himself, Marx (son of comedian Groucho Marx) has added insight into his subject.

John R. Holmes

Cross-References

Variety Shows Dominate Television Programming (1948), p. 1383; "Mr. Television," Milton Berle, Has the Top-Rated Show (1948), p. 1394; Television Enters Its Golden Age (1950's), p. 1465; *The Tonight Show* Becomes an American Institution (1954), p. 1623; *Rowan and Martin's Laugh-In* Is the Top Show on Television (1968), p. 2115; *The Sonny and Cher Comedy Hour* Brings Glitz to Television (1971), p. 2244; *Saturday Night Live* Is First Broadcast (1975), p. 2355.

I LOVE LUCY DOMINATES TELEVISION COMEDY

Category of event: Television and radio
Time: October 15, 1951-September 24, 1961
Locale: New York, New York, and Hollywood, California

Innovative in its manner of filming and use of sound techniques as well as strengthened by superb writing and acting, I Love Lucy *consistently ranked among the most popular shows of its era*

Principal personages:
LUCILLE BALL (1911-1989), an established film actress and radio personality who became the female lead on *I Love Lucy*
DESI ARNAZ (DESIDERIO ALBERTO ARNAZ Y DE ACHA III, 1917-1986), the Cuban entertainer who played the male lead on *I Love Lucy*
VIVIAN VANCE (1912-1979), the female costar who portrayed Lucy's neighbor, friend, and coconspirator
WILLIAM FRAWLEY (1887-1966), the Hollywood character actor who costarred as neighbor, landlord, and friend to Lucy and Desi
JESS OPPENHEIMER (1913-   ), the head writer during the early years of the show
KARL FREUND (1890-1969), the chief cinematographer for Desilu Productions

Summary of Event

Television was in its infancy in 1950, when the Columbia Broadcasting System (CBS) network notified Lucille Ball of its desire to transfer her successful radio program, *My Favorite Husband*, to television. Although only four million television sets were in American households at the time, this number represented a quadrupling of the number from the previous year. It was obvious that entertainment was shifting to the new visual medium.

An astute businessperson, Ball quickly recognized the growth potential of television and strongly favored the move. It was her desire, however, that the male lead in the show be portrayed by Desi Arnaz, a Cuban entertainer and bandleader who was Ball's real-life husband.

The network was reluctant to hire Arnaz for the part, for several reasons. First, there was concern about his ability to act. There was also a fear that the public would not accept a Cuban as Ball's husband. Ball's answer was simple and straightforward: "We *are* married!" To overcome the network's reluctance, Ball and Arnaz decided to perform a show on tour. Forming Desilu Productions in 1950, the pair traveled and displayed their act before live audiences. Cut short by Lucy's miscarriage, the show nevertheless demonstrated the popularity of the duo. The reviews of a pilot film, shot live on March 2, 1951, convinced the network that the show could be a success. CBS also created *My Favorite Husband* as a television show modeled more closely on Ball's radio program. It starred Barry Nelson and Joan Caulfield and aired from 1953 to 1957.

I Love Lucy became an immediate hit. Although the initial reviews were modest, by the end of the first season (1951-1952) the show was watched weekly in nearly eleven million homes, more than two-thirds of the households believed to own television sets. During the course of the six years in which original half-hour telecasts were shown (179 episodes), the show never ranked below third in popularity among television programs. An additional thirteen specials broadcast over the next three seasons proved equally popular.

The theme of the show was simple. Ball played Lucy Ricardo, an American of Scottish ancestry married to Ricky Ricardo, a prominent Cuban bandleader. Most episodes were built around Lucy's attempts to break out of the stereotypical housewife mold. Ricky, on the other hand, was quite happy with things as they were. The premise was simple, with the hilarity of plots built around superb writing and acting, particularly the slapstick comedy of Lucille Ball.

The Ricardos' neighbors and friends, Fred and Ethel Mertz, portrayed by Vivian Vance and William Frawley, were an integral part of the show. Ethel continually would be drawn into Lucy's mischief. Vance was an established stage actress prior to joining the show but had limited experience in performing before a camera. During World War II, she was among the first entertainers sent to a combat theater. Suffering a nervous breakdown after her return, Vance had been semiretired when she auditioned for *I Love Lucy*.

Frawley had been a character actor (and a singer, in his youth) for several decades, generally portraying gruff yet kindly personages, extensions of his own personality. As Fred Mertz, he was as often as not a victim of whatever mischief Lucy had concocted. Frawley was twenty-five years older than Vance, a fact that was at times a source of tension between the actors. Nevertheless, the two portrayed a couple that could be anyone's neighbors.

The essence of the show was its basis in reality. It often used slapstick comedy, but the comedy never stretched the boundaries of realism. Events would make sense. One could use as an example events portrayed in a show called "Job Switching," broadcast September 15, 1952. Lucy and Ethel switch roles with their husbands and end up working as candy makers. In a scene reminiscent of a children's food fight, Lucy becomes involved in a chocolate war. In a later scene, her job is to wrap candy as it goes by on a conveyor belt. Rather than having the belt speed up and slow down, as might be expected in a routine comedy act, the writers had the belt move slightly too fast for Lucy and Ethel to keep up. Anyone who ever worked on an assembly line can empathize with such a situation. Lucy and Ethel end up stuffing excess candy into blouses, mouths, and hats in an attempt to keep up with the moving line. The situation was silly but not divorced from reality.

One of the most popular events on the show, with a counterpart in real life, was the birth of Little Ricky on January 19, 1953. The same night, Lucille Ball gave birth to her son, and second child, Desi IV. The character of Little Ricky proved popular through the course of the show.

With the end of filming for the 1956-1957 season, Desilu Productions ceased production of the show as a weekly series. *I Love Lucy* still ranked as the second most popular program on television, but both Lucy and Desi hoped to cut back on their work loads and to branch into other types of productions. A series of one-hour specials, underwritten in part by Westinghouse, was planned under the title of *Desilu Playhouse*. Ultimately, thirteen shows were produced over the next three seasons.

With the completion of the original episodes, prime-time reruns of *I Love Lucy* continued to be shown on the CBS network for two years, with the last airing on September 24, 1961. Daytime reruns were shown on CBS until 1967. In 1960, Ball and Arnaz were divorced, their marriage strained by forced separations during earlier years and troubles aggravated by Arnaz's drinking and womanizing. They continued to run Desilu Productions jointly until Ball purchased Arnaz's shares in 1962. In 1967, Gulf and Western purchased Desilu Productions for $17 million in stock, officially dissolving the company.

Impact of Event

The level of success associated with *I Love Lucy* remains unparalleled in the history of television. When the show was telecast, America literally came to a halt. The show ranked in the number-one position four months after its inception. As noted by writer Bart Andrews, telephone companies reported substantial reductions in calls during its time slot (Mondays at 9:00 P.M. for most of its first-run showings). Taxicabs became difficult to find, as cabbies went into bars to watch the show. The large Marshall Field's department store in Chicago changed its evening hours from Monday to Thursday in response to the loss of business. Leaders of the Parent-Teacher Association (PTA) in Massachusetts demanded that the CBS affiliate broadcast the show earlier than 9:00 P.M. so children would go to bed at an earlier hour. Presidential candidate Adlai Stevenson earned wrath from the public by cutting into one broadcast with five minutes of advertising during the 1952 campaign.

The decision to film the episodes, rather than relying on kinescope as was the case with most early television, was an important development early in the evolution of the show. Arnaz and Ball wanted to film in Hollywood, near their home, while the network was broadcasting from New York City. Because the coast-to-coast coaxial cable was not yet in use, the only alternative was the use of low-quality kinescopes, or motion pictures made from images on a picture tube. The decision was made to use 35-millimeter film for the filming and broadcast. Al Simon, associate producer of the program, had discussed this issue with Ball, who suggested that he contact Karl Freund for advice. Freund had worked with Ball earlier in her film career, and he was known as a master at innovative sound and photography.

Simon explained their idea to film the program using three or four 35-millimeter cameras in front of a live audience, much as one would film a stage play. Freund immediately saw the problem: the different lighting required for shooting from different angles at the same time. Freund suggested the use of a system of "flat light-ing," an overhead lighting system in which the entire stage would be lit uniformly. The method would later become routine in film studios.

Other innovations used on the show eventually would become routine in the tele-vision industry. Tim Brooks and Earle Marsh, in their reviews of television history, suggested that Freund also developed the three-camera method used in filming *I Love Lucy*. This was not the case, however, as the system had been used for other television broadcasts. What was unique, however, was the development of "the mon-ster," a four-headed Moviola capable of holding four reels of film simultaneously. Previously, film editors were forced to spend an inordinate amount of time combin-ing rough cuts of film, since the standard Moviola could hold only a single reel at a time.

Some changes were not so much technical as practical. Filming of the initial shows was carried out from start to finish, without a significant break. Arnaz and Jess Oppenheimer, the show's head writer, decided that the program could be run much like a stage play, with breaks between scenes. In this manner, the use of set and costume changes could become routine. During breaks, Arnaz or others enter-tained and talked with the studio audience.

Because the show was to be filmed, a proper film studio became necessary. Simon discovered a seven-and-a-half-acre lot owned by General Service Studios in Hol-lywood. Desilu and CBS rented the facility and carried out extensive renovations to the stage. The set literally was rebuilt from the ground up and became the center-piece for Desilu Productions. Stage manager Herb Browar suggested the installation of permanent bleachers for seating an audience of three hundred. The bleachers were still standing nearly thirty years later when the studio was purchased by Fran-cis Ford Coppola.

I Love Lucy made household names out of four somewhat obscure actors and actresses. Lucille Ball was the major force on the show. Born in 1911, she showed an early interest in show business. Following several roles in chorus jobs, she studied modeling and once portrayed the Chesterfield cigarette girl. Through a chance meet-ing with a friend in 1933, she was brought to Hollywood by musical director Busby Berkeley. While there, Ball appeared in numerous films, eventually earning as much as fifteen hundred dollars a week. In 1940, she met and married a young singer and bandleader from Cuba, Desi Arnaz.

Arnaz had fled Cuba in 1933, settling in Miami, Florida. He worked at a number of jobs, including the cleaning of canary cages, until being discovered by Xavier Cugat while singing at a hotel. He had a number of bit parts before his marriage to Ball. Arnaz's impact on the show is easily underestimated. Both he and Ball worked closely with their writers, among the best available. If Arnaz believed that a scene lacked impact, it was removed. At least one script was shelved for personal reasons. That script was built around Ricky Ricardo cheating on his income tax. Proud of his Amer-ican citizenship, Arnaz refused to act out that script. Although his close scrutiny sometimes resulted in arguments among the staff, Arnaz always had the final say.

The Desilu empire became a Hollywood powerhouse. In addition to *I Love Lucy*, it produced such programs as *Make Room for Daddy, December Bride,* and *The Untouchables.* The production facilities were responsible for a large number of quality programs, ranging from comedy to drama, as part of the Westinghouse Desilu Playhouse from 1958 to 1960.

With the end of the series and the breakup of the Ball-Arnaz marriage, each principal in the show went his or her own way. Frawley had a starring role for five years in *My Three Sons,* but poor health forced his retirement in 1964. Lucille Ball temporarily retired from television, until her marriage to Gary Morton in 1962. Morton convinced her to return to television, which she did in 1962 with *The Lucy Show,* a Desilu Production produced by Desi Arnaz. Vivian Vance also starred on the program for three years. *The Lucy Show* ran for six years under that title, continuing as *Here's Lucy* for an additional six years. Although successful in this endeavor, Ball never was divorced completely from her previous roles in the eyes of her fans. Despite retirement, Ball returned to television with periodic specials until her death in 1989. Lucie Arnaz, Desi and Lucy's daughter, continued in the family entertainment tradition.

Desi Arnaz retired in 1962, later remarrying. Returning to television as an independent producer, he became involved with several television pilots. The most successful became *The Mothers-in-Law,* which ran from 1967 to 1969. Always a heavy smoker, Arnaz died from lung cancer in 1986.

Bibliography

Andrews, Bart. *The "I Love Lucy" Book.* Garden City, N.Y.: Doubleday, 1985. A revised and updated version of Andrews' previous work, it is the best story of the subject on the market. Numerous photographs are included, as well as a description of each episode of the show.

_____. *Lucy and Ricky and Fred and Ethel: The Story of "I Love Lucy."* New York: E. P. Dutton, 1976. A top-notch history of the show. Well written and anecdotal, it is the first major book on the subject.

Brooks, Tim, and Earle Marsh. *The Complete Directory to Prime Time Network TV Shows: 1946-Present.* New York: Ballantine Books, 1979. Includes a history of television networks. The authors provide a synopsis for each show aired on prime-time television beginning in 1946.

Harris, Warren G. *Lucy and Desi.* New York: Simon & Schuster, 1991. An excellent biography of the principal actor and actress on the show. Well written and detailed, though perhaps a bit dramatic in its presentation. Numerous photographs.

McNeil, Alex. *Total Television.* 3d ed. New York: Penguin Books, 1991. A programming guide to television programs from 1948 on. Contains a list of "special occasions" and a program guide that begins in 1948.

Richard Adler

Cross-References

Television Enters Its Golden Age (1950's), p. 1465; Television Family Comedy Becomes Extremely Popular (1950's), p. 1470; *The Honeymooners* Enchants Audiences of All Ages (1955), p. 1673; Situation Comedies Dominate Television Programming (1960's), p. 1835; *The Dick Van Dyke Show* Popularizes Situation Comedy (1961), p. 1908.

DRAGNET IS THE FIRST
WIDELY POPULAR POLICE SHOW

Category of event: Television and radio
Time: December 16, 1951
Locale: The United States

Dragnet *became the prototype for all realistic drama series and introduced the "docudrama" to American television*

Principal personages:
> JACK WEBB (1920-1982), the creator, star, and driving force behind the *Dragnet* series
> BARTON YARBOROUGH (1911-1951), the costar of the television pilot and the radio series
> BEN ALEXANDER (1911-1969), Webb's costar throughout most of the first run
> HARRY MORGAN (1915-   ), Webb's costar in the return of the show between 1967 and 1970

Summary of Event

On Sunday, December 16, 1951, the pilot episode of *Dragnet*, entitled "The Human Bomb," was aired on the National Broadcasting Company (NBC) television network. The series became one of the most popular programs in the early days of television, with an estimated thirty-eight million viewers per week, regularly putting the show among the top five in ratings. It also is credited with bringing realism to television, along with establishing numerous new production techniques.

Since 1949, *Dragnet* had been a popular radio show. In this medium, Jack Webb, the show's creator, played Sergeant Joe Friday and Barton Yarborough was his partner, Ben Romero. Webb got the idea for a realistic police drama from a conversation with technical adviser Marty Wynn on the film set of *He Walked by Night* (1948), a police drama in which Webb acted. With the growth in popularity of television, *Dragnet* joined other successful radio shows in switching to the new medium.

Beginning with the pilot, Webb introduced to television audiences the "docudrama," a fact-based story with some fictional characterization. Webb's voice-over narrative gave viewers a highly believable personal account while taking them through the steps of crime solving. In Webb's view, authenticity must never be sacrificed, and he emphasized the meticulous nature of police work. He gained a reputation as a workaholic and perfectionist.

In the attempt to depict realism and also to save on production costs, the pilot was filmed on location at Los Angeles City Hall. This set the precedent for future *Dragnet* shows. The episode began when, backed by the *Dragnet* theme, a narrator uttered the now-famous line (moved in later episodes to a spot after a brief introduction) assuring the audience of the story's validity: "The story you are about to see is true. The names have been changed to protect the innocent." Then, Webb's voice-over stated, "This is the city." After a brief description of Los Angeles and its City Hall, Webb then went into his account of the date, weather conditions, and the specific circumstances surrounding the episode. Webb and Yarborough reprised their radio roles as Friday and Romero, while Raymond Burr portrayed Chief of Detectives Thad Brown. Stacy Harris played Vernon Carney, who threatened to detonate an explosive device in City Hall unless his brother was released from prison. Throughout the remainder of the program, viewers witnessed the tense and dangerous but nevertheless realistic disarming of the bomb carrier. In what became another *Dragnet* tradition, the accused, looking somber and somewhat contrite, appeared on the screen at the show's conclusion. At this point, another narrator stated the nature of the court's decision. In the case of Vernon Carney, confinement to a state institution for the criminally insane was the sentence.

The popularity of the pilot ensured *Dragnet* a spot as a midseason replacement on NBC. On January 3, 1952, the series began its regular run, with Webb and Yarborough appearing as the main characters. Yarborough, however, had died on December 19, 1951, after filming only two episodes. Webb tried a number of replacements before choosing former child star Ben Alexander as his new partner, Officer Frank Smith. Both on the set and in the story line itself, the easygoing Alexander proved to be the perfect counterpoint for the intense and driven Webb. Over the next seven years, Webb and Alexander would appear together in more than 250 episodes.

Webb's desire for authenticity was achieved by using actual cases from the Los Angeles Police Department and having the participating police officers utilized as technical advisers. Adherence to the legal framework of police procedures, painstaking fact-finding, and teamwork were stressed. The episodes ranged from more common cases, such as an investigation of hit-and-run drivers and the solving of a liquor store robbery, to the more unusual, including a man strangled with his own necktie and a probe into swindlers preying upon military families. Only one episode was not based on actual police files. The annual Christmas story relating the investigation of a church's missing Christ child was fictitious.

Dragnet was one of the highest-rated shows during the early and mid-1950's. Normally, it placed second or third in the ratings. *I Love Lucy* could be counted on to gain the top spot, and only Arthur Godfrey's talent shows and later *The Honeymooners* regularly challenged *Dragnet*. As early as 1954, however, the restless Webb considered leaving the series. The demanding production schedule, the belief that viewers would soon tire of the program, and his interest in other projects were responsible for this attitude. Webb was criticized for neglecting *Dragnet* in favor of *Pete Kelly's Blues*, a 1959 summer series he had developed. Despite these problems, the show continued. By the late 1950's, the popularity of *Dragnet* began to drop, and it was barely breaking the top twenty in ratings. In 1959, after 278 episodes, Webb voluntarily canceled the series.

After a successful television movie in 1966, *Dragnet* returned as a midseason replacement on NBC in 1967. In order to preclude any perception that reruns were being aired, the show was titled *Dragnet '67*, with later years' episodes also dated. Citing the public's increased interest in urban crime, Webb hoped to combine the old formula with contemporary subjects. Webb would repeat his role as Joe Friday, but since Ben Alexander was already featured in another crime drama, *Felony Squad*, Webb chose Harry Morgan as his new partner, Officer Bill Gannon. Friday, who had risen to the rank of lieutenant in the old series, returned as a sergeant. Once again citing his desire for authenticity, Webb stated that the higher rank would have kept the character from participating in field investigations and thus limited the plot potential.

Although the new series continued to feature the more common types of police investigations, such as robbery, fraud, and missing persons, an emphasis was placed on such issues as race relations and illegal drugs. The first episode on *Dragnet '67* focused on the growing drug culture in Los Angeles and a young man who became a victim of this phenomenon. Other episodes focused on police relations with minority groups. Despite a growth of violence on police dramas, *Dragnet* avoided any tendency in this direction. Although Webb received praise for these efforts, others criticized his characterizations. Sergeant Friday was seen as one-dimensional and too close to perfection. The series was perceived by some as condescending, preachy, and somewhat out of step with the reality of inner-city life.

By the fall of 1970, the new show had run its course, and Webb was involved in other projects. On September 10 of that year, the final episode was shown. First-run episodes of *Dragnet* thus aired on American television for more than ten years. In the process, the series garnered more than one hundred awards from within and outside the entertainment business, including three Emmys.

Impact of Event

Dragnet had a major impact upon the development and style of television programming. It also had a variety of effects on the American public. Its impact and effects ranged from easily definable new production techniques to the more complex relationships between the program and its audience.

Jack Webb was responsible for a number of innovations in the television industry. Along with *I Love Lucy*, *Dragnet* was one of the few early shows to opt for filmed programming instead of live performances. Prior to the success of these shows, filmed television was seen as second rate and was used primarily as "fill-in" material. When industry executives and viewers saw that quality programs need not be live, filming became the principal means of presentation. *Dragnet* took this process one step further in December of 1953, when it became the first series to broadcast regularly in color.

Dragnet also was a major impetus for making Los Angeles the center of the television industry. Most early programs originated from New York. Since the major networks were headquartered in that city and many shows were done live in the studios, this was a logical choice. When *Dragnet* and *I Love Lucy* began to use film, television could take advantage of the facilities in Hollywood. Increasingly, new shows used the Los Angeles area as their base of operation.

Another impact that *Dragnet* had upon the entertainment business and the American public was in its use of music and dialogue. The famous *Dragnet* theme, with its powerful nine-note beginning, was composed by Walter Schumann. The theme proved to be so popular that during 1953 a version of it by Ray Anthony and His Orchestra rose to number three on the *Billboard* chart. Even long after the conclusion of the series, *Dragnet*'s musical introduction symbolized the crime-drama genre. Joe Friday's narrative and clichés also filtered into the popular culture. Although the frequency of their use on the series was somewhat exaggerated, such terms as "just the facts" were often used in everyday speech. These were among the first examples of television's ability to affect other forms of entertainment and to influence American popular culture.

Jack Webb is given credit for establishing a sense of realism in the new medium of television. Most other early programs were vaudeville-type comedies or variety shows, or presented heroes who were detached from the average viewer. Webb attempted to avoid stereotypes and portrayed people as they really behaved, including all of their good and bad points. This characterization extended to the police officers themselves. Although the police usually were portrayed in a favorable light, Webb often delved into the conflicts and misconduct of department members. Such topics as family problems, the taking of bribes, and unprofessional behavior often were presented. His success demonstrated that television programs could be realistic and still gain a large viewership.

In creating the first realistic crime drama on television, Webb broke with the tradition of the romantic lone investigator. Instead of relying on superior intellect or a tough image, the police officers in *Dragnet* depended on hard work and solid research as the means of solving cases. The audience was shown characters who used acceptable means to help society. The show also reinforced the adage that crime did not pay. By using these techniques, Webb was able to identify with the average viewer, supporting such traditional values as the work ethic and good citizenship. *Dragnet* episodes were often shown to school and civic groups to reinforce these themes. It is difficult to determine the success of such efforts.

Another area in which *Dragnet* attempted to influence the American public was with regard to a sense of justice. There was no doubt that Joe Friday was a law-and-order conservative. He never stepped beyond the bounds of the Constitution, however, relying upon the law to determine what was right, not some form of street justice. By the 1970's, individual codes of justice and working around the law had become the norm in police dramas. Even with regard to civil rights issues, Webb tried to convey a sense of fairness. At times, these efforts were a bit awkward and one could question whether such justice really existed. Despite these shortcomings, *Dragnet* did serve as an example of respect for Constitutional law.

The docudrama style, first used on television by *Dragnet*, was soon copied by a number of shows, such as *Medic*, *The Lineup*, and *Justice*, all shows of the 1950's.

Dragnet's popularization of the crime drama would, by 1953, result in the creation of more than twenty new shows in that genre. In the late 1960's and early 1970's, Webb utilized this style to create two new popular shows, *Adam 12* and *Emergency*. By this period, docudramas had become one of the major means of presenting television drama.

Dragnet was the prototype for many aspects of modern television. Its production methods, including a Los Angeles base and filmed and color episodes, became standards in the business. The dialogue and music transcended the medium and became part of popular culture. Its images had so infused American culture that film audiences could identify immediately with the 1987 parody of the show. Perhaps most important, *Dragnet* and Jack Webb infused realism into television.

Bibliography

Castleman, Harry, and Walter J. Podrazik. *Watching TV: Four Decades of American Television*. New York: McGraw-Hill, 1982. Although this is an overview of television history, it devotes a great deal of space to discussing both the development of *Dragnet* and its role in American television history. It gives a solid account of the series' format and its impact upon both the television industry and the public in general.

Fireman, Judy, ed. *TV Book: The Ultimate Television Book*. New York: Workman, 1977. This book presents separate and brief articles on a variety of subjects in television history. Although it is useful in placing *Dragnet* in the context of early television, specific information on the series is limited.

Grossberger, Lewis. "Jack Webb: 1920-1982." *Rolling Stone* (February 17, 1983): 68. Obituary of Webb describing Sergeant Joe Friday as a perfect hero for the 1950's.

Kaminsky, Stuart M., with Jeffrey H. Mahan. *American Television Genres*. Chicago: Nelson-Hall, 1985. Although its discussion of the series is brief, the work does present a comparison of the *Dragnet* detectives with other investigators in literary and motion-picture history. The book also includes a good analysis of the crime-drama genre.

Tregaskis, Richard. "The Cops' Favorite Make-Believe Cop." *The Saturday Evening Post* (September 26, 1953): 24-25+. This article offers a look at the process that led to the making of *Dragnet* and discusses the show's early history. It also gives an insight into Jack Webb's personality and work habits.

Paul J. Zbiek

Cross-References

The Sherlock Holmes Film Series Begins (1939), p. 1131; *The Maltese Falcon* Establishes a New Style for Crime Films (1941), p. 1223; Television Enters Its Golden Age (1950's), p. 1465; Violent Action-Adventure Television Series Flourish (1975), p. 2330; *Hill Street Blues* Defines Hard-Reality Television (1981), p. 2470.

AMAHL AND THE NIGHT VISITORS PREMIERES
ON AMERICAN TELEVISION

Categories of event: Television and radio; music
Time: December 24, 1951
Locale: The United States

On Christmas Eve, 1951, Gian Carlo Menotti's Amahl and the Night Visitors, *the first opera commissioned especially for television, was premiered by the National Broadcasting Company*

Principal personages:
  GIAN CARLO MENOTTI (1911-   ), a celebrated American composer whose appealing operas rank among the world's most popular musical dramas
  SAMUEL BARBER (1910-1981), a noted American composer and Menotti's lifelong friend, who helped Menotti to orchestrate *Amahl and the Night Visitors*
  SAMUEL CHOTZINOFF (1889-1964), a Russian-American pianist and critic who commissioned Menotti to write *Amahl and the Night Visitors*
  ROSARIO SCALERO (1870-1954), an eminent composer and teacher whose composition students at Philadelphia's Curtis School of Music included Menotti, Barber, and Lukas Foss
  THOMAS SCHIPPERS (1930-1977), a gifted American conductor who presided over the orchestra for *Amahl and the Night Visitors'* debut

Summary of Event

When Gian Carlo Menotti's *Amahl and the Night Visitors* was telecast by the National Broadcasting Company (NBC) on December 24, 1951, the event marked the premiere of the first opera commissioned specifically for television. Like many of Menotti's works, though, the one-act Christmas musical drama had a difficult birth. Though the opera was commissioned by NBC in early 1951 for broadcast on Christmas Eve of the same year, Menotti started composing in earnest only on Thanksgiving Day, after calling NBC executive music director Samuel Chotzinoff, who had commissioned the work for the network, to announce that he at last had a title for the project: *Amahl and the Night Visitors.* Created in a tumult of furious composition, orchestration, and rehearsal, *Amahl and the Night Visitors* was, in spite of the last-minute nature of its creation, an unqualified success.

Indeed, almost immediately following its debut broadcast, *Amahl and the Night Visitors* was deemed a classic. The critics loved it. So, too, did the public; in response, NBC made the program a Christmas television tradition for fourteen consecutive years. The work was translated into dozens of foreign languages, and by

1960, *Amahl and the Night Visitors* had become America's most beloved and most performed opera.

The inspiration for the work came from several sources—Menotti's childhood in Italy, where there was no tradition of Santa Claus and where gifts to children were instead brought by the Three Kings; Menotti's love for children and his devotion to creating works for them; and Menotti's conceptualization of opera as musical theater in which the basic elements of dramaturgy—plot, character, and action—are of an aesthetic weight equal to that of the music.

These aspects coalesced in galvanizing fashion just a few days before Thanksgiving in 1951, when Menotti, fretting over the impending deadline and his inability to come up with even a shred of an idea for the libretto, walked despondently through the galleries of the Metropolitan Museum of Art. Suddenly he found himself confronting *The Adoration of the Kings*, the masterpiece by noted Flemish Renaissance painter Hieronymous Bosch. At once, Menotti "heard" a "weird" song of the Three Kings that he had remembered from his youth. For the composer, it was clear that a miracle had happened. The Three Kings, as they did in childhood, had brought Menotti a wondrous gift—this time, the basic subject matter for his new opera.

Another childhood incident figured prominently into the limning of Amahl, the opera's youthful protagonist. As a boy in Italy, Menotti, as the result of an unknown malady, had been crippled for several weeks. When modern medicine failed to provide a remedy, Menotti's concerned nurse took him to the sanctuary of Sacro Monte near his hometown of Cadegliano to seek the help of a venerated Madonna image that was believed capable of performing miracles. In front of the Madonna, the young Menotti's leg was blessed. Amazingly, it mended quickly, and thereafter Menotti was able to walk normally. He was also able to transpose that indelible experience, the apparently supernatural healing of his own crippled condition, into *Amahl and the Night Visitors'* narrative structure, in which a similar miracle functions to resolve the opera's dramatic conflicts.

With the opera's central characters and plot line finally set, Menotti, in a frenzy of activity, managed to write, score, and rehearse *Amahl and the Night Visitors* in a matter of weeks. He also wrote the work's compelling libretto. Messengers made daily trips from New York City to Capricorn, Menotti's country home in Mount Kisco, New York, for a page or two of manuscript so that it could be copied and delivered to the performers, who had started rehearsals in early December. As the deadline loomed, Samuel Barber—Menotti's friend since the late 1920's, when they had studied together at Philadelphia's Curtis Institute of Music under Rosario Scalero—assisted by helping with the orchestration. Rehearsals intensified, and Menotti took a direct hand as stage director working alongside NBC television director Kirk Browning. Somehow, in spite of the self-inflicted pressures of the seemingly impossible schedule, Menotti—ably abetted by his many colleagues—achieved an artistic miracle.

Menotti's commission for the opera resulted from his relationship with Samuel Chotzinoff, the NBC executive in charge of the ambitiously visionary NBC Television Opera Theater. In 1939, Chotzinoff had commissioned Menotti to write an opera in English for radio. The result was *The Old Maid and the Thief*, which premiered on NBC's Blue Network in April, 1939; the work was the first opera commissioned specifically for radio. It was also Menotti's first commission of any kind, as well as the composer's first libretto in English. Most significant, it was a success, and after its first stage performance in 1941, *The Old Maid and the Thief*, like *Amahl and the Night Visitors* a decade later, became one of the most frequently performed operas in the standard repertory. Its popularity stemmed from its libretto in English, its use of a small orchestra, its accessible musicality, and—no small matter—its gripping story, highlighted by lifelike characters and Menotti's overall sense of compelling dramatic construction. When NBC sought to commission and produce the first original opera written specifically for the then-young television medium, it was not surprising that the network would turn to Gian Carlo Menotti.

Impact of Event

Menotti's libretto for *Amahl and the Night Visitors* is deceptively simple. Set near Bethlehem at the time of Christ's birth, the tale concerns a crippled boy, Amahl, and his mother, who live in abject poverty. The Three Kings, on their way to Bethlehem, stop to rest in the little family's wretched hovel. As they tell of the generous gifts they are taking to the newborn Christ, Amahl's mother becomes desperate and asks herself why her own child should go without food. After the kings fall asleep, the mother, risking all to save her son, steals from the kings. She is caught, but she is quickly forgiven. As the kings tell of the wondrous child they seek, Amahl offers his most precious possession, his own rough-hewn crutch, as his gift to the infant Christ. Miraculously, Amahl finds that he can now walk without it. Amahl begs his mother to allow him to accompany the kings and take the crutch to the infant Christ himself. The mother accedes, and as the hopeful band departs for Bethlehem, the screen fades to black.

Menotti's music is also deceptively simple. In keeping with Menotti's declaration that the work is "an opera for children," the vocal requirements for the principals are essentially nonvirtuosic. Yet they are artful and a testament to Menotti's gift as a Pucciniesque melodist. The vocal parts for the one-act opera can perhaps best be regarded as freely interpreted and sparsely accompanied recitatives, a strategy that enables Menotti's *Verismo* lyrics to "speak" clearly. For example, when the mother, exasperated by her son's propensity for embellishing the truth, declaims, "Oh! Amahl, when will you stop telling lies? Here we have nothing to eat and all you do is worry your mother with fairy tales," viewers share her frustration—while at the same time empathizing with Amahl's rich imaginative powers.

Menotti's melodic writing is essentially diatonic, with folklike flavorings. In all, the score is a work of great tonal charm. In contrast to the darkness and dissonance of so much so-called modern music, moreover, Menotti centers his opera in C major, a key associated with connotations of optimism and happiness. The small-scale orchestral palette—flute, two oboes, clarinet, bassoon, horn, trumpet, harp, percussion, and strings—further enhances the ethereal transparency of Menotti's fairy-tale-like music and story.

Amahl and the Night Visitors' initial success owed much to its original cast: twelve-year-old Chet Allen as Amahl, Rosemary Kuhlmann as Amahl's mother, Andrew McKinley as King Kaspar, David Aiken as King Melchior, Leon Lishner as King Balthazar, and Francis Monachino as the page. It also owed much to Thomas Schippers' spirited and sensitive conducting, the expert orchestral players of NBC's musical staff, the settings and costumes of Eugene Berman, and the spartan yet highly effective "live" television direction of NBC's Kirk Browning.

The NBC broadcast of the opera received rave reviews in the major newspapers and weekly newsmagazines. Olin Downes, in an unprecedented front-page review in *The New York Times* on Christmas morning, wrote that "Mr. Menotti with rare art has produced a work that few indeed could have seen and heard last night save through blurred eyes and with emotions that were not easy to conceal. It may be said at once that television, operatically speaking, has come of age." Even a judge as stern as maestro Arturo Toscanini praised *Amahl and the Night Visitors* as Menotti's finest opera.

Interestingly, the fact that *Amahl and the Night Visitors* had made television history seemed to be of little consequence to Menotti. Indeed, the composer recalled that as he was composing the work, the thought of television never really entered his mind. "To me," Menotti has said, "cinema, television and radio seem rather pale substitutes for the magic of the stage. This is why I intentionally disregarded the mobility of the screen and limited myself to the symbolic simplicity of the stage."

Amahl and the Night Visitors was given its stage premiere on April 9, 1952, by the New York City Opera; virtually all the principals from the NBC broadcast were carried over. Again, the critics and public raved. With the "launch" provided by the New York City Opera production and the availability of the score from Menotti's publisher, *Amahl and the Night Visitors* began its rapid ascent to the status of America's most frequently performed and, arguably, most beloved opera.

Amahl and the Night Visitors' lasting appeal is the consequence of several factors, including the work's association with the Christmas season, its modest casting and accompanying requirements, its artfully conceived and nonvirtuosic nature, which makes the work capable of production by even amateur and school groups, and its fifty-minute length.

The character of Amahl is also central to the opera's durability. Indeed, in almost Dickensian fashion, Menotti specified that Amahl must be "a naughty little boy—a little devil. The character should be impish. He tells lies, he is disobedient." He also is caring and generous, and is literally and figuratively transformed by the prospect of taking his crutch to the Christ child. In the score, Menotti expressed further concern about the casting of Amahl: "It is the wish of the composer that the role of Amahl should always be performed by a boy. Neither the musical nor the dramatic concept of the opera permits the substitution of a woman, costumed as a child." This point was essential to Menotti, who viewed the action, and even the characteristics of the adult figures, as being dictated by Amahl's point of view. In Menotti's words: "All these must be interpreted simply and directly in terms of a child's imagination."

It might be concluded that the opera's ultimate appeal lies in the fact that it is family entertainment par excellence. Although the work was intended by Menotti as "an opera for children," the opera's dramatic as well as musical focus, along with the composer's masterful mix of naïveté and sophistication, has made *Amahl and the Night Visitors* a work attractive and accessible to all ages and virtually all tastes.

Bibliography

Archibald, Bruce. "Amahl and the Night Visitors." In *The New Grove Dictionary of Opera*. Vol. 1, edited by Stanley Sadie. New York: Grove's Dictionaries of Music, 1992. An overview of the plot of *Amahl and the Night Visitors* and an appreciation of the opera's enduring appeal.

_____. "Gian Carlo Menotti." In *The New Grove Dictionary of American Music*. Vol. 3, edited by H. Wiley Hitchcock and Stanley Sadie. New York: Grove's Dictionaries of Music, 1986. A concise yet critical review of Menotti's career, with a useful listing of Menotti's compositions. Bibliography.

Ardoin, John. *The Stages of Menotti*. New York: Doubleday, 1985. Ardoin's indispensable and comprehensive treatment focuses on the composer's work in chapters such as "The Television Stage." Lavishly illustrated with an excellent collection of photos edited by Gerald Fitzgerald. Includes a complete chronology of Menotti's varied works, a discography, and a highly useful bibliography.

Graf, Herbert. *Producing Opera for America*. New York: Atlantis Books, 1961. Opera producer Graf, in describing possibilities for producing opera in America, cites *Amahl and the Night Visitors* in several visionary discussions of "Opera on Television" and "Opera on Film."

Gruen, John. *Menotti: A Biography*. New York: Macmillan, 1978. Gruen's compelling biography is a mine of revealing insights connecting the often convoluted links between Menotti's personal and artistic lives. Extensive discussion of *Amahl and the Night Visitors* is included in the chapter entitled "The Gorgon." Illustrated.

Menotti, Gian Carlo. *Amahl and the Night Visitors: Opera in One Act*. New York: G. Schirmer, 1952. The complete score for *Amahl and the Night Visitors* is arranged here for piano rather than orchestra.

Charles Merrell Berg

Cross-References

Gershwin's *Porgy and Bess* Opens in New York (1935), p. 1016; Television Enters Its Golden Age (1950's), p. 1465; Joplin's *Treemonisha* Is Staged by the Houston Opera (1975), p. 2350; *Einstein on the Beach* Is a Triumph of Minimalism (1976), p. 2375; Adams' *Nixon in China* Premieres (1987), p. 2599.

ELLISON'S *INVISIBLE MAN* IS PUBLISHED

Category of event: Literature
Time: April, 1952
Locale: New York, New York

Ralph Ellison published Invisible Man, *a complex portrayal of the role of blacks in the United States that won recognition as one of the best post-World War II novels*

Principal personage:
RALPH ELLISON (1914-   ), the author whose novel *Invisible Man* opened new themes for later black authors

Summary of Event

Ralph Waldo Ellison was born in Oklahoma City, Oklahoma, on March 1, 1914, the son of Lewis and Ida Ellison and the grandson of slaves. He received a good education in Oklahoma and in 1933 moved to Alabama to study at Tuskegee Institute. He studied classical music and read avidly, devouring the works of major Western literary and intellectual masters.

In July, 1936, Ellison went to New York and was captivated by the city's vibrant cultural life. Writing soon replaced music as his main interest, and he began to write reviews, essays, and short stories. He worked for the Federal Writers' Project and as managing editor of *Negro Quarterly*, and in 1945 he was awarded a Rosenwald Fellowship to write a novel. The result, *Invisible Man*, took nearly seven years to write and was published by Random House in 1952.

Ellison's book is narrated by a nameless "Invisible Man," who, in a prologue, explains that he has literally gone underground, where he lives in a sealed-off basement in a whites-only apartment building bordering Harlem. He has become invisible, he says, as a result of having accepted other people's names and labels for himself: "I was looking for myself and asking everyone except myself questions which I, and only I, could answer." The Invisible Man then recounts the incidents that have brought him to his current state.

As a child in the South, the narrator encounters several wise people who try to teach him that he alone is responsible for his destiny. The young man's dying grandfather tells his family that he has been "a spy in the enemy's country." The grandfather advises the narrator how to deal with whites: "Live with your head in the lion's mouth. I want you to overcome 'em with yeses, undermine 'em with grins, agree 'em to death and destruction, let 'em swoller you till they vomit or bust wide open." Carrying out such a strategy in the "enemy country," though, requires self-knowledge that the young man does not have.

When he is a senior in high school, a group of prominent white men invite him to speak to them. He feels honored, seeing himself as a race spokesman in the manner of Booker T. Washington. The white men, though, let him speak only after subjecting him to ritual humiliation. His speech is a naïve parody of Booker T. Washington's message: that blacks should accept social segregation, renounce political agitation, and win acceptance from whites through hard work. The drunken white men then give him a briefcase and a scholarship to a college for blacks.

That night, the young man dreams that his grandfather appears and shows him a document inside the new briefcase. "To Whom It May Concern," the document reads, "Keep This Nigger-Boy Running." The narrator awakens to the sound of his grandfather's laughter.

The Invisible Man learns that the enemy country contains blacks as well as whites. He goes to a famous college for blacks (much like Tuskegee) that is run by Dr. Herbert Bledsoe, a Booker T. Washington-like figure. Bledsoe uses his influence with rich white Northerners to exercise great power; the Invisible Man, though, describes his ambiguous view of a statue of the college's founder lifting a veil from the face of a slave: "I am standing puzzled, unable to decide whether the veil is really being lifted, or lowered more firmly in place; whether I am witnessing a revelation or a more efficient blinding." He then meets a wise man, a veteran, who tells him, "Be your own father, young man. And remember, the world is possibility if only you'll discover it." The narrator, though, does not yet understand the message.

The young man goes north to Harlem, long a symbol to blacks of freedom and cultural vitality. He intends to take advantage of New York's freedom and wealth to achieve success, but he soon finds that he is everywhere met with a more polite version of his grandfather's dream-letter: "Keep This Nigger-Boy Running."

The Invisible Man comes to a clearer understanding of the enemy country, but he still cannot fathom how to fight on this terrain. He has to learn a few more hard lessons. He meets Brother Jack, a white man who controls the Brotherhood, a radical political organization. The Invisible Man joins the Brotherhood, but he finds that he is expected to sacrifice the people of Harlem for some larger ideological goal. The Invisible Man thus learns that political leaders turn people into abstractions and exploit their trust.

The Invisible Man also comes into contact with Ras the Exhorter, a black nationalist. Ras challenges the young man to confront the meaning of his own blackness, but the Invisible Man comes to see that Ras, like Brother Jack, uses people to enhance his personal power.

The Invisible Man at last finds one person who has mastered the terrain of the enemy's country. B. P. (Bliss Proteus) Rinehart assumes different forms to fit his environment. Some people see him as a minister, some as a gambler and numbers runner, some as an underworld boss and corrupter of the police, some as a lover. "His world was possibility and he knew it," the Invisible Man says. "He was years ahead of me and I was a fool. I must have been crazy and blind. The world in which we lived was without boundaries." Now he understands the message of the veteran: One can, in fact, be one's own father, remaking oneself as one desires. The narrator recalls that the revelation at first frightened him: "The world seemed to flow before my eyes. All boundaries down, freedom was not only the recognition of necessity, it was the recognition of possibility."

Finally, trapped in a riot in Harlem, caught between agents of the Brotherhood and Ras the Exhorter, and chased by white racists, the Invisible Man pops into a hole and finds protection in the surrounding darkness.

As the book ends, the Invisible Man is not hiding in his basement but hibernating. He will emerge, he says, with the wiliness of Br'er Rabbit and the strength of Br'er Bear. When he emerges, his message will not be one of abstractions and hate but one of love, based on his understanding of shared humanity and culture.

Impact of Event

When it was published in 1952, *Invisible Man* quickly established its reputation as one of the most important and influential post-World War II novels. Random House recognized the book's potential and sent advance copies to reviewers equipped to deal with such a challenging work. The novel received favorable reviews from such major literary figures as Saul Bellow, Wright Morris, Delmore Schwartz, and Langston Hughes and won the National Book Award in 1953.

The literary establishment readily accepted Ellison. Although he faced criticism for not being outspoken during the Civil Rights movement, *Invisible Man* survived all changes in political moods and movements, and Ellison continued to receive recognition as a major cultural figure. He received the Medal of Freedom and in 1964 was appointed to the American Institute of Arts and Letters. By the 1990's, *Invisible Man* was firmly established in the American literary canon.

While black civil rights leaders mobilized masses of people to wage a political and moral battle against racism and segregation, Ellison fought for freedom on another battlefield. His victory helped to free young black authors from limiting racial labels. Previous black writers, including Ellison's friend Richard Wright, were frequently given such condescending labels as "black author," "race spokesman," or "protest novelist."

Some reviewers went too far and ignored Ellison's race altogether. Ellison, however, explored ways in which blacks were subjected to social segregation, political manipulation, and economic exploitation. He wrote from a black point of view and drew from black culture. It was black folklore and music that gave characters such as the Invisible Man's grandfather their moral and intellectual strength. The Invisible Man was a product of the same racist society as Richard Wright's famous character, the culturally impoverished Bigger Thomas. In contrast to Wright, though, Ellison saw a richness in black culture that nourished its people and allowed them to transcend the limitations of their surroundings while giving them the strength to fight for change.

While Ellison explored racial discrimination, he raised deeper questions about American culture and the role of black writers within it. Ellison argued that his culture could be described neither as African nor as an American subculture. He wrote as a Westerner, as an heir to all the rich complexity of Western civilization. Whites had tried to confine blacks but had failed; blacks had absorbed all the richness of American and Western culture. Blues music, for example, was distantly related to African music, but it was much more closely related to Western religious music, European ballads, and Southern musical traditions, enriched in theme by black folklore and cultural concerns.

Ellison did not see himself limited in his literary ancestry to black writers such as Langston Hughes and Richard Wright. Homer, Dante Alighieri, and Vergil were as much his ancestors as they were for any Western writer. If Ellison introduces blues and jazz references in *Invisible Man*, he also alludes to Homer, William Shakespeare, and Walt Whitman. From the opening line of the novel, Ellison carries on a continuous dialogue with such predecessors as Shakespeare, Edgar Allan Poe, Herman Melville, Fyodor Dostoevski, James Joyce, T. S. Eliot, and Ernest Hemingway. The novel itself draws on symbolic, realistic, and surrealistic traditions in Western literature. In later decades, it was seen as an example of Magical Realism, a style usually associated with post-World War II Latin American writers, and as an early example of postmodernist writing.

Ellison's work allowed later writers, white and black, to free themselves from the one-dimensional approach that often characterized works about black men and women. While Ellison showed readers the pain and humiliation that blacks faced in the United States, he also celebrated the diversity and democratic chaos of American culture that prevented blacks from being turned into creatures of the whites. Whites could never prevent blacks from enjoying the cultural richness that was part of the American heritage.

At another level, Ellison helped to bring into postwar American literature the existential themes shaping European literature. Ellison dealt with the plight of a young man thrust into the chaos of the world. He was concerned with the way that men and women of all races met their individual doom. He explored the fictional structures that people imposed on a world that had no structure. The world had many names, Ellison said, and they all spelled chaos. Before humans could discover even one of those names, they must name themselves. This was the trial that the Invisible Man faced: to name himself before he began his ambiguous struggle for freedom in the world. Ellison wrote that life is a formless sea into which humans are thrust; art is the ship that reduces it to form and course.

Ellison was a major influence on the experimental fiction of white and black writers after World War II. His approach to the novel influenced white writers such as Joseph Heller and freed black writers from the confines of the protest novel. Younger black writers explored the territory opened by Ellison, carried on their own dialogues with him in their fiction, and adopted his experimental mode of writing. Ellison left such later black writers as Ishmael Reed, Alice Walker, and Toni Morrison a richer literary terrain than the one that he had inherited from Richard Wright.

Bibliography

Benston, Kimberly W., ed. *Speaking for You: The Vision of Ralph Ellison.* Washington, D.C.: Howard University Press, 1987. A collection of nearly thirty articles on aspects of Ralph Ellison's life and works, focusing on *Invisible Man.* Includes several interviews with Ellison, who is one of the best critics of his own work.

Busby, Mark. *Ralph Ellison.* Boston: Twayne, 1991. The best short introduction to Ellison's life and work. Busby introduces readers to the major critical approaches to Ellison's work and provides an up-to-date bibliography of Ellison's writings and studies of him.

Covo, Jacqueline. *The Blinking Eye: Ralph Waldo Ellison and His American, French, German, and Italian Critics, 1952-1971.* Metuchen, N.J.: Scarecrow Press, 1974. An interesting work; Covo summarizes international biographical and bibliographical sources on Ellison and provides a chronological summary of the principal reviews of *Invisible Man.*

Hersey, John, ed. *Ralph Ellison: A Collection of Critical Essays.* Englewood Cliffs, N.J.: Prentice-Hall, 1974. Hersey includes studies of *Invisible Man* by some major literary critics and writers, including Robert Penn Warren, Saul Bellow, Irving Howe, and Tony Tanner.

Nadel, Alan. *Invisible Criticism: Ralph Ellison and the American Canon.* Iowa City: University of Iowa Press, 1988. A fine, close reading of *Invisible Man* focusing on Ellison's brilliant and subtle use of allusion, which draws into *Invisible Man* virtually the whole canon of American literature.

O'Meally, Robert G. *The Craft of Ralph Ellison.* Cambridge, Mass.: Harvard University Press, 1980. A biographical overview of Ellison's life, as well as a critical examination of all of his work up to 1980. O'Meally focuses on black folklore as a key to understanding Ellison's work.

_____, ed. *New Essays on "Invisible Man."* Cambridge, England: Cambridge University Press, 1988. Contains excellent essays, including insightful studies by O'Meally, Thomas Schaub, and others.

Reilly, John M., ed. *Twentieth Century Interpretations of "Invisible Man."* Englewood Cliffs, N.J.: Prentice-Hall, 1970. Includes provocative studies of motifs in *Invisible Man*, Ellison's attitude toward black leadership, and his use of satire and the absurd. Includes essays by Robert Bone, Charles Glicksberg, and Esther Merle Jackson.

William E. Pemberton

Cross-References

The Harlem Renaissance Celebrates African-American Culture (1920's), p. 480; Eliot Publishes *The Waste Land* (1922), p. 539; Wright's *Native Son* Depicts Racism in America (1940), p. 1185; Baldwin Voices Black Rage in *The Fire Next Time* (1963), p. 1929; Baraka's *Dutchman* Dramatizes Racial Hatred (1964), p. 2000; *The Autobiography of Malcolm X* Is Published (1965), p. 2022.

CAGE'S *4' 33"* PREMIERES

Category of event: Music
Time: August 29, 1952
Locale: New York, New York

John Cage's 4' 33", the most famous work by a leading advocate of musical inde-terminacy and minimalism, celebrated the randomness and incoherence of life

Principal personage:
JOHN CAGE (1912-1992), the composer whose theories about sound and indeterminacy made him arguably the most influential composer of the late twentieth century

Summary of Event

When asked to enumerate the outstanding musical event of the twentieth century, listeners may suggest the riot that accompanied the 1913 premiere of Igor Stravinsky's *The Rite of Spring*, the arrival of Arnold Schoenberg's twelve-tone music, or even the first Beatles concert in America. A case could well be made, though, for the most famous and audacious piece of the American composer John Cage, a work with a title that concisely describes its duration: *4' 33"*.

For this piece, a pianist seats himself at the keyboard, opens the score, and turns the pages at precisely indicated intervals; what he does not do is play a single note. An audience unfamiliar with the piece or with Cage's intention or general reputation will grow restless, amused, irritable, or annoyed, but it is not likely to be bored. At the end of the piece, when the pianist rises to bow, the audience will respond with applause, laughter, or boos; but each member of the audience will have heard a musical event of his or her own making. There is unlikely to have been complete silence for the listener (unless he is profoundly deaf); the listener may have heard a fly buzz or the usual annoyances of concert halls, such as coughing, paper crinkling, and chairs squeaking. If the hall is quiet, he may have heard the hum of the air conditioning or simply supplied words and tunes in his own brain. The listener has to agree that there has been sound, even of his own devising, and that there has been a performance.

One need not agree with Allan Kozinn's description of the effect of *4' 33"* in his obituary of Cage in *The New York Times*; Kozinn wrote that "listeners were forced to focus on nonmusical sounds, or . . . on the quality of silence itself." Absolute silence is virtually unavailable; the ever-active human ear, even on the quietest horizon, invariably picks up messages from over the threshold. If the world seems increasingly noisy, that did not evoke a complaint from Cage, who late in life argued that "I think it is true that sounds are, of their nature, harmonious, and I would extend that to noise. There is no noise, only sound." (He drew the line only at sounds that frighten or cause pain.)

Born in 1912, Cage lived a life that took him from the West Coast—particularly Los Angeles, where he was born and formulated his musical theories—to New York, where he lived from World War II until his death in August, 1992. He showed early interest in two of his abiding passions, rhythm and dance. He showed much less interest in conventional harmony and the Western serious musical tradition than in the interrelationship of music and sound, specifically in rejecting the customary distinction between music and noise. He studied in his youth with the great German composer Arnold Schoenberg, when the latter taught at the University of California at Los Angeles (UCLA) after his exile from Europe in the 1930's. Cage invariably considered Schoenberg's dismissal of his pupil's compositional efforts as a compliment; Cage, said Schoenberg, is "not a composer but an inventor of genius."

In 1937, Cage wrote a prescient youthful essay entitled "The Future of Music: Credo," which sketched the outline of Cage's long career as a composer, performer, and musical theorist. "Whatever we are, what we hear is mostly noise," he explained. "When we listen to it, we find it fascinating. The sound of a truck at fifty miles an hour. Static between the stations. Rain. . . . Whereas, in the past, the point of disagreement has been between dissonance and consonance, it will be, in the immediate future, between noise and so-called musical sounds." Cage never wavered from his belief in the ability of human listeners to mediate among sounds and take pleasure from them.

In his studies with Schoenberg, he showed greater interest in rhythm than in harmonization, and he developed his lifelong interest in dance from his early job as a dance-rehearsal pianist. His early music, such as *Bacchanale* (1938), shows his interest in the intermingling of musical sounds (specific pitches) and noise (non-pitched sounds). Like Henry Cowell before him and George Crumb after, he showed awareness of the potential of the "prepared piano," in which objects are inserted between a piano's strings, which may be strummed like guitar strings.

Following his move to New York during World War II, Cage was attracted to Eastern philosophy. He studied Zen Buddhism at Columbia University and became intrigued by the *I Ching*, the Chinese "Book of Changes," which reinforced his belief in the role of indeterminacy and chance in human affairs. He showed a lifelong interest in the principles of Dada, the art form associated with Marcel Duchamp; the "found objects" that Duchamp utilized in his art had their analogies in the random and unanticipated sounds in Cage's musical scores.

Cage's fascination with the collision of sounds and the potency of silence bore fruit not only in *4' 33"* but also in his frequent collections of writings, the most famous of which remains the cogently titled *Silence* (1961). *Silence* revealed his creative awareness of Eastern thought and religion, sounds and music, dance, art, and poetry.

Impact of Event

By acceding to the elements of chance and incoherence in daily life, by asking the listener to contemplate the congruence of music and noise, and by being willing to appear ridiculous in defense of his theories of art, John Cage became a guru to several generations of American composers, performers, and audiences. When asked angrily if he were a charlatan, Cage is said to have replied, "No, I was born in 1912." For his willingness to court the scorn of the musical academy and for maintaining his faith in the validity of his theories over a long career, Cage became something of an American original and an artistic icon.

During a mid-1960's concert of his music at the University of Illinois in which Cage gargled into a microphone and chopped vegetables in a blender, even Cage was startled when an elderly member of the music faculty started tossing chairs from the wings of the auditorium onstage. Muttering about what a disgrace Cage was and that, indeed, if Cage was saying that all noise is music, then here was music, the old academic succeeded only in playing into the hands of the wily innovator. Cage cheerfully accepted the criticism as part of the performance. Within a few years of this occasion, Cage found himself anointed a prophet of the antiwar, counterculture movement of the late 1960's, when the message of his theories was perceived as "if it sounds good, do it." In the 1960's, he was seen as a champion of the "circus concert," in which many musical events would happen spontaneously and simultaneously, and of the "happening," in which people would converge in an unplanned, memorable confluence of people, sounds, and good fun. By the end of his life in the final decade of the twentieth century, when assaults on the human ear seemed less musical and more and more threatening, Cage seemed almost a cheerful prophet of doom.

While Cage was frequently called a "minimalist," the term more recently has been appropriated by a very different school of composers such as Steve Reich and Philip Glass, who favor simple, nonprogressive harmonies and repeated rhythmic patterns (borrowed from Javanese and other "exotic" non-Western musical traditions)—emphases quite different from Cage's concern with indeterminacy. In their eagerness to garner attention and to thumb their noses at the mainline musical tradition, however, they are clearly indebted to Cage's example.

Cage had always forced audiences to reconsider the relationship between the notes on the score, the sounds emerging from instruments and tools, the intention of the composers and performers, and the actual result that occurred when music and sounds merged and collided in the human ear. He was a cheerful phenomenologist who passed the mantle of creativity from the composer and the performer to the listener, who had to sort out the jumble of sounds and sensations and decide whether the result was pleasing or repellent. Cage may have overestimated the goodwill of listeners if he thought that the buzz of a noxious insect or the sound of a jackhammer could be perceived as pleasant or even as a kind of spontaneous music, but he was right to demand, as American musical innovators such as Charles Ives and Henry Cowell had, that listeners be far more attentive to sounds and use their ears in a creative way.

To the musical establishment, Cage was often seen as an anarchist, scuttling the musical language and rules that had developed over many centuries; to enthusiasts of the serious music repertory, Cage was seen as a kind of terrorist, robbing the composer of his privileged position as philosopher and arbiter of musical taste and handing over the composer's functions to the listener. In *4' 33"*, Cage could be said to have returned musical self-negation on the part of the composer and performer to a point of modesty that even the most self-effacing medieval monk could envy. To Cage's critics, the piece seemed the height of arrogance and charlatanry, since listeners at a concert are punished with four and half minutes of silence, during which many will simply fume at Cage's presumption and egotism.

During the duration of the piece, with the composer sitting at the piano and turning the pages at specified points, a noisy or rambunctious audience may enjoy the composer's chutzpah or simply take the occasion as an opportunity to chat; a quiet audience may sit nervous and uncomfortable. Whatever happens, the audience itself is creating the event and inventing, in its ears, the music. Cage's musical output generally may strike listeners as a cold shower, an act of discipline, or even presumption and outright fraud, but an audience is unlikely to go home indifferent or unchanged in its attitudes.

Earlier composers claimed variously to have drawn their music directly from God (like Johann Sebastian Bach) or from their own titanic grapplings with their imaginations (like Ludwig van Beethoven). Cage once wrote, "In an older view, and my own, it is the artist's duty to imitate in his work not the appearance of nature, but her manner of operation." Such an approach could lead to the self-effacing claim of Edward Elgar, the British composer, that the air was full of music and that the composer simply wrote it down, or to the approach of Cage, who believed that "music" was nothing more or less than the random, indiscriminate collision of sounds, and that it was the responsibility of the listener, not the composer, to make sense of this variety. In *4' 33"*, Cage achieved his musical masterpiece, and he marked a turning point in the human perception of music, by offering unmediated access to the world of sounds.

Bibliography

Cage, John. *Silence: Lectures and Writings.* Middletown, Conn.: Wesleyan University Press, 1961. Arguably the best known and most influential of Cage's theoretical writings; sparked the late 1960's fascination with Cage. Despite the ironic title, Cage's writings celebrate the ubiquity of unexpected, pleasing sounds.

Hoover, Kathleen, and John Cage. *Virgil Thomson: His Life and Music.* New York: Thomas Yoseloff, 1959. Cage's admiring study of Thomson's equally "American" music, which was based on hymn tunes and homely material rather than on indeterminacy. Places Thomson among the pantheon of composers who "have done what they had to do without pretense and in defiance of the general run of Teutonism and neo-classicism."

Kostelanetz, Richard, ed. *John Cage.* New York: Praeger, 1970. A collection of facts and opinions about the composer.

Rockwell, John. *All-American Music.* New York: Alfred A. Knopf, 1983. Notes admiringly Cage's assimilation of European and Eastern ideas and commends him for his genius, but crankily complains about Cage's alleged "disturbing indifference to how his music actually sounds"—a statement that oddly ignores Rockwell's repeated point about the listener's role in creating music from Cage's do-it-yourself packages.

Thomson, Virgil. *A Virgil Thomson Reader.* Boston: Houghton Mifflin, 1981. Contains Thomson's essay "Cage and the Collage of Noises." Although Cage had written a sensitive study of Thomson's music, Thomson attacks Cage as an opportunistic hustler and his music as a "one-way tunnel leading only to the gadget-fair."

Byron Nelson

Cross-References

Duchamp's "Readymades" Challenge Concepts of Art (1913), p. 349; The Dada Movement Emerges at the Cabaret Voltaire (1916), p. 419; Minimalism Emphasizes Objects as Art (1963), p. 1949; Cunningham Stages His First Dance "Event" (1964), p. 2011; Laurie Anderson's *United States* Popularizes Performance Art (1983), p. 2517.

THE MOUSETRAP BEGINS A RECORD-BREAKING RUN

Category of event: Theater
Time: November 25, 1952
Locale: Ambassadors' Theatre, London, England

Agatha Christie's The Mousetrap, *a well-constructed, well-publicized, and well-managed whodunit, makes theater history because of its longevity*

Principal personages:

AGATHA CHRISTIE (1890-1976), a celebrated writer of mystery novels and plays who was created Dame of the Order of the British Empire in 1971

PETER SAUNDERS (1911-   ), the presenter of *The Mousetrap* and many other plays written by Christie

RICHARD ATTENBOROUGH (1923-   ), an actor, producer, and director who played the part of Detective Sergeant Trotter in the first performance of *The Mousetrap*

PETER COTES (1912-   ), an author, lecturer, play producer, and stage, film, and television director, the first producer of *The Mousetrap*

Summary of Event

Agatha Christie's career as a writer of mystery stories and thrillers began modestly with the publication of *The Mysterious Affair at Styles* in 1920. By the late 1930's, she was recognized as the preeminent writer in the genre. As of 1980, it was estimated that four hundred million copies of her books had been sold worldwide. Similarly, she experienced only modest success with her first play, *Black Coffee*, which was produced in 1930, but greater success followed with her adaptations of her own novels for the stage productions of *Ten Little Indians* (1943), *Appointment with Death* (1945), *Murder on the Nile* (1945), and *The Hollow* (1951). Christie attained the height of success as a dramatist during the 1953-1954 theater season, when three of her plays ran concurrently in London's West End: *Witness for the Prosecution* ran for 468 performances, *The Spider's Web* ran for 774 performances, and *The Mousetrap* continued its astonishing run.

Whodunits had been popular in the English theater since their introduction in the nineteenth century. During the 1920's and 1930's, Edgar Wallace's thrillers, which depended heavily on melodrama much like their predecessors, were among the most popular. Early adaptations of Christie's work by other authors were similarly melodramatic. Dissatisfied with such dramatic versions of her works as *Alibi* (1928), *Love from a Stranger* (1936), and *Peril at End House* (1940), Christie decided to adapt her work for the theater herself, improving it by simplifying sets, using smaller casts of characters, and eliminating the extremes of melodrama. She retained detective story conventions and formulas while ingeniously and continuously varying them.

The Mousetrap opened at the Theatre Royal in Nottingham on October 6, 1952, and then had its first performance in London at the Ambassadors' Theatre on November 25. On March 25, 1974, the production moved to St. Martin's Theatre without breaking its run. When the play opened, Hubert Gregg, an actor and director, described it as "a jolly good little whodunit, no more, no less." Peter Saunders, the presenter, predicted a successful run of fourteen months, and Agatha Christie more modestly predicted an eight-month run. Noting its longevity thirteen years later, she wrote, "No doubt about it, miracles happen."

The Mousetrap's great success ultimately remains an enigma. *Ten Little Indians* is recognized as her technically most complex play, while *Witness for the Prosecution* is generally considered her best. Like many of her other plays, *The Mousetrap* is based on an earlier work, "The Three Blind Mice," a radio play that she wrote in 1947 at the request of the British Broadcasting Corporation (BBC) to celebrate Queen Mary's eightieth birthday. Yet unlike adaptations of her novels, which required simplification, adaptation of the radio play required expansion—"extra characters, a fuller background and plot, and a slow working up to the climax"—to fulfill the requirements of a two-act stage play. Christie noted that the proportions of "The Three Blind Mice" made for "good construction" in *The Mousetrap*.

The Mousetrap exemplifies the qualities that made Christie's other plays successful. The setting, typically, isolates the characters. Giles and Mollie Ralston's very first guests arrive at Monkswell Manor Guesthouse during a snowstorm that cuts them off from the rest of the world. Like many of Christie's characters, they are stereotypes, easily identifiable through speech patterns, mannerisms, and appearances.

The outline of the plot is simple. In act 1, scene 1, the guests arrive. In act 1, scene 2, which takes place on the following afternoon, Sergeant Trotter skis to the guesthouse to warn the inhabitants that a homicidal maniac intends to kill one or possibly two of them. Shortly afterward, Mrs. Boyle, a guest, is murdered. At the beginning of act 2, Sergeant Trotter interrogates the Ralstons and their guests and tells them that one of them is a murderer and will strike again. Suspense builds as characters become enmeshed in fear, mutual suspicion, and accusations. Then Sergeant Trotter gathers everyone together to reenact the murder. The play reaches a climax when a second murder is averted and the character who has always been assumed innocent, Sergeant Trotter, is identified as the murderer. He had set out to avenge crimes committed against his family in the past. The denouement follows at a rapid pace, providing answers to unanswered questions and turning the play world from tragedy to comedy.

Because of its phenomenal run, *The Mousetrap* has become a monument in theater history. After seeing its twenty-fifth anniversary performance, critic Eric Shorter wrote: "Whether those seeds [of immortality] are to be found in the text, in the performance, the theatre or its position, its management or its publicity, is a question which nobody can answer for sure." Agatha Christie has long pleased her audiences with plays built on conventions and formulas to which she gives twists and surprises. By negative example, her play *Verdict*, produced in 1958, proves her success in meeting audience expectations. An examination of character rather than a detective story or thriller, *Verdict* was booed off the stage; however, her next play, *The Unexpected Guest*, also produced in 1958, returned Christie to the good graces of the audience. One reviewer wrote that Christie had "reverted to the old 'whodunit' formula that has paid her so well in *The Mousetrap.*"

Peter Saunders, who has been described as a "super-ingenious barker," carefully managed and publicized the play from its beginning. *The Mousetrap* opened with an excellent cast, including Richard Attenborough in the part of Sergeant Trotter; however, the most famous name associated with the production, that of Agatha Christie, occupied the largest space on the theater marquee. On the play's fifth anniversary, Peter Saunders held a party that was televised after the performance at the Ambassadors' Theatre. The press was also invited to the spectacular seventh anniversary party, held at the Savoy Hotel, to which Saunders invited a thousand guests. Beginning with the production's eighth year, Saunders changed the cast and had the production restaged by a new director on the anniversary of its opening. Christie, who ordinarily eschewed publicity, participated in promoting the play. She attended parties, had her picture taken with new casts, and donated the "Mousetrap Cup" as a prize for horse racing. In 1965, Saunders formed the Mousetrap Club for people who have been connected with the play in any way. Since the late 1950's, *The Mousetrap* has become a tourist attraction and a piece of nostalgia. People return to it to commemorate various anniversaries. The long run itself has generated interest in the play, which in turn has extended its run.

In her autobiography, Agatha Christie wrote that "people are always asking me to what I attribute the success of *The Mousetrap*," and noted that her answer was "ninety per cent luck, at least." She was probably too modest; in addition to luck, the play's success stems from its author's uncanny ability to please audiences.

Impact of Event

Agatha Christie's *The Mousetrap* obviously is not an innovative work; rather, it is the epitome of the mystery play. Such plays typically feature well-constructed plots, stereotypical characters, and formulaic motifs such as isolated country houses, hidden identities, conflicting testimonies about the past, shots in the dark, blackouts, and reenactments of the crime that lead to the detection of the murderer.

Because of Christie's expert handling of these elements and the play's outstanding success, *The Mousetrap* has exerted an important influence on late twentieth century drama in both simple and complex ways. Popular playwrights such as Anthony Shaffer and Ira Levin have borrowed her construction and motifs to create successful mystery plays, while more learned and experimental dramatists such as Peter Shaffer, Harold Pinter, and Tom Stoppard have used Christie's work as a springboard for the creation of more sophisticated metaphysical mysteries.

Anthony Shaffer is thoroughly versed in mystery conventions, having collaborated on two detective novels with his twin brother Peter and having written the screenplay for the 1978 film version of Christie's *Death on the Nile*. He is best known for his first play, *Sleuth* (1970), which broke box-office records at the St. Martin's Theatre, where

The Mousetrap has played since 1974. Shaffer also wrote the screenplay for the 1973 film version of *Sleuth*, starring Laurence Olivier and Michael Caine and directed by Joseph Mankiewicz. *Sleuth* is an ingenious thriller filled with multiple reversals. Andrew Wyke, a consummate game player and mystery novelist, determines to punish his wife's lover, Milo Trundle. He engages Milo in a series of mystery-novel scenarios that ultimately lead to Milo's murder and Andrew's arrest.

In 1979, the American author Ira Levin, who also wrote *Rosemary's Baby* (1967) and *The Boys from Brazil* (1976), published his play *Deathtrap*, which was filmed in 1982 in a production starring Michael Caine and Christopher Reeve and directed by Sidney Lumet. *Deathtrap*, like *Sleuth*, is a roller-coaster thriller during which Sidney Bruhl, a blocked mystery writer, seemingly kills his rival playwright to steal his play. Sidney's wife joins in the murder cover-up after the fact, but she subsequently dies from shock when the "dead" Clifford rises from the grave. In fact, Sidney and Clifford are lovers who have planned the wife's death, but Clifford kills Sidney to take possession of the play they fabricated, which he now wants produced. Clifford, however, is arrested; the family lawyer sends the play off to Broadway, where it has success as *Deathtrap*—thus completing the series of art-reality twists similar to those of *Sleuth*.

Peter Shaffer utilized Christie's mystery-plot techniques in his collaborations with his brother, but he employed them in a more ambitious and complex manner in *Equus* (1974) and *Amadeus* (1979). Winner of five major awards and filmed in 1977 in a production starring Richard Burton and directed by Sidney Lumet, *Equus* is a psychological mystery play, or "whydunit." A psychiatrist, Dysart, tries to uncover the reasons for the blinding of six horses by a troubled adolescent, Alan Strang. The play is a lengthy and textured investigation of the nature of ritualized violence, but no easy explanations are provided.

With *Amadeus*, Shaffer won a Tony Award for best drama; he won an Academy Award for best screenplay when the play was made into a 1984 film by director Milos Forman. The play contains well-wrought murder-mystery techniques, but with a difference: the audience knows who the prospective murderer is and watches the composer Salieri slowly destroy his genius rival, Wolfgang Amadeus Mozart.

The most enigmatic of the complex school of Christie's heirs are Harold Pinter and Tom Stoppard. In the 1950's, Pinter was an actor who played in Christie's *Murder at the Vicarage* (1959), *Ten Little Indians*, *The Spider's Web* (1954), *Love from a Stranger* (1936), *Witness for the Prosecution*, and *Peril at End House* (1940). Pinter borrowed many of her stock techniques to create his works. Menaced, isolated characters are used in Pinter's *The Caretaker* (1960), *No Man's Land* (1975), and *The Birthday Party* (1959); conflicting testimonies about the past and about characters' identities appear in *Old Times* (1971); and melodramatic action at the closing of the curtain takes place in *The Dumb Waiter* (1960) and *The Room* (1960). The difference between Pinter and Christie is that Pinter does not resolve the mysteries; menace and enigma remain.

A similar situation prevails in Tom Stoppard's *The Real Inspector Hound* (1968), which is a parodic revision of *The Mousetrap*. Stoppard satirizes the convention of the detective as crime solver by making him a murderer also. Major Mangus, like Major Metcalf in *The Mousetrap*, is the real detective, Inspector Hound, but he is also the murderer Puckeridge, a third-rate journalist, who is also Albert Muldoon, the long-missing owner of Muldoon Mansion. Through the proliferation of identities, Stoppard satirizes how dramatists fashion their characters after hackneyed ones like those in *The Mousetrap*.

Although Agatha Christie's *The Mousetrap* is not innovative, it does represent the epitome of the conventional mystery play, which by its recognizable and popular formulas influenced later dramatists in both simple and complex manners. In both their emulation and their parodying of her techniques, these writers pay tribute to Christie's achievement.

Bibliography

Christie, Agatha. *An Autobiography*. New York: Dodd, Mead, 1977. Christie engagingly creates a sense of her life-style and values. She describes her interest in games and puzzles, love of literature and the theater, and her lifelong pleasure with the world of her imagination. Her decision to omit information about her traumatic disappearance in December, 1926, might disappoint some readers.

Gregg, Hubert. *Agatha Christie and All That Mousetrap*. London: William Kimber, 1980. A director of some of Christie's most successful plays, Gregg discusses his experience in working with her and with Peter Saunders. Although slight, this highly personal account, which is often irreverent, offers a unique perspective on Christie's plays. Gregg's book includes excerpts of play reviews and general comments about the London theater during the 1940's and 1950's.

Morgan, Janet. *Agatha Christie: A Biography*. New York: Alfred A. Knopf, 1985. Morgan's book, the authorized biography, is a detailed study packed with names and dates, often useful in placing and filling out events that Christie wrote about in her more casual autobiography. Morgan's book includes good portraits of Colonel Archibald Christie, Agatha's first husband, and Sir Max Mallowan, her second husband.

Osborne, Charles. *The Life and Crimes of Agatha Christie*. London: William Collins Sons, 1982. Osborne provides detailed summaries of Christie's novels, plays, nonfiction, poetry, and films. He relates her work to events in her life, provides information about the production of plays, comments on actors' performances, and provides contemporary reviews. His book, which is dense with facts, names, and dates, is written in a lucid and flowing style.

Riley, Dick, and Pam McAllister, eds. *The Bedside, Bathtub, and Armchair Companion to Agatha Christie*. New York: Frederick Ungar, 1979. A compendium of useful information, this book includes biographical and literary material as well as an outstanding bibliography. Essays of both serious and satiric nature provide statistics about *The Mousetrap* and Christie's overall popularity and give glimpses of her actual and fictional worlds.

Frank Ardolino

Cross-References

The Mysterious Affair at Styles Introduces Hercule Poirot (1920), p. 496; *The Maltese Falcon* Introduces the Hard-Boiled Detective Novel (1929), p. 793; Hitchcock Becomes England's Foremost Director (1934), p. 946; The Sherlock Holmes Film Series Begins (1939), p. 1131; *The Maltese Falcon* Establishes a New Style for Crime Films (1941), p. 1223.

ROSENBERG DEFINES "ACTION PAINTING"

Category of event: Art
Time: December, 1952
Locale: New York, New York

Harold Rosenberg's article "The American Action Painters" in the December, 1952, issue of Art News *gave a name to the controversial painting style of Jackson Pollock and others*

Principal personages:
> HAROLD ROSENBERG (1906-1978), a lawyer, poet, and onetime Marxist who became an influential art critic
> JACKSON POLLOCK (1912-1956), an abstract expressionist painter and the unnamed target of Rosenberg's 1952 article
> CLEMENT GREENBERG (1909-   ), another powerful art critic and a supporter of Pollock
> WILLEM DE KOONING (1904-1988), an abstract expressionist painter whom Rosenberg preferred to Pollock

Summary of Event

Harold Rosenberg was a lawyer, a poet, a painter, and a critic of literature and art. He had been a Trotskyite Marxist in the 1930's and was always an admirer of—and advocate for—Surrealism and other French movements in art and ideas. His long years on the Advertising Council had given him a knack for the catchy phrase. (He had helped invent Smokey the Bear.) His 1952 *Art News* article "The American Action Painters" was noteworthy not because it led to important developments in the techniques or theories of artists but because it gave a vivid name to the practices of certain abstract expressionist painters, notably Jackson Pollock. The genius of the article lies in its title, for the essay itself is opaque in its abstractness and its oblique approach to its putative topic. Moreover, Rosenberg mentions no painters, leaving his readers to guess at his targets, and the article was dismissed contemptuously by many knowledgeable art critics.

Yet behind Rosenberg's labored obscurity lies a raucous chapter in the history of the whole abstract expressionist movement. The story began in the summer of 1952, with a dinner that Harold and May Rosenberg held at their home and to which they invited Jackson Pollock and his wife and fellow painter, Lee Krasner. Pollock got drunk, sneered at the pretentiousness of Rosenberg's talk about art, and went upstairs to sleep. Krasner then attacked Rosenberg for his remarks about Pollock, and the evening ended sourly.

One thing that especially grated on Rosenberg was Pollock's boost to fame by Clement Greenberg, a fellow critic whom Rosenberg detested. Not only were Greenberg and Pollock a critical and creative team hostile to Rosenberg, Greenberg had feuded with Willem de Kooning, Pollock's greatest rival in abstract expressionism and a painter whose work Rosenberg had promoted. Thus, the stage was set for a manifesto in which Rosenberg would vanquish his enemies.

What would his approach be? Rosenberg had by this time moved on from his 1930's Marxism, but he still railed against the suppression of genius in a capitalist economy that spawned a vulgar mass culture. Always enamored of all things French, Rosenberg fastened on the modishness of post-World War II existentialism and its preachments of self-creation. (Other artists, such as Robert Motherwell and Richard Huelsenbeck, had asserted similar heroic visions in the 1940's.) Rosenberg himself had already written in 1948 of the artist as revolutionary hero, free and unalienated and "making a new self through his actions." By the time Rosenberg came to write "The American Action Painters," then, other artists (including Barnett Newman and Clyfford Still), embittered by their failure to win a public for their paintings, had sour-graped their obscurity by blaming a philistine public and proclaiming that only the act itself of painting had value. Mimicking this line, Pollock had himself held forth to Rosenberg on the holy act of painting.

Rosenberg announces in his essay that "at a certain moment the canvas began to appear to one American painter after another as an arena in which to act. . . . What was to go on the canvas was not a picture but an event." He adds that the big moment came when it was decided to paint. . . . Just *to paint*. The gesture on the canvas was a gesture of liberation from value—political, aesthetic, moral." The main idea here is simple and clear. The trouble begins with Rosenberg's condemnation of the laziness that infects much of the practice and his scorn for "never so many unearned masterpieces!" A corollary of this laziness is a frequent "megalomania," and he comments that the "mystical dissociation of painting as an ineffable event has made it common to mistake for an act the mere sensation of having acted—or of having been acted upon."

Rosenberg is clearly not only identifying a phase of abstract expressionism but also pointing an accusing finger at artists he perceives as phonies. His vagueness encourages speculation: Some readers have identified Willem de Kooning as the unnamed central figure of the polemic, but Rosenberg generally liked de Kooning and probably even wanted to establish his preeminence over Pollock. The argument for Pollock makes better sense, especially in light of the difficult relationship between Pollock and Rosenberg. The coyness of the article, for example, is understandable when Rosenberg's dilemma is understood: He has a thesis to present, but the painter whose work illustrates it best is Jackson Pollock—whom Rosenberg deeply dislikes and at whose paintings he sneers.

A sensational article in *Life* magazine for August 8, 1949, had made Pollock famous for his drip-painting technique, and his name was probably the first that would leap to most readers' minds with the use of the term "action painting." He also suited Rosenberg's ideological purpose well, for action painting must dramatize its creator's intense inner personal revolt and signify the growth of an existential self constantly feeding on its creative overflow. Acting on the canvas and nurturing the self are insufficient, though; the artist must be sincere (one of modish existential-ism's most cherished attributes), and it is easy to read Pollock into the essay at this point. He is the artist with "megalomania" whose "daily annihilation" in his art is only "apocalyptic wallpaper." Rosenberg pronounces: "The man who started to re-make himself has made himself into a commodity with a trademark."

The implications of Rosenberg's obscure, puzzling article escaped most readers even if tenacity took them all the way through it, but the painter Paul Brach attacked Rosenberg directly. "I think you wrote that article just to tear down Jackson," Brach insisted. In reply, Rosenberg told Brach that he was "a smart kid." The upshot of it all was that "The American Action Painters" became a sensational success. The phrase had just the right cachet to provoke the New York art cenacles (as Tom Wolfe has called them) to excited, if superficial, controversy. For the artists themselves, "action painter" suggested life lived on the edge, a macho style that often justified years of chaotic subsistence and verbal—and physical—brawling.

Rosenberg denied that the article was about Pollock, but he insisted that even though Pollock had used the term "action painting" first, he had done so only after Rosenberg "had put the idea in Jackson's mouth." Rosenberg's description of Pol-lock "painting like a monkey" unleashed a war of the wives, with Lee Krasner charging de Kooning with "craving recognition at Jackson's expense" and Rosen-berg of "pushing Jackson out of the way to get de Kooning in." May Rosenberg responded that Krasner wanted to "destroy everybody except for Jackson." Pollock's own response to the uproar over Rosenberg's article is caught nicely in a story told by a onetime neighbor of Pollock's, Charles Boultenhouse, who arrived at Pollock's home one day to find the painter drunk and in a great ire over the whole subject: "Jackson had this huge kitchen knife, great for dicing and mincing, which he was playing with and muttering 'action painting' with utter hatred, and Lee [Krasner] was standing behind him, stroking his head and trying to soothe him, saying, 'Now, you know you've gotten over that, Jackson, you've gotten over that.'"

Impact of Event

"The American Action Painters" did not herald a nascent movement in American art as much as it provided a noisy benediction for a moribund one. The whole action painting chapter in American art history is a phase of abstract expressionism, best understood in terms of what preceded it and what evolved out of it.

In its spontaneity, action painting has affinities with Leonardo da Vinci's insight into the use of stains, or blots, as the inspirational starting point for creativity. The Russian-born Englishman Alexander Cozens took da Vinci's stains a bit further in his eighteenth century "blot drawings." Cozens began with a cluster of haphazard blots and developed them into finished compositions. For both Leonardo and Coz-ens, though, blots were mere means, never ends in themselves, and neither of them saw a blank canvas as the setting to dramatize the struggle of the emerging self. The French word *tache*, for "blot" or "stain," was used to describe a technique (known as *tachisme*) that went beyond the efforts of da Vinci and Cozens and was in fact very much like Pollock's style.

One of the German abstract expressionists, Wassily Kandinsky, who divided his life between Moscow and Germany, painted abstract works before 1914 that greatly resemble Pollock's drip paintings. Indeed, the term "Abstract expressionism" was first used by the critic Alfred Barr in reference to Kandinsky's work. Relating the German movement to the American is difficult, however, and the attempt to define artists in relation to such movements often tends merely to obscure the individuality of the artists involved.

One significant figure in art theory looms behind the abstract expressionists: John Graham. In 1937, Graham published *System and Dialectics of Art*, in which he made the following claim: "No technical perfection or elegance can produce a work of art. A work of art is neither the faithful nor distorted representation, it is the immediate and unadorned record of an authentic intellecto-emotional REACTION of the artist set in space." Graham's doctrine was almost certainly known to Arshile Gorky, de Kooning, Pollock and others of the soon-to-be abstract expressionists, and it is hard to believe that Graham was not a powerful influence on them. For Pollock, particularly, who was always sensitive about his weak draftsmanship and whose personality was charged with tensions, a theory such as Graham's that stressed a "flow of feeling" would have been especially reassuring.

The New York School included not only Gorky, de Kooning, and Pollock, but also Clyfford Still, Robert Baziotes (a favorite of Rosenberg's), Mark Rothko, and Adolph Gottlieb, among others. Their roots were in Surrealism, and their works revealed psychological themes more than the emotional subject matter of the expressionists, but they became known by the name that still designates them collectively—abstract expressionists. By the end of the 1940's, however, their Surrealistic phase had worn itself out.

In the period from 1947 to 1950, Pollock was executing his drip paintings, standing over his canvases and letting paint drip onto their surface in a creative mode that stressed the "automatic." For this technique, exemplified in such famous works as "One (Number 31)" (1950) and "Echo" (1951), Pollock was sometimes referred to as "Jack the Dripper." It is the paintings of Pollock's from this period that constitute the second phase of abstract expressionism and that are defined in Rosenberg's disquisition on "action painting." One feature of these works is their "all-overness," that is, their even distribution of design without a sense of beginning or climax. This is the quality that Rosenberg probably had in mind when he sneered at the "apocalyptic wallpaper" of the spurious action painters.

The third and final phase of abstract expressionism, overlapping with the second, occurred with Mark Rothko, Adolph Gottlieb, and Barnett Newman. Their paintings of the middle to late 1950's often display a preoccupation with hues presented in rectangles, blotches, and other nonrepresentational figures. These works clearly represent the end of a movement, and with them the stage is set for the pop art of Roy Lichtenstein and the creations of Jasper Johns, Robert Rauschenberg, Andy Warhol, and others in the 1960's.

Action painting did not reach far beyond its own immediate circle of artists and critics, but there is a tenuous link to a group of New York poets, including James Schuyler, John Ashbery, and Kenneth Koch. Schuyler himself has stressed the influence of the action painters on poetry and has offered his own perhaps too baffling definition of action painting: "the finding of the painting in the act of painting it, and leaving a sufficient record of the search: an autobiography whose past is the present of its creation, a now whose linkage to the past is often reduced to a series of repudiations." Despite these late skirmishes on the critical front, though, action painting, whatever the ultimate judgment on its practitioners, faded away into a few paragraphs in the history of American art.

Bibliography

Horvath, Brooke. "James Schuyler's Early Art Criticism and the Poetics of Action Poetry." *Denver Quarterly* 24 (Spring, 1990): 53-67. Horvath relates Rosenberg's article to the tenets of those he judges to be action poets: Schuyler, Kenneth Koch, and John Ashbery. A useful introduction to a little-known subject; has a good bibliography.

Naifeh, Steven, and Gregory White Smith. *Jackson Pollock: An American Saga.* New York: Clarkson N. Potter, 1989. This excellent biography tells for the first time the whole story of the events behind Rosenberg's article. Chapter 41, "Against the World," is indispensable.

Rose, Barbara. *American Painting: The Twentieth Century.* Rev. ed. New York: Rizzoli, 1986. Rose's chapter on "The New York School" is especially informative. She identifies John Graham as a probable influence on the action painters and sorts out the whole abstract expressionist movement into three identifiable phases.

Rosenberg, Harold. "The American Action Painters." In *The Art World: A Seventy-Five-Year Treasury of Art News,* edited by Barbaralee Diamonstein. New York: Art News Books, 1977. The famous essay that began the controversy.

Wolfe, Tom. *The Painted Word.* New York: Farrar, Straus & Giroux, 1975. A witty but hostile view of the claustrophobic New York art scene dominated by Greenberg, Rosenberg, and the abstract expressionists. Wolfe does not get everything quite right (he mistakenly identifies de Kooning as the object of Rosenberg's malice in his article), but the chapter "Greenberg, Rosenberg & Flat" should not be missed.

Frank Day

Cross-References

The Dada Movement Emerges at the Cabaret Voltaire (1916), p. 419; *De Stijl* Advocates Mondrian's Neoplasticism (1917), p. 429; The Formation of the Blue Four Advances Abstract Painting (1924), p. 583; *Abstract Painting in America* Opens in New York (1935), p. 1001; Peggy Guggenheim's Gallery Promotes New American Art (1942), p. 1239.

LAURA ASHLEY AND HER HUSBAND FOUND A FASHION COMPANY

Category of event: Fashion and design
Time: 1953
Locale: London, England

Laura Ashley promoted a simple, traditional life-style through her fashions and designs

Principal personages:
LAURA MOUNTNEY ASHLEY (1925-1985), a fashion designer
BERNARD ASHLEY (1926-   ), her husband and business partner

Summary of Event

Laura Mountney Ashley was born in Wales, into a lower-middle class but respectable family with high moral standards and a desire for self-improvement. Even as a child, she learned to find means of creating her own sanctuary or place of peace, calm, and safety, an oasis vital to her own life. Her Aunt Elsie introduced her to an orderliness and peacefulness that she did not have at home, as well as to the world of books and dresses from Liberty, the famous department store in London that was known for its role in the Arts and Crafts movement. Cleanliness and orderliness were important to Ashley, even as a child. She grew to love church; had goals of industry, loyalty, obedience, cheerfulness, and respectability; and admired novels by Jane Austen and Anthony Trollope, as well as others that depicted close family life. The disorder she experienced at home made her Aunt Elsie's house and its English tidiness all the more attractive.

Ashley never finished high school, but she constantly read, and learned, and she explored libraries and antiques shops. She believed in industry, traditional values, and family life. She preferred the company of her family to activities outside the family, and she believed in traditional roles for women and a traditional type of femininity.

Ashley had been part of the first Women's Royal Naval Service party to go to the Continent after D day. This woman who believed that a woman's first place was in the home thus had an adventure during which she wore a duffle coat, bell-bottom naval trousers, and a navy-blue square rig shirt and jersey. Ashley's expression of naval motifs later on in her clothes surely comes from this era. After the war, Ashley became secretary to the first secretary at the Pakistan High Commission and attended courses run by the Women's Institute. In March, 1952, the Women's Institute organized a show of traditional handicrafts at the Victoria and Albert Museum, including embroidery, hand-printed fabric, hand-woven material, patchwork, and quilts. Ashley discovered that crafts produced by home-based women could still be of museum quality. This stimulated her to start printing with "potato," or "lino," cuts. She borrowed several library books on how to build a silk screen, and her husband Bernard built a textile-printing screen stencil. Bernard and Laura were living in Chelsea, and he contacted a teacher from the Chelsea Art College so that he might learn more about printing methods.

About this time, there was a popular film called *Roman Holiday* (1953). In this film, Audrey Hepburn wore a simple scarf with her sweater. Laura and Bernard had a holiday in Italy in 1953, during which they observed that Italian girls were wearing scarves similar to Hepburn's. The Ashleys brought some home. Since they already had set up printing equipment, they were ready to cut, hem, and print their own scarves. Bernard also sold six linen table mats with a two-color African print to a handicraft shop in Ludgate Circus. At this time, not long after the war, there was pent-up desire for luxury goods, and there were not enough producers of quality merchandise. Laura Ashley rode a bus to John Lewis' store in Oxford Street and conquered her shyness to talk to the buyer after an employee at the store praised her scarves. She sold dozens of scarves that day to John Lewis.

Soon the Ashleys established a business pattern. After Bernard came home from work at night, they would stay up all night making scarves to fill orders for the company they formed in 1953. Bernard would deliver them on his motorcycle on his way to work in the morning. Laura became pregnant with the couple's first child. Instead of giving up work to await the birth, Laura hemmed the cotton squares, attached a small label that said "ashley," and packed, invoiced, and performed other tasks involved in the business. She was even good at sales, although she hated it. Bernard continued to run the financial side of the business, as he had from the beginning.

By September of 1953, Bernard had decided to leave his job in London in time for the Christmas season, so that he could maximize production of the company's scarves. Unfamiliar with the printing methods that they were using, they burned a large proportion of them, but even their "seconds," or damaged merchandise, sold. Although Laura had high blood pressure, brought on by her pregnancy, she continued to work, and Bernard and Laura's first daughter, Laura Jane, was born on October 1, 1953. When Laura came home from the hospital, she saw that the flat in Chelsea had been turned into a factory.

Laura and Bernard moved their growing family to the country. The month that they moved, *House & Garden* ran an article entitled "Good Mixers," featuring Bernard Ashley's cotton "Plaza" design, in which charcoal-colored jigsaw forms were silhouetted against a white background. The 36-inch-wide fabric sold for fifteen shillings a yard.

On March 19, 1954, Laura and Bernard formed Ashley Mountney Company "to carry on all or any businesses of manufacturers, dealers in textile and fibrous fabrics and substances of all kinds." Among the early customers were the P & O shipping lines, for their cruise ships, and Terence Conran, an extremely creative furniture designer. The postwar period was one both of pent-up desire for luxury goods and of a return to the traditional. As early as the mid-1950's, Bernard and furniture designer

Peter Brunn contemplated designing and selling wall-paper. The Ashleys' company began printing linen tea towels with Victorian themes, a huge and immediate success.

House & Garden continued to give Bernard Ashley Fabrics regular coverage. In the October, 1955, issue, the editor praised Ashley Mountney table mats and household linens. A tablecloth with thick, black, irregular stripes on white linen was one of the gifts suggested for good looks, quality, and value.

The free advertising and publicity from *House & Garden* was of such value that, by the end of 1955, the Ashleys had two hundred accounts and frequent requests from overseas. They had no real showroom, so they decided to take one on Old Burlington Street, in the heart of London's wholesale textile trade. Bernard made the rooms impressive and hired a secretary. In the first days the showroom was open, a buyer from San Francisco placed a standing order for the complete collection of Victorian tea towels. Laura found Victorian images in old books, posters, and theater bills, using them for new designs. Ashley Mountney bar towels won a gold medal for design at the Sacramento Trade Fair. Harrod's and Fortnum and Mason's department stores asked the company to print special runs with their own names and images. The Ashleys also designed a gardening apron, which led to a gardening overall or smock with an identical back and front sewn together, with three large patch pockets added at the front. The wastage from the scooped neck provided enough fabric for oven gloves. The smock became a basic, inexpensive dress.

The first floral motif the company used was unlike the later small patterns that would characterize, and almost define, Laura Ashley's work. It was a simple daisy with four petals printed in two bright primary colors. It was immediately successful, and the Ashleys reacted by printing more adventurous florals. Laura tried, with her easy charm and desire to please, to make anything for which she was asked. When she moved back to Wales, she and her Cornish designer dreamed up a shirtdress, more shirt designs, and a Victorian nightdress as "Laura Ashley" designs.

Impact of Event

The 1960's were an age of free sex and the new "mod" look, but a large segment of society remained traditional. Romantic, nostalgic Laura Ashley appealed to this segment. Old-fashioned values and the continuance of the English country life, respectability, and conservation were values found in Ashley life and products. Hot pants and miniskirts were not for everyone all the time. The 1960's also idealized the dream of country living, with homemade bread and pottery, natural wood furniture, and the "simple life." This idealization brought further success to Laura Ashley. She always insisted that her clothes were not fashion but merely an alternative to jeans. Her simple, long-skirted "milkmaid" dresses in flower-printed calico or insets of coarse lace, as well as her pinafores and frilly blouses, were bought eagerly throughout this period. A similar mood was caught by Yves St. Laurent in 1964 with Provençal cotton print skirts and headscarves. Even Oscar de la Renta in New York presented cotton dresses with matching head scarves and frilly petticoats in 1971.

Ashley was, by then, far ahead of him in incorporating the "hippie" back-to-nature look of long-skirted dresses.

White calico garments, full petticoats, frilled blouses, and nightdresses were some of the items Ashley considered as she spent time poring over the old books she constantly sought in thrift stores, libraries, and museums. The endpapers of novels, old plates, and teapots were also influences for her prints. Laura opened a shop in Bath, where her "milkmaid" style flourished, as did the Victorian nursery-maid style.

There are several versions of how Laura Ashley began printing Victorian themes. Laura herself once said that no one remembers. Later she said that Bernard saw an old theater playbill, liked its typeface, and decided to print it. After that, Laura did research in visits to booksellers in Charing Cross Road. Later, living in the countryside made Laura more interested in rural life forms, wildflowers, gardening, the church, children and their relationship with their mothers, and the rural ideal that had always held such charm for the English. She began employing local women, as she would later in Wales, to sew at home, as she approved of women being able to stay home.

Many of the Victorian motifs Laura mixed with her country wildflower prints included items such as theater bills. A tea towel showed some refined Edwardian gentlemen with the words "Anyone for washing up?" below. The Edwardian was fashionable. It was deliberately unfashionable people, however, who were to change the fashion industry with their smocks, petticoats, calico flowers, and mother-and-daughter dresses with matching hats and gloves. People were influenced by Laura, and women would do their hair in her "peasant" style and copy her apparel.

Laura was pushed to increase the range of products sold, partly because wholesalers began to expect different clothes every season. When the company and the family moved to Wales from Kent, they began to be influenced by the countryside. Laura adored being asked to make traditional Welsh flannel costumes with shawls and hats. The location of the company and the family, their romantic old house, the mountains, and the Victorian prints added an air of nostalgia and further romanticized the notions of the company. The company was nevertheless interested in modern machinery and in cutting the time it took to make samples; Bernard Ashley always had been interested in engineering and technology.

Keeping her family and other families together was Laura's most cherished ideal. She tried to create clothes that told of a purer life than that being lived in the London of the 1960's and 1970's. She had moved away from the primary colors of the early 1960's in her London flat and was using colors more reminiscent of old-fashioned vegetable dyes, rustic shades of mushroom brown, sage green, and almost a faded blue, colors that complemented the style of her dresses and nightdresses.

As Laura, Bernard, and their family moved to larger and larger houses, (they eventually moved into a chateau in France), she saw herself as a faithful wife helping other women develop an aesthetic that illustrated an ethic. Laura herself wore a working wardrobe of plain colors, often navy or beige, with cardigans often full of holes in the elbow. When she died at the age of sixty, after tripping on her long nightgown and falling down the cellar steps, it was the end of an age for the company. She had begun giving up many of her roles in the company to Bernard, their son Nick, and others so that she could be a more active grandmother, so the company was able to endure.

Bibliography

Foltz, Kim. "The Laura Ashley Touch." *Newsweek* 104 (September 17, 1984): 66. Describes planned changes in the management of the company, including adding to the number of shops in the United States and expanding operations into the Far East. By 1984, the company earned almost half of its profits in the United States.

Gandee, Charles. "Nick Ashley: Life After Laura." *House & Garden* 163 (April, 1991): 212. Nick Ashley, son of the acclaimed designer Laura Ashley, assumed design control of her company. Since her death, he had been responsible for 475 Laura Ashley stores in fifteen countries and a product range of about twenty-five thousand items, ranging from fashion to furniture.

Melcher, Richard A. "A Pennsylvania Yankee in Laura Ashley's Court." *Business Week* (December 23, 1991): 80+. Describes the efforts of James Maxmin as chief executive officer of Laura Ashley Holdings. The company had faced bankruptcy a year prior to this article and had had two other chief executive officers in the same period. Maxmin intended to license more home furnishings to increase the visibility of Ashley designs and to add trendy designs to the traditional floral patterns in an attempt to attract younger customers and career women.

Murphy, Rhonda Jaffin. "Laura Ashley: A Synonym for Prettiness." *House Beautiful* 133 (March, 1991): 150. Laura Ashley is profiled here. Her designs, characterized by gentle floral prints and pastel colors, are explained as being synonomous with the romantic Victorian image.

Sebba, Anne. *Laura Ashley: A Life by Design.* London: George Weidenfeld and Nicolson, 1990. The best work on the life of Laura Ashley and her company. It does not deal with her influence on other designers and is largely a biography rather than a study of the influences on her design. A must for anyone studying the designer.

Merrilee Cunningham

Cross-References

Brooks Brothers Introduces Button-Down Shirts (1900), p. 24; Chanel Defines Modern Women's Fashion (1920's), p. 474; Dior's "New Look" Sweeps Europe and America (1947), p. 1346; Quant Introduces the Miniskirt (Early 1960's), p. 1824; Punk's Antifashion Style First Appears (1974), p. 2299; Madonna Revolutionizes Popular Fashion (1980's), p. 2449.

MARILYN MONROE CLIMBS TO STARDOM

Category of event: Motion pictures
Time: 1953-1955
Locale: Hollywood, California

The star of three motion pictures in 1953, Marilyn Monroe went on to become the ultimate Hollywood sex symbol and to capture the imagination of America

Principal personages:
MARILYN MONROE (NORMA JEAN MORTENSON, 1926-1962), the ultimate Hollywood sex symbol, who became an American icon
HENRY HATHAWAY (1898-   ), the director of *Niagara* (1953), Monroe's first starring vehicle
HOWARD HAWKS (1896-1977), the director of *Gentlemen Prefer Blondes* (1953), who helped Monroe establish the comedic dimensions of the sex symbol
JOHN NEGULESCO (1900-   ), the director of *How to Marry a Millionaire* (1953), who continued the Hawks style of direction while focusing on an element of vulnerability in Monroe's persona
JOE DIMAGGIO (1914-   ), the baseball great who married Monroe on January 14, 1954
BILLY WILDER (1906-   ), the director of *The Seven Year Itch* (1955), who completed the work of Hawks and Negulesco in portraying Monroe's sweet and comic sexuality

Summary of Event

With the release of *The Seven Year Itch* on June 3, 1955, Marilyn Monroe capped a three-year buildup as Twentieth Century-Fox's biggest box-office star and as Hollywood's ultimate sex symbol. The filming of *The Seven Year Itch* had been accompanied by tremendous publicity, including enormous press coverage of the movie's skirt-blowing scene, which had been filmed on location in New York City in front of a crowd of several thousand people. When the movie opened in New York City, a several-stories-high poster of Monroe with her skirts rising was attached to a tall Manhattan building in the theater district; in subsequent promotional newsreels, people in the street were asked about the image.

Beginning in 1953, Monroe began to receive awards as the newest, freshest personality in Hollywood, and by the end of that year was the top box-office draw for her studio, Twentieth Century-Fox. In part, her appeal had been created by her studio's employment of her in a number of small but exploitative roles in *All About Eve* (1950), *As Young as You Feel* (1951), *Love Nest* (1951), and *We're Not Married* (1952), in which she played, respectively, an aspiring actress, a secretary, a glamorous girl-next-door, and a beauty-contest winner. Her work at other studios in *Love Happy* (1949), in which she saunters suggestively past Groucho Marx, *The Asphalt Jungle*

(1950), a memorable crime picture that displays her curled up on a sofa, the mistress of a corrupt attorney, and *Clash by Night* (1952), in which she played a feisty and sexy fish-cannery worker, solidified her appeal as the younger woman about to over-take an earlier generation of sex symbols such as Betty Grable. It was during filming of *Clash by Night* that Monroe admitted to having appeared in a nude calendar, confirming a story that a Hollywood journalist was about to release. Monroe ex-plained that she had posed for fifty dollars in order to pay the rent and keep her career alive in the days before her stardom. Monroe's prompt, simple explanation endeared her to fans, who were already bombarding her studio with requests for her photographs. Throughout this period, still photographs of her perpetuated a volup-tuous image often more provocative than her early supporting roles, especially in shots of her by renowned photographers such as Phillipe Halsman, who helped create the sex-symbol image of dreamy, beckoning, half-closed eyes and half-open mouth, with an hourglass figure swathed in the satiny folds of tight-fitting gowns.

Henry Hathaway was the first movie director to employ the full resources of the cinema to showcase Monroe as a sex symbol. Again, still photography was used—this time in the promotion of *Niagara*, in which an image of Monroe as femme fatale was almost surrealistically draped horizontally across Niagara Falls to project an image of her sexuality as a force of nature. The movie featured tight close-ups of her face and emphasized the singularity of her rhapsodic involvement with her own sensuality. Using wide-angle lenses, Hathaway followed Monroe across the movie frame as a subject for ogling—as in the celebrated tracking shot of Monroe sham-bling down a cobblestone street while wearing high heels that accentuated every movement of her derriere. Although the studio and the star received some protests over this flaunting of her figure, most of her audience was taken with her uninhibited relish in the attraction she knew she was provoking.

In *Gentlemen Prefer Blondes*, director Howard Hawks capitalized on and accentu-ated Monroe's appeal by teaming her with another sex symbol, Jane Russell, who served as a kind of older sister and chaperon to the emerging star. Monroe, however, went beyond what any director could do for her by showing a distinctive flair for comedy, exaggerating her sexual appeal as a joke and at the same time playing the innocent and unworldly woman with a logic that was simple and direct. As Lorelei Lee, Monroe acts as a nightclub performer whose business it is to be charming and whose uncomplicated nature makes it easy for her to render her roles without taking them too seriously.

How to Marry a Millionaire added one more element to Monroe's version of the sex symbol: vulnerability. Her director, John Negulesco, a painter and a well-read man, empathized with Monroe and saw that, though she was ambitious, she was also full of doubt and fragile, with a yearning to be assured of her worth. Negulesco helped her to express such feelings in the role of Pola, an aspiring model uncertain of her intelligence and scared that her wearing of glasses will ruin her physical appeal.

With three huge box-office successes behind her in 1953, Monroe began the new year by marrying Joe DiMaggio on January 14, 1954. At the height of his fame, having recently retired from a great career with the New York Yankees, DiMaggio had been linked with Monroe in the press for more than a year. Their marriage was attended by stupendous press notices, especially since their honeymoon was spent in Japan (where Monroe was already a big star, and where baseball was popular) and in Korea, where Monroe entertained the troops and received more publicity than any other star had been accorded for a comparable event.

The DiMaggio-Monroe marriage and divorce (after only nine months of marriage), made memorable by a tearful, distraught Monroe's appearance before newsreel cameras, was more significant than the mediocre parts Fox forced upon her in *River of No Return* (1954) and *There's No Business Like Show Business* (1954). She appeared as an earnest and earthy young woman (a dance-hall singer and a musical-comedy entertainer) in both films—roles that sustained her image as a fantasy figure by combining innocence and sex appeal. In *River of No Return*, acting opposite Robert Mitchum and the juvenile actor Tommy Rettig (playing Mitchum's son), she was able to display womanly and maternal qualities that broadened, slightly, the range of roles she could perform while maintaining her sex-symbol image.

In *The Seven Year Itch*, director Billy Wilder and screenwriter George Axelrod exploited all the elements of the sex symbol while writing lines with Monroe directly in mind. She did not play a character so much as a fantasy, emphasized by the fact that she is referred to as "The Girl," never given any other name, and is featured in key scenes as clearly the product of the overheated imagination of her pursuer, played by Tom Ewell. She is direct, innocent, and accepts Ewell's pass at her as normal, for she has had to fend off many interested males. She treats such attentions matter-of-factly while tenderly handling the middle-aged, plain-faced Ewell's advances. As sex symbol, Monroe's image is universalized to appeal to virtually any male.

Impact of Event

One immediate result of the buildup of Marilyn Monroe as sex symbol was the promotion of a spate of imitators. Mamie Van Doren, Jayne Mansfield, Diana Dors, Kim Novak, and others all attempted to copy the sweet, simpering, nonthreatening, fun-loving image that Monroe projected so perfectly, although none of these actresses matched Monroe's grace, sincerity, and comic timing.

For some women, Monroe's exaggerated rendition of the sex symbol was an embarrassment. Gloria Steinem, for example, has written about how Monroe's obvious need to please men bothered her; at the same time, Steinem and other women were drawn to Monroe's energy and to the kind of shrewdness she exhibited in some of her performances. There was a strength, even a daring quality, in Monroe that young actresses such as Ellen Burstyn admired.

There is no doubt, however, that Monroe herself worried over the image of women she projected in both her on-screen and off-screen appearances. Like some members of her audience, she wondered whether she was doing her own talent justice in taking on "dumb blonde" roles; there is no question that her male audience often equated the blonde and the highly sexed with low intelligence, even when films such as *Gentlemen Prefer Blondes* mocked male stereotyping of women. As Monroe's character says in that film, she can be smart when she wants to be, but most men do not like it. In retrospect, in an age more sensitive to feminism, the sexism of 1950's films and those movies' sly attacks on male chauvinism are more recognizable than they were at the time of release.

In the long term, the process by which Marilyn Monroe became a sex symbol has taken on added significance. From the late 1950's to the early 1970's, Monroe's own talent was insufficiently appreciated, and she was viewed as merely the product and the victim of a studio system that could make and destroy stars. In subsequent decades, however, critics have asked more searching questions about Monroe and the phenomenon of the sex symbol, wondering why she came to so dominate the stereotype. The wave after wave of books on Monroe, of narratives that recount her rise to stardom, suggest the enduring nature of her appeal. What Monroe did for herself as an ambitious but also deeply flawed and vulnerable woman began to dominate discussions of her career.

Monroe as sex symbol became an icon—literally a focus of worship, as in Ken Russell's movie *Tommy* (1977), which features a cathedral scene with a group of Monroe look-alike acolytes carrying a statue of Monroe with skirts flying. Similarly, in the 1980's and 1990's, singing star Madonna offered several tributes to Monroe in the way she dressed and engaged in Monroe poses for still photographers.

The story of Marilyn Monroe as sex symbol can be used to probe the contradictions of popular culture, which simultaneously glorifies individuality—stardom—and yet emphasizes conformity, repetition, and sameness. What excites the audience is that it knows exactly what it is going to get; what satisfies the performer is a socially sanctioned—or, at least, popularly applauded—role. As Monroe showed, however, becoming a symbol, engaging in certain expected, almost ritualistic gestures, takes a toll on a performer's identity that cannot be recouped by the pleasures of stardom.

Bibliography

Guiles, Fred L. *Legend: The Life and Death of Marilyn Monroe.* New York: Stein & Day, 1984. A revision of *Norma Jean: The Life of Marilyn Monroe* (1969). Still the most factually correct and comprehensive biography. Based on interviews with Monroe's closest friends and associates; particularly informative on Monroe's early years. Guiles does an admirable job of sorting fact from fiction. Photographs.

Mailer, Norman. *Marilyn: A Biography.* New York: Grosset & Dunlap, 1973. Controversial but provocative on the subject of Monroe's acting and her love affairs—particularly with the Kennedys. Mailer is also shrewd on the subject of Monroe's use of publicity, on how acting appealed to her fragile sense of identity, and on her last completed movie, *The Misfits* (1961). While Mailer did some important interviews, his narrative relies heavily on the work of Guiles and Maurice Zolotow. Photographs, annotated bibliography.

Mellen, Joan. *Marilyn Monroe.* New York: Pyramid, 1973. A critical, sometimes harsh view of the Hollywood studio system and Monroe's efforts to surmount it by hard work and talent. Some excellent analysis of Monroe's movies from a feminist point of view. Photographs, filmography, bibliography.

Rollyson, Carl E., Jr. *Marilyn Monroe: A Life of the Actress.* Ann Arbor: University of Michigan Research Press, 1986. The only biography to analyze carefully Monroe's development as an actress. Extensive discussion of her roles, her studies as an actress, her reading, and how her professional and personal lives influenced each other. Relies heavily on the work of Guiles and Zolotow for biographical facts, with some new interviews. Monroe's last important interview is also included as an appendix. Photographs, extensive bibliography.

Rosten, Norman. *Marilyn: An Untold Story.* New York: Signet Books, 1973. The best reminiscence of Monroe, by her friend Norman Rosten, a poet who gives a loving glimpse of what she was like away from the screen—sitting in Rosten's Brooklyn kitchen, conversing with him and his wife Hedda, reading poetry, dating and marrying Arthur Miller. A sensitive and complex portrait of a divided woman. Photographs.

Steinem, Gloria. *Marilyn.* New York: Henry Holt, 1986. A sympathetic feminist reading of Monroe's career. Adds little by way of new facts, but probes Monroe's femininity and the possibilities that her life might have been different had her career and her times not been so dominated by a male power structure. Demonstrates profound empathy for Monroe's plight and meditates informatively on her significance. Photographs.

Summers, Anthony. *Goddess: The Secret Lives of Marilyn Monroe.* New York: Macmillan, 1985. The first half of the biography is a rehash of earlier biographies, but the second half brings to light much new information on Monroe's career, her relationships with the Kennedys, the last days of her life, and the murky circumstances in which she died. Photographs.

Wagenknecht, Edward, ed. *Marilyn Monroe: A Composite View.* Philadelphia: Chilton, 1969. Contains Monroe's last two interviews, memories by Hollis Alpert, Flora Rheta Schreiber, Edith Sitwell, several of her photographers, Adele Whitely Fletcher, and Norman Rosten; reflections by Cecil Beaton, Lee Strasberg, Lincoln Kirstein, Diana Trilling, David Robinson, Alexander Walker, and Wagenknecht. Photographs.

Zolotow, Maurice. *Marilyn Monroe.* New York: Bantam Books, 1961. Written while Monroe was still alive and based on several interviews with her and her directors. Especially revealing are Zolotow's re-creations of Monroe's behavior on movie sets. He is one of the first biographers to take her seriously while still writing within the ethos of her own time. Though Zolotow relies a great deal on secondary sources, parts of his analysis of her character are psychologically acute. Photographs.

Carl Rollyson

Cross-References

Pickford Becomes "America's Sweetheart" (1909), p. 224; The Classic Screwball Comedy Reaches Its Height in Popularity (1934), p. 951; The Hollywood Studio System Is Transformed (1946), p. 1307; Dean Becomes a Legend in *Rebel Without a Cause* (1955), p. 1640; Presley Becomes a Rock-and-Roll Sensation (1956), p. 1705.

WAITING FOR GODOT EXPRESSES THE EXISTENTIAL THEME OF ABSURDITY

Category of event: Theater
Time: January 5, 1953
Locale: Paris, France

Samuel Beckett's controversial play Waiting for Godot *broke with traditional dramatic forms by introducing the theme of nothingness and by innovating the techniques of the Theater of the Absurd*

Principal personages:
　　SAMUEL BECKETT (1906-1989), a playwright, author of *Waiting for Godot*
　　FRIEDRICH WILHELM NIETZSCHE (1844-1900), a German philosopher who
　　　proclaimed "God is dead" and introduced cultural nihilism
　　EUGÈNE IONESCO (1912-　　), a playwright born in Romania, a contem-
　　　porary of Beckett also classified as a leading exemplar of the Theater
　　　of the Absurd
　　JEAN-PAUL SARTRE (1905-1980), a French novelist and playwright who
　　　depicted the "bad faith" inherent in human existence
　　ALBERT CAMUS (1913-1960), a French essayist, playwright, and existen-
　　　tial author who dealt with the theme of absurdity
　　JAMES JOYCE (1882-1941), an Irish novelist and friend of Beckett who
　　　influenced Beckett's use of language

Summary of Event

Waiting for Godot, an avant-garde tragicomic play, was written by Samuel Beckett between 1947 and 1949, and published as *En attendant Godot* in 1952. First performed on January 5, 1953, in Paris, the play soon gained worldwide attention, as did Beckett and the Theater of the Absurd. The play's immediate reception ranged from boredom and disgust to wild enthusiasm. The Paris production was championed by many critics as a revolutionary breakthrough in modern drama.

The first review of the Paris production, by Sylvain Zegel, was representative. He predicted that the play would be discussed for a long time. Zegel described the play as "an inexplicable miracle" and heralded Beckett as "one of today's best playwrights." Zegel sensed that the two tramps in the play represented all of humanity and that audience members had been confronted with a deep image of their own emptiness. Many reviewers after Zegel amplified on the manner in which *Waiting for Godot* contains universal existential dilemmas, surreal communications, and a consciousness-raising confrontation of the audience's own self-deception.

Many critics and audience members found the play too unconventional and walked away in boredom or disgust. Beckett's break with traditional theater forms appalled some critics and viewers. Beckett's experimental theater, which combined elements of vaudeville, existentialism, and what was later to be called deconstructionism, was too radical for some. The first American reviewer, Marya Mannes, seeing a London performance, doubted whether she ever had seen a worse play. She characterized the play as "typical of the self-delusion of which certain intellectuals are capable, embracing obscurity, pretense, ugliness, and negation as protective coloring for their own confusions." The dialogue was characterized as "gibberish" between two "symbolic maniacs." Her review ended by quoting this line from the play: "Let us hang ourselves." She quipped that the line was unhappily not acted upon.

In 1956, a large portion of the viewers at a performance in Miami, Florida, left in disgust during the intermission, enacting an early line in the play itself: "I have had better entertainment elsewhere." The audience had been misled by the play's billing as the "laugh sensation of two continents." Critics and audience alike complained that nothing happens in the play. In this assessment, the play's critics came closer to sensing the actual meaning of the play than they realized. The fact that nothing happens was the main point in the play; moreover, defenders of *Waiting for Godot* would argue that nothing happens in the lives of the audience. Proponents of what was to become the Theater of the Absurd contended that the more popular plays following a formula, such as boy meets girl, problem-climax-resolution, or heroic action, were actually superficial. These proponents suggested that traditional theater provides mere escapist fantasies that serve to anesthetize the individual and help avoid the pain of truth. Beckett's formula—or, better yet, his cyclical equation—of born-troubled-died denuded the bourgeois drama formulas. The lack of scenery, plot, action, and character development in *Waiting for Godot* actually draws the audience member into an existential encounter with his or her own truth. The ensuing vacuum created between the audience and the stage forces an encounter between the audience members with the absurdity of their own lives.

Beckett's *Waiting for Godot*, although nominally about a pair of Rabelaisian existential tramps waiting for a mysterious Mr. Godot, actually encapsulates post-World War II Europe, seen as godless and lost in the void. Through the dialogue of two clownish tramps, Beckett enacts the essential concerns and futility of the midcentury human condition. The breakdown in the very foundation of culture is allegorized: Midcentury humanity stood in a crisis in the areas of epistemology, religion, family, sex, government, and economics. The fact that *Waiting for Godot* touches on each of these ultimate human concerns has prompted thousands of productions and translations into more than twenty languages. A brief description of the play and its inaction will help make several points clear.

The setting is a place where there is nothing but one scrawny tree, where two tramps engage in fruitless conversations while waiting for rescue from their misery. The rescue is to come from a mysterious Godot, who never arrives. It is worth noting that the word "God" is part of Godot's name. In the very opening line of the play, Estragon, while unsuccessfully trying to pull his boot off, states "nothing to be done" and then gives up trying. Later, Estragon decides that it is time to go. This prompts Vladimir to remind him that they cannot go, since they are "waiting for Godot." The expectation that Godot will come and that things will improve may be a thinly veiled Christian allegory. The cycle of vain discussions, philosophical musings, arguments, and antics followed by the upshot that they must wait for Godot is repeated, over and over again, throughout the remainder of the two-act play. By this monotonous repetition, Beckett turns theater into life and shows life to be the illusion. Estragon and Vladimir consider hanging themselves in each of the two acts but decide that it is safer to not do anything. They obviously are filling time, fighting boredom while waiting for Godot.

Two strangers appear on the scene, a cruel master, Pozzo, and a placating intellectual slave, Lucky. Pozzo is a powerful tyrant who is proven to be as dependent on his slave as he is in control of him. The master-slave relationship of Pozzo and Lucky puts Vladimir and Estragon's democratic relationship into amiable relief. Although Vladimir and Estragon disparage each other, they do it as equals, lending an affectionate quality to their bantering. At the end of act 1, Lucky and Pozzo leave, and a messenger from Godot arrives. The messenger is a youthful goatherd who reports that Godot will come the next evening. Act 2 is essentially the same, except that Lucky has been struck dumb while Pozzo is blind. This might be seen as a positive development, with an unhealthy relationship proven self-destructive while the two existential tramps are proven to be survivors. The otherwise monotonous repetition in act 2 enhances the effect that nothing happens.

Impact of Event

The impact of *Waiting for Godot* in the areas of experimental theater, philosophy, theology, and cultural criticism has been revolutionary. The Theater of the Absurd was practically defined by the play. Traditionally, theater has attempted to provide a standard intellectual and emotional catharsis for the audience and has acted as an agent that helps maintain social control by defusing untoward human emotions that might cause disruption of the status quo. In *Waiting for Godot*, rather than providing an emotional safety valve for the audience, Beckett deemed it more authentic and artistic to build up those pressures and help make them unbearable for the audience. In the absurdity of the play, the audience is brought face to face with its own spiritual schizophrenia. The viewer is confronted with the madness of the human condition. In observing two seedy tramps waste their lives waiting in vain for a Mr. Godot who never comes, viewers catch a reflection of the dull routine and self-deception of their own lives.

Prior to *Waiting for Godot*, the essence of a play was believed to be in its text. In Beckett's play, concrete language, repetition, inaction, and confusion create a surreal mode of communication that transcends rational dialogue and dramatic movement. The textual content of the play becomes a prop that serves no central significance in the total impression. This use, or nonuse, of text represented a revolution in theatrical form.

The play's impact on the history of modern theater is equally striking. Beckett's use of non sequiturs rather than coherent dialogue, his mixture of vaudeville and existentialism, and his unorthodox use of plot and props stimulated some of the most important dramaturgical experiments of the next thirty years. The repetitious movements and unique blend of structure and theme account for the startling impact of the play, which rightly earned Beckett a place as one of the great theatrical pioneers of the modern period. Even thirty-five years after the Paris production, Geoffrey Strickland, a critic who argued that the play was a disappointment, conceded that art as original as this runs the risk of total failure. The play continued to receive mixed reactions.

Waiting for Godot reflects an era in which traditional frames of reference were no longer viable. Friedrich Wilhelm Nietzsche introduced the concept of the death of God, and people have had to struggle with new theologies. The existential themes of alienation and emptiness are mirrored in the play. Beckett's play fits into the post-World War II French existential movement also represented by Albert Camus and Jean-Paul Sartre. Beckett's play is a signpost proclaiming the end of humanity's spiritual heteronomy.

By confronting the audience with an image of its own unrepressed disintegration, *Waiting for Godot* facilitates the individual in integrating the forces that would dissociate him or her. Viewing the play resembles a cultural therapeutic session in which the patient's denial of dysfunction is exposed. Through the differing worldviews represented by the four characters, Beckett has rendered an analysis of several different approaches to human fulfillment. Jungian analyst Eva Metman has suggested that the approaches taken by Estragon and Vladimir will fail because the act of waiting for Godot functions to keep them unconscious. Although the brutal materialism displayed by Pozzo and Lucky rejects any myth of salvation, they fail stupendously in their sadomasochistic dance, which leads to their deterioration and collapse in act 2. The possibility of a third approach, searching for fulfillment in himself, is implied by Vladimir, but the implication is not followed through. Many contemporary thinkers of the existential, new age, humanistic psychology, and Eastern religious movements might concur with this third approach. It is a mistake, however, to look for a single correct interpretation of *Waiting for Godot*, since the play captures the inherent ambiguity of life itself.

Waiting for Godot will be remembered as Beckett's most significant play and a major contribution to his winning the Nobel Prize in Literature in 1969. The play continues to be regarded as one of the most controversial works of twentieth century theater, and it certainly is seen as seminal. Its minimalist approach to dramatic form and imagery, tangential dialogue, and theme of insignificance helped shape and define the Theater of the Absurd and modern theater. Whether critics denounced the play or acclaimed it, it was a landmark event in twentieth century Western culture and an expression of the crisis of the midcentury human condition. If, as is often believed, artists are the antennae of the race, Beckett proved prophetic in indicating the need for a new alternative. The old myths are obsolete; the new ones have not yet arrived, so we wait.

Although the play has elicited diverse interpretations ranging from orthodox Christian to nihilistic atheist, most critics identify the play with post-World War II existentialism. In spite of the fact that Beckett did not identify himself as an existentialist, his plays express existentialism clearly and consistently, better, in fact, than proponents of existentialism who recommend it while not following their own recommendation. Theatergoers will continue to wait in line to see *Waiting for Godot* not because it diagnoses some cultural crisis or implies a solution but rather because it mirrors—with all of its concreteness, ambiguity, and mystery—the process and integrity of life itself. Relentless seeking, questioning, and reaching for a better future is perhaps the irreducible kernel of the human condition.

Bibliography

Cohn, Ruby, ed. *Casebook on "Waiting for Godot."* New York: Grove Press, 1967. The impact of Beckett's modern classic play is reviewed, analyzed, and interpreted. This collection of thirty classic reviews and essays provides the reader with an excellent grasp of the diversity of opinion on the play. A humbled Norman Mailer's recanting second review, written seven years after his first scathing one, graphically depicts the ability of the play to hold a viewer until either the viewer or the play changes.

Cousineau, Thomas. *"Waiting for Godot": Form in Movement.* Boston: Twayne, 1990. Superb graduate-level work for the serious student of Beckett and theater. This book includes an annotated, up-to-date bibliography covering twenty-one secondary book-length works and seventeen articles on the subject. The author provides a very insightful handling of the dramaturgical, philosophical, and broad historical implications of the play.

Esslin, Martin, ed. *Samuel Beckett.* Englewood Cliffs, N.J.: Prentice-Hall, 1965. A collection of critical essays including Esslin's own, which places the play in historical context. A rare recorded interview of Beckett being questioned about his views on art is included. Thirteen authors contributed to provide a fairly diverse coverage of issues and views on topics ranging from the Beckett hero to the implicit philosophy of Beckett's works.

Matuz, Roger. "Beckett." In *Contemporary Literary Criticism*, vol. 57. Detroit: Gale, 1990. This is a fifty-one-page review of the criticism on *Waiting for Godot.* This review contains contributions from forty of the world's foremost experts on the play.

Miller, James, and Bonnie Nelson. *Samuel Beckett's "Waiting for Godot."* New York: Simon & Schuster, 1971. Although somewhat dated, this work provides an excellent introductory exposition of Beckett's structure, style, symbolism, and impact on future theater. The authors include a detailed treatment of the philosophical and psychological significance of *Waiting for Godot.* Especially recommended for the person who has time to read only one work on the subject.

Paul August Rentz

Cross-References

Sartre and Camus Give Dramatic Voice to Existential Philosophy (1940's), p. 1174; Sartre's *Being and Nothingness* Expresses Existential Philosophy (1943), p. 1262; Beckett's Trilogy Pushes Against the Frontiers of Fiction (1951), p. 1498; Ionesco's *Rhinoceros* Receives a Resounding Worldwide Reception (1959), p. 1812; Esslin Publishes *The Theatre of the Absurd* (1961), p. 1871; Tawfiq al-Hakim Introduces Absurdism to the Arab Stage (1961), p. 1893; *The American Dream* Establishes Albee as the Voice of Pessimism (1961), p. 1903.

FULLER'S FIRST INDUSTRIAL GEODESIC DOME IS ERECTED

Category of event: Architecture
Time: April, 1953
Locale: Dearborn, Michigan

A geodesic dome designed by R. Buckminster Fuller was constructed to cover the Rotunda Building of the Ford Motor Company, and the project's huge success initiated a widespread demand for such domes

Principal personages:
R. BUCKMINSTER FULLER (1895-1983), an American inventor, architect, and engineer whose life was dedicated to improving human welfare by advancing modern technology through the application of nature's structural principles
ANNE HEWLETT FULLER (1896-1983), an architect's daughter and Fuller's wife, who encouraged her husband's efforts in architecture and design
HENRY FORD II (1917-1987), the Ford Motor Company president who commissioned Fuller to design the dome for the Rotunda Building

Summary of Event

"Dymaxion" was a word that R. Buckminster Fuller liked. Developed through an interaction between Fuller and an advertising specialist, this word became the hallmark of some of his most famous inventions, including the Dymaxion House, the Dymaxion Car, and the Dymaxion Map. He once defined "dymaxion"—a combination of "dynamic," "maximum," and "ion"—as "maximum gain of advantage from minimum energy input," and it came to mean technologies that provided maximum performance from available knowledge. Although many of Fuller's early inventions were excellent embodiments of the idea of dymaxion, it was not until he built his geodesic dome, designed when he was in his early fifties, that he had his first great success. He felt strongly that such constructions as the Empire State Building and Rockefeller Center were heavy and inefficient and that the structures of such innovators as Le Corbusier and the Bauhaus architects failed to make the best use of modern technology. He believed that his geodesic dome, in contrast, used to the fullest new materials and the insights of modern science and technology.

Fuller's geodesic dome grew out of his studies of systems of forces in nature that produce maximum strength with minimal material. He was especially fascinated with the icosahedron, a geometrical shape with twenty equilateral triangular faces that repeatedly recurs in nature, for example, in the protein shells of certain viruses and in the faceted eyes of certain insects. Fuller was also familiar with the ancient and medieval domes that roofed tombs, mosques, and churches, but to him these structures were extremely inefficient, essentially made by the clever piling up of heavy stone blocks. He was attracted to the dome because of its ability to enclose vast volumes of space in relation to surface area, but conventional domes, because of their great weight, were unable to span large distances. Fuller's light geodesic domes could.

When Fuller began to build model geodesic domes in the 1940's, they were basically networks of spherical triangles, that is, triangles the three sides of which were arcs of great circles. Indeed, the term "geodesic" had been defined by geometers as the arc on a spherical surface representing the shortest distance between any two points. Fuller, who named his dome after this relationship, viewed his geodesic dome as a three-way grid of great circles.

During the late 1940's and early 1950's, Fuller developed practical prototypes of geodesic domes through student projects at various universities and technical schools. In this way, he produced a variety of highly sophisticated domes in a fraction of the time that commercial companies would have required. For example, at Black Mountain College in North Carolina, Fuller and some students used venetian-blind slats to construct a forty-eight-foot-diameter hemispherical dome that was much stronger than a traditional dome made with much more material. They also made a small dome that could be folded into a flat package and opened into a structure strong enough to support eight people. Fuller's first large-scale geodesic dome was erected in December, 1950, by some of his former students at the Chicago Institute of Design for the Fuller Research Foundation. Through these and other projects, Fuller's geodesic domes began to become widely known. To protect his invention, he filed for a patent on December 12, 1951 (the patent was eventually issued to him on June 29, 1954).

In 1952, the Ford Motor Company became the first industrial organization licensed to build a geodesic dome under Fuller's patent. As the centerpiece of the company's fiftieth anniversary in June, 1953, Henry Ford II wanted to carry out the wish of his grandfather, the first Henry Ford, by erecting a dome over the court of the Rotunda Building at the company's River Rouge plant in Dearborn, Michigan. When he learned that a conventional steel dome would weigh 160 tons, much more than the light walls of the Rotunda Building could support, Ford turned to Fuller, who believed that a geodesic dome could be designed, produced, tested, and installed in the short time available. Fuller regarded his signing the contract for the Ford dome as the fulfillment of a promise he had made early in his career to discover the universe's principles and forge this knowledge into inventions that would benefit his fellow human beings.

Because of all of his previous design work on domes, Fuller and a young engineer, Don Richter, were quickly able to work out the detailed geometry of the ninety-three-foot-diameter geodesic dome that would be erected atop the Rotunda Building. The dome would be assembled from 19,680 aluminum struts, each about three feet long and five ounces in weight. Since, to increase the strength of the riveted assembly, the struts would be spaced to an accuracy of five one-thousandths of an inch, Fuller had to reduce the error tolerated by the automobile industry's relatively crude machine tools from one-hundredth to one-thousandth of an inch. The actual construction of the dome was straightforward: Workmen riveted the struts into triangles, then joined the triangles into arrays, starting at the apex and jacking the completed sections up as its structure developed, ring by ring. The completed geodesic dome, which was covered with a translucent plastic skin, weighed only eight and a half tons, a mere two and a half pounds for each square foot it roofed (in comparison, the dome of the Vatican's St. Peter's Cathedral weighs 1,350 pounds per square foot of floor covered). The construction of the Rotunda dome took only four months, a tremendously short time for a job of such magnitude, and the result was an immediate success; the public found the splendor of sunlight streaming through the curved honeycomb of triangles magnificent to behold. Architects were also impressed, for the design advantages of the dome were clearly apparent. In a very short time, the geodesic dome had made Fuller famous.

Impact of Event

Fuller's 1954 patent for the geodesic dome put him in control of any and all geodesic structures to be built. He therefore organized corporations to handle licenses for the use of this and his other patents. Geodesics, Incorporated, dealt with government and armed-services applications of Fuller's work, and Synergetics, Incorporated, oversaw all design and research for private industry. Fuller hired some of his young disciples as designers and managers for these companies, and because of the great interest in geodesic domes, they soon had much work to do.

The first important business for Fuller's companies after the Ford Rotunda came not from industry but from the military. The United States Marine Corps needed inexpensive but strong mobile shelters (the tents and semipermanent structures then in use were flimsy and expensive). Fuller responded to this need by designing geodesic domes with wood frames and plastic skins that could be picked up by helicopters and hauled anywhere (the first such airlift and transport of a Fuller dome, which was successful, occurred in February, 1954). For the Marine Corps, he designed a series of geodesic structures ranging from large domes for aircraft hangars to small, expendable paperboard shelters for a few men. The Marines tested some of the large domes—one the largest plastic structure ever built—and found that they could be assembled in only fourteen hours yet could withstand wind velocities in excess of 220 miles per hour. The Marine Corps tested various geodesic-dome prototypes for more than two years and concluded that Fuller's domes were the first basic improvement in mobile military shelters in the past 2,600 years. The report also stated that the structures had only 3 percent of the weight of previous shelters, 6 percent of the packaged volume, and 14 percent of the cost. As a consequence, the Marine Corps purchased more than three hundred of Fuller's domes and used them all over the world, even in the Antarctic.

Another notable military use of the geodesic domes was along the Distant Early Warning (DEW) Line. Because of the Cold War between the United States and the Soviet Union during the 1950's, the United States and Canada felt a need to defend themselves against a sudden nuclear attack over the polar regions. In response to this threat, officials in the U.S. Defense Department decided to set up a three-thousand-mile line of radar installations across the Arctic Circle in Alaska and Canada. Because of harsh and violent weather along the DEW Line, radar installations had to be housed in structures that could withstand winds above 200 miles per hour and yet be made from materials that would not interfere with the radar's microwave beam. The structures would also have to be deliverable by air and capable of being assembled quickly on the ground. Fuller accepted the challenge of designing such a structure, and with the help of his associates, he came up with a plastic radar dome, later nicknamed "radome," that could be delivered by plane in a knocked-down form. This dome was first tested on the peak of Mount Washington in New Hampshire, where it successfully endured winds of 182 miles per hour. This test passed, Fuller's radomes were built, flown to the stipulated locations along the DEW Line, and erected by Eskimo labor in a very short time.

While working for the military, Fuller was able to augment international recognition of his geodesic dome's value by participating in the Tenth International Design Exhibition, widely known as the Triennale, held in Milan, Italy, in 1954. He submitted two geodesic domes made of paperboard and plastic, one of which won the exhibition's grand prize. Further international fame followed when Fuller designed a geodesic dome for the United States Pavilion in the 1956 International Trade Fair in Kabul, Afghanistan. This dome, then the world's largest geodesic structure, was erected by local labor in two days and was the hit of the fair. It attracted more attention than all the other exhibits, including those from the Soviet Union and China. Capitalizing on this great success, the U.S. government had the dome flown to other cities throughout the Orient, where it served to dramatize American ingenuity, imagination, and technological creativity.

Aiding this large-scale manufacturing and marketing of the domes was Henry J. Kaiser, owner of one of the world's great aluminum companies, who became interested in geodesic domes through one of Fuller's former students. He decided that his hotel complex, the Hawaiian Village, in Honolulu needed a concert auditorium, and he obtained a license from Fuller to manufacture a geodesic dome to cover a two-thousand-seat hall. Fuller designed a 145-foot-diameter dome for Kaiser, who had it manufactured in Oakland, California, and shipped to Honolulu in February, 1957. Workers there assembled the aluminum-skinned dome, which weighed only thirty tons, in the surprisingly short time of twenty-two hours. This domed concert hall had excellent acoustics, and its success so excited Kaiser that, with Fuller's permission, he began making aluminum geodesic domes in his West Coast plant. Kaiser Aluminum produced domes in a variety of sizes and costs for such uses as theaters, banks, and community centers.

By 1971, when Fuller's patent for the geodesic dome expired, more than fifty thousand licensed domes existed worldwide, a figure that does not include the many "outlaw" domes built on back lots and in other infrequently visited areas. Fuller, whom critics called a naïve romantic, foresaw even more extensive and grandiose uses of his invention. He envisioned a dome two miles in diameter and a mile high covering a large part of New York City. Because domes could create their own environment, he predicted that they would be used in the Antarctic, at the bottom of the oceans, and on the moon. On the other hand, many architects found Fuller's proposals fanciful and impractical, and city planners thought that his geodesic domes looked out-of-place amid the rectangular building blocks of traditional cities. Despite these criticisms, Fuller maintained his faith in geodesic domes as a new type of habitable space able to differentiate human ecological patterns from those of nature and traditional technology.

Fuller's geodesic domes now cover more ground than the buildings of any architect in history, but his overall achievement cannot be judged solely on the basis of them. For him, the geodesic dome was simply a step in the development of technology that would make the good life available to everyone. He worked from the assumption that creative intelligence is limitless and that technological progress can provide every human being with a rich and satisfying life. Fuller, who introduced the term "Spaceship Earth," advocated using the world's resources wisely and fairly. Wealth, he felt, was not measured by the amounts of money in banks or gold in vaults, but by the creative human energy that could be unleashed to solve the many problems connected with making the earth work for its inhabitants. The geodesic dome was the result of the creative energy of one man, and what one man could do, many others could do. In this light, Fuller's most lasting contribution was not to design the geodesic dome but to send people into the future with the conviction that each has the capability to do something toward creating a better world.

Bibliography

Fuller, R. Buckminster. *Inventions: The Patented Works of R. Buckminster Fuller.* New York: St. Martin's Press, 1983. This book, which Fuller wrote just before he died, is organized around the most significant of his more than two thousand patents, including those related to the geodesic dome. He wrote the book to show others what they can do if they have "absolute faith in the eternal cosmic intelligence we call God." A large-format volume, with many photographs, detailed figures, and diagrams.

Hatch, Alden. *Buckminster Fuller: At Home in the Universe.* New York: Crown, 1974. Hatch, a close friend of Fuller for sixty years, has written an affectionate biography that interprets the designer's life in the classic pattern of early troubles, persistent struggles, and ultimate triumph. Intended for general audiences, this biography presents Fuller as a visionary, inventor, and educator with a magnificent power to persuade.

Kenner, Hugh. *Bucky: A Guided Tour of Buckminster Fuller.* New York: William Morrow, 1973. The purpose of Kenner's book is to make Fuller's ideas and inventions accessible to a wide variety of readers. He uses biography, geometry, poetry, and other disciplines to clarify the complexities of Fuller's writings. The appendices include a helpful glossary. Annotated bibliography and index.

Marks, Robert, and R. Buckminster Fuller. *The Dymaxion World of Buckminster Fuller.* Garden City, N.Y.: Anchor Books, 1973. This is a revised version of a book originally published in hardcover by Southern Illinois University Press in 1960. The intent of the authors is to give a clear verbal and pictorial explanation of Fuller's most important concepts and creations. This extensively illustrated volume also includes a good treatment of several of his most important geodesic domes. Index.

Rosen, Sidney. *Wizard of the Dome: R. Buckminster Fuller, Designer for the Future.* Boston: Little, Brown, 1969. Written by a popularizer of science, this account of Fuller's life and career is meant to simplify his ideas for novices with little previous knowledge about the man or his work. Illustrated with many diagrams and a packet of photographs. Bibliography and index.

Snyder, Robert, ed. *R. Buckminster Fuller: An Autobiographical Monologue/Scenario.* New York: St. Martin's Press, 1980. Snyder, Fuller's son-in-law, draws on a film he made about Fuller's life and work, and on material from the Fuller family archives, to give an interesting personal account. Numerous photographs.

Robert J. Paradowski

Cross-References

German Artists Found the Bauhaus (1919), p. 463; Le Corbusier's Villa Savoye Redefines Architecture (1931), p. 869; Prouvé Pioneers the Prefabrication of Buildings (Late 1930's), p. 1021; Expo 67 Presents Innovative Architectural Concepts (1967), p. 2081; Disney Emerges as an Architectural Patron (Early 1990's), p. 2646.

GOLDING'S *LORD OF THE FLIES* SPURS EXAMINATION OF HUMAN NATURE

Category of event: Literature
Time: 1954
Locale: London, England

A study of the human capacity for evil, this parable about a group of boys marooned on an island has proved to have great resonance, not only for adult readers—its original intended audience—but also for younger readers

Principal personage:
WILLIAM GOLDING (1911-1993), the author, whose World War II experiences led to his awareness of human aggressive instincts and to the writing of this book

Summary of Event

Soon after *Lord of the Flies* was published in the United States in 1955, it became a campus phenomenon. *Time* magazine called it "Lord of the Campus" and identified it as one in a series of underground literary favorites that were challenging the required reading lists of the traditional humanities curriculum. Before Golding's surprise best-seller, it was common knowledge that students were reading "unauthorized books," especially J. D. Salinger's *The Catcher in the Rye* (1951), in spite of (and frequently because of) their condemnation by "the establishment." The existence of a serious subliterature with an intelligent, dedicated readership flourishing in the midst of the conventional curriculum was something unprecedented on college campuses.

In *Lord of the Flies*, Golding postulates a future time and an imaginary island. What he tells readers about that time—planes, warships, and atomic bombs—is an extension of the very real present; he does not suggest weapons or machines or circumstances that are still in the fantasy stage. His threats are real even if his setting is not. It is the very deceptiveness of the setting that gives his tale its unique character. What could be further removed from the threat of death and devastation than an exotic tropical island, the sort of paradise that holiday dreams are made of, a land of love and sweet indulgence? Golding's island becomes a grim microcosm of the monstrous world that surrounds it and that introduces evil to it after a plane carrying refugees from an English boys' school crashes during what seems to be a third world war.

Golding is carefully selective of details, but those he provides are not the trappings of a fairy-tale world. The island at first seems as innocent as any island one might find in the Caribbean or the South Pacific. It has palm trees and fruit trees, sunshine and sandy shores, peace and quiet. At first, the boys behave the way one would expect of children who are temporarily without adult supervision. They horse around and tease one another, offering insults in the language of the playground;

neglectful of their appearance, they are unaware that as the sun burns their faces and the salt water bleaches their hair, their clothes are disintegrating and they are looking and acting more and more like savages.

The scene grows ominous as it dawns on the boys that there are no adults around to intervene, nor are there likely to be. It is at this point that their "play" takes on sinister overtones. At the end of the book, when adults come "just in time," it comes more as a shock than as a relief, for readers know that the boys' warfare has been interrupted by adults who are participating in a deadlier warfare of their own, and on a much larger scale. It is not until the naval officer smiles indulgently at the little rascals and mutters something about "fun and games" that the full extent of the horror of what is happening really hits. Although the boys have been halted temporarily in their regression to barbarism, the sleek cruiser lying peacefully at anchor on the horizon is waiting to transport them back to a world that, like their island, is already going up in flames.

When Golding, as a sailor on duty in the North Atlantic during World War II, saw the ecstasy on the faces of his fellow sailors as they returned the fire of the enemy or launched an attack, he realized with a shock of recognition that the beast of gratuitous aggression was within almost everyone, waiting to break through the fragile veneer of civilization. Golding reveals that reason is subservient to humanity's depraved instincts and that the moment people forget why they have constructed a rational social structure to protect themselves, these instincts will clamor for release and destroy that structure. At that point, one dominant order arises that demands total fidelity. Once this order becomes oppressive, however, or fails to nourish the depraved instincts of the loyal, loyalty falters, restlessness takes root, and reason limps forth to offer at least temporary balance.

On Golding's island, order lasts only until the boys become aware that there is no one to enforce it but themselves. Because they have never known the reason behind order, they have no reason to respect its function. What they feel is a sense of freedom: freedom from restraint, from discipline, from rules they never understood and that seemed to be imposed only to keep them from enjoying whatever they wanted to enjoy. Freedom for them is freedom from reason, or freedom to indulge instincts.

These instincts, according to Golding, are aggressive. The boys kill primarily for the sake of killing, and after that, for sacrifice. Killing for food runs a poor third. Their killing is mixed up with power, sex, and fear. They are driven by the desire to dominate, to violate, and to feel threatened by mysterious forces. Their feelings are, of course, the basic impulses behind political, social, and religious institutions, and their recrudescence is to the earliest known manifestation of these impulses: the primitive hunting society, led by a fierce oligarchy, circumscribed by a rigid code of social obligation, and dedicated to the pacification through worship of and sacrifice to a mysterious, threatening force.

Slowly, irresistibly, the supporters of Ralph, who represents the social order of the outside world, are drawn toward the charismatic Jack, who becomes the virtual dictator of the other boys. Finally there are only four holding out: Ralph, Piggy (a nearsighted, thoughtful boy), and the twins Sam and Eric. Then the twins are captured and Piggy is killed. Ralph is alone, a civilized man alone against the powers of darkness. Readers are left with the awful suspicion that he remains "civilized" only because Jack must have an enemy, and Ralph must be that enemy. Excluded forever from Jack's group, Ralph encourages exaggerated sympathy because he is so terribly alone; a victim always seems somehow more civilized than his tormentors. Nevertheless, much of the power of the book derives from the fact that one's sympathies must be with Ralph and that readers therefore can feel the vulnerability, the awful weakness, of flimsy rationality at the mercy of a world gone mad. There is no place to run, no place to hide, no exit. Rescue is only temporary and is perhaps ultimately more horrible than quick and early death.

Impact of Event

Readers who were attracted to *The Lord of the Flies* in the 1950's were at odds with a world that was sinking into complacency as a reaction to half a century of economic and political upheaval, punctuated by wars of unprecedented horror. They saw a world that they feared was recycling itself for more disaster. They were concerned about social inequalities that festered but were ignored, and they were worried about the atomic bomb. Golding's book gave them the explanations for which they were looking. It made human selfishness and indifference a cold fact of human nature, and it made the metaphor of the burning island only too relevant to fears of a world in radioactive flames.

The book also spoke to confusion about the world's shifting and baffling political alliances. Americans who once had been convinced that the Germans and the Japanese were less than human were beginning to suspect that these people were not really monsters. They were even more puzzled by the Russian bear, who was suddenly chasing about the world gobbling up the defenseless and threatening his former keepers. Whom could you trust? No one, said Golding, and especially not yourself. A knowledge of the human heart of darkness, however, cold comfort as it might be, was at least some defense against dread. Those who could admit common beastliness could perhaps do something to contain it.

Golding appealed to those who were deeply suspicious of humanity and who believed that human instincts required constant restraint. Unfortunately, when they neglected to include themselves among the tainted, they tended to assume the kind of lofty attitude the book unfortunately encouraged. Golding's thesis is an absolute that allows no room for balanced judgment. One can either deny one's own depravity or sit back and wait for it to ruin oneself.

The discomfort that the boys willingly endure in *Lord of the Flies* is exceeded only by the pain they enjoy inflicting on one another. It is the politics of pain at its most basic: One is either a giver or a receiver of pain. The boys in *Lord of the Flies* accept Jack's tyranny because it excuses their own licentiousness. Their minds are possessed by fear and by the handmaidens of fear, which are hate, lust, and anger.

Those who took Golding's thesis to heart were able to torture themselves by searching out their own depravity and either exaggerating it or capitulating to it—or both. To them, this unalterable truth about their own natures soured every deed and thought. They grew suspicious of their own intentions and found in everything they did a selfish motive. To them, civilization was a fraud, an artfully constructed façade designed to deceive both oneself and others while the forces of self-aggrandizement were at work. Smiles, cooperation, and united goals were also masks for the advancement of the self, and this advancement meant nothing more than self-gratification.

Golding's most ardent followers turned reactionary. Humanity's depravity had been revealed to the world most horribly and visibly in the two world wars of the first half of the twentieth century, and there was every reason to believe that it was necessary to retreat to the safer ground of an earlier order, if only to postpone the inevitable Armageddon. Power was too diffuse, society too open, religion too ineffectual, education too liberal to retard the decline.

Governments had to be stronger, and there was even an upsurge of interest in the machinations of recent dictators, not to rejoice over their failures but to learn how not to go wrong. If the world gave in to leaders like Jack, the world deserved them. How could Jack be blamed if others submitted so willingly? Recent world dictators might be called depraved; Jack was simply shrewd. At worst, he was the one-eyed king in the land of the blind; at best, he was a model of the leader responsible only unto himself and not to those who chose to follow him instead of his example.

Bibliography

Babb, Howard S. *The Novels of William Golding*. Columbus: Ohio State University Press, 1970. Lucidly written but tentative. Its attempt to assess a career in midstream is necessarily limited, but what it says about *Lord of the Flies* remains remarkably relevant.

Baker, James R. "The Decline of *Lord of the Flies*." *South Atlantic Quarterly* 69 (1970): 446-460. Attributes the decline of the book's reputation to the mood of the 1960's and views about Vietnam, Aquarianism, a naïve view of humanity, and rejection of original sin. An original if debatable thesis, well argued and provocative, and interesting for its close-up look at the 1960's.

_____. *William Golding: A Critical Study*. New York: St. Martin's Press, 1965. The first major critical study of Golding, scholarly but readable. What Baker has to say about *Lord of the Flies* is both profound and prophetic.

Carey, John, ed. *William Golding: The Man and His Books*. New York: Farrar, Straus & Giroux, 1987. A satisfying overview of Golding's life and works and the peculiar relationship between the two. Avoids the abstractions of the textual critic in favor of the substantive virtues of biographical and psychological criticism.

Meitcke, W. *William Golding's "Lord of the Flies."* Woodbury, N.Y.: Barron's, 1984. A good, readable consensus of mainstream responses to Golding's most famous novel. Very good for any reader encountering the novel for the first time.

Nelson, F. William, ed. *William Golding's "Lord of the Flies": A Source Book*. New

York: Odyssey Press, 1963. A splendid toolbox for anyone interested in the fascinating background of a novel that is very much in the tradition of the boys' adventure genre.

Scott, James B. *Golding's "Lord of the Flies": A Critical Commentary.* New York: Barrister, 1966. A good, early commentary that remains curiously undated in spite of all the criticism that has followed. Addresses most of the issues that have either puzzled or provoked critics, without sounding like the last word.

Whitley, John S. *Golding: "Lord of the Flies."* London: Edward Arnold, 1970. A sophisticated study guide in the Studies in English Literature series. Especially good for its historical value as a challenging piece of earlier criticism.

Thomas Whissen

Cross-References

Huxley's *Brave New World* Reflects Fears About the Future (1932), p. 896; *Nineteen Eighty-Four* Portrays Totalitarianism and Mind Control (1949), p. 1421; Young Readers Embrace *The Catcher in the Rye* (1951), p. 1493; *Catch-22* Illustrates Antiwar Sentiment (1961), p. 1866; Vonnegut's *Cat's Cradle* Expresses 1960's Alienation (1963), p. 1939.

JASPER JOHNS PAINTS THE AMERICAN FLAG

Category of event: Art
Time: 1954
Locale: New York, New York

Jasper Johns's portrayal of a national symbol as a work of art sparked controversy and helped lead to a revival of figurative painting

Principal personages:
JASPER JOHNS, JR. (1930-   ), a New York artist whose depictions of flags, targets, and other common objects became landmarks of modern art
ROBERT RAUSCHENBERG (1925-   ), a friend and artistic colleague of Johns who earned fame for his collages
PHILIP JOHNSON (1906-   ), a celebrated architect who purchased some of Johns's most important early work

Summary of Event

When Jasper Johns had a dream about painting a large American flag one night in 1954, he instinctively imagined a new means of expression for his work. Struck by this vivid image, Johns subsequently executed his first flag painting some days later, though it would be several years before the work would be formally exhibited. In choosing the iconic image of the American flag, the artist selected an instantly recognizable object that was imbued with many layers of meaning. The flag was a preconditioned sign with complex associations, familiar, symbolic, and sacrosanct; it was an object that viewers already knew. As a symbol of the United States, the flag was intricately tied to the values and intentions of the nation. In choosing this image, Johns selected an emotionally charged subject to depict and to deconstruct.

In 1954, less than a decade after the end of World War II, the United States had become a superpower embroiled in international Cold War politics. The country was staunchly conservative and was largely retrenching and rebuilding for the future. Americans saw their international role as global defenders of freedom; on the home front, they were in hot pursuit of the American Dream. U.S. citizens were both optimistic about the future and fiercely nationalistic. Although the worst paranoia of the Joseph McCarthy era had passed, a climate of fear and suspicion still prevailed, and the specter of international communism was regarded as a major threat to the American way of life. The image of the flag thus took on added resonance, as the primary symbol of freedom around the world and as a beloved emblem of national pride at home. This reverence for the flag was used by Johns as a cultural subtext that he subverted through the cool, abstract, and analytical style of his painting.

Johns undertook paintings of flags, targets, and numbers—instantly recognizable things that would be accepted into a viewer's consciousness without scrutiny—and explored the universal possibilities inherent in these visual signs. In these works, Johns broke with standardized perception and dislocated the subjects of his paintings, challenging viewers to see them in a new way.

Born in Augusta, Georgia, in 1930, Johns moved to New York City after being discharged from the U.S. Army. One of the first people he met in New York was Robert Rauschenberg, who was pursuing his own artistic experiments, principally the creation of highly individual collages. Johns and Rauschenberg soon became fast friends, sharing ideas and even living in the same building. Both artists began experimenting with the use of "found" objects in their work, thus breaking with abstract expressionism's emphasis on the sublime elements of abstraction by introducing figural elements into contemporary avant-garde art. By combining the techniques of abstract expressionism with images of common, everyday objects, the two young artists added another dimension to the abstract—a new layering of meaning, rooted in the experience of contemporary life, that called for a cultural engagement with their works.

Along with Rauschenberg, Johns worked as a window display artist for such New York department stores as Bonwit Teller and Tiffany's, sometimes using his paintings as backgrounds for the display of merchandise. Two of his early flag paintings, *Flag on Orange Field* and *White Flag*, were shown in late 1957 in a Bonwit Teller window; the display of the works in such a context emphasized the "objectness" of the paintings and challenged ingrained notions of cultural symbolism. In these early, proto-pop art paintings, Johns questioned the basic notion of assigning distinct roles to an object and to the painting of the object. Through their use as props or backdrops for commercial consumerism, the paintings also blurred the distinction between "high" and "low" art, thus subtly questioning the role of fine art and its authenticity. Moreover, in using recurring images of flags, targets, numbers, and letters, Johns elevated the impression of the object as an entity in and of itself, without narrative context or structure, as a valid subject for painting.

Johns's flags were flat, rigid, and frontally depicted. They were not objects, but paintings of objects. The flag was thus neutralized and abstracted, a paradox. By removing the potent patriotic meaning from the depiction, Johns subverted and dislocated the flag; he destroyed its uniqueness and made it merely another sign. In choosing the iconic image of the flag, Johns selected an object that was often seen but that was not really looked at or understood. By casting that image in abstract terms and taking it into another realm of perception and understanding, the artist jarred his viewers into responding. The mythic quality of the flag was contested, and viewers were forced to rethink the emotional responses it engendered. Johns simplified the complex contextual underpinnings inherent in the depiction of the flag and presented it anew and devoid of emotion.

In his representations of the flag, Johns took a neutral position. He painted it in a distanced manner, as an observer. He presented the elements of discourse without offering commentary of his own. This position of neutrality would become central to pop art; viewers were allowed to make associations with objects that were laden with meaning, but they were prevented from drawing firm conclusions about the artists' attitudes toward their subjects.

This sense of coolness, of removal from the charged imagery of his works, was achieved through the medium with which Johns rendered his paintings. Johns at first attempted to execute his works in enamel paint, but he found enamel to be too slow-drying for his purposes. He began to experiment with the encaustic technique, a painting method in which a mixture of pigment and hot wax was applied to a canvas, producing a thick, translucent surface. The artist's hand was in evidence in the soft layers of the final product; the waxy glaze had a shimmering glow to it, giving the color an added depth.

Johns's use of the encaustic process allowed him to produce layers of color and imagery and thus to make the painting process a key element in his work. Many of the flag paintings began with a layer of newspaper collage that bled through the translucent layers of wax pigment, giving the works more complex inner visual structures and adding an additional layer of contextual meaning, as words bled through to the surface to conjure new associations. By using the underlying layer of collage, Johns extended the appropriation of the image itself—in a sense, a painted collage—and further removed the image from its original intention as an iconic object.

The status of the flag paintings as objects in their own right was further emphasized by their static, frontal presentation. The flags in the paintings did not seem to furl in an imagined breeze; instead, they appeared unbending, hard, and immobile. In Johns's refashioning of the object, the flags stood apart from themselves, integrally connected to the spatial ground while unconnected in context. Johns thus implicitly asked questions about the flag and its meaning, but he gave no answers. Unlike Marcel Duchamp and other Dada artists who decisively influenced Johns's work, Johns and the pop artists who followed him were not directly critical of their society or culture. Instead, they opened the discussion without commentary and offered no solutions. Johns's work was thus often described as ambiguous and mysterious. There was no strident political agenda evident in his work, only a sense of inquiry. He was not contemptuous of his society, merely ambivalent.

Impact of Event

The first formal showing of Johns's flag and target paintings took place at an exhibition entitled "Artists of the New York School: Second Generation," held at the Jewish Museum in New York from March 10 to April 28, 1957. Art dealer Leo Castelli saw the show, and several months later, while visiting Rauschenberg's studio, he asked if he could meet Johns. Castelli was so impressed with Johns's work that he offered the young artist a one-man show at his gallery. On January 20, 1958, the first exhibition of Johns's work opened at the Castelli Gallery, where the flag and target paintings were viewed by a stunned public.

The exhibition of Johns's work broke the abstract expressionists' stranglehold on the New York avant-garde art scene. In a nearly unprecedented publicity coup, *ARTnews* magazine carried a reproduction of Johns's *Target with Four Faces* on its January,

1958, cover, giving the show enormous publicity. The show itself, though, served as the real launching pad for Johns's career. Some viewers were outraged by the imagery of the flags and targets, but many were simply impressed. Alfred H. Barr, an official of New York's Museum of Modern Art, visited the exhibition and stayed for three hours. Barr and the museum's curator, Dorothy Miller, arranged to buy four of Johns's paintings, including *Flag*, Johns's original 1954 vision, for the museum's permanent collection. The purchase of *Flag*, however, proved politically problematic; Barr resolved the dilemma by persuading the renowned architect Philip Johnson to purchase the work and later donate it to the museum. Barr thus protected himself and the Museum of Modern Art from potential criticism for purchasing what some regarded as an unpatriotic depiction of a national icon.

Johns refuted the uniqueness of the flag by making it merely another sign in a system of signs; he thus undercut the emotional connotations of the flag image and rendered it anonymous and tenuous. He presented the flag without reverential connections and with an emphasis on its "thingness." Viewers of Johns's flag paintings were thus put off-balance by the depiction of the familiar object, on one hand, and by the implied ambivalence toward it, on the other. The critic Max Kozloff has noted that Johns reduced his flags and targets to "merely so many abstract forms upon which social usage had conferred meaning, but which now, displaced into their new context, cease to function socially." In Johns's paintings, the flag lost its power to command, and it retained only vestigial trappings of past meaning.

Despite the controversy the flag image generated, Johns would rework it many times over the years. In 1958's *Three Flags*, for example, Johns used a reverse perspective to depict a small flag receding into a second, larger flag, with a third, still larger flag behind both. The resulting subversion of traditional perspective created a visual pun that denied not only the spatial illusion of the three-dimensional object— the flag—in a pictorial space but that also denied the status of the object as a bona fide painted illusion. By bringing the smallest flag to the foreground, with the larger flags overlapping it from behind, Johns also jarred his viewers' perceptions; the larger flags seemed to push forward. The painting seemed to imply a succession of such flags stretching into infinity, thus extending the visual aspects of the painting into a mental construct of limitless images of the object. This treatment was further augmented by the layering of the encaustic technique, which added to the visual emphasis on the work's surface and created a depth of field.

The abstract expressionists' quest for the heroic and the sublime in art was suddenly superseded by the efforts of a new wave of artists led by Rauschenberg and Johns. Abstract expressionism was the artistic expression of a personal search for the inner self; philosophically rooted in existentialism, it relied on individual experience and insisted on its practitioners' ultimate control of and responsibility for their actions. Abstract expressionism called for its adherents to leap "into the void," wrote critic Irving Sandler, "retrieving it and making the act transcendent." Through their angst, these artists sought to achieve a personal art that transcended twentieth century alienation; through the artistic application of their own determination and spirit, they hoped to emerge as heroes.

Between Johns's first exhibition in 1958 and the full-fledged emergence of pop art in the early 1960's, a new aesthetic was born. Moving away from the deeply felt emotionalism of the abstract expressionists, Johns and the pop artists created works that were cool, removed, and devoid of emotion. They produced dispassionate paintings of common objects and of images gleaned from advertising and popular culture. The pop artists coolly and objectively evaluated their society by portraying images common to everyday experience. Their work, with its emphasis on objects, was thus a radical critique of abstract expressionism and its tenets. Rejecting abstraction, Johns and his cohorts demythologized art and offered instead a straightforward look at American culture.

With his flag paintings, Johns both presented a new "reading" of the flag image and instigated a new inquiry into what constitutes a work of art. His dislocation of the cultural meaning inherent in the flag created a conflict between the object and the painting of the object; using a familiar and emotionally charged symbol, he denied a connection between art objects and the psychological framework from which they come. Moreover, by challenging abstract expressionism's dominance of the avant-garde art scene, Johns helped to inspire a return to the depiction of objects and a renewal of the artistic connection to the world of tangible things.

Bibliography

Alloway, Lawrence. *Topics in American Art Since 1945.* New York: W. W. Norton, 1975. A compendium of postwar American art that offers insight into the development of modern art, from the work of the abstract expressionists to the later "Earthwork" artists. Succinctly places Johns in his proper context as a link between abstract expressionism and pop art.

Francis, Richard. *Jasper Johns.* New York: Abbeville Press, 1984. An excellent book on Johns's work and his development as an artist. Francis gives the reader a clear understanding of the period and also undertakes a personal exploration of the artist.

Hoffman, Katherine. *Explorations: The Visual Arts Since 1945.* New York: Harper-Collins, 1991. An excellent history of the period. Details the development of the various postwar movements and the artists who shaped them. Hoffman's section on Johns is highly informative; her discussion of his flag paintings is especially good.

Hughes, Robert. *The Shock of the New.* New York: Alfred A. Knopf, 1980. Produced as the companion to a widely acclaimed television series narrated by Hughes. Although the book contains only a small section on Johns, it explicates his use of common objects in a new sign system. The entire text provides an excellent background on the development of modern art and Johns's place in its evolution.

Kozloff, Max. "American Painting During the Cold War." In *Pollock and After*, edited by Francis Franscina. New York: Harper & Row, 1985. An excellent essay on Johns's work. Kozloff has a full understanding of Johns's art. The other essays in the book give a useful account of the art and politics of the period.

Tomkins, Calvin. *Off the Wall: Robert Rauschenberg and the Art World of Our Time.* New York: Penguin Books, 1981. A free-wheeling account of the lives of Johns and Rauschenberg. A must for those interested in the works of either artist.

Nancy Malloy

Cross-References

Duchamp's "Readymades" Challenge Concepts of Art (1913), p. 349; The New Objectivity Movement Is Introduced (1925), p. 631; Rosenberg Defines "Action Painting" (1952), p. 1557; Minimalism Emphasizes Objects as Art (1963), p. 1949; Warhol's *The Chelsea Girls* Becomes a Commercial Success (1966), p. 2053.

1596

LA STRADA SOLIDIFIES FELLINI'S RENOWN
AS A BRILLIANT DIRECTOR

Category of event: Motion pictures
Time: 1954
Locale: Venice, Italy

By moving beyond the limits of both Italian neorealism and linear modes of story-telling, Federico Fellini's film La Strada *consolidated its director's international fame*

Principal personages:
FEDERICO FELLINI (1920-), an Italian filmmaker whose highly personal and episodic films invigorated the medium
GIULIETTA MASINA (1920-), the actress-wife of Fellini and star of *La Strada* whom the director called his muse
ANTHONY QUINN (1915-), the Irish-Mexican male lead of *La Strada* who represented brutish masculinity in the film
RICHARD BASEHART (1914-1984), an American actor who played the Fool of *La Strada*
ROBERTO ROSSELLINI (1906-1977), an influential neorealist director for whom the young Fellini worked

Summary of Event

When Federico Fellini's film *La Strada* opened at the Venice Film Festival on September 11, 1954, its director was relatively well known in Italy and Europe, but he had not yet achieved true international status. This situation, however, changed very quickly once *La Strada* won the festival's prestigious Grand Prize and became both a critical and a commercial success.

Fellini had come to film as a screenwriter in 1941, turning out entertainment fare. After the fall of the Fascists in 1943, he met both his future wife, the actress Giulietta Masina, and the accomplished director Roberto Rossellini, who made Fellini assistant director and cowriter for his *Roma, città aperta* (1945; *Rome, Open City*). The story of an Italian resistance fighter captured and tortured by Nazis, Rossellini's film stunned America with its ultrarealistic, semidocumentary view of war-torn Italy. Seen and loved by a worldwide audience, *Rome, Open City* founded the international reputation of Italian neorealism and shaped the aesthetics of postwar Italian cinema.

When *La Strada* opened in Venice, Fellini's work for Rossellini had already given him a shared Oscar for his contributions to the script of *Paisà* (1946; *Paisan*) a film about a woman war refugee stranded among Italian fishermen. Since 1951, Fellini had directed his own films, finishing three comedies, of which the latest, *I vitelloni* (1953), had received a very warm critical welcome. Fellini was seen as a promising new director, closely linked to neorealism, and critics were keen to follow his career.

La Strada tells the story of a young woman, Gelsomina, played brilliantly by

Giulietta Masina, who ultimately sacrifices her life for her unresponsive lover, the brutish Zampano (Anthony Quinn), who lives by performing a one-man circus act based on his physical strength. Sold by her mother to accompany Zampano on his travels across Italy's roads, Gelsomina likes the strongman despite his primitive behavior. She discovers, however, that Zampano's base nature drives him to promiscuity and violence.

After two affairs, which nearly cost him Gelsomina's love, Zampano accidentally murders a fellow performer, the Fool (Richard Basehart). The Fool, a melancholy highwire artist, had taken a brotherly interest in the naïve Gelsomina and had tried to help her love Zampano. After his death, Gelsomina goes mad and leaves Zampano, who years later returns to the village where she died of sorrow. Perhaps realizing what he has lost, and discovering that she really died for him, Zampano breaks down on the nearby beach, a place similar to the seaside cottage from which he once took Gelsomina.

It was not primarily the story that entranced Fellini's Venetian audience, but the way in which he told it. What most intrigued American and British critics was *La Strada*'s highly episodic structure, or free-form narrative, which rejected the conventional idea that tight plotting determines the narration of a film.

Gelsomina and Zampano's time together is presented through many individual episodes that are not closely linked together by cause and effect but that instead offer many glimpses of the couple's complicated relationship. Indicative of this approach is also the fact that many minor characters, such as the members of a lovingly filmed wedding party or the nuns of a Franciscan convent, suddenly appear and disappear without directly influencing the ending, as they would have had to in classical Hollywood cinema.

Similarly startling for critics used to American movies, *La Strada* included surrealistically composed scenes reminiscent of the empty landscapes of the Italian protosurrealist painter Giorgio de Chirico. While Zampano has his first extramarital affair, Gelsomia sits through the night in a deserted village square; suddenly, a riderless horse appears and gallops away.

Italian and French critics also noticed—and did so, with the exception of the Marxists, with enthusiasm—that Fellini's individualized characters contradicted the emphasis neorealism generally placed on social, rather than individual, struggles. To add to this deviation, Fellini gave *La Strada* an unmistakably autobiographical touch and moved toward a mystical, personalized view of the human condition, which he presented with great imaginativeness. Not only did Fellini claim that Zampano had his real-life counterpart in a brutal pig-gelder he had met as a child, but he also established a symbolic connection between his three central characters and the elements of sea (Gelsomina), earth (Zampano), and air (Fool). Such symbolism decisively violated the tenets of neorealism.

Despite his success at Venice, and perhaps because of Marxist criticism, which saw *La Strada* as a betrayal, Fellini's next film, *Il bidone* (1955; *The Swindle*), offered a bitter, realistic portrayal of two swindlers who, dressed as priests, cheat the poor. A year later, Fellini's *Le notti di Cabiria* (1957; *The Nights of Cabiria*) reintroduced his more personal, imaginative vision. Cabiria, played again by Giulietta Masina, is a lively, joyful, but hapless streetwalker who finds spiritual redemption despite her real-life disappointments.

While Fellini was still filming *The Nights of Cabiria*, *La Strada*'s delayed opening in America (where it would run for more than three years) on July 16, 1956, suddenly brought him an explosion of international fame. Back to back, Fellini received two Oscars for best foreign-language film: *La Strada* won in 1956, and *The Nights of Cabiria* in 1957. Worldwide, *La Strada* earned a rough total of fifty awards.

Buoyed by this international success, Fellini felt free to abandon neorealism completely, to move his production into a studio, and to pursue highly personal, tightly controlled projects. His next two films, *La Dolce Vita* (1960; released under its Italian title, which means "the sweet life"), and *Otto e mezzo* (1963; *8½*), the latter another Oscar winner, received worldwide acclaim. Through a remarkable series of outstanding films, Fellini had earned an indisputable reputation as a major international filmmaker.

Impact of Event

When *La Strada* opened in Venice in 1954, Federico Fellini had already left his mark on American culture. For as Rossellini's *L'Amore* (1948; *Woman* and *Ways of Love*) was about to be released in America, the film was indicted for its allegedly blasphemous episode "Il miracolo" ("the miracle"). Written by Fellini, the episode tells the story of a stranger, played by Fellini himself, who is mistaken for St. Joseph by a naïve peasant girl, whom he impregnates and quickly deserts.

After taking up the case, the U.S. Supreme Court ruled in a landmark 1952 decision that motion pictures were capable of possessing artistic merit, and thus that films, including Fellini's episode, deserved protection under the First Amendment. The ruling reversed a 1915 decision that had held that films were "business, pure and simple." By attracting the eye of the censors, Fellini had brought the American film industry a major victory.

Ironically, it was not until April 25, 1956, that American filmgoers would see their first full-length feature by Fellini, who had directed four films by then. Riding on the wave of *La Strada*'s international acclaim, Fellini's second film, *Lo sceicco bianco* (1952; *The White Sheik*), made it to America just three months ahead of its famous successor. A lighthearted comedy, *The White Sheik* intrigued America with its realistic portrait of middle-class Italian society. *La Strada*'s American success also ensured that Fellini's next films (with the exception of the bitter *The Swindle*) were shown in America with little delay, feeding the flames of his rising fame.

Fellini's climb to fame was aided by the fortunate fact that his artistic triumph, solidified by *La Strada*, coincided with a deep crisis in the American film industry. His star rose at the moment when America's film leaders began to look abroad for inspiration to help combat the threats posed by the nascent medium of television, a declining audience, and the brain-drain caused by the anti-Communist witchhunts of the 1950's. Many eyes fell on Fellini, who stoked the embers of the neorealist movement of which he had been part and who promised still more innovations.

Since Rossellini's *Rome, Open City*, which marked the beginning of Fellini's serious work, Italian neorealism had left its mark on American film. William Wyler's *The Best Years of Our Lives* (1946), which included a disabled World War II veteran among its cast of returning soldiers trying to readjust to civilian life, was as influenced by this new trend toward uncomfortable realism as was Elia Kazan's masterpiece *On the Waterfront* (1954). The Italian neorealists' influence even touched American theater, which increasingly produced plays of a gritty realism such as Arthur Miller's *Death of a Salesman* (1949).

In 1956, however, neorealism had lost some of its luster. "It sometimes seemed as if the neorealists thought they could make a film only if they put a shabby man in front of the camera," Fellini noted. Now his *La Strada* promised reinvigoration. His introduction of special and socially atypical characters and his addition of symbolic and imaginative meaning to the still-observed formal elements of neorealism—such as the use of real locations and a nonprofessional supporting cast—led to profound changes in both Italian and world cinema.

Until his 1970's drift into the deeply subjective and inaccessible, Fellini remained the admired exemplar for filmmakers trying to find a middle way between artistic and commercial cinema. Indeed, *La Strada* stands at the beginning of a rare moment in film history, when, for roughly fifteen years, Italian cinema, under the leadership of Fellini and others, produced an impressive body of films which, like *La Dolce Vita* and *8½*, combined artistic accomplishment with box-office success.

Fellini's trademark episodic style together with his successful fusion of neorealism and personal vision influenced a whole group of young American filmmakers. Many, like, Robert Altman, viewed *La Strada* as a model; Altman's interest in nonlinear storytelling led to his surprise hit *M*A*S*H* (1970), which depicts, in loose form, the tribulations of the staff of a field hospital during the Korean War. His highly individualistic style also endeared Fellini to the directors of the French New Wave, who looked to him as a prominent European auteur, or author of his own films.

Fellini's free-form narrative led to international experimentation with that form and enriched independent American filmmaking during the 1960's and 1970's. It even freed the imagination of Hollywood directors. Francis Ford Coppola's *Apocalypse Now* (1979), for example, gains much from the cumulative effect of the individual episodes that occur during the film's hero's quest for a renegade soldier.

La Stada was a masterpiece that vitalized not only Italian but also international cinema at a time when Hollywood, the world's leading film industry, had foundered. In turn, Federico Fellini achieved indisputable international status as one of the century's greatest directors.

Bibliography

Bondanella, Peter. *Italian Cinema: From Neorealism to the Present.* Rev. ed. New

York: Continuum, 1990. A readable and comprehensive account that underlines Fellini's major position in Italian film. Sees *La Strada* as Fellini's decisive break with neorealism and as a major artistic step forward. Sharply outlines Fellini's development as a director. Illustrations, notes, selected bibliography on Italian cinema, and rental information about distributors of Italian films in America.

_____, ed. *Federico Fellini: Essays in Criticism.* New York: Oxford University Press, 1978. Five excellent individual essays that deal with *La Strada.* Selected bibliography and Fellini filmography up to 1976. Illustrated.

Burke, Frank. *Federico Fellini: "Variety Lights" to "La Dolce Vita."* Boston: Twayne, 1984. Covers the films indicated by the title, with a useful, concise chapter on *La Strada.* Introduction places Fellini in the context of his national cinema. Illustrated, filmography of films covered, and an annotated bibliography.

Costello, Donald P. *Fellini's Road.* Notre Dame, Ind.: University of Notre Dame Press, 1983. Begins with a well-illustrated discussion of *La Strada*; combines character analysis with a debate on Fellini's themes. Arguing that it contains key concerns of Fellini's, Costello returns to *La Strada* throughout. Makes references to other critics, but differs from most in his negative judgment of the film's ending. Notes.

Marcus, Millicent. "Fellini's *La Strada*: Transcending Neorealism." In *Italian Film in the Light of Neorealism.* Princeton, N.J.: Princeton University Press, 1986. Excellent advanced discussion of *La Strada.* The best study for those already familiar with the film; discusses its themes, meanings, and context in Italian cinema. Jargon-free; credits Fellini with bringing new vigor to film. Some illustrations, footnotes, bibliography.

Murray, Edward. *Fellini the Artist.* Rev. ed. New York: Frederick Ungar, 1985. Detailed synopses of Fellini's films up to *E la nave va* (1983; *And the Ship Sails On*) are embedded in a biography, critical overview, and conclusion. The discussion of *La Strada* emphasizes Fellini's camerawork and his editing and gives many concrete examples of both. Good introduction to the film and its director, but the advanced reader soon longs for more critical discussion. Illustrated; filmography with main credits, brief bibliography.

Stubbs, John C., with Constance D. Markey and Marc Lenzini. *Federico Fellini: A Guide to References and Resources.* Boston: G. K. Hall, 1978. Nearly a thousand annotated entries cover primary and secondary sources from 1950 to 1977. Also lists Fellini's screenplays. Detailed synopses of all films up to 1976, with full credits and notes, are most valuable. Begins with a biography, which follows Edward Murray, and a critical overview.

R. C. Lutz

Cross-References

Renoir Marks the High Point of Prewar Filmmaking (1937), p. 1073; The Italian New Wave Gains Worldwide Acclaim (1942), p. 1228; Kurosawa's *Rashomon* Wins the Grand Prize at Venice (1951), p. 1476; *A Streetcar Named Desire* Brings Method Acting to the Screen (1951), p. 1487; The French New Wave Ushers in a New Era of Cinema (1956), p. 1710; Bergman Wins International Fame with *The Seventh Seal* (1957), p. 1742; Godard's Expressionistic *À bout de souffle* Revolutionizes Film (1960), p. 1845.

TAYLOR ESTABLISHES HIS OWN DANCE COMPANY

Category of event: Dance
Time: 1954
Locale: New York, New York

Paul Taylor founded his own dance company, which showcased his diversity as a choreographer and established him as one of the most acclaimed choreographers of his generation

Principal personages:

PAUL TAYLOR (1930-), a choreographer of international renown who, before his retirement from performing in 1974, was also an acclaimed modern dancer

CAROLYN ADAMS (1943-), a dancer who joined the Taylor company in 1965 and performed many featured roles in the Taylor repertory

BETTIE DE JONG (1933-), a dancer with Taylor's company who originated many roles in the Taylor repertory

DANIEL WILLIAMS GROSSMAN (1942-), a dancer with the Taylor company during the 1960's who went on to found his own company

SHARON KINNEY, a dancer with the Taylor company during the 1960's who premiered roles in "Aureole," "Piece Period," and "Party Mix"

DAN WAGONER (1932-), a dancer with Paul Taylor's company from 1959 until 1969 who left the company to found his own company

Summary of Event

Paul Taylor's career as a dancer and choreographer is not one that can be easily summarized. From his early experiments in avant-garde choreography in the 1950's to his attainment of critical acclaim in the 1990's, Taylor has been one of the brightest lights in American modern dance. His company has been home to a panoply of celebrated dancers, many of whom went on to great acclaim as choreographers in their own right. Spanning decades, his choreographic longevity rivals that of his early mentors, Martha Graham and Merce Cunningham. His awards include a French knighthood, three Guggenheim Fellowships, a MacArthur Fellowship, Capezio Awards, several honorary degrees, and selection to honorary membership in the Academy and Institute of Arts and Letters. His company has performed in hundreds of cities in the United States and has made dozens of overseas tours, and works by Taylor are in the repertories of major dance companies, including the Royal Danish Ballet, American Ballet Theatre, the Joffrey Ballet, the San Francisco Ballet, the Paris Opera Ballet, and the London Contemporary Dance Theatre.

Born in Pennsylvania, Taylor grew up in and around Virginia, Maryland, and Washington, D.C. An art student at Syracuse University, where he was also a member of the swimming team, Taylor grew dissatisfied with painting and fell in love with dance. In his 1987 autobiography *Private Domain*, Taylor described the "flash of recognition" in which he realized that he would become a dancer: "All at once and seemingly without warning, my future becomes clear. The flash, or whatever it is, is telling me that I'm to become a dancer—not any old dancer, but one of the best." Taylor's instincts were right—he was destined to be one of the world's best dancers, and he would also be hailed as a choreographic genius.

Having started dance instruction in his twenties (already considered late for training a dancer's body), Taylor nevertheless almost immediately began performing with various dance companies, including those of Pearl Lang, Merce Cunningham, and Martha Graham. From 1955 to 1961, he was a leading soloist in the Graham company. Graham created several important roles for him, notably Aegisthus in *Clytemnestra*, Hercules in *Alcestis*, and Samson in *Samson Agonistes*; he also danced lead roles in *Night Journey* and *Embattled Garden*. Taylor danced with Merce Cunningham in 1953 and 1954 and was also selected by George Balanchine for a solo variation in *Episodes* in 1959. While performing in the works of Cunningham and Graham might have been fulfillment enough for most young dancers, Taylor had the urge to create his own dances, and in 1954 he formed his own company.

Taylor referred to that original group, which was intended primarily as a vehicle for gaining performance experience, as a "loosely formed fly-by-night group" and stated that he was "not the least interested in leaving monuments to the future." Many of the company's works, such as *Jack and the Beanstalk* (choreographed in 1953 and performed in 1955), were never performed twice. Taylor worked with acquaintances and classmates in those early concerts. Artist friends Robert Rauschenberg, Jasper Johns, and Alex Katz designed sets and costumes for Taylor; in return, he helped Rauschenberg and Johns with window displays.

Four pieces created between 1956 and 1962 attest to the scope and diversity of Taylor's early choreography. *Four Epitaphs* (created in 1956, but later renamed *Three Epitaphs* for a 1960 premiere), *Epic* (1957), *Insects and Heroes* (1961), and *Aureole* (1962) range from the sardonic to the sublime. All masterpieces in their own ways, each dance contributes to a deeper understanding of Taylor's genius.

Three Epitaphs was first performed at the Festival of Two Worlds in Spoletto, Italy, by Taylor, Akiko Kanda, Mabel Robinson, and Kathleen Stanford. It featured costumes designed by Robert Rauschenberg that covered the dancers from head to foot in black, with tiny reflective bits attached to the all-black head coverings. The dancers looked, one critic noted, like "marionettes with the strings gone slack" and "slag in human form dotted with shiny bits of mica." The total effect on the audience, according to Rauschenberg, was either "the saddest or the funniest thing you ever saw." The dancers slouched, pivoted, shambled, lurched, waved their forearms like clocks gone awry, hesitated, gathered, and followed one another. Their odd gait and abrupt stops were alternately comic, pathetic, and deeply touching.

Epic was first performed by Taylor in New York City on October 20, 1957. Taylor, in a business suit, performed a series of complicated postures and gestures to the accompaniment of a telephone time recording. *Epic* and the six other pieces Taylor presented made him the darling of the avant-garde but incurred the wrath of dance critic Louis Horst, who responded to Taylor's concert by printing a blank review: the name, date, and location of the concert followed by empty space, with Horst's initials at the bottom. Taylor's experiments with everyday gesture and action as the basis for dance predated much of the avant-garde choreography of the 1960's; in the same concert, during *Events 1*, two female dancers waited, sat down, stood up, and walked around, until one left. While bringing Taylor more notoriety than notice, the concert nevertheless was an invaluable lesson for the young choreographer, and he continued his exploration of movement with a vengeance, albeit from a more kinetic approach.

The year 1961 was a turning point for Taylor. He left the Graham company while still at the peak of his performing career, was invited with his company to be in residence at the American Dance Festival, and created *Insects and Heroes* and *Junction*. His company's personnel began to stabilize, and his recognition as a highly original choreographer garnered him his first Guggenheim Fellowship. *Insects and Heroes* is considered a pivotal piece for Taylor; in it, the darkness of his vision of humanity is evident. Within every human, the work states, there dwells both an insect and a hero. For Taylor, both aspects are viable subjects for dance. The first of Taylor's dances to illustrate his fascination with the duality of human existence, *Insects and Heroes* was ambiguous and provoking, but somewhat inaccessible.

Heralded as one of the most beautiful dances ever created, *Aureole* was first performed at the American Dance Festival in New London, Connecticut, in 1962. A lyric contrast to the starkness of *Epic*, the tragicomedy of *Epitaphs*, and the skewered ambiguity of *Insects and Heroes*, *Aureole* is the closest thing to a ballet blanc found in modern dance. Set to music by George Frideric Handel, the piece featured Taylor, Elizabeth Walton, Dan Wagoner, Sharon Kinney, and Renee Kimball in lilting, joyous movement. The women wore white dresses, the men white tights; the atmosphere was of rarified light, lively abandon, and heavenly play. The dancers skimmed, turned, leaped, circled, undulated, and hopped ecstatically. Nothing could have surprised audiences more from Paul Taylor than his lyrical balletic piece, but they loved it.

Impact of Event

Paul Taylor has created more than one hundred dances for his company since its inception. Recognized throughout the world as a major choreographer, Taylor has created works that are considered among the finest in modern dance. Dancers who have been in his company include many celebrated performers, and several, including Dan Wagoner, Danny Grossman, Twyla Tharp, Senta Driver, Pina Bausch, David Parsons, Laura Dean, Elizabeth Keen, and Cliff Keuter, have gone on to critical acclaim as choreographers in their own right. By 1992, Taylor's company had grown to seventeen dancers, and a junior company had been established. Taylor's school in New York City continued to attract young dancers.

Taylor's company was one of the first to feature an eclectic and appealing blend of dance that could be classically lyrical while simultaneously demonstrating the weighted vigor of modern dance. Each piecè revealed a new vocabulary and a new aesthetic, and Taylor's choreography was always unique: Uninterested in codifying a technique or recognizable dance language, Taylor was free to create works that confounded expectations. What emerged was a startling array of diverse dances and a singularly expressive style of dancing.

Taylor's insistence on the individuality of his dancers has also been noteworthy. Dance writer Don McDonagh credits Taylor with having been "the first modern dancer to reflect on a sustained scale an approach to choreography that was attuned to the personalities of his dancers while maintaining many of the formal traditions of historic modern dance." McDonagh suggests that this approach to a large extent accounts for the popularity of Taylor's company both in the United States and abroad. Taylor has explained that in selecting his dancers, he looks for more than skill and attractiveness. "I want individuals that form a team," he has remarked. "I like a variety of shapes, sizes, colors, and types."

Taylor can always be expected to surprise. His choice of musical accompaniment ranges from electronic to classical; it is impossible to fit his work into a single category, musically, stylistically, or artistically. His collaborations with artists Robert Rauschenberg, Alec Katz, Rouben Ter-Arutunian, and others have made for pieces that are visually unique and recall the celebrated early twentieth century Ballets Russes collaborations of Alexandre Benois, Léon Bakst, and Pablo Picasso with choreographers Michel Fokine, Leonid Massine, and Vaslav Nijinsky. In Taylor's company as in the Ballets Russes productions, the works of the artists have not merely provided set decoration or attractive costuming but have combined with the dancing to form a powerful totality.

Critics often note the opposites apparent in Taylor's repertory, a chiaroscuro of choreographic statements. While his sunny dances such as *Aureole, Esplanade*, and *Airs* are beloved by audiences everywhere, it is the dark, twisted, or sardonic pieces such as *Cloven Kingdom, Big Bertha*, and *Speaking in Tongues* that linger in the mind of the viewer. Anna Kisselgoff, senior dance reviewer of *The New York Times*, has written, "There are four Paul Taylors. One choreographs dark pieces, another creates light comic works, a third favors homemade rituals and the last seems to invent pure dance pieces inspired by music."

Paul Taylor is a choreographer of great talent, formidable artistic longevity, and admirable creative energy. His works are imbued with a depth of insight that belies easy classification; always evocative, often ambiguous, they afford the viewer a richness of experience that is seldom equaled in contemporary dance.

Bibliography

McDonagh, Don. "Advanced Ideas and Conventional Theatre." In *The Rise and Fall and Rise of Modern Dance*. Pennington, N.J.: a capella books, 1990. McDonagh presents a thoughtful analysis of Taylor's career and choreographic sympathies. Included is a brief history of modern dance, with special emphasis on modern dance in the 1960's.

Mazo, Joseph H. "Nikolais, Ailey, Taylor: Three Specialists." In *Prime Movers: The Makers of Modern Dance in America.* Princeton, N.J.: Princeton Book Company, 1977. Mazo gives a concise history of Taylor's career and influences, including summaries of major pieces choreographed prior to 1976. Mazo's writing is light and informative, and the text is well illustrated by photographs.

Rosen, Lillie F. "Talking with Paul Taylor." *Dance Scope* 13 (Winter/Spring, 1979): 82-92. Rosen's interview with Taylor focuses on the art of choreography and Taylor's views on creativity. An interesting insight into how the choreographer's mind works and what he thinks about his dances, dancers, and company.

Taylor, Paul. "Down with Choreography." In *The Modern Dance: Seven Statements of Belief,* edited by Selma Jeanne Cohen. Middletown, Conn.: Wesleyan University Press, 1966. Cohen's book is an early collection of essays by choreographers on dance. Taylor's contribution is a homage to the dancers in his company, followed by a wandering essay on a hypothetical piece of choreography. Written in 1966; interesting to compare with later articles on Taylor's choreographic ideas and artistic aesthetics.

_____. *Private Domain.* New York: Alfred A. Knopf, 1987. A friendly, rambling book full of anecdotes and behind-the-scenes glimpses into the world of the dancer/choreographer. An engaging and charming memoir, yet its lack of specific dates and details makes it frustrating to serious researchers. In spite of his apparent candor, Taylor actually says very little about his choreography.

Cynthia J. Williams

Cross-References

Graham Debuts *Appalachian Spring* with Copland Score (1944), p. 1284; Balanchine and Kirstein Make New York a World Center for Ballet (1946), p. 1301; Ailey Founds His Dance Company (1958), p. 1774; Cunningham Stages His First Dance "Event" (1964), p. 2011; Tharp Stages *Deuce Coupe* for the Joffrey Ballet (1973), p. 2288.

TOLKIEN PUBLISHES *THE LORD OF THE RINGS*

Category of event: Literature
Time: 1954-1955
Locale: Oxford, England

An Oxford professor's epic fantasy became an unexpected best-seller and sparked a long-term resurgence of fantasy literature

Principal personages:

JOHN RONALD REUL TOLKIEN (1892-1973), a professor of English at the University of Oxford who created the fantasy world of "Middle Earth" as a lifelong preoccupation

RAYNER UNWIN (1926-   ), the son and successor of publisher Stanley Unwin, who dealt long and patiently with Tolkien over *The Lord of the Rings*

CLIVE STAPLES LEWIS (1898-1963), a close friend of Tolkien for many years who encouraged him to continue his fantasy writing

CHRISTOPHER TOLKIEN (1924-   ), Tolkien's third son, who oversaw the posthumous publication of much of his father's work

Summary of Event

The first publication of *The Lord of the Rings* in three volumes was preceded by a long gestation period. The book's origins can be traced as far back as 1917, when Tolkien was invalided out of active combat duty toward the end of World War I. An early fascination with languages (Old and Middle English, Norse, Welsh, and Finnish, among others) led him to create two languages of his own, based on Welsh and Finnish, and to create legends and myths that might, as it were, have been written in those languages originally. The first of such stories was called "The Fall of Gondolin"; other early stories were "The Children of Hurin" and "Beren and Luthien." The two languages evolved as the "Elvish" languages of Quenya and Sindarin.

By the late 1920's, these stories were already being revised and edited under the title of *The Silmarillion*. In the early 1930's, C. S. Lewis, Tolkien's colleague both at Oxford and in the "Inklings," a discussion group formed mainly of Oxford academics, had listened to parts of *The Silmarillion* and had urged Tolkien to finish the volume with a view to publication.

Tolkien was a perfectionist and preferred to rework his material, filling out the languages and geography of his mythic world. He also attempted a verse account of several of the stories. At the time, moreover, Tolkien had a growing family of four children, for whom he invented numerous fantasy stories with illustrations. Tom Bombadil became a character in one of these, and Tolkien's later book *Farmer Giles of Ham* (1949) grew out of another.

The most famous of these stories is *The Hobbit: Or, There and Back Again*, which was first drafted by 1931. Over the next few years, Tolkien added elements of his mythology to it until, almost by chance, it was shown to an editor of the British publishers George Allen & Unwin in 1936. Tolkien was persuaded to add several missing chapters and to submit the book for publication. The publisher, Stanley Unwin, asked his ten-year-old son Rayner to read it as a test. The boy reported favorably on Tolkien's book, leading to its publication in September, 1937, and the subsequent publication of a U.S. edition by Houghton Mifflin. *The Hobbit* received a good reception on both sides of the Atlantic; the first edition was sold out by Christmas, and the *New York Herald Tribune* awarded it a prize as the best juvenile book of the season.

Inevitably, Unwin wanted a sequel; Tolkien submitted several of his other children's stories and also part of *The Silmarillion*. Unwin was not happy with any of these but suggested that some stories could be quarried from the latter text. In considering this, Tolkien was struck by the idea of a return of the ring found by Bilbo, the protagonist of *The Hobbit*. A preliminary chapter done the next year met with a favorable reception.

As work proceeded on the new story, Tolkien finally saw a way of incorporating his original idea of a "mythology for England" with *The Hobbit*'s setting, the country of the Shire (based on the countryside of Oxfordshire). Such a move shifted the new book's style and matter decisively away from children's literature toward the heroic romance style of *The Silmarillion*. During World War II, Tolkien was writing intermittently as the concept of the magically powerful ring, the quest for its destruction, and the adventures of the book's heroes grew in his mind. He read many of the chapters to the Inklings, Lewis especially being again very encouraging. Lewis was shown the final typed-up version of some half million words in 1949.

Further delays to publication were caused by Tolkien's abortive search for a publisher who would publish both *The Lord of the Rings*, as the story had come to be called, and *The Silmarillion*. In the end, Rayner Unwin, who had succeeded his father at Allen & Unwin, decided to publish *The Lord of the Rings* in three volumes, each with a separate title, at twenty-one shillings each (four dollars approximately); Tolkien was offered a half-profits agreement. Unwin expected both small sales and profits. The print run for the book's first volume, *The Fellowship of the Ring*, released in June, 1954, was 3,500. Slightly fewer copies of the second volume, *The Two Towers*, and the third volume, *The Return of the King*, were printed. *The Two Towers* was released in October, 1954, but *The Return of the King*, delayed by Tolkien's inability to finish a series of appendices for the book, did not appear until October of 1955. Houghton Mifflin published the American edition of *The Lord of the Rings* beginning in October of 1954.

Initial reviews were favorable on the whole, with Lewis the most enthusiastic British critic and W. H. Auden the book's leading champion in the United States. A British Broadcasting Corporation (BBC) dramatization (done without Tolkien's approval) also helped make the work known. Tolkien's first half-profits check in early 1956 came to more than his annual professorial salary.

Although Tolkien was surprised by even this modest success, the immediate effect of the book's publication on him was not great. He had committed himself not to retire until he was sixty-seven, which meant that, even with his new income, he was obligated to Oxford until 1959. He had put off publishing a number of academic works for which he now had time, and he continued to work on *The Silmarillion.* He did take seriously the fan mail that began to arrive and to give selective interviews. A film about him and a biography were produced in the early 1960's, and reprintings of *The Hobbit* kept up with regular hardback reprintings of *The Lord of the Rings.*

Impact of Event

The real impact of *The Lord of the Rings* was not felt until the mid-1960's, when the book was printed in paperback. Response to the book took two distinct forms, an immediate "cultic" form and a longer-term literary one.

By the mid-1960's, Tolkien's popularity was, if anything, greater in the United States than in Great Britain. Tolkien societies had been set up in New York and elsewhere, much to Tolkien's "alarm and despondency," as he put it. The 1965 printing of an American paperback edition was controversial; a small publisher (Ace) went ahead with a pirated edition before Houghton Mifflin, in association with Ballantine Books, could bring out a revised, copyrighted version. In the end, Tolkien, with American writers and supporters, forced Ace to pay royalties and promise not to reprint. The controversy attracted national publicity, and while Ace sold more than a hundred thousand copies, Ballantine sales soon reached a million.

Already a popular best-seller, *The Lord of the Rings* then spawned a campus cult. By the end of 1966, the book topped sales at Yale University and Harvard University. Lapel badges reading "Frodo Lives," "Gandalf for President," and "Come to Middle Earth," referring to characters and places in the book, mushroomed, as did the psychedelic magazine *Gandalf's Garden*, aimed at hippies particularly. More Tolkien societies sprang up in California and New York. Tolkien remained horrified by the whole phenomenon, seeing it as a distortion of his own vision. He put it down to the different mental climate of America, which, he felt, had become polluted and impoverished. Other explanations have been sought in the ecological, antimachine bias of *The Lord of the Rings*, which expressed Tolkien's reaction to and rejection of modern civilization. The best explanation for the book's astonishing success probably lies in the sense of "cosmic insecurity" of much of the youth of the 1960's, together with the generation's widespread desire for a new consciousness and a new value system; such things need a new mythology and a new language. Tolkien's "fellowship" also promised new possibilities of heroic community and extended family, a renewing of aspects of the American Dream.

The longer-term impact was literary: to establish fantasy as a major genre in modern literature, one for which publishers and writers could confidently expect a large audience. Previously, fantasy and children's literature in the United States had been marginalized (in Great Britain, children's fantasy had always been popular). The immediate impact was to move popular writers such as Andre Norton and Ursula K. Le Guin, whose *Wizard of Earthsea* appeared in 1968, from science fiction to fantasy. New fantasy writers appeared and have continued to do so—Anne Mc-Caffrey, Stephen Donaldson, Peter Beagle, Poul Anderson, David Eddings, and Robert Silverberg, to name but a few. Publishers specializing in fantasy, including Ballantine, grew enormously, and other publishers developed fantasy sections.

Few writers have managed to establish the concrete reality of Tolkien's Middle Earth or to maintain the rhythms and style of his prose. Some have merged science fiction features with their high fantasy. There has been a simultaneous drift among fantasy devotees toward horror and even fantasy games—something totally alien to Tolkien's own philosophy of myth as true reality. The drift to occult settings would doubtless have been deplored by Tolkien, a devout Catholic. Other fantasy writers such as Lloyd Alexander have received more indirect inspiration, preferring to keep to more traditional Arthurian themes. Such general popularity of high fantasy can even be seen as reflecting a profound shift in the Puritan, materialistic, and enlightenment ethics and outlooks of the Western world, and as a turning away from America as consoling dream toward imaginary lands.

The Tolkien phenomenon continued unabated after the 1960's. In 1990 alone, 150,000 copies of *The Hobbit* were sold. Despite many initial difficulties on Tolkien's part, translations of his work now exist in twenty-five languages. Four years after Tolkien's death in 1973, his son Christopher was finally able to bring out *The Silmarillion*, having sorted through the many versions and corrections his father had made. Since then, Christopher Tolkien has edited a number of volumes of *The History of Middle Earth*, a series intended to include all the unpublished work on Middle Earth written by Tolkien. In 1992, to mark the centenary of Tolkien's birth, his publishers brought out new editions, including an illustrated edition of *The Lord of the Rings*. By that date, more than fifty million copies of Tolkien's works had been sold, and sales of *The Lord of the Rings* stood at more than ten million.

Bibliography

Brooke-Rose, Christine. *A Rhetoric of the Unreal*. New York: Cambridge University Press, 1981. A difficult theoretical book on fantasy in general, but contains a useful chapter on *The Lord of the Rings* in which other theoretical views are also discussed. Bibliography, index.

Carpenter, Humphrey. *J. R. R. Tolkien: A Biography*. New York: Houghton Mifflin, 1977. The "official" family biography, charting Tolkien's life from his birth in South Africa, through his time as an academic at Leeds and Oxford, to his retirement and death. Deals sympathetically with his marriage and Catholicism. Four appendices, index, and photographs.

Day, David. *Tolkien: The Illustrated Encyclopedia*. London: Mitchell Beazley, 1991. Brought out to coincide with the centenary of Tolkien's birth. More lavish, but not better, than Robert Foster's production.

Foster, Robert. *The Complete Guide to Middle Earth: From "The Hobbit" to "The Silmarillion."* New York: Ballantine, 1978. The most highly praised encyclopedia of Middle Earth, bringing together facts and information about names, languages, and history.

Isaacs, Neil D., and Rose A. Zimbardo, eds. *Tolkien and the Critics.* Notre Dame, Ind.: University of Notre Dame Press, 1968. The first attempt at a critical evaluation of *The Lord of the Rings,* including C. S. Lewis' and W. H. Auden's essays. Though written at the height of the campus cult, manages to retain sufficient objectivity to make it a worthwhile contribution to literary criticism. Indexes.

Kocher, Paul. *Master of Middle-Earth: The Achievement of J. R. R. Tolkien in Fiction.* Boston: Houghton Mifflin, 1972. Discusses Tolkien's literary merits in light of his theory of fairy story and also in light of some of the earlier negative criticism. Notes and index.

Salu, Mary, and Robert T. Farrell, eds. *J. R. R. Tolkien, Scholar and Storyteller: Essays In Memoriam.* Ithaca, N.Y.: Cornell University Press, 1979. Collection of essays about Tolkien's work that contains particularly important pieces by Derek Brewer on romance, William Davie on theology, and T. K. Shippey on philology. Bibliography of all Tolkien's works.

Strachey, Barbara. *Journeys of Frodo: An Atlas of J. R. R. Tolkien's "The Lord of the Rings."* New York: Ballantine, 1981. A series of fifty maps, derived from close reading of the text, each with an exact description of distances traveled by the characters. Illustrates Tolkien's perfectionist desire for accuracy in his text.

Tolkien, J. R. R. *The Letters of J. R. R. Tolkien.* Edited by Humphrey Carpenter. London: Allen & Unwin, 1981. Selections from 354 of Tolkien's letters written from 1914 to 1973. A valuable backup to Carpenter's biography. Full notes, introduction, appendix.

——————. "On Fairy Stories." In *The Tolkien Reader.* New York: Ballantine, 1966. Originally given as a lecture at the University of St. Andrews in 1938, this much-reprinted essay sets out Tolkien's own literary credo on the power of myth and the status of fantasy writer as subcreator.

David Barratt

Cross-References

American Science Fiction Enjoys Its Golden Age (1938), p. 1094; Disney's *Fantasia* Premieres and Redefines the Boundaries of Animation (1940), p. 1195; Heinlein Publishes *Stranger in a Strange Land* (1961), p. 1883; Syndication Turns *Star Trek* into a Cult Classic (1972), p. 2260; The *Star Wars* Trilogy Redefines Special Effects (1977), p. 2391.

ABC MAKES A LANDMARK DEAL WITH DISNEY

Category of event: Television and radio
Time: April, 1954
Locale: New York, New York, and Hollywood, California

American popular culture was changed by an agreement to make a long-running television series and construct a new type of amusement park

Principal personages:

WALT DISNEY (1901-1966), the creative head of a small Hollywood studio who linked filmmaking, television production, and a new style of theme park

ROY DISNEY (1893-1971), the financial head of the small Disney studio, chairman of the Walt Disney Company from 1966 to 1971

LEONARD GOLDENSON (1905-   ), the man who built ABC television into one of the three dominant American networks

FESS PARKER (1925-   ), the actor who played Davy Crockett on television

Summary of Event

From its beginnings in 1923 as a small film studio through the close of World War II, the Disney corporate enterprise grew from a marginal operation to a successful niche filmmaking company. Walt and his older brother Roy Disney represented but one of the many sets of film entrepreneurs trying to make it in an industry dominated by eight major studios. Throughout the 1930's and 1940's, the Disney brothers failed to make theirs a major Hollywood studio even though they produced some successful films.

Initially the postwar expansionary economic environment disagreed with the Walt Disney Company. During 1948 and 1949, losses appeared on its balance sheets. Throughout the early 1950's, problems began to mount. In 1953, they came to a crest when the new owner of Radio-Keith-Orpheum (RKO), the major Hollywood studio that had long distributed Disney films, broke its agreement. The new owner, billionaire Howard Hughes, dismantled his company and sent Disney out on its own.

Walt and Roy Disney had to ante up millions of dollars to form their own film distribution arm, Buena Vista. The Disney company also turned from producing animated films such as *Snow White and the Seven Dwarfs* (1937), *Fantasia* (1940), and *Pinocchio* (1940) to a greater concentration on mainstream live-action adventure films aimed at a family audience, beginning with *Twenty Thousand Leagues Under the Sea* (1954). This attempt by the Disney studio to try to grow into a Hollywood powerhouse initially met with little success. The Disney brothers struggled to fill their new channel of distribution. The Disney filmmaking operation could not grind out feature films fast enough to support its new distribution arm. Disney needed to do something else to ensure corporate survival.

In April, 1954, the Walt Disney Company in Hollywood and the American Broadcasting Company (ABC) in New York City announced plans for a Disney television series. Network television was a new outlet for Disney but not the company's only plan for expansion. Sensing a new audience being created by the baby boom and a new means of access in the widespread sale of automobiles, Walt and Roy Disney wanted to build a new type of theme park for families in the suburbs. Roy Disney had approached banks with the idea but could not convince conservative bank officers that Disney would build more than "another Coney Island." The conservative financial institutions turned Roy Disney down; they wanted no part of the proposed "Disneyland."

Walt and Roy Disney tried a new tactic. David Sarnoff at the National Broadcasting Company (NBC) and William Paley at the Columbia Broadcasting System (CBS) were not interested in the proposed theme park; they turned down the Disneys cold. Leonard Goldenson of ABC, with a bankroll of millions of dollars from theaters he had been forced to sell, agreed to back Disneyland if the Disney company would produce a one-hour television series for the then-struggling ABC-TV. Goldenson, who had merged the former Paramount theaters with ABC-TV, was desperately looking for program suppliers and agreed to pay $500,000 plus $50,000 per show.

The *Disneyland* television show went on the air on Wednesday nights on ABC beginning in October, 1954; it moved (as *Walt Disney Presents*) to Friday nights in 1958 and then to Sunday nights in 1960. It would remain a Sunday-night fixture for more than two decades, becoming *Walt Disney's Wonderful World of Color* when it moved to NBC in 1961, then *The Wonderful World of Disney* in 1969 and *Disney's Wonderful World* in 1979. CBS took over the show in 1981, as *Walt Disney*, and showed it for several years, on either Tuesday or Saturday nights.

The show gave ABC-TV its first top-twenty ratings hit. The show finished sixth in the ratings for the television season that ran from September, 1954, through May, 1955. Thereafter, the Disney television show rarely fell out of the top ten. It finished fourth in 1955-1956 and thirteenth in 1956-1957. Its appearance in the top twenty from 1964 through 1975 signaled one of the great successes in television's history.

This pioneering television series was designed to kindle interest in the Disneyland theme park, which opened in July, 1955. ABC-TV took a one-third financial interest in the park as well as all profits from food concessions for the first ten years in exchange for providing financing. Disneyland proved to be an instant hit, forever transforming the Disney company. Walt and Roy Disney sought to follow up with an even more popular park. They began the complex in Orlando, Florida, but Disney World would not open until October, 1971, years after Walt's death and only months before Roy's. The Walt Disney Company and ABC-TV worked to cross-promote their products. The *Disneyland* television series served as a weekly advertisement for the Disneyland park and later for Disney World.

At first, the *Disneyland* show featured animation and live-action films from the Disney film library in addition to "specials" centered in the theme parks. The show's four-part rotation even reflected the divisions of the California park: "Frontierland," "Fantasyland," "Tomorrowland," and "Adventureland." One segment of the Disney television effort on ABC-TV surpassed all expectations. The December, 1954, "Davy Crockett, Indian Fighter" episode, shown during "Frontierland," created a national obsession of enormous proportions. Two more episodes about Crockett aired in January and February of 1955, with Crockett killed in the second of these. By mid-1955, "The Ballad of Davy Crockett" had become a pop music hit, coonskin caps were the rage among children, and actor Fess Parker had become one of television's first true stars. Disney made several more Davy Crockett episodes, depicting incidents earlier in his life, when the company recognized the popularity of the first three episodes.

The ABC-TV deal proved to be the cornerstone of the new Disney corporate empire. There was one more important new corporate strategy: the regular rereleases of classic feature-length Disney films. In approximately seven-year cycles, heralded on Disney's television show, the company put *Snow White and the Seven Dwarfs* and *Pinocchio*, among other films, back onto the theater screens of the world. Other studio films might be shown on television, but Disney feature-length animation classics could be seen only during the holidays in theaters. The results of the rereleases often were spectacular. For example, *Snow White and the Seven Dwarfs* was rereleased in 1952, 1958, and 1967 and earned nearly fifty million dollars more from worldwide markets.

Impact of Event

Walt Disney died in 1966 and Roy Disney five years later. Walt had become famous and both brothers had become rich, based largely on their initial contract with ABC-TV and the resulting exploitation of television and theme parks. In stark contrast, Leonard Goldenson stood in the background, remaining head of his television network well into the 1980's. Goldenson was known only to insiders in the television business. Only they knew that he ranked with David Sarnoff of NBC and William Paley of CBS as the men who created American network television.

The Disney-ABC deal merged television and Hollywood. Prior to this arrangement, Hollywood studios had been trying to take over television, seeking ways to own and operate stations. The studios resisted helping television unless they could also own the stations. ABC proved that former radio networks would and could operate the stations and networks, and that Hollywood would have to be satisfied producing programs.

In the years immediately following the success of the *Disneyland* show, Warner Bros., a major studio, moved directly into television production. The other major Hollywood studios soon followed. By 1960 television production was almost entirely on film, principally produced in Hollywood. The days of live television drama done from New York City were over. Disney and ABC made Hollywood the center of television production and the major Hollywood studios the locus of that production.

Fess Parker perhaps was not the first person to reach the national consciousness based solely on television fame, but he certainly was among the first. Previously, it took fame in the movies to launch a career; after Parker's success playing Davy Crockett, television more and more became the means to achieve fame and fortune. Disney and ABC-TV proved that the small screen found in increasing numbers of homes was a mass communication apparatus of massive power.

It should not be forgotten that the Disney brothers frequently made corporate misjudgments. For example, the company never replicated Davy Crockett's success, despite Walt and Roy Disney's efforts. Few remember their television efforts in line with the Davy Crockett shows such as *The Saga of Andy Burnett* or *The Nine Lives of Elfego Baca*. Even Fess Parker could not make a success of his next series, *Westward Ho! The Wagons.* Leslie Nielsen as the "Swamp Fox" sported a foxtail three-cornered hat, but few children pressed their parents to buy a facsimile. Television enabled the Disney brothers to move their operation into the big time, but it did not make them infallible. The "Fantasyland" segments allowed exposure of Disney cartoon characters such as Mickey Mouse and Donald Duck. *The Mickey Mouse Club*, a children's show featuring a cast of child members of the fan club in addition to cartoons and other recurring elements, began airing in 1955. The *Disneyland* show surely helped to develop the Mickey Mouse fan club phenomenon.

Disney changed the nature of amusement parks. Prior to Disneyland, amusement parks had been located at the ends of trolley or subway lines, seeking to promote ridership. Most were on a small scale. No one would mistake Disneyland for Coney Island. Disneyland was not located at the end of a New York subway line but at the edge of the then-suburbanized mecca of Los Angeles. One traveled to Disneyland by automobile, not trolley.

Disneyland offered a fantasy world. Parts looked back to the glories of America's past. "Tomorrowland" looked to a future that included space travel. Disney created a world in which there was no dirt and no poverty. Everybody could have a good time and forget their troubles in the wonderful world of Disneyland, "The Happiest Place on Earth."

Disney World would change the nature of American vacation patterns. Prior to its opening in 1971, few journeyed to Orlando, Florida, for vacations. Miami was the locus of the Florida tourist trade. By the 1980's, Disney World had become the most popular tourist attraction in the United States. The success of it and Disneyland spawned parks in Japan and France. Disney changed the proper way to vacation with a family, with the parks as focal points for vacations.

The long-run Disney corporate "magic" focused on meshing all these elements, forming an entertainment conglomerate. The Walt Disney Company, at first in partnership with ABC, symbiotically promoted its theme parks, films, and television series so as to create a corporate image of having fun. The popular culture of the United States—indeed, of the world—has never been the same.

Bibliography

Goldenson, Leonard H. *Beating the Odds.* New York: Charles Scribner's Sons, 1991. A candid autobiography by the man who created ABC-TV. The deal with Disney is described in some detail, as is the impact on ABC-TV in particular and on the television industry in general. Should be read in conjunction with *Inside ABC* by Sterling Quinlin.

Grover, Ron. *The Disney Touch.* Homewood, Ill.: Business One Irwin, 1991. Offers a business perspective on the fascinating history of the Disney company, from its founding to the late 1980's. This is no corporate puffery but rather an objective analysis of why the Walt Disney Company succeeded and was able to maintain its success.

Maltin, Leonard. *The Disney Films.* New York: Popular Library, 1978. The definitive filmography for the Walt Disney Company during Walt Disney's lifetime. Contains a great deal of information on the changing Disney output during the 1950's. A first-rate book.

Quinlin, Sterling. *Inside ABC: American Broadcasting Company's Rise to Power.* New York: Hastings House, 1979. A serious history of ABC, tendered by a former vice president of the company. Offers significant detail on the ABC-TV and Disney deal. Should be read in conjunction with *Beating the Odds.*

Schickel, Richard. *The Disney Version.* New York: Simon & Schuster, 1968. The first outsider history of the Disney company. Especially valuable for its frank evaluation of the corporate culture. A critique rather than a corporate public relations tale.

Thomas, Bob. *Walt Disney: An American Original.* New York: Simon & Schuster, 1976. Sympathetically examines the rise of Walt Disney as a cultural entrepreneur. Uncritical and often fawning in its praise. Often reads like a public relations puff piece but still contains a great deal of valuable information.

Douglas Gomery

Cross-References

Disney Releases *Snow White and the Seven Dwarfs* (1937), p. 1053; Disney's *Fantasia* Premieres and Redefines the Boundaries of Animation (1940), p. 1195; ABC Begins Its Own Network Television Service (1948), p. 1368; Television Enters Its Golden Age (1950's), p. 1465; Disney Emerges as an Architectural Patron (Early 1990's), p. 2646.

THE FIRST NEWPORT JAZZ FESTIVAL IS HELD

Category of event: Music
Time: July 17 and 18, 1954
Locale: Newport, Rhode Island

The 1954 Newport Jazz Festival symbolized jazz's popular and commercial revival and marked another stage in its curious and exciting evolution

Principal personages:
CHARLIE CHRISTIAN (1916-1942), a pioneer jazz guitarist
LESTER YOUNG (1909-1959), a superb saxophonist and a founder of the style of "cool" jazz
ROY ELDRIDGE (1911-1989), a trumpeter and bass player who helped to revolutionize jazz
JIMMY BLANTON (1918-1942), a bass player who changed his instrument's role in jazz
CHARLIE PARKER (1920-1955), an outstanding alto saxophonist and composer
"DIZZY" GILLESPIE (1917-1993), a pioneering trumpeter
LENNIE TRISTANO (1919-1978), a blind pianist and a founder of the cool school of jazz
GERRY MULLIGAN (1927-   ), a versatile saxophonist and a leading exponent of West Coast cool jazz
OSCAR PETERSON (1925-   ), a sophisticated pianist and leader of a jazz trio
MILES DAVIS (1926-1991), a leading and brilliant explorer of cool jazz

Summary of Event

The fortunes and visibility of jazz's varied styles and players, and public acceptance of them, have swung almost cyclically since the 1890's. Jazz began in parochial obscurity as an apparent musical and cultural eccentricity endemic to groups of musicians in New Orleans, St. Louis, Memphis, Kansas City, Oklahoma City, San Francisco, and New York City from the 1880's through the early 1900's. It emerged into national prominence as ragtime, blues, and Dixieland music, and the various styles had become widely known as "jazz" by 1917. While purists and some music historians exclude all such styles but Dixieland from classification as early jazz, performers in each instance knew that it was still jazz that they were singing or playing.

Intended as a "four-letter" word, always intentionally shocking to the non-jazz musical world, jazz derived from and thrived upon dispute and divisions among its own devotees as well as upon a measure of social disrepute. Consequently, its varied temporal currents—including ragtime, Dixieland, blues, Chicago jazz, swing, boogie-woogie, Kansas City jazz, bop, hard bop, and cool jazz—have enjoyed their greatest popularity when the general public has undergone significant social and generational changes (among them altered racial attitudes), when dominant musical styles become stale, or when public taste overtakes the products of jazz musicians' ingenuity. Jazz historians and musicians can therefore conveniently trace the evolution of jazz by charting its preeminent styles—with a due reckoning of subtle, long-term developments—almost decade by decade.

The late 1940's and 1950's were marked by the partial consummation of a jazz revolution, notable for its stylistic diversity but more particularly for the early dominance of the styles of bop and cool jazz—as well as for the novel commercial attraction of large audiences through live and recorded performances. Such was the broad context into which the Newport Jazz Festival of July, 1954, fit. Sponsored by the Newport Chamber of Commerce, by town residents such as Louis and Elaine Lorillard, and by Boston impresario George Wein, the festival was an outgrowth of the tremendous successes of Norman Granz. A serious jazz fan, Granz had in the 1940's and early 1950's introduced the jazz concert, often in conjunction with philharmonic orchestras, to various parts of the country. His self-described motives were to improve race relations—contractually, all audiences had to be unsegregated—to offer great jazz, and to turn a profit. He realized something of all three objectives, in the process becoming a multimillionaire.

When musicians and performers gathered on the Newport Casino's tennis courts on the evening of July 17, 1954, jazz was in the midst of another its transitions, in this instance away from its roots toward bop music (a rapid, complex style of jazz variously known as "bebop" and "rebop") and its many distinctive substyles. Bop, of course, had not sprung full-blown from jazzmen's instruments; it had sunk roots of its own decades earlier in the unique or experimental playing of Charlie Christian, Lester Young, Jimmy Blanton, Roy Eldridge, and Bix Beiderbecke. These experiences were passed to or absorbed by Lennie Tristano, Miles Davis, Lee Konitz, Gil Evans, Dizzy Gillespie, and, among still others, Stan Getz, Gerry Mulligan, Charlie Mingus, and Thelonious Monk. The playing of all these men rhythmically departed from the solid beat of hot jazz and swing; harmonically, chords were more ambitious, forming new progressions away from familiar sequences; and, accordingly, melody often was shifted away from singable or even recognizable tunes, and the focus was typically on a series of short-duration notes. Such jazz was more complex and required more abstract comprehension from its listeners than did earlier styles; indeed, the new approach alienated many audiences, just as its counterparts in fine arts, classical music, and architecture had done as those disciplines, too, were revolutionized during the first half of the twentieth century.

At Newport's inaugural jazz festival, the billing made a propitiatory bow toward various styles of jazz. Stan Kenton, the former leader of the first great West Coast jazz band, acted as master of ceremonies and recited a history of jazz. Trumpeter Bobby Hackett, bandleader Eddie Condon, clarinetist Pee Wee Russell, and the magnificent—and versatile—singer Ella Fitzgerald were on hand to symbolize the fading "swing" era. Yet it was the modern—particularly the "cool"—jazz musicians who dominated the two evenings of performances. The already popular Modern Jazz Quartet, which had sprung from Dizzy Gillespie's orchestra in 1952, with vibra-harpist Milt Jackson, pianist John Lewis, drummer Connie Kay, and bassist Percy Heath, performed to acclaim. So too did famed Canadian pianist Oscar Peterson, Chicago saxophonist Lee Konitz (who had worked with Claude Thornhill's and Kenton's bands as well as with Miles Davis and Lennie Tristano), and Gerry Mulligan, a baritone saxophonist, composer, and arranger of cool West Coast jazz. Nearly fourteen thousand people attended the festival, and the profits reportedly exceeded twenty-five thousand dollars—a measure of acceptance adequate to drive forward plans for further festivals.

In addition to Norman Granz's managerial abilities, several other factors accounted for the first festival's success. Certainly, a wartime ban on recordings and audience boredom with reiterations of swing-band music from the 1930's and the World War II years created an immense demand for novel musical styles. The new forms of jazz grew enormously in popularity; nightclubs featuring jazz proliferated. Newspapers and magazines began treating jazz seriously, hiring specialists to review its evolution. Bookstores offered comprehensive encyclopedias and specialized studies on jazz and its personalities. In addition, a number of radio stations—notably FM stations—accorded jazz an accepted place alongside mainstream music, while recording companies produced spates of jazz records. These developments were paralleled by the emergence of a new generation of highly trained jazz musicians who were anxious in their own right to experiment freely and break with old routines. At least equally important, as concerts and the Newport festival confirmed, jazz at last appealed to a mass paying audience.

Impact of Event

Despite popular impressions to the contrary in the United States, the Newport Festivals were not the first jazz shows of their kind, even in America. Trying to make jazz respectable, for example, bandleader Paul Whiteman had attempted something similar in New York City's Aeolian Hall in 1924 with his introduction of George Gershwin's *Rhapsody in Blue*; and overseas, as jazz became a special American export, jazz shows were familiar events. There had been festival-like shows in Australia in 1946, in Nice, France, in 1948 (a show that had featured Louis Armstrong, Earl Hines, Baby Dodds, Pops Foster, Barney Bigard, and Jack Teagarden, among others), and in Paris—a show featuring Miles Davis, Sidney Bechet, and Charlie Parker—in 1949. Relative to the Newport festivals and other later shows, however, these were modest affairs.

In this regard, there is no question that the context in which the first Newport festival occurred was a unique one. Indeed, it was amid a veritable popular jazz revival, evidenced by newspaper, magazine, book, and radio coverage and promotion, that Newport sponsors organized their initial presentation. The success of the first festival encouraged more. In 1955, a three-day event held in a Newport football stadium that accommodated fifteen thousand people reported profits in excess of fifty thousand dollars. By 1956, when saxophonist Paul Gonsalves, under the direction of the enduring and remarkable Duke Ellington, performed successive choruses of "Diminuendo and Crescendo in Blue," the crowd danced in the aisles—and profits rose above the previous year's.

The 1957 festival, not surprisingly, thus became a four-day affair, and for added interest even featured non-jazz performances by the New York City Ballet and popular singer and dancer Eartha Kitt. Again, profits soared. Regardless of the performers—the 1958 and 1959 festivals, for instance, included international jazz talents as well as the Stockholm Opera Company—the commercial success continued, not only at Newport, but also elsewhere in the United States and Canada, where appetites of audiences and promoters alike had been whetted. Nationally, by the end of the 1950's, nine festivals were reported having grossed nearly one million dollars.

Profits notwithstanding, by 1960, disillusionment with Newport's festivals—and with some imitative gatherings elsewhere—became increasingly apparent, chiefly for two reasons. First, as festival promoters catered to larger audiences, they drew in constituencies of people to whom the event itself was more important than the music presented. Rowdyism broke out in 1959, and alcohol-fueled riots disrupted the third night of a five-day festival in 1960. Newport's city council, previously lax in its enforcement of liquor laws, closed the festival, causing its organizers losses of more than $100,000. Reopened under stricter law enforcement, the festival still encountered the same difficulties, largely because of the fans drawn to the event. Riots occurred again in 1961, 1969, and 1970, with the result that operations were transferred to New York City in 1972. Newport's experience through the decade had a dampening effect on festivals and concerts elsewhere. Mass-audience jazz events at New York City's Randall's Island, at the Hollywood Bowl in Los Angeles, and at Quaker City, Philadelphia, all thereafter caused significant financial losses for their sponsors. Meanwhile, smaller jazz concerts that attracted fewer but more-devoted fans to such places as Monterey, California, and Long Island, continued to prosper. Yet the steam had gone out of Newport-style festivals by the close of the 1960's.

There was further disillusionment with large festivals among jazz musicians themselves. Many, like Miles Davis, found "jazz supermarkets" offensive. Others complained, as did Oscar Peterson, about redundant programming and about the modest—often exceedingly brief—playing time allotted to even headline performers. Moreover, despite accrued experience with festivals, organizers often did little to improve basic facilities such as sound, lighting, staging, and timing. Similarly, Newport and other "festivals" scarcely lived up to their names as such, concentrating instead almost exclusively on jazz numbers and not upon other jazz-related festivities. There were exceptions; though the music was roundly criticized, the President's Music Committee's so-called International Jazz Festival of 1962 did sponsor an event in Washington, D.C., that was notable for the scope of its jazz entertainments, which ranged from films to ballet.

In other areas, however, the impetus lent to jazz by Newport and by comparable festivals continued. Hundreds of thousands of people had listened to live jazz concerts, and nearly eighty million dollars in jazz recordings had been sold by the end of the 1960's. Moreover, jazz poetry had gained a foothold on the West Coast and in New York, and jazz playing was welcomed into the services and other activities of many churches eager to take advantage of the revival. Jazz musicians, who were often more comfortable playing for themselves, for one another, or for small but devoted audiences, remained divided between traditionalists—who played "hot" music—and those whose training and interpretations of tradition kept them experimenting with cooler, freer, and more esoteric forms.

Bibliography

Dale, Rodney. *The World of Jazz.* Birmingham, England: Basinghall Books, 1979. A fine introduction to nearly all the major figures associated with Newport and other jazz festivals, along with excellent thumbnail sketches of their specialties, accomplishments, and contributions to jazz. Good brief historical materials on jazz's evolution. Scores of photos, two appendices, directory of musicians, brief index.

Hentoff, Nat. *The Jazz Life.* New York: Dial Press, 1961. Popularly written. Hentoff supplied Stan Kenton with his history of jazz for recitation at the first Newport festival and was the author of numerous works on the jazz scene. An informative read on the jazz elites. Some photos, no notes; brief bibliography, index.

Hodeir, André. *Jazz: Its Evolution and Essence.* Translated by W. David Noakes. New York: Grove Press, 1961. A major work; an authoritative and well-balanced discussion of jazz rather than an analysis of its social or historical contexts. Notes, bibliography, and index.

Tirro, Frank. *Jazz: A History.* New York: W. W. Norton, 1977. Excellent, if no more definitive than other histories of jazz. A splendid employment of historical, sociological, and cultural anthropological perspectives. Excellent on the "jazz revolution." Photos and scores. Ample chapter notes, fine annotated bibliography, discography, and an excellent triple-columned index.

Ulanov, Barry. *A History of Jazz in America.* New York: Viking Press, 1955. Authoritative, readable, reliable, and informative. Long a standard work, if by later standards lacking in broader sociocultural perspectives. Some photos, notes; a somewhat dated bibliography; good index.

Wilson, John S. *Jazz: The Transition Years, 1940-1960.* New York: Appleton-Century-Crofts, 1966. Superb, concise, yet filled with carefully chosen materials. The author was a former jazz critic for *The New York Times,* so the emphasis is on the analytical and interpretative study of jazz's transition from swing through bop to cool. Useful information on Newport festivals. Short, but still an outstanding, perceptive work. Essential reading. No photos. Useful glossary, brief discography, and even briefer bibliography. Fine double-columned index.

Clifton K. Yearley

Cross-References

Parker's Playing Epitomizes Bebop (1946), p. 1318; Davis' *Birth of the Cool* Recordings Spawn 1950's Cool Jazz (1949), p. 1438; The Monterey Pop Festival Inaugurates the "Summer of Love" (1967), p. 2104; Davis' *Bitches Brew* Vitalizes Jazz-Rock Fusion (1969), p. 2153; The Woodstock Music Festival Marks the Climax of the 1960's (1969), p. 2180; Wynton Marsalis Revives Acoustic Jazz (1980's), p. 2454.

THE TONIGHT SHOW BECOMES
AN AMERICAN INSTITUTION

Category of event: Television and radio
Time: September 27, 1954
Locale: New York, New York, and Burbank, California

The Tonight Show, *evolving from an idea by television programming pioneer Sylvester "Pat" Weaver, became a late-night American institution under the successive tenures of Steve Allen, Jack Paar, and Johnny Carson*

Principal personages:

SYLVESTER "PAT" WEAVER (1908-   ), the programming genius whose belief in the potential of late-night television was vindicated with the successful introduction of *Tonight!* in 1954

STEVE ALLEN (1921-   ), the celebrated comic, author, and musician whose multiple talents coalesced in his successful three-year stewardship as the show's host

JACK PAAR (1918-   ), the master monologuist and heart-on-sleeve host who steered the program to a more conversational, rather than comic, format

JOHNNY CARSON (1925-   ), the endearing and durable host whose thirty-year reign made him American television's most recognized and beloved icon

ED MCMAHON (1923-   ), Carson's longtime sidekick, announcer, cheerleader, and pitchman

DOC SEVERINSEN (1927-   ), a noted trumpeter and one of Carson's favorite comic foils

JAY LENO (1950-   ), a noted stand-up comic who took the show's reins from Carson

Summary of Event

The Tonight Show had its genesis with the mercurial Sylvester "Pat" Weaver, a programming genius for the National Broadcasting Company (NBC). In the late 1940's, Weaver expressed his faith in the entertainment and profit potential of live, late-night television entertainment. To test the premise, Weaver introduced *Broadway Open House*, with nightclub comic Jerry Lester and gag-writer Morey Amsterdam alternating as hosts. With its melange of vaudeville routines and musical diversions, the sixty-minute *Broadway Open House* was an immediate success and proof of late-night television's starmaking powers. Lester, Amsterdam, bandleader Milton DeLugg, and buxom blonde Dagmar catapulted to fame.

With success, though, came friction. Lester, who had discovered Dagmar, grew restive over her increasing popularity. Inflated by his own newfound celebrity, Lester also made untenable salary and scheduling demands. Eventually, the clash of egos sapped the show's vitality, and on August 24, 1951, network television's first regularly scheduled late-night variety show gasped its last breath. Nevertheless, the show's fifteen-month run proved Weaver's concept a money-maker. Weaver decided that his next late-night venture should be more relaxed than the antic slapstick of Lester and Amsterdam. With the appearance of *The Steve Allen Show*, a production of WNBT-TV, NBC's owned-and-operated New York station, in June, 1953, Weaver had at last found a standard-bearer for his revised concept. Securing the support of NBC's affiliates, Weaver promoted Allen's local show to the network. *Tonight!*, with an expanded 105-minute time slot, debuted on September 27, 1954, and was seen as far away as Omaha, then the westernmost terminus of NBC's coaxial cable.

Allen, a veteran of early television, was a convivial, witty, and multitalented performer who established the essential parameters of the show's enduring format: the opening monologue, segments involving the studio audience such as "Stump the Band," a spartan set with a desk and chair for the host and a couch for guests, comedy skits, a brassy band to punctuate segues, a group of regulars, and a compelling mix of human interest and low-key comedy arising from Allen's spirited interactions with an ever-varying roster of guests.

In contrast to Jack Paar's and Johnny Carson's shows, Allen's *Tonight!* was permeated by music. Allen, an accomplished pianist and composer, featured singers Steve Lawrence, Eydie Gorme, and Andy Williams. His unabashed enthusiasm for jazz led to appearances by such musical legends as tenor saxophonist Coleman Hawkins and trumpeter Louis Armstrong.

In June, 1956, NBC put Allen into a big-budget variety hour opposite Ed Sullivan, the ratings blockbuster of the Columbia Broadcasting System (CBS). Though *The Steve Allen Show* seldom topped Sullivan, the genial host created enough havoc to warrant NBC's continued support. To ease the pressure of Allen's back-breaking schedule, Ernie Kovacs was brought in to host *Tonight!*'s Mondays and Tuesdays. Allen soon dropped his late-night commitment to concentrate on his epic battle with Sullivan. On January 25, 1957, Allen gaveled his last *Tonight!* The series' first epoch had come to a close.

Without the inspired guidance of Weaver, who in 1955 had been shunted from the NBC presidency in favor of Robert Sarnoff, NBC introduced *Tonight: America After Dark* on January 28, 1957. Featuring correspondents Bob Considine and Earl Wilson in New York and Irv Kupsinet in Chicago, the ersatz mix of news and entertainment was a flop. Faced with plummeting ratings, affiliates dropped out in favor of more lucrative local programming. At NBC, the search for a new host who could revive the format—and success—of Allen's *Tonight!* began in earnest.

On July 29, 1957, NBC introduced *Tonight*, without the exclamation mark of the Allen era. At the helm was the bright yet idiosyncratic Jack Paar. A conversationalist who could tell a joke rather than an out-and-out comic, the brash and petulant Paar, in spite of his protestations, seemed to thrive on controversy. There were feuds with Ed Sullivan (now an NBC tradition), Dorothy Kilgallen, Walter Winchell, and even

Steve Allen. Galvanized by the new host's mercurial temperament, a growing legion of Paar fans pushed *Tonight* back to the top of the late-night ratings. NBC, pleased with Paar's doubling of affiliates and the show's soaring advertising rates, redubbed the series as *The Jack Paar Tonight Show.*

Paar's supporting cast was also appealing. There was sidekick-announcer Hugh Downs and bandleader Jose Melis. There was daffy Dody Goodman, "weather girl" Tedi Thurman, and Bil and Cora Baird's puppets. Semiregulars included French chanteuse Genevieve, British raconteur Alexander King, and Washington hostess Elsa Maxwell, as well as entertainers Zsa Zsa Gabor, Peggy Cass, and Cliff (Charley Weaver) Arquette. The main attraction, though, was the host.

Paar's appeal was multidimensional. There was his thin-skinned tempestuousness, which *Newsweek* aptly described as "Russian roulette with commercials." Also, there was Paar's willingness to share even his most private moments. When he revealed to the country that his daughter Randy had gotten her first bra, he cried. It was a "performance" capitalizing on television's affinity for intimacy and Paar's own gut-wrenching confessions. Paar, though, seemed anxious, and as early as 1958 contemplated retirement.

On February 11, 1960, after NBC censors had cut a "water closet" joke without consulting Paar, the obviously vexed host announced his displeasure with the network's action and made a teary farewell to his nonplussed nation. Paar soon returned after entreaties from NBC's brass, but two years later again announced his retirement when NBC refused to reduce *Tonight*'s 105-minute length. Paar told the press, "I don't want more money, I just want less time." On March 29, 1962, Paar, at the apex of his popularity, sobbed three times and said goodnight, thus leaving America to ponder his replacement.

The Tonight Show's third era began with Carson's debut on October 1, 1962. Carson brought with him the redoubtable Ed McMahon. On the premiere, as Skitch Henderson's band blared Paul Anka's freshly penned "Johnny's Theme" and McMahon boomed "Heeeerrre's Johnny," Carson offered his first late-night monologue and bantered with Rudy Vallee, Groucho Marx, Joan Crawford, Mel Brooks, and Tony Bennett. Reviews were positive, and the show's already good ratings, a significant part of Paar's heritage, began a steady climb to even loftier heights.

Impact of Event

While building on the framework bequeathed by Steve Allen and Jack Paar, *The Tonight Show* has become inextricably linked to Johnny Carson by dint of his amazingly protean three-decade tenure. By finding a distinct and instantly recognizable "voice" within the show's basic concept, Carson successfully won the hearts and, sometimes, even the minds of the American public.

In show business, timing, as it is often said, is everything. At one level, Carson was a fortunate beneficiary of larger forces swirling about him. First, he began on *The Tonight Show* just as the wiring of America's television system was being completed. By 1962, the coaxial cable girded the continental United States. With the successful launching of cable systems and broadcast satellites, Carson had a technologically derived advantage enabling him to enter virtually every home in America, an edge not enjoyed by his predecessors.

Unlike either Allen or Paar, who viewed *Tonight* as a stepping-stone to bigger things, Carson had the prescience to realize that he had found a special niche as "King of the Night." There were forays into prime-time to host Academy Award shows and specials, but late-night was where he felt most comfortable. In protecting his turf, Carson took pleasure in knocking off such would-be competitors as Joey Bishop and Dick Cavett as well as abortive comeback attempts by Allen and Paar. No triumph, though, was more keenly felt than his 1986 decimation of Joan Rivers, his former "permanent" guest host; Carson had felt betrayed when Rivers left NBC, unannounced, to host her own show for the fledgling Fox Network.

Timing was also a trump card of Carson's comedic style. Whether he was doing a Jack Benny double-take or delivering a double entendre with wide-eyed innocence, Carson's pacing was always a marvel. Even in the show's campy skits, Carson's self-reflexive reactions to his hokey material put the bits over. As in the monologues, Carson created the impression of being at one with his audience, an aspect enhanced by his "gee whiz" midwestern background and seemingly easygoing demeanor.

Carson, in spite of fame and fortune, successfully took on the mantle of "everyman," a quality embellished by his casual demeanor. When Carson spoke, people listened. They also believed, demonstrating a kind of trust that, for example, created unintended chaos when, in 1973, an offhand mention of a possible toilet-paper shortage created a consumer run on the product. Similarly, Carson, like Will Rogers, served as an effective deflator of American foibles and political pomposity. Though he always sought a middle-of-the-road, nonconfrontational posture, his seemingly benign remarks had devastating consequences for such figures as Richard Nixon, Gerald Ford, and Dan Quayle.

Tonight's impact can be further gauged in Carson's decision to move the show from New York to Burbank in 1972, a tacit recognition that America's cultural center was shifting westward. The move further blurred the line separating entertainment and unabashed hucksterism. As Carson himself noted, his show had become a virtual nonstop promotional parade where the main item of business was the spotlighting of guests pitching their latest films, shows, records, books, and ideas. The show was both an influence and a mirror in setting the agenda of topics for public and private discussion, and it was a forerunner of such news and promotional mixes as *Entertainment Tonight* and MTV.

Carson, though a feared show-business figure, was perhaps most appreciated by talented newcomers looking for a break—which, from the outset of Carson's tenure, came to mean a spot on *The Tonight Show*. The "halo effect" emitted by Carson extended to announcer-sidekick Ed McMahon, America's most indefatigable pitchman, and trumpeter Doc Severinsen, the virtuosic leader of the Tonight Show Orchestra from 1967 to 1992.

The four decades of *Tonight* with Steve Allen, Jack Paar, and Johnny Carson promise to stand as one of the unparalleled successes of American television. When Carson stepped down in May, 1992, in favor of longtime substitute and guest host Jay Leno, the episode seemed more like a changing of the guard than mere show business as usual. The show has served as a veritable beacon of American popular culture, a barometer reflecting, and sometimes even galvanizing, the tidal shifts in America's cultural, social, and political affairs.

Bibliography

Allen, Steve. *The Funny Men.* New York: Simon & Schuster, 1956. Includes Allen's penetrating chapters on "A Few Thoughts on TV Humor" and "A Few More Thoughts on TV Humor," as well as sections devoted to such funnymen as Jack Benny, Milton Berle, Sid Caesar, Jackie Gleason, and Red Buttons.

Cox, Stephen. *Here's Johnny: Thirty Years of America's Favorite Late-Night Entertainment.* New York: Harmony Books, 1992. A useful if roughly assembled scrapbook focusing on Carson's stewardship of *The Tonight Show.* Though marred by an overly adulatory tone, there are memorable photos of Carson at work, and "guest chapters" by Neil Shister, Joe Rhodes, and John Lofflin.

De Cordova, Frederick. *Johnny Came Lately: An Autobiography.* New York: Simon & Schuster, 1988. A whimsical yet informative autobiography by *The Tonight Show*'s executive producer, with numerous and witty references to Carson.

Galanoy, Terry. *Tonight!* Garden City, N.Y.: Doubleday, 1972. A brisk and highly informative chronicle of America's most popular late-night show, with particularly good coverage of Allen's and Paar's tenures. Galanoy's incisive criticisms add perspective. Includes photos.

Leamer, Laurence. *King of the Night: The Life of Johnny Carson.* New York: William Morrow, 1989. A well-written account of the stormy interfaces between Carson's professional persona and private life. Includes candid coverage of Carson's often aloof relations with wives, sons, ex-lawyer Henry Bushkin, and associates Ed McMahon, Doc Severinsen and Fred de Cordova.

McNeil, Alex. "The Tonight Show." In *Total Television: A Comprehensive Guide to Programming from 1948 to the Present.* 2d ed. New York: Viking Penguin, 1984. McNeil's vast and valuable compendium of American television includes a concise and informative entry on *The Tonight Show,* as well as its predecessors.

Metz, Robert. *The Tonight Show.* Chicago: Playboy Press, 1977. A carefully researched yet lively account of *The Tonight Show* and its principal personalities. Based on extensive interviews with *Tonight Show* writers, directors, and stars.

Paar, Jack. *P.S. Jack Paar.* Garden City, N.Y.: Doubleday, 1983. Paar's warm and witty reminiscences include revealing chapters entitled "The Tonight Show" and "Plumbing Can Make You Famous," the latter about the infamous joke that led to Paar's clash with NBC's censors and his subsequent walkout.

Rico, Diana. *Kovacsland: A Biography of Ernie Kovacs.* San Diego: Harcourt Brace Jovanovich, 1990. A scrupulously researched biography of the iconoclastic comic, with detailed coverage of Kovacs' uncomfortable, yet often scintillating, tenure as the show's part-time host in 1956 and 1957.

Smith, Ronald L. *Johnny Carson: An Unauthorized Biography.* New York: St. Martin's Press, 1987. A lively account of the interconnections between Carson's personal and public lives.

Charles Merrell Berg

Cross-References

Variety Shows Dominate Television Programming (1948), p. 1383; "Mr. Television," Milton Berle, Has the Top-Rated Show (1948), p. 1394; Television Enters Its Golden Age (1950's), p. 1465; *The Red Skelton Show* Becomes a Landmark on Network Television (1951), p. 1520; *Saturday Night Live* Is First Broadcast (1975), p. 2355.

VARÈSE PREMIERES *DÉSERTS*

Category of event: Music
Time: December 2, 1954
Locale: Paris, France

The classical music world was divided when Edgard Varèse incorporated taped electronic sounds into one of his already radical compositions, but for a younger generation of composers, he was pointing the way to the future

Principal personages:

EDGARD VARÈSE (1883-1965), a radical composer who dreamed of liberating sound from the timbres, scales, and structures of the conventional orchestra and previous composers

FERRUCCIO BUSONI (1866-1924), an Italian-German composer, pianist, and music theorist whose calls for a new music were an important influence on Varèse

LE CORBUSIER (CHARLES-ÉDOUARD JEANNERET, 1887-1965), a renowned modernist architect responsible for Varèse's commission to do *Poème électronique*

PIERRE SCHAEFFER (1910-   ), a French pioneer of tape music in whose studio Varèse mixed *Poème électronique*

YANNIS XENAKIS (1922-   ), Le Corbusier's assistant, a composer whose explanations of sound masses and the possibilities of rhythm were influenced by Varèse's work

Summary of Event

At the end of World War II, Edgard Varèse was an isolated, eccentric figure, a composer who had stopped writing in the mid-1930's because no one would perform his work. Varèse was a stubborn visionary who in 1916 told a newspaper, "I refuse to submit myself to sounds that have already been heard. What I am looking for are new technical mediums which can lend themselves to every expression of thought." He dreamed of a music liberated from scales and conventional instruments, and he found support for his ideas in the writings of music theoretician Ferruccio Busoni, whom he met in Berlin.

In his compositions written in the 1920's, Varèse stressed percussion and brassy blocks of tuneless sound in his search for a new musical language. A great believer in the possibilities of science, he also used sirens and primitive electronic instruments while dreaming of a more sophisticated electronic music. In 1922, he had told *The Christian Science Monitor* that "the composer and the electrician will have to labor together." Most of his work was greeted with hostility, however, and few conductors were willing to commit their prestige to conducting Varèse's music.

Music had changed greatly in the first decades of the twentieth century with the advent of the twelve-tone system of Arnold Schoenberg, the rhythmic experiments of Igor Stravinsky, and the serialism of Anton Webern. Nevertheless, partly as a result of the rise of radio, most composers were placing more emphasis on accessibility for a popular audience than they had been at the beginning of the century.

It was only after World War II that an audience existed for Varèse's radical vision—along with the technology and equipment necessary for him to pursue the electronic music of which he dreamed. Electronic music studios were founded in Paris by Pierre Schaeffer and at Princeton University, and Varèse was invited to use them. Encouraged by the changing cultural climate and the advances in technology that made these studios possible, Varèse began composing *Déserts* in 1950.

Although a few younger composers began to use electronics shortly before Varèse did, *Déserts* is considered by many to be the first real work of electronic music. Focusing on evocations of the "déserts," or wilderness, the piece alternates between four orchestral and three taped electronic passages.

Like much of Varèse's earlier work, *Déserts* was concerned with rhythm and with volumes and densities of sound. Recognizable melody is entirely absent. Rather than unfolding themes, the sound takes on physical form, sonic planes that seem to move and unfold as the timbres of the different instruments blend together and pull apart. Startling rhythms sound unpredictably from five groups of percussion instruments; the sharp attack of the wind instruments is also used rhythmically.

The orchestral section of *Déserts* is scored for two flutes, two clarinets, two horns, three trumpets, three trombones, two tubas, a piano used as a resonator, and five groups of percussion instruments. The taped sounds tend to be harsh and industrial and include screeches and sharp electronic tones. Varèse's use of the wind instruments, which often emit shrill blasts, complements the tapes.

Varèse composed the instrumental sections first, finishing them in 1952. He then recorded the three taped interludes, gathering sounds from factories, sawmills, and airports. The mixing process was finished, in stereo, at the Paris studio of Pierre Schaeffer in 1954. As electronic sound technology rapidly improved, Varèse went back and tinkered with the tapes, redoing his work three times before he was satisfied with the final version, which was completed in 1962.

Déserts received the same hostile reception that most of Edgard Varèse's other compositions were given. Its premiere in Paris provoked some audience members to stand up and shout at the orchestra to stop.

The premiere took place at the Théâtre des Champs-Élysées, the same theater in which a riot had occurred following the premiere of Igor Stravinsky's *The Rite of Spring* forty years earlier. *Déserts* was played between Wolfgang Amadeus Mozart's *B-flat Overture* and Peter Ilich Tchaikovsky's *Pathétique* symphony (pieces that could not be more unlike Varèse's) by the Orchestra of Radio-Televisions Française and was broadcast live in stereo. The audience nearly rioted, with some members of the audience screaming at the orchestra to stop. One critic wrote that "what our electro-symphonist needs is a trip to the electric chair."

Yet Varèse also had his partisans who applauded enthusiastically after the performance. Many poets, writers, and younger composers considered the work a revolutionary masterpiece, as did a few older composers such as Stravinsky. Despite the negative reaction of the audience. *Déserts* brought Varèse back to public attention. He received a number of awards, and *Déserts* was soon performed in the United States.

The aging composer's star continued to rise as many younger composers who were influenced by him began to make their mark. Colleges invited Varèse to lecture, and newspapers and magazines interviewed him. In 1956, the modernist French architect Le Corbusier was commissioned to build the Philips pavilion for the 1958 Brussels World's Fair. Despite numerous objections by Philips, Le Corbusier insisted that Varèse do the music for the pavilion.

As a result Varèse was finally able to begin creating the music he had envisioned for decades. The electronic sections of *Déserts* point the way to this final work, the entirely electronic *Poème électronique*, a repeating tape 480 seconds long played through 150 loudspeakers. Electronically filtered choruses and voices, transformed bells and piano chords, and studio-made recordings were combined to create *Poème électronique*. The pavilion received two million visitors during the fair.

Varèse became ill soon after and died in 1965, at the age of eighty-two, without completing another work. He had, however, gained the recognition that had always eluded him.

Impact of Event

When Varèse surrounded electronic and taped sounds with orchestral music in *Déserts*, he implicitly said that the new medium was as serious and worthy of attention as the old. Rather than being a curiosity, as it was before World War II, electronic music became one of the most important new areas of exploration in music throughout the 1960's and 1970's.

The call of the young Varèse for the invention of a new musical language was answered by a full spectrum of composers after World War II, and many consider Varèse one of the most important founding fathers of experimental music. Varèse preferred to characterize his work as "organized sound" rather than music, and his rejection of conventional scales has been widely followed by composers such as Yannis Xenakis and Karlheinz Stockhausen.

During the Brussels World's Fair, a photograph was taken of the composers Henri Pousseur, Mauricio Kagel, Luciano Berio, Stockhausen, and John Cage at the Le Corbusier pavilion. All were influenced by Varèse to some degree and continued the investigation of themes Varèse explored in his work. Stockhausen composed the electronic portion of his *Kontakte* from 1958 to 1960. The piece is mainly taped electronics, but one version calls for live percussion and piano to be played with the tape.

Stockhausen must certainly have been thinking of *Déserts*, but *Poème électronique* also influenced him. *Poème électronique* took a large number of sources, reflecting the diversity of the city, and ran them together. Stockhausen's *Hymnen* and *Tele-*

musik, from 1966, do the same thing on a worldwide scale. For composers such as Stockhausen, electronics have become part of the equipment of the modern orchestral composer. While *Déserts* and other works by Varèse were not the only influence on such pieces, his work is an important precursor.

Pieces involving live instruments and taped material began pouring forth after *Déserts* and soon became commonplace. In 1958, Otto Luening was writing *Synthesis for Orchestra and Electronic Sound* and Pierre Boulez was writing *Poésie pour pouvoir*, both of which mixed tapes with live instrumentation. In 1967, the Pulitzer Prize for music was awarded to Leon Kirschner's String Quartet No. 3, which combined electronic sounds with live performance of acoustic instruments.

Varèse's views have also left their mark in rock music. In his taped pieces for *Déserts* and *Poème électronique*, Varèse took full advantage of the new medium of stereo. Sounds come from one speaker or the other or flow back and forth between them, a technique used by rock musicians beginning in the late 1960's.

Composer and musician Frank Zappa has cited Varèse as one of his formative influences and has conducted performances of Varèse's work. Varèse's work has influenced Zappa's songs less than his composed pieces and tape collages, on which Varèse's influence is unmistakable. Sections of the rock band Pink Floyd's 1969 album *Ummagumma* sound much like *Poème électronique*, and the band's next album, 1970's *Atom Heart Mother*, has sections that alternate between "live" music and tape interpolations.

The primary reason Varèse limited the electronic music of *Déserts* to taped interludes was that it was not possible to play electronic music live with the technology available at the time. The invention of the Moog synthesizer and drum machines in the 1960's made possible the live performance of electronic music. Live electronic concerts, ranging from the performances of composers such as Philip Glass to groups such as Tangerine Dream, have become common.

Varèse's belief that all audible phenomena are material from which to make music was an important spur to composer John Cage, who in his *4'33"* used the sounds of people sitting in a room watching a performer sit before a piano without playing it. Varèse was perhaps the first composer to investigate the boundary between noise and music. Certainly, works such as Cage's *Cartridge Music*, in which turntable cartridges and contact microphones are manipulated in ways that create unpredictable bursts of sound, owe a philosophical debt to Varèse. Many noisy rock recordings probably are not directly influenced by Varèse, but ultimately they are continuing Varèse's investigation of the music/noise border.

Varèse's preoccupation with rhythm was also influential. The central role of rhythm in his work, best seen in the rhythmic cells he used in the works of his middle period, point the way to the work of Steve Reich and other minimalists, who frequently built pieces around evolving rhythmic cells. Varèse's heavily percussive piece *Ionisation*, from 1931, is the precedent for almost every percussion work that came thereafter. Stockhausen, for example, composed *Zyklus* for percussion in 1959, continuing Varèse's exploration of total rhythm and no melody, while Xenakis has composed other works centering on rhythm.

This elevation of rhythm was an important turning point in Western art music, turning the prior privileging of melody on its head. Partly under the influence of Varèse's work, composers such as Boulez and Stockhausen spent some time composing pieces that refused to use any rhythmic regularity. The use of toys as a source of sound by the Art Ensemble of Chicago and others has its origin in part in Varèse's music and its use of all available sound sources.

At a lecture given in 1936 in Santa Fe, New Mexico, Varèse predicted that timbre would move from being an incidental concern in music to becoming an integral part of it; postwar music confirmed his prediction. Varèse's use of tonal colors, sound masses, and sound densities gave rise to the walls of sound and texture in the compositions of Gyorgi Ligeti, Yannis Xenakis, and Kristof Penderecki. The slowly building walls of sound favored by Glen Branca in his symphonies for percussion and electric guitar also have their precedent in Varèse's masses of sound.

Finally, the invention of the sampler, which literally makes it possible to compose with anything as a sound source, represents the final liberation of sound that Varèse longed for as a young man.

Bibliography

Griffiths, Paul. *A Guide to Electronic Music.* London: Thames and Hudson, 1979. An excellent overview of the history of electronic music, beginning with theories and inventions of the early years of the twentieth century but primarily focused on the postwar period. The sections on Varèse are short, but clearly show his integral role in the evolution of electronic music.

Ouellette, Fernand. *Edgard Varèse.* Translated by Derek Coltman. New York: Orion Press, 1968. Written shortly after Varèse's death, this biography lacks true perspective on his work. As a full record of Varèse's life and the evolution of his thought and compositions written by someone who knew him, however, it is indispensable.

Peyser, Joan. *The New Music: The Sense Behind the Sound.* New York: Delacorte Press, 1971. Focuses primarily on the major schools of music in the first half of the century: Arnold Schoenberg's twelve-tone school and Igor Stravinsky's neoclassical school. Varèse is given nearly equal billing, and his work is examined as a more radical break from the past than the work of Schoenberg or Stravinsky.

Russcol, Herbert. *The Liberation of Sound.* Englewood Cliffs, N.J.: Prentice-Hall, 1972. Contains a chapter on Varèse and also much information on other experimental and electronic composers from the early twentieth century until the 1960's. Includes brief biographies of postwar composers, lists of their most important pieces, and a glossary of electronic music terms.

Van Sokema, Sherman, ed. *The New Worlds of Edgard Varèse.* New York: Institute for Studies in American Music, 1979. A short book containing essays by composers Elliott Carter, Robert P. Morgan, and Chou Wen-chung. Carter provides an overview of the importance of Varèse's use of rhythm and atonality, while the other two focus on specific works by Varèse and go through them nearly measure for measure.

Scott M. Lewis

Cross-References

Busoni's *Sketch for a New Aesthetic of Music* Is Published (1907), p. 166; Schoenberg Breaks with Tonality (1908), p. 193; Cage's *4′33″* Premieres (1952), p. 1546; The First Successful Synthesizer Is Completed (1959), p. 1785; *Einstein on the Beach Is a Triumph of Minimalism* (1976), p. 2375.

CHRONOLOGICAL LIST OF EVENTS

VOLUME I

VOLUME II

VOLUME III

VOLUME IV

VOLUME V